Crises in the Twentieth Century

VOLUME I
Handbook of International Crises

Crises in the Twentieth Century

VOLUME I
Handbook of International Crises

by

MICHAEL BRECHER
McGill University

JONATHAN WILKENFELD
University of Maryland, College Park

SHEILA MOSER

PERGAMON PRESS
OXFORD · NEW YORK · BEIJING · FRANKFURT
SÃO PAULO · SYDNEY · TOKYO · TORONTO

U.K.	Pergamon Press, Headington Hill Hall, Oxford OX3 0BW, England
U.S.A.	Pergamon Press, Maxwell House, Fairview Park, Elmsford, New York 10523, U.S.A.
PEOPLE'S REPUBLIC OF CHINA	Pergamon Press, Room 4037, Qianmen Hotel, Beijing, People's Republic of China
FEDERAL REPUBLIC OF GERMANY	Pergamon Press, Hammerweg 6, D-6242 Kronberg, Federal Republic of Germany
BRAZIL	Pergamon Editora, Rua Eça de Queiros, 346, CEP 04011, Paraiso, São Paulo, Brazil
AUSTRALIA	Pergamon Press Australia, P.O. Box 544, Potts Point, N.S.W. 2011, Australia
JAPAN	Pergamon Press, 8th Floor, Matsuoka Central Building, 1-7-1 Nishishinjuku, Shinjuku-ku, Tokyo 160, Japan
CANADA	Pergamon Press Canada, Suite No. 271, 253 College Street, Toronto, Ontario, Canada M5T 1R5

First edition 1988

Library of Congress Cataloging-in-Publication Data
Brecher, Michael.
Crises in the twentieth century
1. World politics—20th century.   I. Wilkenfeld,
Jonathan.   II. Moser, Sheila.   III. Title.
D443.B713   vol. 1   909.82 s   87-8323
[D445]   [909.82]

British Library Cataloguing in Publication Data
Brecher, Michael
Crises in the twentieth century.
1. International relations
I. Title   II. Wilkenfeld, Jonathan
III. Moser, Sheila
327   JX4471
ISBN 0-08-034981-1

Reproduced, printed and bound in Great Britain by Hazell Watson & Viney Limited Member of BPCC plc Aylesbury Bucks

Contents

LIST OF FIGURES AND TABLES   vii

PREFACE   xi

Part I   **Framework**   1

Prologue   1

Conceptualization   3

Actor–System Linkages   9

Controls   12

Notes   16

Part II   **Methodology**   19

Case List   19

Codebooks and Variables   24

Coder Training and Reliability   28

Summaries   29

Statistical Procedures   29

Controls   31

Notes   32

List of International Crises 1929–79   35

Part III   **Variables**   59

Breakpoint (Trigger) to International Crisis   60

Triggering Entity of Crisis   63

Duration of International Crisis   65

Gravity of Value Threatened   67

Crisis Management Technique   70

Centrality of Violence   73

Intensity of Violence   76

Timing of Violence   77

Intra-War Crisis   79

Number of Involved Actors   81

Content of Great Power/Superpower Activity   83

Effectiveness of Great Power/Superpower Activity   86

Most Effective Great Power/Superpower Activity   90

Source of Global Organization Involvement   93

Global Organization Organ Most Active in Crisis   94
Content of Global Organization Involvement   97
Effectiveness of Global Organization Involvement   99
Most Effective Global Organization Organ   101
Most Effective Global Organization Involvement   103
Source of Regional/Security Organization Involvement   105
Regional/Security Organization Most Active in Crisis   106
Content of Regional/Security Organization Involvement   108
Effectiveness of Regional/Security Organization Involvement 109
Most Effective Regional/Security Organization   110
Perceived Content of Outcome   111
Form of Outcome   113
Extent of Satisfaction about Outcome   115
Escalation or Reduction of Tension   117

Part IV   Severity   119

Concepts and Data   119

Index of Severity   123

Data Analysis   127

Part V   Summaries   143

List of Figures and Tables

FIGURES

I.1.A	Conceptual Map: Macro-Level	6
I.1.B	Conceptual Map: Micro-Level	7
I.2	Unit- and System-Level Crisis Components	10
I.3	Static and Dynamic Concepts of Crisis	10
IV.1	Indicators of Severity—Network of Effects	124

TABLES

II.1	Geographic Location of International Crises	22
II.2	Location of International Crises in Time and Space	22
II.3	Conflict Setting of International Crises	23
II.4	Involvement by the Powers in International Crises	23
II.5	Sources of Data: Periods	30
II.6	Sources of Data: Geography	30
II.7	List of International Crises 1929–79, with Select Attributes	35
III.1.A	Breakpoint (Trigger) to International Crisis: Types	61
III.1.B	Breakpoint (Trigger) to International Crisis: Geography	61
III.1.C	Breakpoint (Trigger) to International Crisis: Polarity	61
III.1.D	Breakpoint (Trigger) to International Crisis: System Level	62
III.1.E	Breakpoint (Trigger) to International Crisis: Power Discrepancy	62
III.1.F	Breakpoint (Trigger) to International Crisis: Involvement by Powers	62
III.2.A	Triggering Entity of Crisis	64
III.2.B	Triggering Entity of Crisis: Polarity	64
III.2.C	Triggering Entity of Crisis: System Level	65
III.2.D	Triggering Entity of Crisis: Conflict	65
III.3.A	Duration of International Crisis: Geography	66
III.3.B	Duration of International Crisis: System Level	66
III.3.C	Duration of International Crisis: Conflict	66
III.4.A	Value Threatened: Geography	68
III.4.B	Value Threatened: Polarity	68
III.4.C	Value Threatened: System Level	68
III.4.D	Value Threatened: Conflict	68
III.4.E	Value Threatened: Power Discrepancy	69
III.5.A	Crisis Management Technique: Geography	71
III.5.B	Crisis Management Technique: Polarity	71
III.5.C	Crisis Management Technique: System Level	71
III.5.D	Crisis Management Technique: Power Discrepancy	71
III.5.E	Crisis Management Technique: Involvement by Powers	72
III.6.A	Centrality of Violence: Geography	74
III.6.B	Centrality of Violence: Polarity	74
III.6.C	Centrality of Violence: System Level	74
III.6.D	Centrality of Violence: Power Discrepancy	75
III.6.E	Centrality of Violence: Involvement by Powers	75
III.7.A	Intensity of Violence: Geography	76
III.7.B	Intensity of Violence: Polarity	77
III.7.C	Intensity of Violence: System Level	77
III.8.A	Timing of Violence: Geography	78
III.8.B	Timing of Violence: Polarity	78
III.8.C	Timing of Violence: System Level	79
III.8.D	Timing of Violence: Power Discrepancy	79

III.9.A	Intra-War Crisis: Geography	81
III.9.B	Intra-War Crisis: Polarity	81
III.9.C	Intra-War Crisis: System Level	81
III.10.A	Number of Involved Actors: Frequencies	82
III.10.B	Number of Involved Actors: Geography	82
III.10.C	Number of Involved Actors: Polarity	83
III.11.A	Content of US/USSR Activity: Geography	84
III.11.B	Content of GP/US/USSR Activity: Polarity	85
III.11.C	Content of GP/US/USSR Activity: Conflict	85
III.12.A	Effectiveness of US/USSR Activity: Geography	87
III.12.B	Effectiveness of GP/US/USSR Activity: Polarity	88
III.12.C	Effectiveness of GP/US/USSR Activity: System Level	88
III.13.A	Most Effective US/USSR Activity: Geography	91
III.13.B	Most Effective GP/US/USSR Activity: Polarity	91
III.13.C	Most Effective GP/US/USSR Activity: System Level	92
III.13.D	Most Effective GP/US/USSR Activity: Conflict	93
III.14.A	Source of Global Organization Involvement: System Level	94
III.15.A	Global Organization Organ Most Active in Crisis: Geography	95
III.15.B	Global Organization Organ Most Active in Crisis: Polarity	95
III.15.C	Global Organization Organ Most Active in Crisis: System Level	96
III.15.D	Global Organization Organ Most Active in Crisis: Conflict	96
III.15.E	Global Organization Organ Most Active in Crisis: Involvement by Powers	96
III.16.A	Content of Global Organization Involvement: Geography	98
III.16.B	Content of Global Organization Involvement: Polarity	98
III.16.C	Content of Global Organization Involvement: System Level	99
III.16.D	Content of Global Organization Involvement: Conflict	99
III.17.A	Effectiveness of Global Organization Involvement: Geography	100
III.17.B	Effectiveness of Global Organization Involvement: Conflict	101
III.17.C	Effectiveness of Global Organization Involvement: Involvement by Powers	101
III.18.A	Most Effective Global Organization Organ: Polarity	102
III.18.B	Most Effective Global Organization Organ: System Level	102
III.18.C	Most Effective Global Organization Organ: Conflict	103
III.18.D	Most Effective Global Organization Organ: Involvement by Powers	103
III.19.A	Most Effective Global Organization Involvement: Polarity	104
III.19.B	Most Effective Global Organization Involvement: Conflict	105
III.19.C	Most Effective Global Organization Involvement: Power Discrepancy	105
III.19.D	Most Effective Global Organization Involvement: Involvement by Powers	105
III.20.A	Source of Regional/Security Organization Involvement: System Level	106
III.21.A	Regional/Security Organization Most Active in Crisis: Polarity	107
III.21.B	Regional/Security Organization Most Active in Crisis: Conflict	107
III.22.A	Content of Regional/Security Organization Involvement: Polarity	109
III.22.B	Content of Regional/Security Organization Involvement: System Level	109
III.22.C	Content of Regional/Security Organization Involvement: Involvement by Powers	109
III.23.A	Effectiveness of Regional/Security Organization Involvement: Conflict	110
III.24.A	Most Effective Regional/Security Organization: Polarity	111
III.25.A	Perceived Content of Outcome: Polarity	112
III.25.B	Perceived Content of Outcome: System Level	112
III.25.C	Perceived Content of Outcome: Conflict	112
III.26.A	Form of Outcome: Geography	113

III.26.B	Form of Outcome: Polarity	114
III.26.C	Form of Outcome: Conflict	114
III.26.D	Form of Outcome: Involvement by Powers	114
III.27.A	Extent of Satisfaction about Outcome: Geography	116
III.27.B	Extent of Satisfaction about Outcome: Polarity	116
III.27.C	Extent of Satisfaction about Outcome: System Level	116
III.27.D	Extent of Satisfaction about Outcome: Conflict	116
III.28.A	Escalation or Reduction of Tension: Geography	117
III.28.B	Escalation or Reduction of Tension: Polarity	118
IV.1	International Crises 1929–79: Components of Overall Severity	128
IV.2	Index of Severity, 1973–74 Middle East Crisis	134
IV.3	Average Overall Severity Scores for International Crises, 1929–79: Geography, Polarity, Conflict	134
IV.4	Most Severe International Crises, 1929–79: Time, Space, Overall Severity	135
IV.5	Average Overall Severity of Most Severe Crises, 1929–79	136

Preface

The *Handbook of International Crises* and its companion *Handbook of Foreign Policy Crises* encompass the 50-year period 1929–79. Together with a related volume of analysis, they constitute the aggregate or mapping dimension of the International Crisis Behavior (ICB) Project. The primary objective of these *quantitative* studies in *breadth*, as with the *qualitative* studies in *depth* in this project, is to illuminate a crucial phenomenon in twentieth-century world politics.

The first *Handbook* volume focuses on the macro-level of analysis, the second on the micro-level. Definitions of crisis at both levels, along with conceptual maps, are provided in Part I of the *Handbook of International Crises*. This is followed by a discussion of methodology and a list of the 278 international crises during the half-century with key select attributes. Part III of the first *Handbook* presents macro-level data, variable by variable, with decision rules for coding and tables containing the frequency distributions of all 278 international crises. Additional tables for some of the variables indicate the distribution of cases using controls for geography, polarity, system level, protracted conflict, power discrepancy and major power involvement. Brief descriptive analyses of the most salient findings follow each table. Part IV examines the severity or intensity of all international crises for the half-century under inquiry. Part V provides summaries of background material and of crucial aspects of each case.

The *Handbook of Foreign Policy Crises* follows the same format regarding framework, methodology and data presentation at the actor level. In addition, this volume examines actor profiles for the half-dozen most crisis-prone states, and provides a portrait of patterns of crisis. It also focuses on the subset of intra-war crises.

The primary function of the two *Handbooks* is informational, namely, to present the data on 278 international crises and 627 foreign policy crises, with a description of the findings deriving from the application of the control variables to the data sets. The data described in these two *Handbooks* are available from the International Relations Archive of the University of Michigan. The *Handbooks* will be followed by an *Analysis of International Crises*. This will explore the meaning of crises during much of the twentieth century by a set of overarching studies of enduring intellectual issues in international relations and the impact of crises thereon.

The collection of data for the ICB's aggregate study of crises took 10 years, 1975–85. For their skill, devotion and tireless efforts to generate a body of reliable and comprehensive data, the authors are indebted to a large number of research assistants: Hemda Ben Yehuda, Gerald Bichunsky, Mark Boyer, Diana Brecher, Doreen Duffy, Ofra Einav, Robert Einav, Alex Forma, Etel Goldmann, Sharon Greenblatt (who also assembled the Bibliography), Steve Hill, Patrick James, Cindy Kite, Maureen Latimer, Eileen Long, Rutie Moser, Hanan Naveh, Arie Ofri, Lily Polliak, (the late) Mordechai Raz, Michel Reichman, André Rosenthal, Joel Schleicher, Bruce Slawitsky, and Sara Vertzberger.

Many scholars gave generously of their time and their knowledge as regional specialists, with much benefit to the ICB enterprise: Douglas Anglin (Carleton), Alexandre de Barros (Rio de Janeiro), Robert A. Baumann (Missouri), Luigi Bonanate (Turino), Thomas Bruneau (McGill), Karen Dawisha (Maryland), Richard H. Dekmejian (SUNY-Binghamton), Jorge I. Dominguez (Harvard), Alan Dowty (Notre Dame), Benjamin Geist (Jerusalem), Alexander L. George (Stanford), Galia Golan (Jerusalem), Kjell Goldmann (Stockholm), Ehud Harari (Jerusalem), Barbara Haskel (McGill), Naomi Hazan (Jerusalem), Charles F. Hermann (Ohio State), Karl Jackson (University of California-Berkeley), Ellis Joffe (Jerusalem), Nelson Kasfir (Dartmouth), Paul Kattenburg (South Carolina), Edy Kaufman (Jerusalem), Jacob Landau (Jerusalem), E. S. Milenky

(Washington), Guy Pauker (RAND), Frederic S. Pearson (Missouri), Leo Rose (University of California-Berkeley), Martin Rudner (A.N.U.), Filippo Sabetti (McGill), Amnon Sella (Jerusalem), Yaacov Shimoni (Jerusalem), Shlomo Slonim (Jerusalem), Saadia Touval (Tel Aviv), Yaacov Y. I. Vertzberger (Jerusalem), Robert Vogel (McGill), and George T. C. Yu (Illinois).

Valuable ideas and comments on earlier drafts of *Crises in the Twentieth Century* were made by Yehudit Auerbach, Hemda Ben Yehuda, Davis B. Bobrow, Avraham Diskin, Patrick James, Joe Oppenheimer, Raymond Tanter, Yaacov Y. I. Vertzberger and Avner Yaniv.

Jacqueline Lieberthal and Sharon Greenblatt in Jerusalem, Regina Cunningham, Lynn Stanton, Sheila Owens and Brigid Driscoll at Maryland, and Judy Warnock at McGill showed endurance and exceptional ability in transforming a myriad of drafts and tables into the final typescript.

Two Canadian institutions provided generous financial support to the ICB Project from 1975 to 1985: the Killam Program of the Canada Council and the Social Sciences and Humanities Research Council of Canada. McGill University contributed to this enterprise in two respects: annual leaves of absence to Michael Brecher; and substantial funds at a critical point in the preparation of these *Handbooks*. Computational and other types of support were provided by the Computer Science Center and the Office of Graduate Studies and Research of the University of Maryland.

The international dimension of this inquiry into world politics is also evident in the physical dispersal of the authors. Brecher spent the autumn term at McGill University in Montreal, where he introduced ICB concepts, data and research methods to graduate students. For most of each year he directed, and was intimately involved in, every aspect of the ICB enterprise in Jerusalem. Wilkenfeld was based in Washington, D.C., where he set up an ICB team at the University of Maryland to handle the design for data collection, validation, processing and conversion into machine-readable form. Moser, the senior research assistant, administered the project in Jerusalem and worked on data collection with student assistants from the Hebrew University. In addition, Wilkenfeld, who joined this aggregate research project as co-director in 1978–79 while in Jerusalem, made annual visits there between 1980 and 1985. Over the years the authors had many intensive sessions together in Montreal, Jerusalem and Washington to plan policy and work through problems. Nevertheless, physical distance caused some delays and misunderstandings. These difficulties were largely overcome by visits, long-distance telephone conversations and a voluminous correspondence. Moreover, the benefits derived from the multinational aspect of the three locations should not be minimized. The three sets of students and the professionals served to check and balance one another, added different perspectives, and provided diverse sources of talent and material.

MICHAEL BRECHER
Montreal/Jerusalem

JONATHAN WILKENFELD
Washington, D.C.

SHEILA MOSER

1 Framework

Prologue

More than four decades have passed since the publication of Quincy Wright's seminal volume, *A Study of War* (1942); a comparable work on the related phenomenon of international crisis has not yet appeared. There are, to be sure, studies of high quality: the Stanford Group's analysis of the crucial link between perceptions and decisions in the 1914 Crisis;[1]* McClelland's (1964, 1972) examination of quantitative data pertaining to actions and responses by the contending parties in two "conflict arenas," Berlin from 1948 to 1963, and the Taiwan Straits from 1950 to 1964; Paige's (1968) "guided reconstruction" of America's response to the outbreak of the Korean War in 1950; Allison's (1971) use of three paradigms – rational actor, bureaucratic politics and organizational process – to explore US behavior in the Cuban Missile Crisis; George and Smoke's (1974) "focused comparison" of deterrence in 11 crises for the United States, from the Berlin Blockade in 1948 to the Missile Crisis in 1962; Snyder and Diesing's (1977) dissection of the bargaining process in 16 international crises, from the Anglo-French dispute over Fashoda in 1898 to the Middle East conflagration in 1973, along with Leng *et al.*'s (1979, 1982, 1983) quantitative studies of bargaining in these and other twentieth-century crises; Stein and Tanter (1980) on Israel's multiple paths to choice in the 1967 Middle East Crisis; and Lebow's (1981) analysis of 26 cases, from Cuba in 1897–98 to the events preceding the 1967 Arab–Israel War, with emphasis on misperceptions, cognitive closure and crisis management. At a more general level, Hermann (1972) presented the collective wisdom of behavioral research into crisis in the late 1960s.[2]

Together, these studies illuminated several aspects of international crisis: the images and behavior of great powers in one grave global crisis; a demonstration of the merits of macro-quantitative research into two prolonged conflicts, including a sequence of crises; decision-making by one superpower in several high-profile crises; one type of crisis management (the practice of deterrence) by the same superpower; a few dimensions of crisis behavior (bargaining between adversaries, cognitive closure and crisis management) in a nonrepresentative sample of cases; and, in the volume edited by Hermann, evidence of the embryonic but promising state of the art.

In the mid-1980s there is still little systematic knowledge about crisis perceptions and the decision-making style of the USSR;[3] the myriad of twentieth-century crises in regions other than Europe (with few exceptions);[4] crises experienced by weak international actors;[5] the role of alliance partners in crisis management; the immediate triggers of crises; crisis outcomes; and the consequences of crises for the power, status, behavior and subsequent perceptions of participant states. Nor is there a widely shared theory of crisis.[6]

It was an awareness of these *lacunae*, despite the impressive scholarly contributions noted above, that led to the initiation of the International Crisis Behavior (ICB) Project in 1975. Underlying the Project are three assumptions: first, that the destabilizing effects of crises, like conflicts and wars, are dangerous to global security; second, that understanding the causes, evolution, actor behavior, outcomes and consequences of crises is possible by systematic investigation; and third, that knowledge can facilitate the avoidance of crises, or their effective management, so as to minimize the adverse effects on world order.

The aim of the ICB Project and of the *Handbooks* is, in the largest sense, to shed light on a pervasive phenomenon of twentieth-century world politics. There are four specific objectives: the accumulation and dissemination of knowledge about

*Superscript numbers refer to Notes at the end of Parts.

international crises between 1929 and 1979; the generation and testing of hypotheses about the effects of crisis-induced stress on coping and choice by decision-makers; the discovery of crisis patterns focusing on the dimensions of crisis – onset, actor behavior and crisis management, superpower activity, involvement by international organizations and outcome; and the application of the lessons of history to the advancement of international peace and world order.

To attain these ends we undertook a large-scale inquiry – the sources, processes and outcomes of military–security crises of all international (state) actors over a 50-year period and across all continents, cultures and political and economic systems in the contemporary era.[7] Its methods are both qualitative and quantitative: studies in depth of perceptions and decisions by a single state;[8] and studies in breadth of aggregate data on approximately 100 variables for a total population of 278 international crises comprising 627 crisis actors.

The ICB Project concentrates on inter-state crises and on the behavior of states under externally generated stress. In so doing, it continues in the tradition associated with, among others, the scholars noted above. At the same time, it analyzes in detail the multiple roles of supra-state actors (League of Nations, United Nations, regional organizations) in crisis management, as well as the (often significant) roles of sub-state actors (e.g., nationalist movements, tribal groups in Africa) as triggering entities, stimuli to state behavior, etc. Moreover, the activity of non-state actors is discussed in the summaries of the 278 international crises in Part V below.

The *raison d'être* for our aggregate study of crises in the twentieth century is both theoretical and policy-oriented in nature. The rationale goes beyond the goal of the traditional crisis literature, sometimes articulated, sometimes implicit, namely, to lessen the probability of *any* violence, that is, to move from "war-like" to "peaceful" crisis management. It is argued here that the presence or absence of violence is only one of many core questions about crises in which academicians and policy-makers should be interested. Many crises do not involve violence, as the ICB *Handbooks* will amply demonstrate. One of the significant questions is why some do – and some do not – escalate to military hostilities. Another focuses on the types of situational changes during a war which lead to more intense violence and its consequences. Thus the rationale for research on crises is not simply the issue of non-violence or violence. Rather, it is the phenomenon of change in the international system, with crisis serving as the master analytical key. Some of those changes are induced, or are accompanied, by violence; some are not. In short, our primary concept is crisis, not violence. And our principal focus is change.

The links between crisis and change are threefold. Crisis erupts from change in the environment. Crisis engenders change in state behavior. And crisis often leads to change in an international system. These links draw attention to the phenomenon of crisis at both unit and system levels which serve as the parallel frameworks of analysis for *Handbooks I* and *II*. These links also help to integrate the distinct concepts of crisis, conflict and war.

Crisis, as the *Handbooks* will reveal, is a much broader phenomenon than war. In fact, war is a subset of crisis, not the reverse; that is, all wars result from crises, but not all crises lead to war. There are, however, crises which occur during a war, that is, intra-war crises. Similarly, crises may occur within, or outside, the setting of a protracted conflict between adversaries. These concepts will be defined and elaborated below.

In the theoretical realm, our inquiry is also designed, as noted earlier, to generate knowledge about all facets of crises, from onset to termination, across time and space. The data on 50 years of crises will facilitate the testing of many hypotheses and thereby contribute to the framing of core generalizations about world politics.

Several policy benefits may also derive from our study of crisis: improved crisis management; control over escalation; and reliable crisis anticipation. If the data support propositions regarding international crises and state behavior, we will have acquired a valid basis for anticipating the likely profile of future crises: those which may occur prior to, or outside the setting of, inter-state war; those which may erupt during a war; and those which may take place within, or outside of, a protracted conflict. An assessment of the relative potency of crisis attributes and dimensions in causing crisis oucomes will enable decision-makers, major powers and international organizations to manage future crises more effectively. Moreover, an understanding of the behavior patterns which accompany the stress generated by crisis situations – in all of those settings – will assist in reducing the likelihood of escalation, from non-violence to violence in crisis management generally and, during a war, from less intense to more acute, more destructive and more widespread violence by the protagonists.

Conceptualization

The first task was to construct definitions at both micro- and macro-levels aspiring to universality in time and space. The goal was to formulate definitions of crisis that are valid and analytically comprehensive. These definitions should incorporate the crucial concepts related to change which permeate the literature. Moreover, it is essential that viable definitions differentiate the two levels of analysis, yet relate them to each other.

> A *foreign policy crisis*, that is, a crisis viewed from the perspective of an individual state, is a situation with three necessary and sufficient conditions deriving from a change in a state's external or internal environment. All three are perceptions held by the highest level decision-makers of the actor concerned: a *threat to basic values*, along with the awareness of *finite time for response* to the external value threat, and a *high probability of involvement in military hostilities*.[9]

A foreign policy crisis is triggered by an event, act or situational change (e.g., the movement of Anglo-American and Yugoslav (Partisan) forces in the vicinity of Trieste, triggering crises for the UK, US and Yugoslavia on 1–2 May 1945; the shelling of the islands of Quemoy and Matsu by the People's Republic of China beginning 3 September 1954, triggering a crisis for the Republic of China on Taiwan and the United States; and Egypt's nationalization of the Suez Canal on 26 July 1956, triggering a crisis for France and the UK). These developments generated the necessary crisis conditions of perceived threat, time constraint and war likelihood. The termination of foreign policy crises is evidenced by the reduction of these stress-creating perceptions towards the pre-crisis level. In the cases noted above, these were, respectively: the withdrawal of Yugoslav troops on 11 June 1945, ending the Trieste Crisis for all three actors; an offer by China's Premier Chou En-lai on 23 April 1955 to negotiate, reducing stress for the US and the PRC; and the acceptance of a cease-fire by Britain and France in the Suez Canal Zone on 6 November 1956, following a Soviet threat to bomb London and Paris.

In all of these illustrations, it must be emphasized, trigger and termination are perceptual in character; that is, a crisis for a state derives from the decision-makers' image of pressures to cope with stress; so too, termination is associated with the awareness of declining turmoil and stress; both are subjective in focus. By contrast, an international crisis is based upon objective behavioral data about conflictual interaction among states within an international system.

> An *international crisis* is a situational change characterized by two necessary and sufficient conditions: (1) distortion in the type and an increase in the intensity of *disruptive interactions* between two or more adversaries, with an accompanying high probability of *military hostilities*, or, during a war, an *adverse change* in the *military balance*; and (2) a *challenge* to the existing *structure* of an international system – global, dominant or subsystem – posed by the higher-than-normal conflictual interactions.

An international crisis erupts with a breakpoint event, act or change, that is, a disturbance which creates a (foreign policy) crisis as defined above for one or more actors. Some illustrations may be noted: the Soviet-supported attempt by Iran's *Tudeh* Party on 23 August 1945 to take over the Azerbaijan capital of Tabriz, the beginning of the Azerbaijan Crisis; the crossing of the Thag La Ridge in the North East Frontier Agency by Chinese forces on 8 September 1962, setting in motion the Sino-Indian Border Crisis; and the dispatch of Egypt's 4th Armored Division into Sinai on 17 May 1967, along with its overflight of Israel's nuclear research center at Dimona the same day, leading to the crisis period of the Six Day War Crisis. These events indicated distortion in existing patterns of inter-state inter-action. International crises end with exitpoints, that is, events which denote a significant reduction in conflictual activity. In the cases noted above, these were, respectively: the withdrawal of Soviet troops from Iran on 9 May 1946; the unilateral declaration of a cease-fire by Beijing on 1 December 1962; and the end of the Six Day War on 11 June 1967.[11]

Every international crisis contains one or more crises for an individual state. Thus international crises which occur in a pre-war setting (Entry into World War II, 1939), during a war (Dien Bien Phu, 1954, with France, the UK and the US as crisis actors, including the serious consideration of using nuclear weapons), or post-war setting (Turkish Straits, 1946), do not differ with respect to the generic conditions of a crisis, namely, disruptive interactions, destabilization, and the military dimension (either the likelihood of an outbreak of military hostilities or of a change in the military balance).

It is these disruptive interactions, accompanied by the likelihood of violence or, during a war, the escalation of violence, and the challenge posed by these crises to the stability of international systems, which are at the heart of these *Handbooks* and the in-depth case studies. Stated differently, a major focus of ICB research is system discontinuities that affect decision-making processes. Thus intra-war crises (IWCs) – like defeat in a major battle (Stalingrad in 1943) or the dropping of an atomic bomb on Japan in 1945, leading to its surrender – profoundly affected the decisions of German and Japanese leaders during World War II. So too did the Tet Offensive in 1968 for the United States. Indeed, the effects were more significant in terms of the sweep of world politics than the consequences of many non-IWC crises on behavior and subsequent events. It is precisely the relationship between the stress of crisis, on the one hand, and decisions, on the other, whether the stress is created in a non-war setting or during a war, that is a central focus of our inquiry.

Since IWCs share the generic conditions of crisis, as noted above, they are integrated into the overall set of 278 international crises from 1929 to 1979 – for purposes of data presentation in Part III below. At the same time, intra-war crises have one distinctive attribute, the setting of a war in process. Thus they can be separated from the pre-war cases and analyzed as a distinctive subset of crises, as can other segments of a vast and multifaceted body of data, such as everything related to the geographic dimension of crises, or a specific time/polarity frame, e.g., crises in the bipolar system 1945–62, or subsystem crises or superpower cases, etc. Readers are encouraged to impose a variety of cuts on the data for purposes of testing a wide range of hypotheses relating to crisis, conflict and war. The authors themselves will analyze several such subsets of data in *Handbook II*, including a comparison of pre-war and intra-war crises.

Comparative analyses across region, polarity, power discrepancy, level of system, protracted conflict and other salient features to be examined in *Handbook I* are aimed at enriching our understanding of crises at the international level. Such questions as (1) the relationship between the attributes of actors and their propensity for crisis involvement; and (2) the relationship between the type of trigger and the duration and outcomes of crises, are among those to be explored in *Handbook II*.

The aggregate study of international crises has two distinguishing characteristics. First, it is cross-national in scope. Second, it is quantitative in form.

More than 100 states appear as crisis actors at least once during the period under inquiry; some states experienced frequent crises (e.g., the US, 47), leading to a total of 627 actor-cases. Two types of analysis probe the cross-national nature of the data set. One, explicitly descriptive, explores the temporal distributions of various crisis phenomena. Basic attributes of crisis will be examined, such as sources, or triggers, the issue-areas into which certain types of crises tend to cluster, the gravity of threat in crises, crisis management techniques and their outcomes. The other seeks to describe the nature of the international system at the time of the crisis, the extent and type of great power/superpower activity, international and/or regional organization involvement and similar systemic considerations.

The second major characteristic of the aggregate data set, known as CRISBANK, is its quantitative form, which will permit the use of statistical techniques to search for patterns of relations in subsequent volumes of analysis. This facilitates our move beyond crisis description to the testing of propositions in the international relations literature, in an effort to explain the occurrence of various crisis phenomena.

In searching for the optimal block of time for the analysis of crises we selected 1929–79. Several considerations shaped our choice of this time frame. First, it maximizes the bases for comparison: crises in multipolar, bipolar and polycentric international systems with diverse global and regional organizations. Second, by incorporating the hundred new actors emerging at the end of the European imperial era, we achieve great variation in such characteristics of states as their age, size of territory, population, regime type, regime duration, belief system, economic development and so forth. Third, we can thereby explore the crisis-laden years of Germany's reascent to major power status and the approach of World War II, 1933–39, as well as the profusion of crises in Africa during the last half of the 1970s. Finally, the set of cases to be generated would be large enough to permit statistical analysis of the aggregate data.

For the half-century under inquiry, every international crisis falls within one of the following periods of system polarity:

multipolar	1929–39
World War II	1939–45
bipolar	1945–62
polycentric	1963–79

One of these periods is complete, with unquestioned onset and termination dates, namely, World War II (1939–45). While it is similar to the preceding decade, with many centers of power, it also resembles the succeeding period, with two coalitions of power in direct confrontation. In essence, it stands apart from both, for it is characterized by extreme inter-bloc hostility and intra-bloc cohesion, in a hegemonic war of the most intense violence. Another of the four system-periods, bipolarity (1945–62), accords with recognized demarcation points in twentieth-century world politics, beginning with the emergence of the US and the USSR as hegemonic powers in the aftermath of global war and ending with the 1962 Cuban Missile Crisis. The decade 1929–39 is part of the inter-war multipolar system. And the polycentric system (1963–79) continues into the 1980s. (The rationale for the four periods is elaborated below in the discussion of polarity as a control.) The choice of 1979 as the terminal date was dictated by the paucity of data on later cases. As for 1929, the enormity of our data collection and our judgment that a decade of multipolarity provided sufficient data for comparative analysis led to closure with half a century of international crises.

Data have been collected on four sets of variables, two at the micro/state level, two at the macro/international level: actor attributes and actor-case dimensions; crisis attributes and crisis dimensions. Data on the first two sets relate to the year of the crisis for each crisis actor, that is, every state whose decision-makers perceive as directly relevant to them the conditions of threat, time and war likelihood, noted above. A codebook was designed for that purpose. Research has yielded a set of descriptive data on 627 actor-cases in the period 1929–79. In addition, a separate codebook was designed to tap crisis attributes and crisis dimensions at the international level. The contents of the macro-level codebook and the macro-level data are set out in Parts II and III below. Their micro-level counterparts are presented in the companion *Handbook*.

All variables within this inquiry are incorporated into a two-level conceptual scheme. For the international crisis as a whole, that is, at the macro-level (Figure I.1.A), there are seven clusters of Crisis Dimensions – Setting, Breakpoint–Exitpoint, Crisis Management Technique, Great Power/Superpower Activity, International Organization Involvement, Outcome and Severity. Each variable cluster contains one or more specific variables, as indicated in the Map. There are also six controls – Geography, Polarity, System Level, Conflict, Power Discrepancy, Involvement by Powers – to be elaborated in the pages that follow.

As is evident in Figure I.1.B., there are five clusters of Crisis Dimensions at the actor level – Trigger, Actor Behavior, Great Power/Superpower Activity, International Organization Involvement and Outcome. There is an array of controls, both context and type – the macro-level controls noted above, along with war – and six clusters of Actor Attributes as controls – Age, Territory, Regime, Capability, Values and Conditions. For purposes of explanatory analysis, the assumption is that national attributes, as well as contextual variables, will condition both the propensity to become involved in crises and behavior patterns exhibited in those crises.[12] For example, actor behavior incorporates four components – namely, the crisis actor's major response, its technique(s) of crisis management, and the centrality

CRISIS DIMENSIONS

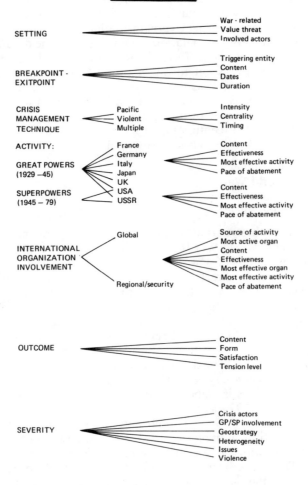

CONTROLS

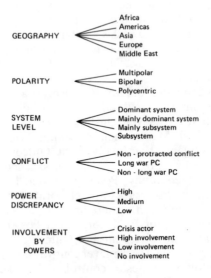

FIGURE I.1.A. Conceptual Map: Macro-Level.

CRISIS DIMENSIONS

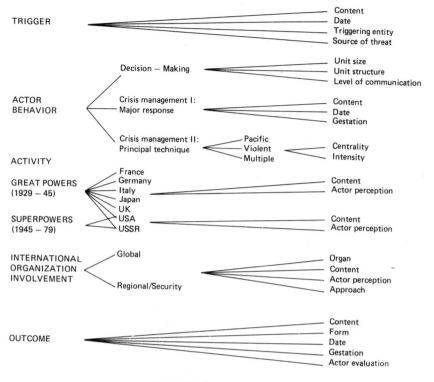

CONTROLS

A. CONTEXT

B. ACTOR ATTRIBUTES

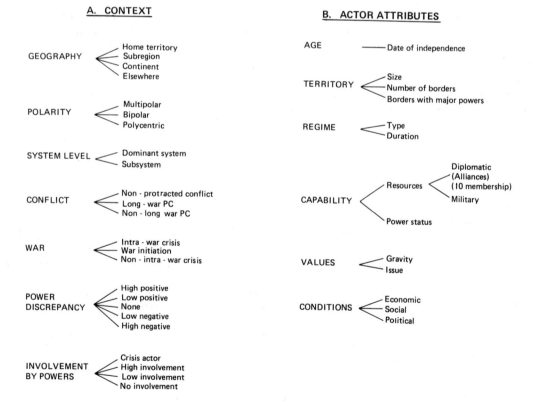

FIGURE I.1.B. Conceptual Map: Micro-Level.

and intensity of violence where it occurs. (Definitions and coding rules for attributes and dimensions at the macro-level are provided in Part III below; definitions and coding rules at the micro-level are contained in *Handbook II*.)

Figure I.1.A. implies a focus on certain macro-level questions which guided our investigation. Some of these may now be elucidated.

Setting	— Did a crisis occur during a war, that is, was it an intra-war crisis (IWC), or did it erupt ouside the context of a war? — What was the highest value perceived to be threatened by any crisis actor in an international crisis, along a scale from a threat to existence to a limited threat to population and/or property? — How many states were involved in a crisis, as perceived by the crisis actor?
Breakpoint–Exitpoint	— Which state(s) or non-state actor(s) triggered an international crisis by generating a crisis situation for the first actor in a crisis cluster? — What was the specific event(s), act(s) or situational change(s) which catalyzed disruptive interactions between two or more adversaries by generating the three perceptual conditions of crisis – threat, time and war likelihood – for the first crisis actor in the international crisis? — When did the first breakpoint, that is, the trigger for the first crisis actor, occur? — When did the international crisis end, that is, a decline in perceived threat by the last actor to exit the crisis? — What was the duration of the crisis – from the first breakpoint to the last exitpoint?
Crisis Management Technique (CMT)	— Of all the primary CMTs used by the crisis actors, what was the highest, along a scale from violence to non-violent military, non-military pressure, adjudication, arbitration, mediation and negotiation?
Great Power/Superpower Activity	— To what extent was a great power/US/USSR involved in the crisis?[13] — How effective was its activity in abating the crisis, that is, in preventing hostilities or contributing to the termination of the crisis? — Which activity by a power was most effective in crisis abatement? — Did the activity by a power affect the rapidity of crisis abatement?
International Organization Involvement[14]	— Who initiated third party intervention by the global or regional organization in the crisis as a whole? — Which organ of the League/UN – or regional organization – was most active in the crisis as a whole? — What was the most intense type of involvement by the League/UN/regional organization? — How effective was this involvement in abating the crisis? — What was the most effective type of international organization involvement in the crisis? — Did international organization involvement affect the rapidity of abatement of the crisis as a whole?[15]
Outcome	— What was the outcome of the crisis as a whole—ambiguous or definitive? — What was the form of outcome of the crisis between the adversaries? — Was there a consensus about the outcome or was there a mixed reception by the adversaries? — How did the crisis outcome affect the tension level between the adversaries during the 5 years following the termination of the crisis – was there escalation or reduction?

Severity — How many states were direct participants in the crisis?
— What was the extent of great power/superpower adversarial involvement in the crisis—from aloofness to direct military intervention?
— How broad was the geostrategic salience of the crisis – from one subsystem to the global system?
— How many attribute differences were there between the adversaries (military capability, economic development, political regime, culture)?
— How many – and which – issues were the foci of contention in the crisis?
— What was the extent of violence – from none to full-scale war?[16]

In sum, our aggregate research at the macro-level is designed to describe seven clusters of crisis dimensions as delineated in the Map: setting (IWC/non-IWC, value threat, number of involved actors); breakpoint–exitpoint (content, dates, duration); crisis management techniques; activity by the powers and international organizations (content and effectiveness in crisis abatement); outcome (content, form, legacy); and severity (number of crisis actors, major power involvement, geostrategy, heterogeneity, issues and violence). So too with five clusters of actor-case dimensions at the micro-level: trigger (content, date, source); actor behavior (major response, techniques of crisis management and the centrality and intensity of violence); the activity of great powers/superpowers and international organizations in a specific state's crisis (content, and the crisis actor's perception thereof); and outcome (substance, form and evaluation by the crisis actor).

Actor–System Linkages In all branches of knowledge there are several levels of analysis, each with distinct concepts, research questions and methodologies. Every level is capable of illuminating a segment of knowledge within a discipline, but no more. To provide insights into a part of any whole is admirable. However, the ultimate challenge is to link the findings at all levels into an aggregate of the whole and its parts in order to comprehend as much as possible of the total universe of knowledge in any field.[17]

Our point of departure is the conviction that the focus on a single level of analysis is inadequate. To examine the two levels of crisis – unit and system – would enable us to move beyond the position of blind men attempting to grasp the elephant. North's (1967: 394) advice for the IR field in general is apt:

> As research scholars and would-be theorists in international relations we might all derive at least three useful lessons from the old fable about the blind men and the elephant. The first is that the elephant [crisis] presumably existed; the second is that each of the groping investigators at the unit and system levels, despite sensory and conceptual limitations, had his fingers on a part of reality; and the third is that if they had quieted the uproar and begun making comparisons, the blind men might – all of them – have moved considerably closer to the truth.

It is in this spirit that we approach the task of linking the unit (micro-) and system (macro-) levels of crisis analysis.

The focus of the unit level is images held, and actions taken, by the decision-makers of one state. The focus of the system level is interactions among states in an international crisis. There is no one-to-one relationship between actor and systemic crisis: the former occurs for a single state; the latter is predicated upon the existence of distortion in the pattern of interaction between two or more adversaries in a system.

At the unit level there are crisis actors, that is, states whose decision-makers perceive the three conditions of crisis. There are parallel concepts at the system level. For the threat component the counterparts are values of decision-makers and structure of the system. Basic values, such as existence, influence in the global and/or regional systems, territorial integrity, economic welfare, and others are the elements which guide goals, decisions and actions of states. Similarly, at the system level, structure provides the setting for continuity in interaction processes. Threat at the actor level indicates (subjective) perceptions by decision-makers. Challenge at the system level means an (objective) possibility of change in the structure. A

Component	Level	
	Unit (Perception)	System (Reality)
Threat	threat to basic values	challenge to system structure
Time	finite time for decisions	*
Violence	increase in war likelihood	increase in disruptive interaction

* Time is relevant to, but is not a *necessary condition* of, an international crisis, unlike "finite time," that is, the awareness by decision-makers of time constraints on their response to perceived threat, in a unit-level definition of crisis. At the macro-level, time does not have an analogous function. It merely designates the duration of an international crisis, from the first breakpoint event, a disturbance to the system in the form of a trigger to a crisis for one or several states, to the final exitpoint, which denotes a significant reduction in conflictual activity within the system, as indicated in the text illustrations above of the Azerbaijan Crisis in 1945–46, the Sino-Indian Border Crisis in 1962, and the 1967 Six Day War.

FIGURE I.2. Unit- and System-Level Crisis Components.

challenge to the structure may or may not materialize, just as a threat to basic values may or may not be realized (Figure I.2).

In the 1948–49 Berlin Blockade Crisis, the threat to Soviet and US–UK–France influence in Germany and, more generally, in the international system, generated a sharp increase in conflictual interaction. This distortion, the counterpart of an increase in perceived likelihood of military hostilities, posed a challenge to the existing structure of the system, namely, to the number of actors (two or more Germanies) and the tighter polarization around the superpowers as a result of the crisis.

A crisis may thus be addressed in macro- and micro-terms. While the former deals with an international crisis as a whole, the latter focuses on each crisis actor. There are situational changes in which only one state perceives a crisis for itself, that is, action(s) by one (or more) state(s) which trigger(s) images of threat, time pressure and war likelihood for a single actor (e.g., the massing of Indian demonstrators on the border with Goa in 1955, creating a crisis for Portugal). In other instances, two or more states experience a crisis over the same issue, as with the Western Powers and the USSR over Berlin in 1948–49, 1957–59 and 1961.

The link between unit- and system-level concepts of crisis may be illustrated by two different cases: when a crisis for all actors is identical in time; and when their crises overlap but are not identical in time. Establishing this link requires the clarification of static and dynamic concepts at both levels. The former are trigger/termination at the unit level and breakpoint/exitpoint at the system level. The latter are escalation/de-escalation and distortion/accommodation, respectively (Figure I.3).

Nature of concept	Level	
	Unit	System
Static	trigger/termination	breakpoint/exitpoint
Dynamic	escalation/de-escalation	distortion/accommodation

FIGURE I.3. Static and Dynamic Concepts of Crisis.

At the actor level, a trigger, a static act, is defined as the catalyst to a crisis. In the 1948–49 Berlin Blockade Crisis the trigger to the Soviet Union's crisis was the publication by the Western Powers on 7 June 1948 of the recommendations of the March London Conference for the integration of their three zones of occupation. The trigger for the United States, Britain and France was the Soviet decision on 24 June to block all Western transportation into and out of Berlin. In terms of a dynamic process, a trigger denotes an escalation in perceived threat, time pressure and the likelihood of military hostilities.

The termination of a crisis at the actor level is the point in time when decision-makers' perceptions of threat, time pressure and war likelihood decline to a level approximating that which existed prior to the crisis trigger. In the Berlin case, the termination date for each of the Four Powers was 12 May 1949, when an agreement regarding West and East Germany as separate entities was signed. Thus the triggers did not coincide, but the termination dates for the various actors did so.

In dynamic process terms, termination for crisis actors marks the final de-escalation in perceived threat, time pressure and war likelihood during a crisis.

At the macro-level, parallel notions exist—breakpoint and exitpoint as counterparts of trigger and termination. A breakpoint is a disturbance to the system created by the entry of an actor into a crisis. An international crisis, as noted, erupts with an initial breakpoint event, such as the Western Powers' challenge to Moscow on 7 June 1948 regarding the integration of their zones of occupation. In dynamic terms, this change denoted distortion in the pattern of East–West interaction. Similarly, an exitpoint refers to a significant reduction in conflictual activity, such as the formal agreement among the Four Powers on 12 May 1949 about the future of Germany and the lifting of the blockade. This change indicates accommodation, that is, a shift to a less intense level of hostile interaction than that during the crisis.

The duration of an international crisis is measured from the first breakpoint to the last exitpoint which, in unit-level terms, means from the trigger for the first actor to termination for the last actor. For the initial breakpoint to occur there must be two or more adversarial actors in higher-than-normal conflictual interaction. Both or all may become crisis actors simultaneously, a rare occurrence, for this requires triggers on the same day, as in the 1965 India–Pakistan Crisis over Kutch. More often, they comprise one crisis actor and one adversary who triggers the crisis; the latter may later become a crisis actor, as with Belgium and the Congo in the 1960 Congo Crisis,[18] or it may not. A variant is one initial crisis actor and one adversary, with the latter joined by another in the process of becoming crisis actors, as with the US and the USSR-cum-Cuba in the 1962 Missile Crisis.[19] Another variation is one crisis actor at the outset with several adversaries who later become crisis actors simultaneously, as with the USSR and the US–UK–France in the 1948–49 Berlin Blockade Crisis. As for the winding down of an international crisis, the majority of cases reveal a simultaneous termination for all crisis actors and, therefore, simultaneous accommodation by the system, as in the Berlin and India–Pakistan cases noted above.

Distortion may be gradual or rapid; so too with accommodation. In general, international crises are characterized by initial and subsequent breakpoints, that is, gradual distortion and, by contrast, few exitpoints, that is, rapid accommodation. The reason is that the onset of an international crisis is usually a process in which crisis actors cumulatively challenge one another. The result is that breakpoints tend to differ in time, and, therefore, distortion is gradual. Accommodation, however, usually requires agreement, either formal or tacit. Thus exitpoints tend to coincide in time. However, as long as any crisis actor has not terminated its crisis, accommodation has not yet been completed: termination of the unit-level crisis for the last participant and the end of the international crisis are identical in time.

Breakpoints and exitpoints also indicate the entry or departure of actors in an international crisis. Each breakpoint denotes an increase in conflictual interaction relative to the pre-crisis phase whereas exitpoints signal accommodation at the system level. Linking the unit analysis to the system analysis, the effects of trigger/termination on breakpoints/exitpoints are immediate and direct; that is, a trigger at the unit level always denotes a breakpoint at the system level and thus a further distortion in international interaction. In the Berlin case, both 7 June and 24 June 1948, which were triggers at the unit level for the Soviet Union and the Western Powers, respectively, were also immediate breakpoints in the macro-level crisis. However, when international crisis is linked downward to actors, the effects of exitpoints on de-escalation are immediate and direct for some but may be delayed and indirect for others. Stated differently, not all system-level changes affect all units at once and equally in a readily identifiable way. The Berlin Blockade Crisis provides an example of direct and immediate effects: the last systemic exitpoint on 12 May 1949 denotes final de-escalation for the Four Powers. In general, international crises have more significant effects than unit-level crises because they pose a dual danger, namely, to the structure of the system and to its actors, whereas unit-level crises affect actors only.

In summary, an international crisis requires behavioral change on the part of at least two adversarial actors leading to more intense conflictual interaction. Although a crisis is catalyzed by behavioral actions, these actions, the trigger to an actor-level crisis, can always be traced to their perceptual origin. Here lies the organic link between the two levels of crisis.

Controls

The macro-level data for 50 years of international crises will be presented and analyzed, variable by variable, in *Handbook I*. The data at the micro-level on individual crisis actors will be presented in *Handbook II*. In the course of our dissection of the system-level data, it has become apparent that this is often aided by the introduction of control variables. Such controls allow us to highlight patterns which are often obscured when data across 50 years and 278 cases are aggregated. Six control variables have been utilized in the descriptive analysis of the data for international crises: Geography, Polarity, System Level, Conflict, Power Discrepancy and Involvement by Powers. The conceptual basis of these controls will now be discussed. (Rules governing the use of these controls are set out in Part II below.)

The first control variable in the analysis of ICB data is *Geography*. Each international crisis can be identified in space: e.g., the Chinese Eastern Railway Crisis of 1929 in East Asia; the Austria Putsch Crisis of 1934 in Central Europe; the Israel Independence Crisis of 1948–49 in the Middle East; the Ethiopia–Somalia Crisis of 1977–78 in East Africa; and the Beagle Channel Crisis of 1978–79 in South America. Initially, each crisis is located in one of 18 geographic sub-regions. For purposes of analysis these are collapsed into five regions, namely, Africa, Americas, Asia, Europe and the Middle East (see Tables II.1 and II.2 below).

Whether an international crisis occurs in one region or another will impinge on its configuration; many crisis dimensions are likely to be affected by this spatial aspect – crisis management techniques, great power/superpower activity, international organization involvement and outcomes. So too will some crisis attributes, as delineated in the Conceptual Map. Herein is the rationale for using geography as a control variable.

Polarity, as used in this inquiry, refers to the number of power centers in a relevant international system. Theoretically, a system may be unipolar, bipolar or multipolar, with variations like polycentric.

A *unipolar* structure is characterized by an overwhelming concentration of military capability in one entity which thereby shapes the rules of the system, dominates relations among its lesser actors and asserts its suzerainty at will from its acknowledged position at the apex of the power pyramid. Rome at the height of its power and authority was a notable example of unipolarity in the international system. The Ch'in Empire in China (221–207 B.C.) was another. Although neither the global system nor the dominant international system exhibited unipolarity during the half-century under inquiry, the Americas approximated a unipolar structure throughout this period, with the United States as the hegemonial power, as did Eastern Europe since 1948, under Soviet hegemony. Moreover, like the unit-veto system[20] or other theoretical constructs, unipolarity may pervade world politics in the future.

Bipolarity indicates a concentration of power in two relatively equal actors. They may be individual units in a system, loose or tight coalitions, or variations thereof (e.g., the Ch'i- and Ch'u-led alliances of north and south states during the later phase of the "Spring and Autumn" period of the Chinese state system, 771–483 B.C.; the Athens-led bloc and the Sparta-led Peloponnesian League in the Greek city-state system from 431 B.C. onwards; the Triple Alliance and the Triple Entente in the early twentieth century). Bipolarity in an international political system is not the exact counterpart of duopoly in an economic system, just as unipolarity denotes less than a monopoly of power. Nevertheless, the two polar centers possess recognized preeminence in determining the essential rules of the system, the conditions of stability, the limits of independent behavior by bloc members or unaffiliated actors, and the outcomes of major wars in the system.

Bipolarity, in the sense of two concentrations of military power, has characterized the global system since the end of World War II. However, in the wider meaning of hostile centers of power and decision the term applies to the period 1945 to late 1962. And even within that time frame there have been distinct phases: embryonic bipolarity, from the end of World War II to the summer of 1948, when the power preeminence of the US and the USSR (and the emerging bloc structure) had not yet fully crystallized; tight bipolarity, referring to two centers of decision, as well as power, an emergent reality with two "turning-point" developments closely related in time – Communist hegemony in Czechoslovakia

(February 1948) and the eruption of the Berlin Blockade Crisis (June 1948), culminating in the formal creation of NATO in 1949 and the Warsaw Pact in 1955; the entry of the Soviet Union into the nuclear club in 1949, superimposed upon its conventional military power, marked the advent of bipolarity in the power sense; and loose bipolarity was ushered in by the passive cooperation of the superpowers in the Suez Crisis (October–November 1956).

Multipolarity signifies a diffusion of power among several relatively equal units within an international system, at least three (tripolar), usually more (e.g., long stretches of time during the Chou dynasty in China, 1122–221 B.C.; the Greek city-state system prior to the Peloponnesian War, with Athens, Sparta, Corinth, Thebes and others dominating the behavior of weaker units; Italy in the fifteenth century, the principal units being Venice, Milan, Genoa, Florence and Naples; and most of the Western state system, 1648–1919). The diffusion of power led to a flexible alliance configuration and the ubiquity of violence in "international" relations.

The decade from 1929 to 1939, in fact the entire inter-World War period, was a multipolar system *par excellence*, with seven relatively equal great powers recognized by each other and by all other members of the system as sharing the apex of the power pyramid: France, Germany, Great Britain, Italy, Japan, the Soviet Union and the United States. For most of that period Great Britain was first among equals, and Italy was the weakest of the seven. However, unlike unipolarity and bipolarity, the structure of the inter-World War system was characterized by flexibility in alliance pattern, multiple centers of power and decision and uncertainty about behavior by the other great powers in the system.

The period 1939–45 was, as noted, essentially a self-contained transition from the multipolar system of the 1930s to the bipolar system after 1945; that is, it exhibits many centers of decision, resembling the former, along with intense inter-coalition conflict and intra-coalition cohesion, like the latter. There were, too, some changes in the power hierarchy: France ceased to be a great power from June 1940 until the end of the War; so too did Italy from 1943 onwards; and Germany replaced Great Britain as the preeminent member of the group, effectively a superpower from the fall of Western Europe in the spring of 1940 until the defeat at Stalingrad in early 1943. An additional reason for treating World War II (1 September 1939–2 September 1945) as a distinctive block of time in terms of polarity is that nearly all international crises during that period were intra-war crises, whose principal dimensions – trigger (breakpoint), actor behavior, great power activity and outcome – were affected by the setting of an ongoing war of very great intensity.

Polycentrism identifies a hybrid structure with two preeminent centers of power and multiple centers of autonomous decision. As such, it resembles both bipolarity and multipolarity. This duality was present in earlier international systems (e.g., Napoleonic France and the coalition of traditional European powers – England, Austria, Prussia and Russia – exhibiting power bipolarity, but with each state a separate decisional unit). The term polycentrism, however, began to emerge in the late 1950s, during the phase of loose bipolarity. Its two notable manifestations were China's withdrawal from the Soviet bloc from 1957 onwards and France's military disassociation from NATO, a process dating from soon after de Gaulle's return to power in 1958. Both were slow to mature and were accompanied by the development of two self-consciously independent centers of power, though qualitatively inferior to the military capability of the superpowers. These were symbolized by France's determined retention of her nuclear strike force, the *force de frappe*, and China's first nuclear explosion in 1964. While a precise date marking the onset of polycentrism is uncertain, we have chosen the immediate aftermath of the Cuban Missile Crisis and the Sino-Indian border war, both in October–November 1962: in the former, the superpowers withdrew from the brink of nuclear war, dramatizing the constraints on overwhelming military capability; in the latter, the deepening Sino-Soviet split became irrevocable. Together they indicated that power bipolarity and decision bipolarity are not synonymous and that other centers of decision in the international system could no longer be controlled by the US and the USSR.[21] These developments point up conceptual distinctions and similarities. Multipolarity is characterized by wide dispersion among many centers of power, while polycentrism retains the essential bipolar centralization of power in the hands of the US and the USSR. They are similar in that they both have many centers of decision.

The underlying assumption in the selection of polarity as a control variable is that the structural configuration of power and decision in an international system will affect the dimensions of crisis and crisis behavior, from trigger (breakpoint) to outcome.[22]

A third control variable in the analysis of ICB data is *System Level*. Every international crisis occurs – exclusively or primarily – within the dominant system or in one of several regional subsystems, which together constitute the global international system. The dominant system is identified by many international relations theorists with interaction among the great powers in world politics or, in the Singer–Small formulation (1972: 381), with "the most powerful, industrialized, and diplomatically active members of the interstate system, generally coinciding with the 'European state system'." For the half-century of our study, this meant the European great powers, the US and Japan in the 1930s, the US–USSR inter-bloc system since 1945. The two most frequently recognized attributes of a subsystem are geographic proximity and regular interaction among its members. Others cited are intra-relatedness, external recognition as a distinctive region, self-identification, shared bonds, inferior military capability, evidence of integration, etc. M. Haas (1970: 101), drawing on Brecher's earlier (1963) formulation, specified delimited scope, with primary emphasis on a geographical region, at least two actors and a "relatively self-contained network of political interactions between the members, involving such activities as goal attainment, adaptation, pattern maintenance, and integration and dealing with power relations and military interaction."[23]

The Chaco Crises of 1928–29 and 1932–35 took place in the South American subsystem. There were also crises which were predominantly subsystem in focus, but with a spillover to the dominant system, usually when one or more great power(s)/superpower(s) was a crisis actor: an illustration is Angola in 1975–76 (Southern Africa). Crises may also be classified as primarily dominant system level in focus, for example, the Ussuri River Crisis in 1969. And finally, there were many dominant system crises *per se*, such as the Berlin Crises of 1948–49, 1957–59 and 1961. Underlying the choice of system level as a control is the expectation that this contextual aspect of a crisis, namely, the level at which a crisis occurs, will, like geography and polarity, affect many of its dimensions and attributes, including extent of violence, the effectiveness of third party intervention, the form of outcome, etc.

Some international crises occur in a setting unburdened by long-term hostility. Others erupt in a context of prolonged dispute between two or more actors over several issues, with a legacy of periodic violence and the spillover effects of cumulative crises between the same adversaries on other domains of their relationship, in short, an environment of protracted *Conflict*. According to Azar *et al.* (1978: 53), a protracted conflict is characterized by: extended duration; fluctuating interaction; spillover of hostility into all aspects of relations; strong forces tending to restore equilibrium, and indefinite continuation of the conflict.

This definition was applied by Azar *et al.* to the Arab–Israel Conflict, now 40 years old, with a highly conflictual relationship punctured by six major outbursts of violence (1948–49, 1956, 1967, 1969–70, 1973–74, 1982), with persistent hostility over political, cultural, economic and territorial issues, and a slow painful process towards accommodation, highlighted by a formal peace agreement between one pair of adversaries, Egypt–Israel. The Arab–Israel Conflict, however, is not unique in recent world politics. There are comparable conflicts between China and Japan, East and West (the US- and USSR-led blocs), India and Pakistan, the two Vietnams, Ethiopia and Somalia, Greece and Turkey, etc. All are lengthy, some of them lasting several decades or more. All have fluctuated in intensity: many have moved from war to partial accommodation and back to violence (e.g., India and Pakistan since 1947); others have been characterized by continuous war, but of varying severity (Vietnam 1964–75). All have aroused intense animosities among the actors, with spillover to a broad spectrum of issues. Marginal disputes have been highly salient to the adversaries. And conflict termination has yet to occur in most of them.

The distinction between crises which are context-specific and those occurring within a protracted conflict provides the rationale for this control variable. More precisely, it is assumed that there are differences between crises within and outside of protracted conflicts, and that the multiple attribute of protractedness affects all of the dimensions of an international crisis: type of breakpoint; value threatened; crisis management, in particular, the role of violence; involvement by the great powers/superpowers and its effects; the activity and effectiveness of international organizations in crisis abatement; and the substance and form of crisis outcomes. The use of protracted conflict as a control on our data will uncover the effects of long-term, multiple-issue hostility on other crisis dimensions.[24]

Power Discrepancy refers to the capability gap between adversaries, whether they be individual states or coalitions. As with polarity and other controls, the rationale for using power discrepancy as a control variable is the assumption that differences in capability – and the extent of the gap – will affect some, perhaps all, crisis dimensions after the breakpoint: that is, the crisis management behavior of the more – and less – powerful; the type and degree of third party intervention by great powers/superpowers and international organizations, and its effectiveness; and the substance and form of outcome.

As an operational control in the analysis of crisis, discrepancy derives from the concept of potential power or capability which determines the power of an actor relative to a specific international crisis. Capability incorporates several types of resources: human (size of population); economic (a composite of several components, notably GNP); diplomatic (alliance relationships *vis-à-vis* great powers/superpowers); geographic (size of territory); and military (conventional and nuclear weapons, as well as military expenditure).

The extent of Power Discrepancy in a crisis ranges from none, when all adversaries are at the same level of capability (e.g., Rwanda-Burundi Crisis 1964), to maximal discrepancy, when the principal adversaries are a superpower and a small power (e.g., Mayaguez Crisis 1975 between the US and Cambodia).

Involvement by Great Powers or *Superpowers* in international crisis incorporates two elements – content and effectiveness. Superpowers possess all component-resources of power – human, economic, diplomatic, geographic and military – in such quality and quantity as to give them, in the nuclear age, a veto over the survival of the system and all its members (US, USSR).[25] The great powers' composite of the five components gives to their foreign policy decisions a far-reaching impact on crisis outcomes in their region and on global politics other than the survival of the system.

The content of activity by one or more of the powers takes one of several forms: political (e.g., President Kennedy's dispatch of a special envoy in an effort to restore disrupted transit and trade between Afghanistan and Pakistan in 1961); economic – financial aid or withholding of aid (an economic and technical aid agreement between the USSR and Afghanistan during the latter's 1961 crisis with Pakistan); semi-military – such as the dispatch of military aid or advisors, without direct participation in the fighting (the US airlift of military aid to India in November 1962, during its border war with China); and direct military intervention (the USSR invasion of Czechoslovakia, August 1968).

Effectiveness of superpower/great power activity for crisis abatement extends from the most positive to negative: the single most important contributor (e.g., British mediation in the 1932 Shanghai Crisis between China and Japan); an important impact (the Soviet role of mediation in the second Kashmir Crisis of 1965, culminating in the Tashkent Agreement); a marginal effect (the UK–France–Italy protest note to Lithuania during the Kaunas Trials Crisis in March 1935); and escalation of the crisis (the US–UK announcements, on 8 October 1953, of their intention to withdraw their troops and relinquish their administration of Trieste to the Italian Government, in the crisis between Yugoslavia and Italy).

The dynamics of an international crisis cannot be impervious to the extent of participation by the powers, ranging from a role as crisis actors to aloofness. What the powers do is also likely to affect the role of international organizations. The outcome of a crisis, too, will be influenced by the activity of great powers/superpowers. And other aspects of a crisis may be shaped by the activity or inactivity of the most powerful members of the system. These assumptions underlie our choice of great power/superpower behavior as one of the controls in the data analysis to follow.

The framework for this *Handbook* has been introduced, along with core definitions, key research questions, an approach to linkage of the macro- and micro-levels of analysis and the controls to be applied to the data.[26] In the following chapter, the procedures used in data collection and related methodological questions will be discussed. Thereafter, a guide to the entire macro-level data set will be provided in the form of a master table containing eight attributes, from duration to outcome, for each of the 278 international crises.

Notes

1. The first of many data-based publications – by North, O. R. Holsti, Brody, Zinnes and others – was by Zinnes, North and Koch (1961). The principal quantitative findings were incorporated in Holsti (1972). A companion volume by Nomikos and North (1976) presented a detailed narrative of events.

2. This volume contains papers prepared following a symposium in April 1967 sponsored by the Center of International Studies at Princeton University. Authors include Hermann, Holsti, McClelland, Paige, and Snyder, noted above, as well as James A. Robinson, Howard H. Lentner, Thomas W. Milburn, David C. Schwartz, Dina A. Zinnes, Joseph L. Zinnes, and Robert D. McClure.

3. For attempts to overcome this *lacuna* see Dawisha (1984), George (1983), Horelick (1964), Kaplan (1981), Triska and Finley (1968), Valenta (1979), and Wilkenfeld and Brecher (1982).

4. See, for example, Stremlau (1977) and Whiting (1960).

5. This is indirectly explored in M. Singer (1972).

6. For insightful surveys of the theoretically oriented literature see O. R. Holsti (1979), Hopple and Rossa (1981), Tanter (1979) and M. Haas (1986).

7. One of the major constraints on research into crises has been the paucity of reliable data about their range, volume and content in any historical era or geographic region. This has been partly overcome by some recently published inventories of international crises and related phenomena – conflicts, incidents and militarized disputes: Blechman and Kaplan (1978); Butterworth (1976); Donelan and Grieve (1973); E. Haas (1983); Hazlewood and Hays (1976); Kaplan (1981); Maoz (1982); Moore *et al.* (1975); and Zacher (1979).

8. The ICB studies in depth published so far are : Brecher with Geist (1980); A. I. Dawisha (1980); Shlaim (1983); Dowty (1984); K. Dawisha (1984); and Jukes (1985).

9. For an elaboration see Brecher (1979). Our point of departure was Hermann's (1969: 414) widely-accepted view of a crisis for a state as "a situation that (1) threatens high-priority goals of the decision-making unit, (2) restricts the amount of time available for response before the decision is transformed, and (3) surprises the members of the decision-making unit by its occurrence." Extensive discussions led to a compelling case for revision. The ICB definition incorporates five specific changes: (a) the deletion of *surprise*, in light of the discovery that many threat-time situations were not unanticipated (e.g., the 1961 Berlin Wall Crisis for the United States); (b) the addition of *perceived probability of war*, or, more precisely, perceived likelihood of military hostilities, without which crisis-induced stress leading to effects on coping and choice is absent or marginal; this condition of crisis is also emphasized by Snyder and Diesing (1977: 6–7): "The centerpiece of (the) definition is 'the perception of a dangerously high probability of war' by the governments involved.. . . The perceived probability must at least be high enough to evoke feelings of fear and tension to an uncomfortable degree;" (c) the replacement of short time by *finite time* for the major response, since many responses to crises occur weeks or months after the trigger date (e.g., the Soviet Union's Berlin Deadline Crisis 1957-59: it was triggered by a NATO announcement on 15 December 1957 regarding an intended deployment of nuclear missiles; and it responded on 10 November 1958 with a declared intention to transfer control over East Berlin to the GDR; (d) the inclusion of *internal* environmental changes as potential triggers to crises (e.g., a military coup against Archbishop Makarios on 15 July 1974 triggered a crisis for Cyprus and Turkey (Cyprus III, 1974–75), and (e) the shift from high-priority goals to *basic values* such as existence as the object of threat. For an elaboration of these differences see Brecher with Geist (1980: 2–6). ICB focuses on military-security crises. We recognize – but do not explore in these *Handbooks* – other types of crises, such as political, economic and cultural.

10. Definitions of international or systemic crisis, based upon concepts related to international systems, can be classified into two groups, process and combined interaction–structure.

   Process definitions view systemic crisis as a turning point at which there occurs an unusually intense period of conflictual interactions. According to McClelland (1968: 160–161), "a crisis is, in some way, a 'change of state' in the flow of international political actions. . . ." Similarly, for Azar (1972: 184), "Interaction above the . . . upper critical threshold . . . for more than a very short time implies that a crisis situation has set in."

   Combined structural–interaction definitions view an international crisis as a situation characterized by basic change in processes which might affect structural variables of a system. Thus Young (1968: 15) identified "a crisis in international politics (as) a process of interaction occurring at higher levels of perceived intensity than the ordinary flow of events and characterized by . . . significant implications for the stability of some system or subsystem. . . ."

   A problem common to systemic crisis definitions is the mixture of unit- and system-level concepts. A striking illustration is Wiener and Kahn's (1962) 12 generic dimensions of crisis. Among them are system-level indicators such as a turning point in a sequence of events, a new configuration of international politics as a crisis outcome and changes in relations among actors. There are also unit-level indicators: a perceived threat to actor goals; a sense of urgency, stress and anxiety among decision-makers; increased time pressure, and so forth; see also Young (1968: 10, 14). For a discussion of 25 definitions of crisis at both the macro- and micro-levels, see M. Haas (1986: 25–33).

In summary, our definition of international crisis emerged from an extensive review of concepts and is designed to resolve several difficulties with existing, system-level formulations. First, the available definitions are not fully integrated with the body of literature devoted to systems and subsystems. Thus prominent concepts such as change in interaction and type of structure do not receive adequate attention. Second, existing definitions of international crisis are more descriptive than analytical in character. They describe processes of interaction, but do not focus on the impact of crises on the properties of a system. Third, they mix system concepts with unit-level components such as perception, stress and values. Finally, unit- and system-level definitions are inadequately linked.

It was in an effort to overcome these weaknesses that we formulated a new definition of international crisis based upon a revised concept of system and system properties. For an elaboration of this critique and of the new definition of system see Brecher and Ben Yehuda (1985).

11. It may be argued that economic processes can produce no less, perhaps more, significant changes at the international level than military-security issues. Although the present definition focuses on dilemmas of war and peace, at least some international crises will reflect the prior and cumulative impact of conflicting economic interests. Cod War I in 1973, a crisis that involved Iceland and the UK, is a useful example. This crisis, which included the use of violence, had a prior basis in a conflict over fishing rights. Further instances of military-security crises resulting from clashing economic interests are noted in the ICB *Handbooks*. Hence the proposed definition does not exclude economic issues, although it is true that these factors can bring about change in ways other than through a military-security international crisis. Above all, it is hoped that these *Handbooks* will encourage new approaches to the study of international economic crises.

12. Many variables in the Conceptual Map have been explored in the international relations literature of the past three decades.

Actor attributes have been examined by proponents of the decision-making approach. More specifically, the concepts of age of a state, its regime, military and economic resources (capability), domestic conditions and territorial size and location—and their effects on foreign policy behavior—were analyzed by, among others, Andriole *et al*. (1975), East (1973), East and Hermann (1974), Hopple *et al*. (1977), Rosenau (1966), Rummel (1968, 1969), Ward and Widmaier (1982), and Wilkenfeld *et al*. (1980).

The decision-making unit—its size, structure and rank of participants; their values and issues at stake; information processing; and various effects on decision-making and crisis management—have been dissected by Allison (1969, 1971), Brecher (1969, 1980), George (1980), Hermann (1963, 1969), Stein and Tanter (1980), Vertzberger (1984), and others.

The crisis dimension of actor behavior was a major focus of the works noted at the beginning of this chapter—the Stanford Group, McClelland, Paige, Allison, George and Smoke, Snyder and Diesing, Lebow, and Hermann, as well as Allan (1983), Bueno de Mesquita (1981, 1985), Frei (1982), and Goldmann (1983).

Finally, crucial system characteristics and their impact on state behavior have been illuminated by students of the macro-level of international relations, notably Azar (1972), Cannizo (1978), Deutsch and Singer (1964), Kaplan (1957), McClelland (1964, 1968, 1972), Rosecrance (1963, 1966), Singer and Small (1968), Waltz (1979), and Young (1967).

All have contributed insights into one or several aspects of crises.

13. There are various degrees of involvement in an international crisis. States which perceive a situational change as triggering a crisis for themselves are *crisis actors*. However, other states (and, frequently, transnational [non-state] actors) may be involved to a lesser extent: they may provide verbal, political, economic, semi-military or direct military support to a crisis actor or its adversary; and they may be perceived by a crisis actor as involved in the crisis; that is, they are *involved actors*. The crucial distinction is that one or more of the three necessary conditions of a unit-level crisis do not apply to them.

14. The inclusion of international organization variables in *Handbook I* is designed to replicate for crisis management the role of the League/UN and regional organizations in conflict management, as reported in E. Haas, Nye and Butterworth (1972) and E. Haas (1983). For a preliminary attempt in this direction see Wilkenfeld and Brecher (1984).

15. The phrasing of the questions regarding crisis abatement should not be interpreted as bias in favor of the status quo. As noted, the *Handbooks* focus on change. Stability is preferred only in the Hobbesian sense of the desirability of avoiding inter-state anarchy, since this would generate intolerable costs for all members of an international system.

16. Figure I.1.B. implies a concern with similar questions about a crisis from the perspective of an individual state. These guided our research at the micro-level and are indicated in Part I of *Handbook II*.

17. Among the pioneers of systems theory in the social sciences, Boulding (1956: 202, 201) introduced the idea of system rungs or levels. Deutsch (1974: 152–156) set out a ten-level political system, including four levels in international politics. McClelland (1955: 34; 1958) was perhaps the first to specify levels in the study of world politics. The "level-of-analysis problem" was first given explicit formulation by Singer (1961; also 1971). See also Andriole (1978).

18. The crisis trigger for Belgium, on 5 July 1960, was a mutiny among soldiers of the Congolese *Force Publique*, which rapidly turned into a general movement against Belgian and other European residents. Belgium responded on the 8th by announcing its intention to send military reinforcements to the Congo. A crisis was triggered for the Congo 2 days later when Belgian troops went into action.

19. The Missile Crisis for the United States was triggered on 16 October 1962 when photographic evidence of the presence of Soviet missiles in Cuba was presented to President Kennedy. The US major response, on 22 October, was a decision to blockade all offensive military equipment en route to Cuba. This, in turn, triggered crises for the Soviet Union and Cuba.

20. As indicated by Kaplan (1957: 50), who coined the term, the sole condition of a unit-veto system is "... the possession by all actors of weapons of such a character that any actor is capable of destroying any other actor that attacks it even though it cannot prevent its own destruction."

21. The multidimensional character of polarity has also been noted by others. Bueno de Mesquita (1975, 1978) referred to three attributes of polarity: the number of poles or clusters of states; their tightness and discreteness; and the degree of inequality in the distribution of power. Rapkin, Thompson with Christopherson (1979) distinguished between polarity (the distribution of power) and polarization (the tendency for actors to cluster around the system's most powerful states). Wayman (1984) differentiated power polarity (power distribution) from cluster polarity (alliance clustering). Hart (1985: 31), too, distinguished between polarity – "the number of autonomous centers of power in the international system" – and polarization – "the process by which a power distribution is altered through alignment and coalition formation." And Wallace (1985: 97) defined polarization in terms of two key structural attributes of a system: the distribution of military capability and the configuration of military alliances within it.

22. A similar assumption about polarity and war has been the basis of a celebrated – and continuing – debate. Among the participants are Morgenthau (1948); Kaplan (1957); Deutsch and Singer (1964); Waltz (1964, 1967); Rosecrance (1966); M. Haas (1970); Singer, Bremer and Stuckey (1972); Wallace (1973); Bueno de Mesquita (1975, 1978); Rapkin, Thompson with Christopherson (1979); Wayman (1984); Garnham (1985); and Levy (1985).

23. The concepts of dominant system and subsystem are elaborated in Brecher and James (1986: Part I.1).

24. For an attempt to assess the impact of protracted conflicts on crises see Brecher (1984).

25. There were no superpowers as defined above before World War II. However, the category great powers, comprising Britain, France, Germany, Italy, Japan, the US and the USSR, stood at the apex of the global power pyramid. Thus it will serve, for the 1929–45 period, as the analytical equivalent of superpowers from 1945 to 1979.

26. We recognize that scholars frequently disagree about how best to translate a concept into a precise definition and that some of the concepts in the ICB framework manifest conflicting definitions in the international relations literature, such as foreign policy crisis, international crisis, intra-war crisis, multipolarity, polycentrism, power discrepancy and power status. The definitions of concepts discussed above seem to us to meet the criteria specified earlier. They are valid. They are analytically comprehensive. They incorporate concepts related to change. And they have operational utility, as will be amply demonstrated in Parts III and IV below.

II Methodology

The conversion of the concepts discussed in Part I of this *Handbook* into procedures for the collection and operationalization of data required meticulous care. The first task was to design methods to compile a list of crises which adhere rigorously to the ICB definition of an international crisis, to specify the state actors in each crisis and to construct a set of variables which would generate a reliable data set.

The identification of distinguishing characteristics of crises for a diverse set of actors across a 50-year period entailed certain methodological difficulties. The most serious was the inability to develop quantitative indicators for certain kinds of information on a uniform cross-national basis. At the outset of this project we realized that it would make a distinctive contribution to crisis research only if we adopted a creative approach to variable operationalization. While many of our variables can be thought of as "hard" – geographic location, number of actors, extent of violence, global organizations' involvement – others are "softer" in nature. This latter category includes such variables as content and extent of satisfaction about outcome, effectiveness of third parties in crisis abatement and values threatened. Here we consulted often with regional experts while relying on the coders' ability to reach conclusions based upon their research on the case in question. While readers may differ in interpretation, it is hoped that errors were kept to a minimum.

The problem of "Western prejudice" was dealt with as honestly as possible. It was aggravated by the abundance of source materials in English – a large majority of which was presented by American or British authors with their own prejudices. We endeavored to offset this in three ways. First, we made extensive use of regional specialists whose knowledge of the crises under inquiry was broad and detailed.[1] This task was made easier by our association with three different universities. Secondly, we sought and achieved a diversity of language skills among the coders; students were able to research cases from source materials published in English, French, German, Hebrew and Spanish. And thirdly, the ICB case list was carefully compared to lists of conflicts, wars, disputes, incidents, armed acts, etc., in the international relations literature.[2] Despite these compensatory efforts, much information, particularly for recent crises, as well as for those pertaining to the Soviet bloc, China and African states, was not as abundant as desired.

In some cases crucial information was not reported because of its secret nature. This is particularly so in states with severe security problems or where government censorship does not permit the publication of troop movements, reserve call-ups, etc. Difficulties and problems notwithstanding, the project was set in motion in the mid-seventies.

Case List

An initial set of crises for the 30-year period 1945–75 was compiled by two doctoral students in 1975–76, using two sources – the *New York Times* and *Keesing's Contemporary Archives*. The preliminary data on situations that conformed to the definition of international crisis set out in Part I were first integrated into a global set which consisted of approximately 175 cases. In 1980 the time period under study was expanded to 50 years – from 1929 to 1979.

Once crises had been identified, we sought to identify the participating states. These actors had to conform to three basic criteria. First, they had to be sovereign states and recognized members of the international system. Second, there had to be persuasive evidence that the decision-makers of those states perceived the three conditions of a foreign policy crisis as defined in Part I – a threat to basic values, finite time in which to make a decision and a probability of military hostilities, all resulting from a change in a state's external or internal environment. And, third, there had to be a clear indication that the adversary was another sovereign state.

The requirement of sovereignty for crisis actors and adversaries excluded all international crises involving campaigns for independence. To be sure, Algeria's 8-year struggle to achieve independence from France (1954–62) involved several crises both for France and for an FLN-led non-independent Algeria. These crises, as well as many others, such as those between Portugal and Mozambique, or India's struggle for independence from Britain, were not included in the final case list because they lacked an adversarial relationship between two or more independent states. Similarly, crises involving terrorist or nationalist groups only were omitted. However, in the crisis over an Air France plane hijacked to Uganda (1976), an adversarial relationship was created between Israel and Uganda when the latter refused to withdraw its support from PLO guerrillas, who had triggered the crisis and were holding Israeli citizens hostage in Entebbe. Civil wars which did not include other states as crisis actors, such as Nigeria's internal conflict over Biafra, were also excluded. On the other hand, Yemen's 5-year civil war (1962–67), in which Saudi Arabia and Egypt allied themselves with Royalist and Republican Yemen, respectively, did appear on the final ICB list of crises. And in Greece's long civil war from 1944 to 1949, two external crises were included: the first in 1944, as a crisis for Britain, when its influence in the area was threatened by a possible Communist takeover in Greece; and the second for Greece in 1946, when infiltrators from Yugoslavia, Albania and Bulgaria threatened severe setbacks to the Greek Government's struggle against Greek Communist guerrillas.

The principal qualification for inclusion, as noted, was the presence of a threefold perception (threat–time–war likelihood) by a state's decision-makers. In cases where decision-makers articulated these perceptions, as in memoirs, statements to the press, or proceedings of the legislature or executive, the decision for exclusion or inclusion was simplified. When reliable perceptual data were not available, a state's behavioral response was used to indicate the presence of perceptions of all three crisis components; an example is the movement of troops ordered by Tanzania's President Nyerere and Uganda's President Idi Amin in the 1971 crisis between the two countries. In other cases, inclusion was determined according to the logic of the situation; for example, Finland's crises over Soviet diplomatic notes in 1948 and 1961 were inferred from the historical context of Soviet–Finnish relations. A state initiating a crisis for another actor is not necessarily a crisis actor experiencing threat, time pressure and increased probability of military hostilities, though it may acquire these perceptions later, as a consequence of the response by the initial crisis actor. Nevertheless, the many single-actor cases in our data confirm that adversaries need not be crisis actors.

Although economic, political and status crises among states abound, prudence led us to limit the inquiry to the military-security issue-area alone. Indeed, in many cases the disputed issue may be economic or political; but if no evidence existed about the perceived possibility of military hostilities between the adversaries, those cases were excluded. Empirical data on any or all of the excluded categories may be collected, classified, compared and measured, for it is abundantly clear that, with slight modification, a framework and research program now exists for inquiry into other areas of inter-state conflict.

Another decision rule in generating the case list was that decision-makers could experience more than one crisis for their state within the duration of an international crisis. The termination of an actor's crisis was identified as the time when perceptions of threat, time pressure and likelihood of military hostilities had declined to the pre-crisis norm. Nonetheless, it is conceivable that, before an international crisis reaches final termination, the same actor can once more perceive the three conditions of crisis. The duration of an international crisis is measured from the trigger for the first actor to the termination for the last actor. Thus, in the first international crisis over Cyprus, which began on 30 November 1963 and ended on 10 August 1964, Turkey's decision-makers perceived three separate crises: from 30 November to 29 December 1963; from 27 May to 5 June 1964; and from 4 to 10 August 1964. Greece's decision-makers perceived two distinct threat–time–war likelihood situations, from 6 December 1963 to 27 March 1964, and from 7 to 10 August 1964. And Cyprus's crisis began on 6 December 1963 and ended on 10 August 1964. Thus during the first international crisis over Cyprus (1963–64) there were six crisis actors: Turkey, three times; Greece, twice;

and Cyprus, once. In other words, when crisis perceptions decreased to pre-crisis levels, a state's foreign policy crisis was deemed to have terminated. When fresh perceptions of threat, time and war probability were discovered during an overall international crisis, we considered that the relevant state was experiencing another foreign policy crisis.

The number of "failed cases," that is, disputes which did not qualify for inclusion in the final ICB case list, is large.[3] This dimension of the process of case selection may be clarified by an illustration. Tibet's declaration of independence from Chinese suzerainty in 1949 was never recognized by the international community. Thus neither China's invasion and annexation of Tibet in 1950–51 nor the flight of the Dalai Lama in 1959 constituted ICB crises as defined by an adversarial relationship between two or more independent state actors. Exceptions to this decision rule were made in one category only – those states whose crises began before formal independence but terminated after its achievement, for example, Indonesia from 1945 to 1949, Bangladesh in 1971, or Angola in 1975.

Regional experts consulted about our tentative list of cases suggested 94 others. All were explored. Some, like the crisis between Japan and Holland over Japanese penetration of the Dutch East Indies in 1930, were omitted because the points of contention were exclusively economic. In that instance, The Netherlands imposed trade restrictions and negotiated a settlement with Japan. A Dutch military-security crisis erupted only in December 1942 when Japan's assault on Pearl Harbor threatened Holland's Indonesian colonies as well. Others were political-diplomatic in nature: in 1965 Togo closed its border with Ghana after accusing it of harboring anti-government guerrillas. In both cases, as in many others, there was an extremely low perceived probability of military hostilities between the adversaries.

Some cases were omitted from the ICB crisis list because of the absence of an external threat. The serious and violent demonstrations which began in Gdansk in 1970 and subsequently spread throughout Poland constituted a domestic crisis for the Polish Government. The Soviet Union extended political support to the Government of Poland but did not become – and was not perceived as likely to become – militarily involved. And on a smaller scale, the internal problems resulting from a coup in Gabon in 1964 were quickly suppressed with French assistance, and Leon Mba was reinstated as Gabon's President within a matter of days. As noted earlier, civil wars, unless they involved external threats to sovereign states, were excluded.

Potential, near-crises between the superpowers provide ample material for the study of US–USSR relations, but not all confrontations or incidents were classified as crises. One example was an aborted crisis between the Soviet Union and the United States in late 1978 over the deteriorating situation in Iran. General Secretary Brezhnev warned the US that any military interference in Iran's internal affairs would be regarded as affecting Soviet interest in the stability of the region. Notwithstanding early US avowed intentions not to interfere, the US aircraft carrier *Constellation* was ordered to leave its base in the Philippines to signal US concern over possible Soviet military moves in the Persian Gulf. President Carter decided against sending a task force to Iranian waters and thus forestalled a foreign policy crisis for the US until the following year when American diplomats were taken hostage in Iran.

Finally, there is no dearth of incidents or crisis-like situations within protracted conflicts, where exclusion or inclusion in the case list had to be determined. The Arab–Israel conflict, for example, has witnessed 40 years of hostilities. Thus its "normal" tension level is much higher than that characterizing relations between Canada and the United States, for example. Within that Middle East conflict, only 22 cases were included in the ICB data set. Israeli military reprisals constituted a particularly serious problem in the task of selection. Blechman (1972) lists 101 Israeli reprisal raids into Jordan, Egypt or Syria between 1949 and 1969. These were in response to hostile Arab acts inside Israeli territory. Within this setting of increased violence, infiltration and reprisals were identified as crisis situations for Israel and/or its neighboring Arab states when evidence was found of state behavior beyond standard operating procedures, that is, decision-making at the highest political level, in order to deal with the situation of change within this protracted conflict. Consequently, only four appear on the ICB case list: Tel Mutillah, 1951 (Israel/Syria); Qibya, 1953 and Qalqilya, 1956 (Jordan); and the Gaza Raid, 1955 (Egypt). Similarly, during extended wars the criterion of non-standard operating procedures, as well as other indicators listed in the types of intra-war crises in Part III of this *Handbook*, were applied. In World War II, for example, the case list consisted of those crises where a state entered into, or exited from, the ongoing war, and turning points which strongly influenced the war's outcome, such as the battles of El Alamein, Stalingrad or Saipan. From the declaration of war by the UK and its allies in September 1939 to the signing of the treaty of Japanese surrender in September 1945, 31 cases were included.

The distribution of international crises from 1929 to 1979, in space, time, conflict setting and involvement by the powers, is presented in Tables II.1, II.2, II.3, and II.4 below.

TABLE II.1. Geographic Location of International Crises

Region	Freq.	%
AFRICA		
North Africa (Egypt, Libya, Tunisia, Algeria, Morocco)	15	5.4%
East Africa (Ethiopia, Somalia, Kenya, Tanzania, Uganda, Sudan)	15	5.4%
Central Africa (Rwanda, Burundi, Zaire, Cameroun, Central African Republic Chad, Niger, etc.)	10	3.6%
West Africa (from Nigeria, through Ghana, Guinea, Senegal to Mauritania)	7	2.5%
Southern Africa (Angola, Botswana, Mozambique, Rhodesia/Zimbabwe, South Africa, Zambia)	17	6.1%
AMERICAS		
North America (Canada, USA, Mexico)	0	0.0%
Central America (south of Mexico, north of Colombia)	24	8.6%
South America (from Colombia to Argentina)	9	3.3%
ASIA		
East Asia (China, Japan, Koreas, Mongolia, Taiwan)	25	9.0%
Southeast Asia (Burma, Laos, Cambodia, Vietnams, Thailand, Malaysia, Singapore, Indonesia, Philippines)	29	10.4%
South Asia (India, Pakistan, Bangladesh, Afghanistan, Sri Lanka, Nepal)	15	5.4%
EUROPE		
North Europe (Scandinavian states)	7	2.5%
East Europe (Baltic states, Poland, Romania, Bulgaria, USSR)	19	6.8%
Central Europe (Czechoslovakia, Germany, Austria, Hungary, Switzerland)	15	5.4%
West Europe (UK, France, Benelux)	2	0.7%
South Europe (Portugal, Spain, Italy, Greece, Albania, Cyprus)	14	5.0%
MIDDLE EAST		
Middle East (Israel, Jordan, Lebanon, Syria, Iraq, Iran, Turkey, Gulf States, S. Arabia, Yemens)	55	19.8%
AUSTRALASIA		
Australasia (Australia, New Zealand)	0	0.0%
Total	278	100%

TABLE II.2. Location of International Crises in Time and Space

Period	Africa		Americas		Asia		Europe		Middle East		Total	
	Freq.	%	Freq.	%	Freq.	%	Freq.	%	Freq.	%	Freq.	%
1929–39	3	8%	7	19%	10	26%	16	42%	2	5%	38	14%
1939–45	2	6%	1	3%	7	23%	17	55%	4	13%	31	11%
1945–62	12	13%	12	13%	31	33%	17	18%	21	23%	93	33%
1963–79	47	41%	13	11%	21	18%	7	6%	28	24%	116	42%
Total	64	23%	33	12%	69	25%	57	20%	55	20%	278	100%

TABLE II.3. Conflict Setting of International Crises

	First crisis/ conflict duration	Non-long-war- protracted conflict	Long-war- protracted conflict	Total
AFRICA				
Rhodesia	(1965–80)	2	9	11
Western Sahara	(1975–)	3	4	7
Angola	(1975–)	5	–	5
Chad–Libya	(1971–)	1	3	4
Ethiopia–Somalia	(1960–)	3	–	3
Ethiopia–Italy	(1934–45)	2	–	2
Rwanda–Burundi	(1963–)	1	–	1
AMERICAS				
Chaco	(1928–35)	1	1	2
Essequibo	(1968–)	1	–	1
ASIA				
Indo–China	(1953–)	8	9	17
Sino–Japanese	(1931–45)	3	8	11
Indo–Pakistani	(1947–)	7	–	7
PRC–Taiwan	(1948–)	4	–	4
Indonesia	(1945–49)	3	–	3
Pushtunistan	(1949–)	3	–	3
Korea	(1950–)	–	3	3
Sino–Soviet	(1969–)	1	–	1
EUROPE				
World War II	(1939–45)	–	18*	18
Greece–Turkey	(1963–)	4	–	4
Trieste	(1945–53)	2	–	2
MIDDLE EAST				
Arab–Israel	(1947–)	22	–	22
Yemen	(1962–)	2	4	6
MULTIREGIONAL				
East–West	(1945–)	18	–	18
Total		96	59	155**

* Four of these crises occurred in North and East Africa and the Middle East.
** The other 123 international crises occurred outside of protracted conflicts.

TABLE II.4. Involvement by the Powers in International Crises

	Africa		Americas		Asia		Europe		Middle East		Total	
Great power participation, * *1929–1939*												
	Freq.	%	Freq.	%	Freq.	%	Freq.	%	Freq.	%	Freq.	%
Low or No	0	0%	6	35%	2	12%	8	47%	1	6%	17	45%
High	3	14%	1	5%	8	38%	8	38%	1	5%	21	55%
Total	3	8%	7	19%	10	26%	16	42%	2	5%	38	100%
Great power participation, * *1939–1945*												
Low or No	0	0%	1	14%	0	0%	4	57%	2	29%	7	23%
High	2	8.3%	0	0%	7	29.2%	13	54.2%	2	8.3%	24	77%
Total	2	6%	1	3%	7	23%	17	55%	4	13%	31	100%
Superpower participation, ** *1945–1979*												
Low or No	52	34.7%	19	12.7%	31	20.7%	12	8%	36	24%	150	72%
High	7	12%	6	10%	21	36%	12	20%	13	22%	59	28%
Total	59	28%	25	12%	52	25%	24	12%	49	23%	209	100%

* *Great power participation*
  Low = One or more powers direct military, semi-military, or covert; or all powers political, economic, or none.
  High = One or more powers as crisis actors.
** *Superpower participation*
  Low = Both SPs political, economic, or none; or one SP direct military, semi-military or covert.
  High = One or both SPs crisis actors; or both SPs direct military, semi-military or covert.

The most striking geographic change over time (Table II.2) is the decline of Europe as the locus of international crises, from its preeminence in the thirties and World War II to a marginal 6% of cases during the sixties and seventies, the lowest by far among the five continents/regions. Even in the 1945–62 period, Europe ranked ahead of Africa and the Americas in this dimension of crisis. This downward trend reflects: (a) the general decline of Europe as the center of world politics; but, even more, (b) the process of integration in both Western (EEC, NATO, etc.) and Eastern (COMECON, Warsaw Pact, etc.) Europe and (c) the stable coexistence between the two (US- and USSR-led) blocs of European states, making international crises among actors of both blocs a rare occurrence.

There was virtually no change in the proportion of international crises which occurred in the Americas and the Middle East during the post-World War II periods. Asia, as well as Europe, experienced a substantial decline. Africa, by contrast, witnessed a fivefold increase of crises to a high of 41% of the total in the 1960s and 1970s. This explosion of crises in Africa was one of several consequences of the marked increase in the number of independent states in that continent, from four in 1956 to more than 40 in 1979. Apart from the accompanying instability of political and economic systems in post-colonial Africa, the marked growth in the number of potential adversarial pairs and coalitions of states accounts for the large increase in the Africa-located crises from 1963 onwards.

Table II.3 excludes international crises which occurred within a long war where one of the two principal parties was not a sovereign state, e.g., the Spanish Civil War 1936–39, the Greek Civil War 1944–49, the Lebanese Civil War 1975 ff., etc. Almost half of the 155 crises within protracted conflicts occurred during four conflicts, namely, Arab–Israel, East–West, Allied–Axis (World War II), and Indo-China. The gap by region was very large, from three cases in the Americas to 49 in Asia. Africa followed Asia with 33 cases. There were 28 crises in the Middle East. And Europe, including four extra-European Allied/Axis cases during World War II, accounted for 24. Two of the conflicts with the largest concentration of international crises, Arab-Israel (22) and East-West (18), are still unresolved. In fact, of the 23 protracted conflicts in the data set, only seven have terminated.

As is evident in Table II.4, the great powers were highly involved in almost two-thirds of the international crises from 1929 to 1945. In regional terms, high participation was concentrated in Europe- and Asia-located crises, reflecting both the pervasiveness of World War II crises in these two regions, with all seven great powers – Britain, France, Germany, Italy, Japan, the US, and the USSR – highly involved, and the fact that six of the seven were located in Europe and Asia. In the Americas, by contrast, great power involvement was high in only one of eight cases.

This table also reveals that, overall, the superpowers – the US and USSR – were much less active in international crises since World War II than were the great powers prior to 1945; they were uninvolved or little involved in 72% of the cases compared to 35%, an indication of the *caution and prudence characteristic of US and Soviet crisis behavior*. In no region were the SPs highly involved in more than half of the crises– in only half of Europe's cases and 40% of those in Asia. They exhibited high participation in one-fourth of the crises in the Middle East and the Americas and in only 12% of Africa-located crises. Clearly, they rarely regarded African crises as salient to their vital interests, with European crises, followed by those in Asia, the most salient. Among the 59 post-1945 high SP involvement cases, Asia was the most prominent, accounting for 36% of these crises, the Middle East accounting for 22% of those cases and Europe for 20%. Those were the regions of greatest concern to the US and USSR: Europe, because it was the geographic center of the superpower dominant system; Asia, because of the reemergence of a powerful China and the prolonged US participation in the Indo-China conflict zone; and the Middle East, because it was a "grey" area of vital resources and geostrategic significance in the global struggle for power and influence.

Codebooks and Variables

The first codebook was assembled in 1977. The variables contained therein went through five revisions before its final form in 1981. There were several problems. Some of the variables did not contain a complete set of alternative values, as became evident in preliminary coding. Occasionally the answer to the question posed by the variable did not fit into any of the alternatives provided. Sometimes the variable was revised – did the US declaration of non-intervention at the outset of the Spanish Civil War in 1936 constitute activity or inactivity? An appropriate value – declaration of non-intervention – was added to variables dealing with great power/superpower activity during a crisis. And sometimes difficulties arose in choosing among alternatives – did the 1968 Soviet bloc invasion of Czechoslovakia escalate, and delay the termination of, the crisis, or was it the single most important contributor to crisis abatement, contributing as well to the more rapid termination of the crisis? The coders opted for the former.

We attempted to minimize the problem of missing data by specifying a set of variables for which data were available for the vast majority of states. Even so, data were missing, and as we moved back in time, particularly to the pre-World War II period, this problem was aggravated. We compensated for the scarcity of earlier data by the extensive use of sources other than the standard cross-national statistical abstracts and, at times, extrapolated the information from what was available.[4]

Initial coding instructions were not always precise, and coders had different interpretations as to what information was being sought. What was meant by escalation or reduction of tension level? Arbitrary rules had to be fixed; for example, escalation or reduction in terms of that particular variable meant whether or not the adversaries perceived another crisis within a 5-year period after the termination of the crisis being coded. A number of variables proved too awkward to code. Difficulties in translating soft information into hard data became apparent. And the first codebooks contained some variables pertaining to the international crisis as a whole, especially those dealing with the role of global and regional organizations. Initially, this required identical scores for these variables for each crisis actor. This problem was eliminated when we moved to parallel research at the micro- and macro-levels – to be dealt with below.

The ICB codebooks were designed to uncover relevant information, amenable to quantification, about crisis attributes and dimensions and actor attributes and dimensions (see Figures I.1.A and I.1.B in Part I above). Macro-data on variables pertaining to the systemic domain tap the first two realms and have been incorporated into a codebook on *International Crises*. Microdata on variables pertaining to the attributes and dimensions of each actor in an international crisis are contained in another codebook entitled *Foreign Policy Crises*.

The codebook on foreign policy crises contains 27 variables concerning actor attributes. These variables describe state conditions at the time of the onset of the crisis: the assumption is that national attributes will affect both the propensity to become involved in crises and behavior patterns during those crises. In addition, 30 variables on actor dimensions describe the characteristics of the crisis and the types of behavior by the crisis actors. These variables relate, in particular, to the crisis management techniques employed, the participation of third parties in the crisis and the crisis outcome – all from the perspective of the crisis actor. Most of these variables are described in full in Part III of the companion volume, *Handbook of Foreign Policy Crises (Handbook II)*, together with the aggregate findings.

A second set of variables was designed to generate a complementary data bank on international crises as a whole. These variables are based upon the definition of an international crisis as a situational change characterized by higher-than-normal conflictual interaction which poses a challenge to the structure of an international system – as specified in Part I of this *Handbook*. The 49 macro-level variables locate the actor-case within the international system at the time of its occurrence. These variables, with a key to their operationalization, are listed below;[5] and, along with frequency distributions and statistical control of data and the analysis of findings, they are set out in detail in Part III below.[6]

Crisis Dimensions
1. *Intra-war Crisis* – the type of situational change triggering a crisis during an ongoing war.
2. *Value Threatened* – the gravest threat perceived by any of the crisis actors, ranging from threat to existence to a limited threat to population and property.
3. *Number of Involved Actors* – the total number of states perceived by all crisis actors, separately, to be involved in any way in an international crisis.
4. *Triggering Entity* – the state(s) or any other actor(s) which triggered a crisis for the first crisis actor.

5. *Breakpoint (Initiation) of Crisis* – the specific event(s) or situational change perceived by the decision-maker(s) of the first crisis actor as a threat to basic values, with finite time for response and a high probability of military hostilities.
6. **Date of Breakpoint* – the date of the trigger for the first crisis actor.
7. **Date of Exitpoint* – the date of termination for the last crisis actor to leave the crisis.
8. *Duration* – the elapsed time from the first breakpoint (trigger) to the last actor's exit from the crisis, measured in number of days.
9. **Major Response* – the most disruptive act in an entire crisis, along a scale from compliance to violent military.
10. *Crisis Management Technique (CMT)* – the highest primary CMT employed by any crisis actor, along a scale from negotiation to violence, is coded as the primary CMT for an international crisis as a whole.
11. *Intensity of Violence as a CMT* – the most intense use of violence by any crisis actor during a crisis, from no violence through minor clashes to serious clashes to full-scale war.
12. *Centrality of Violence as a CMT* – the highest relative importance attributed by any crisis actor to its use of violence in order to obtain goals during a crisis, ranging from preeminent, important, minor to none.
13. *Timing of Violence* – the first occurrence of violence, if any, prior to, at the onset of, or during a crisis.

Superpower Activity

United States
14. *Activity* – the highest type of US activity as perceived by any of the crisis actors, coded along a scale from none to direct military activity.
15. *Effectiveness* – measures the US contribution to crisis abatement, if any, for an entire crisis, from the single most important contributor to US escalation of a crisis.
16. *Most Effective US Activity* – determined on the basis of the activity assessed in the preceding variable (political, economic, covert, semi- or direct military).
17. **US Activity and Pace of Abatement* – the impact of US activity, if any, on the rapidity of crisis abatement, ranging from hastening termination to no effect, to delay of termination.
18–21. *Soviet Union* (the identical variables to the four for the United States).

International Organization Involvement–Global

22. *Source* of Global Organization Involvement – if the League of Nations or the United Nations was approached, was it by crisis actor(s), superpower(s), third party(ies), or was activity initiated by the global organization?
23. Global Organization *Organ Most Active* in Crisis – Secretary-General, (General) Assembly, (Security) Council or general UN or League activity.
24. *Content* of Global Organization Involvement (by the most active organ) – from good offices to emergency military forces.
25. *Effectiveness* of Global Organization Involvement – contribution to abatement of a crisis by prevention of hostilities or by termination, from the single most important, important or marginal contribution, to no effect, to escalation of a crisis.
26. *Most Effective Global Organ* – the organ which made the highest contribution to crisis abatement, as distinct from the most intense activity during a crisis – (General) Assembly, (Security) Council, etc.
27. *Most Effective Global Organization Involvement* – the activity of the most effective global organ, as identified in variable 26 above, ranging from discussions, fact-finding, through mediation to observers or emergency military forces.[7]
28. **Global Organization Involvement and Pace of Abatement* – the impact of global organization activity, if any, on the rapidity of crisis abatement, from more rapid termination to delay.

*These variables are not subjected to analysis in Part III below. However, the raw data are part of the ICB set, which can be obtained from the Consortium at the University of Michigan; see note 6.

International Organization
Involvement–Regional

29. *Source* of Regional Organization Involvement – coded as in variable 22 above.
30. *Most Active* Regional Organization – the most (or coequally) active regional/security organization in a crisis – among OAS, SEATO, NATO, WTO, LAS, OAU, CENTO, other.
31. *Content* of Regional Organization Involvement – coded as in variable 24.
32. *Effectiveness* of Regional Organization Involvement – coded as in variable 25.
33. *Most Effective Regional Organization* – in terms of which organization made the highest contribution to crisis abatement.
34. **Most Effective Regional Organization Involvement* – coded as in variable 27.
35. *Regional Organization Involvement and *Pace of Abatement* – coded as in variable 28.

Outcome

36. *Perceived Content* of Crisis Outcome – the outcome of an international crisis, identified as ambiguous or definitive, based upon a combination of the crisis actors' perceptions as to the outcome; a mixture of two or more among defeat, victory, stalemate or compromise indicates ambiguous, while defeat and/or victory indicate a definitive outcome.
37. *Form* of Outcome – from formal or semi-formal agreement, through tacit understanding, unilateral act, to other kinds of non-agreement.
38. *Extent of Satisfaction* about Outcome – based upon the combined satisfaction or dissatisfaction of each of the crisis actors.
39. *Escalation or Reduction of Tension* – indicated by the presence (escalation) or absence (reduction) of one or more crises among the adversarial actors in the 5 years following the termination of a crisis.

Severity

(The following six variables will be examined as components of the overall severity of an international crisis in Part IV below.)
40. *Number of Crisis Actors* – the number of states whose decision-makers perceive a threat to values, time pressure and the likelihood of involvement in military hostilities during a crisis.
41. *Extent of Involvement by Powers* – the adversarial behavior by the superpowers since 1945 (or, for 1929–45, the great powers), from no involvement through low (political or economic support), or high involvement (direct military, semi-military or covert activity), to the great powers/superpowers as crisis actors.
42. *Geostrategic Salience* – the significance of the location of a crisis in terms of its natural resources, distance from power centers, etc., measured by the level and number of international systems – global, dominant, subsystem – which are affected by a crisis.
43. *Heterogeneity* among adversarial actors – measured by the number of attribute differences between the most heterogeneous pair of adversaries within an international crisis, the attributes being military capability, political regime, economic development and culture (belief system, ideology, language, etc.).
44. *Issues* – coded according to the principal issue-area for each crisis actor (military-security, political-diplomatic, economic-developmental, and cultural-status), and any change during a crisis.
45. *Violence* – the extent of violence in an international crisis, ranging from no violence, through minor clashes, serious clashes, to full-scale war. (This variable differs from other indicators of violence in the ICB data set in that it measures extent of violence during a crisis as a whole, regardless of its use or non-use by a specific actor as a crisis management technique, as in variable 10 above).

Importance

Change in the structure of an international system, as a result of an increase in disruptive interaction between two or more adversaries, is indicated by four components of importance, measured for the period of 3 years after the termination of a crisis. For the data on importance see Brecher and James (1986).
46. **Change in Actors* – comprises both regime change, whether in orientation or

type, and a more basic structural shift, namely, the emergence or disappearance of one or more independent states as a result of an international crisis.

47. *Change in Alliances* – shifts in the structure or functioning, or the elimination, of an alliance, from the entry (or exit) of one or more actors into (or from) a formal or informal alliance, to an increase or decrease of cohesiveness in an existing alliance, to no change in alliance configuration.

48. *Change in Power Balance* – in both the number of power centers and the hierarchy of power, from change in the composition of states at the apex of a power pyramid, through change in rank among the five most powerful states within the dominant system or a subsystem, to change in relative power, but not in power rank, to no change in relative power among adversarial actors.

49. *Change in Rules of the Game* – those norms, derived from law, custom, morality or self-interest, which serve as guidelines for behavior by actors in a system, from the creation or elimination of codified or tacit rules, through the increase or decrease in actor consensus about codified-institutionalized rules, to an increase or decrease in actor consensus about tacit rules, to no change in rules.

Coder Training and Reliability

At an early stage of case list and codebook formation, a group of 12 graduate students in International Relations at the Hebrew University of Jerusalem was assembled for coding. These students were carefully selected in terms of background, education, language skills and, above all, perspicacity. Several long and arduous training sessions ensued. The coders were initiated into the framework and concepts underlying the ICB Project. Each variable was reviewed for clarity of language and singularity of meaning. Suggestions for revision, addition or deletion of variables to the codebook, as well as objections and differences of opinion, were thoroughly discussed. And finally, despite generous support by the Killam Program of the Canada Council and the Social Sciences and Humanities Research Council of Canada, financial limitations had to be imposed upon our student assistants engaged in data collection. A rough guideline was determined: 25 hours of research per case for each of two students working independently, with additional time allocated for debriefing sessions. Naturally, we retained a great deal of flexibility; some complex or enigmatic cases required more time for research, others less.

Once agreement was reached on the codebook variables and the case list, an international crisis, containing information on an approximate time period and a list of probable crisis actors was assigned to two coders. Each was instructed to research the crisis without prior consultation with the other coder. The students also received a codesheet containing an abbreviated name for each variable, with space allotted for the entering of numbers corresponding to the values set forth in the codebook. After these sheets were completed by each coder separately, they met to compare their findings, marking differences of opinion for an inter-coder reliability test. The next step was the development of a unified coding for each actor-case, in a debriefing session comprising the two coders and at least one of the senior project staff. It was during these early sessions that codebook inadequacies were discerned, rules of coding consistency formulated and procedures for data collection systematized. Biweekly seminars were instituted to air recommendations, test reliability and improve understanding. The five revisions of Codebook I referred to earlier were the result of such discussions. Once early stumbling blocks had been dealt with, formal coding was set in motion in 1977. Cases were assigned to pairs of coders, with care to the formation of as many combinations of coder pairs as possible in order to take into account dissimilar backgrounds and outlooks. Inter-coder reliability reached .85. Debriefing sessions, while often turbulent and lengthy, did produce agreement on final combined coding, which was subsequently punched into our computer files.[8]

During the prolonged quest for systematic and consistent coding of actor-cases, i.e., foreign policy crises, the second codebook tapping macro-level data on international crises was introduced. This, too, required frequent seminar sessions to explain, develop and clarify concepts and procedures for data collection. Revisions were made and tested, after which coders were required to address two sets of variables in two separate codebooks which dealt, simultaneously, with the collection of micro- and macro-data about specific cases. And throughout the entire period of aggregate research (1975–85) the original case- and actor-lists were revised whenever coders and senior staff agreed that early suggestions for inclusion or rejection were unwarranted, according to ICB specifications of an international or foreign policy crisis. In addition, while the core of ICB personnel remained constant, students, as is their wont, completed degrees, moved on to other interests and distant lands and new coders were introduced into the Project, requiring more training and group molding. The end result is a case list of 278 international crises comprising 627 crisis actors for the 1929–79 period.

Summaries

In addition to macro- and micro-coding of each international and foreign policy crisis, one of every pair of coders was assigned the task of preparing a draft summary of the case. As the ICB Project focused on crisis, not on conflict as a whole, a reflection of this unique perspective was required. Student assistants were instructed to provide a brief background of the dispute which led to the crisis, together with a chronological account and description of the major events, including the dates of the trigger, response and termination for each crisis actor. Further, the summary includes an indication of involved actors as differentiated from crisis actors, a specification of the major issues, values threatened, techniques of crisis management and outcomes for each crisis actor, as well as any unique circumstances of the crisis. Summaries also include reference to all previous and subsequent related crises involving substantially the same set of actors. If a state's decision-makers experienced escalation of tension during a crisis, that is, a perception of more threat and/or an increase in one or both of the other two components of crisis – time salience and the probability of military hostilities – this, too, is explicated. And the draft summary was to reflect points of disagreement between coders, that is, variables which were coded with coder reservations.

A revised version of these summaries, standardized and abbreviated, along with a bibliography of the major sources consulted, is presented as Part V of this *Handbook*.

Statistical Procedures

Two types of analysis of the cross-national data set are contained in this *Handbook*. The first, explicitly descriptive, is presented in the Summaries, noted above. The second is quantitative. The collection of quantitative data permitted the use of statistical techniques designed to enhance the search for patterns of relations, for example, between internal traits and the propensity for crisis involvement; among the trigger, duration and outcome attributes of various types of crises or crisis actors; and the impact of differences between high and low involvement by superpowers or global organizations on crisis abatement.

Several sources were used for the data collection. As noted, the *New York Times* and *Keesing's Contemporary Archives* were the starting point for information-gathering in every case. The National and Hebrew University Library in Jerusalem provided the bulk of the materials, with additional sources obtained from Project and private collections. Other relevant historical sources were consulted, including newspapers, scholarly articles, books, memoirs and official documents. In cases where information was abundant, all of the above were researched to enable the coder to choose among the several alternatives posed for each variable. In most cases, however, some combination of the available source material provided sufficient information for coding.

Tables II.5 and II.6 present frequency distribution for categories of sources of data used by the coders. These categories range from the most extensive, a combination of documents, memoirs, chronologies, books and articles, to the least extensive, only chronologies. Overall, multiple sources were used for 82% of the cases. With regard to time-periods, it is generally the case that the earlier the crisis, the more extensive the sources. As might be expected, the World War II period presented the most extensive sources to the coders (68%), while 33% of all post-1962 crises were coded on the basis of chronologies alone.

In Table II.6 we note that the most extensive sources are available for cases in Asia (51%), Europe (42%) and the Middle East (38%). Once again, the African cases, most of which occurred in the 1963–79 period, showed a high reliance on chronologies alone (36%).

All sources used to collect the data in the *Handbooks* are listed in the bibliography at the end of *Handbook II*. The list of *General Sources. 1929–79*,

TABLE II.5. Sources of Data: Periods

Period	All sources		All sources excluding documents or memoirs or articles		All sources excluding documents and memoirs		Chronologies only		Total	
	Freq.	%	Freq.	%	Freq.	%	Freq.	%	Freq.	%
1929–39	15	40%	10	26%	10	26%	3	8%	38	14%
1939–45	21	68%	7	23%	3	9%	0	0%	31	11%
1945–62	38	41%	25	27%	20	21%	10	11%	93	33%
1963–79	26	22.4%	26	22.4%	26	22.4%	38	32.8%	116	42%
Total	100	36%	68	25%	59	21%	51	18%	278	100%

TABLE II.6. Sources of Data: Geography

Geography	All sources		All sources excluding documents or memoirs or articles		All sources excluding documents and memoirs		Chronologies only		Total	
	Freq.	%	Freq.	%	Freq.	%	Freq.	%	Freq.	%
Africa	12	19%	9	14%	20	31%	23	36%	64	23%
Americas	8	24%	7	21%	10	31%	8	24%	33	12%
Asia	35	51%	17	25%	14	20%	3	4%	69	25%
Europe	24	42%	22	39%	7	12%	4	7%	57	20%
Middle East	21	38%	13	24%	8	14%	13	24%	55	20%
Total	100	36%	68	25%	59	21%	51	18%	278	100%

contains 56 items which were widely used. A specific list, entitled *Handbooks I and II, Variables, Severity and Summaries*, gives the complete citation for every reference used to gather data for the 50-year period of our inquiry. An abbreviated form of these sources is provided with the summary of each case. When no specific citation is indicated, only general sources were used.

Data preparation used the following procedure: the combined codesheets for each crisis were sent to the University of Maryland, where all computer work was centralized. Two raw data files were established, one for international crises ($N = 278$) and one for foreign policy crises ($N = 627$). Two master data handling programs were written for SPSS, including routines for recoding variables, creating indices and outputting lists of cases and frequency distributions.

Data on newly coded international crises continued to be collected in Jerusalem and sent to Maryland over a 6-year period (1979–85). Reliability checks were run on each new case prior to its incorporation into the two data sets. Subsequent checks revealed several types of error – from coding, to data entry, to analysis. The task of minimizing error required enormous effort. Each time a change in coding procedure was adopted, all earlier coding had to be reviewed and corrected. Newly published or hitherto unconsulted information about state decisions, perceptions and/or behavior during crises often required coding changes. Some variables proved more prone to error than others and had to be checked for every case. Countless hours were devoted to the task of cleaning the data; however, despite our most valiant efforts, we have come to recognize that perfection, alas, is unattainable.

The data presentation of the aggregate numbers and frequency distributions for each of the macro-variables describing international crises is contained in Part III below. They are based on the coding for the 278 crises (and the 627 actor-cases) which occurred between 1929 and 1979. Illustrations for each variable category are provided. Where convenient, options were collapsed into broader categories, for example, non-violent state behavior (mediation, negotiation, non-violent military, etc.). The tables, with collapsed categories, follow the presentation of simple frequencies.

Controls

Crises occur in diverse geographical and strategic settings and generate varying degrees of major power participation. They may be part of an ongoing conflict or war. They take place at the global, dominant or subsystem level, with varying power among the adversaries. Data on each variable in the ICB set are thus presented in additional tables using controls for geography, polarity, system level, conflict, power discrepancy and involvement by the powers. Detailed explanations and illustrations of control variables were presented in Part I above. The statistical procedures used to apply controls are discussed below.

Geography – cases were grouped into 18 sub-regions according to where a crisis took place (see Table II.1). In subsequent analyses these were collapsed into five regions, with the following distribution of international crises: Africa (64), Americas (33), Asia (69), Europe (57) and Middle East (55). The distribution by time within each region may be found in Table II.2.

Polarity – each of the 278 international crises was placed into one of the three system-periods, multipolar 1929–39 (38), bipolar 1945–62 (93) and polycentric 1963–79 (116), with a separate category for the 6-year period of World War II (31), according to the breakpoint of the crisis (i.e., the trigger date for the first crises actor).

System Level – every international crisis was classified according to the system level at which the crisis took place. These were subsystem (168 cases), mainly subsystem (46), mainly dominant (30) or dominant system (34). Combined judgment of three independent coders was used to determine the system level assigned to each case.

Conflict – all 278 crises were divided into three categories of conflict setting: long-war-protracted conflict (59 cases), non-long-war-protracted conflict (96) and non-protracted conflict (123) (see Table II.3).

Power Discrepancy (PD) – a three-step procedure was used. First, power was computed for each crisis actor and its adversary, for the year the crisis began. The power score was the sum of six separate scores on scales measuring the size of population, GNP, territorial size, alliance capability, military expenditures and nuclear capability. Second, the difference between the combined power scores for the members of each adversarial coalition represented the raw power discrepancy score. With the exception of World War II cases, the scores were then collapsed into three categories. There were 85 cases with PD scores above 9 (high), 79 cases between 3 and 8 (medium) and 83 cases with PD scores from 0 to 2 (low).

Great Power/Superpower Involvement – two scales were devised to measure major power involvement in a crisis. The first, for the 1945–79 period, extends from the participation of both the US and the USSR as crisis actors to low or no involvement by both superpowers. Low involvement refers to political or economic, while high involvement refers to direct military, semi-military or covert activity. These same categories were applied to great power participation during the 1929–45 periods. As indicated in Table II.4, there were 150 cases where the involvement of both superpowers was low or none (1945–79) and 59 cases where they were highly involved. The comparable figures for the great powers for 1929–39 were high involvement (21) and low/no involvement (17).

Some or all of the above controls were applied to each variable in Part III below.

Data on several of the macro-variables, such as breakpoint (trigger), outcome and crisis management technique, were derived from individual actor coding presented in *Handbook II*. The micro-level, to be discussed there, deals with state attributes and actor dimensions of 627 actor-cases. The methodology pertaining to those cases is set out in Part II of that volume.

The potential use of the ICB data bank is vast. Our research program covers several essential aspects of the relationship of crisis to change and stability in the international system; disorders within that system, such as conflict and war; the effects of power discrepancy on the behavior of adversaries and on crisis outcomes; the effectiveness of third party intervention by major powers or global organizations; and links between crisis attributes and crisis outcomes, in content and form.

More sophisticated statistical techniques are required for these types of analyses. The ICB data bank offers basic information on international and foreign policy crises. Multivariate analysis provides insights into linkages among crisis components. As indicated in Part III below, as well as in Part III of *Handbook II*, preliminary research has uncovered associations between such crisis dimensions as types of triggers or values threatened, on the one hand, and actor behavior, responses, and crisis management techniques, as well as outcomes, on the other; between perceptions of value threat and actor attributes; and between effectiveness of third party intervention, actor attributes, threatened values and the use of violence.

Part II of this *Handbook* is followed by the *List of International Crises 1929–79, with Select Attributes.*[9] This Master Table (Table II.7) lists all 278 international crises and includes information on crisis actors, duration, triggering entity, triggering act, highest value threat, intensity of violence, major power activity, global organization involvement and form of outcome. These cases form the basis for the frequency distributions and analysis in Parts III and IV below.

Notes

1. A list of regional experts is contained in the Preface to this volume.
2. The lists consulted, along with types of disruptive interactions, period covered (from 1929 onward) and number of cases are as follows:

Authors	Focus	Period	No. of cases
Blechman and Kaplan (1978)	US use of military force	1946–75	215
Butterworth (1976)	interstate security conflicts	1945–74	310
CACI (1978)	international crises for USSR	1946–75	386
Carroll (1968)*	wars	1946–68	65
Deitchman (1964)*	military engagements	1945–62	30
Greaves (1962)*	wars, revolts, coups, crises	1945–62	55
Holsti (1966)	international conflicts	1929–65	58
(1983)	international conflicts	1929–79	74
Kaplan (1981)	Soviet use of military force	1944–79	190
Kellogg (n.d., *circa* 1965)*	wars, coups, crises	1945–64	38
Kende (1968)*	wars	1945–67	69
(1971)	local wars	1945–70	95
(1978)	wars	1945–76	120
Leiss and Bloomfield (1967)*	local conflicts, limited wars	1945–65	27
Maoz (1982)	militarized interstate disputes	1929–76	95**
Richardson (1960)*	deadly quarrels	1946–54	13
Singer and Small (1972)	international wars	1931–65	19
Siverson and Tennefoss (1982)	conflict events	1931–65	114
Small and Singer (1982)	interstate and extra-systemic wars	1931–79	37
Snyder and Diesing (1977)	international crises	1938–62	8
Wainhouse (1966)*	global organization peace activities	1946–65	21
Wood (1968)*	conflicts	1946–67	53
Wright (1965)*	international and civil wars	1945–64	13
Zacher (1979)	international conflicts	1946–77	116

* These 10 lists, from 1945 to 1968, are contained in SIPRI (1969).
** A random sample of cases; Gochman and Maoz (1984) refer to an (unpublished) list of 960 interstate militarized disputes from 1816 to 1976, of which 393 are from 1946 to 1976.

3. The following list comprises disputes, incidents, etc., which were on the preliminary ICB case list and were subsequently dropped because they did not meet one or more of the necessary conditions of an international crises as defined in Part I above. The list is not exhaustive.

Soviet Military Threat Against Romania	1930
Japan/Dutch East Indies	1930
Bulgaria/Greece Border Dispute	1931
Ethiopia/French Somaliland Border Dispute	1932
UK Ultimatum to Afghanistan	1933
Austria Domestic Nazi Unrest	1935
Peking	1935
Japan Threat to China	1935
USSR/Japan Border Clash	1935
Argentina/Bolivia Clash	1935
German Military Concentration on Austria Border	1936
German Demands re Sudetenland	1936
Chaco	1938
Ecuador/Peru Border Dispute	1938
Romania/Germany	1939
Cambodia/Thailand Border Dispute	1941
Mexico/Brazil	1942
UK–France/Lebanon	1943
France/Italy Border Dispute	1945
Communist Threat to British Burma	1945
Austria/Italy Border Dispute	1945–46
Corfu Mining	1947

Vietminh Offensive in Vietnam	1950
China's Occupation of Tibet	1950
Iran Oil Nationalization	1953
Jordan/Libya	1953
Bureimi Oasis	1955
Pilsen Riots	1956
Iceland Fisheries	1958
Tibet Revolt	1959
U2 Incident – Pakistan	1960
U2 Incident – Turkey	1960
Togo – Conspiracy against President	1961
Bolivia/Chile	1962
Gabon Coup	1964
Niger/Ghana	1964
French Intervention in Gabon	1964
Ghana/Togo	1965
Sudan/Chad	1965
Syrian Coup	1966
Biafra	1967
Beagle Channel	1967
Hong Kong Riots	1967
Mercenary Invasion of Zaire	1967
Hijacking of El Al Airliner	1968
African Secession Attempts	1970
Poland – Gdansk Riots	1970
Tupamaro Insurgency in Uruguay	1971
Iran Takeover of Gulf Islands	1972
Oman/South Yemen	1976
France/Somalia	1976
Egypt/Libya	1976
Uruguay/Venezuela	1976
Honduras/El Salvador Border Dispute	1976
North Korea/South Korea	1976
Chile/Peru	1976
Malagasy Republic/South Africa	1977
Iraq/Syria	1977
Ethopia/Sudan	1977
Bolivia/Chile	1978
Ecuador/Peru	1978
Indonesia/Netherlands Hostages	1978
Iran/US/USSR	1978
French Intervention in Central African Republic	1979
Lesotho/South Africa	1979
Terrorism in Mecca	1979

Omitted from this list of excluded cases are a large number of "independence" crises, e.g., Cyprus (1954), Algeria (1954–62), Kenya (1963); civil wars, e.g., Sudan; guerrilla wars; many cross-border retaliation raids and a multitude of incidents.

4. Users of the ICB data bank, CRISBANK, will note several instances when variables were coded as missing data in cases where information was not readily available and could not be traced in more obscure sources. This is particularly noticeable in our inability to compute power discrepancy for the cases covering World War II.
5. A comparable listing of the micro-level variables is to be found in *Handbook II*.
6. The data on micro- and macro-level variables will be stored in the International Relations Archive at the University of Michigan and will be available from the Inter-University Consortium for Political and Social Research. Further inquiries may be addressed to Professor Michael Brecher at the Department of Political Science, McGill University, or Professor Jonathan Wilkenfeld, at the Department of Government and Politics, University of Maryland.
7. A word to the perplexed reader is in order here. The attempt to differentiate the most intense from the most effective global organization involvement may be clarified by the example of the 1967 Six Day War between Israel and its Arab neighbors. The UN organ most active in the crisis was the Security Council, which passed resolutions calling for a cease-fire. The organ which affected the outcome of the crisis, however, was the Secretary-General, whose decision to withdraw the emergency military force (UNEF) from the Sinai allowed the armies of Israel and Egypt to confront one another. Thus the UN organ *most active* in that crisis was the *Security Council*, and the substance of its activity was a *call for action*. The *most effective* UN organ was the *Secretary-General*, whose most effective activity was the removal of the *Emergency Military Force*. His contribution to the pace of abatement was negative – he *escalated the crisis*.
8. Coder reliabiltiy was computed on the basis of the number of disagreements between the two coders, as a percentage of the total number of variables being coded for that case. While a figure of .85 is high in itself, it should also be borne in mind that all instances of coder disagreement were discussed in the debriefing sessions, where each coder was asked to justify his/her coding. More often than not, since the coders had used different sources, such coding discrepancies were resolved during these discussions. Thus, while coder reliability was not recomputed after debriefing sessions, had we done so, it would have been even higher.
9. The first case listed was the Chaco War between Bolivia and Paraguay which began in December 1928. It is included in the set because most of the crisis took place in 1929.

Code for Table II.7

Crisis actor = a sovereign state whose decision-maker(s) perceive(s) a high threat to one or more basic values, finite time for response to the value threat, and a high probability of involvement in military hostilities; all three perceptions derive from a change in the state's external or internal environment.

Duration = the elapsed time in days between the first breakpoint (the date on which the earliest crisis actor perceived threat, time pressure and war likelihood) and the last exitpoint (the date on which the last actor perceived crisis termination).

Triggering entity = the state(s) or non-state actor which triggered the crisis.

Triggering act = the specific event or situational change which catalyzed the three crisis perceptions noted above:

Political (verbal) act – protests, threats, accusations, demands, etc.

Political act – subversion, alliance of adversaries, diplomatic sanctions, severance of diplomatic relations, violation of treaties, etc.

Economic act – embargo, dumping, nationalization of property, withholding of economic aid, etc.

External change – intelligence reports, change in specific weapon, weapon system, offensive capability, change in global system or regional subsystem, challenge to legitimacy by international organization, etc.

Other non-violent

Internal verbal or physical challenge to regime or elite – incitement by media, proclamation of new regime, fall of government, *coup d'état*, sabotage act, terrorism, assassination, riot, demonstration, strike, arrest, martial law, execution, mutiny, revolt.

Non-violent military – show of force, war games or maneuvers, mobilization, movement of forces, change of force posture to offensive.

Indirect violent act – revolt in another country, violent act directed at ally, friendly state, or client state.

Violent act – border clash, border crossing by limited forces, invasion of air space, sinking of ship, sea–air incident, bombing of large target, large-scale military attack, war.

Highest value threat = the gravest threat perceived by the decision-maker(s) of any of the crisis actors during the course of an international crisis.

Low threat – limited threat to population and property, threat to the social system such as forced emigration, change of ethnic equilibrium, challenge to legitimacy of belief system, threat to economic interest such as control of another actor's economy, requisition of resources, loss of markets, blocked access to resources or markets.

Threat to political system – threat of overthrow of regime, change of institutions, replacement of elite, intervention in domestic politics, subversion.

Threat to territorial integrity – threat of integration, annexation of part of a state's territory, separatism.

Threat to influence in the international system or regional subsystem – threat of declining power in the global system and/or regional subsystem, diplomatic isolation, cessation of patron aid.

Threat of grave damage – threat of large casualties in war, mass bombings.

Threat to existence – threat to survival of population, genocide, threat to existence of entity, of total annexation, colonial rule, occupation.

Intensity of violence = the intensity of hostile physical interaction in the crisis as a whole.

No violence.

Minor clashes involving few or no deaths or injuries.

Serious clashes short of full-scale war.

Full-scale war.

Great power/superpower activity = any substantive verbal or physical activity during an international crisis by the US and/or the USSR (from 1945 to 1979) and by one or more of the seven great powers (from 1929 to 1945).

No activity.

Political – statements of approval or disapproval by authorized government officials.

Economic – financial aid, or the withholding of aid from an actor, etc.

Covert – support for anti-government forces, etc.

Semi-military – military aid or advisors, without participation in actual fighting.

Direct military – dispatch of troops, aerial bombing of targets or naval assistance to a party in a war.

Global organization involvement = the substance of activity by the United Nations or the League of Nations during the course of an international crisis.

General.

Discussion without resolution.

Fact-finding.

Good offices – minimal involvement in both the content and the process of resolving the dispute.

Condemnation – includes implied or explicit demand to desist, request for member aid to victim of hostile activity.

Call for action by adversaries – includes call for cease-fire, withdrawal, negotiation, member action to facilitate termination.

Mediation – includes proposing a solution, offering advice, and conciliation of differences.

Arbitration – formal binding settlement by arbitral body.

Sanctions.

Observers.

Emergency military force.

Form of outcome = the form in which an international crisis ends.

Agreement – treaty, cease-fire, semi-formal agreement including letter, oral declaration.

Tacit – mutual understanding by adversaries, neither stated nor written.

Unilateral act.

Other/no agreement – crisis fades with no known termination date and no known agreement among the adversaries.

The numbers within brackets and the numbers beside each state are internal ICB code numbers. The former refer to the international crisis, the latter to the crisis actors.

Table II.7. List of International Crises, 1929–79, with Select Attributes

Case and crisis actors		Duration	Triggering entity	Triggering act	Highest value threat	Intensity of violence	Great power activity	Global organization involvement	Form of outcome
1 (0155)	Chaco I	05/12/28–12/09/29	Paraguay	Violent	Existence	Minor clashes	USA	Good offices	Agreement
0075	Bolivia	05/12/28–12/09/29							
0076	Paraguay	14/12/28–12/09/29							
2 (0165)	Chinese Eastern Railway	13/07/29–22/12/29	USSR	Political (verbal)	Political regime	Serious clashes	France, Germany, Japan, UK, USA, USSR	None	Agreement
0080	China	13/07/29–22/12/29							
3 (0170)	Haiti Unrest	04/12/29–28/06/30	Non-state actor	Indirect violent	Low threat	Minor clashes	USA	None	Unilateral
0090	USA	04/12/29–28/06/30							
4 (0180)	Mukden Incident	18/09/31–	Japan	Violent	Territory	Serious clashes	Japan, UK, USA, USSR	Fact-finding	Unilateral
0101	China	18/09/31–							
0100	Japan	18/09/31–18/02/32							
5 (0182)	Shanghai	24/01/32–05/05/32	Japan	Political (verbal)	Territory	Serious clashes	France, Italy, Japan, UK, USA	Condemnation	Agreement
0106	China	24/01/32–05/05/32							
0105	Japan	29/01/32–05/05/32							
6 (0185)	Chaco II	18/06/32–12/06/35	Bolivia	Violent	Existence	War	France, Germany, Italy, UK, USA, USSR	Sanctions	Agreement
0111	Paraguay	18/06/32–12/06/35							
0110	Bolivia	18/07/32–12/06/35							
7 (0190)	Leticia	08/09/32–25/05/33	Peru	Violent	Territory	Serious clashes	UK, USA	Mediation	Agreement
0122	Colombia	08/09/32–25/05/33							
0120	Peru	27/12/32–25/05/33							
8 (0196)	Jehol Campaign	23/02/33–31/05/33	Japan	Violent	Territory	War	Italy, Japan, UK, USA	Discussion	Agreement
0128	China	23/02/33–31/05/33							
9 (0195)	Saudi/Yemen War	18/12/33–20/05/34	Yemen	Violent	Influence	War	France, Italy, UK	None	Agreement
0124	Saudi Arabia	18/12/33–20/05/34							
0125	Yemen	22/03/34–20/05/34							
10 (0205)	Austria Putsch	25/07/34–31/07/34	Internal Austria	Non-violent military	Influence	Minor clashes	France, Germany, Italy, UK	None	Tacit
0135	Austria	25/07/34–31/07/34							
0138	Czechoslovakia	25/07/34–31/07/34							
0137	Italy	25/07/34–31/07/34							
0136	Yugoslavia	25/07/34–31/07/34							
11 (0220)	Assassination/ King Alexander	09/10/34–10/12/34	Non-state actor	Internal challenge	Influence	No violence	France, Italy	Call for action	Agreement
0150	Yugoslavia	09/10/34–10/12/34							
0151	Hungary	22/11/34–10/12/34							
12 (0225)	Wal-Wal	06/12/34–	Italy	Violent	Existence	Minor clashes	France, Italy, UK	Good offices	No agreement
0156	Ethiopia	06/12/34–							
0155	UK	00/08/35–22/10/35							
13 (0235)	Bulgaria/ Turkey I	06/03/35–10/03/35	Turkey	Non-violent military	Influence	No violence	None	None	Tacit
0166	Bulgaria	06/03/35–10/03/35							
0165	Turkey	08/03/35–10/03/35							

Table II.7. *Continued*

Case and crisis actors		Duration	Triggering entity	Triggering act	Highest value threat	Intensity of violence	Great power activity	Global organization involvement	Form of outcome
14 (0230)	Kaunas Trials	28/03/35–25/09/35	Germany ✓	Economic	Existence	No violence	France, Germany, Italy, UK	None	Tacit
0160	Lithuania	28/03/35–25/09/35							
15 (0236)	Bulgaria/ Turkey II	03/08/35–31/08/35	Turkey ✓	Non-violent military	Territory	No violence	None	None	Agreement
0167	Bulgaria	03/08/35–31/08/35							
16 (0240)	Ethiopian War	02/10/35–05/05/36	Italy	Violent	Existence	War	France, Italy, UK	Sanctions	Unilateral
0175	Ethiopia	02/10/35–05/05/36							
0176	France	07/10/35–03/03/36							
0177	Italy	06/11/35–03/03/36							
17 (0265)	Marañon I	01/11/35–30/11/35	Ecuador ∨	Violent	Territory	No violence	None	None	Tacit
0189	Peru	01/11/35–30/11/35							
18 (0255)	Remilitarization of Rhineland	07/03/36–16/04/36	Germany ✓	Non-violent military	Grave damage	No violence	France, Germany, Italy, UK, USSR	Discussion	Unilateral
0174	Belgium	07/03/36–23/03/36							
0178	Czechoslovakia	07/03/36–23/03/36							
0179	Poland	07/03/36–23/03/36							
0167	Romania	07/03/36–23/03/36							
0180	Yugoslavia	07/03/36–23/03/36							
0172	France	07/03/36–16/04/36							
0173	UK	07/03/36–16/04/36							
19 (0260)	Spanish Civil War	17/07/36–28/03/39	Internal Spain	Internal challenge	Grave damage	War	France, Germany, Italy, UK, USSR	Call for action	Unilateral
0181	Spain	17/07/36–28/03/39							
0185	USSR	18/07/36–30/09/38							
0183	France	20/07/36–27/02/39							
0182	UK	30/07/36–27/02/39							
0184	Spain	00/11/38–28/03/39							
20 (0295)	Alexandretta	09/09/36–23/06/39	France	Political	Influence	Minor clashes	France, Italy, UK	Arbitration	Agreement
0115	Turkey	09/09/36–27/01/37							
0116	France	07/01/37–27/01/37							
0117	France	03/06/37–04/07/37							
0118	France	29/10/37–29/01/38							
0119	France	04/06/38–04/07/38							
0199	France	05/04/39–23/06/39							
21 (0283)	Amur River Incident	22/06/37–04/07/37	USSR ✓	Violent	Territory	Minor clashes	Japan, USSR	None	Agreement
0194	Japan	22/06/37–04/07/37							
0193	USSR	28/06/37–04/07/37							
22 (0285)	Marco Polo Bridge	08/07/37–16/01/38	Japan	Violent	Existence	War	France, Germany, Italy, Japan, UK, USA, USSR	Condemnation	Unilateral
0195	China	08/07/37–13/12/37							
0196	Japan	09/07/37–16/01/38							
23 (0313)	Postage Stamp Crisis	00/08/37–10/12/37	Nicaragua	Political	Territory	No violence	USA	None	Agreement
0210	Honduras	00/08/37–10/12/37							
0211	Nicaragua	30/08/37–10/12/37							
24 (0290)	Haiti/Dominican Republic	05/10/37–31/01/38	Dominican Republic	Violent	Political regime	Minor clashes	USA	None	Agreement
0198	Haiti	05/10/37–31/01/38							

Case and crisis actors		Duration	Triggering entity	Triggering act	Highest value threat	Intensity of violence	Great power activity	Global organization involvement	Form of outcome
25 (0289)	Panay Incident	12/12/37–26/12/37	Japan	Violent	Low threat	Minor clashes	France, Japan, UK, USA	None	Agreement
0197	USA	12/12/37–26/12/37							
26 (0315)	Anschluss	12/02/38–14/03/38	Germany	Political (verbal)	Existence	No violence	France, Germany, Italy, UK	None	Agreement
0215	Austria	12/02/38–14/03/38							
0216	Germany	09/03/38–14/03/38							
27 (0305)	Polish Ultimatum	13/03/38–19/03/38	Poland	Political (verbal)	Existence	Minor clashes	France, Germany, UK, USSR	Good offices	Agreement
0193	Lithuania	13/03/38–19/03/38							
28 (0301)	Czech May Crisis	19/05/38–23/05/38	Germany	Non-violent military	Existence	No violence	France, Germany, UK, USSR	None	Agreement
0185	Czechoslovakia	19/05/38–23/05/38							
0188	France	19/05/38–23/05/38							
0187	UK	19/05/38–23/05/38							
0186	Germany	20/05/38–23/05/38							
29 (0320)	Changkufeng Incident	13/07/38–11/08/38	USSR	Non-violent military	Territory	Serious clashes	Japan, USSR	None	Agreement
0219	Japan	13/07/38–11/08/38							
0218	USSR	31/07/38–11/08/38							
30 (0321)	Munich	07/09/38–00/10/38	Internal Czechoslovakia	Internal challenge	Existence	No violence	France, Germany, UK, Italy, USA, USSR	None	Agreement
0233	Czechoslovakia	07/09/38–30/09/38							
0231	France	12/09/38–30/09/38							
0232	UK	12/09/38–30/09/38							
0230	USSR	19/09/38–00/10/38							
31 (0310)	Italian Colonial Demands	30/11/38–31/03/39	Italy	Political	Territory	No violence	France, Germany, Italy, UK, USA	None	Unilateral
0173	France	30/11/38–31/03/39							
32 (0327)	Czechoslovakia Annexation	14/03/39–15/03/39	Germany	Political (verbal)	Existence	No violence	France, Germany, UK	None	Agreement
0245	Czechoslovakia	14/03/39–15/03/39							
33 (0331)	Memel	15/03/39–22/03/39	Germany	External change	Existence	No violence	Germany	None	Agreement
0255	Lithuania	15/03/39–22/03/39							
34 (0323)	Danzig	21/03/39–06/04/39	Germany	Political (verbal)	Existence	No violence	France, Germany, UK, USSR	None	No agreement
0235	Poland	21/03/39–06/04/39							
35 (0333)	Invasion of Albania	25/03/39–13/04/39	Italy	Political (verbal)	Existence (verbal)	War	France, Germany, Italy, UK	None	No agreement
0260	Albania	25/03/39–08/04/39							
0263	Greece	07/04/39–13/04/39							
0262	France	07/04/39–13/04/39							
0261	UK	07/04/39–13/04/39							
36 (0329)	Nomonhan	28/05/39–15/09/39	Japan	Indirect violent	Territory	War	Japan, USSR	None	Agreement
0246	USSR	28/05/39–15/09/39							
0247	Japan	18/06/39–15/09/39							
37 (0337)	Tientsin	14/06/39–00/08/39	Japan	Economic	Influence	No violence	France, Japan, UK, USA	None	Agreement
0275	UK	14/06/39–00/08/39							

Table II.7. *Continued*

Case and crisis actors		Duration	Triggering entity	Triggering act	Highest value threat	Intensity of violence	Great power activity	Global organization involvement	Form of outcome
38 (0343)	Entry World War II	20/08/39–28/09/39	Germany and USSR	Political	Existence	War	France, Germany, Italy, Japan, UK, USA, USSR	None	No agreement
0312	Latvia	20/08/39–01/09/39							
0321	Japan	21/08/39–28/08/39							
0311	UK	21/08/39–03/09/39							
0322	USSR	21/08/39–28/09/39							
0323	Luxemburg	22/08/39–31/08/39							
0310	Switzerland	22/08/39–31/08/39							
0301	Denmark	22/08/39–01/09/39							
0313	Estonia	22/08/39–01/09/39							
0300	Finland	22/08/39–01/09/39							
0309	Norway	22/08/39–01/09/39							
0324	Romania	22/08/39–01/09/39							
0295	Sweden	22/08/39–01/09/39							
0318	Lithuania	22/08/39–02/09/39							
0320	Australia	22/08/39–03/09/39							
0303	Belgium	22/08/39–03/09/39							
0304	France	22/08/39–03/09/39							
0306	Netherlands	22/08/39–03/09/39							
0308	New Zealand	22/08/39–03/09/39							
0307	Canada	22/08/39–10/09/39							
0305	Poland	22/08/39–17/09/39							
0319	South Africa	01/09/39–06/09/39							
39 (0350)	Soviet Occupation/ Baltic	26/09/39–10/10/39	USSR	Political (verbal)	Existence	No violence	Germany, USSR	None	Agreement
0396	Estonia	26/09/39–28/09/39							
0397	Latvia	03/10/39–05/10/39							
0395	Lithuania	03/10/39–10/10/39							
40 (0351)	Finnish War	06/10/39–13/03/40	USSR	Political (verbal)	Grave damage	War	France, Germany, Italy, UK, USA, USSR	Condemnation	Agreement
0340	Finland	06/10/39–13/03/40							
0344	Sweden	27/12/39–13/03/40							
0345	France	14/01/40–13/03/40							
0341	UK	14/01/40–13/03/40							
41 (0353)	Invasion of Scandinavia	08/04/40–10/06/40	Germany	Non-violent military	Existence	War	France, Germany, UK	None	Agreement
0380	Norway	08/04/40–10/06/40							
0381	Denmark	09/04/40–09/04/40							
0382	Netherlands	09/04/40–27/04/40							
0379	France	09/04/40–08/06/40							
0375	UK	09/04/40–08/06/40							
42 (0357)	Fall of Western Europe	10/05/40–22/06/40	Germany	Violent	Existence	War	France, Germany, Italy, UK, USA	None	Agreement
0356	Luxemburg	10/05/40–10/05/40							
0361	Netherlands	10/05/40–15/05/40							
0355	Belgium	10/05/40–28/05/40							
0360	UK	10/05/40–17/06/40							
0357	France	10/05/40–22/06/40							
43 (0358)	Burma Road Closure	24/06/40–14/07/40	Japan	Political (verbal)	Grave damage	No violence	Japan, UK, USA	None	Agreement
0370	UK	24/06/40–14/07/40							
44 (0367)	Romanian Territories	26/06/40–07/09/40	USSR	Political (verbal)	Territory	Minor clashes	Germany, Italy, UK, USSR	None	Agreement
0400	Romania	26/06/40–02/07/40							
0402	Romania	01/07/40–30/08/40							
0401	Romania	00/07/40–07/09/40							
45 (0359)	Battle of Britain	10/07/40–15/09/40	Germany	Violent	Existence	War	Germany, UK, USA	None	No agreement
0390	UK	10/07/40–15/09/40							

Case and crisis actors		Duration	Triggering entity	Triggering act	Highest value threat	Intensity of violence	Great power activity	Global organization involvement	Form of outcome
46 (0372)	East African Campaign	19/08/40–17/05/41	Italy	Violent	Influence	War	Italy, UK, USA	None	Agreement
0419	UK	19/08/40–17/05/41							
0420	Italy	27/03/41–17/05/41							
47 (0369)	Balkan Invasions	28/10/40–01/06/41	Italy	Violent	Existence	War	Germany, Italy, UK, USA	None	Unilateral
0412	Greece	28/10/40–21/11/40							
0415	Yugoslavia	28/10/40–21/11/40							
0410	UK	28/10/40–22/11/40							
0411	Turkey	28/10/40–17/02/41							
0413	Italy	21/11/40–23/04/41							
0429	Germany	21/11/40–01/06/41							
0427	Yugoslavia	04/03/41–17/04/41							
0428	Greece	06/04/41–23/04/41							
0426	UK	06/04/41–01/06/41							
48 (0378)	Middle East Campaign	29/04/41–14/07/41	UK	Non-violent military	Influence	Serious clashes	Germany, Italy, UK, USA	None	Agreement
0432	Iraq	29/04/41–30/05/41							
0430	UK	29/04/41–14/07/41							
0433	Germany	14/05/41–06/06/41							
0431	Vichy France	08/06/41–14/07/41							
49 (0379)	Barbarossa	22/06/41–05/12/41	Germany	Violent	Existence	War	Germany, Italy, UK, USA, USSR	None	Unilateral
0445	USSR	22/06/41–05/12/41							
50 (0384)	Marañon II	05/07/41–29/01/42	Peru	Violent	Territory	Serious clashes	USA	None	Agreement
0463	Ecuador	05/07/41–29/01/42							
51 (0385)	Occupation of Iran	25/08/41–29/01/42	UK and USSR	Violent	Existence	Serious clashes	UK, USA, USSR	None	Agreement
0465	Iran	25/08/41–29/01/42							
52 (0387)	Pearl Harbor	26/11/41–07/06/42	USA	Political	Existence	War	Germany, Italy, Japan, UK, USA	None	Unilateral
0469	Japan	26/11/41–15/02/42							
0473	UK	07/12/41–15/02/42							
0476	Netherlands	07/12/41–05/03/42							
0475	Australia	07/12/41–08/05/42							
0471	New Zealand	07/12/41–08/05/42							
0470	Canada	07/12/41–07/06/42							
0474	USA	07/12/41–07/06/42							
0483	Thailand	08/12/41–10/12/41							
0477	Germany	08/12/41–15/02/42							
0478	Italy	08/12/41–15/02/42							
53 (0391)	El Alamein	23/10/42–13/05/43	UK	Violent	Grave damage	War	Germany, Italy, UK, USA	None	Agreement
0485	Germany	23/10/42–13/05/43							
0486	Italy	23/10/42–13/05/43							
54 (0393)	Stalingrad	19/11/42–02/02/43	USSR	Violent	Grave damage	War	Germany, Italy, USSR	None	Agreement
0491	Germany	19/11/42–02/02/43							
55 (0395)	Fall of Italy	10/07/43–11/09/43	Allies	Violent	Existence	War	Germany, Italy, UK, USA	None	Unilateral
0504	Italy	10/07/43–08/09/43							
0507	Germany	25/07/43–11/09/43							
56 (0397)	German Occup./ Hungary	13/03/44–19/03/44	Germany	Non-violent military	Existence	No violence	Germany, USA, USSR	None	Unilateral
0512	Hungary	13/03/44–19/03/44							

Table II.7. *Continued*

Case and crisis actors		Duration	Triggering entity	Triggering act	Highest value threat	Intensity of violence	Great power activity	Global organization involvement	Form of outcome
57 (0398)	Soviet Occupation/ East Europe	26/03/44–13/02/45	USSR	External change	Grave damage	War	Germany, UK, USA, USSR	None	Unilateral
0517	Romania	26/03/44–12/09/44							
0518	Germany	23/08/44–22/09/44							
0521	Hungary	22/09/44–13/02/45							
0520	Germany	15/10/44–13/02/45							
58 (0399)	D-Day	06/06/44–07/05/45	Allies	Violent	Existence	War	Germany, UK, USA, USSR	None	Agreement
0522	Germany	06/06/44–07/05/45							
59 (0396)	Saipan	09/07/44–18/07/44	USA	External change	Grave damage	War	Japan, USA	None	No agreement
0510	Japan	09/07/44–18/07/44							
60 (0476)	Iran	26/09/44–09/12/44	USSR	Political (verbal)	Low threat	No violence	UK, USA, USSR	None	No agreement
1561	Iran	26/09/44–09/12/44							
61 (0401)	Leyte and Luzon	20/10/44–24/02/45	USA	Violent	Grave damage	War	Germany, Japan, UK, USA, USSR	None	Unilateral
0495	Japan	20/10/44–26/12/44							
0525	Japan	09/01/45–24/02/45							
62 (0478)	Greek Civil War I	03/12/44–15/01/45	Internal Greece	Indirect violent	Influence	Serious clashes	UK, USSR	None	Agreement
1770	UK	03/12/44–15/01/45							
63 (0400)	Final Soviet Offensive	11/01/45–07/05/45	USSR	Violent	Existence	War	Germany, UK, USA, USSR	None	Agreement
0496	Germany	11/01/45–07/05/45							
64 (0407)	Iwo Jima	19/02/45–16/03/45	USA	Violent	Grave damage	War	Japan, UK, USA	None	Unilateral
0530	Japan	19/02/45–16/03/45							
65 (0475)	Communism in Romania	24/02/45–06/03/45	Internal Romania	Indirect violent	Influence	Minor clashes	USA, USSR	None	Unilateral
1604	USSR	24/02/45–06/03/45							
1603	Romania	28/02/45–06/03/45							
66 (0408)	Okinawa	01/04/45–21/06/45	USA	Violent	Grave damage	War	Japan, UK, USA, USSR	None	Unilateral
0531	Japan	01/04/45–21/06/45							
67 (0540)	Trieste I	01/05/45–11/06/45	Yugoslavia	Non-violent military	Influence	No violence	UK, USA	None	Agreement
1851	UK	01/05/45–11/06/45							
1852	USA	02/05/45–11/06/45							
1840	Yugoslavia	02/05/45–11/06/45							
68 (0406)	Syria/Free French Forces	17/05/45–03/06/45	France	Non-violent military	Grave damage	Serious clashes	UK, USA, USSR	None	Agreement
0526	Syria	17/05/45–03/06/45							
0527	France	28/05/45–03/06/45							

Case and crisis actors	Duration	Triggering entity	Triggering act	Highest value threat	Intensity of violence	Superpower activity USA	USSR	Global organization involvement	Form of outcome
69 (0479) Kars-Ardahan	07/06/45–05/04/46	USSR	Political (verbal)	Territory	No violence	Semi-military	Semi-military	None	Unilateral
1764 Turkey	07/06/45–05/04/46								
70 (0405) End of WWII	06/08/45–02/09/45	USA	Violent	Existence	War	(Japan, UK)	(USA, USSR)	None	Agreement
0541 Japan	06/08/45–02/09/45								
71 (0491) Azerbaijan	23/08/45–09/05/46	Internal Iran	Internal challenge	Influence	No violence	Political	Military	Call for action	Agreement
1560 Iran	23/08/45–00/09/45								
1730 Iran	16/11/45–09/05/46								
1790 UK	16/11/45–09/05/46								
1830 USA	04/03/46–09/05/46								
1740 USSR	09/03/46–09/05/46								
72 (0610) Indonesia Independence I	29/09/45–25/03/47	Internal Indonesia	Political	Existence	Serious clashes	None	Political	Discussion	Agreement
1961 Netherlands	29/09/45–25/03/47								
2361 Indonesia	02/10/45–25/03/47								
73 (0565) Communism in Poland	30/06/46–19/01/47	Internal Poland	Other	Influence	No violence	Political	Political	None	Unilateral
1863 USSR	30/06/46–19/01/47								
74 (0480) Turkish Straits	07/08/46–26/10/46	USSR	Political (verbal)	Influence	No violence	Semi-military	Political	None	Unilateral
1760 Turkey	07/08/46–26/10/46								
1762 USA	07/08/46–26/10/46								
75 (0501) Greek Civil War II	13/11/46–28/02/47	Internal Greece	Internal challenge	Political	War	Political	Semi-military	Fact-finding	No agreement
1710 Greece	13/11/46–28/02/47								
76 (0570) Communism in Hungary	10/02/47–01/06/47	Hungary	External change	Influence	No violence	Political	Military	None	Unilateral
1883 USSR	10/02/47–01/06/47								
1882 Hungary	26/02/47–01/06/47								
77 (0485) Truman Doctrine	21/02/47–22/05/47	UK	Political (verbal)	Influence	No violence	Economic	Political	Discussion	Unilateral
1768 Greece	21/02/47–22/05/47								
1765 Turkey	21/02/47–22/05/47								
1870 USA	21/02/47–22/05/47								
78 (0576) Marshall Plan	04/07/47–10/07/47	Czechoslovakia	Political	Influence	No violence	Political	Political	None	Unilateral
1902 USSR	04/07/47–10/07/47								
1900 Czechoslovakia	09/07/47–10/07/47								
79 (0611) Indonesia Independence II	21/07/47–17/01/48	Netherlands	Violent	Existence	War	Political	Political	Good offices	Agreement
2362 Indonesia	21/07/47–17/01/48								
1960 Netherlands	31/07/47–17/01/48								
80 (0580) Dominican Republic/Cuba	26/07/47–28/09/47	Cuba	Non-violent military	Political regime	No violence	None	None	None	Unilateral
1910 Dom. Republic	26/07/47–28/09/47								
81 (0590) Junagadh	17/08/47–24/02/48	Non-state actor	Political	Territory	Minor clashes	None	None	None	Unilateral
1940 India	17/08/47–09/11/47								
1970 Pakistan	01/11/47–24/02/48								
82 (0592) Kashmir I	24/10/47–01/01/49	Pakistan	Indirect violent	Territory	War	None	None	Observer group	Agreement
1950 India	24/10/47–01/01/49								
2070 Pakistan	27/10/47–01/01/49								

Table II.7. *Continued*

Case and crisis actors		Duration	Triggering entity	Triggering act	Highest value threat	Intensity of violence	Superpower activity USA	USSR	Global organization involvement	Form of outcome
83 (0600)	Palestine Partition	29/11/47–17/12/47	UN	External change	Influence	Minor clashes	Political	Political	Call for action	Unilateral
1894	Egypt	29/11/47–17/12/47								
1895	Iraq	29/11/47–17/12/47								
1896	Lebanon	29/11/47–17/12/47								
1893	Syria	29/11/47–17/12/47								
84 (0577)	Communism in Czechoslovakia	13/02/48–25/02/48	Czechoslovakia	Political	Influence	No violence	Economic	Political	None	Unilateral
1906	USSR	13/02/48–25/02/48								
1904	Czechoslovakia	19/02/48–25/02/48								
85 (0575)	Soviet Note to Finland I	22/02/48–06/04/48	USSR	Political (verbal)	Political regime	No violence	None	Political	None	Agreement
1884	Finland	22/02/48–06/04/48								
86 (0640)	Israel Independence	15/05/48–20/07/49	Israel	External change	Existence	War	Political	Political	Call for cease-fire	Agreement
2131	Iraq	15/05/48–18/07/48								
2130	Egypt	15/05/48–24/02/49								
2170	Lebanon	15/05/48–23/03/49								
2160	Jordan	15/05/48–03/04/49								
2140	Israel	15/05/48–20/07/49								
2230	Syria	15/05/48–20/07/49								
87 (0644)	Berlin Blockade	07/06/48–12/05/49	Western powers	Political	Influence	No violence	Military	Military	Mediation	Agreement
2210	USSR	07/06/48–12/05/49								
2282	France	24/06/48–12/05/49								
2281	UK	24/06/48–12/05/49								
2280	USA	24/06/48–12/05/49								
88 (0645)	Hyderabad	21/08/48–18/09/48	Non-state actor	Political (verbal)	Territory	Minor clashes	None	None	Discussion	Unilateral
2071	India	21/08/48–18/09/48								
89 (0660)	China Civil War	23/09/48–08/12/49	Non-state actor	Indirect violent	Influence	War	Political	Political	Call for action	Tacit
2290	USA	23/09/48–26/10/48								
2340	China	01/10/49–08/12/49								
90 (0665)	Costa Rica/ Nicaragua I	11/12/48–21/02/49	Nicaragua	Violent	Political regime	Minor clashes	Political	None	Call for action	Agreement
2110	Costa Rica	11/12/48–21/02/49								
91 (0667)	Indonesia Independence III	19/12/48–27/12/49	Netherlands	Violent	Existence	War	Economic	Political	Call for cease-fire	Agreement
2360	Indonesia	19/12/48–27/12/49								
2390	Netherlands	23/12/48–27/12/49								
92 (0670)	Sinai Incursion	25/12/48–10/01/49	Israel	Violent	Influence	War	Political	None	Call for cease-fire	Tacit
2311	Egypt	25/12/48–10/01/49								
2312	UK	25/12/48–10/01/49								
2310	Israel	31/12/48–10/01/49								
93 (0680)	Pushtunistan I	00/03/49–05/10/50	Pakistan	Non-violent military	Influence	Serious clashes	None	None	None	Unilateral
2320	Afghanistan	00/03/49–31/07/49								
2550	Pakistan	30/09/50–05/10/50								
94 (0685)	Luperon	19/06/49–21/06/49	Non-state actor	Violent	Political regime	Minor clashes	None	None	None	Tacit
1911	Dom. Republic	19/06/49–21/06/49								

Case and crisis actors		Duration	Triggering entity	Triggering act	Highest value threat	Intensity of violence	Superpower activity USA	USSR	Global organization involvement	Form of outcome
95 (0690)	Soviet Bloc/ Yugoslavia	19/08/49–	USSR	Political (verbal)	Political regime	Minor clashes	Economic	Political	General	No agreement
2450	Yugoslavia	19/08/49–								
96 (0710)	Korean War I	25/06/50–30/09/50	North Korea	Violent	Existence	War	Military	Semi-military	Emergency military force	Unilateral
2532	South Korea	25/06/50–29/09/50								
2530	USA	25/06/50–29/09/50								
2534	PRC	27/06/50–00/07/50								
2535	Taiwan	28/06/50–30/09/50								
97 (0715)	Korean War II	01/10/50–10/07/51	South Korea	Violent	Existence	War	Military	Military	Call for cease-fire	Agreement
2531	North Korea	01/10/50–10/07/51								
2536	USSR	07/10/50–26/12/50								
2537	PRC	07/10/50–10/07/51								
2538	USA	31/10/50–10/07/51								
2539	South Korea	26/12/50–10/07/51								
98 (0760)	Tel Mutillah	15/03/51–14/05/51	Israel	Political	Territory	Serious clashes	Political	None	Call for cease-fire	Agreement
2620	Syria	15/03/51–14/05/51								
2610	Israel	04/04/51–14/05/51								
99 (0763)	Punjab War Scare	07/07/51–00/08/51	Pakistan	Non-violent military	Territory	No violence	Political	None	Good offices	Tacit
2673	India	07/07/51–00/08/51								
2675	Pakistan	10/07/51–00/08/51								
100 (0780)	Suez Canal	30/07/51–30/01/52	UK	Political (verbal)	Influence	Serious clashes	Political	None	Fact-finding	Agreement
2590	Egypt	30/07/51–27/01/52								
2660	UK	08/10/51–30/01/52								
101 (0795)	Catalina Affair	16/06/52–00/07/52	USSR	Violent	Low threat	Minor clashes	Political	Military	None	Tacit
2693	Sweden	16/06/52–00/07/52								
102 (0785)	Burma Infiltration	08/02/53–15/10/54	Taiwan	Internal challenge	Political regime	Serious clashes	Political	None	Call for action	Unilateral
2505	Burma	08/02/53–15/10/54								
103 (0790)	Invasion of Laos I	24/03/53–	North Vietnam	Non-violent military	Influence	Serious clashes	Semi-military	None	None	No agreement
2745	France	24/03/53–								
2740	Laos	05/04/53–								
104 (0716)	Korean War III	16/04/53–27/07/53	North Korea and PRC	Violent	Existence	War	Military	Political	Discussion	Agreement
2540	USA	16/04/53–27/07/53								
2543	North Korea	22/05/53–27/07/53								
2541	PRC	22/05/53–27/07/53								
2542	South Korea	08/06/53–27/07/53								
105 (0781)	East Berlin Uprising	17/06/53–11/07/53	Internal GDR	Indirect violent	Influence	Minor clashes	Political	Military	None	Unilateral
2665	USSR	17/06/53–11/07/53								
106 (0800)	Trieste II	08/10/53–05/12/53	UK and USA	Political	Territory	No violence	Political	None	Discussion	Agreement
2760	Yugoslavia	08/10/53–05/12/53								
2720	Italy	10/10/53–05/12/53								
107 (0810)	Qibya	14/10/53–	Israel	Violent	Political regime	Serious clashes	Political	None	Condemnation	No agreement
2730	Jordan	14/10/53–								

Table II.7. *Continued*

Case and crisis actors		Duration	Triggering entity	Triggering act	Highest value threat	Intensity of violence	Superpower activity USA	USSR	Global organization involvement	Form of outcome
108 (0820)	Guatemala	12/12/53–29/06/54	USA	Political	Influence	Serious clashes	Semi-military	Semi-military	General	Unilateral
2810	Guatemala	12/12/53–29/06/54								
2770	USA	10/02/54–29/06/54								
7090	Honduras	18/05/54–29/06/54								
109 (0880)	Dien Bien Phu	13/03/54–21/07/54	Non-state actor	Violent	Influence	War	Political	Political	None	Agreement
2875	France	13/03/54–21/07/54								
2874	USA	20/03/54–08/05/54								
2876	UK	11/04/54–27/04/54								
110 (0830)	Taiwan Straits I	00/08/54–23/04/55	Taiwan and USA	Political	Existence	Serious clashes	Semi-military	Political	Discussion	Agreement
2780	PRC	00/08/54–00/11/54								
2790	Taiwan	03/09/54–02/12/54								
2839	USA	03/09/54–02/12/54								
2852	PRC	02/12/54–23/04/55								
2850	Taiwan	10/01/55–25/03/55								
2851	USA	10/01/55–23/04/55								
111 (0850)	Costa Rica/ Nicaragua II	08/01/55–20/01/55	Venezuela	Non-violent military	Political regime	Serious clashes	Semi-military	None	None	Agreement
2860	Costa Rica	08/01/55–20/01/55								
2900	Nicaragua	16/01/55–20/01/55								
112 (0920)	Baghdad Pact	24/02/55–00/10/55	Iran, Iraq, Pakistan, Turkey, UK	Political	Influence	No violence	Political	Semi-military	None	No agreement
2940	Egypt	24/02/55–00/10/55								
113 (0860)	Gaza Raid	28/02/55–23/06/56	Israel	Violent	Grave damage	Serious clashes	Political	Semi-military	Mediation	No agreement
2870	Egypt	28/02/55–28/09/55								
2970	Israel	28/09/55–23/06/56								
114 (0870)	Pushtunistan II	27/03/55–00/11/55	Pakistan	Political	Territory	No violence	None	Economic	None	No agreement
2840	Afghanistan	27/03/55–00/11/55								
2910	Pakistan	29/03/55–14/10/55								
115 (0890)	Goa I	10/08/55–06/09/55	India	Political (verbal)	Political regime	Minor clashes	None	None	None	Tacit
2920	Portugal	10/08/55–06/09/55								
116 (0940)	Suez Nationalization	26/07/56–06/11/56	Egypt	Economic	Influence	War	Political	Semi-military	Emergency military force	Agreement
3020	France	26/07/56–06/11/56								
3120	UK	26/07/56–06/11/56								
117 (0925)	Qalqilya	13/09/56–00/10/56	Israel	Violent	Territory	Serious clashes	Political	None	Discussion	No agreement
3050	Jordan	13/09/56–00/10/56								
3000	Israel	12/10/56–15/10/56								
118 (0930)	Poland Liberalization	00/10/56–22/10/56	Poland	External change	Influence	No violence	Political	Political	None	Agreement
3110	USSR	00/10/56–22/10/56								
3080	Poland	18/10/56–22/10/56								
119 (0960)	Hungarian Uprising	23/10/56–14/11/56	Hungary	External change	Influence	Serious clashes	Political	Military	Call for action	Unilateral
3090	USSR	23/10/56–14/11/56								
3040	Hungary	01/11/56–04/11/56								

Case and crisis actors		Duration	Triggering entity	Triggering act	Highest value threat	Intensity of violence	Superpower activity USA	USSR	Global organization involvement	Form of outcome
120										
(0970)	Suez–Sinai Campaign	29/10/56–12/03/57	Israel	Violent	Grave damage	War	Political	Semi-military	Emergency military force	Agreement
3100	USSR	29/10/56–08/11/56								
3010	Egypt	29/10/56–12/03/57								
3142	France	05/11/56–06/11/56								
3141	UK	05/11/56–06/11/56								
3140	USA	05/11/56–08/11/56								
3070	Israel	05/11/56–12/03/57								
121										
(0990)	Nicaragua/ Honduras	26/02/57–09/05/57	Honduras	Political	Territory	Minor clashes	Political	None	None	Agreement
3200	Nicaragua	26/02/57–05/05/57								
3150	Honduras	18/04/57–09/05/57								
122										
(1040)	Jordan Regime	04/04/57–03/05/57	Internal Jordan	Internal challenge	Political regime	Minor clashes	Semi-military	Covert	None	Unilateral
3172	Jordan	04/04/57–03/05/57								
123										
(1071)	Tunisia/ France I	31/05/57–27/06/57	France	Violent	Low threat	Minor clashes	None	None	None	Agreement
3240	Tunisia	31/05/57–27/06/57								
124										
(1030)	Syria/Turkey Border	18/08/57–29/10/57	Syria	Political	Influence	No violence	Semi-military	Semi-military	Discussion	Tacit
3170	Turkey	18/08/57–29/10/57								
3175	USA	18/08/57–29/10/57								
3160	Syria	07/09/57–29/10/57								
125										
(1000)	Ifni	23/11/57–	Non-state actor	Violent	Territory	Serious clashes	Political	None	None	No agreement
3220	Spain	23/11/57–								
126										
(1050)	West Irian I	01/12/57–	Indonesia	Economic	Low threat	No violence	Political	None	Discussion	No agreement
3190	Netherlands	01/12/57–								
127										
(1135)	Berlin Deadline	15/12/57–15/09/59	NATO	Political (verbal)	Grave damage	No violence	Political	Political	General	Agreement
3541	USSR	15/12/57–15/09/59								
3544	France	27/11/58–30/03/59								
3545	FRG	27/11/58–30/03/59								
3543	UK	27/11/58–30/03/59								
3542	USA	27/11/58–30/03/59								
128										
(1061)	Formation of UAR	01/02/58–14/02/58	Egypt and Syria	Political	Existence	No violence	None	None	None	Unilateral
3337	Iraq	01/02/58–14/02/58								
3336	Jordan	01/02/58–14/02/58								
129										
(1070)	Tunisia/ France II	08/02/58–17/06/58	France	Violent	Political regime	Minor clashes	Political	None	Discussion	Agreement
3250	Tunisia	08/02/58–17/02/58								
3360	Tunisia	24/05/58–17/06/58								
130										
(1060)	Sudan/Egypt Border	09/02/58–25/02/58	Egypt	Non-violent military	Territory	No violence	None	None	Discussion	Tacit
3340	Sudan	09/02/58–25/02/58								
131										
(1105)	Indonesia- Aborted Coup	21/02/58–20/05/58	USA	Non-violent military	Political regime	Serious clashes	Covert	Political	None	Unilateral
3235	Indonesia	21/02/58–20/05/58								
132										
(1080)	Lebanon/Iraq Upheaval	08/05/58–00/10/58	Internal Iraq	Internal challenge	Influence	Serious clashes	Military	Semi-military	Observer group	No agreement
3320	Lebanon	08/05/58–14/10/58								
3400	USA	14/07/58–14/10/58								
3310	Jordan	14/07/58–00/10/58								
3390	UK	14/07/58–00/10/58								

Table II.7. *Continued*

Case and crisis actors	Duration	Triggering entity	Triggering act	Highest value threat	Intensity of violence	Superpower activity USA	USSR	Global organization involvement	Form of outcome
133 (1120) Taiwan Straits II	17/07/58–23/10/58	PRC	Non-violent military	Grave damage	Serious clashes	Semi-military	Political	Discussion	Tacit
3350 Taiwan	17/07/58–23/10/58								
3420 USA	23/08/58–14/09/58								
3260 PRC	27/08/58–30/09/58								
134 (1100) Cambodia/ Thailand	24/07/58–06/02/59	Cambodia	Political	Political regime	Minor clashes	None	Political	Mediation	Agreement
3432 Thailand	24/07/58–06/02/59								
3430 Cambodia	01/09/58–06/02/59								
135 (1130) Mexico/Guatemala Fishing Rights	29/12/58–01/02/59	Mexico	Economic	Low threat	Minor clashes	None	None	None	Agreement
7110 Guatemala	29/12/58–01/02/59								
3500 Mexico	31/12/58–12/01/59								
136 (1170) Cuba/Central America I	25/04/59–00/12/59	Non-state actor	Violent	Political regime	Minor clashes	Semi-military	None	General	No agreement
3520 Panama	25/04/59–04/05/59								
3510 Nicaragua	01/06/59–14/06/59								
3450 Dom. Republic	14/06/59–00/12/59								
3620 Haiti	13/08/59–05/09/59								
137 (1160) India/China Border I	25/08/59–19/04/60	India	Non-violent military	Territory	Minor clashes	Political	Political	None	Agreement
3481 PRC	25/08/59–19/04/60								
3480 India	28/08/59–19/04/60								
138 (1180) Shatt-al-Arab I	28/11/59–04/01/60	Iran	Political (verbal)	Territory	Minor clashes	Political	Political	None	Tacit
3630 Iraq	28/11/59–04/01/60								
3680 Iran	02/12/59–04/01/60								
139 (1190) Rottem	15/02/60–08/03/60	Israel	Non-violent military	Territory	No violence	None	Political	None	Tacit
3640 Egypt	15/02/60–01/03/60								
7150 Israel	23/02/60–08/03/60								
140 (1200) Ghana/Togo Border	00/03/60–01/04/60	Togo	Political	Territory	No violence	None	None	None	Unilateral
3600 Ghana	00/03/60–01/04/60								
141 (1230) Assassin. Attempt/ Venezuela Pres.	24/06/60–00/09/60	Internal Venezuela	Internal challenge	Political regime	No violence	Economic	Political	General	No agreement
3760 Venezuela	24/06/60–20/08/60								
3590 Dom. Republic	25/06/60–00/09/60								
142 (1240) Congo I: Katanga	05/07/60–15/02/62	Non-state actor	Violent	Grave damage	Serious clashes	Political	Semi-military	Emergency military force	Agreement
3570 Belgium	05/07/60–15/07/60								
3581 Congo	10/07/60–15/07/60								
3580 Congo	11/07/60–15/02/62								
143 (1260) Mali Federation	20/08/60–22/09/60	Senegal	Internal challenge	Territory	No violence	None	Political	Discussion	Unilateral
7482 Mali	20/08/60–22/09/60								
7481 Senegal	20/08/60–22/09/60								
144 (1175) Cuba/Central America II	09/11/60–07/12/60	Cuba	Violent	Political regime	Minor clashes	Semi-military	None	General	Tacit
3650 Nicaragua	09/11/60–07/12/60								
3610 Guatemala	13/11/60–07/12/60								

Case and crisis actors		Duration	Triggering entity	Triggering act	Highest value threat	Intensity of violence	Superpower activity USA	USSR	Global organization involvement	Form of outcome
145										
(1220)	Ethiopia/ Somalia	26/12/60–	Somalia	Violent	Grave damage	Serious clashes	None	None	None	No agreement
3700	Ethiopia	26/12/60–								
146										
(1350)	Pathet Lao Offensive I	09/03/61–16/05/61	Non-state actor	Indirect violent	Influence	Serious clashes	Semi-military	Political	None	Agreement
3940	USA	09/03/61–16/05/61								
4120	Thailand	10/04/61–16/05/61								
147										
(1270)	Bay of Pigs	15/04/61–24/04/61	Non-state actor & Cuba	Violent	Influence	Serious clashes	Semi-military	Political	Call for action	Unilateral
3790	Cuba	15/04/61–19/04/61								
3930	USA	15/04/61–24/04/61								
148										
(1330)	Pushtunistan III	19/05/61–29/01/62	Afghanistan	Violent	Territory	Serious	Political clashes	Economic	None	Agreement
3859	Pakistan	19/05/61–00/06/61								
3861	Afghanistan	23/08/61–29/01/62								
3860	Pakistan	30/08/61–29/01/62								
149										
(1290)	Kuwait Independence	25/06/61–13/07/61	Iraq	Political (verbal)	Existence	No violence	None	None	Discussion	Agreement
3872	Kuwait	25/06/61–13/07/61								
3910	UK	30/06/61–13/07/61								
150										
(1300)	Bizerta	17/07/61–29/09/61	Tunisia	Political (verbal)	Grave damage	Serious clashes	None	Economic	Condemnation	Agreement
3820	France	17/07/61–29/09/61								
7460	Tunisia	19/07/61–29/09/61								
151										
(1320)	Berlin Wall	29/07/61–17/10/61	Internal GDR	Internal challenge	Grave damage	No violence	Military	Military	None	Unilateral
3830	GDR	29/07/61–13/08/61								
3835	USSR	29/07/61–17/10/61								
3810	France	13/08/61–17/10/61								
3840	FRG	13/08/61–17/10/61								
3920	UK	13/08/61–17/10/61								
3960	USA	13/08/61–17/10/61								
152										
(1351)	Vietcong Attack	18/09/61–15/11/61	Non-state actor	Internal challenge	Influence	Minor clashes	Semi-military	Covert	None	Unilateral
3971	South Vietnam	18/09/61–15/11/61								
3970	USA	18/09/61–15/11/61								
153										
(1370)	West Irian II	26/09/61–15/08/62	Netherlands	Political (verbal)	Influence	Minor clashes	Political	Semi-military	Good offices	Agreement
4060	Indonesia	26/09/61–15/08/62								
4070	Netherlands	19/12/61–15/08/62								
154										
(1340)	Breakup of UAR	28/09/61–05/10/61	Internal UAR	Internal challenge	Influence	Minor clashes	Political	None	None	Agreement
3874	Egypt	28/09/61–05/10/61								
155										
(1277)	Soviet Note to Finland II	30/10/61–24/11/61	USSR	Political (verbal)	Political regime	No violence	None	Political	None	Agreement
4189	Finland	30/10/61–24/11/61								
156										
(1377)	Goa II	11/12/61–19/12/61	India	Political (verbal)	Territory	Minor clashes	Political	Political	Discussion	Agreement
2925	Portugal	11/12/61–19/12/61								
157										
(1379)	Mauritania/ Mali	29/03/62–18/02/63	Mali	Internal challenge	Territory	Minor clashes	None	None	None	Agreement
7490	Mauritania	29/03/62–18/02/63								
158										
(1380)	Taiwan Straits III	22/04/62–27/06/62	Taiwan	Political (verbal)	Political regime	Minor clashes	Political	None	None	Tacit
4175	PRC	22/04/62–27/06/62								

Table II.7. *Continued*

Case and crisis actors		Duration	Triggering entity	Triggering act	Highest value threat	Intensity of violence	Superpower activity USA	USSR	Global organization involvement	Form of outcome
159 (1352)	Pathet Lao Offensive II	06/05/62–12/06/62	Non-state actor	Indirect violent	Influence	Serious clashes	Semi-military	Political	None	Tacit
4165	Thailand	06/05/62–12/06/62								
4160	USA	06/05/62–12/06/62								
160 (1390)	India/China Border II	08/09/62–23/01/63	PRC	Violent	Grave damage	War	Semi-military	Political	None	Unilateral
4050	India	08/09/62–23/01/63								
4010	PRC	04/10/62–21/11/62								
4051	India	16/11/62–01/12/62								
161 (1395)	Yemen War I	26/09/62–15/04/63	Non-state actor	Indirect violent	Influence	War	Semi-military	Economic	Fact-finding	Agreement
4101	Jordan	26/09/62–15/04/63								
4100	Saudi Arabia	26/09/62–15/04/63								
4140	Egypt	01/10/62–15/04/63								
4150	Yemen	01/10/62–15/04/63								
162 (1400)	Cuban Missiles	16/10/62–20/11/62	USSR	Non-violent military	Grave damage	Minor clashes	Military	Semi-military	Mediation	Agreement
4180	USA	16/10/62–20/11/62								
4031	Cuba	22/10/62–20/11/62								
4090	USSR	22/10/62–20/11/62								
163 (1460)	Malaysia Federation	11/02/63–09/08/65	Indonesia	Political (verbal)	Existence	Minor clashes	Economic	Political	Fact-finding	No agreement
4260	Malaysia	11/02/63–05/08/63								
4300	Indonesia	09/07/63–05/08/63								
4301	Indonesia	14/09/63–09/08/65								
4261	Malaysia	15/09/63–09/08/65								
164 (1440)	Jordan Internal Challenge	21/04/63–04/05/63	Internal Jordan	Indirect violent	Influence	No violence	Semi-military	None	None	Unilateral
4330	Israel	21/04/63–04/05/63								
165 (1430)	Dominican Republic/Haiti	26/04/63–03/06/63	Haiti	Political	Political regime	No violence	Semi-military	Political	Discussion	Tacit
4220	Dom. Republic	26/04/63–14/05/63								
4240	Haiti	27/04/63–03/06/63								
166 (1470)	Algeria/ Morocco Border	01/10/63–04/11/63	Morocco	Non-violent military	Territory	Serious clashes	None	None	None	Agreement
4210	Algeria	01/10/63–04/11/63								
4310	Morocco	08/10/63–04/11/63								
167 (1510)	Venezuela/Cuba	01/11/63–01/12/63	Internal Venezuela	Internal challenge	Political regime	No violence	Political	None	None	No agreement
4360	Venezuela	01/11/63–01/12/63								
168 (1500)	Kenya/Somalia	13/11/63–04/03/64	Somalia	Violent	Territory	Minor clashes	None	None	None	Tacit
4500	Kenya	13/11/63–04/03/64								
169 (1520)	Cyprus I	30/11/63–10/08/64	Cyprus	Political (verbal)	Grave damage	Serious clashes	Political	Political	Emergency military force	Agreement
4320	Turkey	30/11/63–29/12/63								
4230	Greece	06/12/63–27/03/64								
4211	Cyprus	06/12/63–10/08/64								
4550	Turkey	27/05/64–05/06/64								
4420	Turkey	04/08/64–10/08/64								
4460	Greece	07/08/64–10/08/64								
170 (1540)	Jordan Waters	11/12/63–05/05/64	Israel	Political (verbal)	Grave damage	No violence	Political	Political	General	Tacit
7181	Egypt	11/12/63–05/05/64								
7170	Jordan	11/12/63–05/05/64								
7160	Lebanon	11/12/63–05/05/64								
7180	Syria	11/12/63–05/05/64								
4480	Israel	16/01/64–05/05/64								

Case and crisis actors	Duration	Triggering entity	Triggering act	Highest value threat	Intensity of violence	Superpower activity USA	USSR	Global organization involvement	Form of outcome
171 (1480) Dahomey/Niger	21/12/63–04/01/64	Dahomey	Non-violent military	Territory	No violence	None	None	None	Agreement
7475 Niger	21/12/63–04/01/64								
7470 Dahomey	22/12/63–04/01/64								
172 (1465) Rwanda/Burundi	21/12/63–00/04/64	Non-state actor	Violent	Territory	Serious clashes	None	None	Fact-finding	No agreement
7352 Rwanda	21/12/63–00/04/64								
7353 Burundi	22/01/64–00/04/64								
173 (1530) Panama Canal	09/01/64–12/01/64	USA	Internal challenge	Influence	Minor clashes	Political	None	General	Agreement
4565 Panama	09/01/64–12/01/64								
4560 USA	10/01/64–12/01/64								
174 (1575) East Africa Rebellions	19/01/64–30/01/64	Internal Tanganyika	Indirect violent	Influence	Minor clashes	None	None	None	Unilateral
4534 UK	19/01/64–30/01/64								
175 (1550) Ogaden I	07/02/64–30/03/64	Somalia	Violent	Territory	Serious clashes	Semi-military	Semi-military	Good offices	Agreement
4430 Ethiopia	07/02/64–30/03/64								
4520 Somalia	08/02/64–30/03/64								
176 (1401) Yemen War II	00/05/64–08/11/64	Non-state actor & Saudi Arabia	Violent	Influence	War	None	None	Observer force	Agreement
4141 Egypt	00/05/64–08/11/64								
4151 Yemen	00/05/64–08/11/64								
4111 Saudi Arabia	00/08/64–08/11/64								
177 (1638) Gulf of Tonkin	02/08/64–00/08/64	North Vietnam	Violent	Grave damage	Serious clashes	Military	Political	Discussion	Unilateral
4433 USA	02/08/64–07/08/64								
4435 North Vietnam	04/08/64–00/08/64								
178 (1570) Congo II	04/08/64–30/12/64	Internal Congo	Internal challenge	Influence	Serious clashes	Military	Semi-military	Call for action	Unilateral
4410 Congo	04/08/64–30/12/64								
4390 Belgium	26/09/64–29/11/64								
4580 USA	26/09/64–29/11/64								
7240 USSR	24/11/64–17/12/64								
179 (1402) Yemen War III	03/12/64–25/08/65	Non-state actor & Saudi Arabia	Violent	Influence	War	Political	Semi-military	General	Agreement
4142 Egypt	03/12/64–25/08/65								
4152 Yemen	03/12/64–25/08/65								
4112 Saudi Arabia	23/01/65–25/08/65								
180 (1639) Pleiku	07/02/65–02/03/65	North Vietnam	Violent	Grave damage	Serious clashes	Military	Semi-military	General	Unilateral
4663 USA	07/02/65–02/03/65								
4665 North Vietnam	07/02/65–02/03/65								
181 (1590) Rann of Kutch	08/04/65–30/06/65	India	Violent	Territory	Serious clashes	Political	Political	General	Agreement
4710 Pakistan	08/04/65–30/06/65								
4630 India	08/04/65–30/06/65								
182 (1580) Dominican Republic	24/04/65–31/08/65	Internal Dominican Republic	Indirect violent	Influence	Minor clashes	Military	Political	Call for cease-fire	Agreement
4860 USA	24/04/65–31/08/65								
183 (1591) Kashmir II	05/08/65–10/01/66	Pakistan	Violent	Territory	War	Political	Political	Call for cease-fire	Agreement
7030 India	05/08/65–10/01/66								
4650 Pakistan	25/08/65–10/01/66								
4640 India	16/09/65–21/09/65								

Table II.7. *Continued*

Case and crisis actors	Duration	Triggering entity	Triggering act	Highest value threat	Intensity of violence	Superpower activity USA	USSR	Global organization involvement	Form of outcome
184 (1620) Guinea Regime	09/10/65–00/12/65	Internal	Internal challenge	Political regime	No violence	None	None	Good offices	Tacit
4731 Guinea	09/10/65–00/12/65								
185 (1610) Rhodesia UDI	05/11/65–27/04/66	Rhodesia	Political	Existence	No violence	Economic	Political	Condemnation	Unilateral
4690 Zambia	05/11/65–27/04/66								
186 (1403) Yemen War IV	14/10/66–26/09/67	Non-state actor	Violent	Influence	War	Political	Semi-military	Good offices	Agreement
4113 Saudi Arabia	14/10/66–26/09/67								
4143 Egypt	24/10/66–26/09/67								
4153 Yemen	24/10/66–26/09/67								
187 (1660) El Samu	12/11/66–15/11/66	Jordan	Violent	Grave damage	Minor clashes	Political	None	Good offices	Unilateral
4725 Israel	12/11/66–15/11/66								
4720 Jordan	13/11/66–15/11/66								
188 (1685) Ché Guevara	23/03/67–10/10/67	Non-state actor	Internal challenge	Political regime	Serious clashes	Semi-military	None	None	Unilateral
4745 Bolivia	23/03/67–10/10/67								
189 (1690) Six Day War	17/05/67–11/06/67	Egypt	Non-violent military	Existence	War	Political	Political	Call for cease-fire	Agreement
4820 Israel	17/05/67–11/06/67								
4800 Egypt	05/06/67–11/06/67								
4830 Jordan	05/06/67–11/06/67								
4950 USA	06/06/67–11/06/67								
4920 Syria	09/06/67–10/06/67								
4900 USSR	09/06/67–11/06/67								
190 (1710) Cyprus II	15/11/67–04/12/67	Cyprus	Indirect violent	Influence	Minor clashes	Political	None	Mediation	Agreement
4850 Turkey	15/11/67–01/12/67								
4845 Greece	17/11/67–01/12/67								
4840 Cyprus	17/11/67–04/12/67								
191 (1730) Pueblo	22/01/68–23/12/68	North Korea	Violent	Influence	Minor clashes	Semi-military	Political	Discussion	Agreement
5050 USA	22/01/68–23/12/68								
192 (1720) Tet Offensive	30/01/68–31/03/68	North Vietnam	Violent	Grave damage	War	Military	Semi-military	Mediation	Unilateral
5090 South Vietnam	30/01/68–24/02/68								
5040 USA	27/02/68–31/03/68								
193 (1740) Karameh	18/03/68–22/03/68	Jordan	Violent	Grave damage	Serious clashes	Political	Political	Discussion	Unilateral
4980 Israel	18/03/68–21/03/68								
4985 Jordan	18/03/68–22/03/68								
194 (1750) Prague Spring	09/04/68–18/10/68	Czechoslovakia	Political	Influence	Minor clashes	Political	Military	Discussion	Agreement
5022 GDR	09/04/68–20/08/68								
5021 Poland	09/04/68–20/08/68								
5024 Bulgaria	08/05/68–20/08/68								
5023 Hungary	08/05/68–20/08/68								
5020 USSR	27/06/68–18/10/68								
4970 Czechoslovakia	20/08/68–18/10/68								
195 (1682) Essequibo Territory	09/07/68–00/08/68	Venezuela	Political (verbal)	Territory	No violence	Political	None	Good offices	No agreement
5304 Guyana	09/07/68–00/08/68								

Case and crisis actors	Duration	Triggering entity	Triggering act	Highest value threat	Intensity of violence	Superpower activity USA	USSR	Global organization involvement	Form of outcome
196									
(1770) Pre-War of Attrition	07/09/68–07/11/68	Egypt	Violent	Low threat	Serious clashes	None	Semi-military	None	Unilateral
5010 Israel	07/09/68–07/11/68								
197									
(1780) Beirut Airport	28/12/68–00/01/69	Israel	Violent	Low threat	Minor clashes	Political	Political	Condemnation	No agreement
5000 Lebanon	28/12/68–00/01/69								
198									
(1829) Vietnam Spring Offensive	22/02/69–08/06/69	North Vietnam	Violent	Existence	Serious clashes	Military	None	None	No agreement
5157 USA	22/02/69–18/03/69								
5156 South Vietnam	12/05/69–08/06/69								
199									
(1790) Ussuri River	02/03/69–20/10/69	PRC	Violent	Influence	Serious clashes	Political	Military	None	Agreement
5200 USSR	02/03/69–20/10/69								
5120 PRC	15/03/69–20/10/69								
200									
(1799) War of Attrition I	08/03/69–28/07/69	Egypt	Violent	Low threat	War	Political	Political	Observer force	Unilateral
5170 Israel	08/03/69–28/07/69								
201									
(1805) EC-121 Spy Plane	15/04/69–26/04/69	North Korea	Violent	Influence	Minor clashes	Military	Political	None	Unilateral
5412 USA	15/04/69–26/04/69								
202									
(1782) Shatt-al-Arab II	15/04/69–30/10/69	Iraq	Political (verbal)	Territory	No violence	None	None	Discussion	Agreement
5232 Iran	15/04/69–30/10/69								
5231 Iraq	19/04/69–30/10/69								
203									
(1820) Football War	15/06/69–30/07/69	Honduras	Violent	Territory	War	Political	None	Good offices	Agreement
5140 El Salvador	15/06/69–30/07/69								
5150 Honduras	14/07/69–30/07/69								
204									
(1821) Cairo Agreement	22/10/69–03/11/69	Syria	Non-violent military	Political regime	Serious clashes	Political	Political	None	Agreement
5152 Lebanon	22/10/69–03/11/69								
205									
(1800) War of Attrition II	07/01/70–07/08/70	Israel	Violent	Grave damage	War	Political	Military	Call for cease-fire	Agreement
5330 Egypt	07/01/70–07/08/70								
5415 USSR	22/01/70–07/08/70								
5380 Israel	19/03/70–07/08/70								
206									
(1850) Invasion of Cambodia	13/03/70–22/07/70	Cambodia	Political (verbal)	Influence	War	Military	Political	Mediation	Unilateral
5590 North Vietnam	13/03/70–30/06/70								
5260 Cambodia	23/03/70–22/07/70								
5580 South Vietnam	10/04/70–22/07/70								
5520 USA	21/04/70–30/06/70								
207									
(1860) Black September	15/09/70–29/09/70	Jordan	Political	Influence	War	Semi-military	Political	None	Agreement
5480 Syria	15/09/70–29/09/70								
5560 USA	15/09/70–29/09/70								
5400 Israel	19/09/70–29/09/70								
5430 Jordan	19/09/70–29/09/70								
208									
(1865) Cienfuegos Base	16/09/70–23/10/70	USSR	External change	Grave damage	No violence	Political	Semi-military	None	Agreement
5485 USA	16/09/70–23/10/70								
209									
(1870) Portuguese Invasion of Guinea	22/11/70–11/12/70	Non-state actor	Violent	Political regime	Serious clashes	Economic	Political	Call for action	Tacit
5360 Guinea	22/11/70–11/12/70								

Table II.7. *Continued*

Case and crisis actors		Duration	Triggering entity	Triggering act	Highest value threat	Intensity of violence	Superpower activity USA	USSR	Global organization involvement	Form of outcome
210 (1900)	Invasion of Laos II	08/02/71–25/03/71	South Vietnam & USA	Violent	Grave damage	War	Military	Political	General	Unilateral
5690	Laos	08/02/71–25/03/71								
5880	North Vietnam	08/02/71–25/03/71								
211 (1890)	Bangladesh	25/03/71–17/12/71	Pakistan	Violent	Existence	War	Semi-military	Political	Discussion	Agreement
5630	Bangladesh	25/03/71–17/12/71								
5710	Pakistan	26/03/71–17/12/71								
5633	India	12/10/71–17/12/71								
5730	Pakistan	21/11/71–17/12/71								
212 (1910)	Chad/Libya I	24/05/71–17/04/72	Chad	External change	Influence	No violence	None	None	None	Agreement
7509	Libya	24/05/71–17/04/72								
7510	Chad	27/08/71–28/08/71								
213 (1920)	Caprivi Strip	05/10/71–12/10/71	South Africa	Violent	Territory	Minor clashes	None	None	Condemnation	No agreement
7520	Zambia	05/10/71–12/10/71								
214 (1935)	Uganda/ Tanzania I	20/10/71–25/11/71	Uganda	Violent	Territory	Minor clashes	None	None	None	Agreement
7535	Tanzania	20/10/71–25/11/71								
6025	Uganda	24/10/71–25/11/71								
215 (1930)	Vietnam–Ports Mining	30/03/72–19/07/72	North Vietnam	Violent	Influence	War	Military	Political	Discussion	Agreement
5920	South Vietnam	30/03/72–19/07/72								
7130	USA	30/03/72–19/07/72								
6030	North Vietnam	08/05/72–19/07/72								
216 (1940)	Uganda/ Tanzania II	17/09/72–05/10/72	Non-state actor	Violent	Political regime	Minor clashes	None	None	None	Agreement
6020	Uganda	17/09/72–05/10/72								
7530	Tanzania	18/09/72–05/10/72								
217 (1942)	North/South Yemen I	26/09/72–28/11/72	North and South Yemen	Violent	Territory	War	None	None	None	Agreement
6115	North Yemen	26/09/72–28/11/72								
6110	South Yemen	26/09/72–28/11/72								
218 (1931)	Christmas Bombing	23/10/72–27/01/73	USA	External change	Existence	War	Military	Political	None	Agreement
2147	South Vietnam	23/10/72–27/01/73								
7140	USA	04/12/72–27/01/73								
7145	North Vietnam	17/12/72–27/01/73								
219 (1962)	Zambia	19/01/73–03/02/73	South Africa	Violent	Territory	Minor clashes	None	None	Call for action	Unilateral
6134	Zambia	19/01/73–03/02/73								
220 (1950)	Libyan Plane	21/02/73–21/02/73	Libya	External change	Grave damage	Serious clashes	None	None	None	Unilateral
6160	Israel	21/02/73–21/02/73								
221 (1960)	Iraq Invasion– Kuwait	20/03/73–08/06/73	Iraq	Violent	Territory	Minor clashes	None	None	None	Agreement
6220	Kuwait	20/03/73–08/06/73								
222 (1980)	Israel Mobilization	10/04/73–00/06/73	Egypt	Political (verbal)	Grave damage	No violence	None	None	None	Tacit
6180	Israel	10/04/73–00/06/73								

Case and crisis actors		Duration	Triggering entity	Triggering act	Highest value threat	Intensity of violence	Superpower activity USA	USSR	Global organization involvement	Form of outcome
223 (2000)	Cod War I	14/05/73–13/11/73	Iceland	Violent	Low threat	Minor clashes	Political	Semi-military	None	Agreement
6310	UK	14/05/73–13/11/73								
6140	Iceland	19/05/73–13/11/73								
224 (2030)	Oct.–Yom Kippur War	05/10/73–31/05/74	Egypt and Syria	Non-violent military	Grave damage	War	Semi-military	Semi-military	Call for cease-fire	Agreement
6210	Israel	05/10/73–31/05/74								
6300	Syria	10/10/73–31/05/74								
6340	USA	12/10/73–31/05/74								
6130	Egypt	18/10/73–18/01/74								
6270	USSR	22/10/73–31/05/74								
225 (2035)	South Yemen/ Oman	18/11/73–11/03/76	South Yemen	Violent	Territory	Serious clashes	Semi-military	Semi-military	None	Agreement
6368	Oman	18/11/73–11/03/76								
226 (2040)	Cyprus III	15/07/74–24/02/75	Internal Cyprus	Internal challenge	Grave damage	War	Political	Semi-military	Call for cease-fire	Unilateral
6360	Cyprus	15/07/74–24/02/75								
6400	Turkey	15/07/74–24/02/75								
6390	Greece	20/07/74–24/02/75								
227 (2065)	Final N. Vietnam Offensive	14/12/74–30/04/75	North Vietnam	Violent	Political regime	War	Economic	Semi-military	Good offices	Unilateral
7594	South Vietnam	14/12/74–30/04/75								
7592	Cambodia	01/01/75–17/04/75								
228 (2080)	Mayaguez	12/05/75–15/05/75	Cambodia	Violent	Influence	Serious clashes	Military	None	Good offices	Unilateral
7800	USA	12/05/75–14/05/75								
7900	Cambodia	13/05/75–15/05/75								
229 (2070)	War in Angola	12/07/75–27/03/76	Non-state actor	Indirect violent	Influence	War	Semi-military	Semi-military	Condemnation	Agreement
7590	Zambia	12/07/75–18/02/76								
7580	Zaire	12/07/75–28/02/76								
7570	South Africa	08/08/75–27/03/76								
6420	Angola	15/08/75–24/02/76								
7475	Cuba	15/08/75–24/02/76								
7476	USSR	15/08/75–24/02/76								
7600	USA	01/09/75–19/12/75								
230 (2060)	Moroccan March– Sahara	16/10/75–14/11/75	Morocco	Political (verbal)	Territory	No violence	Political	None	Mediation	Agreement
7350	Spain	16/10/75–14/11/75								
7550	Morocco	02/11/75–14/11/75								
231 (2037)	Belize I	01/11/75–30/11/75	Guatemala	Non-violent military	Low threat	No violence	None	None	Call for action	Agreement
6465	UK	01/11/75–30/11/75								
232 (2063)	Sahara	14/11/75–00/04/76	Morocco	Political	Influence	Serious clashes	Semi-military	Covert	Mediation	No agreement
7540	Algeria	14/11/75–06/03/76								
7560	Mauritania	10/12/75–00/04/76								
7553	Morocco	27/01/76–14/04/76								
233 (2150)	Cod War II	23/11/75–01/06/76	Iceland	Internal challenge	Low threat	Minor clashes	Political	None	Discussion	Agreement
7791	UK	23/11/75–01/06/76								
7790	Iceland	25/11/75–01/06/76								
234 (2103)	East Timor	28/11/75–17/07/76	Non-state actor	Political	Influence	Serious clashes	None	Covert	Call for action	Unilateral
6444	Indonesia	28/11/75–17/07/76								
235 (2110)	Lebanon Civil War I	18/01/76–30/09/76	Non-state actor	Indirect violent	Influence	Serious clashes	Political	Political	Good offices	Unilateral
7740	Syria	18/01/76–30/09/76								

Table II.7. *Continued*

Case and crisis actors	Duration	Triggering entity	Triggering act	Highest value threat	Intensity of violence	Superpower activity USA	USSR	Global organization involvement	Form of outcome
236 (2160) Uganda Claims	15/02/76–24/02/76	Uganda	Political (verbal)	Territory	No violence	None	None	None	Agreement
7810 Kenya	15/02/76–24/02/76								
237 (2180) Operation Thrasher	22/02/76–00/04/76	Mozambique	Violent	Political regime	Serious clashes	Political	Semi-military	Condemnation	Unilateral
7840 Rhodesia	22/02/76–00/03/76								
7841 Mozambique	24/02/76–00/04/76								
238 (2200) Nouakchott I	08/06/76–08/06/76	Non-state actor	Violent	Political regime	Serious clashes	None	None	None	Unilateral
7845 Mauritania	08/06/76–08/06/76								
239 (2115) Iraqi Threat	09/06/76–17/06/76	Iraq	Non-violent military	Political regime	No violence	None	None	None	Unilateral
7740 Syria	09/06/76–17/06/76								
240 (2210) Entebbe Raid	30/06/76–04/07/76	Non-state actor	Other	Low threat	Minor clashes	None	None	None	Unilateral
7911 Israel	30/06/76–04/07/76								
241 (2230) Sudan Coup Attempt	02/07/76–15/07/76	Internal Sudan	Internal challenge	Political regime	Minor clashes	None	None	None	Unilateral
7940 Sudan	02/07/76–15/07/76								
242 (2220) Aegean Sea	07/08/76–25/09/76	Turkey	Political	Territory	No violence	Semi-military	Political	Call for action	Unilateral
7845 Greece	07/08/76–25/09/76								
243 (2211) Nagomia Raid	09/08/76–00/11/76	Rhodesia	Violent	Low threat	Minor clashes	Economic	Political	Fact-finding	Unilateral
7913 Mozambique	09/08/76–00/11/76								
244 (2213) Syria Mobilization	21/11/76–13/12/76	Syria	Non-violent military	Influence	No violence	Political	None	None	Tacit
7916 Israel	21/11/76–13/12/76								
245 (2181) Operation Tangent	20/12/76–31/03/77	Rhodesia	Political (verbal)	Low threat	Serious clashes	None	Political	Condemnation	Unilateral
7917 Botswana	20/12/76–31/03/77								
246 (2350) Shaba I	08/03/77–26/05/77	Angola	Violent	Political regime	Serious clashes	Semi-military	Semi-military	None	No agreement
9000 Zaire	08/03/77–26/05/77								
9005 Angola	08/03/77–25/05/77								
247 (2182) Mapai Seizure	29/05/77–30/06/77	Rhodesia	Violent	Low threat	Serious clashes	Political	None	Call for action	No agreement
7918 Mozambique	29/05/77–30/06/77								
248 (2400) Belize II	25/06/77–28/07/77	Guatemala	Non-violent military	Territory	No violence	Political	None	None	Agreement
9100 UK	25/06/77–28/07/77								
249 (2393) Nouakchott II	03/07/77–00/07/77	Non-state actor	Violent	Political regime	Serious clashes	None	None	None	No agreement
9042 Mauritania	03/07/77–00/07/77								
250 (2392) Libya/Egypt Border	14/07/77–10/09/77	Egypt	Violent	Political regime	Serious clashes	Semi-military	Semi-military	None	Agreement
9025 Libya	14/07/77–10/09/77								
9026 Egypt	19/07/77–10/09/77								

Case and crisis actors	Duration	Triggering entity	Triggering act	Highest value threat	Intensity of violence	Superpower activity USA	USSR	Global organization involvement	Form of outcome
251									
(2390) Ogaden II	22/07/77 – 14/03/78	Somalia	Violent	Territory	War	Semi-military	Military	None	Unilateral
9040 Ethiopia	22/07/77 – 14/03/78								
9045 Somalia	21/01/78 – 14/03/78								
252									
(2372) Rhodesia Raids	31/08/77 – 14/08/78	Rhodesia	Violent	Grave damage	Serious clashes	Political	None	Condemnation	Agreement
9024 Zambia	31/08/77 – 14/08/78								
253									
(2395) Vietnam Invasion of Cambodia	24/09/77 – 00/01/78	Cambodia and Vietnam	Violent	Existence	War	None	Semi-military	None	Unilateral
9046 Cambodia	24/09/77 – 00/01/78								
9047 Vietnam	24/09/77 – 00/01/78								
254									
(2476) French Hostages	25/10/77 – 23/12/77	Non-state actor	Indirect violent	Low threat	Minor clashes	None	Political	Call for action	Unilateral
9157 France	25/10/77 – 23/12/77								
9158 Algeria	29/10/77 – 23/12/77								
255									
(2470) Chimoio Tembue Raids	23/11/77 – 22/03/78	Rhodesia	Violent	Low threat	War	Political	None	Call for action	Unilateral
9150 Mozambique	23/11/77 – 22/03/78								
256									
(2565) Beagle Channel I	05/12/77 – 20/02/78	Argentina	Non-violent military	Low threat	No violence	Political	None	None	Agreement
9236 Chile	05/12/77 – 20/02/78								
9237 Argentina	05/01/78 – 20/02/78								
257									
(2520) Chad/Libya II	22/01/78 – 27/03/78	Chad	External change	Influence	War	None	None	None	Agreement
9204 Libya	22/01/78 – 24/02/78								
9205 Chad	28/01/78 – 27/03/78								
258									
(2525) Lebanon Civil War II	07/02/78 – 20/02/78	Lebanon	Violent	Influence	Serious clashes	None	None	None	Unilateral
9216 Syria	07/02/78 – 20/02/78								
259									
(2500) Sino/Vietnam War	09/02/78 – 15/03/79	Vietnam	Violent	Existence	War	Political	Semi-military	Discussion	Unilateral
9183 Thailand	09/02/78 – 07/01/79								
9180 Vietnam	15/12/78 – 07/01/79								
9185 Cambodia	25/12/78 – 07/01/79								
9181 PRC	25/12/78 – 15/03/79								
9182 Vietnam	17/02/79 – 15/03/79								
260									
(2550) Litani Operation	14/03/78 – 13/06/78	Israel	Violent	Territory	Serious clashes	Political	Political	Call for action	Unilateral
9230 Lebanon	14/03/78 – 13/06/78								
261									
(2710) Chad/Libya III	15/04/78 – 29/08/78	Internal Chad	Indirect violent	Influence	War	None	None	None	Unilateral
9363 France	15/04/78 – 00/07/78								
9364 Libya	18/05/78 – 00/07/78								
9365 Chad	22/06/78 – 29/08/78								
262									
(2575) Cassinga Incident	03/05/78 – 17/05/78	Non-state actor	Violent	Influence	Serious clashes	Political	Semi-military	Condemnation	Tacit
9262 South Africa	03/05/78 – 17/05/78								
9261 Angola	04/05/78 – 06/05/78								
263									
(2570) Shaba II	11/05/78 – 30/07/78	Angola	Violent	Influence	Serious clashes	Semi-military	Semi-military	None	Agreement
9255 Zaire	11/05/78 – 30/07/78								
9250 Angola	11/05/78 – 30/07/78								
9257 Belgium	14/05/78 – 22/05/78								
9258 USA	14/05/78 – 22/05/78								
9256 France	14/05/78 – 25/05/78								

Table II.7. *Continued*

Case and crisis actors		Duration	Triggering entity	Triggering act	Highest value threat	Intensity of violence	Superpower activity USA	USSR	Global organization involvement	Form of outcome
264 (2625)	Air Rhodesia Incident	03/09/78–31/10/78	Zambia	Violent	Grave damage	Serious clashes	Political	None	Condemnation	Unilateral
9289	Rhodesia	03/09/78–31/10/78								
9290	Zambia	19/10/78–23/10/78								
265 (2640)	Nicaraguan Civil War	10/09/78–17/07/79	Non-state actor	Violent	Political regime	War	Semi-military	None	Condemnation	Unilateral
9310	Nicaragua	10/09/78–25/09/78								
9305	Costa Rica	12/09/78–17/07/79								
9311	Nicaragua	27/05/79–17/07/79								
266 (2645)	Beagle Channel II	16/10/78–08/01/79	Argentina	Non-violent military	Low threat	Minor clashes	Political	None	Discussion	Agreement
9316	Chile	16/10/78–08/01/79								
9317	Argentina	16/12/78–08/01/79								
267 (2630)	Fall of Amin	30/10/78–10/04/79	Uganda	Violent	Influence	War	Political	Political	Good offices	Unilateral
9295	Tanzania	30/10/78–10/04/79								
9300	Uganda	31/10/78–10/04/79								
9296	Libya	25/02/79–09/04/79								
268 (2635)	Angola Invasion Scare	07/11/78–14/11/78	South Africa	External change	Grave damage	No violence	None	None	General	Unilateral
9312	Angola	07/11/78–14/11/78								
269 (2666)	Tan Tan	28/01/79–00/03/79	Non-state actor	Violent	Territory	Serious clashes	None	None	None	No agreement
9337	Morocco	28/01/79–00/03/79								
270 (2729)	Raids on ZIPRA	12/02/79–31/05/79	Zambia	Violent	Low threat	Serious clashes	None	None	Condemnation	Unilateral
9427	Rhodesia	12/02/79–31/05/79								
9426	Angola	26/02/79–10/05/79								
9425	Zambia	13/04/79–12/05/79								
271 (2600)	North/South Yemen II	24/02/79–30/03/79	North and South Yemen	Violent	Territory	War	Semi-military	Semi-military	None	Agreement
9270	North Yemen	24/02/79–30/03/79								
9265	South Yemen	24/02/79–30/03/79								
272 (2730)	Raids on SWAPO	06/03/79–28/03/79	South Africa	Violent	Low threat	Minor clashes	None	None	Condemnation	No agreement
9430	Angola	06/03/79–28/03/79								
273 (2731)	Chad/Libya IV	12/04/79–10/11/79	Chad	Political	Influence	War	None	None	General	Unilateral
9373	Libya	12/04/79–10/11/79								
9375	Chad	25/06/79–10/11/79								
9376	France	25/06/79–10/11/79								
274 (2725)	Goulimime–Tarfaya Road	01/06/79–25/06/79	Non-state Actor	Violent	Territory	Serious clashes	None	None	Discussion	Unilateral
9371	Morocco	01/06/79–25/06/79								
9372	Algeria	06/06/79–25/06/79								
275 (2726)	Soviet Threat to Pakistan	01/06/79–03/07/79	USSR	Political (verbal)	Low threat	No violence	Political	Political	None	Agreement
9374	Pakistan	01/06/79–03/07/79								
276 (2780)	Rhodesian Settlement	15/07/79–04/03/80	Internal Rhodesia	Internal challenge	Political regime	Serious clashes	Political	Semi-military	Condemnation	Agreement
9436	Rhodesia	15/07/79–04/03/80								
9437	Botswana	08/08/79–21/12/79								
9438	Mozambique	05/09/79–21/12/79								
9435	Zambia	17/11/79–31/01/80								

Case and crisis actors	Duration	Triggering entity	Triggering act	Highest value threat	Intensity of violence	Superpower activity USA	USSR	Global organization involvement	Form of outcome
277									
(2735) Raid on Angola	28/10/79-02/11/79	South Africa	Violent	Low threat	Minor clashes	None	None	Condemnation	Tacit
9380 Angola	28/10/79-02/11/79								
278									
(2860) US Hostages in Iran	04/11/79-20/01/81	Iran	Political	Political regime	Minor clashes	Military	Political	Call for action	Agreement
9335 USA	04/11/79-20/01/81								
9340 Iran	24/04/80-20/01/81								

III Variables

Variables*	Tables	Page
1 Breakpoint (Trigger) to International Crisis	III.1	61
2 Triggering Entity of Crisis	III.2	64
3 Duration of International Crisis	III.3	66
4 Gravity of Value Threatened	III.4	68
5 Crisis Management Technique	III.5	71
6 Centrality of Violence	III.6	74
7 Intensity of Violence	III.7	76
8 Timing of Violence	III.8	78
9 Intra-War Crisis	III.9	81
10 Number of Involved Actors	III.10	82
11 Content of Great Power/Superpower Activity	III.11	84
12 Effectiveness of Great Power/Superpower Activity	III.12	87
13 Most Effective Great Power/Superpower Activity	III.13	91
14 Source of Global Organization Involvement	III.14	94
15 Global Organization Organ Most Active in Crisis	III.15	95
16 Content of Global Organization Involvement	III.16	98
17 Effectiveness of Global Organization Involvement	III.17	100
18 Most Effective Global Organization Organ	III.18	102
19 Most Effective Global Organization Involvement	III.19	104
20 Source of Regional/Security Organization Involvement	III.20	106
21 Regional/Security Organization Most Active in Crisis	III.21	107
22 Content of Regional/Security Organization Involvement	III.22	109
23 Effectiveness of Regional/Security Organization Involvement	III.23	110
24 Most Effective Regional/Security Organization	III.24	111
25 Perceived Content of Outcome	III.25	112
26 Form of Outcome	III.26	113
27 Extent of Satisfaction about Outcome	III.27	116
28 Escalation or Reduction of Tension	III.28	117

* The ordering of variables in Part III follows a sequence from the outbreak of a crisis to its termination. This necessitated the treatment of the three setting variables – war-related, value threat, and involved actor – after the discussion of the onset of the crisis.

Breakpoint (Trigger) to International Crisis (BREAK)

The breakpoint to an international crisis is that event, act or situational change which catalyzes a crisis for the earliest crisis actor, that is, which leads decision-makers to perceive a threat to basic values, time pressure for response and heightened probability of involvement in military hostilities. The date of this trigger thus becomes the initiation date for the entire international crisis.

Breakpoints do not occur in a vacuum. Rather, crises erupt in diverse international settings. They generate varying degrees of major power participation. Breakpoints and the crises which ensue may or may not be part of an ongoing conflict or war. They take place within the dominant international system or a subsystem. And the power relationship between the adversaries will vary. Thus the data on breakpoints will be presented and analyzed in relation to six control variables: geography; polarity; system level; conflict; power discrepancy; and involvement by the powers.

Breakpoint is an attribute of an international crisis as a whole. However, it is based upon the coding of the trigger for a particular crisis actor. Hence the reader should refer to the treatment of this variable (TRIGGR) in *Handbook II*.

Coding Rules and Raw Frequencies, with Illustrations

1   **Political (verbal) act** ($N = 39$; 14%) – protests, threats, accusations, demands, etc. (Archbishop Makarios, President of the Cypriot Republic, made proposals, in the form of a memorandum, for the amendment of the constitution to change Cyprus to a unitary state, triggering a crisis for Turkey on 30 November 1963, the onset of the Cyprus I Crisis).

2   **Political act** ($N = 30$; 11%) – subversion, alliance of adversaries, diplomatic sanctions, severance of diplomatic relations, violation of treaties (On 8 October 1953 the UK and the US announced their intention to relinquish their administration of Trieste to the Italian Government, triggering a crisis for Yugoslavia, beginning the Trieste II Crisis).

3   **Economic act** ($N = 5$; 2%) – embargo, dumping, nationalization of property, withholding of economic aid (In response to the Kaunas trials of Nazis in Lithuania, Germany closed the border and imposed economic sanctions, triggering a crisis for Lithuania on 28 March 1935, the start of the Kaunas Trials Crisis).

4   **External change** ($N = 14$; 5%) – intelligence reports, change in specific weapons, weapon system, offensive capability, change in global system or regional subsystem, challenge to legitimacy by international organization (The UN General Assembly vote on 29 November 1947, calling for the partition of Palestine into separate Arab and Jewish states, triggered a crisis for Egypt, Iraq, Lebanon and Syria, in the Palestine Partition Crisis).

5   **Other non-violent** ($N = 2$; 1%) (A pre-election referendum in Poland showing the Peasant Party to be strongest triggered a crisis for the USSR on 30 June 1946, catalyzing the Communism in Poland Crisis).

6   **Internal verbal or physical challenge to regime or elite** ($N = 22$; 8%) – incitement by media, proclamation of new regime, fall of government, *coup d'état*, sabotage acts, terrorism, assassination, riots, demonstrations, strikes, arrests, martial law, executions, mutiny, revolt (In the Congo, the National Liberation Committee established a Revolutionary Council in Stanleyville, triggering a crisis for the Congo Government on 4 August 1964, in the Congo II case).

7   **Non-violent military act** ($N = 34$; 12%) – show of force, war games or maneuvers, mobilization, movement of forces, change of force posture to offensive (A crisis was triggered for India on 7 July 1951, when Pakistan moved a brigade to 15 miles from the Kashmir district of Poonch, setting in motion the Punjab War Scare Crisis).

8   **Indirect violent act** ($N = 17$; 6%) – revolt in another country, violent act directed at ally, friendly state, or client state (Supporters of Juan Bosch overthrew the military junta in the Dominican Republic, triggering a crisis for the US on 24 April 1965, the onset of the Dominican Republic Crisis).

9   **Violent act** ($N = 115$; 41%) – border clashes, border crossings by limited forces, invasion of air space, sinking of ships, sea–air incidents, bombing of large targets, large-scale military attack, war (A Chinese ambush of Soviet forces on the Ussuri River on 2 March 1969 triggered a crisis for the USSR, the beginning of the Ussuri River Crisis).

Analysis of Breakpoints (Triggers)

Almost half (48%) of all international crises from 1929 to 1979 were triggered by direct or indirect violence (see Table III.1.A). Non-violent military acts accounted for another 12% of breakpoints. Thus, the military component, especially in its violent form, was preeminent in catalyzing international crises.

Viewed in terms of geographic location, the regions vary from a low of 12% of crises in the Americas to a high of 25% in Asia and 23% in Africa (Table III.1.B). Violent breakpoints were preponderant in the region of the youngest political systems (in 64% of Africa cases), with Europe, the region of the oldest independent states, exhibiting the lowest proportion of crises initiated by violence (25%); conversely, the absence of violence in any form as a crisis trigger was preeminent in Europe's crises (51%), compared to 22% of Africa cases. This suggests a meaningful association between the age of actors and their proneness to violent initiation of crises. Non-violent military breakpoints, such as mobilization, alert and the movement of troops, were the most frequent, relatively, in the Americas.

From the perspective of international systems (see Table III.1.C), the post-1962 polycentric system exhibited the highest proportion of cases with violent breakpoints – 60%. This figure stands in sharp contrast to both the 1930s multipolar system and the 1945–62 bipolar system, and reinforces the findings on the conspicuous increase in violence in late twentieth-century international relations. A

TABLE III.1.A. Breakpoint (Trigger) to International Crisis: Types

	Frequency	%
Non-violent (categories 1–5)	90	32% ✓
Internal challenge (category 6)	22	8%
Non-violent military (category 7)	34	12% ✓
Direct and indirect violent (categories 8–9)	132	48%
Total	278	100%

TABLE III.1.B. Breakpoint (Trigger) to International Crisis: Geography

Region	Non-violent		Internal challenge		Non-violent military		Direct and indirect violent		Total	
	Freq.	%	Freq.	%	Freq.	%	Freq.	%	Freq.	%
Africa	14	22%	6	9%	3	5%	41	64%	64	23%
Americas	7	21%	4	12%	7	21%	15	46%	33	12%
Asia	22	32%	2	3%	7	10%	38	55%	69	25%
Europe	29	51%	6	10%	8	14%	14	25%	57	20%
Middle East	18	33%	4	7%	9	16%	24	44%	55	20%
Total	90	32%	22	8%	34	12%	132	48%	278	100%

TABLE III.1.C. Breakpoint (Trigger) to International Crisis: Polarity

System	Non-violent		Internal challenge		Non-violent military		Direct and indirect violent		Total	
	Freq.	%	Freq.	%	Freq.	%	Freq.	%	Freq.	%
Multipolar (1929–39)	14	37%	3	8%	6	16%	15	39%	38	14%
World War II (1939–45)	8	26%	0	0%	5	16%	18	58%	3	11%
Bipolar (1945–62)	42	45%	10	11%	12	13%	29	31%	93	33%
Polycentric (1963–79)	26	22%	9	8%	11	10%	70	60%	116	42%
Total	90	32%	22	8%	34	12%	132	48%	278	100%

TABLE III.1.D. Breakpoint (Trigger) to International Crisis: System Level*

Level of system	Non-violent		Internal challenge		Non-violent military		Direct and indirect violent		Total	
	Freq.	%	Freq.	%	Freq.	%	Freq.	%	Freq.	%
Subsystem	47	28%	15	9%	21	12%	85	51%	168	60%
Mainly subsystem	18	39%	3	6%	4	9%	21	46%	46	17%
Mainly dominant	11	37%	1	3%	5	17%	13	43%	30	11%
Dominant system	14	41%	3	9%	4	12%	13	38%	34	12%
Total	90	32%	22	8%	34	12%	132	48%	278	100%

* For the derivation of the four system-level values, see the discussion of this control variable in Parts I and II above.

TABLE III.1.E. Breakpoint (Trigger) to International Crisis: Power Discrepancy*

Power discrepancy	Non-violent		Internal challenge		Non-violent military		Direct and indirect violent		Total	
	Freq.	%	Freq.	%	Freq.	%	Freq.	%	Freq.	%
Low	19	23%	9	11%	11	13%	44	53%	83	34%
Medium	27	34%	5	6%	8	10%	39	50%	79	32%
High	36	42%	8	9%	10	12%	31	37%	85	34%
Total	82	33%	22	9%	29	12%	114	46%	247**	100%

* For explanations of low, medium, and high discrepancy, see the discussion of control variables in Part II.
** Does not include World War II cases because of the difficulties associated with computing power discrepancy scores while a world war was in progress.

TABLE III.1.F. Breakpoint (Trigger) to International Crisis: Involvement by Powers

Involvement	Non-violent		Internal challenge		Non-violent military		Direct and indirect violent		Total	
*Great power participation, 1929–39										
	Freq.	%	Freq.	%	Freq.	%	Freq.	%	Freq.	%
Low or No	7	41%	1	6%	2	12%	7	41%	17	45%
High	7	33%	2	10%	4	19%	8	38%	21	55%
Total	14	37%	3	8%	6	16%	15	39%	38	100%
*Great power participation, 1939–45										
Low or No	3	43%	0	0%	1	14%	3	43%	7	23%
High	5	21%	0	0%	4	17%	15	62%	24	77%
Total	8	26%	0	0%	5	16%	18	58%	31	100%
**Superpower participation, 1945–79										
Low or No	46	31%	14	9%	19	13%	71	47%	150	72%
High	22	37%	5	8%	4	7%	28	48%	59	28%
Total	68	33%	19	9%	23	11%	99	47%	209	100%

* Great power participation
Low = One or more powers direct military, semi-military or covert; or all Powers political, economic, or none.
High = One or more powers as crisis actors.
** Superpower participation
Low = Both SPs political, economic, or none; or one SP direct military, semi-military or covert.
High = One or both SPs crisis actors; or both SPs direct military, semi-military or covert.

plausible explanation is the large number of new states in the global system in the 1960s and 1970s, many of which were born in violence and, of necessity, carried that violence into their post-independence relations. Many of these new states were internally disunited, with unstable regimes and leaders who may have sought to offset domestic opposition and dissatisfaction by external adventures.

System does not seem to affect the frequency of internal challenges as triggers to crises; there is virtually no variation except during World War II when external threats were ubiquitous and internal challenges disappeared altogether.

Subsystem crises account for 60% of all international crises for the 50-year period (see Table III.1.D). Among these, violent breakpoints occurred almost twice as often as non-violent (non-military) breakpoints (51% to 28%), a disparity which is not evident in any other level of system category. This is one indicator of a greater proneness to violence in subsystem interstate relations than among actors in the dominant system.

The extent of power discrepancy between adversaries and the type of crisis breakpoint are clearly related (see Table III.1.E): where the power discrepancy is low, there is a much higher tendency to violent breakpoints (53%), with a low propensity to non-violent breakpoints (23%); where the power gap is high, the tendency to violent breakpoints is lowest (37%). This suggests that crises between relatively equal powers are more destabilizing – precisely because the greater uncertainty about their capability *vis-à-vis* their adversary provides a greater inducement to use violence, whereas a large power gap makes violence in break-points unnecessary, unproductive in terms of goals, and therefore less likely for all adversaries.

Level of involvement by superpowers (see Table III.1.F) does not covary with the type of breakpoint; that is, the extent of SP participation in crises does not vary with type of trigger.

Triggering Entity (TRIGENT)

Which entity triggered an international crisis, i.e., initiated the act(s) which was (were) perceived by the earliest crisis actor in the cluster as involving a threat to basic values, a heightened probability of military hostilities and finite time for response? In addition to nation-states, crises may be internally-generated or catalyzed by non-state actors (such as OPEC, the PLO, mercenaries, etc.). Crises can also be triggered by more than one nation-state.

Analysis of Triggering Entity of Crisis

Table III.2.A presents a breakdown of triggering entities of international crises. Ten states which triggered six or more crises during the 1929–79 period, accounting for 93 crises, are listed individually, while all other triggering states are grouped under "Other States."

As evident in Table III.2.B, the clusters of states which were the most frequent triggering entities, including multiple cases, vary considerably over time and type of international system. All 23 crises in the multipolar system of the 1930s were catalyzed by four states, Germany, Japan, Italy (the Axis revisionist powers) and the Soviet Union. During World War II, the US and USSR set in motion the most intra-war crises, followed by the UK and Germany. The picture changes drastically following World War II. The three former Axis powers did not trigger a single crisis from 1945 to 1979. Israel and the USSR were the most frequent state triggering entities during the bipolar period, with Egypt, North Vietnam and Rhodesia (Zimbabwe) sharing that role in the polycentric system, another of many indicators of the dispersion of conflict in the post-1945 transformed global international system.

Almost two-thirds of the 114 international crises in the high-frequency triggering entity group occurred at the subsystem/mainly subsystem level (Table III.2.C). Of the high-frequency states, all of Rhodesia's and Pakistan's cases occurred at the purely subsystem level; so too with most of the cases triggered by Egypt and Israel, along with North Vietnam-initiated crises at the overall subsystem level. At the other extreme, as expected, all of the dominant system cases were catalyzed by Germany, the US, the USSR and the UK. And only those four major powers catalyzed crises at all four system levels.

The high-frequency group of cases were almost equally divided among the three conflict categories (see Table III.2.D). As for states within this group, the USSR and Germany together accounted for almost two-thirds of the 31 cases which

TABLE III.2.A. Triggering Entity of Crisis

Triggering entity	Number of crises triggered*
USSR	19
Israel	12
Germany	12
USA	10
Japan	8
Egypt	7
North Vietnam	7
Italy	6
Rhodesia (Zimbabwe)	6
Pakistan	6
Other states	114
Internal trigger	24
Non-state actor	33
Multiple	14**
Total	278

* When the multiple cases are considered, the frequencies for some of the above triggering entities increase as follows:

USSR	19 + 2 multiple = 21
Germany	12 + 1 multiple = 13
USA	10 + 6 multiple = 16
Egypt	7 + 2 multiple = 9
(UK	4 + 6 multiple = 10)

** The following international crises had multiple triggering entities:

Entry into World War II	20/08/39	Germany, USSR
Occupation of Iran	25/08/41	UK, USSR
Fall of Italy	10/07/43	US, UK
D-Day	06/06/44	US, UK
Berlin Blockade	07/06/48	US, UK, France
Korean War III	16/04/53	North Korea, PRC
Trieste II	08/10/53	UK, US
Taiwan Straits I	00/08/54	Taiwan, US
Baghdad Pact	24/02/55	Iran, Iraq, Pakistan, Turkey, UK
Formation of UAR	01/02/58	Egypt, Syria
Invasion of Laos II	08/02/71	South Vietnam, US
North/South Yemen I	26/09/72	North and South Yemen
October–Yom Kippur War	05/10/73	Egypt, Syria
Vietnam Invasion of Cambodia	24/09/77	Vietnam, Cambodia
North/South Yemen II	24/02/79	North and South Yemen

TABLE III.2.B. Triggering Entity of Crisis: Polarity

Triggering entity	1929–39		1939–45		1945–62		1963–79		Total	
	Freq.	%	Freq.	%	Freq.	%	Freq.	%	Freq.	%
USSR	4	19%	8	38%	7	33%	2	10%	21	19%
USA	0	0%	8	50%	5	31%	3	19%	16	14%
Germany	8	62%	5	38%	0	0%	0	0%	13	12%
Israel	0	0%	0	0%	8	67%	4	33%	12	11%
Egypt	0	0%	0	0%	3	33%	6	67%	9	8%
UK	0	0%	5	50%	5	50%	0	0%	10	8%
Japan	7	88%	1	12%	0	0%	0	0%	8	7%
N. Vietnam	0	0%	0	0%	1	14%	6	86%	7	6%
Italy	4	67%	2	33%	0	0%	0	0%	6	5%
Rhodesia (Zimbabwe)	0	0%	0	0%	0	0%	6	100%	6	5%
Pakistan	0	0%	0	0%	4	67%	2	33%	6	5%
Total	23	20%	29	25%	33	29%	29	26%	114*	100%

* In this and the following tables for triggering entity, multiple triggering entities are added in. Thus, for example, the USSR had 19 single cases plus two multiple (Entry into World War II and Occupation of Iran).

TABLE III.2.C. Triggering Entity of Crisis: System Level

Triggering entity	Subsystem		Mainly subsystem		Mainly dominant		Dominant		Total	
	Freq.	%	Freq.	%	Freq.	%	Freq.	%	Freq.	%
USSR	2	9%	7	33%	6	29%	6	29%	21	19%
USA	2	12.5%	4	25%	2	12.5%	8	50%	16	14%
Germany	1	7.7%	1	7.7%	1	7.7%	10	77%	13	12%
Israel	10	83.3%	1	8.3%	1	8.3%	0	0%	12	11%
Egypt	6	67%	2	22%	1	11%	0	0%	9	8%
UK	1	10%	2	20%	2	20%	5	50%	10	8%
Japan	3	38%	5	62%	0	0%	0	0%	8	7%
N. Vietnam	3	43%	4	57%	0	0%	0	0%	7	6%
Italy	0	0%	4	67%	2	33%	0	0%	6	5%
Rhodesia (Zimbabwe)	6	100%	0	0%	0	0%	0	0%	6	5%
Pakistan	6	100%	0	0%	0	0%	0	0%	6	5%
Total	40	35%	30	26%	15	13%	29	26%	114	100%

TABLE III.2.D. Triggering Entity of Crisis: Conflict

Triggering entity	Non-protracted conflict		Protracted conflict		Long-war-protracted conflict		Total	
	Freq.	%	Freq.	%	Freq.	%	Freq.	%
USSR	12	57%	4	19%	5	24%	21	19%
USA	2	12%	4	25%	10	63%	16	14%
Germany	7	54%	0	0%	6	46%	13	12%
Israel	0	0%	12	100%	0	0%	12	11%
Egypt	4	44%	5	56%	0	0%	9	8%
UK	2	20%	3	30%	5	50%	10	8%
Japan	2	25%	3	37.5%	3	37.5%	8	7%
N. Vietnam	0	0%	1	14%	6	86%	7	6%
Italy	2	33.3%	2	33.3%	2	33.3%	6	5%
Rhodesia (Zimbabwe)	0	0%	1	17%	5	83%	6	5%
Pakistan	0	0%	6	100%	0	0%	6	5%
Total	31	27%	41	36%	42	37%	114	100%

occurred outside of a protracted conflict setting. All of the high-frequency states except Germany triggered one or more crises within a non-long-war-protracted conflict setting; among them Israel was preeminent – all of the 12 crises which it set in motion fall into that category; so, too, did all of Pakistan's six cases. Three long-war-protracted conflicts account for almost all of the 42 cases in that category – World War II, Vietnam, Rhodesia.

Duration of International Crisis (BREXIT)

The duration of an international crisis is defined in terms of the elapsed time in days between the first breakpoint and the last exitpoint. The first breakpoint is that date on which the earliest crisis actor perceived threat to basic values, finite time for response and heightened probability of involvement in military hostilities (see variable BREAK). The last exitpoint is the date on which the last actor perceived crisis termination, i.e., a decline in stress associated with the three factors above to the pre-crisis norm.

Crises vary considerably in duration. For purposes of presentation here, the cases will be collapsed into three broad categories.

Coding Rules and Raw Frequencies with Illustrations
1 **Short: 1–31 days** ($N = 82$; 31%) (The merger of Egypt and Syria into the United Arab Republic triggered a crisis for Jordan and Iraq on 1 February 1958; a joint proclamation by Jordan and Iraq establishing the Arab Federation on 14 February 1958 terminated the crisis – duration = 14 days).

2 **Medium: 32–60 days** ($N = 35$; 13%) (A crisis between El Salvador and Honduras began on 15 June 1969, in the aftermath of riots occurring at a football game between the national teams of the two countries; a compromise settlement was reached on 30 July 1969, terminating the crisis – duration = 46 days).

3 **Long: 61+ days** ($N = 150$; 56%) (On 22 July 1977 Somalia mounted a full-scale attack into the Ogaden, triggering a crisis for Ethiopia; on 14 March 1978 Somalia completed a withdrawal from the Ogaden, terminating the crisis for both actors – duration = 236 days).

Analysis of Duration of International Crisis

Overall, international crises from 1929 to 1979 exhibited a tendency to "long" duration: 56% of the 267 crises with known termination dates, including half or more of the cases in each region except Europe, lasted at least 2 months (see Table III.3.A). In general, too, crises tended to be long or short – not of medium duration. The largest proportion of crises of short duration (a month or less), and the smallest proportion of relatively long crises, occurred in Europe. The situation is just the opposite for Asia, where only 21% of the crises terminated within 31 days, while 70% lasted 61 days or more. Medium-length crises (1–2 months) were most frequent in the Americas.

Crises occurring at the mainly dominant system level stand out, with the largest proportion of longer crises and a much smaller percentage of cases of short duration (see Table III.3.B). This suggests that, when major powers are participants in subsystem crises over global issues, it takes longer to reconcile conflicting interests.

TABLE III.3.A. Duration of International Crisis: Geography

Region	1–31 days		32–60 days		61+ days		Total	
	Freq.	%	Freq.	%	Freq.	%	Freq.	%
Africa	19	32%	10	17%	30	51%	59	22%
Americas	8	25%	7	22%	17	53%	32	12%
Asia	14	21%	6	9%	47	70%	67	25%
Europe	22	40%	8	15%	25	45%	55	21%
Middle East	19	35%	4	7%	31	58%	54	20%
Total	82	31%	35	13%	150	56%	267*	100%

* For 11 cases, the precise termination date could not be determined.

TABLE III.3.B. Duration of International Crisis: System Level

Level of system	1–31 days		32–60 days		61+ days		Total	
	Freq.	%	Freq.	%	Freq.	%	Freq.	%
Subsystem	52	32.5%	24	15%	84	52.5%	160	60%
Mainly subsystem	15	33%	4	9%	26	58%	45	17%
Mainly dominant	3	11%	2	7%	23	82%	28	10%
Dominant system	12	35%	5	15%	17	50%	34	13%
Total	82	31%	35	13%	150	56%	267	100%

TABLE III.3.C. Duration of International Crisis: Conflict

Conflict setting	1–31 days		32–60 days		61+ days		Total	
	Freq.	%	Freq.	%	Freq.	%	Freq.	%
Non-protracted conflict	51	43%	13	11%	54	46%	118	44%
Protracted conflict	21	23%	14	15%	56	62%	91	34%
Long-war-protracted conflict	10	17%	8	14%	40	69%	58	22%
Total	82	31%	35	13%	150	56%	267	100%

As Table III.3.C indicates, crises which occurred outside of protracted conflicts tended to be shortest in duration. As expected, 69% of the crises within long-war-protracted conflicts continued for over 60 days, as compared with 62% of the cases in non-long-war-protracted conflicts and 46% for non-protracted conflicts. Medium duration, that is, more than one month but not more than two, was the least frequent in all these conflict settings.

Gravity of Value Threatened (GRAVCR) This variable identifies the object of gravest threat, as perceived by the principal decision-makers of any of the crisis actors during the course of an international crisis. It need not be the value threat perceived by the earliest actor in a crisis.

While gravity of threat is an attribute of a crisis as a whole, it is based upon the coding of value threat for each crisis actor. Hence the reader should also refer to the treatment of this variable in *Handbook II*.

Coding Rules and Raw Frequencies, with Illustrations
1   **Low threat** ($N = 26$; 9%) – limited threat to population and property, threat to the social system such as forced emigration, change of ethnic equilibrium, challenge to legitimacy of belief system, threat to economic interests such as control of other actor's economy, requisition of resources, loss of markets, blocked access to resources or markets (An economic threat to Britain and Iceland during the Cod War I Crisis, 14 May to 13 November 1973).
2   **Threat to political system** ($N = 39$; 14%) – threat of overthrow of regime, change of institutions, replacement of élite, intervention in domestic politics, subversion (Crises for Nicaragua, Panama, the Dominican Republic, and Haiti, generated by Cuba-assisted invasions by exiles of these states from 25 April to December 1959 in the Cuba/Central America I Crisis).
3   **Threat to territorial integrity** ($N = 58$; 21%) – threat of integration, annexation of part of a state's territory, separatism (Japanese military operations in China, ultimately resulting in the Japanese unilateral declaration of independence of Manchuria, as a territorial threat to China, the Mukden Incident beginning 18 September 1931 and fading some time in 1932).
4   **Threat to influence in the international system or regional subsystem** ($N = 70$; 25%) – threat of declining power in the global system and/or regional subsystem, diplomatic isolation, cessation of patron aid (Egypt's nationalization of the Suez Canal on 26 July 1956, as a threat to the global and regional influence of Britain and France, in the Suez Nationalization Crisis).
5   **Threat of grave damage** ($N = 39$; 14%) – threat of large casualties in war, mass bombings (The PRC build-up of forces in the coastal areas around Quemoy and Matsu was perceived by Taiwan as a threat of grave damage on 17 July 1958, in the Taiwan Straits II Crisis).
6   **Threat to existence** ($N = 46$; 17%) – threat to survival of population, genocide, threat to existence of entity, of total annexation, colonial rule, occupation (Italy's invasion of Ethiopia and the war which ensued, 2 October 1935 to 5 May 1936).

Analysis of Gravity of Value Threatened The level of threat in international crises for the 50-year period as a whole was high: 77% of all cases involved important values – territorial integrity, influence in the global and/or regional system, the avoidance of grave material damage and existence. The last two, the most basic values, were threatened in almost one-third of all international crises between 1929 and 1979.

Two regions, Europe and Asia, stand out in terms of the concentration of crises involving threats to existence; together, they accounted for 36 of the 46 cases with the highest value threat, that is, 78% of the total (Table III.4.A). It is also interesting to note that the vast majority of the European cases of threat to existence occurred in the multipolar and World War II systems, 1929–45, while most of the Asian cases of threat to existence occurred in the bipolar and polycentric systems, 1945–79. At the other extreme, low threats were conspicuous in Africa and the Americas, while medium threats (to political regime, territory and influence), taken together, were predominant in the Americas (73%), Africa (69%) and the Middle East (64%). In Europe, boundaries had crystallized by the 1920s, making threats to territory a rare occurrence compared to Africa-located crises.

TABLE III.4.A. Value Threatened: Geography

Region	Low		Political		Territory		Influence		Grave damage		Existence		Total	
	Freq.	%	Freq.	%	Freq.	%	Freq.	%	Freq.	%	Freq.	%	Freq.	%
Africa	10	15%	12	19%	19	30%	13	20%	7	11%	3	5%	64	23%
Americas	5	15%	12	37%	8	24%	4	12%	2	6%	2	6%	33	12%
Asia	3	5%	7	10%	16	23%	16	23%	11	16%	16	23%	69	25%
Europe	3	5%	4	7%	4	7%	17	30%	9	16%	20	35%	57	20%
Middle East	5	9%	4	7%	11	20%	20	37%	10	18%	5	9%	55	20%
Total	26	9%	39	14%	58	21%	70	25%	39	14%	46	17%	278	100%

TABLE III.4.B. Value Threatened: Polarity

System	Low		Political		Territory		Influence		Grave damage		Existence		Total	
	Freq.	%	Freq.	%	Freq.	%	Freq.	%	Freq.	%	Freq.	%	Freq.	%
Multipolar (1929–39)	2	5%	2	5%	11	29%	6	16%	2	5%	15	40%	38	14%
World War II (1939–45)	1	3%	0	0%	2	7%	5	16%	10	32%	13	42%	31	11%
Bipolar (1945–62)	4	4%	19	20%	20	22%	30	32%	10	11%	10	11%	93	33%
Polycentric (1963–79)	19	16%	18	15%	25	22%	29	25%	17	15%	8	7%	116	42%
Total	26	9%	39	14%	58	21%	70	25%	39	14%	46	17%	278	100%

TABLE III.4.C. Value Threatened: System Level

Level of system	Low		Political		Territory		Influence		Grave damage		Existence		Total	
	Freq.	%	Freq.	%	Freq.	%	Freq.	%	Freq.	%	Freq.	%	Freq.	%
Subsystem	22	13%	33	20%	48	29%	33	20%	16	9%	16	9%	168	60%
Mainly subsystem	4	9%	3	6%	9	20%	16	35%	8	17%	6	13%	46	17%
Mainly dominant	0	0%	3	10%	1	3%	14	47%	3	10%	9	30%	30	11%
Dominant system	0	0%	0	0%	0	0%	7	21%	12	35%	15	44%	34	12%
Total	26	9%	39	14%	58	21%	70	25%	39	14%	46	17%	278	100%

TABLE III.4.D. Value Threatened: Conflict

Conflict setting	Low		Political		Territory		Influence		Grave damage		Existence		Total	
	Freq.	%	Freq.	%	Freq.	%	Freq.	%	Freq.	%	Freq.	%	Freq.	%
Non-protracted conflict	15	12%	30	24%	30	24%	29	24%	6	5%	13	11%	123	44%
Protracted conflict	6	6%	4	4%	26	27%	29	30%	18	19%	13	14%	96	35%
Long-war-protracted conflict	5	9%	5	9%	2	3%	12	20%	15	25%	20	34%	59	21%
Total	26	9%	39	14%	58	21%	70	25%	39	14%	46	17%	278	100%

TABLE III.4.E. Value Threatened: Power Discrepancy

Power discrepancy	Low		Political		Territory		Influence		Grave damage		Existence		Total	
	Freq.	%	Freq.	%	Freq.	%	Freq.	%	Freq.	%	Freq.	%	Freq.	%
Low	6	7%	20	24%	30	36%	11	13%	7	9%	9	11%	83	34%
Medium	10	13%	11	14%	24	30%	15	19%	8	10%	11	14%	79	32%
High	9	11%	8	9%	2	2%	39	46%	14	17%	13	15%	85	34%
Total	25	10%	39	16%	56	23%	65	26%	29	12%	33	13%	247*	100%

* Does not include World War II cases.

There is a striking difference in the relative frequency of threats to existence in the multipolar system before World War II (40%) and the post-1945 bipolar/polycentric systems (11%/7% or 9% for the entire 1945–79 period) (see Table III.4.B). This suggests that an international system characterized by a diffusion of power protects its members much less effectively than does a system with a concentration of power in two states, and/or that a bipolar system has a greater interest in the continued existence of member-states. Alternatively stated, the evidence on values threatened indicates that a bipolar structure is more conducive to stability in the international system than a multipolar structure.

Political threats are almost exclusively found in the bipolar/polycentric systems, 37 of 39 cases. There are two possible explanations: (a) in the post-1945 systems many states are of recent creation and their regimes have not yet crystallized, whereas in the 1930s most states had been in existence for a long time; (b) ideology was more influential in the bipolar/polycentric systems, in the form of a direct USA/USSR confrontation of democracy vs. communism, than it was in the 1930s, with seven more or less co-equal system leaders.

The level of system has a marked relationship with values threatened (see Table III.4.C). Thus, the highest value threats were much more frequent in the dominant system than in a subsystem: existence, 44% to 9%; grave damage, 35% to 9%. Conversely, threats to lesser values predominated in subsystem crises: territory, 29% to 0%; political, 20% to 0%; low, 13% to 0%.

Crises within the dominant system are, in short, more threatening, more dangerous and more destabilizing than those within a subsystem. The principal reason would seem to be the preeminent role of the great powers or superpowers in the dominant system and their greater capability for destructive violence. High value threats, combined with high violence capability, constitute a grave danger to system stability.

Sharp contrasts exist between long-war-protracted conflict crises and non-protracted conflict crises (see Table III.4.D). Long-war cases are characterized much more by high value threats (existence, 34% to 11%; grave damage, 25% to 5%). In crises outside protracted conflicts, by contrast, lesser values are more visible (territory, 24% to 3%; political, 24% to 9%; low, 12% to 9%). In short, the most threatening – and destabilizing – international crises are those which occur during a prolonged violent conflict. The persistence of a conflict and the continued resort to violence by the adversaries make the stakes high, with a high probability (59%) that a crisis erupting in such an environment will threaten core values of one or another actor, either its very existence or the danger of grave damage. The protractedness of conflict and the ubiquity of war not only manifest this likelihood but also explain it: hostility deepens over time, and with it mutual fear and growing inability to compromise; conflicting interests are accentuated, and shared interests become blurred and are submerged; the perpetuation of the conflict strengthens the negative and antagonistic forces in the relationship.

The most frequent value threatened in crises characterized by high-power discrepancy among the adversaries was influence (46%), more than double any other value; in low-discrepancy cases, threat to territory was the most visible, 36% (see Table III.4.E). Generally, the higher the power discrepancy, the higher the value threat.

Crisis Management Technique (CRISMG)

Crisis actors employ a variety of management techniques when coping with crises. This variable identifies the primary crisis management technique used by the crisis actors. Values for this variable – for individual crisis actors – are scaled from techniques involving negotiation and mediation through those involving violence. Hence the reader should refer to the treatment of this variable in *Handbook II*.

The crisis management technique selected for the international crisis as a whole is the highest crisis management technique used by any actor along a scale from pacific techniques to violence.

Coding Rules and Raw Frequencies, with Illustrations
1 **Negotiation** (N = 43; 16%) – formal, informal, bilateral, multilateral, international, diplomatic exchange (In the crisis between Poland and the USSR in October 1956, negotiations took place between the parties attending the Polish Plenum).
2 **Mediation** (N = 7; 3%) – by global or regional organization, ally, or alliance personnel (In the Rann of Kutch Crisis between India and Pakistan, from 8 April to 30 June 1965, both parties agreed to mediation by Britain).
3 **Multiple not including violence** (N = 29; 10%) – (In the Shatt-al-Arab I Crisis from 28 November 1959 to 4 January 1960, Iran placed its troops on full alert, moved troops to the Iraqi border, and engaged in negotiations, the latter ultimately leading to resolution of the crisis).
4 **Non-military pressure** (N = 3; 1%) – e.g., withholding of promised economic aid (In a crisis involving Dahomey and Niger between 21 December 1963 and 4 January 1964, Dahomey closed its rail and road links with Niger, thus cutting off the Dahomeyan Port Cotonou from landlocked Niger).
5 **Non-violent military** (N = 41; 15%) – physical acts (maneuvers, redisposition of forces); verbal acts (oral and written statements by authorized leaders or agencies threatening to use violence) (Yugoslavia placed its forces on alert and conducted military maneuvers, in response to a Soviet ultimatum perceived as a possible prelude to military invasion, in the Soviet Bloc/Yugoslavia Crisis, beginning 19 August 1949).
6 **Multiple including violence** (N = 76; 27%) – (In the 1951–52 Suez Canal Crisis, Britain reinforced its forces in Egypt and engaged in serious clashes with Egyptian troops; it also prohibited the export of arms to Egypt).
7 **Violence** (N = 79; 28%) – (The US and South Korea attempted to manage the 1950 Korean War I Crisis by full-scale military action).

Analysis of Crisis Management Technique

Overall, violence plays a very important role in the management of international crises. No less than 55% of all crises showed violence or multiple including violence as the primary crisis management technique (CMT). In an additional 15% of all crises, non-violent military techniques were preeminent. By contrast, negotiation as the primary CMT was evident in only 16% of international crises. And non-military pressure, along with mediation, were rarely used in managing crises.

Violence as the primary CMT was most frequently used in Asia-located crises – and rarely in the Americas (Table III.5.A). When one adds cases with multiple CMTs including violence, the primacy of violence for Asia is even more marked (71%), but Europe (38%) replaces the Americas (46%) as the least prone to violence in crisis management. There is little variation among the five regions in terms of the resort to negotiation as the primary CMT. Mediation and non-military pressure were very rare. However, the Americas reveal the most frequent reliance on multiple non-violent CMTs, and on pacific crisis management techniques generally (42%), followed closely by Europe (37%). While violence or multiple including violence was the most frequent primary CMT for crises in four regions (Africa, Asia, Americas and Middle East), the most frequent CMT in Europe-located crises was military acts of a non-violent nature such as mobilization or alert of armed forces.

Clearly, the period of World War II has the highest proportion of crises in which violence was employed as the primary crisis management technique (see Table III.5.B). Not surprisingly, the probability of multiple techniques including violence, and non-violent military, are lower for the war period than for any of the other periods examined. However, if we add together the three categories of violence, multiple including violence and non-violent military, we find the period of World

TABLE III.5.A. Crisis Management Technique: Geography

Region	Negotiation		Mediation		Multiple no violence		Non-military pressure		Non-violent military		Multiple including violence		Violence		Total	
	Freq.	%	Freq.	%	Freq.	%	Freq.	%	Freq.	%	Freq.	%	Freq.	%	Freq.	%
Africa	8	12%	0	0%	6	9%	1	2%	9	14%	19	30%	21	33%	64	23%
Americas	4	12%	3	9%	7	21%	0	0%	4	12%	12	37%	3	9%	33	12%
Asia	11	16%	2	3%	3	4%	0	0%	4	6%	19	28%	30	43%	69	25%
Europe	11	19%	1	2%	9	16%	0	0%	14	25%	10	17%	12	21%	57	20%
Middle East	9	16%	1	2%	4	7%	2	4%	10	18%	16	29%	13	24%	55	20%
Total	43	16%	7	3%	29	10%	3	1%	41	15%	76	27%	79	28%	278	100%

TABLE III.5.B. Crisis Management Technique: Polarity

System	Negotiation		Mediation		Multiple no violence		Non-military pressure		Non-violent military		Multiple including violence		Violence		Total	
	Freq.	%	Freq.	%	Freq.	%	Freq.	%	Freq.	%	Freq.	%	Freq.	%	Freq.	%
Multipolar (1929–39)	8	21%	2	5%	5	13%	0	0%	6	16%	13	34%	4	11%	38	14%
World War II (1939–45)	5	16%	1	3%	2	6.5%	1	3%	2	6.5%	4	13%	16	52%	31	11%
Bipolar (1945–62)	17	18%	2	2%	10	11%	1	1%	18	19%	22	24%	23	25%	93	33%
Polycentric (1963–79)	13	11%	2	2%	12	10%	1	1%	15	13%	37	32%	36	31%	116	42%
Total	43	16%	7	3%	29	10%	3	1%	41	15%	76	27%	79	28%	278	100%

TABLE III.5.C. Crisis Management Technique: System Level

Level of system	Negotiation		Mediation		Multiple no violence		Non-military pressure		Non-violent military		Multiple including violence		Violence		Total	
	Freq.	%	Freq.	%	Freq.	%	Freq.	%	Freq.	%	Freq.	%	Freq.	%	Freq.	%
Subsystem	27	16%	7	4%	17	10%	1	1%	23	14%	51	30%	42	25%	168	60%
Mainly subsystem	6	13%	0	0%	7	15%	1	2%	4	9%	14	30.5%	14	30.5%	46	17%
Mainly dominant	3	10%	0	0%	2	6.7%	0	0%	5	16.7%	8	26.7%	12	40%	30	11%
Dominant system	7	21%	0	0%	3	9%	1	3%	9	26%	3	9%	11	32%	34	12%
Total	43	16%	7	3%	29	10%	3	1%	41	15%	76	27%	79	28%	278	100%

TABLE III.5.D. Crisis Management Technique: Power Discrepancy

Power discrepancy	Negotiation		Mediation		Multiple no violence		Non-military pressure		Non-violent military		Multiple including violence		Violence		Total	
	Freq.	%	Freq.	%	Freq.	%	Freq.	%	Freq.	%	Freq.	%	Freq.	%	Freq.	%
Low	11	13%	3	4%	8	10%	1	1%	12	14%	35	42%	13	16%	83	34%
Medium	15	19%	3	4%	11	14%	0	0%	9	11%	20	25%	21	27%	79	32%
High	12	14%	0	0%	8	10%	1	1%	18	21%	17	20%	29	34%	85	34%
Total	38	16%	6	2%	27	11%	2	1%	39	16%	72	29%	63	25%	247*	100%

* Does not include World War II cases.

TABLE III.5.E. Crisis Management Technique: Involvement by Powers

Involvement	Negotiation		Mediation		Multiple no-violence		Non-military pressure		Non-violent military		Multiple including violence		Violence		Total	
	Freq.	%	Freq.	%	Freq.	%	Freq.	%	Freq.	%	Freq.	%	Freq.	%	Freq.	%
Great power participation, 1929–39																
Low or No	5	29%	2	12%	2	12%	0	0%	2	12%	6	35%	0	0%	17	45%
High	3	14.3%	0	0%	3	14.3%	0	0%	4	19%	7	33.3%	4	19%	21	55%
Total	8	21%	2	5%	5	13%	0	0%	6	16%	13	34%	4	11%	38	100%
Great power participation, 1939–45																
Low or No	2	29%	1	14%	1	14%	1	14%	2	29%	0	0%	0	0%	7	23%
High	3	12%	0	0%	1	4%	0	0%	0	0%	4	17%	16	67%	24	77%
Total	5	16%	1	3%	2	6.5%	1	3%	2	6.5%	4	13%	16	52%	31	100%
Superpower participation, 1945–79																
Low or No	26	17.3%	4	2.7%	17	11.3%	1	0.7%	23	15.3%	41	27.3%	38	25.3%	150	72%
High	4	7%	0	0%	5	8%	1	2%	10	17%	18	30%	21	36%	59	28%
Total	30	14%	4	2%	22	11%	2	1%	33	16%	59	28%	59	28%	209	100%

War II almost indistinguishable from the two subsequent periods. Thus, while the intensity of violence was quite different in the post-war periods, the extent to which military CMTs were employed was no different in exclusively war and predominantly non-war periods. This suggests that the ubiquity of military techniques, especially violence, from 1939 to 1945 became an accepted "rule of the game" after World War II, one of its important legacies to international political behavior.

Violence alone was less prominent as the primary CMT in the multipolar system of the thirties, with seven great powers, than in the post-1945 bipolar/polycentric systems, 11% and 25%/31%, respectively. If violence and multiple including violence are combined, then violence in crisis management was much less prominent in the multipolar system than in the polycentric system, 45% to 63% of the cases. The explanation for these findings, especially the much lower rate of violence alone in crisis management during the multipolar system, lies partly in the comparative effectiveness of security regimes. The "rules of the game" are much less ambiguous in a multipolar than in a polycentric system. This, in turn, is due to the sharper awareness, in a multipolar system, of the power discrepancy between the strong and the weak. Thus a security regime, as an informal consensus about the rules of the game, is more effective in limiting disruptions, that is, containing instability, in a multipolar system. Moreover, self-imposed constraint on the use of violence by crisis actors is more likely to occur and to be effective in a balance-of-power type of international system of relatively equal powers, that is, multipolarity, than among weak states on the periphery of an international system dominated by two equal power blocs, who are unable or unwilling to constrain violent behavior by the unaligned, that is, polycentrism.

Negotiation as the primary CMT declined over time from 1929 to 1979. In structural terms, it moved from 21% of all cases in the multipolar system to 11% of the cases in the polycentric system. This is the obverse of the increasing use of violence as the primary CMT from the multipolar to the polycentric system and is one of several indicators of the general decline of pacific CMTs over the half-century. One possible explanation is the sharp increase in the number of state actors from the multipolar to the polycentric system: other things being equal, the larger the number of autonomous actors, the greater the likelihood of conflictual interaction and the greater the likelihood of resort to violence in crisis management. The decline in resort to negotiation as the primary CMT may also reflect the predominance of appeasement within the foreign policy behavior of many great powers in the 1930s, specifically, their preoccupation with the avoidance of war.

Two findings are noteworthy with regard to level of system (see Table III.5.C). First, there was a much more frequent reliance on multiple techniques including violence at the subsystem level than at the dominant system level. This disposition of subsystem actors to multiple CMTs may be due to their greater sense of dependence on superpowers or great powers, using pressure through negotiation or mediation or granting or withholding of aid to/from clients.

The second finding is the greater reliance on non-violent military acts to manage crises at the dominant system level than at the subsystem level – 26% to 14%, or 43% to 23% for the extended dominant system and subsystem cases. This suggests that, in a dominant system crisis, threatened action may be sufficient to constrain the adversary.

The frequencies for power discrepancy present interesting paradoxes (see Table III.5.D). On the one hand, we find that when we are concerned with the primary use of violence as a crisis management technique, greater use of violence is associated with higher power discrepancy. On the other hand, when we are concerned with multiple techniques including violence, we find the reverse trend – the lower the power discrepancy, the greater the tendency to multiple techniques including violence. This may be an indication that when the power gap is narrow, adversaries seek various methods of coping with a crisis before resorting to violence.

The contrast between multipolar and bipolar/polycentric systems, in terms of crisis actors' reliance on violence as their primary CMT, is also evident when the great powers and superpowers are highly involved in a crisis, 19% and 36%, respectively (see Table III.5.E); that is, superpowers were less effective in constraining the resort to violence in crisis management within a bipolar system than were great powers in a multipolar system. During the post-war period crises with low superpower participation were again more likely than high participation cases to exhibit pacific CMTs (31% versus 15%), although the data clearly suggest that these techniques were less used in the latter period in general.

In post-1945 crises there was a greater disposition to negotiate when the US and/or USSR were not involved or only moderately involved in a crisis. In the multipolar system of the 1930s, crisis actors were more inclined to mediation or negotiation when the powers were less involved. Thus, in both systems, high involvement by the powers was accompanied by a high resort to violence in crisis management, in 52% (multipolar) and 65% (bipolar/polycentric) of high involvement cases.

Centrality of Violence (CENVIOSY)

For those crises in which violence was employed as a primary crisis management technique (CMT), the present variable identifies the centrality of that violence. This refers to the relative importance which decision-makers attached to their use of violence in order to obtain their goals in a crisis.

In a specific international crisis it is likely that the various actors differed in the extent of violence employed. The present variable identifies the most extensive use of violence as the primary crisis management technique by any of the crisis actors. The reader should refer to the treatment of this variable at the individual actor level (CENVIO) in *Handbook II*.

Coding Rules and Raw Frequencies, with Illustrations
1 **No violence as crisis management technique** ($N = 96$; 35%).
2 **Minor violence** ($N = 26$; 9%) – violence occurred but played a minor role relative to other, non-violent crisis management techniques (During the Uganda/Tanzania I Crisis of 1971 Ugandan Air Force jets bombed a Tanzanian military camp allegedly used for training anti-Amin forces).
3 **Violence important** ($N = 74$; 27%) – violence was important, but was supported by other crisis management techniques (In the Ogaden I Crisis of 1964 Ethiopia responded to a Somali attack on a frontier post with military resistance, together with a declaration of a state of emergency, a call for a meeting of the OAU, and a protest to the USSR chargé d'affaires in Addis Ababa).
4 **Violence preeminent** ($N = 82$; 29%) (Violence was the preeminent crisis management technique employed in the Korean War crises of 1950–53).

Analysis of Centrality of Violence

Violence as a crisis management technique was preeminent or important in 56% of all international crises between 1929 and 1979. The Asia region ranks first in terms of the proportion of cases in which violence was the primary crisis management technique: it was preeminent in 45% and was extensively used in 74% of Asia-located cases (Table III.6.A). Violence was also prominent in crisis management within Africa and the Middle East, in 63% and 51% of those regions' crises, respectively. Crises occurring in Europe during the 50-year period under analysis reflect the unique history of that region: a high proportion of crises which involved no violence as a CMT (54%), characterizing the period subsequent to World War II, and a relatively high proportion of crises with violence as preeminent or important (39%), characterizing the World War II period. The Americas exhibit the lowest proportion of crises (9%) in which violence was the preeminent crisis management technique.

The preeminent use of violence as a crisis management technique was least in evidence during the multipolar period (see Table III.6.B). In an environment of global war, actors did not resort to violence as a CMT in 22% of the cases. In the post-war era, we note an increase in the tendency toward the centrality of violence in crises from the bipolar to the polycentric system, both as an important and as the preeminent CMT.

The dominant system is distinctive in terms of the pattern for violence as a crisis management technique (see Table III.6.C). Violence was employed as a CMT in

TABLE III.6.A. Centrality of Violence: Geography

Region	No violence		Violence minor role		Violence important		Violence pre-eminent		Total	
	Freq.	%	Freq.	%	Freq.	%	Freq.	%	Freq.	%
Africa	18	28%	6	9%	19	30%	21	33%	64	23%
Americas	14	43%	4	12%	12	36%	3	9%	33	12%
Asia	12	17%	6	9%	20	29%	31	45%	69	25%
Europe	31	54%	4	7%	9	16%	13	23%	5	20%
Middle East	21	38%	6	11%	14	25.5%	14	25.5%	55	20%
Total	96	35%	26	9%	74	27%	82	29%	278	100%

TABLE III.6.B. Centrality of Violence: Polarity

System	No violence		Violence minor role		Violence important		Violence pre-eminent		Total	
	Freq.	%	Freq.	%	Freq.	%	Freq.	%	Freq.	%
Multipolar (1929–39)	19	50%	2	5%	13	34%	4	11%	38	14%
World War II (1939–45)	7	22%	4	13%	3	10%	17	55%	31	11%
Bipolar (1945–62)	37	40%	11	12%	21	22%	24	26%	93	33%
Polycentric (1963–79)	33	28%	9	8%	37	32%	37	32%	116	42%
Total	96	35%	26	9%	74	27%	82	29%	278	100%

TABLE III.6.C. Centrality of Violence: System Level

Level of system	No violence		Violence minor role		Violence important		Violence pre-eminent		Total	
	Freq.	%	Freq.	%	Freq.	%	Freq.	%	Freq.	%
Subsystem	55	33%	18	11%	51	30%	44	26%	168	60%
Mainly subsystem	14	30.4%	4	8.7%	14	30.4%	14	30.4%	46	17%
Mainly dominant	8	27%	3	10%	7	23%	12	40%	30	11%
Dominant system	19	56%	1	3%	2	6%	12	35%	34	12%
Total	96	35%	26	9%	74	27%	82	29%	278	100%

only 44% of the dominant system cases, as compared with a 70% average for the other three systems. When violence was employed as a CMT in dominant system cases it was as the preeminent crisis management technique (12 of 15 cases or 80%, as compared to 70 of 167 cases or 42% for the other three system-levels). It is interesting to note that 23 of the 34 dominant system crises occurred prior to or during World War II.

An interesting pattern emerges in terms of how the power discrepancy among the major adversaries in a crisis relates to the use of violence as the primary crisis management technique (see Table III.6.D). The higher the power discrepancy, the greater the likelihood that the role of violence in crisis management will predominate. However, it is also the case that the higher the power discrepancy, the greater the likelihood that no violence will be employed as a CMT.

In Table III.6.E we examine the centrality of violence under conditions of low and high great power/superpower participation. In all three periods high participation by the major powers in crises was more closely associated with the predominant role of violence in crisis management: 19% to 0% (1929–39); 71% to 0% (1939–45); and 37% to 26% (1945–79). During the multipolar period, crises with low participation on the part of great powers had a rather low probability of violence as compared to crises with high great power participation – 35% versus 62%. During the post-war period, we note both a trend toward lower participation on the part of the superpowers – 72% of all crises after World War II exhibited low involvement compared to 45% from 1929 to 1939 – and a greater trend toward violence in these low involvement cases – 67% from 1945 to 1979, compared to 35% in the thirties. This would seem to be due to two factors: the decline in intra-bloc cohesion and ineffective control over client behavior by the US and the

TABLE III.6.D. Centrality of Violence: Power Discrepancy

Power discrepancy	No violence		Violence minor role		Violence important		Violence pre-eminent		Total	
	Freq.	%	Freq.	%	Freq.	%	Freq.	%	Freq.	%
Low	27	33%	7	8%	36	43%	13	16%	83	34%
Medium	27	34%	10	13%	20	25%	22	28%	79	32%
High	35	41%	5	6%	15	18%	30	35%	85	34%
Total	89	36%	22	9%	71	29%	6	26%	247*	100%

For explanations of low, medium, and high discrepancy, see the discussion of control variables in Part II.
* Does not include World War II cases.

Table III.6.E. Centrality of Violence: Involvement by Powers

Involvement	No violence		Violence minor role		Violence important		Violence pre-eminent		Total	
Great power participation 1929–39										
	Freq.	%	Freq.	%	Freq.	%	Freq.	%	Freq.	%
Low or No	11	65%	0	0%	6	35%	0	0%	17	45%
High	8	38%	2	10%	7	33%	4	19%	21	55%
Total	19	50%	2	5%	13	34%	4	11%	38	100%
Great power participation, 1939–45										
Low or No	4	57%	3	43%	0	0%	0	0%	7	23%
High	3	12.5%	1	4%	3	12.5%	17	71%	24	77%
Total	7	22%	4	13%	3	10%	17	55%	31	100%
Superpower participation, 1945–79										
Low or No	50	33%	19	13%	42	28%	39	26%	150	72%
High	20	34%	1	2%	16	27%	22	37%	59	28%
Total	70	33%	20	10%	58	28%	61	29%	209	100%

USSR; and, more significant, the growth in the number of non-aligned state actors from the 1960s onward.

Intensity of Violence (INTVIOSY)

For those crises in which violence was employed as a primary crisis management technique, the present variable identifies the intensity of that violence. In a specific international crisis, it is likely that the actors differ in terms of the degree of intensity of violence employed. The present variable identifies the most intense use of violence as the primary crisis management technique by any of the crisis actors. The reader should refer to the treatment of this variable at the individual actor level (INTVIO) in *Handbook II*.

Both the intensity of violence (INTVIOSY) and the centrality of violence (CENVIOSY), the previous variable in this analysis, are actor-focused within an international crisis. They differ from the extent of violence in a crisis (VIOL), which refers to the intensity of hostile physical interaction in the crisis as a whole, rather than the centrality or intensity of violence used by actors as the primary crisis management technique. The extent of violence, an indicator of the overall intensity of a crisis, is discussed in Part IV below.

Coding Rules and Raw Frequencies, with Illustrations
1 **No violence** ($N = 96$; 35%).
2 **Minor clashes** ($N = 44$; 16%) (On 20 August 1968, during the Prague Spring Crisis, troops of the Warsaw Pact invaded Czechoslovakia; they met only token resistance and acquired total control of Czech territory within 36 hours).
3 **Serious clashes** ($N = 71$; 25%) (On 8 April 1965 India launched an attack on a Pakistani police post in the disputed part of the Rann of Kutch, provoking a counter-attack by Pakistan).
4 **Full-scale war** ($N = 67$; 24%) (The Japanese attack and Chinese counter-attack at the Marco Polo Bridge in early July 1937 were the initial moves in the long war between these two countries).

Analysis of Intensity of Violence

Overall, one-fourth of the 278 international crises from 1929 to 1979 witnessed the resort to full-scale war as the primary crisis management technique. At the same time, violence in any form was not so employed in 35% of the cases. As noted, the European region had a high proportion of crises with no violence (55%), as well as a relatively high proportion of cases with full-scale war as the primary crisis management technique (28%) (Table III.7.A); almost all of the latter were intra-war crises during World War II. Combining full-scale war and serious clashes as high intensity of violence in crisis management, Asia ranks first (68%), followed by Africa (56%) and the Middle East (51%). The Americas were at the other extreme in terms of the intensity of violence – no violence or minor clashes in 76% of their cases, with only 9% involving full-scale war.

Table III.7.B focuses on the degree of violence employed in the four system-periods. It is noteworthy that the relative frequency of full-scale war and minor clashes as the primary CMT was identical in the multipolar and polycentric systems; the basic difference in intensity of violence for these two systems is that half of all crises in the former exhibited no violence, whereas one-third of the crises in the latter showed serious clashes.

TABLE III.7.A. Intensity of Violence: Geography

Region	No violence		Minor clashes		Serious clashes		Full-scale war		Total	
	Freq.	%	Freq.	%	Freq.	%	Freq.	%	Freq.	%
Africa	18	28%	10	16%	27	42%	9	14%	64	23%
Americas	14	43%	11	33%	5	15%	3	9%	33	12%
Asia	12	17%	10	15%	23	33%	24	35%	69	25%
Europe	31	55%	7	12%	3	5%	16	28%	5	20%
Middle East	21	38%	6	11%	13	24%	15	27%	55	20%
Total	96	35%	44	16%	71	25%	67	24%	278	100%

TABLE III.7.B. Intensity of Violence: Polarity

System	No violence		Minor clashes		Serious clashes		Full-scale war		Total	
	Freq.	%	Freq.	%	Freq.	%	Freq.	%	Freq.	%
Multipolar (1929–39)	19	50%	5	13%	5	13%	9	24%	38	14%
World War II (1939–45)	7	23%	2	6%	5	16%	17	55%	31	11%
Bipolar (1945–62)	37	40%	21	22%	22	24%	13	14%	93	33%
Polycentric (1963–79)	33	28%	16	14%	39	34%	28	24%	116	42%
Total	96	35%	44	16%	71	25%	67	24%	278	100%

TABLE III.7.C. Intensity of Violence: System Level

Level of system	No violence		Minor clashes		Serious clashes		Full-scale war		Total	
	Freq.	%	Freq.	%	Freq.	%	Freq.	%	Freq.	%
Subsystem	55	33%	32	19%	51	30%	30	18%	168	60%
Mainly subsystem	14	31%	7	15%	12	26%	13	28%	46	17%
Mainly dominant	8	27%	4	13%	8	27%	10	33%	30	11%
Dominant system	19	56%	1	3%	0	0%	14	41%	34	12%
Total	96	35%	44	16%	71	25%	67	24%	278	100%

Full-scale war as the most intense form of violence in crisis management within the international system becomes more probable as we move from the subsystem level to the dominant system level, that is, to more complex crises – 18% to 41% (see Table III.7.C). Interestingly, the dominant system crisis cluster was divided almost entirely between full-scale war (41%) and no violence (56%), with only one of the 34 dominant system crises exhibiting either minor or serious clashes. At the subsystem level, on the other hand, 49% of all crises involved minor or serious clashes as the most intense CMT.

Timing of Violence (TIMVIO)

This variable indicates the point at which violence (if any) occurred in an international crisis. The reference is to violence in general, not to violence as a technique of crisis management (discussed above under centrality and intensity of violence); hence the discrepancy between the number of cases without violence in timing, on the one hand, and centrality/intensity, on the other.

Coding Rules and Raw Frequencies, with Illustrations
1 **Violence prior to the crisis period** ($N = 122$; 44%) – (Violence between the French and Vietminh forces had been going on for 7 years prior to the crisis over Dien Bien Phu which began on 13 March 1954).
2 **Violence triggered the crisis period** ($N = 64$; 23%) – (The Bay of Pigs Crisis was triggered on 15 April 1961 by the bombing of Cuban military and civilian centers by US-supplied B-26 aircraft).
3 **Violence subsequent to initiation of the crisis period** ($N = 37$; 13%) – (In a crisis over the Chinese Eastern Railway, which began on 13 July 1929, violence between Soviet and Chinese troops broke out on 12 August with the Soviet occupation of three strategic towns in north China).
4 **Violence did not occur** ($N = 55$; 20%) – (On 10 April 1973 Israel placed its forces on full alert, anticipating an attack by Egyptian forces. The attack never occurred, and the Israel Mobilization Crisis subsided in late June of that year).

Analysis of Timing of
Violence

As was to be expected, violence occurred either before or during 80% of all international crises from 1929 to 1979; that is, most crises of the military-security type were accompanied by violence at some point in time – before, at the onset of, or during, a crisis.

Crises erupted within a setting of preexisting violence in 44% of the cases, almost twice as frequent as any other timing of violence category in international crises for the half-century.

Among the 92 cases where violence was not present prior to, or at the beginning of, a crisis, violence did not occur at all in 60% of these crises. This indicates a striking collective misperception by decision-makers of various states, for there was a marked discrepancy between their perception – at the outset of the crisis – of the likelihood of military hostilities, a necessary condition of an international crisis, and the reality of violence during crises.

Violence was present prior to the crisis period in a large proportion of crises in Africa, Asia and the Middle East, the bulk of the Third World. This is in sharp contrast to crises in the Americas, the oldest Third World region, as well as in Europe (Table III.8.A). In America-located crises, the first violence was most likely to have been the triggering event itself, much more so than in any other region. Europe stands apart as the region with least violence (39%). The contrast is particularly sharp with Asia-located crises, of which only 4% were violence-free.

The setting for international crises in the bipolar system was much less violent than in either the polycentric or multipolar systems – 29%, 55% and 45% of the cases, respectively, in which violence occurred prior to a crisis (see Table III.8.B).

Crises within the polycentric system (1963–79) were clearly the most violence-prone: 55% occurred in a violent setting, as noted; 87% were associated with violence at some point in time; and the proportion of cases without violence (13%) was well below the percentage of non-violent cases for either the multipolar or bipolar periods.

There was virtually no difference in the proportion of cases triggered by violence during the four system-periods under inquiry (Table III.8.B). This suggests that the structure of a system does not affect the probability of a violent or non-violent onset of a crisis.

TABLE III.8.A. Timing of Violence: Geography

Region	Prior to trigger		Trigger		After trigger		No violence		Total	
	Freq.	%	Freq.	%	Freq.	%	Freq.	%	Freq.	%
Africa	36	56%	13	20%	6	10%	9	14%	64	23%
Americas	7	21%	12	37%	5	15%	9	27%	33	12%
Asia	39	57%	14	20%	13	19%	3	4%	69	25%
Europe	16	28%	11	19%	8	14%	22	39%	57	20%
Middle East	24	44%	14	25%	5	9%	12	22%	55	20%
Total	122	44%	64	23%	37	13%	55	20%	278	100%

TABLE III.8.B. Timing of Violence: Polarity

System	Prior to trigger		Trigger		After trigger		No violence		Total	
	Freq.	%	Freq.	%	Freq.	%	Freq.	%	Freq.	%
Multipolar (1929–39)	17	45%	8	21%	4	10%	9	24%	38	14%
World War II (1939–45)	14	45%	7	23%	5	16%	5	16%	31	11%
Bipolar (1945–62)	27	29%	20	21.5%	20	21.5%	26	28%	93	33%
Polycentric (1963–79)	64	55%	29	25%	8	7%	15	13%	116	42%
Total	122	44%	64	23%	37	13%	55	20%	278	100%

TABLE III.8.C. Timing of Violence: System Level

Level of system	Prior to trigger		Trigger		After trigger		No violence		Total	
	Freq.	%	Freq.	%	Freq.	%	Freq.	%	Freq.	%
Subsystem	79	47%	38	22%	23	14%	28	17%	168	60%
Mainly subsystem	19	41%	13	28%	5	11%	9	20%	46	17%
Mainly dominant	9	30%	7	23%	8	27%	6	20%	30	11%
Dominant system	15	44%	6	18%	1	3%	12	35%	34	12%
Total	122	44%	64	23%	37	13%	55	20%	278	100%

TABLE III.8.D. Timing of Violence: Power Discrepancy

Power discrepancy	Prior to trigger		Trigger		After trigger		No violence		Total	
	Freq.	%	Freq.	%	Freq.	%	Freq.	%	Freq.	%
Low	36	43%	20	24%	10	12%	17	21%	83	34%
Medium	41	52%	19	24%	11	14%	8	10%	79	32%
High	31	37%	18	21%	11	13%	25	29%	85	34%
Total	108	44%	57	23%	32	13%	50	20%	247*	100%

* Does not include World War II cases.

The system level at which a crisis occurred during the half-century under inquiry (see Table III.8.C) had no perceptible effect on the proneness to violence prior to a crisis – 47% for the subsystem level to 44% for the dominant system level, or as the essential characteristic of the trigger (22% to 18%). By contrast, crises within a mainly dominant system manifested post-trigger violence twice as often, proportionately, as subsystem crises and almost nine times as frequently as in crises within the dominant system alone. This may be explained by the reluctance of major powers, especially superpowers since 1945, to engage in violence in the central international system once a crisis has unfolded because the costs of escalation were perceived as much higher than any possible benefits of direct violent confrontation. In mainly dominant system crises, however, they had fewer compunctions about violent conflict between their client or vassal states; on the contrary, these were encouraged to serve various superpower interests, including battlefield testing of new weapons.

The absence of violence was conspicuously higher in dominant system crises than in all other system-level categories, largely for the reason noted above, namely, costs far outweighed benefits. Stated differently, mutual deterrence was an effective constraint on violence.

The association between the extent of power discrepancy among crisis adversaries and the timing of violence (see Table III.8.D) is weak: a violent setting for crises was somewhat more frequent, proportionately, in conditions of medium power discrepancy, 52% to 43% (low) to 37% (high discrepancy); and the absence of violence was more frequent in cases of high than of low or medium discrepancy, 29%, 21% and 10%, respectively.

Intra-War Crisis (IWC)   Intra-war crisis (IWC) is an attribute of an international crisis as a whole; that is, it is characterized by an increase in the intensity of disruptive interaction and incipient change within the structure of an international system. It differs from all other international crises only in the setting in which it occurs, namely, during an ongoing war. Nevertheless, as in other international crises, disruptive interactions are more acute, and a challenge to the structure of an international system is posed.

War-initiated crisis refers to an environmental change which accords not only with the necessary conditions of an international crisis, as noted earlier (see Part I);

it is also the first crisis in an ongoing war. And its intensity of violence, as distinct from that of the war itself, may be less than "full-scale war," namely, serious clashes.

An international crisis is identified as an IWC when three conditions obtain: (1) the crisis is an integral part of an ongoing war; (2) at least one of the principal adversaries is a continuing actor in that war; and (3) it is an inter-state war, not a civil or purely guerrilla war.

This variable identifies eight types of environmental changes which trigger intra-war crises (categories (3)–(10) below). Not every incident or battle during every war from 1929 to 1979 was designated an IWC; only "turning point" environmental changes were included in the data set. The counterpart IWC at the micro-level is a situation in which an environmental change, during a state of war, generates a perceived threat to basic values, an awareness of finite time to respond and a perceived adverse change in one's military capability or the military balance. Hence the reader should refer to the more elaborate treatment of this variable in *Handbook II*.

Coding Rules and Raw Frequencies, with Illustrations

1 **Not an intra-war crisis** ($N = 181$; 65.1%)
2 **Initiation of a war** ($N = 34$; 12.1%) – (On 25 June 1950 North Korean forces invaded South Korea).
3 **Perceived high probability that a major power will exit from a war** ($N = 1$; .4%) – (On 23 October 1972 South Vietnam learned of agreements reached between the US and North Vietnam (the Paris Accords), which could have resulted in the exit of the US from the war – in the Christmas Bombing Crisis).
4 **Entry of a major actor into an ongoing war** ($N = 4$; 1.4%) – (Military campaigns in the Middle East by Germany and Italy triggered intra-war crises for Britain, Iraq and Vichy France from 29 April to 14 July 1941).
5 **Technological escalation of a war** ($N = 4$; 1.4%) – any introduction of new weapons in a war (German aerial bombing of the UK, between 10 July and 15 September 1940, constituted the Battle of Britain intra-war crisis).
6 **Major escalation of a non-technological type** ($N = 41$; 14.7%) – invasion, major battle (On 30 March 1972 North Vietnam launched a spring offensive, initiating the Vietnam–Ports Mining intra-war crisis).
7 **Defeat in a significant battle** ($N = 5$; 1.8%) – (The Soviet defeat of the German Army at the Battle of Stalingrad triggered an IWC for Germany).
8 **Perceived high probability that a major power will enter a war** ($N = 1$; .4%) – (Israel's crisis in November 1956 arose from the Soviet threat to intervene in the Sinai–Suez War).
9 **Internal deterioration leading to reduced capability to wage war** ($N = 2$; .7%) – economic strength, political stability, social cohesion (In March 1944 Hungarian leaders perceived that German troops massing on its borders were about to occupy Hungary).
10 **Other** ($N = 5$; 1.8%).

Analysis of Intra-War Crisis Almost one-fourth of all international crises from 1929 to 1979 occurred during an ongoing war. If crises which initiated a war are added, the proportion of war-linked crises rises to 35% (Table III.9.A). Asia ranks highest among the five regions in terms of the proportion of IWCs (39%); most of these occurred during the three long-war-protracted conflicts – the Pacific War 1937–45, the Korean War 1950–53, the Vietnam War 1964–75. The Americas are at the other extreme, with no IWCs. Surprisingly, IWCs comprise only 13% of Middle East crises, not because there were no – or few – wars, but rather because almost all Middle East wars were very short. The 12 Europe-located IWCs all occurred during World War II. In Africa, by contrast, the IWCs were brief eruptions in ongoing, relatively low-level wars, such as over Rhodesia. The Middle East and Asia exhibited the highest proportions of war-initiated crises among all regions, 18% and 16%, respectively. At the other extreme were the Americas and Europe, 6% and 7%, respectively.

The bulk of IWCs occurred in two periods: World War II (23 crises) and the polycentric period (28 crises) (Table III.9.B). By contrast, both the multipolar and

TABLE III.9.A. Intra-War Crisis: Geography

Region	Not IWC		War-initiated crisis		IWC		Total	
	Freq.	%	Freq.	%	Freq.	%	Freq.	%
Africa	40	62%	7	11%	17	27%	64	23%
Americas	31	94%	2	6%	0	0%	33	12%
Asia	31	45%	11	16%	27	39%	69	25%
Europe	41	72%	4	7%	12	21%	57	20%
Middle East	38	69%	10	18%	7	13%	55	20%
Total	181	65%	34	12%	63	23%	278	100%

TABLE III.9.B. Intra-War Crisis: Polarity

System	Not IWC		War-initiated crisis		IWC		Total	
	Freq.	%	Freq.	%	Freq.	%	Freq.	%
Multipolar (1929–39)	26	68%	8	21%	4	11%	38	14%
World War II (1939–45)	7	23%	1	3%	23	74%	31	11%
Bipolar (1945–62)	78	84%	7	7%	8	9%	93	33%
Polycentric (1963–79)	70	60%	18	16%	28	24%	116	42%
Total	181	65%	34	12%	63	23%	278	100%

TABLE III.9.C. Intra-War Crisis: System Level

Level of system	Not IWC		War-initiated crisis		IWC		Total	
	Freq.	%	Freq.	%	Freq.	%	Freq.	%
Subsystem	119	71%	21	12%	28	17%	168	60%
Mainly subsystem	26	57%	7	15%	13	28%	46	17%
Mainly dominant	19	64%	4	13%	7	23%	30	11%
Dominant system	17	50%	2	6%	15	44%	34	12%
Total	181	65%	34	12%	63	23%	278	100%

bipolar periods show relatively few intra-war crises. The marked increase in the number of intra-war crises and of war-initiated crises from the bipolar to the polycentric period (respectively, 9% to 24% and 7% to 16%) indicates an important transformation in the structure of the global international system.

In Table III.9.C we examine the extent to which the frequency of intra-war crises differs among system levels. The contrast is particularly sharp between crises at the subsystem level, which exhibit only 17% IWCs, and the other three systems, which combine to produce an intra-war crisis rate of about 32%. As we have seen in Table III.7.C, crises involving full-scale war are least common at the subsystem level, and hence the finding of a lower incidence of IWCs is consistent.

Number of Involved Actors (NOACTR)

How many states were perceived by the crisis actors to be involved in an international crisis, including the crisis actors themselves? Where objective evidence exists of substantial involvement without an articulated perception by a crisis actor, these states were included as involved actors. Substantial involvement refers to any one of the following types of activity: direct military; semi-military; covert; economic; and political other than mere statements of approval or disapproval by officials. This variable is aggregated from the actor-level data (excluding overlaps).

Analysis of Number of Involved Actors   Table III.10.A presents a detailed breakdown of frequencies of involved actors. In Table III.10.B the data are collapsed into four categories: 2–3 actors, 4–5 actors, 6–10 actors, and 11+ actors. There is a marked contrast between the Americas and Asia, on the one hand, and the Middle East and Europe, on the other, in terms of the number of involved actors in international crises. The former reveal a high proportion of cases with only two to three involved actors (41% and 38%, respectively); this is infrequent in the latter (9%, 14%). At the other extreme, there were six or more involved actors in slightly more than half of the crises in Africa, the Middle East and Europe, but in only a third of the cases in Asia and the Americas. For Africa and Europe the explanation may be the active involvement of the international organization (OAU, League of Nations), with many states in these regions participating, at least in discussions on crisis resolution, and thereby generating perceptions of widespread involvement. In the Middle East, most crises are part of the protracted Arab–Israel Conflict, in which the latter perceives many Arab states as involved.

During the multipolar period prior to World War II, there was a relatively high frequency of crises in the 6–10 actor range (54%), compared to 27% for the bipolar period and 34% for the polycentric period. This finding is even more impressive when account is taken of the relatively small size of the international system in the pre-World War II period, as compared with the post-1945 periods (see Table III.10.C).

TABLE III.10.A. Number of Involved Actors: Frequencies

Number of involved actors	Frequency	%
2	36	13%
3	35	13%
4	38	14%
5	43	16%
6	38	14%
7	18	7%
8	16	6%
9	11	4%
10	11	4%
11	6	2%
12	6	2%
13	5	2%
14	3	1%
15	3	1%
16	1	0%
17	1	0%
18	1	0%
21	2	1%
22	1	0%
24	1	0%
32	1	0%
Total	277*	100%

* One case with missing data.

TABLE III.10.B. Number of Involved Actors: Geography

Region	2–3 actors		4–5 actors		6–10 actors		11+ actors		Total	
	Freq.	%	Freq.	%	Freq.	%	Freq.	%	Freq.	%
Africa	19	30%	13	20%	22	34%	10	16%	64	23%
Americas	13	41%	8	25%	9	28%	2	6%	32	11%
Asia	26	38%	21	30%	15	22%	7	10%	69	25%
Europe	8	14%	20	35%	25	44%	4	7%	57	21%
Middle East	5	9%	19	35%	23	42%	8	14%	55	20%
Total	71	26%	81	29%	94	34%	31	11%	277*	100%

* One case with missing date.

TABLE III.10.C. Number of Involved Actors: Polarity

System	2–3 actors		4–5 actors		6–10 actors		11+ actors		Total	
	Freq.	%	Freq.	%	Freq.	%	Freq.	%	Freq.	%
Multipolar (1929–39)	6	16%	8	22%	20	54%	3	8%	37	13%
World War II (1939–45)	6	19%	13	42%	10	32%	2	7%	31	11%
Bipolar (1945–62)	33	36%	29	31%	25	27%	6	6%	93	34%
Polycentric (1963–79)	26	22%	31	27%	39	34%	20	17%	116	42%
Total	71	26%	81	29%	94	34%	31	11%	277*	100%

* One case with missing data.

The number of involved actors is, *inter alia*, an indicator of the scope and complexity of an international crisis. Thus the multipolar system was characterized by a pattern of great breadth in terms of crisis interaction. So too was the polycentric system which accounted, proportionately, for more than twice as many cases with 11 or more involved actors as the multipolar or bipolar systems (17%, 8%, 6%). Moreover, crises with 11 or more involved actors in the polycentric system comprised 20 of 31 such cases, that is, 64%. Many of these were Africa-located crises where the OAU and African states manifested a strong tendency to seek crisis resolution within that continent of newly-independent states. By contrast, bipolar system crises were prone to minimal involvement – almost half of all two to three involved actors (33 of 71) and over a third of all bipolar cases. One possible explanation is that the presence of seven relatively equal great powers in the multipolar system and the consequent uncertainty of alliance configuration made them more prone to involvement in crises so as to enhance their interests and reduce the danger from potential adversaries. As for the polycentric system, its structural similarity to the multipolar system, along with the existence of a very large number of states, may explain multiple involvement by state actors in international crises.

Content of Great Power/Superpower Activity (GPINV30, USINV, SUINV)

Three variables, one for the great powers in the 1929–39 period, and one each for the US and the USSR in the post-World War II period, assess great power/superpower activity in crises. Activity is defined as any substantive verbal or physical act, regardless of whether the great power/superpower was itself a crisis actor. If more than one form of great power/superpower activity occurred, the most intense was identified.

The small number of international crises during the multipolar period (1929–39) does not justify a separate breakdown for each of the great powers – France, Germany, Italy, Japan, the UK, the US and the USSR. Therefore, these data have been collapsed in such a way that the highest level of activity exhibited by any great power in a crisis was taken as the value for the entire crisis. In addition, the World War II cases were excluded entirely from this analysis.

Coding of these variables was based upon the coding for individual actor-cases and refers to the most intense great power/superpower activity as perceived by any of the crisis actors. Hence the reader should refer to the treatment of these variables in *Handbook II*. The reader should also refer to the GPINV and SPINV variables in Part IV of *Handbook I*, where a composite great power/superpower involvement variable is discussed in conjunction with the Severity Index.

Coding Rules and Raw Frequencies, with Illustrations
1 **GP/US/USSR not active** (GP N = 3; 8%, US N = 62; 30%, USSR N = 90; 43%) – (None of the great powers was involved in the Bulgaria/Turkey Crises of March and August 1935; the US was not involved in the second Pushtunistan Crisis between Afghanistan and Pakistan, 27 March–November 1955; and the USSR was not involved in the Qalqilya Crisis between Israel and Jordan, from 13 September to October 1956).

2 **Low-level GP/US/USSR activity** (GP N = 12; 32%, US N = 91; 43%, USSR N = 67; 32%) – political activity, including statements of approval or disapproval by authorized government officials; economic involvement, e.g., financial aid, or the withholding of aid from an actor; and propaganda involvement, e.g., increase in Voice of America broadcasts beamed at a particular country (There was low-level activity by France and Italy in the crisis over the assassination of Yugoslavia's King Alexander, from 9 October to 10 December 1934; the US was involved politically in the Congo I: Katanga Crisis of 1960–62; and the USSR was involved politically in the Dominican Republic Crisis of 1965).

3 **GP/US/USSR covert or semi-military activity** (GP N = 8; 21%, US N = 36; 17%, USSR N = 40; 19%) – covert activity, e.g., support for anti-government forces; and military aid or advisors, without participation in actual fighting (Italy rushed troops to the border with Austria in the July 1934 Austria Putsch Crisis; US and USSR activity in the October-Yom Kippur War of 1973 was semi-military, by virtue of their arms shipments to Israel, and to Egypt and Syria, respectively).

4 **GP/US/USSR direct military activity** (GP N = 15; 39%, US N = 20; 10%, USSR N = 12; 6%) – dispatch of troops, aerial bombing of targets or naval assistance to a party in a war (On 29 June 1937 Japanese forces bombed and sank a Soviet gunboat during the Amur River Incident; US activity in the various Vietnam crises between 1964 and 1973; and USSR involvement in the 1970 War of Attrition between Egypt and Israel).

Analysis of Content of Great Power/Superpower Activity

There are many contrasts between US and USSR activity in international crises, both within different regions for one superpower and between the superpowers in a specific region. US activity in crises ranged from 92% in Europe, 84% in the Americas and 81% in Asia, to 75% in the Middle East and only 43% of Africa-located crises (Table III.11.A). In Europe, US low-level activity was predominant (79% of cases). In the Americas, the US was heavily involved in both low-level (economic and political aid) and semi-military activity, that is, military aid and support for one of the crisis actors. The highest concentration of direct US military activity was in Asia-located crises, both in Korea from 1950 to 1953 and in Indo-China from 1961 to 1975. Yet even in Asia the US relied more on low-level activity – and even more so, relatively, in all four other regions. In fact, low-level US activity was the largest single category of US activity in crises (43%), more than double the proportion of semi-military activity and four times as frequent as direct military activity.

TABLE III.11.A. Content of US/USSR Activity: Geography

Region	No activity		Low-level		Semi-military		Military		Total	
US activity										
	Freq.	%	Freq.	%	Freq.	%	Freq.	%	Freq.	%
Africa	34	57%	17	29%	7	12%	1	2%	59	28%
Americas	4	16%	11	44%	8	32%	2	8%	25	12%
Asia	10	19%	19	37%	10	19%	13	25%	52	25%
Europe	2	8.3%	19	79.2%	1	4.2%	2	8.3%	24	12%
Middle East	12	25%	25	51%	10	20%	2	4%	49	23%
Total	62	30%	91	43%	36	17%	20	10%	209*	100%
USSR activity										
Africa	38	64%	8	14%	12	20%	1	2%	59	28%
Americas	18	72%	4	16%	3	12%	0	0%	25	12%
Asia	13	25%	29	56%	8	15%	2	4%	52	25%
Europe	3	12.5%	11	46%	3	12.5%	7	29%	24	12%
Middle East	18	37%	15	31%	14	28%	2	4%	49	23%
Total	90	43%	67	32%	40	19%	12	6%	209*	100%

* Includes cases for 1945–79 only.

TABLE III.11.B. Content of GP/US/USSR Activity: Polarity*

System	No activity		Low-level		Semi-military		Military		Total	
GP activity										
	Freq.	%	Freq.	%	Freq.	%	Freq.	%	Freq.	%
Multipolar (1929–39)	3	8%	12	32%	8	21%	15	39%	38	100%
US activity										
Bipolar (1945–62)	23	25%	45	48%	18	19%	7	8%	93	44%
Polycentric (1963–79)	39	34%	46	40%	18	15%	13	11%	116	56%
Total	62	30%	`91	43%	36	17%	20	10%	209	100%
USSR activity										
Bipolar (1945–62)	34	36%	36	39%	15	16%	8	9%	93	44%
Polycentric (1963–79)	56	48%	31	27%	25	22%	4	3%	116	56%
Total	90	43%	67	32%	40	19%	12	6%	209	100%

* World War II cases were excluded.

TABLE III.11.C. Content of GP/US/USSR Activity: Conflict*

Conflict setting	No activity		Low-level		Semi-military		Military		Total	
GP activity										
	Freq.	%	Freq.	%	Freq.	%	Freq.	%	Freq.	%
Non-protracted conflict	3	11%	9	32%	7	25%	9	32%	28	74%
Protracted conflict	0	0%	2	33%	0	0%	4	67%	6	16%
Long-war-protracted conflict	0	0%	1	25%	1	25%	2	50%	4	10%
Total	3	8%	12	32%	8	21%	15	39%	38	100%
US activity										
Non-protracted conflict	31	35%	37	42%	15	17%	5	6%	88	42%
Protracted conflict	21	24%	44	49%	20	22%	4	5%	89	43%
Long-war-protracted conflict	10	31%	10	31%	1	3%	11	35%	32	15%
Total	62	30%	91	43%	36	17%	20	10%	209	100%
USSR activity										
Non-protracted conflict	49	56%	22	25%	13	15%	4	4%	88	42%
Protracted conflict	27	30%	36	41%	19	21%	7	8%	89	43%
Long-war-protracted conflict	14	44%	9	28%	8	25%	1	3%	32	15%
Total	90	43%	67	32%	40	19%	12	6%	209	100%

* World War II cases were excluded.

The Soviet Union, too, remained aloof from the majority of Africa-located crises (64%) but, unlike the US, from most crises in the Americas as well (72%), one indicator of Soviet recognition of the US primary role in the Western Hemisphere. The two regions of frequent low-level USSR activity were Asia and Europe, much more so than the US in the former, much less so in the latter. The main region for Soviet semi-military activity in crises was the Middle East, slightly higher than US semi-military activity in that region. The principal superpower regional contrast in semi-military activity was in the Americas, 32% to 12% in favor of the US. As for direct military activity, the USSR was much more active in Europe-located crises, 29% to 8%, much less active in Asia, 4% to 25%. Overall, the distribution among the four categories of superpower activity was very similar for both the US and the USSR.

Table III.11.B shows, *inter alia*, the pattern of superpower activity in crises from 1945 to 1979. For the entire post-World War II period the US was active in 70% of all international crises, while the USSR was active in 57%. There was no substantial difference, proportionately, in the extent of activity – low, semi-military, military. Moreover, both superpowers were cautious about direct military activity in international crises – the US was so involved in only 10% and the USSR in only 6% of all 209 cases. They were more prone to the less destabilizing semi-military type of activity, and even more so to low-level political and economic activity. Most significantly, they avoided any form of military activity in three-fourths of all international crises from 1945 to 1979. Stated differently, the wish to minimize the risk of superpower confrontation led both the US and USSR to aloofness or low-level activity in a very large majority of post-World War II crises.

These findings for the superpowers stand in contrast with those for the great powers in the 1929–39 period. There we find the great powers active in 92% of all crises, with some form of military activity characteristic of 60% of all crises for this period. Thus the aloofness exhibited by the superpowers in the post-World War II period differed sharply from the pattern followed by the great powers in the decade prior to the outbreak of that war. If one criterion of the extent of system stability is the scope of military hostilities involving the major powers, this suggests that bipolarity and polycentrism are more conducive than multipolarity to stability in world politics.

Table III.11.C examines the level of great power/superpower activity in relation to conflict. The great powers during the multipolar period of the 1930s exhibited a rather high level of activity in protracted conflicts: 75% of the crises in long-war-protracted conflicts exhibited either semi-military or military activity on the part of the great powers. This contrasts with 38% for the US and 28% for the USSR during the post-World War II period. For non-protracted conflicts, the great powers exhibited an overall 89% activity rate, as compared with a rate of 65% for the US and 44% for the USSR. Once more, the findings indicate greater stability in a bipolar and polycentric than in a multipolar international system. At the same time, the US resorted to direct military activity much more frequently than the USSR during the post-World War II period as a whole.

Effectiveness of Great Power/Superpower Activity (GPEFCT30, USEFCT, SUEFCT)

Three variables, one for the great powers in the 1929–39 period, and one each for the US and the USSR in the post-World War II period, assess the effectiveness of major power activity in abating crises. Effectiveness in crisis abatement is understood in terms of preventing hostilities or otherwise contributing to the termination of an international crisis. This assessment refers only to the role of the great powers, the US, or the USSR, from the first breakpoint (trigger) to the final exitpoint (termination) of an international crisis.

The small number of international crises during the multipolar period (1929–39) does not justify a separate breakdown for each of the great powers – France, Germany, Italy, Japan, the UK, the US and the USSR. Therefore, an entire case is coded as the highest level of effectiveness exhibited by any of the great powers.

Coding Rules and Raw Frequencies, with Illustrations
1 **No GP/US/USSR activity** (GP $N = 3$; 8%, US $N = 62$; 30%, USSR $N = 90$; 43%).
2 **GP/US/USSR activity escalated crisis** (GP $N = 2$; 5%, US $N = 17$; 8%, USSR $N = 33$; 16%) – (German actions during the Memel Crisis in March

1939; the US/UK announcement on 8 October 1953, of their intention to withdraw their troops and relinquish the administration of Trieste to the Italian Government, in the crisis between Yugoslavia and Italy; and the USSR emplacement of missiles in Egypt in the 1970 War of Attrition Crisis between Egypt and Israel).

3 **GP/US/USSR activity did not contribute to crisis abatement** (GP $N = 7$; 18% US $N = 50$; 24%, USSR $N = 54$; 26%) – (British and French efforts to bring about a solution to the Wal-Wal Crisis of 1934–35 between Ethiopia and Italy; the US decision not to send troops to Vietnam, in the Dien Bien Phu Crisis of 1954; and USSR activity in the Baghdad Pact Crisis of 1955).

4 **GP/US/USSR activity contributed marginally to crisis abatement** (GP $N = 6$; 16%, US $N = 16$; 8%, USSR $N = 14$; 7%) – GP/US/USSR activity was not a major factor (The UK–France–Italy protest note to Lithuania during the Kaunas Trials Crisis in 1935; the US action of witholding the Dominican Republic sugar quota and breaking off diplomatic relations in the crisis resulting from the assassination attempt on the Venezuelan President in June–September 1960; and the USSR warning Israel and the Arab states against the use of force in the 1963–64 Jordan Waters Crisis).

5 **GP/US/USSR activity had an important impact on crisis abatement** (GP $N = 16$; 42%, US $N = 45$; 21%, USSR $N = 13$; 6%) – important impact, along with the actions of other international entities (The US, along with other members of the Pan-American Conference on Conciliation and Arbitration, facilitated the signing of a conciliation protocol between Bolivia and Paraguay in the 1928–1929 Chaco I Crisis; US activity in the Lebanon Crisis of 1958, including the landing of Marines in July; and USSR pressure on India to accept the Chinese proposal for talks to end the 1962 Sino-Indian border crisis).

6 **GP/US/USSR activity was the single most important contributor to crisis abatement** (GP $N = 4$; 11%, US $N = 19$; 9%, USSR $N = 5$; 2%) (British mediation efforts during the 1932 Shanghai Crisis between China and Japan; the US action of moving the Seventh Fleet into the area of the Taiwan Straits Crisis of 1958 between the PRC and Taiwan; and Soviet conciliatory moves in the 1957 Syria/Turkey Border Crisis).

Analysis of Effectiveness of Great Power/Superpower Activity As evident in Table III.12.A, the patterns of superpower effectiveness in crisis abatement reveal marked differences. First, the US effectiveness rate as a whole, that is, most important, important and marginal contribution together, far exceeded that of the USSR (38% to 15%). Moreover, while the gap in effectiveness relating to crises in the Americas was enormous (72% to 12%), US effectiveness was only moderately greater than that of the Soviet Union for crises in all other regions: Asia

TABLE III.12.A. Effectiveness of US/USSR Activity: Geography

Region	No activity		Escalated		Did not contribute		Marginal		Important		Most important		Total	
	Freq.	%	Freq.	%	Freq.	%	Freq.	%	Freq.	%	Freq.	%	Freq.	%
US effectiveness														
Africa	34	57%	1	2%	14	24%	4	7%	6	10%	0	0%	59	28%
Americas	4	16%	2	8%	1	4%	4	16%	10	40%	4	16%	25	12%
Asia	10	19.2%	9	17.3%	9	17.3%	1	1.9%	11	21.2%	12	23.1%	52	25%
Europe	2	8%	4	17%	10	42%	2	8%	4	17%	2	8%	24	12%
Middle East	12	24%	1	2%	16	33%	5	10%	14	29%	1	2%	49	23%
Total	62	30%	17	8%	50	24%	16	8%	45	21%	19	9%	209*	100%
USSR effectiveness														
Africa	38	64%	9	15%	10	17%	1	2%	1	2%	0	0%	59	28%
Americas	18	72%	1	4%	3	12%	0	0%	3	12%	0	0%	25	12%
Asia	13	25%	5	10%	21	40%	7	13%	6	12%	0	0%	52	25%
Europe	3	12.5%	12	50%	4	17%	2	8%	0	0%	3	12.5%	24	12%
Middle East	18	37%	6	12%	16	33%	4	8%	3	6%	2	4%	49	23%
Total	90	43%	33	16%	54	26%	14	7%	13	6%	5	2%	209*	100%

* Includes 1945–79 cases only.

TABLE III.12.B. Effectiveness of GP/US/USSR Activity: Polarity

System	No activity		Escalated		Did not contribute		Marginal		Important		Most important		Total	
	Freq.	%	Freq.	%	Freq.	%	Freq.	%	Freq.	%	Freq.	%	Freq.	%
Great power effectiveness														
Multipolar (1929–39)	3	8%	2	5%	7	18%	6	16%	16	42%	4	11%	38	100%
US effectiveness														
Bipolar (1945–62)	23	25%	7	7%	21	23%	5	5%	25	27%	12	13%	93	44%
Polycentric (1963–79)	39	34%	10	9%	29	25%	11	9%	20	17%	7	6%	116	56%
Total	62	30%	17	8%	50	24%	16	8%	45	21%	19	9%	209	100%
USSR effectiveness														
Bipolar (1945–62)	34	37%	20	22%	21	22%	7	8%	6	6%	5	5%	93	44%
Polycentric (1963–79)	56	48%	13	11%	33	29%	7	6%	7	6%	0	0%	116	56%
Total	90	43%	33	16%	54	26%	14	7%	13	6%	5	2%	209	100%

TABLE III.12.C. Effectiveness of GP/US/USSR Activity: System Level

Level of system	No activity		Escalated		Did not contribute		Marginal		Important		Most important		Total	
	Freq.	%	Freq.	%	Freq.	%	Freq.	%	Freq.	%	Freq.	%	Freq.	%
Great power effectiveness														
Subsystem	3	18%	0	0%	0	0%	5	29%	7	41%	2	12%	17	45%
Mainly subsystem	0	0%	1	9%	3	27%	1	9%	5	46%	1	9%	11	29%
Mainly dominant	0	0%	0	0%	1	50%	0	0%	1	50%	0	0%	2	5%
Dominant system	0	0%	1	12.5%	3	37.5%	0	0%	3	37.5%	1	12.5%	8	21%
Total	3	8%	2	5%	7	18%	6	16%	16	42%	4	11%	38	100%
US effectiveness														
Subsystem	61	41%	8	5%	37	25%	14	9%	23	16%	6	4%	149	71%
Mainly subsystem	1	3%	4	14%	6	21%	1	3%	12	42%	5	17%	29	14%
Mainly dominant	0	0%	3	15%	6	30%	1	5%	5	25%	5	25%	20	10%
Dominant system	0	0%	2	18%	1	9%	0	0%	5	46%	3	27%	11	5%
Total	62	30%	17	8%	50	24%	16	8%	45	21%	19	9%	209	100%
USSR effectiveness														
Subsystem	85	57%	12	8%	40	27%	10	6.7%	1	7%	1	7%	149	71%
Mainly subsystem	4	14%	9	31%	7	24%	1	3%	6	21%	2	7%	29	14%
Mainly dominant	1	5%	7	35%	4	20%	2	10%	4	20%	2	10%	20	10%
Dominant system	0	0%	5	46%	3	27%	1	9%	2	18%	0	0%	11	5%
Total	90	43%	33	16%	54	26%	14	7%	13	6%	5	2%	209	100%

– 46% to 25%; Middle East – 41% to 18%; Africa – 17% to 4%; and Europe – 33% to 21%. And thirdly, the contrasting impact of superpower involvement is reinforced by the data on escalation: overall, the USSR exceeded the US in escalation (16% to 8%); in Europe, the gap in escalation of crises was acute (50% to 17%); and only in Asia did the US escalate crises more than the USSR (17% to 10%). In short, US activity was likely to be much more salutary than Soviet activity, in terms of crisis abatement. Set against this contrast is the fact that both superpowers were either inactive or ineffective in the vast majority of crises from 1945 to 1979: the US was effective in 80 cases, or 38% of the total, the USSR in 32 cases, or 15% of the total; in the Americas, however, the effectiveness rate of US involvement was very high (72%) (Tables III.12.A and III.13.A).

Overall, as noted in our discussion of Table III.11.B, great powers were more active in the crises of the multipolar period than were the US and the USSR in post-World War II crises. Perhaps the most outstanding feature of the data for this variable is the sharp differences among the great powers, the US and the USSR in terms of their effectiveness in crisis abatement. The great powers were the most important or an important factor in crisis abatement in 53% of the multipolarity cases, compared with a 30% effectiveness rate for the US and an 8% rate for the USSR in the post-World War II period (see Table III.12.B). Thus, using the criterion of effective crisis management by the major powers, the multipolar system seems more conducive to stability than bipolarity. Of particular interest is the sharp contrast in effectiveness rates for the US and USSR. This contrast is accentuated by the data on crisis escalation: activity by the USSR had an adverse effect on almost twice as many international crises as did US activity, with an even larger difference between escalatory effects of Soviet activity after 1945 and great power activity in the 1930s.

There was a modest decline in effectiveness of both US and USSR activity from the bipolar to the polycentric period, along with a considerable reduction in the escalatory effects of Soviet activity in international crises.

While the superpowers were uninvolved in many post-World War II crises, as noted, this was particularly so in crises at the subsystem level: they accounted for 85 of 90 Soviet no activity cases, and 61 of 62 US cases. Taking the subsystem-level cases as a whole – and they comprise 71% of all cases from 1945 to 1979 – the US was uninvolved in 41%, the USSR in 57% of those crises (see Table III.12.C). It is interesting to note that, while the rate of crisis activity for the great powers was much higher than that for the superpowers, all three of the great power no activity cases occurred at the subsystem level.

There are quite different patterns of superpower effectiveness when one takes account of the system level at which crises occurred. US activity exhibited its greatest effectiveness, either as the most important or an important contributor to crisis abatement, when the crises occurred within the dominant system – 73% effective, compared with 18% for the Soviet Union. Moreover, the data show that the USSR escalated a crisis in 46% of the cases at the dominant system level and in 35% of the cases which were mainly dominant system crises, compared to 18% and 15% for the US, respectively. (In the case of these latter figures, some bias can be explained by the fact that the coders relied largely on Western sources for data on the roles of the superpowers in these crises.) System level appeared to be unrelated to effectiveness for the activity of the great powers during the 1930s.

A second composite variable (GPPACE30, USPACE, SUPACE) was designed to tap a different aspect of the impact of activity by the major powers than GPEFCT30, USEFCT and SUEFCT, namely, its effect on the timing of crisis abatement rather than the content of its effect, both type (positive, negative, neutral) and its extent (marginal, important, most important). The coding was done in terms of content. However, the data as generated reveal a very strong overlap in the frequencies for comparable values of these two variables:

GPPACE30, USPACE, SUPACE
1 **No GP/US/USSR activity** (GP N = 3; 8%, US N = 63; 30%, USSR N = 92; 44%).
2 **GP/US/USSR activity delayed termination** (GP N =2; 5%, US N = 14; 7%, USSR N = 23; 11%).
3 **GP/US/USSR activity had no effect on the timing of termination** (GP N = 10; 26%, US N =61; 29%, USSR N = 62; 30%).

4 **GP/US/USSR activity contributed to more rapid termination** (GP N = 23; 61%, US N =71; 34%, USSR N = 32; 15%).

Thus the reader should consult the tables and analysis of the GPEFCT30, USEFCT and SUEFCT data for knowledge on GPPACE30, USPACE and SUPACE.

Most Effective Great Power/Superpower Activity (GPEFAC30, USEFAC, SUEFAC)

Three variables, one for the great powers in the 1929–39 period, and one each for the US and the USSR in the post-World War II period, identify the most effective type of activity engaged in by the major powers in those crises in which such activity was deemed to have been effective in crisis abatement. The cases included in this analysis are those in which great power, US or USSR activity was identified as the most important, an important, or a marginal contributor to crisis abatement.

The small number of international crises during the multipolar period (1929–39) does not justify a separate breakdown for each of the great powers – France, Germany, Italy, Japan, the UK, the US and the USSR. Therefore, these data have been collapsed so as to identify the activity associated with the most effective great power in a crisis.

Coding Rules and Raw Frequencies, with Illustrations
1 **Effective low-level GP/US/USSR activity** (GP N = 19; 73%, US N = 50; 63%, USSR N = 23; 72%) – political, economic and propaganda activity (US mediation, together with that of Costa Rica and Venezuela, during the Postage Stamp Crisis of 1937 between Nicaragua and Honduras, prevented armed hostilities between the parties; on 7 August 1970 the acceptance by Egypt and Israel of US Secretary of State Rogers' Peace Plan brought the second War of Attrition Crisis to an end; and the USSR announcement that construction had been halted at the Cienfuegos Naval Base in Cuba on 23 October 1970 contributed to crisis abatement).
2 **Effective GP/US/USSR covert and semi-military activity** (GP N = 3; 12%, US N = 21; 26%, USSR N = 6; 19%) – (During the Saudi-Yemen War of 1933–34 the dispatch of British, French and Italian warships to the area had the effect of halting a Saudi advance; during the Cuba/Central America I Crisis of 1959 the US organized a naval mission to patrol the Caribbean waters in order to bar any Communist-led invasion attempt; and the USSR provided massive amounts of arms and equipment to Egypt and Syria during the 1973 October-Yom Kippur War).
3 **Effective GP/US/USSR military activity** (GP N = 4; 15%, US N = 9; 11%, USSR N = 3; 9%) – (Japanese military action in the 1933 Jehol Campaign Crisis induced China to sign an armistice; the US and Belgium dispatched paratroops who occupied Stanleyville and handed control back to the Central Government forces on 19 November 1964 during the Congo II Crisis; and USSR military action terminated the October-November 1956 crisis in Hungary).

Analysis of Most Effective Great Power/Superpower Activity

Although there is a striking similarity in the overall distribution of most effective superpower activity among the three levels – low, semi-military and military – the regional patterns show a good deal of variability (Table III.13.A). In Asia, while 50% of US effective activity occurred at relatively high levels – semi-military and military – all 13 cases of effective Soviet activity in that region were at the lowest level. In Europe, the pattern is reversed, with low-level activity being the norm for effective US involvement (88%), while high-level activity typified effective USSR cases (80%). Despite the fact that 59 of the 209 crises from 1945 to 1979 occurred in Africa (see Table III.12.A), the US was effective in only 10, and the USSR in only two.

We have already noted the sharp differences in effectiveness rates for the great powers and the two superpowers (Table III.12.B). Despite these disparities, the great powers of the 1930s and the superpowers after 1945 did not differ markedly in terms of the type of activity deemed most effective in crisis abatement. Low-level activity, i.e., political, economic and propaganda, accounted for 73% of the effective great power cases, 63% of the effective US cases and 72% of the effective USSR cases, with somewhat more proportional difference for semi-military or military activity. More significantly, low-level activity by great powers and both superpowers was most effective much more frequently than was direct military activity (see Tables III.11.B and III.13.B). In the case of the superpowers this may well be due to the enormous gap in power between the US and USSR, and other states, making it possible for them to affect crisis outcomes with infrequent resort to coercion.

The most conspicuous change in effectiveness over time (Table III.13.B) was that Soviet military activity was the most effective type of involvement in 17% of the bipolarity cases in which it contributed to crisis abatement – but never in the polycentric period. By contrast, the relative effectiveness of US military activity more than doubled from bipolarity to polycentrism; the effectiveness of its semi-military activity declined, proportionately, almost as much.

Table III.13.C presents some significant differences between the superpowers in terms of their effectiveness in crises occurring at different system levels. The data

TABLE III.13.A. Most Effective US/USSR Activity: Geography

Region	Low-level		Semi-military		Military		Total	
US effectiveness								
	Freq.	%	Freq.	%	Freq.	%	Freq.	%
Africa	7	70%	2	20%	1	10%	10	13%
Americas	11	61%	6	33%	1	6%	18	22%
Asia	12	50%	7	29%	5	21%	24	30%
Europe	7	88%	0	0%	1	12%	8	10%
Middle East	13	65%	6	30%	1	5%	20	25%
Total	50	63%	21	26%	9	11%	80	100%
USSR effectiveness								
Africa	1	50%	1	50%	0	0%	2	6%
Americas	2	67%	1	33%	0	0%	3	9%
Asia	13	100%	0	0%	0	0%	13	41%
Europe	1	20%	1	20%	3	60%	5	16%
Middle East	6	67%	3	33%	0	0%	9	28%
Total	23	72%	6	19%	3	9%	32	100%

TABLE III.13.B. Most Effective GP/US/USSR Activity: Polarity

System	Low-level		Semi-military		Military		Total	
Great power effectiveness								
	Freq.	%	Freq.	%	Freq.	%	Freq.	%
Multipolar (1929–39)	19*	73%	3	12%	4	15%	26	100%
US effectiveness								
Bipolar (1945–62)	25	60%	14	33%	3	7%	42	52%
Polycentric (1963–79)	25	66%	7	18%	6	16%	38	48%
Total	50	63%	21	26%	9	11%	80	100%
USSR effectiveness								
Bipolar (1945–62)	12	66%	3	17%	3	17%	18	56%
Polycentric (1963–79)	11	79%	3	21%	0	0%	14	44%
Total	23	72%	6	19%	3	9%	32	100%

* In Table III.11.B, dealing with the content of great power activity, we report 12 cases with low-level activity, while in Table III.13.B, dealing with the most effective great power activity, 19 cases with low-level activity are reported. There were several cases in which the most intense activity differed from the most effective one, i.e., while high-level great power activity was the most intense (Table III.11.B), the activity which was deemed most effective in contributing to crisis abatement (Table III.13.B) was economic or political.

TABLE III.13.C. Most Effective GP/US/USSR Activity: System Level

Level of system	Low-level		Semi-military		Military		Total	
Great power effectiveness								
	Freq.	%	Freq.	%	Freq.	%	Freq.	%
Subsystem	12	86%	1	7%	1	7%	14	54%
Mainly subsystem	3	43%	1	14%	3	43%	7	27%
Mainly dominant	0	0%	1	100%	0	0%	1	4%
Dominant system	4	100%	0	0%	0	0%	4	15%
Total	19	73%	3	12%	4	15%	26	100%
US effectiveness								
Subsystem	33	77%	10	23%	0	0%	43	54%
Mainly subsystem	7	39%	4	22%	7	39%	18	22%
Mainly dominant	5	45%	6	55%	0	0%	11	14%
Dominant system	5	63%	1	12%	2	25%	8	10%
Total	50	63%	21	26%	9	11%	80	100%
USSR effectiveness								
Subsystem	10	83%	2	17%	0	0%	12	38%
Mainly subsystem	6	67%	2	22%	1	11%	9	28%
Mainly dominant	6	75%	1	12.5%	1	12.5%	8	25%
Dominant system	1	33.3%	1	33.3%	1	33.3%	3	9%
Total	23	72%	6	19%	3	9%	32	100%

indicate that the US was most effective at the subsystem level, and that low-level activity was most effective. While low-level USSR activity, too, was effective at the subsystem level, there were only 10 Soviet cases compared to 33 US cases. The two superpowers also differed at the mainly subsystem level, where the most effective US activity was equally divided between military and low-level, while the most effective USSR activity was the latter, that is, political or economic. In both these respects the US pattern resembles, and Soviet behavior differs considerably from, that exhibited by the great powers in the 1929–39 period.

There are some rather sharp differences between the great powers in the 1930s and the two superpowers in the post-1945 era, in terms of their most effective activity in crises during non-protracted and protracted conflicts (see Table III.13.D). For the great powers, low-level activity was the most effective in all three crises within long-war-protracted conflicts in the 1930s. The findings are identical for the USSR in the post-1945 period. However, of the six crises during long-war-protracted conflicts in which US activity was effective, 5 fall in the military activity category. For crises within non-protracted conflicts and non-long-war-protracted conflicts, there were few significant differences among the great powers, the US and the USSR. More generally, the combined data for content and most effective type of superpower activity in crises, both controlled for conflict setting (Tables III.11.C and III.13.D), reveal a noteworthy difference: semi-military activity was the most effective in crisis abatement much more frequently for the US than the USSR, in all 3 conflict categories and overall – 20 of 36 cases (55%) for the US, 6 of 40 cases (15%) for the USSR; this contrast is only slightly less evident for the effectiveness of direct military activity, in all but the non-protracted conflict category—9 of 20 cases (45%) for the US, overall, compared to 3 of 12 cases (25%) for the USSR.

TABLE III.13.D. Most Effective GP/US/USSR Activity: Conflict

Conflict setting	Low-level		Semi-military		Military		Total	
Great power effectiveness								
	Freq.	%	Freq.	%	Freq.	%	Freq.	%
Non-protracted conflict	14	70%	3	15%	3	15%	20	77%
Protracted conflict	2	67%	0	0%	1	33%	3	11.5%
Long-war-protracted conflict	3	100%	0	0%	0	0%	3	11.5%
Total	19*	73%	3	12%	4	15%	26	100%
US effectiveness								
Non-protracted conflict	20	65%	9	29%	2	6%	31	39%
Protracted conflict	30	70%	11	25%	2	5%	43	54%
Long-war-protracted conflict	0	0%	1	17%	5	83%	6	7%
Total	50	63%	21	26%	9	11%	80	100%
USSR effectiveness								
Non-protracted conflict	4	50%	2	25%	2	25%	8	25%
Protracted conflict	16	76%	4	19%	1	5%	21	66%
Long-war-protracted conflict	3	100%	0	0%	0	0%	3	9%
Total	23	72%	6	19%	3	9%	32	100%

* In Table III.11.C, dealing with the content of great power activity, we report 12 cases with low-level activity, while in Table III.13.D, dealing with the most effectve great power activity, 19 cases with low-level activity were reported. There were several cases in which the most intense activity differed from the most effective one, i.e., while high-level great power activity was the most intense (Table III.11.C), the activity which was deemed most effective in contributing to crisis abatement (Table III.13.D) was economic or political (low-level).

Source of Global Organization Involvement (SOGLACT)

The following six variables refer to the activity and effectiveness of global organizations (GO) in international crises, from the first breakpoint (trigger) to the last exitpoint (termination). While global organization activity existed prior to 1945 in the form of the League of Nations, such activity was minimal and virtually ceased with the outbreak of World War II. Hence data pertaining only to the UN in the post-1945 period will be reported extensively, while League data will be reported only in summary form.

The first variable addresses the basic question: Which party (if any) approached the League/UN during a crisis? The initial request may have occurred prior to the breakpoint of the crisis period.

Coding Rules and Raw Frequencies, with Illustrations

1 **Global organization not approached** (League $N = 21$; 55%, UN $N = 77$; 39%).
2 **Crisis actor(s)** (League $N = 15$; 39%, UN $N = 76$; 38%) (In the Mukden Incident Crisis, China appealed to the League of Nations following a Japanese invasion on 18 September 1931; India's appeal to the UN Security Council on 1 January 1948 led to a Council Resolution on 17 January calling upon India and Pakistan to maintain the status quo in Kashmir).
3 **Third party** (League $N = 1$; 3%, UN $N = 9$; 4%) – non-crisis actor or actor involved in a crisis, other than a superpower (In the second Sahara Crisis, 1975–76, Spain appealed to the UN for action).
4 **US** (League $N = 0$; 0%, UN $N = 13$; 6%) (The US requested a Security Council meeting during the Gulf of Tonkin Crisis of August 1964).

5 **USSR** (League $N = 0$; 0%, UN $N = 3$; 2%) (The USSR called for a UN Security Council Resolution on OAS sanctions during the crisis between Venezuela and the Dominican Republic in 1960).

6 **Initiation by global organization** (League $N = 1$; 3%, UN $N = 22$; 11%) (During the crisis resulting from the invasion of Laos by North Vietnam in 1971, UN Secretary-General U Thant appealed for negotiations).

Analysis of Source of Global Organization Involvement The League of Nations was approached in only 17 of 38 (45%) international crises occurring during the 1929–39 period, as compared to the UN figure of 123 of 200, or 61% of the crises in the post-World War II period (see Table III.14.A). For both the League and the UN the majority of cases of global organization activity occurred at the subsystem level (64% for the League, 73% for the UN).

The preeminent role of crisis actors in initiating global organization activity in international crises is evident in the data in Table III.14.A: they did so in more than one-third of all crises (91 of 238).

The global organization initiated crisis management activity directly in only 23 cases – in 11% of all crises from 1945 to 1979 and 3% of all crises from 1929 to 1939. This indicates not only a strong tendency of the League/UN to be a responsive third party but also that, if no state actor appealed for its intervention, the global organization was unlikely to attempt to manage a crisis. Almost all the GO-initiated activity occurred in crises at the subsystem level, one of many indicators that global organizations lack the capacity to resolve crises in which either or both of the superpowers are crisis actors – and act accordingly.

Moving up the scale of system level, from crises which were exclusively subsystem in scope to those within the dominant system, there was a steady decline in the proportion of UN cases initiated by the crisis actors themselves.

TABLE III.14.A. Source of Global Organization Involvement: System Level

Level of system	Global organization not approached		Crisis actor		Third party		US		USSR		Global org.		Total	
	Freq.	%	Freq.	%	Freq.	%	Freq.	%	Freq.	%	Freq.	%	Freq.	%
League of Nations 1929–39	21	55%	15	39%	1	3%	0	0%	0	0%	1	3%	38	100%
UN 1945–79 Subsystem	53	36%	62	42%	7	5%	4	3%	3	2%	17	12%	146	73%
Mainly subsystem	10	40%	8	32%	1	4%	4	16%	0	0%	2	8%	25	12%
Mainly dominant	9	50%	4	22%	1	6%	2	11%	0	0%	2	11%	18	9%
Dominant system	5	46%	2	18%	0	0%	3	27%	0	0%	1	9%	11	6%
Total	77	39%	76	38%	9	4%	13	6%	3	2%	22	11%	200*	100%

* There were 9 cases coded multiple.

Global Organization Organ Most Active in Crisis (GLOBORG) Which organ of the global organization was the most active in a crisis? Where more than one organ was very active, perhaps during different stages of a crisis, the highest organ was chosen according to the ranking below.

Coding Rules and Raw Frequencies, with Illustrations

1 **General global organization activity** (League $N = 1$; 7%, UN $N = 13$; 11%) – no data about specific involvement or through a specific organ, or suborgans subject to the General Assembly, specialized agencies such as UNESCO (In the Punjab War Scare Crisis of 1951 between India and Pakistan, the UN Representative for Kashmir was in the area and had discussions with Indian and Pakistani officials).

2 **Secretary-General** (League $N = 0$; 0%, UN $N = 24$; 19%) (During the Cambodia/Thailand Crisis of 1958–59 UN Secretary-General Hammarskjöld appointed a retired Swiss diplomat as a mediator).

3 **(General) Assembly** (League $N = 5$; 36%, UN $N = 16$; 13%) (During the Suez Canal Nationalization Crisis, July-November 1956, the UN General Assembly voted to send an emergency military force to the region).

4 **(Security) Council** (League $N = 8$; 57%, UN $N = 70$; 57%) (After sending a fact-finding mission to the crisis area the Security Council called for an end to the invasion of the Republic of Guinea in November 1970 by mercenaries from Portuguese Guinea).

Analysis of Global Organization Organ Most Active in Crisis

As anticipated by the UN Charter, the Security Council was the most active organ in international crises in which the United Nations became involved; so, too, was the League of Nations Council (both 57%). The General Assembly was even less active in crisis management than the Secretary-General; and it was the primary UN organ less than one-fourth as often as the Security Council. This was due partly to intent (Charter provisions) and partly to its size, making the General Assembly a cumbersome instrument of crisis management, more suitable as a forum for the expression of state aspirations and opinions. However, this figure masks some regional variations (see Table III.15.A). The Security Council was the most active in only 44% and 47% of the crises in Asia and the Americas, respectively. On the other hand, for Europe and Africa the Security Council was the most active in 69% and 66% of the crises, respectively.

(Security) Council involvement remained constant across the three periods under consideration here (Tables III.15.A and B). This was so despite the fact that the UN handled a larger number of crises in the polycentric period than in the bipolar period or the League in the multipolar period. In Table III.15.B we also note that the crisis management role of the Secretary-General steadily increased in importance, especially in the polycentric period, while there was a parallel decline in the role of the General Assembly. In most of the 24 cases where the Secretary-General displayed the greatest activity it was he who initiated UN involvement, under the

TABLE III.15.A. Global Organization Organ Most Active in Crisis: Geography

Region	General		Secretary-General		(General) Assembly		(Security) Council		Total*	
	Freq.	%	Freq.	%	Freq.	%	Freq.	%	Freq.	%
League of Nations 1929–39	1	7%	0	0%	5	36%	8	57%	14	100%
UN 1945–79										
Africa	4	11%	5	14%	3	9%	23	66%	35	28%
Americas	3	20%	3	20%	2	13%	.7	47%	15	12%
Asia	4	12%	9	28%	5	16%	14	44%	32	26%
Europe	0	0%	2	15.4%	2	15.4%	9	69.2%	13	11%
Middle East	2	7%	5	18%	4	14%	17	61%	28	23%
Total	13	11%	24	19%	16	13%	70	57%	123*	100%

* In this and subsequent tables relating to global organization involvement, only those cases in which GO activity took place were analyzed (i.e., 14 of the 38 cases for the 1929–39 period, 123 of the 209 cases for the 1945–79 period).

TABLE III.15.B. Global Organization Organ Most Active in Crisis: Polarity

System	General		Secretary-General		General Assembly		Security Council		Total*	
	Freq.	%	Freq.	%	Freq.	%	Freq.	%	Freq.	%
Bipolar (1945–62)	6	12%	5	10%	11	21%	29	57%	51	42%
Polycentric (1963–79)	7	10%	19	26%	5	7%	41	57%	72	58%
Total	13	11%	24	19%	16	13%	70	57%	123	100%

* See note to Table III.15.A.

TABLE III.15.C. Global Organization Organ Most Active in Crisis: System Level

Level of system	General		Secretary-General		General Assembly		Security Council		Total*	
	Freq.	%	Freq.	%	Freq.	%	Freq.	%	Freq.	%
Subsystem	12	14%	19	22%	6	7%	50	57%	87	71%
Mainly subsystem	0	0%	3	16%	4	21%	12	63%	19	15%
Mainly dominant	1	9%	0	0%	6	55%	4	36%	11	9%
Dominant system	0	0%	2	33%	0	0%	4	67%	6	5%
Total	13	11%	24	19%	16	13%	70	57%	123	100%

* See note to Table III.15.A.

TABLE III.15.D. Global Organization Organ Most Active in Crisis: Conflict

Conflict setting	General		Secretary-General		General Assembly		Security Council		Total*	
	Freq.	%	Freq.	%	Freq.	%	Freq.	%	Freq.	%
Non-protracted conflict	6	15%	6	15%	6	15%	22	55%	40	33%
Protracted conflict	6	10%	9	16%	6	10%	37	64%	58	47%
Long-war-protracted conflict	1	4%	9	36%	4	16%	11	44%	25	20%
Total	13	11%	24	19%	16	13%	70	57%	123	100%

* See note to Table III.15.A.

TABLE III.15.E. Global Organization Organ Most Active in Crisis: Involvement by Powers

Involvement	General		Secretary-General		General Assembly		Security Council		Total*	
	Freq.	%	Freq.	%	Freq.	%	Freq.	%	Freq.	%
Superpower participation										
Low or No	12	14%	17	19%	8	9%	51	58%	88	72%
High	1	3%	7	20%	8	23%	19	54%	35	28%
Total	13	11%	24	19%	16	13%	70	57%	123	100%

* See note to Table III.15.A.

provisions of Article 99 of the Charter. The General Assembly tended to become the decisional forum in rare but significant crises, namely, when draft resolutions in the Security Council were blocked by a permanent member's veto (e.g., Korean War II 1950–51, Suez-Sinai Campaign 1956–57). The increase in UN membership, coupled with a decline in control of its organs by the superpowers, contributed to the decline in General Assembly activity and the rise in personal diplomacy on the part of the Secretary-General.

As is evident in Table III.15.C, the bulk of crises in which the UN became involved occurred at the subsystem level (71%). This is particularly interesting since, as we noted previously, only 60% of crises in general occurred at the subsystem level (Table III.8.C). In the UN, the Security Council played a central role in crisis management at all system levels with the exception of the mainly dominant level, where the General Assembly was the most active organ in 55% of the crises.

Table III.15.D examines the involvement of UN organs in the context of protracted conflict. Specifically, the data show that in crises during long-war-protracted conflicts the Secretary-General and the Security Council exhibited considerable activity, while crises during both non-protracted conflicts and non-long-war-protracted conflicts show the Security Council as the most active organ by far (55% and 64%, respectively). This finding is particularly interesting since it demonstrates important differences in UN crisis management during the two types of protracted conflict. In general, the UN was least active in crises during long-war-protracted conflicts.

Table III.15.E indicates that the UN was active in crisis management much more frequently when superpower participation was low or nil than when it was high (72% to 28%). However, the level of superpower participation in a crisis was not strongly related to the type of UN organ most active in a crisis. We do note a tendency for the General Assembly to take a more important role when the level of superpower participation was high, and for general UN activity to be in evidence when there was low or no superpower participation.

Content of Global Organization Involvement (GLOBACT)

This variable identifies the content of global organization involvement during the course of an international crisis.

Coding Rules and Raw Frequencies, with Illustrations

1   **Discussion without resolution** (League $N = 2$; 14.3%, UN $N = 27$; 22%) (During the crisis which resulted from the Israeli retaliatory raid on the Jordanian village of Karameh in March 1968, the UN Security Council discussed the matter but failed to pass a resolution).

2   **Fact-finding** (League $N = 1$; 7.1%, UN $N = 6$; 5%) (The initial crisis over the Malaysian Federation between Indonesia and Malaysia in 1963–65 terminated when they agreed that the UN would send a fact-finding mission to assess the views of the people).

3   **Good offices** (League $N = 3$; 21.4%, UN $N = 13$; 11%) – minimal involvement in both the content and process of resolving a dispute (In the Mayaguez Crisis between the US and Cambodia in May 1975 the UN Secretary-General offered his good offices to settle the dispute).

4   **Condemnation** (League $N = 2$; 14.3%, UN $N = 16$; 13%) – includes an implied or explicit demand to desist, a request for member aid to victim of hostile activity (The UN Security Council condemned Israel for its commando raid on the Beirut Airport on 28 December 1968).

5   **Call for action by adversaries** (League $N = 2$; 14.3%, UN $N = 28$; 23%) – includes call for cease-fire, withdrawal, negotiation, member action to facilitate termination (In the Zambia Crisis of 1973 the UN Security Council passed a resolution calling upon Britain to convene a conference to bring about self-determination and independence for Rhodesia).

6   **Mediation** (League $N = 1$; 7.1%, UN $N = 9$; 7%) – includes proposing a solution, offering advice, and conciliation of differences (Secretary-General Waldheim's mediation efforts in the Moroccan March-Sahara Crisis of 1975 contributed substantially to crisis abatement).

7   **Arbitration** (League $N = 1$; 7.1%, UN $N = 0$; 0%) – formal binding settlement by arbitral body (The League Council, in January 1937, placed Alexandretta under Syrian control and drafted a Statute of Fundamental Law of the Sanjak).

8   **Sanctions** (League $N = 2$; 14.3%, UN $N = 1$; 1%) (The League of Nations adopted a resolution to maintain an arms embargo against Paraguay and to lift it from Bolivia, on 16 January 1935 during the second Chaco Crisis).

9   **Observer group** (League $N = 0$; 0%, UN $N = 4$; 3%) (During the Lebanon/Iraq Crisis of 1958 the Security Council adopted a resolution dispatching an observer group to Lebanon to ensure that there was no infiltration across its border).

10 **Emergency military forces** (League $N = 0$; 0%, UN $N = 5$; 4%) (In July 1960 the Security Council passed a resolution establishing a UN emergency military force for the Congo in the Congo I: Katanga Crisis).

11 **General-other** (League $N = 0$; 0%, UN $N = 14$; 11%).

Analysis of Content of Global Organization Involvement

Examination of the data on League of Nations and United Nations involvement (raw frequencies) reveals several patterns. Overall, the UN was involved in a much higher proportion of crises than was the League (123 of 209, 59%/14 of 38, 37%) (see Tables III.11.B and III.16.A). For the League, activities spanned a wide range of categories. For the UN, discussion without resolution (low level), condemnation and call for action accounted for 58% of GO action. At the highest level, the League was most likely to use sanctions and arbitration, while the UN was most likely to use observers and emergency military forces.

The content of UN involvement in international crises after 1945 was almost equally divided between low and medium, with only rare excursions into high activity, including the dispatch of observers and emergency military forces (8%) (Table III.16.A). Of the 10 cases of high involvement, four related to Middle East crises. Overall, the Middle East and Africa were the regions of "medium" and UN activity, particularly in the form of condemnations, calls for action and mediation, 47% and 57%, respectively. At the other extreme of the content of activity spectrum were Asia and the Americas, where the UN engaged in low-level involvement, such as discussion without resolution, fact-finding and good offices, in 66% and 60% of those regions' cases, respectively.

The data on content of global organization involvement and polarity indicate that the UN was more active in the polycentric than in the bipolar system. However, the League showed a greater tendency than the UN toward high-level involvement (see Tables III.16.A and B). As noted, all of this activity was in the form of sanctions and arbitration. For the UN, there was little difference between the bipolar and polycentric systems in terms of low-level involvement. However, there was a stronger tendency to medium-level activity in the latter (49% to 35%).

The data in Table III.16.C indicate that the four system-levels differed only slightly in terms of the proportion of crises exhibiting low involvement by the global organization. It is in the realm of medium activity – condemnation, calls for action,

TABLE III.16.A. Content of Global Organization Involvement: Geography

Region	Low*		Medium		High		Total	
	Freq.	%	Freq.	%	Freq.	%	Freq.	%
League of Nations 1929–39	4	29%	7	50%	3	21%	14	100%
UN 1945–79								
Africa	12	34%	20	57%	3	9%	35	28%
Americas	9	60%	6	40%	0	0%	15	12%
Asia	21	66%	9	28%	2	6%	32	26%
Europe	7	54%	5	38%	1	8%	13	11%
Middle East	11	39%	13	47%	4	14%	28	23%
Total	60	49%	53	43%	10	8%	123	100%

* Low involvement includes discussion without resolution, fact-finding, good offices and general-other.
Medium involvement includes condemnation, call for action by adversaries, mediation.
High involvement includes arbitration, sanctions, observers and emergency military forces.

TABLE III.16.B. Content of Global Organization Involvement: Polarity

System	Low*		Medium		High		Total	
	Freq.	%	Freq.	%	Freq.	%	Freq.	%
Bipolar (1945–62)	27	53%	18	35%	6	12%	51	42%
Polycentric (1963–79)	33	46%	35	49%	4	5%	72	58%
Total	60	49%	53	43%	10	8%	123	100%

* See note to Table III.16.A.

TABLE III.16.C. Content of Global Organization Involvement: System Level

Level of system	Low*		Medium		High		Total	
	Freq.	%	Freq.	%	Freq.	%	Freq.	%
Subsystem	44	50%	38	44%	5	6%	87	71%
Mainly subsystem	7	37%	10	53%	2	10%	19	15%
Mainly dominant	6	55%	2	18%	3	27%	11	9%
Dominant system	3	50%	3	50%	0	0%	6	5%
Total	60	49%	53	43%	10	8%	123	100%

* See note to Table III.16.A.

TABLE III.16.D. Content of Global Organization Involvement: Conflict

Conflict setting	Low*		Medium		High		Total	
	Freq.	%	Freq.	%	Freq.	%	Freq.	%
Non-protracted conflict	25	62%	12	30%	3	8%	40	33%
Protracted conflict	23	40%	31	53%	4	7%	58	47%
Long-war-protracted conflict	12	48%	10	40%	3	12%	25	20%
Total	60	49%	53	43%	10	8%	123	100%

* See note to Table III.16.A.

mediation – that the similarity breaks down: crises occurring at the mainly dominant system level had a much lower incidence of medium involvement, proportionately, than crises at the other three levels. Variation is also marked at the highest level of GO involvement, with 27% of the mainly dominant system cases falling into this category, but none among the dominant system crises. Thus, while high UN involvement increased from subsystem to mainly subsystem to mainly dominant system cases, there were no instances of high UN involvement at the purely dominant system level.

As evident in Table III.16.D, crises during protracted conflicts and long-war-protracted conflicts exhibited similar patterns. It would appear that in non-protracted conflicts, where the interests of the major powers were less affected, and the danger to the stability of the international system was low, the UN tended to take relatively low-level action (62%). Conversely, the UN was more prone to involvement in crises occurring during a protracted conflict (47%); and it is there, among the non-long-war-protracted conflicts that the UN had the greatest potential for more substantive, that is, medium-level activity. As will be noted in Table III.18.C below, 60% of all cases in which UN activity was effective occurred among these same non-long-war-protracted conflicts.

Effectiveness of Global Organization Involvement (GLOBEFCT)

This variable assesses the effectiveness of global organization (GO) activity in abating international crises. Effectiveness in crisis abatement is understood in terms of preventing hostilities or otherwise contributing to the termination of an international crisis. This assessment refers to the role of the GO from the first breakpoint until the final exitpoint of an international crisis.

Coding Rules and Raw Frequencies, with Illustrations
1 **Global organization involvement escalated crisis** (League $N = 0$; 0%, UN $N = 4$; 3%) (The dispatch of a UN Observer Group to Lebanon in 1958 exacerbated that crisis and delayed its termination, since the group was too small to cover the entire border area).

2 **Global organization involvement did not contribute to crisis abatement** (League N = 8; 57.1%, UN N = 76; 62%) (The UN Security Council became involved in the 1945-47 Indonesia Independence I Crisis but its activity did not contribute to the resolution of that crisis).

3 **Global organization involvement contributed marginally to crisis abatement** (League N = 3; 21.4%, UN N = 18; 15%) (During the first War of Attrition Crisis in 1969, UN Observer Forces and Big Four talks under UN auspices contributed marginally to crisis abatement).

4 **Global organization involvement had an important impact on crisis abatement** (League N = 3; 21.4%, UN N = 21; 17%) (The active participation of the UN Secretary-General (and the US Government) in the West Irian Crisis of 1961–62 had an important impact on crisis abatement).

5 **Global organization involvement was the single most important contributor to crisis abatement** (League N = 0; 0%, UN N = 4; 3%) (Zambia's crisis with South Africa over the Caprivi Strip in 1971 terminated when the UN Security Council passed a resolution condemning South Africa and calling on it to respect the sovereignty of Zambia).

Analysis of Effectiveness of Global Organization Involvement

As noted previously, the League of Nations became involved in 14 of 38, or 37% of international crises from 1929 to 1939, and the UN in 123 of 209, or 59% of crises during the period 1945 to 1979. Despite the lower rate of League activity, it was judged to have been effective – marginal, important, most important – in 6 of 14 cases, or 43%, as compared to 43 of 123 cases, or 35%, for the UN (see Table III.17.A).

Africa stands out as the region in which the UN was particularly effective: all four cases in which the involvement of the global organization was the most important contribution to crisis abatement occurred in Africa; and the overall UN effectiveness rate – most important, important and marginal – was 51% in Africa-located crises (Table III.17.A). The Americas show the lowest effectiveness rate, only 13%, probably because of the more active role of the regional organization, the OAS, in that region's crises. Europe ranked second to Africa in terms of UN effectiveness – but never was it the most important contributor to crisis abatement in a Europe-located case. Finally, the UN's negative role (escalation) was most evident in Middle East crises (three of four cases).

In Table III.17.B we evaluate the effectiveness of global organization involvement in crises in the context of conflict. If marginal, important and most important roles in terms of crisis abatement are combined, we find rather strong trends. The UN was effective in 28% of crises in which it became involved when these crises occurred in non-protracted conflicts, and it played an important – or the most important – role in 20% of these cases. In a non-long-war-protracted conflict setting UN effectiveness reached 45%, in more than half the cases as an important – or the most important – factor, while crises during long-war-protracted conflicts showed only 24% UN effectiveness.

TABLE III.17.A. Effectiveness of Global Organization Involvement: Geography

Region	Escalated		Did not contribute		Marginal		Important		Most important		Total	
	Freq.	%	Freq.	%	Freq.	%	Freq.	%	Freq.	%	Freq.	%
League of Nations 1929–39	0	0%	8	57.1%	3	21.4%	3	21.4%	0	0%	14	100%
UN 1945–79												
Africa	0	0%	17	49%	11	31%	3	9%	4	11%	35	28%
Americas	0	0%	13	87%	0	0%	2	13%	0	0%	15	12%
Asia	1	3%	21	66%	3	9%	7	22%	0	0%	32	26%
Europe	0	0%	8	61%	1	8%	4	31%	0	0%	13	11%
Middle East	3	10.7%	17	60.7%	3	10.7%	5	17.9%	0	0%	28	23%
Total	4	3%	76	62%	18	15%	21	17%	4	3%	123*	100%

* See note to Table III.15.A.

TABLE III.17.B. Effectiveness of Global Organization Involvement: Conflict

Conflict setting	Escalated		Did not contribute		Marginal		Important		Most important		Total	
	Freq.	%	Freq.	%	Freq.	%	Freq.	%	Freq.	%	Freq.	%
Non-protracted conflict	1	2.5%	28	70.0%	3	7.5%	7	17.5%	1	2.5%	40	33%
Protracted conflict	2	3%	30	52%	11	19%	14	24%	1	2%	58	47%
Long-war-protracted conflict	1	4%	18	72%	4	16%	0	0%	2	8%	25	20%
Total	4	3%	76	62%	18	15%	21	17%	4	3%	123*	100%

* See note to Table III.15.A.

TABLE III.17.C. Effectiveness of Global Organization Involvement: Involvement by Powers

Involvement	Escalated		Did not contribute		Marginal		Important		Most important		Total	
	Freq.	%	Freq.	%	Freq.	%	Freq.	%	Freq.	%	Freq.	%
Superpower participation												
Low or No	1	1%	50	57%	16	18%	17	19%	4	5%	88	72%
High	3	9%	26	74%	2	6%	4	11%	0	0%	35	28%
Total	4	3%	76	62%	18	15%	21	17%	4	3%	123*	100%

* See note to Table III.15.A.

In Table III.17.C we note that 37 of the 43 cases of UN effectiveness were situations in which there was either low or no activity on the part of the superpowers. Thus it seems safe to conclude that there is an inverse relationship between superpower activity and UN effectiveness. In substantive terms, when the superpowers were active militarily or semi-militarily, the UN ability to contribute to crisis abatement declined markedly.

A second variable, Global Organization Involvement and Pace of Abatement (GLOBPACE), was designed to tap a different aspect of the impact of global organization involvement than GLOBEFCT, namely, its effect on the timing of crisis abatement rather than the content of its effect. However, the data as generated reveal a very strong overlap in the frequencies for comparable value of these two variables:

GLOBPACE
1 **GO activity delayed termination** (League $N = 0$; 0%, UN $N = 2$; 2%).
2 **GO activity had no effect on the timing of termination** (League $N = 11$; 79%, UN $N = 85$; 69%).
3 **GO activity contributed to more rapid termination** (League $N = 3$; 21%, UN $N = 36$; 29%).

Thus the reader should consult the tables and analysis of the GLOBEFCT data for knowledge on GLOBPACE.

Most Effective Global Organization Organ (GLOBEFOR)

This variable addresses those crises in which global organization involvement was deemed to have been effective in crisis abatement. Specifically, it identifies the organs which were coded as marginally effective, important or most important in terms of crisis abatement, as reported in the effectiveness variable (GLOBEFCT).

Coding Rules and Raw Frequencies, with Illustrations
1 **Secretary-general** (League $N = 0$; 0%, UN $N = 10$; 24%) (During the Rwanda/Burundi Crisis of 1963-64 the UN Secretary-General appointed a Representative to investigate the refugee problem).

2 **(General) assembly** (League $N = 2$; 33%, UN $N = 6$; 14%) (In the Suez-Sinai Crisis of 1956–57 the General Assembly decided to send an emergency military force to the region).

3 **(Security) council** (League $N = 4$; 67%, UN $N = 26$; 62%) (In the Cyprus III Crisis of 1974–75, the Security Council took a leading role in crisis abatement; it arranged and supervised cease-fires and facilitated talks among the parties to the crisis).

Analysis of Most Effective Global Organization Organ

As evident in Table III.18.A, the (Security) Council was the leading organ in terms of effective crisis abatement, accounting for 67% of the effective League cases and 62% of the effective UN cases. However, there was considerable variation across the two post-World War II periods, with 47% of the bipolarity cases showing the Security Council as most effective, compared to 72% for the polycentric period. The General Assembly, by contrast, had a 24% most effective rate for the bipolar period, but only 8% for the polycentric period. The Secretary-General was the most effective in crisis abatement in 24% of the cases for the UN, but was never active or effective for the League.

The data in Table III.18.B relate to the most effective UN organ in terms of the system level of a crisis. The overwhelming proportion of crises in which the UN was effective in crisis abatement occurred at the subsystem level (79%), and the Security Council was the leading organ in these situations. The role of the Security Council in crises occurring at other system levels was considerably less. By contrast,

TABLE III.18.A. Most Effective Global Organization Organ*: Polarity

System	Secretary-General		(General) Assembly		(Security) Council		Total	
	Freq.	%	Freq.	%	Freq.	%	Freq.	%
League of Nations								
Multipolar (1929–39)	0	0%	2	33%	4	67%	6	100%
UN								
Bipolar (1945–62)	5	29%	4	24%	8	47%	17	40%
Polycentric (1963–79)	5	20%	2	8%	18	72%	25	60%
Total	10	24%	6	14%	26	62%	42**	100%

* Readers should be aware of the precision in procedures used in coding data for this variable and for the Global Organization Organ most active in a crisis (Tables III.15.A, B, C, D, E). Occasionally, the organ most active in a crisis was not identical to the one which contributed most effectively to crisis abatement. In addition, the 13 cases of general UN activity were not included in the presentation of the tables that follow. Thus some small discrepancies may occur in the number of crises relating to some of the categories.
** One case of effective UN action could not be coded on this variable.

TABLE III.18.B. Most Effective Global Organization Organ*: System Level

Level of system	Secretary-General		General Assembly		Security Council		Total	
	Freq.	%	Freq.	%	Freq.	%	Freq.	%
UN								
Subsystem	7	21%	3	9%	23	70%	33	79%
Mainly subsystem	2	67%	0	0%	1	33%	3	7%
Mainly dominant	0	0%	3	75%	1	25%	4	9%
Dominant system	1	50%	0	0%	1	50%	2	5%
Total	10	24%	6	14%	26	62%	42	100%

* See notes to Table III.18.A.

TABLE III.18.C. Most Effective Global Organization Organ*: Conflict

Conflict setting	Secretary-General		General Assembly		Security Council		Total	
	Freq.	%	Freq.	%	Freq.	%	Freq.	%
UN								
Non-protracted conflict	4	36.4%	3	27.3%	4	36.4%	11	26%
Protracted conflict	6	24%	3	12%	16	64%	25	60%
Long-war-protracted conflict	0	0%	0	0%	6	100%	6	14%
Total	10	24%	6	14%	26	62%	42	100%

* See notes to Table III.18.A.

TABLE III.18.D. Most Effective Global Organization Organ*: Involvement by Powers

Involvement	Secretary-General		General Assembly		Security Council		Total	
	Freq.	%	Freq.	%	Freq.	%	Freq.	%
UN								
Superpower participation								
Low or No	8	22%	4	11%	24	67%	36	86%
High	2	33.3%	2	33.3%	2	33.3%	6	14%
Total	10	24%	6	14%	26	62%	42	100%

* See notes to Table III.18.A.

the General Assembly role was most prominent at the mainly dominant system level and the Secretary-General at the mainly subsystem level.

In Table III.18.C we observe that UN involvement was most effective when it dealt with crises in non-long-war-protracted conflicts (60%). The Security Council was the most effective UN organ in 64% of those cases, compared to 36% of crises in non-protracted conflicts and 100% of the few long-war-protracted conflict cases. While the Security Council was the most effective organ in both long-war and non-long-war protracted conflict crises, the effectiveness rate for the three UN organs was almost evenly divided in the non-protracted conflict category.

Table III.18.D compares the effectiveness of UN organs in crisis management across levels of superpower participation. The outstanding finding is that 86% of all cases in which the UN was effective in crisis abatement showed either no superpower activity or activity at a low level. Stated differently, the likelihood of UN effectiveness was six times as great when superpower activity was nil or low (36 to 6 cases). There is no variation in effectiveness by UN organs when the superpowers were highly involved. However, the Security Council was most effective most frequently in the absence of high superpower activity. In Table III.15.E above, we noted that 34 cases in which the UN became involved exhibited high superpower participation; but, as evident in Table III.18.D, only 6 of these cases or 18% showed the UN as effective. Among low participation cases on the other hand, 36 of 89 cases, or 40%, showed effective UN activity.

Most Effective Global Organization Involvement (GLOBEFAC)

This variable addresses those crises in which global organization involvement was deemed to have had a positive effect on crisis abatement. It identifies the specific actions which were coded as marginally effective, important and most important in terms of crisis abatement, that is, positive effect as reported in the effectiveness variable (GLOBEFCT).

Coding Rules and Raw Frequencies, with Illustrations
1 **Low global organization involvement** (League $N = 0$; 0%, UN $N = 9$; 21%) – discussion without resolution, fact-finding, good offices, general-other (Good

offices on the part of the UN Secretary-General helped to bring about an agreement between The Netherlands and Indonesia in their 1961–62 West Irian II Crisis).

2 **Medium global organization involvement** (League $N = 3$; 50%, UN $N = 27$; 63%) – condemnation, call for action by adversaries, mediation (The UN Security Council passed a cease-fire resolution during the third (1948–49) crisis between The Netherlands and Indonesia).

3 **High global organization involvement** (League $N = 3$; 50%, UN $N = 7$; 16%) – arbitration, sanctions, observers, emergency military forces (On 4 March 1963 the Security Council adopted a resolution establishing a UN peace-keeping force in Cyprus).

Analysis of Most Effective Global Organization Involvement

Overall, the global organization effectiveness rate was not inconsiderable – six of 14 (League of Nations) and 43 of 123 (UN), that is, 49 of 137 (36%). It was highest for the League (43%), followed by the UN in the polycentric system (26 of 72, or 36%) and the bipolar period (17 of 51, or 33%) (see Tables III.16.A, B, III.19.A). As evident in Table III.19.A, the majority of crises in which global organization involvement was effective in crisis abatement falls in the category of medium activity: condemnation, call for action, mediation (League – 50%, UN – 63%). For the UN, all three levels of activity exhibited a degree of effectiveness in the bipolar system. For the polycentric system, 73% of all cases of effective UN involvement fell in the medium activity category, with low and high activity represented equally marginally. Clearly, then, in terms of effectiveness, there has been a change over time and type of international system in the degree of effectiveness of various kinds of global organization involvement.

Turning to Table III.19.B, we observe that the preponderance of crises in which the UN was effective (17 of 43 cases, or 40% of the total) exhibit the following characteristics: non-long-war-protracted conflict setting and medium-level UN involvement. It is also worth noting that among non-protracted conflict cases the lowest level of UN activity was more effective than it was among protracted conflict cases.

Table III.19.C focuses on the power discrepancy among the principal adversaries in crises. Medium UN involvement was about equally effective for all three levels of power discrepancy and accounted for more than half of the cases at each level. Crises with low UN involvement exhibited a high proportion of instances in which power discrepancy among the adversaries was low (38%). And where power discrepancy was medium or high in crises, effective UN involvement was more often intense than passive.

Table III.19.D examines the degree of superpower participation in crises and the effectiveness of various levels of UN involvement – low, medium, high. In general, the UN was much more effective when superpower participation was low – 86% to

---

TABLE III.19.A. Most Effective Global Organization Involvement*: Polarity

System	Low		Medium		High		Total	
	Freq.	%	Freq.	%	Freq.	%	Freq.	%
League of Nations								
Multipolar (1929–39)	0	0%	3	50%	3	50%	6	100%
UN								
Bipolar (1945–62)	5	29%	8	47%	4	24%	17	40%
Polycentric (1963–79)	4	15%	19	73%	3	12%	26	60%
Total	9	21%	27	63%	7	16%	43	100%

* Readers should be aware of the precision in procedures used in coding data for this variable and for Content of Global Organization Involvement (Tables III.16.A, B, C, D), in which the most intense activity was recorded. In some cases differences were found in the global organization's most intense involvement and that which most contributed to crisis abatement. Thus the total number of cases in some of the categories may differ from those appearing in the earlier tables.

TABLE III.19.B. Most Effective Global Organization Involvement: Conflict

Conflict setting	Low		Medium		High		Total	
	Freq.	%	Freq.	%	Freq.	%	Freq.	%
UN 1945–79								
Non-protracted conflict	4	36%	5	46%	2	18%	11	26%
Protracted conflict	4	15.4%	17	65.4%	5*	19%	26	61%
Long-war-protracted conflict	1	17%	5	83%	0	0%	6	14%
Total	9	21%	27	63%	7	16%	43	100%

* In Table III.16.D, dealing with the content of global organization involvement, four of the 58 protracted conflict cases showed high GO activity. In Table III.19.B, dealing with the most effective global organization type of involvement, five of the 26 protracted conflict cases showed high GO activity. This apparent discrepancy is explained by the fact, as noted earlier (* note to Table III.13.B), that there were several cases in which the most intense activity differed from the most effective one.

TABLE III.19.C. Most Effective Global Organization Involvement: Power Discrepancy

Power discrepancy	Low		Medium		High		Total	
	Freq.	%	Freq.	%	Freq.	%	Freq.	%
UN 1945–79								
Low	6	38%	9	56%	1	6%	16	37%
Medium	2	11%	13	72%	3	17%	18	42%
High	1	11%	5	56%	3	33%	9	21%
Total	9	21%	27	63%	7	16%	43*	100%

* See note to Table III.19.A.

TABLE III.19.D. Most Effective Global Organization Involvement: Involvement by Powers

Involvement	Low		Medium		High		Total	
	Freq.	%	Freq.	%	Freq.	%	Freq.	%
Superpower participation								
Low or No	9	24%	23	62%	5	14%	37	86%
High	0	0%	4	67%	2	33%	6	14%
Total	9	21%	27	63%	7	16%	43*	100%

* See note to Table III.19.A.

14%. In cases in which their participation was low or nonexistent, 24% exhibited effective low-level UN involvement; when superpower participation was high, low-level UN involvement was never effective in crisis abatement. By contrast, there was virtually no difference in the association between the extent of superpower participation and the proportion of cases with medium-level effective UN involvement.

Source of Regional/Security Organization Involvement (SORACT)

The following five variables refer to the activity and effectiveness of regional/security organizations (RSOs) in international crises, from the first breakpoint (trigger) to the last exitpoint (termination). Since regional/security organization involvement was virtually non-existent prior to 1945 (with the exception of three approaches to the Pan American Union, a predecessor of the OAS), the data we report here pertain only to the post-World War II period.

The first variable addresses the following question: Which party(ies) (if any) approached a regional/security organization during a crisis? The initial approach may have occurred prior to the first breakpoint of the crisis period.

Coding Rules and Raw Frequencies, with Illustrations

1 **Regional/security organization not approached** (N = 112; 54%).
2 **Crisis actor(s)** (N = 44; 21%) (In January 1955 Costa Rica appealed to the OAS in a crisis triggered by the arrival of Costa Rican rebels in Nicaragua via Venezuela).
3 **Third party** (N = 10; 5%) – non-crisis actor or actor involved in a crisis, other than superpower (In the Portuguese Invasion of Guinea Crisis of 1970 Ethiopia, Egypt, Libya and Sudan called for action by the OAU, which ultimately passed a resolution condemning Portugal and demanding reparations for Guinea).
4 **US** (N = 7; 3%) (In the Pathet Lao Offensive II Crisis of 1962 the US initiated action by SEATO forces).
5 **USSR** (N = 2; 1%) (In the Ussuri River Crisis of 1969 the Warsaw Treaty Organization met at the request of the USSR).
6 **Initiation by regional/security organization** (N = 32; 16%) (In the Berlin Deadline Crisis of 1957–59 NATO initiated action).

Analysis of Source of Regional/Security Organization Involvement As noted in Table III.20.A, regional/security organizations were approached in 46% of all international crises in the 1945–79 period, compared with 61% for the United Nations (Table III.14.A). Crises at the subsystem or mainly subsystem level exhibited a much more frequent approach to RSOs than did crises at the mainly dominant or dominant system level (49% versus 26% combined). Among these subsystem or mainly subsystem cases the crisis actors themselves were the most

TABLE III.20.A. Source of Regional/Security Organization Involvement: System Level

Level of system	Regional organization not approached		Crisis actor		Third party		US		USSR		Regional organization		Total	
	Freq.	%	Freq.	%	Freq.	%	Freq.	%	Freq.	%	Freq.	%	Freq.	%
Subsystem	77	52%	35	24%	7	5%	2	1%	0	0%	27	18%	148	72%
Mainly subsystem	12	42.8%	8	28.6%	1	3.6%	3	10.7%	1	3.6%	3	10.7%	28	13%
Mainly dominant	16	80%	0	0%	1	5%	1	5%	1	5%	1	5%	20	10%
Dominant system	7	64%	1	9%	1	9%	1	9%	0	0%	1	9%	11	5%
Total	112	54%	44	21%	10	5%	7	3%	2	1%	32	16%	207*	100%

* Two cases with missing data; 1929–45 cases excluded.

frequent source of approach to RSOs (43 of 95, or 45% of all cases of approach to an RSO), with the organizations themselves initiating activity in 30 of 95, or 32% of these cases. Crisis actors made the initial approach to the regional organization in 21% of post-war crises, as compared to a figure of 38% for actor approach to the global organization.

In short, regional/security organizations were treated as less likely than the global organization to be effective crisis managers. However, they displayed greater initiative than their global counterpart in trying to abate a crisis.

Regional/Security Organization Most Active in Crisis (REGORG)

Regional and/or security organizations, in the geographic area of a crisis or elsewhere, intervene in some crises, autonomously or as the organ of great power/superpower activity. Which organization was most active in a crisis, regardless of form, substance, or alignment?

Coding Rules and Raw Frequencies, with Illustrations

1 **League of Arab States** (N = 26; 28%) (During the Palestine Partition Crisis of November–December 1947, the Arab League announced the decision to keep Palestine as an Arab state and to set up an army of volunteers).

2 **North Atlantic Treaty Organization** ($N = 6$; 6%) (In the Syria/Turkey Border Crisis of 1957, NATO's commander issued a warning to the USSR concerning its intentions regarding Turkey).

3 **Organization of American States** ($N = 14$; 15%) (During the Nicaragua/Honduras Crisis of April–May 1957, an OAS investigating committee succeeded in getting both parties to sign a cease-fire).

4 **Organization of African Unity** ($N = 22$; 23%) (In the Kenya/Somalia Crisis of 1963–64, the OAU Council of Ministers passed a resolution calling for steps to settle the dispute).

5 **Southeast Asia Treaty Organization** ($N = 4$; 4%) (During the Vietcong Attack Crisis of September–November 1961, SEATO military advisors met and issued a communiqué).

6 **Warsaw Treaty Organization** ($N = 4$; 4%) (Warsaw Pact forces invaded Czechoslovakia on 20 August 1968 during the Prague Spring Crisis).

7 **Other** ($N = 5$; 5%).

8 **Multiple** ($N = 14$; 15%).

Analysis of Regional/Security Organization Most Active in Crisis As evident in Table III.21.A, the most active regional/security organizations for the period 1945–79 as a whole were the League of Arab States (LAS), the Organization of African Unity (OAU) and the Organization of American States (OAS): together, they account for 66% of the post-World War II crises in which RSOs became involved. Of the 95 cases of RSO activity, 62 or 65% occurred in the polycentric period. Since only 55% of all international crises from 1945 to 1979 occurred during the polycentric period, this indicates that regional/security organizations played a particularly active role in this system.

For the bipolar system, two regional organizations stood out in terms of their involvement in international crises: the LAS with 40%, and the OAS with 21%. In the polycentric system, the LAS was still an important factor with 21% of all crises. However, the OAU became involved in 36% of all crises, primarily because of the emergence of many independent African states since 1960. Paralleling this sharp increase, the OAS dropped to 11% for the bipolar period.

Table III.21.B reveals a considerable degree of variation in terms of the activity of RSOs in crises within non-protracted and protracted conflicts. The OAS and the

TABLE III.21.A. Regional/Security Organization Most Active in Crisis: Polarity

System	LAS		NATO		OAS		OAU		SEATO		WTO		Other		Multiple		Total*	
	Freq.	%	Freq.	%	Freq.	%	Freq.	%	Freq.	%	Freq.	%	Freq.	%	Freq.	%	Freq.	%
Bipolar (1945–62)	13	40%	3	9%	7	21%	0	0%	2	6%	1	3%	1	3%	6	18%	33	35%
Polycentric (1963–79)	13	21%	3	5%	7	11%	22	36%	2	3%	3	5%	4	6%	8	13%	62	65%
Total	26	28%	6	6%	14	15%	22	23%	4	4%	4	4%	5	5%	14	15%	95	100%

* In this and subsequent tables relating to regional organization involvement, only those cases in which RSO activity took place are analyzed. One case had missing data.

TABLE III.21.B. Regional/Security Organization Most Active in Crisis: Conflict

Conflict setting	LAS		NATO		OAS		OAU		SEATO		WTO		Other		Multiple		Total	
	Freq.	%	Freq.	%	Freq.	%	Freq.	%	Freq.	%	Freq.	%	Freq.	%	Freq.	%	Freq.	%
Non-protracted conflict	12	27%	1	2%	13	30%	5	11%	1	2%	2	5%	3	7%	7	16%	44	46%
Protracted conflict	12	33%	5	14%	1	3%	7	19%	1	3%	1	3%	2	6%	7	19%	36	38%
Long-war-protracted conflict	2	13%	0	0%	0	0%	10	67%	2	13%	1	7%	0	0%	0	0%	15	16%
Total	26	28%	6	6%	14	15%	22	23%	4	4%	4	4%	5	5%	14	15%	95	100%

Arab League were particularly active in non-protracted conflicts, while the OAU was most active in crises during long-war-protracted conflicts.

Content of Regional/Security Organization Involvement (REGACT)

This variable identifies the content of regional/security organization activity during the course of a crisis.

Coding Rules and Raw Frequencies, with Illustrations

1 **Discussion without resolution** ($N = 16$; 16.5%) (During the West Irian I Crisis, the NATO Council met in December 1957 but took no action).

2 **Fact-finding** ($N = 5$; 5.2%) (In the Dominican Republic/Haiti Crisis of 1963 an OAS fact-finding mission shuttled between the two countries in an attempt at de-escalation).

3 **Good offices** ($N = 3$; 3.1%) (The President of the Union Africaine et Malgache offered his good offices in the settlement of a territorial dispute between Niger and Dahomey, in December 1963–January 1964).

4 **Condemnation** ($N = 13$; 13.4%) (In the crises resulting from the assassination attempt on the Venezuelan President in 1960 the OAS passed a resolution condemning the Government of the Dominican Republic and calling on member-states to break off diplomatic relations and impose an arms embargo).

5 **Call for action** ($N = 14$; 14.4%) (During the Indonesia Independence III Crisis of 1948–49 the Arab League passed a resolution calling for Dutch acceptance of a cease-fire).

6 **Mediation** ($N = 14$; 14.4%) (In the Black September Crisis of September 1970 the Arab League played a mediating role in producing a cease-fire between Jordan and Syria).

7 **Arbitration** ($N = 1$; 1.0%) (The OAS arbitrated the dispute between Honduras and El Salvador in the Football War of 1969).

8 **Sanctions** ($N = 3$; 3.1%) (In the Soviet Bloc/Yugoslavia Crisis of 1949, the COMECON imposed sanctions on Yugoslavia).

9 **Observer group** ($N = 1$; 1.0%) (The League of Arab States adopted a resolution to supervise the implementation of a cease-fire between North and South Yemen in March 1979).

10 **Emergency military force** ($N = 3$; 3.1%) (In the Dominican Republic Crisis of 1965 an OAS Resolution called for the dispatch of an Inter-American Peace Force to the Dominican Republic).

11 **Multiple activity** ($N = 13$; 13.4%) (In the Berlin Wall Crisis of 1961 Khrushchev's demand for a settlement of the Berlin problem elicited NATO consultations and WTO endorsement).

12 **General-other** ($N = 11$; 11.3%) (In the Venezuela/Cuba Crisis of November–December 1963 the OAS agreed to investigate Venezuela's charges that Cuba had supplied arms to Communist guerrillas).

Analysis of Content of Regional/Security Organization Involvement

In Table III.22.A we note that there was high-level regional/security organization involvement in only 9% of the crises in which they became involved. This figure is similar to that for high-level UN involvement (see Table III.16.A). Low-level RSO activity was somewhat more likely, proportionately, during the polycentric period, while medium-level RSO involvement was more frequent in the bipolar period.

As is evident in Table III.22.B, 77% of all crises in which regional/security organizations became involved occurred at the subsystem level. Among these 65 cases, 43% exhibited low-level involvement, while only 8% exhibited high-level regional/security organization involvement. Most of the other crises occurred at the mainly subsystem level, where we again find a preponderance of cases exhibiting low-level or medium-level involvement.

Sixty-one of 84 or 73% of all crises in which regional/security organizations became involved exhibited low or no superpower participation (see Table III.22.C). Of these cases, 29 or 47% were characterized by low-level involvement. Among the 23 cases with high superpower participation, only 26% exhibited low-level involvement.

TABLE III.22.A. Content of Regional/Security Organization Involvement: Polarity

System	Low-level*		Medium-level*		High-level*		Total	
	Freq.	%	Freq.	%	Freq.	%	Freq.	%
Bipolar (1945–62)	10	35%	16	55%	3	10%	29	34%
Polycentric (1963–79)	25	45.5%	25	45.5%	5	9%	55	66%
Total	35	42%	41	49%	8	9%	84**	100%

* Low-level involvement includes discussion without resolution, fact-finding, good offices, and general-other.
  Medium-level involvement includes mediation, calls for action, and condemnation.
  High-level involvement includes arbitration, sanctions, observers and emergency military forces.
** Thirteen multiple cases were excluded.

TABLE III.22.B. Content of Regional/Security Organization Involvement: System Level

Level of system	Low-level*		Medium-level*		High-level*		Total	
	Freq.	%	Freq.	%	Freq.	%	Freq.	%
Subsystem	28	43%	32	49%	5	8%	65	77%
Mainly subsystem	5	39%	6	46%	2	15%	13	16%
Mainly dominant	1	25%	2	50%	1	25%	4	5%
Dominant system	1	50%	1	50%	0	0%	2	2%
Total	35	42%	41	49%	8	9%	84	100%

* See * note to Table III.22.A.

TABLE III.22.C. Content of Regional/Security Organization Involvement: Involvement by Powers

Involvement	Low-level*		Medium-level*		High-level*		Total	
	Freq.	%	Freq.	%	Freq.	%	Freq.	%
Superpower participation								
Low or No	29	47%	28	46%	4	7%	61	73%
High	6	26%	13	57%	4	17%	23	27%
Total	35	42%	41	49%	8	9%	84	100%

* See * note to Table III.22.A.

Effectiveness of Regional/Security Organization Involvement (ROEFCT)

This variable assesses the effectiveness of regional/security organization activity in abating a crisis. Effectiveness in crisis abatement is understood in terms of preventing hostilities, or otherwise contributing to the termination of an international crisis. This assessment refers to the role of a RSO from the first breakpoint until the final exitpoint of an international crisis.

Coding Rules and Raw Frequencies, with Illustrations
1 **Regional/security organization involvement escalated crisis** ($N = 8$; 8%) (Warsaw Treaty Organization military exercises during the height of the Prague Spring Crisis of 1968 exacerbated that crisis).
2 **Regional/security organization involvement did not contribute to crisis abatement** ($N = 49$; 52%) (A joint OAU/Arab League effort to abate the 1975–76 Sahara Crisis did not have any effect on that crisis).
3 **Regional/security organization involvement contributed marginally to crisis abatement** ($N = 17$; 18%) (The passage of an OAU resolution calling for a settlement of the Kenya/Somalia Crisis of 1963–64 contributed marginally to crisis abatement).

4 **Regional/security organization involvement had an important impact on crisis abatement** ($N = 12$; 13%) (During the Dominican Republic/Haiti Crisis of 1963, OAS activity, including shuttle diplomacy between the two states and a report, had an important impact on crisis abatement).

5 **Regional/security organization involvement was the single most important contributor to crisis abatement** ($N = 9$; 9%) (The OAS Council played a critical role in abating the second crisis between Costa Rica and Nicaragua, in January 1955, including the sending of observers to the area).

Analysis of Effectiveness of Regional/Security Organization Involvement

Regional/security organizations proved effective in 40% of all international crises in which they became involved (marginal, important, most important) (see Table III.23.A), compared to 35% for the UN (see Table III.17.A). Among the 38 crises in which RSOs were effective to some degree in crisis abatement, 23 or 60% occurred in the context of non-protracted conflicts.

While RSOs showed a 52% effectiveness rate in non-protracted conflicts, the rate was 36% for crises in non-long-war-protracted conflicts and only 13% for cases in long-war-protracted conflicts. The comparable figures for UN effectiveness were 28% of crises in non-protracted conflicts, 45% for non-long-war-protracted conflicts, and 24% for long-war-protracted conflict cases (see Table III.17.B). Thus the RSOs were more effective in crises unburdened by an ongoing conflict or war, while the global organization was more effective in a non-long-war-protracted conflict context.

TABLE III.23.A. Effectiveness of Regional/Security Organization Involvement: Conflict

Conflict setting	Escalated		Did not contribute		Marginal		Important		Most important		Total*	
	Freq.	%	Freq.	%	Freq.	%	Freq.	%	Freq.	%	Freq.	%
Non-protracted conflict	4	9%	17	39%	9	20%	7	16%	7	16%	44	46%
Protracted conflict	4	11%	19	53%	7	19%	4	11%	2	6%	36	38%
Long-war-protracted conflict	0	0%	13	86.6%	1	6.7%	1	6.7%	0	0%	15	16%
Total	8	8%	49	52%	17	18%	12	13%	9	9%	95	100%

* One case missing data.

A second variable (ROPACE) was designed to tap a different aspect of the impact of global organization involvement than ROEFCT, namely, its effect on the timing of crisis abatement rather than the content of its effect. However, the data as generated reveal a very strong overlap in the frequencies for comparable values of these two variables:

ROPACE

1 **Regional organization involvement delayed termination** ($N = 5$; 5%).
2 **Regional organization involvement had no effect on the timing of termination** ($N = 62$; 65%).
3 **Regional organization involvement contributed to more rapid termination** ($N = 29$; 30%).

Thus the reader should consult the tables and analysis of the ROEFCT data for knowledge on ROPACE.

Most Effective Regional/Security Organization (ROBODY)

This variable addresses those crises in which regional/security organization activity was deemed to have been effective in crisis abatement. Specifically, it identifies those organizations which were coded as marginally effective, important and most important in terms of crisis abatement, as reported in the effectiveness variable (ROEFCT).

Coding Rules and Raw Frequencies, with Illustrations
1 **League of Arab States** ($N = 9$; 25%) (Arab League activity in the Jordan Waters Crisis of 1963–64).
2 **North Atlantic Treaty Organization** ($N = 5$; 14%) (NATO activity in the Berlin Deadline Crisis of 1957–59).
3 **Organization of American States** ($N = 12$; 33%) (OAS activity in the Costa Rica/Nicaragua Crises of 1948–49 and 1955).
4 **Organization of African Unity** ($N = 7$; 19%) (OAU activity in the Uganda/Tanzania I Crisis of 1972).
5 **Southeast Asia Treaty Organization** ($N = 2$; 6%) (SEATO activity in the Pathet Lao Offensive Crises of 1961 and 1962).
6 **Other** ($N = 1$; 3%) (Council of Europe activity in the US Hostages in Iran Crisis of 1979–81).

Analysis of Most Effective Regional/Security Organization   Overall, and during the bipolar period, the OAS was the most effective regional/security organization, accounting for 12 of the 36 effective cases or 33% from 1945 to 1979, and seven of the 14 effective cases or 50% in the bipolar system (see Table III.24.A). During the polycentric period, which included 61% of all effective cases, the OAU became the most effective RSO with 32% of the effective cases, followed by the OAS and the LAS with 23% each. While the OAS role declined, that of NATO and the OAU became much more prominent. In part, at least, these figures reflect the changing focus of crises in the international arena.

TABLE III.24.A. Most Effective Regional/Security Organization: Polarity

System	LAS		NATO		OAS		OAU		SEATO		Other		Total	
	Freq.	%	Freq.	%	Freq.	%	Freq.	%	Freq.	%	Freq.	%	Freq.	%
Bipolar (1945–62)	4	29%	1	7%	7	50%	0	0%	2	14%	0	0%	14	39%
Polycentric (1963–79)	5	23%	4	18%	5	23%	7	32%	0	0%	1	4%	22	61%
Total	9	25%	5	14%	12	33%	7	19%	2	6%	1	3%	36*	100%

* Two multiple cases could not be classified on this variable.

Perceived Content of Outcome (SUBOUT)   Perceived content of outcome refers to whether or not the outcome of an international crisis was perceived by the actors to have been definitive or ambiguous. A definitive outcome is one in which all actors perceive victory or defeat in terms of the achievement of basic goals in the context of a specific crisis. An ambiguous outcome occurs when at least one of the crisis actors perceives either stalemate or compromise at the termination point of a crisis.

This variable is based upon the coding for individual crisis actors. Hence the reader should refer to the OUTCOM variable in the actor-level data set, reported in *Handbook II*.

Coding Rules and Raw Frequencies, with Illustrations
1 **Ambiguous outcome** ($N = 136$; 49%) – at least one actor coded as either stalemate – no effect on basic goals, no clear outcome to a crisis, no change in situation – or compromise – partial achievement of basic goals (In the crisis over the formation of the UAR in February 1958 both Jordan and Iraq perceived the substance of the outcome as stalemate).
2 **Definitive outcome** ($N = 142$; 51%) – all actors coded either as victory – achievement of basic goals – or defeat – non-achievement of basic goals (In the Cyprus II Crisis of November-December 1967 Cyprus and Greece perceived the outcome as defeat, while Turkey perceived victory).

Analysis of Perceived Content of Outcome The international crises from 1929 to 1979 were almost evenly divided in terms of ambiguous and definitive outcomes (see Table III.25.A). We also note that there is very little variability across the three non-war periods. Only the period of World War II shows a significant tendency toward definitive rather than ambiguous outcomes.

In Table III.25.B we note that crises occurring at the dominant system level had a greater tendency to terminate with a definitive outcome than did crises occurring at the other three system levels.

Finally, in Table III.25.C, we observe that there is a moderate tendency for crisis outcomes to become more ambiguous and less definitive as we move from non-protracted to non-long-war to long-war-protracted conflict setting.

TABLE III.25.A. Perceived Content of Outcome: Polarity

System	Ambiguous outcome		Definitive outcome		Total	
	Freq.	%	Freq.	%	Freq.	%
Multipolar (1929–39)	19	50%	19	50%	38	14%
World War II (1939–45)	9	29%	22	71%	31	11%
Bipolar (1945–62)	46	50%	47	50%	93	33%
Polycentric (1963–79)	62	53%	54	47%	116	42%
Total	136	49%	142	51%	278	100%

TABLE III.25.B. Perceived Content of Outcome: System Level

Level of system	Ambiguous outcome		Definitive outcome		Total	
	Freq.	%	Freq.	%	Freq.	%
Subsystem	88	52%	80	48%	168	60%
Mainly subsystem	22	48%	24	52%	46	17%
Mainly dominant	14	47%	16	53%	30	11%
Dominant system	12	35%	22	65%	34	12%
Total	136	49%	142	51%	278	100%

TABLE III.25.C. Perceived Content of Outcome: Conflict

Conflict setting	Ambiguous outcome		Definitive outcome		Total	
	Freq.	%	Freq.	%	Freq.	%
Non-protracted conflict	52	42%	71	58%	123	44%
Protracted conflict	50	52%	46	48%	96	35%
Long-war-protracted conflict	34	58%	25	42%	59	21%
Total	136	49%	142	51%	278	100%

**Form of Outcome
(FOROUT)**

This variable refers to the form of the outcome of an international crisis at its termination point. Form of outcome is determined by the configuration of forces operative during a crisis. The form of outcome also has an important bearing on subsequent relations among the parties to a crisis.

In most crises the form of outcome is common to all crisis actors. Where it is not, the form closest to consensus by the actors was coded for the entire crisis. Hence the reader should consult the coding of this variable at the actor level (OUTFOR) in *Handbook II*.

Coding Rules and Raw Frequencies, with Illustrations
1 **Agreement** ($N = 129$; 46%) – formal agreement, including treaties, armistices, cease-fires; semi-formal agreement, including letters, oral declarations (The Postage Stamp Crisis, resulting from the issuance of a Nicaraguan stamp showing a map of Nicaragua including parts of southeast Honduras, terminated when the two parties signed a Pact of Reciprocal Agreement on 10 December 1937).
2 **Tacit** ($N = 27$; 10%) – mutual understanding by adversaries, neither stated nor written (In late 1970 the Republic of Guinea was invaded by mercenaries from several countries, including Portuguese Guinea. A tacit agreement was reached in mid-December to end the crisis).
3 **Unilateral act** ($N = 88$; 32%) – an act by a crisis actor, without the voluntary agreement of its adversary(ies), which terminates a crisis, e.g., military intrusion into an adversary's territory, victory in a battle, severance of diplomatic relations, quelling of riots (Israel's rescue of hostages in Uganda in July 1976, terminating the Entebbe Raid Crisis).
4 **Other/no agreement** ($N = 34$; 12%) – crisis fades with no known termination date and no known agreement among the adversaries, other (The first West Irian Crisis, beginning in December 1957, faded and later erupted into West Irian II in September 1961).

Analysis of Form of Outcome

Overall, almost half of all international crises terminated in some form of agreement, while an additional third terminated in unilateral acts. Table III.26.A presents a regional breakdown of forms of outcome. Africa exhibits the lowest rate of termination through agreement (36%), while the Americas show the highest (58%). Termination through unilateral acts was least common in the Americas – 18% – but accounted for about a third of crisis terminations in the other regions.

Table III.26.B reports the distribution of forms of outcome in terms of polarity. The multipolar system was characterized by the highest rate of termination in agreement – 60% – compared to 42% for the post-World War II systems. The polycentric system exhibited the highest rate of termination through unilateral acts – 39% – contrasting with a low of 18% for the multipolar system.

Table III.26.C indicates that crises in non-protracted conflicts were characterized by a high rate of termination in agreement – 54%. Thus agreements are somewhat easier to achieve in situations of non-protracted conflict, where a crisis is part of a new conflict situation, and where agreement among the parties is not inhibited by a long tradition of hostility. This finding is reinforced by the total absence of long-war-protracted conflict crises terminating in tacit understandings, again

TABLE III.26.A. Form of Outcome: Geography

Region	Agreement		Tacit		Unilateral act		No agreement/ Other		Total	
	Freq.	%	Freq.	%	Freq.	%	Freq.	%	Freq.	%
Africa	23	36%	6	9%	24	38%	11	17%	64	23%
Americas	19	58%	4	12%	6	18%	4	12%	33	12%
Asia	32	46%	6	9%	25	36%	6	9%	69	25%
Europe	29	51%	4	7%	18	32%	6	10%	57	20%
Middle East	26	47%	7	13%	15	27%	7	13%	55	20%
Total	129	46%	27	10%	88	32%	34	12%	278	100%

TABLE III.26.B. Form of Outcome: Polarity

System	Agreement		Tacit		Unilateral act		No agreement/ Other		Total	
	Freq.	%	Freq.	%	Freq.	%	Freq.	%	Freq.	%
Multipolar (1929–39)	23	60.5%	4	10.5%	7	18.4%	4	10.5%	38	14%
World War II (1939–45)	18	58%	0	0%	10	32%	3	10%	31	11%
Bipolar (1945–62)	39	42%	14	15%	26	28%	14	15%	93	33%
Polycentric (1963–79)	49	42%	9	8%	45	39%	13	11%	116	42%
Total	129	46%	27	10%	88	32%	34	12%	278	100%

TABLE III.26.C. Form of Outcome: Conflict

Conflict setting	Agreement		Tacit		Unilateral act		No agreement/ Other		Total	
	Freq.	%	Freq.	%	Freq.	%	Freq.	%	Freq.	%
Non-protracted conflict	66	54%	14	11%	28	23%	15	12%	123	44%
Protracted conflict	38	40%	13	14%	33	34%	12	12%	96	35%
Long-war-protracted conflict	25	42%	0	0%	27	46%	7	12%	59	21%
Total	129	46%	27	10%	88	32%	34	12%	278	100%

TABLE III.26.D. Form of Outcome: Involvement by Powers

Involvement	Agreement		Tacit		Unilateral act		No agreement/ Other		Total	
	Freq.	%	Freq.	%	Freq.	%	Freq.	%	Freq.	%
Great power participation 1929–39										
Low or No	13	76%	3	18%	0	0%	1	6%	17	45%
High	10	48%	1	5%	7	33%	3	14%	21	55%
Total	23	60.5%	4	10.5%	7	18.4%	4	10.5%	38	100%
Great power participation 1939–45										
Low or No	4	57%	0	0%	2	29%	1	14%	7	23%
High	14	58.3%	0	0%	8	33.3%	2	8.3%	24	77%
Total	18	58%	0	0%	10	32%	3	10%	31	100%
Superpower participation 1945–79										
Low or No	60	40%	19	13%	48	32%	23	15%	150	72%
High	28	47%	4	7%	23	39%	4	7%	59	28%
Total	88	42%	23	11%	71	34%	27	13%	209	100%

because of the seriousness of the situation. Among crises occurring in non-long-war-protracted conflicts, on the other hand, agreement is less easy to achieve because the lack of outright warfare does not compel the parties to seek agreement. Unilateral acts are the most common form of termination among long-war-protracted conflicts.

Table III.26.D contains the distribution of forms of outcome in terms of level of great power/superpower participation. High involvement by the major powers in crises throughout the half-century was very rarely associated with a tacit understanding. During the multipolar period, agreement was more likely in crises where great power involvement was low or nil than when it was high (76% versus 48%). This pattern was reversed in the post-World War II period, where low or no superpower involvement was associated with agreement in 40% of the cases, compared with 47% agreement for high superpower involvement. Unilateral acts were uncommon in the 1929–39 period and occurred only when there was high involvement by the great powers. During World War II and the post-war periods, by contrast, termination through unilateral acts was common, regardless of the level of involvement of the great powers/superpowers.

Extent of Satisfaction about Outcome (EXSAT)

The extent of satisfaction about the outcome of an international crisis refers to the evaluation of the outcome from the point of view of the individual crisis actors when a crisis terminates. Hence the reader should refer to the coding of this variable at the actor level (OUTEVL) in *Handbook II*. The macro-variable examined below refers to the extent of satisfaction perceived by the crisis actors.

Only cases with two or more adversarial crisis actors can be coded for this variable. Hence 107 single-actor international crises and 28 multiple-actor cases in which the adversary(ies) was not a crisis actor are excluded (two cases with missing data are also excluded).

Coding Rules and Raw Frequencies, with Illustrations
1   **All satisfied** ($N = 44$; 31%) – cases in which all parties perceived themselves as satisfied with the content of the outcome (India and Pakistan were satisfied with the outcome of the Rann of Kutch Crisis in 1965).
2   **Mostly satisfied** ($N = 25$; 18%) – cases in which more crisis actors were satisfied than dissatisfied (France, the UK and the USA were satisfied, the USSR was dissatisfied, with the outcome of the Berlin Blockade Crisis of 1948–49).
3   **Equally mixed** ($N = 48$; 34%) – cases with an identical number of states which were satisfied and dissatisfied with the crisis outcome (The USSR was satisfied and Hungary dissatisfied with the outcome of the Hungarian Uprising of 1956).
4   **Mostly dissatisfied** ($N = 10$; 7%) – cases in which more crisis actors were dissatisfied than satisfied (Egypt, Iraq, Jordan, Lebanon and Syria were dissatisfied, Israel was satisfied, with the outcome of the Israel Independence Crisis of 1948–49).
5   **All dissatisfied** ($N = 14$; 10%) – cases in which all parties perceived themselves as dissatisfied with the content of the outcome (Angola, Rhodesia and Zambia were all dissatisfied with the outcome of the Raids on ZIPRA Crisis of 1979).

Analysis of Extent of Satisfaction about Outcome

Table III.27.A indicates that, while only 31% of all multi-actor international crises terminated in a manner that all actors perceived as satisfactory, an additional 18% of crises terminated with most parties satisfied. There is considerable variation by region. The Middle East stands out in three respects: it shows the highest proportion of cases where all parties were satisfied (38%); the highest proportion of crises in which most or all parties were dissatisfied (35%); and the lowest proportion of crises which terminated with equally mixed evaluations of the outcome (10%). It should be noted that of the 11 Middle East cases where all parties were satisfied, only 6 occurred within the Arab–Israel conflict. The Americas and Asia exhibited the highest proportion of crises with equally mixed outcomes. In all 5 regions satisfaction with crisis outcomes was more frequent than dissatisfaction: this pattern was most striking in the Americas (37% – 6%) and Europe (62% – 13%); it was least marked in the Middle East (55% – 35%).

The extent of satisfaction with crisis outcomes reveals considerable disparity among the four system-periods (see Table III.27.B). While a low 12.5% of crises during World War II showed all parties as satisfied, a rather high 37.5% showed the

TABLE III.27.A. Extent of Satisfaction about Outcome: Geography

Region	All satisfied		Mostly satisfied		Equally mixed		Dissatisfied*		Total	
	Freq.	%	Freq.	%	Freq.	%	Freq.	%	Freq.	%
Africa	11	33%	5	15%	12	37%	5	15%	33	23%
Americas	5	31%	1	6%	9	57%	1	6%	16	11%
Asia	9	23%	7	18%	18	46%	5	13%	39	28%
Europe	8	33%	7	29%	6	25%	3	13%	24	17%
Middle East	11	38%	5	17%	3	10%	10	35%	29	21%
Total	44	31%	25	18%	48	34%	24	17%	141	100%

* Includes the categories "mostly dissatisfied" and "all dissatisfied."

TABLE III.27.B. Extent of Satisfaction about Outcome: Polarity

System	All satisfied		Mostly satisfied		Equally mixed		Dissatisfied*		Total	
	Freq.	%	Freq.	%	Freq.	%	Freq.	%	Freq.	%
Multipolar (1929–39)	7	37%	3	16%	8	42%	1	5%	19	13%
World War II (1939–45)	1	12.5%	3	37.5%	2	25%	2	25%	8	6%
Bipolar (1945–62)	10	21%	7	14%	23	47%	9	18%	49	35%
Polycentric (1963–79)	26	40%	12	18.5%	15	23%	12	18.5%	65	46%
Total	44	31%	25	18%	48	34%	24	17%	141	100%

* See note to Table III.27.A.

TABLE III.27.C. Extent of Satisfaction about Outcome: System Level

Level of system	All satisfied		Mostly satisfied		Equally mixed		Dissatisfied*		Total	
	Freq.	%	Freq.	%	Freq.	%	Freq.	%	Freq.	%
Subsystem	35	39%	7	8%	30	34%	17	19%	89	63%
Mainly subsystem	6	22%	7	26%	11	41%	3	11%	27	19%
Mainly dominant	1	8.3%	6	50%	4	33.3%	1	8.3%	12	9%
Dominant system	2	15%	5	39%	3	23%	3	23%	13	9%
Total	44	31%	25	18%	48	34%	24	17%	141	100%

* See note to Table III.27.A.

TABLE III.27.D. Extent of Satisfaction about Outcome: Conflict

Conflict setting	All satisfied		Mostly satisfied		Equally mixed		Dissatisfied*		Total	
	Freq.	%	Freq.	%	Freq.	%	Freq.	%	Freq.	%
Non-protracted conflict	19	40%	4	8%	19	40%	6	12%	48	34%
Protracted conflict	19	30%	13	21%	22	35%	9	14%	63	45%
Long-war-protracted conflict	6	20%	8	27%	7	23%	9	30%	30	21%
Total	44	31%	25	18%	48	34%	24	17%	141	100%

* See note to Table III.27.A.

parties as mostly satisfied. Among the three other periods the bipolar system of 1945–62 showed the lowest proportion of cases in which all crisis actors were satisfied – 21% – compared to 40% for the polycentric period and 37% for the multipolar period. On the other hand, the multipolar system exhibited a very low rate of mutual dissatisfaction with outcomes.

Mutual satisfaction was most frequent in crises which occurred at the subsystem level (39%), and least frequent in the mainly dominant and dominant system crises (8% and 15%, respectively) (see Table III.27.C). Fortunately for the international system, this decline in satisfaction from subsystem to dominant system matches a decline in the number of crises at each level. Interestingly, the subsystem level exhibits proportionally few cases in which the parties were mostly satisfied, a category which accounts for a large proportion of crises at the other three system-levels and most particularly in the mainly dominant system level (50%). As with regions, satisfaction with crisis outcomes exceeded dissatisfaction at all four system-levels, ranging from the mainly dominant (58% – 8%) to the dominant level (54% – 23%).

As is evident in Table III.27.D, the extent of satisfaction varied sharply by conflict setting. Mutual satisfaction was highest among non-protracted conflict cases (40%), compared with 30% satisfaction in non-long-war-protracted conflict cases and only 20% in long-war-protracted conflict cases. By contrast, about a quarter of the long-war-protracted conflict cases terminated with most parties satisfied, compared with only 8% of the crises outside protracted conflicts. And dissatisfaction was twice as frequent, proportionally, in crises during long-war-protracted conflicts than in the two other settings. Taking the "all satisfied" and "mostly satisfied" outcomes together, there was virtually no difference among the three conflict settings for this crisis dimension.

Escalation or Reduction of Tension (OUTESR) This variable assesses the effect of a crisis outcome on the tension level among the adversaries.

Coding Rules and Raw Frequencies, with Illustrations
1 **Tension escalation** ($N = 146$; 52%) – crisis recurred among the principal adversaries during the subsequent 5-year period (The Gaza Raid Crisis of 1955–56 between Israel and Egypt was followed in October 1956 by the Suez–Sinai Campaign Crisis).
2 **Tension reduction** ($N = 132$; 48%) – crisis did not recur among the principal adversaries during the subsequent 5-year period (The Panama Canal Crisis of 1964 involving the US and Panama was not followed by a subsequent crisis between these adversaries).

Analysis of Escalation or Reduction of Tension As is evident in Table III.28.A, the entire set of 278 international crises is almost evenly divided between those which led to an escalation of tension (52%) and those which led to tension reduction (48%). The Americas stand out as a region in which the outcomes of crises have not led to tension escalation in subsequent periods (88%). At the other extreme, Africa and, to a somewhat lesser extent, Asia and the Middle East have been characterized by crises whose outcomes have indicated tension escalation. Europe occupies a middle ground, with its 57 crises roughly evenly divided between escalation and reduction of tension.

TABLE III.28.A. Escalation or Reduction of Tension: Geography

Region	Escalation		Reduction		Total	
	Freq.	%	Freq.	%	Freq.	%
Africa	43	67%	21	33%	64	23%
Americas	4	12%	29	88%	33	12%
Asia	42	61%	27	39%	69	25%
Europe	27	47%	30	53%	57	20%
Middle East	30	55%	25	45%	55	20%
Total	146	52%	132	48%	278	100%

TABLE III.28.B. Escalation or Reduction of Tension: Polarity

System	Escalation		Reduction		Total	
	Freq.	%	Freq.	%	Freq.	%
Multipolar (1929–39)	25	66%	13	34%	38	14%
World War II (1939–45)	21	68%	10	32%	31	11%
Bipolar (1945–62)	31	33%	62	67%	93	33%
Polycentric (1963–79)	69	59%	47	41%	116	42%
Total	146	52%	132	48%	278	100%

The bipolar system is unique in that 67% of its crises resulted in tension reduction, compared to an average tension reduction rate of 38% for the other three systems (see Table III.28.B). This finding is especially interesting, since the bipolar system showed no unique characteristics, either in terms of definitiveness of outcome (SUBOUT) or tendency to terminate in agreement (FOROUT). Moreover, crises within the multipolar and polycentric systems, both of which were characterized by diffuse state decision-making centers, exhibited a similar distribution of tension escalation and reduction, unlike the bipolar system.

IV   Severity

Concepts and Data

An international crisis, as noted earlier in this *Handbook*, is characterized by two necessary and sufficient conditions: (1) an increase in the intensity of disruptive interactions among system actors, with a high probability of military hostilities; and (2) incipient change in one or more structural attributes of an international system, namely, power distribution, actors/regimes, rules and alliance configuration. Taken together, the increase in disruptive interactions and the embryonic effects of a crisis constitute a challenge to an international system.

What differentiates the *severity* or intensity of one international crisis from others, for example, crises over the Chinese Eastern Railway (1929), the Austria Putsch (1934), Suez (1956–57), the Prague Spring (1968), the Football War (1969), Bangladesh (1971), Angola (1975–76) or the Iran Hostages (1979–81)? As a basic structural characteristic, the number of crisis actors is certainly relevant, that is, states whose principal decision-makers perceive a situational change as a threat to one or more of their basic values, as requiring a response within a finite time, and as likely to involve them in military hostilities before the challenge has been overcome. Severity also depends upon the extent of heterogeneity among the adversaries. Do they vary in military capability or are they all major or minor powers? Are they states with advanced or premodern economies or do they exhibit various levels of development? Are their political regimes divergent or similar? And do they reflect one or more cultures and belief systems?

There are other indicators of the severity of international crises. What was the extent of involvement by the two post-World War II superpowers or, prior to 1945, the seven great powers in world politics: was it primarily political or economic or military support for one or more of the adversaries, or did the US/USSR (or one or more of the great powers of the pre-1945 multipolar system) engage in direct military intervention? Is the crisis's location of high or low geostrategic salience to one or more members of the international system? What are the issues at stake: are they military, political, economic or cultural, or several of these combined? Is there interstate violence in the crisis; if so, how extensive is it?

These questions relate to the severity of an international crisis from its break-point to its conclusion. The variables concerned, ranging from the number of actors to the role of violence, effectively provide a unit-system linkage in the assessment of severity. The number of crisis actors, i.e., those whose decision-makers perceive threat, time pressure and war likelihood, has an obvious connection to the unit level. Another unit-level factor is superpower involvement, based upon the characteristics of relevant nation-states. At the systemic level, geostrategic salience and the range of issues combine to represent the structural component, while the extent of interstate violence corresponds to process or patterns of interaction. One indicator, heterogeneity, is a synthesis of the two levels, e.g., culture at the unit level and relative military capability at the systemic level. Thus collectively these six indicators encompass a wide range of unit- and system-level sources of crisis intensity.

Now that the indicators have been specified, two tasks are necessary in the search for a precise method to measure the overall severity of an international crisis: first, to elaborate the variables of severity – Actors, Involvement, Geostrategy, Heterogeneity, Issues and Violence – and to provide an ordinal scale for each; and second, to assign weights to the six variables leading to the construction of a composite Index of Severity. Each indicator will be defined in operational terms, with examples provided for the accompanying scale points. The choice of a limited set of variables derives from the conviction that it is necessary to strike a balance between economy and exhaustiveness.

Actors The number of crisis actors in an international crisis is one indicator of its intensity: the participation of more actors signifies more widespread embryonic change during a crisis.

Coding Rules and Raw Frequencies, with Illustrations
1 **One actor** ($N = 107$; 38%) (Kaunas Trials 1935, Goa I 1955).*
2 **Two actors** ($N = 107$; 38%) (Mukden Incident 1931–32, Football War 1969).
3 **Three actors** ($N = 27$; 10%) (Ethiopian War 1935–36, Cyprus III 1974–75).
4 **Four actors** ($N = 20$; 7%) (Austria Putsch 1934, Rhodesian Settlement 1979–80).
5 **Five actors** ($N = 7$; 3%) (Fall of Western Europe 1940, Jordan Waters 1963–64).
6 **Six or more actors** ($N = 10$; 4%) (Israel Independence 1948–49 (6), Entry into World War II 1939 (21)).

Involvement Involvement refers to the extent of superpower or, in the 1930s, great power adversarial behavior in international crises. Clearly, superpower or great power confrontation as crisis actors indicates more intense disruption and incipient structural change than any other combination of their involvement in a crisis. Moreover, high involvement by the powers (direct military or semi-military intervention or covert activity) signifies a greater potential structural change than low involvement (political or economic support for client states). And thirdly, high involvement by both the US and the USSR, or more than two great powers in the thirties, indicates higher severity than a combination of high/low or high/no involvement – or even a combination of one major power as a crisis actor with others marginally or not involved, for in such a case their adversarial roles are muted and the systemic effects thereby lessened. These assumptions generated two six-point scales of combinations of involvement by the major powers in international crises, one for 1929–45, the other for 1945–79.

Coding Rules and Raw Frequencies, with Illustrations
   Great Power Involvement (1929–45)

1 **More than two powers low or no involvement** ($N = 14$; 20%) (Most of the great powers remained aloof from the Leticia Crisis between Colombia and Peru 1932–33).
2 **One or more powers high involvement, the others low or no involvement** ($N = 10$; 14%) (Germany was highly involved in the Czech Annexation Crisis of 1939 while the other great powers did not participate or were marginally involved).
3 **One or two powers as crisis actors, the others low or no involvement** ($N = 17$; 25%) (Japan was a crisis actor in the Mukden Incident of 1931–32 while three of the other great powers were politically involved).
4 **One or two powers as crisis actors, the others high, low or no involvement** ($N = 22$; 32%) (Britain and France were crisis actors in the Remilitarization of the Rhineland Crisis in 1936, while Germany was highly involved).
5 **More than two powers as crisis actors, the others low or no involvement** ($N = 2$; 3%) (Britain, France and Germany were crisis actors in the Czech May Crisis of 1938).
6 **More than two powers as crisis actors, the others high, low or no involvement** ($N = 4$; 6%) (Britain, France, Japan and the Soviet Union were crisis actors in the 1939 crisis leading to World War II, while the other great powers manifested varying degrees of involvement).

Coding Rules and Raw Frequencies, with Illustrations
   Superpower Involvement (1945–79)

1 **Both SPs low or no involvement** ($N = 119$; 57%) (The US was politically involved in, and the USSR remained aloof from, the Punjab War Scare between India and Pakistan in 1951).

*There are, as noted, international crises with only one crisis actor. However, every crisis actor has at least one adversary, usually the state which triggers its crisis. A crisis is generated by disruptive interactions between these adversaries.

2 **One SP high involvement, the other SP low or no involvement** (N = 31; 15%) (The USSR engaged in direct military activity in the Catalina Affair in 1952, shooting down a Swedish flying boat, with the US involvement limited to verbal criticism of the Soviet act by the Secretary of State).

3 **One SP a crisis actor, the other SP low or no involvement** (N = 30; 15%) (The US was a crisis actor in the Taiwan Straits Crisis of 1954–55, supporting Taiwan, while USSR activity was confined to political support for the PRC).

4 **Both SPs high involvement** (N = 7; 3%) (The US provided military aid to Ethiopia, the USSR to Somalia in the Ogaden Crisis of 1964).

5 **One SP a crisis actor, the other high involvement** (N = 11; 5%) (The US was a crisis actor in the Guatemala Crisis of 1953–54 while the USSR was highly involved, dispatching military aid to its client, the Arbenz regime).

6 **Both SPs crisis actors** (N = 11; 5%) (The US and USSR were engaged in a direct confrontation in the Cuban Missile Crisis of 1962).

Geostrategic Salience   Geostrategic salience refers to the *location* of an international crisis in terms of its natural resources, distance from major power centers, etc. Geostrategic assets vary over time: oil- and uranium-producing regions acquired greater salience since the 1950s; coal-producing regions became less salient. Key waterways and choke points like Gibraltar, the Suez Canal, the Straits of Malacca, the Panama Canal, etc., retained their geostrategic relevance over the decades. A combination of assets enhances geostrategic salience, as with the Straits of Hormuz which provide access to and egress from a region which, in the 1970s, produced 40% of the world's oil supply, with vast reserves to increase its geostrategic significance.

A broader geostrategic salience indicates more embryonic structural change during an international crisis. Moreover, a crisis located in a region of geostrategic interest to the dominant system, such as Central Europe since 1929, or the Arab–Israel conflict zone in the Middle East since 1956, will be more severe than one which is salient to a single subsystem, for example, South America. At the same time, the direct participation of one or both superpowers or, prior to 1945, more than two great powers, in an international crisis does not *per se* indicate high geostrategic salience. The latter is determined by the significance of the location and resources of the crisis region for one or more international systems, not by the power of crisis actors. Geostrategic salience and extent of great power/superpower involvement tap two distinct though related components of overall crisis severity. Based upon these propositions a five-point scale was generated to score geostrategic relevance.

Coding Rules and Raw Frequencies, with Illustrations

1 **One subsystem** (N = 161; 58%) (The Chaco Crisis from 1932 to 1935 was salient to the Latin American subsystem only, as were the crises over Pushtunistan in 1949, 1955 and 1961–62 to South Asia only).

2 **More than one subsystem** (N = 35; 13%) (The Indonesian Independence Crises of 1945–47, 1947–48 and 1948–49 were salient to the Southeast Asian and West European subsystems).

3 **Dominant system and one subsystem** (N = 57; 20%) (The Ethiopian War of 1935–36 was salient to the dominant system of Europe, as well as East Africa; the Marshall Plan Crisis of 1947 was directly relevant to the East European subsystem, along with the dominant system).

4 **Dominant system and more than one subsystem** (N = 13; 5%) (The Munich Crisis of 1938 was highly salient to the dominant international system, as well as Eastern and Western Europe; all the Berlin crises (1948–49, 1957–59, 1961) were highly salient to the superpowers and the dominant system of world politics, as well as the Western and Eastern European subsystems, by virtue of their significance in the struggle for Germany, their symbolism for the future of Europe, and the centrality accorded these crises by both the US and the USSR).

5 **Global system** (N = 12; 4%) (The German attack on the Soviet Union in 1941, the Barbarossa Crisis, was salient to the global system, as was the Cuban Missile Crisis in 1962).

Heterogeneity   With respect to heterogeneity, severity is measured by the number, not the intensity, of attribute differences among adversaries. The attributes are military capability, economic development, political regime and culture.

Every actor can be classified in terms of its *military capability* at the time of the crisis under inquiry – super, great, middle and small. In the 1930s there were seven great powers: Britain, France, Germany, Italy, Japan, the Soviet Union and the United States. France lost this status from 1940 to 1945; and Italy ceased to qualify from 1943 onwards. For the period 1945–79, only the US and the USSR qualify as superpowers. During the first decade after World War II there were three great powers: France, the People's Republic of China and the United Kingdom. These were joined by the Federal Republic of Germany, Japan and India during the second and third decades. The number of middle and small powers, too, changed over time. With respect to military capability, heterogeneity is said to be present when any pair of adversarial actors in an international crisis belongs to more than one of the four levels of power.

Actors may also be classified in terms of *economic development*, as post-industrial, developed and developing. Here, too, heterogeneity is regarded as present when adversaries are identified with more than one level of development (e.g., North Vietnam and the US in many Indo-China crises from 1964 to 1973), as absent when the adversaries are at the same level of development (Bolivia and Paraguay in the Chaco crises, Ethiopia and Somalia in all of their crises over the Ogaden).

Heterogeneity also includes *political regime* which, as will be elaborated in *Handbook II*, is classified as democratic, civil authoritarian and military. It is evident in all crises between Nazi Germany and democratic Britain and France from 1933 to 1945, all US–USSR crises, many India–Pakistan crises and almost all Arab–Israel crises. It is absent in most intra-African crises because of widespread military regimes. There may also be heterogeneity with respect to the *cultural* attribute, referring to belief systems, ideologies, languages, etc.

More attribute differences among adversaries in an international crisis point to more cleavages, and, therefore, greater severity. Thus the values for this indicator are scored in ascending order from no heterogeneity, point 1, to total heterogeneity, that is, differences in all four attributes, point 5. In cases where the extent of heterogeneity varies among adversarial pairs, the most heterogeneous pair is used for this variable, for example, the US and North Korea, not the two Koreas, in the Korean War Crisis 1950–51.

Coding Rules and Raw Frequencies, with Illustrations
1   **None** (*N* = 27; 10%) (The adversaries in the 1959–60 crises ensuing from Cuba-inspired invasions of several Caribbean and Central American states were all small powers, with underdeveloped economies, authoritarian regimes and the inheritance of Spanish-American culture. Moreover, intervention in the affairs of neighbors by support for mercenaries or more direct means was an established practice in Latin American relations, though without legal sanction).
2   **One attribute** (*N* = 30; 11%) (There was only one attribute difference between India and Pakistan in their post-partition crises over Junagadh, Kashmir and Hyderabad, 1947–49: the former was primarily influenced by Hindu culture, the latter by Islam).
3   **Two attributes** (*N* = 68; 24%) (In the 1947 Marshall Plan Crisis there were adversary differences in two attributes: political – Western democracy versus a Soviet regime; and military – a small power versus a superpower. The USSR and Czechoslovakia were more akin than different in culture and level of economic development).
4   **Three attributes** (*N* = 60; 22%) (In the Trieste Crisis of 1953 Italy and Yugoslavia differed on all but one attribute of heterogeneity: an economically developed versus a developing economy; a Western democratic versus a Communist political regime; and cultural differences embracing language, religion, history, etc. In terms of military capability both states were middle powers).
5   **All four attributes** (*N* = 93; 33%) (In the 1956–57 Suez Crisis the United Kingdom and France were major powers in global terms, while Egypt was a small power. The former were economically advanced, the latter had a very poor developing economy. The adversaries differed in political regime – Western democracy versus military authoritarianism, and in culture – language, belief system, etc.).

Issues A crisis issue indicates the object of contention in a specific international crisis, such as control over governmental power in the 1948 Communism in Czechoslovakia Crisis. Issues with a shared focus can be grouped into four issue-areas: (a) military-security, incorporating territories, borders, free navigation, change in military balance, military incidents and war; (b) political-diplomatic, including sovereignty, hegemony and international influence; (c) economic-developmental, including the nationalization of property, raw materials, economic pressure such as boycott and sanctions, and foreign exchange problems; and (d) cultural-status, comprising issues of ideology, challenge to non-material values and symbols.

A crisis over a military-security issue alone indicates more severity than a crisis concerned with any other issue-area. Moreover, crises involving multiple issues identify more incipient structural change than those dealing with a single issue. Five points on an issue scale of severity have been generated.

Coding Rules and Raw Frequencies, with Illustrations
1   **One issue other than military-security** ($N = 35$; 13%) (US political control over Haiti was challenged by riots against American citizens on the island in December 1929).
2   **Two issues other than military-security** ($N = 11$; 4%) (Turkey's status in the region was undermined by France's cession of the port of Alexandretta to Syria in September 1936; and several diplomatic crises for France were caused by a series of Turkish attempts to regain control of Alexandretta between 1936 and 1939).
3   **Military-security issue alone** ($N = 133$; 48%) (In the Ogaden Crisis of 1964 Ethiopia and Somalia focused their attention exclusively on that territory).
4   **Two issues, including military-security** ($N = 87$; 31%) (In the 1967 Cyprus Crisis both territory and influence in the eastern Mediterranean were issues between Greece and Turkey).
5   **Three or more issues** ($N = 12$; 4%) (Austria's status as an independent state was challenged when members of the Austrian Nazi Party assassinated Chancellor Dollfuss in July 1934; the danger of a German takeover of Austria created a military-security crisis for Czechoslovakia and a political-diplomatic crisis for Italy).

Violence The extent of violence in an international crisis is the last indicator of its severity. It refers to the intensity of hostile physical interaction in the crisis as a whole, rather than the intensity of violence used by any specific actor as its primary crisis management technique. Clearly, hostile physical acts in a crisis are more severe than hostile verbal acts. Moreover, violence is more disruptive than any other type of crisis interaction. It ranges from no violence, through minor clashes resulting in few or no casualties, to serious clashes short of war, to full-scale war.

Coding Rules and Raw Frequencies, with Illustrations
1   **No violence** ($N = 71$; 25.5%) (Bulgaria/Turkey I 1935, Cienfuegos Base Crisis 1970).
2   **Minor clashes** ($N = 66$; 23.8%) (Amur River 1937, Costa Rica/Nicaragua 1948–49).
3   **Serious clashes** ($N = 70$; 25.2%) (Chinese Eastern Railway 1929, Taiwan Straits I 1954–55).
4   **Full-scale war** ($N = 71$; 25.5%) (Spanish Civil War 1936–39, Bangladesh 1971).

Index of Severity   We now proceed to the construction of a composite Index of Severity, the second task related to the measurement of the intensity of international crises. The Index of Severity is based upon a weighted summation of the indicators. Specifying their potential impact on the structure of an international system, these weights will be derived deductively. An alternative approach would be to obtain weights through an inductive method such as factor analysis. The deductive strategy has been adopted in order to preserve the logical consistency of the general investigation of international crises. Since there are six indicators, and each conceivably could be related in a causal manner to any (or all) of the others, there exists a maximum of

30 potential linkages. In order to preserve the clarity of the Severity Index no effort will be made to incorporate the indirect linkages which may exist: even the inclusion of linkages which have but one intervening indicator would require the analysis of an additional 120 possibilities. The weight assigned to each indicator will be based on the number of linkages it is expected to have with the others and, therefore, its input into overall severity. In formal terms:

$$S = \sum_{k=1}^{6} w_k s_k$$

where S = Severity Index,
s_k = kth indicator ($k = 1, \ldots, 6$),
w_k = weight assigned to kth indicator.

The linkages are presented in composite form in Figure IV.1 and, individually, in Figures IV.1.A–F.

For *actors* (indicator s_1), four linkages are postulated (Figure IV.1.A), while one indicator is independent of its effects. Geostrategic salience is an *a priori* attribute of a given region. For example, the level of significance attributed to the Middle East as a crisis region is based on characteristics such as resource assets and does not rise or fall with the number of actors involved in a crisis there. As an inherent characteristic of a region, geostrategic salience in fact is independent of the other indicators as well. Thus, in the summary of linkages the potential effects of other indicators on geostrategic relevance will not be discussed.

The number of actors is expected to affect heterogeneity: a large n necessarily increases the set of pairwise comparisons between crisis actors which can be made.

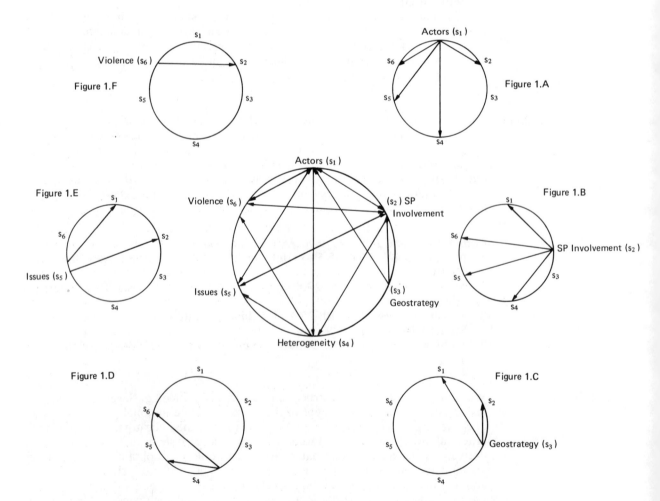

FIGURE IV.1. Indicators of Severity – Network of Effects.

The number of dyads is a quadratic function of the number of crisis actors. The specific form of the function is

$$D = f(n)$$
$$= 1/2(N - 1/2)^2 - 1/8.$$

When there are more dyads there also exist more opportunities for comparing the actors concerned and, potentially, finding highly disparate pairs. Consequently, heterogeneity by and large is expected to be greater in large groups.

Involvement, too, is considered to be sensitive to the number of actors. A larger number of participants makes a given international crisis more salient to the global system. As such the likelihood of superpower (or great power) involvement is expected to be higher because the Soviet Union and United States (or great powers in a multipolar system) will be more concerned with crises which may introduce fundamental changes to the system. Essentially this proposition rests on the assumption that the superpowers (or great powers) tend to act as "system-managers."

Also linked positively to the number of actors is the range of issues in a crisis. A more extensive set of participants has a greater potential to produce different coalition structures. And the more complex coalitional possibilities which result from the entry of new actors will facilitate the linking of issues currently operative in a crisis to others which, until that point, had remained latent. In other words, as the size of the group involved in a crisis increases, so too does the potential scope of bargaining.

Actors may also affect the resort to violence. As a general rule, when a large number of parties is involved in a bargaining sequence, it is more difficult to obtain a solution which will satisfy all concerned. Thus, under such circumstances, there is reason to expect that one (or more) actors will resort to violent means in order to obtain their objectives.

Superpower (or great power) *involvement* (indicator s_2), too, is linked to four other indicators of severity (Figure IV.1.B). When the US or the USSR (or their great power counterparts in the thirties) are active in a crisis, this is expected to lead to involvement by other actors as well; that is, the actions of a superpower (or a great power) will more readily result in "spillover" into the international system. More generally, the behavior of a superpower in a given realm has greater implications for developments elsewhere. For example, when a superpower issues a threat, it may be salient to members of the international polity other than the immediate target.

It is obvious intuitively why greater heterogeneity will result from superpower involvement. The superpowers are qualitatively different from the rest of the members of the international polity. When one of these giants is involved in a crisis it is almost certain that at least one rather disparate dyad will result from the process of pairwise comparison. Thus involvement by a superpower has the effect of raising the probable level of diversity among actors in a crisis setting.

Superpowers have global interests. When they become active in a crisis the range of issues in that crisis may expand. As a result of their panoramic concerns, superpowers can introduce new issues to a process of bargaining – issues which might otherwise have been left out altogether.

There is reason to expect a lower level of violence when superpowers are involved in crises. At the systemic level there are certain behavioral norms which exist with regard to superpower behavior. The US and the USSR have capabilities which dwarf those even of other nuclear powers. Thus their use of violence is expected by system members (and especially each other) to be calibrated carefully with the importance of a conflict, because of the ever-present danger of miscalculation and escalation to the nuclear level. For such reasons superpower crises are expected to be less violent.

Geostrategy (indicator s_3) is expected to have an impact on two other severity indicators, while the remaining three are independent of its effects (Figure IV.1.C). The geostrategic salience of a crisis is likely to affect the number of states which ultimately become crisis actors. Holding *absolute distance* constant, the probability that a state will become involved in a given crisis will increase with the perceived significance of the region in which the crisis occurs.

Crises in locations of high geostrategic salience are more likely to induce superpower activity. The basis for this inference is twofold in nature. The US and USSR are less sensitive than other states to the costs attendant upon involvement in distant crises; that is, a crisis in a significant setting may trigger superpower involvement, even if it is at a great distance physically. Moreover, the previously mentioned concerns for system management are expected to lead to a high level of superpower involvement in crises which occur in strategic settings. For other potential crisis actors a threshold of distance, which is expected to vary from one state to another, may exist beyond which even very high geostrategic salience will not induce involvement.

Any connection between geostrategic salience and the number of issues would be indirect: since more actors are likely in strategically located crises, more issues may be expected as well. There is no reason to expect a direct linkage; in fact, some areas may even be crucial because control over them would provide a virtual monopoly over some single resource. Or it could be the case that a location which is moderately important in several ways also has the potential to evoke "high" salience. Both arguments seem plausible.

There is no clear basis for expecting the level of violence in a crisis to be influenced by geostrategy. On the one hand, those active in a highly sensitive region might be inclined toward prudence in the use of force because of the danger of escalation. On the one hand, they might be more apt to resort to violence in order to achieve goals which are important to them. A parallel analysis could be presented for geostrategically remote locations.

There is no *direct* linkage between geostrategic salience and heterogeneity. Arguably, since geostrategy affects the number of actors and this in turn promotes heterogeneity, indicator s_3 affects heterogeneity indirectly. But, to reiterate, such indirect linkages will not be included in the derivation of weights for the Index of Severity.

Heterogeneity (indicator s_4) is expected to affect two other indicators of severity (Figure IV.1.D). There is good reason to assume that it will have a direct impact on the range of issues. Disparity increases the probability that parties to a crisis will possess different images of their bargaining environment. Consequently, some actors may try to link new issues to those already under consideration. As a general rule, this will tend to increase the range of issues ultimately raised by crisis participants.

Heterogeneity is also expected to lead to a higher level of violence. Members of a diverse group, even if rather small, may experience problems in coordinating their behavior, a challenge which would not confront more homogeneous groups. Failure by them to communicate intentions through subtle means could cause some participants to act violently. In other words, violent crisis management techniques are expected to occur as a result of misperception among members of heterogeneous groups.

Heterogeneity may be linked indirectly to superpower involvement because both are affected similarly by the number of actors. It is hard to imagine why either similarity (or diversity) among parties to a crisis in and of itself would induce (or inhibit) superpower activity. Similarly, it is not expected to have an impact on the number of actors. Instead, as indicated earlier, a larger number of actors will lead to greater diversity.

Issues (indicator s_5), too, have an effect upon two other indicators of severity (Figure IV.1.E). As the range of issues increases, so too will the set of actors drawn into a crisis: a further topic for bargaining may elicit the entry of one or more additional actors, who may have been indifferent to previous points of contention. Moreover, a large number of issues increases the probability of inducing the participation of a given actor. This, in turn, will increase heterogeneity, an indirect link.

Superpower involvement, too, is, in part, a function of the range of issues. Multiple-issue crises have the potential to produce change in more than one facet of international relations. Given their system-wide concerns, the superpowers can be expected to become involved in interactions which potentially have more general implications for the international polity.

There is no reason to expect the number of issues to affect the level of violence one way or the other. A single-issue crisis might cause those involved to focus more intensely on their divergent preferences over that issue, with violence as the outcome. It is also possible that conflict across a range of subject areas could indicate a more pervasive degree of conflict, with the result being violent crisis management. It is unclear which of these possibilities (if either) should take precedence.

Violence (indicator s_6) is expected to affect only one other indicator of severity, namely, superpower involvement (Figure IV.1.F). Crises which have escalated to military confrontation must be viewed as intense. As such, they are likely to gain the attention of one superpower, perhaps both, because of the far-reaching interests of the US and USSR. The superpowers will become concerned with violent crises which have an inherent potential to produce fundamental and long-term changes for their participants and for the system as a whole.

Violence is not expected to have an impact on the number of actors. In some cases it may have a cathartic effect: once it occurs, the intensity of the crisis subsides and as a result uninvolved states stay that way. Under other circumstances violence may exacerbate existing strife and trigger crises for some of those outside the current boundaries of the conflict.

Heterogeneity, too, is independent of violent crisis management. In fact, the causal linkage is in the other direction. It might be conjectured that violent crises will promote heterogeneity because interactions of such intensity could arouse interest among rather diverse outside observers. But the violence also could be the result of intense disagreement over a specific substantive point, with interested parties on the outside sharing certain characteristics associated with concern over that issue. Since arguments can be made either way, there is no justification for linking heterogeneity with violence.

Violence is not linked to issues. The arguments here are much the same as those offered for the case of violence and its potential to produce heterogeneity. On the one hand, violence might raise new issues and expand the domain of conflict. On the other, it could focus attention more directly on a single issue as the cause of the crisis. Thus, there is no general rule for the association of violence with the range of issues considered.

This completes the deductive derivation of linkages among severity indicators. It is now possible to assign values to the weights, with w_1 (actors) = 4; w_2 (involvement) = 4; w_3 (geostrategy) = 2; w_4 (heterogeneity) = 2; w_5 (issues) = 2; and w_6 (violence) = 1.

Data Analysis

The scores for each of the six indicators of severity and the overall severity for all 278 crises from 1929 to 1979 are set out in Table IV.1 below. For ease of exposition the scores for overall severity have been converted to a 10-point scale, with 1.00 as the minimum and 10.00 as the maximum. The linear equation used to transform the scale is as follows, with S' representing the transformed scores:

$$S' = 0.134(S) - 1.$$

The method used to derive the severity scores for all international crises in the data set, 1929–79, can be demonstrated with an exposition of the Middle East Crisis in 1973–74.

The October-Yom Kippur Crisis exhibits high overall severity, 9.18 on a 10-point scale. It began on 5 October 1973, with growing evidence of an impending massive disruption in the then-existing level of conflictual interaction between Israel and its Arab adversaries. A concerted military attack by Egypt and Syria occurred the next day. This event and others that followed posed a serious challenge to the structure of the Middle East subsystem and, towards the end of the crisis, a challenge to the dominant system and other subsystems as well.

There were five *crisis actors:* Egypt, Israel, Syria, the US and the USSR. There were also many involved actors, notably Arab states from the Near East Core such as Iraq and Saudi Arabia, and from North Africa, like Algeria, Libya and Morocco. In terms of actor-participation, this was one of the most severe international crises since the end of World War II.

In terms of *involvement* by the superpowers, too, this crisis ranks very high, point 6 on a six-point scale. Both superpowers were crisis actors in direct confrontation with each other, as demonstrated by the Soviet threat of military intervention in the Sinai and the American counter-threat as expressed in the nuclear alert.

TABLE IV.1. International Crises 1929–1979: Components of Overall Severity

Case number	Name*	Trigger date	Crisis actors**	Geostrategic salience	Heterogeneity	Great power/ superpower involvement	Issues	Violence	Overall severity
1 (0155)	Chaco I	05/12/28	2	1	2	1	3	2	2.48
2 (0165)	Chinese Eastern Railway	13/07/29	1	1	4	2	4	3	3.42
3 (0170)	Haiti Unrest	04/12/29	1	2	5	3	1	2	3.56
4 (0180)	Mukden Incident	18/09/31	2	3	5	3	4	3	5.30
5 (0182)	Shanghai	24/01/32	2	1	5	3	4	3	4.76
6 (0185)	Chaco II	18/06/32	2	1	2	1	3	4	2.75
7 (0190)	Leticia	08/09/32	2	1	2	1	3	3	2.62
8 (0196)	Jehol Campaign	23/02/33	1	1	5	2	3	4	3.56
9 (0195)	Saudi/Yemen War	18/12/33	2	1	1	1	4	4	2.75
10 (0205)	Austria Putsch	25/07/34	4	3	3	3	5	2	5.97
11 (0220)	Assassination/ King Alexander	09/10/34	2	1	2	1	4	1	2.62
12 (0225)	Wal-Wal	06/12/34	2	4	4	3	3	2	4.90
13 (0235)	Bulgaria/Turkey I	06/03/35	2	1	4	1	4	1	3.15
14 (0230)	Kaunas Trials	28/03/35	1	3	4	1	3	1	2.89
15 (0236)	Bulgaria/Turkey II	03/08/35	1	1	4	1	3	1	2.35
16 (0240)	Ethiopian War	02/10/35	3	3	4	3	3	4	5.43
17 (0265)	Maranon I	01/11/35	1	1	1	1	3	1	1.55
18 (0255)	*Remilitarization of Rhineland*	07/03/36	6 (7)	4	5	4	4	1	8.51
19 (0260)	*Spanish Civil War*	17/07/36	4	3	5	6	4	4	8.11
20 (0295)	Alexandretta	09/09/36	2	1	5	3	2	2	4.09
21 (0283)	Amur River Incident	22/06/37	2	1	3	3	3	2	3.82
22 (0285)	Marco Polo Bridge	08/07/37	2	3	5	4	3	4	5.70
23 (0313)	Postage Stamp Crisis	00/08/37	2	1	1	1	3	1	2.08
24 (0290)	Haiti/Dominican Republic	05/10/37	1	1	3	1	1	2	1.68
25 (0289)	Panay Incident	12/12/37	1	1	3	4	1	2	3.29
26 (0315)	Anschluss	12/02/38	2	3	3	3	5	1	4.76
27 (0305)	Polish Ultimatum	13/03/38	1	1	2	1	3	2	1.95
28 (0301)	Czech May Crisis	19/05/38	4	4	3	5	3	1	6.64
29 (0320)	Changkufeng Incident	13/07/38	2	1	3	3	3	3	3.96
30 (0321)	*Munich*	07/09/38	4	4	3	6	4	1	7.44
31 (0310)	Italian Colonial Demands	30/11/38	1	1	3	3	3	1	3.15
32 (0327)	Czech Annexation	14/03/39	1	3	4	2	3	1	3.42
33 (0331)	Memel	15/03/39	1	1	4	2	3	1	2.89
34 (0323)	Danzig	21/03/39	1	3	4	1	3	1	2.89
35 (0333)	*Invasion of Albania*	25/03/39	4	2	5	4	4	4	6.77
36 (0329)	Nomonhan	28/05/39	2	1	3	3	3	4	4.09
37 (0337)	Tientsin	14/06/39	1	1	3	4	1	1	3.15
38 (0343)	*Entry WWII*	20/08/39	6 (21)	5	5	6	3	4	10.00
39 (0350)	Soviet Occup./Baltic	26/09/39	3	1	5	2	3	1	4.23
40 (0351)	Finnish War	06/10/39	4	3	4	4	3	4	6.50
41 (0353)	*Invasion of Scandinavia*	08/04/40	5	3	3	4	3	4	6.77
42 (0357)	*Fall of Western Europe*	10/05/40	5	3	4	4	3	4	7.04
43 (0358)	Burma Road Closure	24/06/40	1	1	3	4	3	1	3.69
44 (0367)	Romanian Territories	26/06/40	1	3	5	2	3	2	3.82
45 (0359)	Battle of Britain	10/07/40	1	5	3	4	3	4	5.16
46 (0372)	East African Campaign	19/08/40	2	3	3	3	3	4	4.63
47 (0369)	*Balkan Invasions*	28/10/40	6	4	5	5	3	4	8.65

*Italics indicate the 26 most severe crises for the entire 1929–1979 period.

**Four international crises had more than six crisis actors: Remilitarization of the Rhineland (7), Entry into World War II (21), Pearl Harbor (10), and War in Angola (7). For World War II and Pearl Harbor, this generated a severity score slightly higher than 10.00. These cases were scaled back to values of 10.00.

Case number	Name*	Trigger date	Crisis actors**	Geostrategic salience	Heterogeneity	Great power/ superpower involvement	Issues	Violence	Overall severity
48 (0378)	Middle East Campaign	29/04/41	4	4	5	3	4	3	6.64
49 (0379)	Barbarossa	22/06/41	1	5	2	4	3	4	4.90
50 (0384)	Maranon II	05/07/41	1	1	1	1	3	3	1.81
51 (0385)	Occupation of Iran	25/08/41	1	3	5	2	4	3	4.23
52 (0387)	*Pearl Harbor*	26/11/41	6 (10)	5	5	6	4	4	10.00
53 (0391)	El Alamein	23/10/42	2	3	3	4	3	4	5.16
54 (0393)	Stalingrad	19/11/42	1	4	3	4	3	4	4.90
55 (0395)	Fall of Italy	10/07/43	2	4	5	4	3	4	5.97
56 (0397)	German Occup./Hungary	13/03/44	1	2	3	2	3	1	2.89
57 (0398)	Soviet Occup./East Europe	26/03/44	3	3	3	4	3	4	5.70
58 (0399)	D-Day	06/06/44	1	5	4	4	3	4	5.43
59 (0396)	Saipan	09/07/44	1	2	3	4	3	1	3.96
60 (0476)	Iran	26/09/44	1	4	4	2	2	1	3.42
61 (0401)	Leyte and Luzon	20/10/44	1	1	3	4	3	4	4.09
62 (0478)	Greek Civil War I	03/12/44	1	3	3	3	1	3	3.42
63 (0400)	Final Soviet Offensive	11/01/45	1	5	2	4	3	4	4.90
64 (0407)	Iwo Jima	19/02/45	1	1	3	4	3	4	4.09
65 (0475)	Communism in Romania	24/02/45	2	3	4	2	1	2	3.56
66 (0408)	Okinawa	01/04/45	1	1	3	4	3	4	4.09
67 (0540)	Trieste I	01/05/45	3	3	5	3	3	1	5.30
68 (0406)	Syria/Free French Forces	17/05/45	2	1	5	3	4	3	4.76
69 (0479)	Kars-Ardahan	07/06/45	1	3	4	4	3	1	4.49
70 (0405)	End of WWII	06/08/45	1	5	3	4	3	4	5.16
71 (0491)	*Azerbaijan*	23/08/45	4	3	5	6	4	1	7.71
72 (0610)	Indonesia Independence I	29/09/45	2	2	5	1	4	3	3.96
73 (0565)	Communism in Poland	30/06/46	1	3	4	3	1	1	3.42
74 (0480)	Turkish Straits	07/08/46	2	3	5	3	3	1	4.76
75 (0501)	Greek Civil War II	13/11/46	1	3	3	2	3	4	3.56
76 (0570)	Communism in Hungary	10/02/47	2	1	5	3	2	1	3.96
77 (0485)	Truman Doctrine	21/02/47	3	3	5	3	5	1	5.83
78 (0576)	Marshall Plan	04/07/47	2	3	3	3	1	1	3.69
79 (0611)	Indonesia Independence II	21/07/47	2	2	5	1	4	4	4.09
80 (0580)	Dominican Republic/Cuba	26/07/47	1	1	1	1	3	1	1.55
81 (0590)	Junagadh	17/08/47	2	1	2	1	4	2	2.75
82 (0592)	Kashmir I	24/10/47	2	1	2	1	3	4	2.75
83 (0600)	Palestine Partition	29/11/47	4	2	4	1	2	2	4.09
84 (0577)	Communism in Czechoslovakia	13/02/48	2	3	3	3	2	1	3.96
85 (0575)	Soviet Note to Finland I	22/02/48	1	1	5	1	1	1	2.08
86 (0640)	Israel Independence	15/05/48	6	2	4	1	5	4	6.24
87 (0644)	*Berlin Blockade*	07/06/48	4	4	4	6	4	1	7.71
88 (0645)	Hyderabad	21/08/48	1	1	2	1	3	2	1.95
89 (0660)	China Civil War	23/09/48	2	3	5	3	4	4	5.43
90 (0665)	Costa Rica/Nicaragua I	11/12/48	1	1	1	1	3	2	1.68
91 (0667)	Indonesia Independence III	19/12/48	2	2	5	1	4	4	4.09
92 (0670)	Sinai Incursion	25/12/48	3	2	4	1	4	4	4.36
93 (0680)	Pushtunistan I	00/03/49	2	1	3	1	4	3	3.15
94 (0685)	Luperon	19/06/49	1	1	1	1	3	2	1.68
95 (0690)	Soviet Bloc/Yugoslavia	19/08/49	1	3	3	2	1	2	2.75
96 (0710)	*Korean War I*	25/06/50	4	3	5	5	4	4	7.58
97 (0715)	*Korean War II*	01/10/50	5	3	5	6	3	4	8.38
98 (0760)	Tel Mutillah	15/03/51	2	1	4	1	3	3	3.15
99 (0763)	Punjab War Scare	07/07/51	2	1	2	1	3	1	2.35
100 (0780)	Suez Canal	30/07/51	2	2	5	1	4	3	3.96
101 (0795)	Catalina Affair	16/06/52	1	2	4	2	3	2	3.29

TABLE IV.1. *Continued*

Case number	Name*	Trigger date	Crisis actors**	Geostrategic salience	Heterogeneity	Great power/ superpower involvement	Issues	Violence	Overall severity
102 (0785)	Burma Infiltration	08/02/53	1	1	5	1	3	3	2.89
103 (0790)	Invasion of Laos I	24/03/53	2	2	5	2	4	3	4.49
104 (0716)	*Korean War III*	16/04/53	4	5	5	3	4	4	7.04
105 (0781)	East Berlin Uprising	17/06/53	1	1	3	3	1	2	2.75
106 (0800)	Trieste II	08/10/53	2	1	4	1	3	1	2.89
107 (0810)	Qibya	14/10/53	1	1	4	1	4	3	2.89
108 (0820)	Guatemala	12/12/53	3	1	5	5	5	3	6.64
109 (0880)	Dien Bien Phu	13/03/54	3	2	5	3	4	4	5.70
110 (0830)	Taiwan Straits I	00/08/54	3	3	5	3	4	3	5.83
111 (0850)	Costa Rica/Nicaragua II	08/01/55	2	1	2	2	3	2	3.02
112 (0920)	Baghdad Pact	24/02/55	1	1	2	2	3	1	2.35
113 (0860)	Gaza Raid	28/02/55	2	2	4	2	4	3	4.23
114 (0870)	Pushtunistan II	27/03/55	2	1	3	1	5	1	3.15
115 (0890)	Goa I	10/08/55	1	2	4	1	1	2	2.22
116 (0940)	Suez Nationalization	26/07/56	2	2	5	2	3	4	4.36
117 (0925)	Qalqilya	13/09/56	2	1	4	1	3	3	3.15
118 (0930)	Poland Liberalization	00/10/56	2	1	3	3	2	1	3.42
119 (0960)	Hungarian Uprising	23/10/56	2	3	3	3	4	3	4.76
120 (0970)	*Suez-Sinai Campaign*	29/10/56	6	5	5	6	4	4	9.72
121 (0990)	Nicaragua/Honduras	26/02/57	2	1	1	1	4	2	2.48
122 (1040)	Jordan Regime	04/04/57	1	1	2	2	1	2	1.95
123 (1071)	Tunisia/France I	31/05/57	1	1	4	1	1	2	1.95
124 (1030)	Syria/Turkey Border	18/08/57	3	1	3	5	1	1	4.76
125 (1000)	Ifni	23/11/57	1	2	5	1	1	3	2.62
126 (1050)	West Irian I	01/12/57	1	2	4	1	2	1	2.35
127 (1135)	*Berlin Deadline*	15/12/57	5	4	4	6	4	1	8.25
128 (1061)	Formation of UAR	01/02/58	2	1	1	1	1	1	1.55
129 (1070)	Tunisia/France II	08/02/58	1	1	4	1	4	2	2.75
130 (1060)	Sudan/Egypt Border	09/02/58	1	1	3	1	3	1	2.08
131 (1105)	Indonesia-Aborted Coup	21/02/58	1	1	5	2	3	3	3.42
132 (1080)	*Lebanon/Iraq Upheaval*	08/05/58	4	3	5	5	2	3	6.91
133 (1120)	*Taiwan Straits II*	17/07/58	3	3	5	5	4	3	6.91
134 (1100)	Cambodia/Thailand	24/07/58	2	1	3	1	4	2	3.02
135 (1130)	Mexico/Guatemala Fishing Rights	29/12/58	2	1	1	1	4	2	2.48
136 (1170)	Cuba/Central America I	25/04/59	4	1	1	2	5	2	4.36
137 (1160)	India/China Border I	25/08/59	2	2	3	1	4	2	3.29
138 (1180)	Shatt-al-Arab I	28/11/59	2	1	3	1	3	2	2.75
139 (1190)	Rottem	15/02/60	2	1	4	1	3	1	2.89
140 (1200)	Ghana/Togo Border	00/03/60	1	1	2	1	3	1	1.81
141 (1230)	Assassin. Attempt/ Venezuela President	24/06/60	2	1	2	1	2	1	2.08
142 (1240)	Congo I: Katanga	05/07/60	2	2	5	2	2	3	3.96
143 (1260)	Mali Federation	20/08/60	2	1	1	1	3	1	2.08
144 (1175)	Cuba/Central America II	09/11/60	2	1	1	2	4	2	3.02
145 (1220)	Ethiopia/Somalia	26/12/60	1	1	3	1	3	3	2.35
146 (1350)	Pathet Lao Offensive I	09/03/61	2	3	5	5	4	3	6.37
147 (1270)	Bay of Pigs	15/04/61	2	1	5	3	4	3	4.76
148 (1330)	Pushtunistan III	19/05/61	2	1	3	1	5	3	3.42
149 (1290)	Kuwait Independence	25/06/61	2	2	5	1	4	1	3.69
150 (1300)	Bizerta	17/07/61	2	2	5	1	3	3	3.69
151 (1320)	*Berlin Wall*	29/07/61	6	4	5	6	5	1	9.32
152 (1351)	Vietcong Attack	18/09/61	2	1	5	5	4	2	5.70

Case number	Name*	Trigger date	Crisis actors**	Geostrategic salience	Heterogeneity	Great power/ superpower involvement	Issues	Violence	Overall severity
153 (1370)	West Irian II	26/09/61	2	2	4	2	4	2	4.09
154 (1340)	Breakup of UAR	28/09/61	1	1	1	1	4	2	1.95
155 (1277)	Soviet Note to Finland II	30/10/61	1	1	5	1	1	1	2.08
156 (1377)	Goa II	11/12/61	1	2	4	1	1	2	2.22
157 (1379)	Mauritania/Mali	29/03/62	1	1	3	1	3	2	2.22
158 (1380)	Taiwan Straits III	22/04/62	1	3	5	1	1	2	2.75
159 (1352)	Pathet Lao Offensive II	06/05/62	2	3	5	3	4	3	5.30
160 (1390)	India/China Border II	08/09/62	2	2	3	2	3	4	3.82
161 (1395)	Yemen War I	26/09/62	4	1	3	2	4	4	4.90
162 (1400)	*Cuban Missiles*	16/10/62	3	5	5	6	3	2	7.58
163 (1460)	Malaysia Federation	11/02/63	2	1	2	1	4	2	2.75
164 (1440)	Jordan Internal Challenge	21/04/63	1	1	3	2	3	1	2.62
165 (1430)	Dominican Republic/Haiti	26/04/63	2	1	2	2	4	1	3.15
166 (1470)	Algeria/Morocco Border	01/10/63	2	1	2	1	3	3	2.62
167 (1510)	Venezuela/Cuba	01/11/63	1	2	3	1	1	1	1.81
168 (1500)	Kenya/Somalia	13/11/63	1	1	4	1	3	2	2.48
169 (1520)	Cyprus I	30/11/63	3	1	4	1	4	3	3.96
170 (1540)	Jordan Waters	11/12/63	5	1	5	1	1	1	4.23
171 (1480)	Dahomey/Niger	21/12/63	2	1	3	1	4	1	2.89
172 (1465)	Rwanda/Burundi	21/12/63	2	1	3	1	4	3	3.15
173 (1530)	Panama Canal	09/01/64	2	3	5	3	1	2	4.36
174 (1575)	East Africa Rebellions	19/01/64	1	1	5	1	1	2	2.22
175 (1550)	Ogaden I	07/02/64	2	1	3	4	3	3	4.49
176 (1401)	Yemen War II	00/05/64	3	1	3	1	4	4	3.82
177 (1638)	Gulf of Tonkin	02/08/64	2	1	5	3	4	3	4.76
178 (1570)	*Congo II*	04/08/64	4	3	5	6	4	3	7.98
179 (1402)	Yemen War III	03/12/64	3	1	3	2	4	4	4.36
180 (1639)	Pleiku	07/02/65	2	1	5	5	4	3	5.83
181 (1590)	Rann of Kutch	08/04/65	2	1	3	1	3	3	2.89
182 (1580)	Dominican Republic	24/04/65	1	1	4	3	2	2	3.29
183 (1591)	Kashmir II	05/08/65	2	1	3	1	4	4	3.29
184 (1620)	Guinea Regime	09/10/65	1	1	1	1	1	1	1.01
185 (1610)	Rhodesia UDI	05/11/65	1	1	4	1	4	1	2.62
186 (1403)	Yemen War IV	14/10/66	3	1	3	2	4	4	4.36
187 (1660)	El Samu	12/11/66	2	1	5	1	3	2	3.29
188 (1685)	Ché Guevara	23/03/67	1	1	3	2	1	3	2.35
189 (1690)	*Six Day War*	17/05/67	6	5	5	6	4	4	9.72
190 (1710)	Cyprus II	15/11/67	3	1	4	1	4	2	3.82
191 (1730)	Pueblo	22/01/68	1	3	5	3	4	2	4.63
192 (1720)	Tet Offensive	30/01/68	2	3	5	5	4	4	6.50
193 (1740)	Karameh	18/03/68	2	1	5	1	3	3	3.42
194 (1750)	*Prague Spring*	09/04/68	6	3	2	3	5	2	6.77
195 (1682)	Essequibo Territory	09/07/68	1	1	4	1	3	1	2.35
196 (1770)	Pre-War of Attrition	07/09/68	1	1	3	4	3	3	3.96
197 (1780)	Beirut Airport	28/12/68	1	1	4	1	3	2	2.48
198 (1829)	Vietnam Spring Offensive	22/02/69	2	1	5	3	3	3	4.49
199 (1790)	Ussuri River	02/03/69	2	3	4	3	3	3	4.76
200 (1799)	War of Attrition I	08/03/69	1	1	4	1	3	4	2.75
201 (1805)	EC-121 Spy Plane	15/04/69	1	3	5	3	3	2	4.36
202 (1782)	Shatt-al-Arab II	15/04/69	2	1	3	1	3	1	2.62
203 (1820)	Football War	15/06/69	2	1	2	1	4	4	3.02
204 (1821)	Cairo Agreement	22/10/69	1	1	4	1	3	3	2.62
205 (1800)	War of Attrition II	07/01/70	3	3	4	3	4	4	5.70

TABLE IV.1. *Continued*

Case number	Name*	Trigger date	Crisis actors**	Geostrategic salience	Heterogeneity	Great power/ superpower involvement	Issues	Violence	Overall severity
206 (1850)	Invasion of Cambodia	13/03/70	4	3	5	3	4	4	6.50
207 (1860)	Black September	15/09/70	4	1	5	3	4	4	5.97
208 (1865)	Cienfuegos Base	16/09/70	1	3	5	5	3	1	5.30
209 (1870)	Portuguese Invasion of Guinea	22/11/70	1	2	3	1	3	3	2.62
210 (1900)	Invasion of Laos II	08/02/71	2	3	5	2	3	4	4.63
211 (1890)	Bangladesh	25/03/71	3	1	4	2	3	4	4.36
212 (1910)	Chad/Libya I	24/05/71	2	1	2	1	4	1	2.62
213 (1920)	Caprivi Strip	05/10/71	1	1	5	1	3	2	2.75
214 (1935)	Uganda/Tanzania I	20/10/71	2	1	3	1	3	2	2.75
215 (1930)	Vietnam--Ports Mining	30/03/72	3	3	5	3	3	4	5.70
216 (1940)	Uganda/Tanzania II	17/09/72	2	1	3	1	3	2	2.75
217 (1942)	North/South Yemen I	26/09/72	2	1	2	1	3	4	2.75
218 (1931)	Christmas Bombing	23/10/72	3	3	5	3	4	4	5.97
219 (1962)	Zambia	19/01/73	1	1	4	1	3	2	2.48
220 (1950)	Libyan Plane	21/02/73	1	2	5	1	3	3	3.15
221 (1960)	Iraq Invasion-Kuwait	20/03/73	1	1	3	1	3	2	2.22
222 (1980)	Israel Mobilization	10/04/73	1	1	4	1	3	1	2.35
223 (2000)	Cod War I	14/05/73	2	4	4	2	1	2	3.82
224 (2030)	Oct.-*Yom Kippur War*	05/10/73	5	5	5	6	4	4	9.18
225 (2035)	South Yemen/Oman	18/11/73	1	1	2	1	3	3	2.08
226 (2040)	Cyprus III	15/07/74	3	1	3	2	3	4	4.09
227 (2065)	Final N. Vietnam Offensive	14/12/74	2	3	5	2	3	4	4.63
228 (2080)	Mayaguez	12/05/75	2	3	5	3	4	3	5.30
229 (2070)	*War in Angola*	12/07/75	6 (7)	3	5	6	4	4	9.18
230 (2060)	Moroccan March-Sahara	16/10/75	2	2	4	1	4	1	3.42
231 (2037)	Belize I	01/11/75	1	2	4	1	3	1.	2.62
232 (2063)	Sahara	14/11/75	3	2	3	4	4	3	5.57
233 (2150)	Cod War II	23/11/75	2	1	2	1	1	2	1.95
234 (2103)	East Timor	28/11/75	1	2	4	2	1	3	2.89
235 (2110)	Lebanon Civil War I	18/01/76	1	1	4	1	1	3	2.08
236 (2160)	Uganda Claims	15/02/76	1	1	2	1	3	1	1.81
237 (2180)	Operation Thrasher	22/02/76	2	1	4	2	4	3	3.96
238 (2200)	Nouakchott I	08/06/76	1	1	1	1	1	3	1.28
239 (2115)	Iraqi Threat	09/06/76	1	1	1	1	3	1	1.55
240 (2210)	Entebbe Raid	30/06/76	1	2	5	1	3	2	3.02
241 (2230)	Sudan Coup Attempt	02/07/76	1	1	1	1	1	2	1.14
242 (2220)	Aegean Sea	07/08/76	1	1	2	2	1	1	1.81
243 (2211)	Nagomia Raid	09/08/76	1	1	4	1	3	2	2.48
244 (2213)	Syria Mobilization	21/11/76	1	1	5	1	3	1	2.62
245 (2181)	Operation Tangent	20/12/76	1	1	5	1	3	2	2.75
246 (2350)	Shaba I	08/03/77	2	1	1	4	3	3	3.96
247 (2182)	Mapai Seizure	29/05/77	1	1	4	1	3	3	2.62
248 (2400)	Belize II	25/06/77	1	1	5	1	3	1	2.62
249 (2393)	Nouakchott II	03/07/77	1	1	1	1	1	3	1.28
250 (2392)	Libya/Egypt Border	14/07/77	2	1	3	1	3	3	2.89
251 (2390)	Ogaden II	22/07/77	2	3	1	4	3	4	4.63
252 (2372)	Rhodesia Raids	31/08/77	1	1	4	1	3	3	2.62
253 (2395)	Vietnam Invasion of Cambodia	24/09/77	2	1	1	1	3	4	2.48
254 (2476)	French Hostages	25/10/77	2	1	5	1	4	2	3.56
255 (2470)	Chimoio Tembue Raids	23/11/77	1	1	4	1	3	3	2.62

Case number	Name*	Trigger date	Crisis actors**	Geostrategic salience	Heterogeneity	Great power/ superpower involvement	Issues	Violence	Overall severity
256 (2565)	Beagle Channel I	05/12/77	2	1	1	1	3	1	2.08
257 (2520)	Chad/Libya II	22/01/78	2	1	3	1	1	4	2.48
258 (2525)	Lebanon Civil War II	07/02/78	1	1	2	1	4	3	2.35
259 (2500)	Sino/Vietnam War	09/02/78	4	2	1	1	4	4	4.09
260 (2550)	Litani Operation	14/03/78	1	1	3	1	4	3	2.62
261 (2710)	Chad/Libya III	15/04/78	3	1	5	1	4	4	4.36
262 (2575)	Cassinga Incident	03/05/78	2	1	5	2	3	3	3.96
263 (2570)	Shaba II	11/05/78	5	1	5	5	4	3	7.44
264 (2625)	Air Rhodesia Incident	03/09/78	2	1	3	1	3	3	2.89
265 (2640)	Nicaraguan Civil War	10/09/78	2	1	2	1	4	4	3.02
266 (2645)	Beagle Channel II	16/10/78	2	1	1	1	3	2	2.22
267 (2630)	Fall of Amin	30/10/78	3	1	3	1	5	4	4.09
268 (2635)	Angola Invasion Scare	07/11/78	1	1	5	1	3	1	2.62
269 (2666)	Tan Tan	28/01/79	1	1	1	1	3	3	1.81
270 (2729)	Raids on ZIPRA	12/02/79	3	1	4	1	3	3	3.69
271 (2600)	North/South Yemen II	24/02/79	2	1	2	4	3	4	4.36
272 (2730)	Raids on SWAPO	06/03/79	1	1	5	1	3	2	2.75
273 (2731)	Chad/Libya IV	12/04/79	3	1	5	1	4	4	4.36
274 (2725)	Goulimime-Tarfaya Road	01/06/79	2	1	1	1	3	2	2.22
275 (2726)	Soviet Threat to Pakistan	01/06/79	1	1	5	1	3	1	2.62
276 (2780)	Rhodesian Settlement	15/07/79	4	1	4	2	5	3	5.30
277 (2735)	Raid on Angola	28/10/79	1	1	5	1	3	2	2.75
278 (2860)	US Hostages in Iran	04/11/79	2	3	5	3	4	2	5.16

The *geostrategic salience* of this crisis was the maximum, that is, point 5 on a five-point scale. Not only was the Suez Canal a key choke point in the transportation nexus between Europe and East Africa-cum-South and Southeast Asia. The vast oil resources of the Gulf region and the embargo imposed by their owners also made this crisis salient to the global system – the dominant (superpower) system and virtually all subsystems which are dependent on a regular supply of imported petroleum.

Heterogeneity among the adversaries – Israel and Egypt (or Syria) – was very high, with differences on the following attributes: political regime (Western democracy versus authoritarianism); level of economic development (modern versus developing); and cultural (Judaism versus Islam). These were accentuated by dissent on rules of the game (non-recognition of Israel's legitimacy and the corresponding Arab right to expunge Israel as a sovereign state, etc.).

There were military and political *issues* in this case, notably territories and borders, hegemony and influence, thus point 4 on the issue scale.

And finally, the indicator of *violence* revealed the highest severity, full-scale war, with the aggravating threat to use nuclear weapons – reportedly by Israel in the early days of setback and implicitly by the US in its nuclear alert.

The crisis continued until 31 May 1974 when an Israel–Syria Disengagement Agreement terminated their war of attrition of several months, denoting the system's adaptation to a new level.

Taken together, these findings lead to an overall score of very high severity, as summarized in Table IV.2.

Table IV.3 provides some summary statistics pertaining to the overall severity scores reported in Table IV.1. In terms of geography, Europe and Asia stand out as the regions with the highest average severity scores, 4.73 and 4.35, respectively, with the Middle East a not-too-distant third (3.98). Even if one excludes the World War II cases, with their high severity scores, Europe and Asia maintain their dominant positions. Regarding polarity, World War II was clearly the system-period with the most severe crises. The multipolar period, which immediately preceded World War II, also ranks high in overall severity, due to such intense crises as the Remilitarization of the Rhineland, the Spanish Civil War, Munich, and

TABLE IV.2. Index of Severity, 1973–74 Middle East Crisis

Indicator	Weight	Assigned Score
Actors	4	5
Involvement	4	6
Geostrategy	2	5
Heterogeneity	2	5
Issues	2	4
Violence	1	4

Severity Index* $= S' = 0.134 \left(\sum_{k=1}^{6} w_k s_k \right) - 1$

$$0.134(4(5) + 4(6) + 2(5) + 2(5) + 2(4) + 1(4)) - 1 = 9.18$$

* The coefficient used in the conversion to a 10-point scale is derived as follows: the lower and upper boundaries (minimal and maximal weighted scores) for severity are 15 and 82: in order to convert these scores to a 10-point scale, it is necessary to multiply by 0.134 and subtract 1 from each value.

TABLE IV.3. Average Overall Severity Scores for International Crises, 1929–79: Geography, Polarity, Conflict

Geography	Average	Frequency	Percent
Africa	3.31	64	23%
Americas	2.97	33	12%
Asia	4.35	69	25%
Europe	4.73	57	20%
Middle East	3.98	55	20%
Total		278	100%
Polarity			
Multipolar (1929–39)	4.17	38	14%
World War II (1939–45)	5.00	31	11%
Bipolar (1945–62)	3.96	93	33%
Polycentric (1963–79)	3.60	116	42%
Total		278	100%
Conflict			
Non-protracted conflict	3.26	123	44%
Protracted conflict	4.34	96	35%
Long-war protracted conflict	4.76	59	21%
Total		278	100%

the outbreak of the War itself. It is also interesting to note that, while the polycentric system accounts for the largest proportion of crises (42%), the average overall severity score for this period is the lowest: that is, in general, there is a downward trend in the severity of international crises over the half-century, except for the World War II period. Finally, the findings for conflict are not surprising, with crises occurring in non-protracted conflicts exhibiting the lowest average severity scores, and crises occurring in long-war-protracted conflicts exhibiting the highest overall severity scores.

Most Severe International Crises

Users of the ICB data on the severity of international crises will have diverse research interests: to compare crises within a specific period/region/protracted conflict, etc., or across periods/regions/protracted conflicts; to test specific hypotheses (e.g., violence level and overall severity), or a more general theory of crisis. The potential use of the ICB data set, as noted, is vast. By way of illustration, we shall explore a subset of the most severe international crises of the half-century under inquiry, to generate a profile or configuration of attributes of these crises of highest severity.

The Most Severe international crises from 1929 to 1979 are the 26 highest overall severity cases out of 278, nearly 10% of the data set: their overall scores range from 10.00 to 6.77 on our 10-point scale (see italicized cases in Table IV.1 above). The distribution of these cases in time and space, along with their individual overall severity score and the average overall intensity by period and region, is presented in Table IV.4.*

Europe was the preeminent *region* of frequent, severe international crises for the half-century under inquiry, accounting for 12 of the 26 Most Severe cases. Europe also showed by far the highest ratio of Most Severe cases to total cases for that region: Europe, 12 of 57 cases (21%); Middle East, five of 55 cases (9%); Asia, five of 69 cases (7%); Africa, three of 64 cases (5%); and the Americas, one of 33 cases (3%). As expected, all five Most Severe crises in the 1930s and three of the four during World War II took place in Europe. Thereafter, the geographical distribution of very high-severity crises becomes diffuse. During the bipolar period (1945–62), four regions were represented – four crises in Asia, three each in Europe and the Middle East and one in the Americas. And in the polycentric period (1963–79), the Most Severe crises were concentrated in the Third World –

TABLE IV.4. Most Severe International Crises, 1929–79: Time, Space, Overall Severity*

	Africa [8.20]**	Americas [7.58]	Asia [7.98]	Europe [7.90]	Middle East [8.65]
1929–39				Rhineland (1936) 8.51 Spanish Civil War (1936–9) 8.11 Munich (1938) 7.44 Invasion of Albania (1939) 6.77 Entry into World War II (1939) 10.00 [8.06]	
1939–45			Pearl Harbor (1941–2) 10.00 [10.00]	Invasion of Scandinavia (1940) 6.77 Fall of Western Europe (1940) 7.04 Balkan Invasions (1940–1) 8.65 [7.49]	
1945–62		Cuban Missiles (1962) 7.58 [7.58]	Korean War I (1950) 7.58 Korean War II (1950–1) 8.38 Korean War III (1953) 7.04 Taiwan Straits II (1958) 6.91 [7.48]	Berlin Blockade (1948–9) 7.71 Berlin Deadline (1957–9) 8.25 Berlin Wall (1961) 9.32 [8.43]	Azerbaijan (1945–6) 7.71 Suez-Sinai (1956–7) 9.72 Lebanon/Iraq Upheaval (1958) 6.91 [8.11]
1963–79	Congo II (1964) 7.98 Angola (1975–6) 9.18 Shaba II (1978) 7.44 [8.20]			Prague Spring (1968) 6.77 [6.77]	Six Day War (1967) 9.72 Yom Kippur War (1973–4) 9.18 [9.45]

* Each of the 26 cases in this table has an overall severity greater than 6.76.
** The numbers in square brackets are the Average Overall Severity by region and time period.

*Some readers may be puzzled by the inclusion of three Africa-located crises, especially Angola (1975–76), whose overall severity ranks among the eight highest for the 50-year period. However, Angola, along with Congo II (1964) and Shaba II (1978), meet all the conditions of high severity, and therefore should have no less claim on our attention than high severity crises in the dominant international system, whether focused on Europe in the 1930s or on the East–West bloc rivalry in the post-1945 period. These three cases demonstrate that crises on the geographic periphery of the global international system can and do exhibit great intensity within their subsystems and must therefore be included in a cluster of Most Severe crises. More generally, they should caution Western scholars to be sensitive to acute disruptive interactions on the geographic periphery of the global system. As for their importance, or consequences, for world politics, Angola and Shaba II rank much lower.

three in Africa and two in the Middle East, with one in Europe. In short, the end of European colonial empires and the trebling of the number of state actors in the global system were accompanied, *inter alia*, by the spread of very high-severity crises beyond the European core to the former geopolitical-economic periphery of Asia, Africa and the Middle East.

Viewed in terms of time, the Most Severe crises declined in frequency from the bipolar to the polycentric period, 11 to six, during identical 17-year time spans. The greatest concentration of these cases was the 3-year period 1956–59 with four crises – Suez, Berlin Deadline, Taiwan Straits II and Lebanon–Iraq Upheaval. In the time domain as well, the proportional distribution of very high-severity crises was stable for the first three periods – 1929–39 (five of 38 cases, that is, one for 7.6 cases), 1939–45 (four of 31, that is, one for 7.75 cases), 1945–62 (11 of 93 cases, that is, one for 8.5 cases). In the polycentric period, 1963–79, there was a sharp decrease (six for 116, that is, one for every 19 cases). In general, this indicates a declining relative frequency of very severe international crises from the onset of polycentrism.

As is evident in Table IV.5, the Most Severe crises from 1929 to 1979 which occurred in the Middle East had the highest average intensity (8.65). Moreover, there were two broad regional groupings in terms of average overall severity of crises: Middle East and Africa (8.65–8.20); and Asia, Europe and the Americas (7.98–7.58). In the time domain, the average score for Most Severe crises was almost identical in 1929–39 and 1939–45, that is, in a period of relative peace and one of global war. The largest concentration of these crises, as noted, occurred in the bipolar period – but their average intensity was the lowest of the four periods. The highest average intensity was in the polycentric period.

TABLE IV.5. Average Overall Severity of Most Severe Crises, 1929–79

	Africa	Americas	Asia	Europe	Middle East	Total
1929–39				8.06		8.06
1939–45			10.00	7.49		8.12
1945–62		7.58	7.48	8.43	8.11	7.92
1963–79	8.20			6.77	9.45	8.38
Total average	8.20	7.58	7.98	7.90	8.65	

Many of the Most Severe crises were linked; that is, they were recurring disturbances in the international system arising from a shared, unresolved issue. Two clusters were located in Europe, one in the 1930s over Germany's challenge to the post-World War I status quo, the other in the bipolar period over Berlin. One cluster focused on the Arab–Israel Conflict. A fourth cluster centered on the Korean War. Altogether, these clusters accounted for 14 of the 26 Most Severe crises. Viewed in terms of *protracted conflicts*, five cases can be identified with the East–West Conflict since 1945 (Azerbaijan, Berlin Blockade, Berlin Deadline, Berlin Wall, Cuban Missiles), three cases with the Arab–Israel Conflict since 1948 (Suez, Six Day War and October-Yom Kippur War), three cases with the Korea Conflict since 1950, and two cases with the Angola Conflict since 1975.

The distribution of Most Severe crises in terms of *power discrepancy* between the adversaries and the *resort to war* is especially instructive. Of the 22 cases (the four IWCs during World War II are excluded because of lack of data), 18 were characterized by high-power discrepancy (e.g., Prague Spring 1968, between the USSR and its Warsaw Pact allies on the one hand, and Czechoslovakia on the other). However, full-scale war was present in only seven of these 18 cases (e.g., Korean War I), while there was no violence in six of them (e.g., Remilitarization of the Rhineland). Conversely, three of the four cases characterized by low-power discrepancy were accompanied by full-scale war (e.g, Korean War II, when the participation of the USSR drastically reduced the power discrepancy between the adversarial coalitions). These findings suggest: (a) that when states know – or believe – they would win a war, they don't have to fight, and (b) that when states know – or believe – they would lose a war, they don't try. Stated differently, *when crises are severe, states are more inclined to fight in a situation of uncertainty about the power balance, indicating a possibility of winning a war.*

We turn now to a brief discussion of the data on the six severity indicators, that is, the components of overall severity, of the Most Severe international crises from 1929 to 1979 as a group. Data on these 26 cases were highlighted in Table IV.1 above.

The minimal number of *crisis actors* was three – in two cases (Cuban Missiles, with the US, USSR and Cuba, and Taiwan Straits II, with the PRC, Taiwan and the US). There were four crisis actors in nine cases, five crisis actors in six cases, and six crisis actors in five cases. In four cases there were more than six crisis actors (Angola (7), Rhineland (7), Pearl Harbor (10), Entry into World War II (21)). By contrast, for the entire set of 278 international crises there was one crisis actor only in 107 cases, and two crisis actors in 107 cases, comprising 76% of all cases.

Until the end of World War II the crisis actors in all Most Severe cases except two (Entry into World War II, Pearl Harbor) were located exclusively in the region where the crisis occurred (e.g., all seven actors in the Remilitarization of the Rhineland case were European states). A change in this respect began with the Azerbaijan Crisis when three regions were represented – the Middle East (Iran), Europe (USSR) and the Americas (US). Multiregional participation in crises continued throughout the bipolar period (four of all 11 crises with actors from three regions, the rest from two regions) and the polycentric period (five of six crises triregional in participants). In short, *severe crises became more multiregional over time*.

Involvement by the Powers was intense in a large majority of the Most Severe crises, 20 of 26 scoring 5 or 6 on the involvement scales. Both superpowers were crisis actors in 11 of these cases (e.g., Korean War II, the three Berlin crises, Suez, Six Day War, October-Yom Kippur War, Cuban Missiles); and in five other cases, during the thirties and World War II, more than two great powers were crisis actors (e.g., Munich, Entry into World War II). In another four Most Severe cases, one superpower was a crisis actor, the other highly involved (e.g., Korean War I, Taiwan Straits II). Among the Most Severe cases with less involvement, there were four with both the US and USSR involved through direct or indirect military aid, or its 1930s counterpart, namely, one or two great powers as crisis actors (e.g., Rhineland). And in two cases, one superpower was a crisis actor, the other was not involved or only marginally so (Korean War III, where the US was a direct participant, the USSR politically involved; Prague Spring, where the USSR was a crisis actor, the US not involved at all). Thus of the six exceptions to our expectation of a very high score for involvement by the powers, four occurred in the 1930s or World War II – Invasion of Albania, Invasion of Scandinavia, Fall of Western Europe, Remilitarization of the Rhineland – while two cases took place after World War II – Korean War III and Prague Spring.

It is noteworthy that, of the four post-World War II Most Severe crises with one superpower as crisis actor and the other highly involved, the pattern was constant, with the US performing the former function, the USSR the latter; *the Soviet Union sent military aid to the US adversary but avoided a direct confrontation*. Moreover, of the 11 cases in which both superpowers were crisis actors, seven occurred during the bipolar period, four in the polycentric period; that is, the change in polarity was accompanied by less direct confrontation between the superpowers. Two issues dominated US–USSR confrontation – Berlin and the Arab–Israel Conflict. At the same time, both superpowers were adversarial crisis actors in all five regions.

As for *geostrategic salience*, all but one of the 26 Most Severe crises had relevance beyond a single international system. Eleven cases were salient to the dominant system (of the great powers in the 1930s and of the superpowers since 1945), as well as one subsystem (e.g., Azerbaijan – Middle East, oil and access to warm water ports for the USSR; Prague Spring – stability of Soviet hegemony in Eastern Europe and East–West European balance). Six of these crises were salient to the dominant system and more than one subsystem (e.g., Rhineland and all three Berlin crises – the balance of power between the great powers and the superpowers, respectively, and influence over Western and Eastern Europe).

Seven of these international crises had global geostrategic salience:

Entry into World War II, because of the worldwide location of its 21 crisis actors and the issues of ideological conflict and global hegemony;

Pearl Harbor, because of the physical globalization of World War II and the struggle for world mastery between the Axis and Allied powers;

Korean War III, because of the implication of the possible use of nuclear weapons by the US for all members of the global system;

Suez, because of the far-reaching significance of the participation of both super-powers and two great powers, France and the UK, and the salience of the Suez Canal to world trade, as well as access to Middle East oil;

Cuban Missiles, because of the near-nuclear confrontation between the US and USSR, and its potential consequences for states and peoples everywhere;

Six Day War and October-Yom Kippur War, because of the intense, adversarial involvement of the superpowers in support of their clients and, in the latter, the oil embargo and the second near-nuclear confrontation between the US and the USSR.

Shaba was the exception to an expected high score in geostrategic salience for the Most Severe cases. However, it scored high in all other elements of severity, sufficient to result in a high score for overall severity. Noteworthy, too, is the evidence that superpower participation in crises as crisis actors does not, *per se*, ensure *global* salience (the three Berlin cases and Azerbaijan).

A large majority of the Most Severe crises, 20 of 26, were characterized by maximal *heterogeneity*; that is, the pair of adversarial actors in a crisis with the widest gap differed on all four attributes – level of military capability, extent of economic development, type of political regime and culture. In three cases there were three attribute differences (Fall of Western Europe – military, political and cultural differences between Germany and Belgium; Berlin Blockade and Berlin Deadline – military, political and cultural differences between Britain or France and the USSR). There were two Most Severe cases with two attribute differences (Munich, Invasion of Scandinavia), and one case with a single attribute difference (military capability between Czechoslovakia and the USSR in the Prague Spring Crisis). All three exceptions to the expectation of a high score for heterogeneity, namely, those with one or two attribute differences, were in Europe.

Only one of the 26 Most Severe crises – Lebanon-Iraq Upheaval – did not focus on a military-security *issue*. Seventeen such cases were over military-security and another type of issue (e.g., Pearl Harbor – military/economic, Suez – military/political, Angola – military/political). Six cases of very high severity focussed on the military-security issue-area alone (e.g., Cuban Missiles). And two crises were multiple-issue in character (Berlin Wall – military/political/status, Prague Spring – military/political/status).

More than half of the Most Severe crises, 14 of 26, involved the highest level of *violence*, namely, full-scale war: in 10 of these cases war preceded – and led to – crisis (e.g., Spanish Civil War); in the other four cases crisis antedated – and culminated in – war (Invasion of Albania, Entry into World War II, Pearl Harbor, Six Day War). It is noteworthy that three of the crisis-leading-to-war cases rank among the highest in overall severity for the entire data set of 278 cases, including the first and second highest severity, Entry into World War II and Pearl Harbor. There were four high-severity cases involving serious clashes (e.g., Taiwan Straits II, Congo II) and two cases with minor clashes (Cuban Missiles). The six exceptions to a high level of violence include many of the celebrated crises in the twentieth century (Rhineland, Munich, Azerbaijan, the three Berlin crises). Notwithstanding the absence of violence, they all scored high in overall severity – because of high scores in most of its other components.

The 26 Most Severe international crises from 1929 to 1979 will now be examined in terms of their frequency distribution along key crisis dimensions: breakpoint (trigger); value threat; crisis management technique; centrality of violence; intensity of violence; duration; involvement by global organization; effectiveness of global organization involvement; substance of outcome; and form of outcome.

Breakpoint (Trigger). Among the 26 Most Severe crises during the half-century under inquiry, half were catalyzed by violent acts; eight were from external sources (e.g., the attack on South Korea by North Korean forces on 25 June 1950, the Korean War I case, and the attack by Soviet-backed MPLA forces against the FNLA headquarters in Luanda on 12 July 1975, triggering the Angola Crisis); the other five were internal physical challenges to the regime of a state (e.g., the revolt against the Spanish Republic by a Franco-led Falange-army coalition on 17 July 1936). Six international crises of very high severity were set in motion by non-violent military acts (e.g., the emplacement of Soviet offensive missiles in Cuba in 1962, triggering the Missile Crisis). Six crises were initiated by political acts (e.g., the publication by the three Western Powers in June 1948 of their March London Conference recommendation to integrate the US, UK and France zones in Germany, triggering the Berlin Blockade Crisis). And one crisis, Berlin Wall 1961, was catalyzed by an external change.

Value Threat. The highest value which actors in each of the 26 Most Severe international crises perceived to be threatened was one of three: existence was at stake in 11 cases (e.g., for Czechoslovakia in the Munich Crisis, and for Israel in the Six Day War Crisis); grave damage was anticipated in eight cases (e.g., by both the PRC and Taiwan in the Taiwan Straits Crisis, 1958, and by Egypt and Israel in the October-Yom Kippur War); and influence was the highest value threatened in seven cases (e.g., by the United States and Britain in the Azerbaijan Crisis, and by the Soviet Union in the Prague Spring Crisis).

Crisis Management Technique. Violence was the pervasive crisis management technique (CMT) in the Most Severe international crises from 1929 to 1979: it was the primary CMT in 12 of the 26 cases and was present in seven others (e.g., the first two Korean War crises, and, for violence as a co-equal CMT with one or more others, the Suez–Sinai War). There were three cases in which non-violent military acts were the primary CMT (e.g., Cuban Missiles); another three with negotiation or a combination of pacific CMTs (e.g., Rhineland Crisis); and one case with non-military pressure as the primary CMT, namely, Azerbaijan.

Centrality of Violence. As for the centrality of violence in crisis management, it was preeminent in 11 of the 26 Most Severe cases (e.g., Pearl Harbor, Six Day War and Shaba). It was important, but supported by other CMTs, in eight other cases of high overall severity (e.g., Invasion of Albania Crisis, Korean War III and Lebanon/Iraq Upheaval). In none of these cases did violence play a minor role. As noted, it was absent as a crisis management technique in seven cases (e.g., Cuban Missiles and the three Berlin crises).

Intensity of Violence. Violence was very intense as the primary crisis management technique in the Most Severe international crises: actors resorted to full-scale war, that is, maximal violence, in half of the 26 cases (e.g., Spanish Civil War, several World War II cases like the Fall of Western Europe, Korean War I and II, Six Day War, October-Yom Kippur War). There were serious clashes in five cases (e.g., Lebanon/Iraq Upheaval), and minor clashes only in the Prague Spring Crisis. The remaining seven cases, as noted, were without violence as a CMT.

Duration. A large majority of the Most Severe crises, 19 of 26, were of long duration, that is, 61 days or more (e.g., Spanish Civil War, almost 3 years; Berlin Blockade, almost a year; Prague Spring, 6 months). There were five medium-duration cases, 32–60 days (Rhineland, Munich, Entry into World War II, Fall of Western Europe, Cuban Missiles). And two of these cases lasted less than 32 days (Invasion of Albania, Six Day War).

Global Organization Involvement. There was no involvement by the global organization in nine of the 26 Most Severe crises (e.g., Munich, Berlin Wall, Shaba II). In three cases the League of Nations or the United Nations engaged in discussion but did not pass a resolution (e.g., Taiwan Straits II). The global organization did pass an operative resolution in eight crises: three UN calls for a cease-fire (e.g., Six Day War); two condemnations (Rhineland, Angola); and three calls for action by member-states (e.g., by the USSR and Iran in the Azerbaijan Crisis). There were two cases of mediation (Berlin Blockade, Cuban Missiles). Emergency military forces were dispatched in two others (Korean War I, Suez). An observer group was sent in one case (Lebanon/Iraq Upheaval). And there was one case of general UN activity (attempted conciliation by the Secretary-General in the Berlin Deadline Crisis).

Global Organization Effectiveness. Global organization involvement in the Most Severe international crises from 1929 to 1979 was ineffective on the whole. There was no League of Nations/UN involvement in nine of 26 cases, as noted. In 10 others their activity did not contribute to crisis abatement (e.g., Rhineland, Berlin Deadline). It had an important, positive effect in three of these crises (Azerbaijan – Security Council pressure on the USSR to reach an amicable withdrawal agreement with Iran; Suez – cease-fire resolutions and the dispatch of an Emergency Military

Force to Sinai; Cuba – mediation by the Secretary-General and UN supervision of the withdrawal of Soviet missiles from the island). However, in three other cases activity by the global organization escalated the crisis (Korean War II – the crossing of the 38th Parallel by UN forces, bringing China into the war; Lebanon/Iraq Upheaval – the dispatch of an inadequate Observer Group whose ineffectiveness in curbing infiltration into Lebanon prolonged that crisis; Six Day War – the withdrawal of UNEF from Sinai, escalating the crisis by removing a 10-year barrier to direct military confrontation between Egypt and Israel). Finally, in one case (October-Yom Kippur War) the UN contributed marginally to crisis de-escalation.

Outcome: Content. A large majority of the Most Severe international crises, 19 of 26, terminated with an ambiguous outcome from all of the crisis actors' perspectives, that is, any combination of defeat, victory, stalemate or compromise between the adversaries, other than a strict defeat–victory pairing. The other seven cases ended definitively, that is, with a defeat–victory pairing. Among them were several celebrated crises of the 50-year period: the Berlin Blockade, with defeat for the USSR and victory for the three Wester Powers; the Cuban Missile Crisis, with a (thinly-concealed) defeat for the Soviet Union and Cuba, and a (self-constrained) victory for the US; and the Six Day War, with a (dramatic) defeat for Egypt, Jordan and Syria, and a victory for Israel.

Outcome: Form. Almost two-thirds of the Most Severe international crises, 15 of 26, ended with a formal or semiformal agreement between the adversaries (e.g., the Munich Agreement among France, Germany, Italy and the UK; a Soviet–Iran withdrawal of forces agreement, based upon a UN Security Council Resolution, in the Azerbaijan Crisis; semi-formal agreements between the Soviet Union and the Western Powers (or the US), ending the Berlin Blockade Crisis and the Cuban Missile Crisis). There was a tacit understanding in one case (Taiwan Straits II). The other 10 cases ended without agreement, seven of them through a unilateral act by the victorious adversary(ies) (e.g., Germany's rejection of any constraint on its remilitarization of the Rhineland, military triumph by the Franco-Germany-Italy coalition in the Spanish Civil War, the USSR's unqualified support for the permanence of the Berlin Wall).

The data on the 26 Most Severe international crises from 1929 to 1979 indicate the following configuration for this subset:

Attribute	Content	Proportion of cases
Trigger (Breakpoint)	Violent Act	50%
Value Threat	Existence, Grave Damage, Influence	100% (42%, 31%, 27%)
Crisis Management Technique	Violence	73.1%
Centrality of Violence	Preeminent or Important	73.1%
Intensity of Violence	Full-Scale War	50.0%
Duration	Long (61 days+)	73.1%
Global Organization Involvement	Non-Involvement, Resolution	65.4% (34.6%, 30.8%)
Global Organization Effectiveness	Inactive or Ineffective	73.1%
Outcome – Content	Ambiguous	73.1%
Outcome – Form	Agreement	57.9%

The rationale for this analytical exercise and the value of the findings, especially the overall severity scores for each international crisis, will now be delineated. Many scholars have affirmed the need to explain change, in world politics as in other domains. However, no consensus exists on guiding themes about change or on the optimal framework.

Our basic assumption is that the concept of international crisis, viewed as a political earthquake, provides the master key to the analysis of change in world politics. To operationalize that key it was essential to devise a method to measure the severity or immediate effects of an international earthquake – and to apply that method to a large and varied body of data over an extended time frame. This task was the focus of the preceding pages. We also assume that crises as earthquakes have long-term consequences for one or more structural components of an international system, such as regimes or alliance configuration, and that the severity of a crisis is closely associated with its importance or impact. Stated differently, we assume that crises induce system change. A crisis-as-earthquake model has been constructed, and we have tested its central postulate, namely, a meaningful association between Severity and Importance, using the data for 278 international crises from 1929 to 1979 (Brecher and James, 1986). The postulated link is supported, marking a major step forward in our ability to anticipate the likely consequences of future crises, a *sine qua non* to effective crisis management.

v Summaries

Part V comprises brief summaries of the 278 international crises in the ICB data set for the period 1929–79. Each summary specifies the crisis actors, that is, the states whose decision-makers perceived a sharp rise in threat to one or more basic values, an awareness of time constraints on decisions and heightened probability of involvement in military hostilities at some point during a crisis. The duration of a crisis is measured from the trigger date for the first actor, that is, the earliest date when the above three perceptions were noted, to the last termination date, namely, when the crisis perceptions of the last actor to leave a crisis decreased to precrisis norms. Relevant background information is noted, such as links to previous crises, and incidents or events which provide the setting in which the international crisis under discussion occurred.

The summary of a crisis proper begins by specifying the first trigger and trigger date, and the triggering entity, that is, the event or action which triggered a crisis for the first actor, when and by which state(s) or non-state actor. A chronological account of events during the crisis follows, including crisis triggers for other actors and the content and date of their major response, namely, the act which captures the major thrust of each state's behavior in response to its crisis. The summary also contains information about the highest value threatened, along a scale from limited threat to population and property, through other value threats such as political regime, to the gravest threat, that is, to the very existence of a state – and crisis management techniques, with special reference to the intensity and centrality of violence. The summary includes a description of how and when a crisis ended for each actor, including the termination of the entire crisis. This refers to both the perceived content of outcome – defeat, victory, stalemate or compromise — and the form of outcome – formal, semi-formal or tacit agreement, unilateral act, or faded. Any superpower or great power activity during the course of an international crisis is also noted. Finally, the summary includes global and/or regional organization involvement to bring about crisis abatement, where relevant.

(1) Chaco I

A crisis between Bolivia and Paraguay occurred between 5 December 1928 and 12 September 1929.

Background

The Chaco Boreal consists of 116,000 square miles of territory which had been claimed by Bolivia and Paraguay for some 150 years. The area is mostly swamp with very few inhabitants, and its agricultural or industrial value was as yet unexplored. It represented the only Bolivian access to the sea. Army patrols and forts were maintained by each country on its side of the Chaco.

Crisis

A crisis for Bolivia was triggered on 5 December 1928 when Paraguayan troops captured and destroyed a Bolivian fort. The Bolivian Government immediately severed diplomatic relations with Paraguay, mobilized its reserve forces and, on 14 December, retaliated with a military attack to reoccupy the captured fort and occupy a second one. This triggered a crisis for Paraguay which regarded Bolivia's military advance as a threat to the very existence of Paraguay. On 17 December, Paraguay proclaimed general mobilization and sent reinforcements north to halt what was believed to be an impending assault.

The adversaries seemed to be on the brink of a war that neither desired. The dispute was submitted by them to the Pan American Conference on Conciliation and Arbitration, a body which had been organized by the Pan American Union, a predecessor of the Organization of American States (OAS). The conference was composed of representatives from the US, Colombia, Cuba, Mexico and Uruguay, as well as the two crisis actors. The activities of the Conference led to a Conciliation Protocol signed in Washington on 3 January 1929. It called for a restoration of the status quo ante and the resumption of diplomatic relations between the two countries, and set up a Commission of Inquiry. The crisis ended on 12 September 1929 when Paraguay and Bolivia ratified a resolution presented by the Commission. The status quo as of December 1928 was restored, but no effort had been made to resolve the basic territorial dispute. The issue erupted again in 1932 (see Case #6). The Council of the League of Nations initiated attempts to mediate the crisis, but withdrew when the Conference of the Pan American Union took up the matter. The United States was the most important contributor to crisis abatement, along with other neutral actors belonging to the Pan American Union.

References Estigarribia 1969; Fagg 1967; Fifer 1972; Ireland 1938; Kain 1938; Klein 1969; Lindsay 1935; Osborne 1965; Pendle 1967; Schurz 1929; Thomas 1956; Warren 1949; Wood 1966; Zook 1960.

(2) Chinese Eastern Railway

A crisis for China began on 13 July 1929 and ended on 22 December 1929.

Background In 1924 an agreement was signed between the USSR and China for the joint management of the Chinese Eastern Railway. During the course of three years the Soviets had almost completely assumed management of the vital railway, and proposals by the Chinese to alter the situation were rejected. Relations between the two countries were strained, and an incident in 1927 in which the Soviet Embassy in Peking (Beijing) was searched did not improve matters. In addition, Chinese Communist activities were being carried out in the railway zone via Soviet diplomatic channels.

On 27 May 1929 the Chinese raided the Soviet Consulate in Harbin, arresting a number of Russian officers and railway employees. Documents seized at the time were subsequently published in the Chinese press and pointed to Soviet interference in China. The Provincial Government, acting in the railway area, on the authority of China's National Government, ordered the takeover of the railway and assumed its management, occupied USSR institutions and arrested Soviet railway officials and citizens. A formal protest by the USSR on 31 May included demands for the immediate release of prisoners and the return of documents and property, which, if not met, would incur the withdrawal of diplomatic privileges to Chinese personnel in the Soviet Union.

Crisis On 13 July 1929 a crisis was triggered for China when the Soviet Ambassador issued an ultimatum demanding the full restoration of the status quo ante *vis-à-vis* the Chinese Eastern Railway. The Chinese were given three days to respond and to agree to a conference to settle problems involving the railway. On 16 July the Chinese, perceiving a threat to their political regime, responded with counter-demands. Moscow broke off diplomatic relations on the 19th, recalled its representatives and sent troops to the border. Military preparations were also made by the Chinese, who published a manifesto regarding Soviet transgressions of the 1924 agreement. Meetings between the Soviet Consul in Harbin and Chinese officials took place on 24 and 28 July and 2 August. Soviet raids into Chinese territory continued throughout the discussions. When proposals advanced by each side were rejected by the other, the crisis took on violent proportions.

On 12 August Soviet troops occupied three strategic towns in China near the border. Six thousand Chinese troops were mobilized on the 15th. Serious clashes occurred. In late December the Soviet advance threatened Harbin. Chinese negotiations with the Soviets led to the signing of a protocol on 22 December 1929 whereby the Chinese capitulated unconditionally to Moscow's demands.

Germany approached the Soviet Union on China's behalf in August and formally offered its good offices to settle the dispute. In October, German attempts to conciliate were once more unsuccessful. During the crisis the United States, Britain and France sent notes to both belligerents requesting a halt to military activities. This received a favorable Chinese response, but the USSR refused any third party mediation. A Japanese recommendation for talks at the local level, too, failed to produce any results.

References Vinacke 1959; Wu 1950.

(3) Haiti Unrest   Unrest in Haiti caused a crisis for the United States from 4 December 1929 to 28 June 1930.

Background   The United States had exercised a protectorate over Haiti since 1915: a diplomatic convention signed by Haiti, under pressure, gave the US control over finance and vocational education and permission to station Marines on the island. The convention also gave foreigners the right to own land and protected them in the same way as native Haitians. The Haitian National Assembly was dissolved in 1917. US interest, based upon the Monroe Doctrine, concerned a sea-passage between the eastern seaboard of the US and the Panama Canal. Haiti resented the domination by foreigners, especially whites, particularly after a century of formal independence. French and American culture vied for Haitian support, with education in Haiti following traditional French emphasis on the humanities. On 12 October 1928 elections scheduled for January 1929 were cancelled by President Borno. On 3 December President Hoover asked Congress to examine US policy in Haiti. At the alleged insistence of the US Director-General of the Services of Agriculture and Vocational Education, the Haitian Government decided to reduce its grant for higher education in the humanities. A wave of strikes in schools and colleges followed, supported by government employees.

Crisis   A crisis for the US was triggered by Haiti on 4 December 1929 when attacks by customhouse employees on US citizens were reported. The US responded the following day with a declaration of martial law by the Marine commander in Haiti. On 6 December five Haitians were killed in a clash with US Marines. US reinforcements were sent to the area on the 7th, and American women and children were evacuated. By 10 December relative order had been restored.

On 7 February a committee was appointed by the US Congress to investigate the situation in Haiti. Another group was formed to study Haiti's educational system. The committee recommended that a neutral president replace Borno until new elections could be held. Some reorganization of the US role in Haiti was suggested to allow for less direct influence and more constructive assistance. There was also a recommendation for co-ordination of vocational education with the entire school system. Finally, the US would appoint an ambassador to Haiti. This was done on 28 June 1930 and ended the crisis for the United States. In subsequent years Haiti did exercise more independent action, and in September 1932 the Haitian Assembly rejected a proposed Treaty of Friendship with the US because of inadequate provisions for the withdrawal of US Marines.

References   See general list, especially *Keesing's Contemporary Archives* 1929, 1930; *New York Times* 1929, 1930.

(4) Mukden Incident   A crisis began for both China and Japan on 18 September 1931 and ended for the latter on 18 February 1932. China's crisis faded, with no known termination date.

Background   On 5 May 1931 a People's National Convention in Nanking adopted a provisional constitution which confirmed the separation of five branches within the Chinese Government. Chinese nationalism had penetrated into China's three eastern provinces, and authority in all of China was fragmented.

Unrest and dissatisfaction with economic conditions in Japan were marked by 1930: the military, while opposing the alliance between government and business, began to assume control. Strong pressure was brought to bear on the government to act positively in defense of Japanese interests in Manchuria, threatened by the policies of the Chinese Nationalists: Manchuria was perceived, in part, as an economic panacea.

Crisis   On the night of 18 September the Japanese Kwantung Army, engaged in night maneuvers at Mukden, used an explosion on the railway as an excuse for the preconcerted seizure, before morning, of the arsenal and of Antung, Yingkow and

Changchun. This triggered a crisis for China and also for the Japanese Government — the invasion being an act by the Japanese Army without previous sanction by the civil authority which was not interested at that time in war with China. China had no choice but to withdraw after serious clashes. On 21 September Kirin was seized. China appealed to the League of Nations and to the US for aid. No serious military response was attempted. On the 24th the Japanese Government called for direct Sino-Japanese negotiations, while rejecting involvement by the League. At the same time Japanese military pressure continued and the northeastern provinces of China were steadily occupied. The Chinese instituted a boycott of Japanese imports into the country.

On 18 February the crisis ended for Japan when it unilaterally declared the independence of the former territory of Manchuria, now called Manchukuo. For China, the crisis faded. It did not regain Manchuria until the end of World War II. During the crisis the League of Nations adopted a resolution and dispatched a fact-finding mission. After the end of Japan's crisis the mission found that the Japanese action of 18–19 September 1931 was not in self-defense and that the creation of Manchukuo did not flow from a "genuine and spontaneous independence movement."

The United States, while condemning Japanese action, continued to follow the principle of non-recognition. Japan viewed the US with hostility and suspicion, while China was dissatisfied with the paucity of the US response. The USSR proposed a non-aggression pact to Japan. Territory previously recognized by Japan to be in the Soviet sphere of influence was now included in its boundaries as the new state of Manchukuo expanded its borders; but Moscow assumed Chinese rights to the Chinese Eastern Railway, which proved to be a continuing source of friction. Great Britain, too, was politically involved. None of the involved actors had any effect on crisis termination.

References Grew 1953; Hane 1972; Hull 1948; Lee 1973; MacNair and Lach 1955; Morley 1974; Ogata 1964; Schurmann and Schell 1967-74; Vinacke 1959.

(5) Shanghai A Sino-Japanese crisis over Shanghai occurred from 24 January to 5 May 1932.

Background At the beginning of the 1930s relations between foreigners and local Chinese authorities were fairly amicable in the "treaty port" of Shanghai. When news of the Japanese takeover in Manchuria reached Shanghai, anti-Japanese sentiment increased markedly. The Chinese, in retaliation, had staged a boycott of Japanese goods, and some Japanese residents in Shanghai were molested (see Case #4). During the first three weeks of January 1932 a number of violent incidents took place.

On 18 January some Japanese residents of Shanghai were attacked by Chinese. Five Japanese demands were presented to the Chinese Mayor of Greater Shanghai, who claimed he was ready to comply with three of these, dealing directly with the incident, but not with the two involving the anti-Japanese movement. The commander of the Japanese fleet in Chinese waters threatened to take direct action; Japanese naval reinforcements were ordered to Shanghai. Twenty thousand Japanese troops arrived on 24 January 1932.

Crisis A crisis was triggered for China on 24 January, when the Japanese notified Mayor Wu T'ieh-ch'eng that, if no reply was forthcoming within a reasonable time or if the reply was unsatisfactory, the Japanese Government reserved the right to take action by 28 January. The Municipal Council of the International Settlement in Shanghai held a meeting on the 28th and declared a state of emergency. Despite the complete acceptance on the 28th of all Japanese demands, military operations began. This territorial threat was met with Chinese armed resistance.

The crisis for Japan occurred on 29 January, when Admiral Shiuzawa concluded that the Japanese forces were inadequate to deal with the developing situation. An aerial bombardment was ordered upon densely-populated sections of the city and additional troops were requested from Tokyo. This was approved by a Cabinet decision on 4 February. Japan's major response on 18 February was an ultimatum requiring the Chinese to withdraw all their troops from Shanghai within two days. The Chinese refused. A Japanese attack followed.

Conditions for a cease-fire were initiated by Great Britain and were agreed to by the adversaries on 28 February, but fighting continued until 3 March when the Chinese had withdrawn to outside the 20 kilometer limit upon which the Japanese had insisted.

At China's request a special session of the League Assembly met to consider the Shanghai incident on 3 March. The US openly condemned Japan at the League. On the 11th a resolution was passed which embodied the doctrine of non-recognition of situations achieved in violation of treaty obligations.

It was largely through British mediation that a settlement between China and Japan was negotiated and an armistice signed on 5 May 1932, establishing a demilitarized zone around Shanghai and terminating the economic boycott.

References See sources for Case #4.

(6) Chaco II

A second crisis over Chaco between Bolivia and Paraguay began on 18 June 1932 and lasted until 12 June 1935.

Background The question of ownership of the vast underdeveloped Chaco region lay in dispute since the crisis of 1928–29 (see Case #1). During the intervening years there were some incidents, but no serious fighting took place. On 11 November 1931 negotiations between the adversaries began on the question of a settlement of their territorial differences. A draft non-aggression pact was under consideration when the second crisis broke out.

Crisis A Bolivian attack and occupation of a fort was reported on 18 June 1932 to the headquarters of the Chief of the Paraguayan General Staff. Paraguay, which perceived a Bolivian threat to its existence, directed its commander in the field to retake the fort at whatever sacrifice. On 15 July Paraguay responded with an attack on a Bolivian fort built after the 18 June incident. Three days later the loss of the fort was reported, triggering a crisis for Bolivia which perceived a threat to its political regime. Bolivia responded during the night of 18 July by holding a special emergency Cabinet meeting where the President ordered a major reprisal and the immediate capture of the areas of Corralo and Toledo. This was done on 27 and 28 July and Boqueron was occupied by Bolivian forces on 31 July 1932.

A Paraguayan counter-attack, during August 1932, succeeded in recapturing these forts and also pushed the Bolivian Army back several miles from the positions held prior to the outbreak of the crisis. A Bolivian counter-attack occurred during November and December 1932.

On 10 May 1933 Paraguay declared war. A truce was proposed in December 1933, but on 6 January 1934 fighting resumed. On 17 November 1934 the Paraguayans captured a principal Bolivian supply base. On 28 May US President Roosevelt issued a proclamation prohibiting the sale of arms to Bolivia and Paraguay. This was eventually agreed to by Germany, the Soviet Union, France, Great Britain and Italy.

The Chaco dispute was placed on the agenda of the 15th Session of the League of Nations Assembly in November 1934, and an inquiry committee was formed to prepare a report. Its recommendations were the cessation of hostilities, withdrawal and demobilization of the armies, and temporary policing of the evacuated zone. They were accepted by Bolivia and rejected by Paraguay.

On 16 January 1935 the Advisory Committee of the Assembly unanimously adopted a recommendation to League members to lift their arms embargo on Bolivia but to maintain it against Paraguay. Paraguay announced its intention to leave the League on 23 February, and the next day the recommendations went into effect. Military advantage began to swing in Bolivia's favor. The final phase of the negotiations for an armistice in the Chaco began on 27 May 1935 when Argentina, Brazil, Chile, Peru, Uruguay and the United States began negotiations with the now exhausted states of Bolivia and Paraguay over a new protocol based upon the League of Nations' recommendations, with some modifications to pacify Paraguay. An agreement was reached on 9 June and signed on 12 June 1935, ending the crisis for both actors. The agreement provided for a cessation of hostilities and the holding of a peace conference. Peace was not formally restored until July 1938.

Mediation was attempted by the neutral Commission of Washington (Colombia, Cuba, Mexico, Uruguay and the US); by the ABCP group (Argentina, Brazil, Chile, Peru); and by the united efforts of all the neutral American states of the Pan American Conference at Montevideo in December 1933.

References   See sources for Case #1.

(7) Leticia   A crisis for Colombia and Peru over Leticia began on 8 September 1932 and terminated on 25 May 1933.

Background   The frontier between Colombia and Peru was in dispute until 1922 when the Salomon-Lozano Treaty was signed by the two countries. The agreement provided that Peru recognize Colombian sovereignty over the Leticia Trapeze – a narrow strip of territory running from the Putumayo River to the Amazon.

During the night of 31 August–1 September 1932 a group of Peruvians attacked and occupied the river port of Leticia, the capital of the Colombian district of the Amazon. During the following week Peru denied responsibility for the attack, citing Communists and enemies of the Peruvian Government as having carried out the invasion. However, rumors of Peruvian President Sanchez Cerro's support for the seizure, as well as for a revision of the Salomon–Lozano Treaty, began to spread.

Crisis   On 8 September 1932 the US Ambassador to Colombia reported to the State Department that Colombian President Olaya perceived the possibility of war with Peru over the latter's support for the occupiers of Leticia. With a view to restoring its control over Leticia, Colombia responded in September 1932 (exact date unknown) by sending a small naval expedition to retake the territory. The expedition had to pass through the Panama Canal and then 2000 miles up the Amazon River. On 22 September the Government of Colombia issued a special loan for national defense. During November Ecuador sent a Note to the League of Nations about the conflict between Colombia and Peru.

On 27 December 1932 the Colombian expedition arrived at the mouth of the Amazon River, triggering a crisis for Peru. At that time Peruvian reinforcements were reported to be assembling near Leticia. Colombia formally asked for League of Nations intervention on 2 January 1933, and again requested a special session on the 21st.

On the 6th General Victor Ramos, commander of the Peruvian forces, cabled a warning to the Colombian Consul in Lima stating that the entry of the Colombian flotilla into the Amazon was a hostile act and he had therefore ordered military measures to prevent its arrival at Leticia. Following a request by the commander of the Colombian expedition to allow him to occupy Tarpaca peacefully, Peru bombed the Colombian gunboats on 14 February 1933. Tarpaca was captured the following day by Colombian forces.

During March and April Colombian troops captured several Peruvian ports. The assassination of President Cerro in Peru on 30 April decreased the possibility of further military clashes. On 2 May direct negotiations began between the new Peruvian President, Benavides, and his close personal friend, Alfonso Lopez, a leader of the Liberal Party in Colombia, who was to become its President the following year. On the 10th the League Council's Advisory Committee submitted a new proposal and on 25 May 1933 an agreement was signed by representatives of Colombia and Peru, transferring control of Leticia from the Peruvian forces to a League Commission of three (United States, Brazil and Spain), terminating the crisis for both actors.

The League Council discussed the Leticia issue on 24 and 26 January 1933 and sent Notes to both parties. In February an Advisory Committee was asked to negotiate with both parties and, on 17 March, it published a report terming Peru the aggressor. The report was adopted unanimously by the Council which also appointed an Advisory Committee to monitor the crisis. The new proposals submitted on 10 May proved to be the basis of negotiations between the adversaries.

The United States responded to a Colombian appeal by sending a Note to Peru asking it to allow the reestablishment of Colombian control over Leticia. Great Britain also applied pressure, mostly on Peru, to cooperate with the League.

References Fluharty 1957; Wood 1966.

(8) Jehol Campaign   China's crisis over the province of Jehol lasted from 23 February to 31 May 1933.

Background The 1932 creation of the State of Manchukuo by Japan (see Case #4) included the territory of China's three northeastern provinces, Jehol and parts of Inner Mongolia. The Japanese/Manchukuon forces had been operating to clear the area of all anti-Japanese and anti-Manchukuo Chinese pockets in Jehol. In order to resist Japanese advances, China resolved to concentrate troops south of the Great Wall at various points in the province of Jehol in December 1932. Despite Japan's repeated warning, three Chinese brigades were moved to Jehol. Japanese forces occupied Shanhaikwan on 3 January 1933 so as to provide a preliminary base for the expected occupation of Jehol. A state of extreme tension prevailed in China, but the Chinese military remained confident of its ability to halt a Japanese advance in Jehol.

Crisis On 23 February 1933 the Japanese issued an ultimatum calling for the evacuation of all Chinese troops from Jehol and warning that no guarantees could be given that military hostilities would not spread to North China. That day 30,000 Japanese and 1000 Manchukuon troops launched an attack on Jehol. The ultimatum was rejected the next day by the Chinese who moved more troops to the area. Jehol fell on 4 March to the Japanese, and by May they had advanced to within three kilometers of Peking (Beijing). On 31 May 1933 the Chinese Government signed a truce at Taugku in accordance with which the Chinese Army withdrew west of Peking and the Japanese undertook to stay north of the Great Wall.

During March 1933 the UK, France and the US were informed that China would not negotiate with Japan and that resistance was its legitimate right as a member of the League of Nations. In February recommendations had been submitted by the League, but China felt that they did not go far enough in sanctioning Japan and withdrew its request. The British then refused to mediate. The US was approached in May; President Roosevelt issued a non-commital statement. Italy strongly condemned Japan. Plans for joint efforts by Italy, the US and Great Britain to settle the fighting in northern China never came to fruition.

References Borg 1964; MacNair and Lach 1955; Thorne 1972; Vinacke 1959.

(9) Saudi/Yemen War   A crisis between Saudi Arabia and Yemen began on 18 December 1933 and ended on 20 May 1934.

Background In 1930 the former protectorate of Asir was incorporated into the Kingdom of Hejaz and Nejd (later, Saudi Arabia), thus extending its territory to the Yemen border. The Imam of Yemen then claimed a number of frontier districts between the two states. Tribes residing in Asir, aided by Yemen, staged a revolt against Ibn Saud. Treaties of friendship had been signed between Saudi Arabia and Great Britain, and between Yemen and Italy.

Crisis On 18 December 1933 the Saudis received information that Yemeni troops had entered Asir. That day Saudi Arabia decided to initiate talks with Yemen. A conference was convened on 16 March 1934, but Yemen refused to withdraw from the disputed area. The Saudis opted for military action and, on 22 March 1934, ordered troops into Asir. This triggered a crisis for Yemen. Saudi troops advanced into the disputed highland and on to Yemen's coastal plain. British, French and Italian warships were sent to the area and their combined political and military pressure succeeded in halting the first Saudi advance.

Yemen resisted the Saudi assault at first but, on 12 April, the Imam cabled Ibn Saud requesting peace and announcing that his troops had been ordered to evacuate Asir. Fighting continued during the talks which centered around the terms of the armistice. On 13 May 1934 Saudi Arabia officially announced an armistice: the Imam had agreed to carry out the Saudi conditions. A peace conference began on 18 May, and on 20 May the crisis ended with the signing of the Treaty of Taif.

References   Carr 1945; Ingrams 1963; Kohn 1934; Wenner 1967.

(10) Austria Putsch   The crisis over the attempted *putsch* in Austria occurred between 25 and 31 July 1934. Austria, Czechoslovakia, Italy and Yugoslavia were crisis actors.

Background   Chancellor Dollfuss began ruling Austria by emergency decrees in March 1932 and built his dictatorship on the anti-Nazi and anti-Marxist principles of the *Heimwehr* (Home Guard) militia. All elections were prohibited after the Nazis won nine of the 20 seats in the Innsbruck municipality. In May 1933 about 100 Austrian Nazis were arrested at a political demonstration. A Nazi campaign of terror led to the formal suppression of the Austrian Nazi Party, the NSDAP. The party went underground. Germany's aggressive policy towards Austria increased in the summer of 1933. Dollfuss's efforts to secure support abroad succeeded in acquiring moral and financial support for Vienna from Britain and France. His appeal to his patron, Mussolini, led to an Italian warning to Hitler on 5 August and subsequent assurances of Italian support. A series of provocative German broadcasts directed at Austria were initiated from the Bavarian capital. Italy, France and Britain sent representatives to Berlin to discuss the cessation of German subversive activity in Austria, with partial success, although the broadcasts continued. On 11 August 1933 there was a shooting incident on the Austro-German frontier. On the 14th alleged documents of the Austrian Nazi Party were published, but their authenticity was denied by the Party. On 3 October there was an unsuccessful assassination attempt on Dollfuss. Attempts at reconciliation between Austria and Germany did not produce results.

On 12 February 1934 the headquarters of the Socialist Party in Linz was stormed. A strike by the electrical workers paralyzed Austria. Arrests of most of the Socialist leaders followed. Three days of heavy fighting between the *Heimwehr* and the Socialists followed. Martial law was proclaimed, together with the dissolution of the Socialist Party, trade unions and all affiliated organizations. On 1 May the Austrian Cabinet declared a new constitution: the country would henceforth be ruled by the clerical Fascists of the *Heimwehr*. Dollfuss assumed the portfolios of Public Security, Foreign Affairs and War, apart from the Chancellorship. Hitler and Mussolini met in Venice on 14 June to discuss the Austrian question. On 12 July the Austrian Cabinet decreed the death penalty for unauthorized possession of explosives following discovery that a new supply of arms was pouring across the German border. A Czech worker was beaten and hung by the police in Vienna on the 24th. A Cabinet meeting was rescheduled for the following day.

Crisis   On 25 July 1934 Austrian Nazis attacked the Chancery and killed Dollfuss, triggering a crisis for Austria, Czechoslovakia and Italy. Austria's response, the same day, was to repress the rebellion and arrest participating members of the SS unit. The Vice-Chancellor took charge of the government. Two days later Czechoslovakia, fearing that a German invasion of Austria would lead to an Italian invasion as well, threatened to move troops in the direction of Vienna to protect its own territory. Italy, determined to prevent an *Anschluss,* responded immediately by rushing troops to the border at the Brenner Pass on 25 July and by warning Hitler that, if the Germans invaded Austria, Italy would cross that border. At that time Dollfuss's family was in Italy, as Mussolini's guests, and were awaiting the Chancellor's arrival on the 27th.

The Italian response of 25 July triggered a crisis for Yugoslavia, which had a long-standing dispute with Italy over Carinthia. Italian troops at the Brenner Pass constituted a serious security problem for Yugoslavia. Its response, that day, was a threat to move forces, mobilization, the strengthening of frontier guards, and the movement of some troops to the Moribor area on the Yugoslav–Austrian border.

The crisis ended for Austria, Czechoslovakia and Italy on 31 July, by which time the Austrian militia had completed the suppression of Nazi uprisings that had belatedly broken out in the provinces. Yugoslavia's crisis ended that day as well, as a result of a unilateral act by Italy – the decision not to send troops into Austria. Germany's decision to pull back from an attempted *Anschluss* constituted a tacit agreement with Italy not to take such action then or later without the latter's approval.

Britain, France and Germany were involved actors. The first two feared a war in Europe as a consequence of a successful *putsch*, while Hitler decried its failure, fearing Western blame for the attempt and not being militarily prepared as yet for a showdown with Britain and France.

References   See sources for Case #26.

(11) Assassination of King Alexander   The international crisis which followed the assassination of Yugoslavia's King Alexander began on 9 October and ended on 10 December 1934. The crisis actors were Yugoslavia and Hungary.

Background   In 1921 King Alexander became the ruler of the Croatian, Serbian and Slovene peoples. In 1929 he proclaimed a royal dictatorship and changed the name of the state to Yugoslavia. A new constitution was proclaimed in 1931, based on the will of the Serbs and the suppression of the minority Croats and Slovenes. Croatian refugees fled to Italy, Bulgaria and especially Hungary where they organized terrorist acts against Alexander's tyranny. The attempt to halt the movement of terrorists led to shooting and border incidents between Yugoslavia and Hungary. Alexander accused Hungary of giving aid to Yugoslavia's enemies. Budapest denied the allegation and brought the Croatian claim before the League of Nations. French Foreign Minister Louis Barthou extended an invitation to King Alexander to visit Paris in October 1934. He wished to confer with the monarch on future policies towards Austria and Italy.

Crisis   On 9 October 1934, hours after King Alexander reached Marseilles, he and Louis Barthou were killed by a Macedonian assassin bearing a Hungarian passport. Leaders of the Croatian terrorist organization were arrested in Italy at the French Government's request, but Rome refused to extradite them to France or allow for their interrogation. Anti-Italian demonstrations broke out in Yugoslav towns. The Quai d'Orsay, on the eve of a Franco-Italian *rapprochement*, persuaded Yugoslavia to minimize the evidence of Italian complicity and to concentrate its anger on Hungary.

The Yugoslav response, and the crisis trigger for Hungary, was a Yugoslav appeal to the League of Nations, alleging that the assassins had been selected at Janka Puszta and had left Hungary freely with Hungarian passports. Budapest denied most of the charges in its response of 24 November.

Threats of war passed, but feelings between the two countries were bitter and angry. A report was presented to the League affirming that certain Hungarian authorities had, at least by negligence, failed to prevent and repress political terrorism, with the result that the task of the assassins had been facilitated. Hungary was asked to make further investigations and report the result. The League discussions ended with a resolution requesting Hungary to "take at once appropriate punitive action in the case of any of its authorities whose culpability may have been established" and to report back to the Council. A commission of experts was set up to study the possibility of an international convention to discourage terrorism. The crisis terminated on 10 December 1934 when both states accepted the League Resolution. In December, too, Belgrade initiated a brutal eviction of several thousand innocent Hungarian peasants from its territory, but stopped when indignant protests were issued from abroad. In January 1935 Hungary informed the Council that a detailed investigation had disclosed no official responsibility for the Marseilles crime.

References   Bullock 1962; Gyula 1979; von Papen 1952; Schuman 1942; Shirer 1964; Walters 1960; Weinberg 1980.

(12) Wal-Wal   A crisis for Ethiopia and Britain over the Wal-Wal incident began on 6 December 1934 and merged into the Ethiopian War (see Case #16).

Background   Italy's entry into East Africa as a colonial power in the late nineteenth century was made possible by a British objective of reducing French influence in the area. Italian penetration continued successfully until they were badly defeated by Abyssinian (Ethiopian) troops at Adowa in 1896. The colony of Eritrea was transferred to Italy by British royal decree in 1899. Mussolini's efforts to control Ethiopia began as early as 1923. In 1928 the two countries concluded a Treaty of Friendship, but Ethiopia refused to live up to its conditions which granted Italy special privileges. In 1932 Mussolini sent his Minister of the Colonies to Eritrea to prepare the colony as a springboard for an invasion of Ethiopia. Thereafter, roads and defenses in Eritrea were built and strengthened. Incidents occurred on the border, as the Ethiopians became more and more apprehensive of Italy's designs. Wal-Wal, a watering site in a loosely-designated border area between Italian and Ethiopian territory, had been used frequently by tribes from British and Italian Somaliland who wandered freely in the area. It became the site of an Italian garrison. In November 1934 a British mission surveying the border between British Somaliland and Ethiopia arrived at the wells of Wal-Wal with an armed Ethiopian escort. Abyssinian tribesmen who gathered around gave the Italian garrison commander the impression that an attack was imminent. He sent for reinforcements, and the British head of the mission withdrew from the area.

Crisis   On 6 December 1934 Ethiopian tribesmen attacked the Italians at Wal-Wal. They were defeated; and Mussolini's demands, the same day, for an unconditional apology, a large indemnity and the punishment of those responsible triggered a crisis for Ethiopian Emperor Haile Selassie who claimed that the dispute fell under the arbitration clause of the 1928 Treaty of Friendship. The UK proposed a conciliatory solution which Italy refused to consider.

The Ethiopian major response was an appeal to the League of Nations on 9 December. When no real progress was forthcoming it requested League intervention on 3 January 1935. The item was removed from the Council's agenda when Italy agreed to bilateral talks. Negotiations began to break down in March in the face of new preconditions by Italy and the build-up of its forces in Eritrea. On 17 March and 3 April there were two more Ethiopian appeals to the League. France, Italy and the UK met on 11–14 April to form the Stresa Front against Germany. Italy then conceded that it would consent to arbitration with Ethiopia under the 1928 Treaty. Further negotiations between the two adversaries and France and Great Britain centered around the 20 May 1935 League Council meeting which adopted two resolutions on the timing and form of arbitration: 25 August was designated as the final date for a ruling. A UK offer of economic concessions to Italy, along with a large part of Ogaden, with an Ethiopian access to the sea through British Somaliland, was refused by Italy in June. The situation was further aggravated by the signing of an Anglo-German naval agreement in June, which allowed German naval expansion to one-third of the British Navy.

A three-power meeting, without Ethiopian participation, began in August 1935. Italy rejected Anglo-French proposals and refused to state its final demands. Sometime during that month a UK perception that Mussolini might attack Britain in retaliation for its support of Ethiopia triggered a crisis for the UK. In response to this perceived threat of a possible war, Britain, on 3 September 1935, reinforced its Mediterranean fleet. It also began a series of negotiations with other Mediterranean powers, especially Yugoslavia and Turkey.

The crisis for Ethiopia continued as negotiations failed to produce any real settlement. On 9 September a League of Nations Committee of Five was appointed to discuss the dispute, as well as Italian claims that Ethiopia was unfit for League membership. League observers were requested to witness increasing Italian mobilization, and when Ethiopia perceived war as imminent it informed the League, on

29 September, of its intentions to mobilize. On 2 October Italy began a full-scale attack on Ethiopia, and the crisis over Wal-Wal merged into the Ethiopian War.

Britain's crisis with Italy continued until after the war between Ethiopia and Italy had broken out. It ended on 22 October 1935 when the UK reasserted its superiority in the area by terminating the neutrality rules for Italian ships calling at British colonial ports.

References See sources for Case #16.

(13) Bulgaria/Turkey I   A crisis between Bulgaria and Turkey occurred between 6 and 10 March 1935.

Background On 8 February 1934 the Balkan Pact was signed by Romania, Turkey, Greece and Yugoslavia, mutually guaranteeing the security of their Balkan borders and promising not to take action with regard to any Balkan non-signatory without previous discussions. Bulgaria refused to recognize the status quo established by the post-World War I peace treaties. On 1 March 1935 the followers of Venizelos in Greece staged an uprising in Athens, Macedonia and Crete as a protest against royalism. Turkish troops began concentrating on their common border with Bulgaria and Greece.

Crisis On 6 March 1935 Bulgaria's Foreign Minister expressed his country's alarm at the concentration of Turkish troops on the border and complained of anti-Bulgarian propaganda in the Turkish press. Bulgaria's response, and the trigger for Turkey, was an aide-mémoire to the League of Nations on 8 March charging Turkey with aggression but not requesting League action. The Turkish response was a press conference denying unfriendly intentions. Turkey declared that its troop concentrations were the result of the situation in Greece and countercharged Bulgarian military preparations along the border while declaring its intention to maintain the status quo in the Balkans.

On 10 March Bulgaria withdrew its memo from the League and asserted its peaceful intentions. This ended the crisis for both actors through a tacit understanding to reduce the level of tension. Five months later another crisis erupted. (see Case #15).

References See General List, especially *New York Times*, and Albrecht-Carrié 1965; Schuman 1942.

(14) Kaunas Trials   Lithuania's crisis with Germany over the Kaunas trials lasted from 28 March to 25 September 1935.

Background The Versailles Treaty following World War I placed the city of Memel under Allied sovereignty. It was occupied by Lithuania in 1923, and the following year the League of Nations awarded Memel a special status under Lithuanian sovereignty. A dissatisfied Germany, which declared its intention to regain the city, was eagerly supported by Memel's German inhabitants. Parallel to the Nazi rise to power in Germany, Nazi and Nazi-front organizations became active in Lithuania. In 1934 an accusation of conspiracy against Lithuania was made against 122 Nazis who were tried in Kaunas. On 26 March 1935 they were found guilty.

Crisis In response to the Kaunas trials Germany closed its border with Lithuania and imposed economic sanctions. This triggered a crisis for Lithuania on 28 March. Even before the trial had ended Memel police and border guards had been alerted to the possibility of an uprising or even an invasion. When Hitler urged the three guarantor powers (Britain, France and Italy) to take action, they handed a protest note to Lithuania together with a threat to bring the issue to the League.

Tension reached its peak when, on 17 May, a Lithuanian appeals court upheld all the sentences except one. That day Germany moved its troops to the border, as did Lithuania while calling up reserve forces. During the period between May and

September tension remained high, with Germany's repeated declarations of hostility. On 25 September elections were held in Memel, and their results led to a temporary reduction of tension. A *détente* between Germany and Lithuania was reached when the latter agreed to new amendments in its electoral laws.

References   Gehase 1946; Gerutis 1969; Schuman 1942; Shirer 1964; Walters 1960; Weinberg 1980.

(15) Bulgaria/Turkey II   Bulgaria's crisis occurred between 3 and 31 August 1935.

Background   Relations between Bulgaria and Turkey remained tense since the crisis of March 1935 (see Case #13). In March Kemal Ataturk was reelected President of Turkey for the next four years. Turkey continued its active policy of rearmament because of distrust of Italy's intentions in the Eastern Mediterranean. In July the Turkish War Ministry ordered the fortification of Kirklareli near Bulgaria's southern border on the Black Sea. Bulgarian nationalists desired an outlet for Bulgaria to the Aegean Sea through the Turkish Gulf of Saros.

Crisis   On 3 August 1935, as the Turkish fortifications at Kirklareli neared completion, Bulgaria's War Council, presided over by King Boris and attended by the leading generals and officers of the Army General Staff, met in emergency session. Bulgaria's response to the crisis was a decision to construct immediately strong permanent fortifications around the southern Bulgarian town of Haskovo. Tension increased in Bulgaria when the Turkish Army began carrying out maneuvers in Eastern Thrace near the border.

On 23 August the Turkish Minister to Bulgaria informed his government of the growing anxiety in Bulgaria regarding Turkish military maneuvers, especially in view of the fact that they were attended by all high-ranking Turkish officers. He also reported on the growing resentment at the anti-Bulgarian articles in the Turkish press. By 25 August the Turkish concentration of troops on the Bulgarian border was reported to have reached the strength of three army corps. Extensive defensive works were under construction along the frontier.

On 31 August, with half of the Turkish Army on maneuvers, the Bulgarian crisis ended with a visit to Sofia by Turkish Foreign Minister Aras which resulted in a joint statement disapproving anti-Bulgarian attacks in the Turkish press.

References   See sources for Case #13.

(16) Ethiopian War   The crisis for Ethiopia, France and Italy, resulting from the Italian invasion of Ethiopia on 2 October 1935, ended on 5 May 1936.

Background   Since the Italian build-up in their colony of Eritrea, bordering on Ethiopia, incidents occurred between the forces of the two countries. One such incident at Wal-Wal was exploited by Italy to raise issues of Italian interests in Ethiopia (see Case #12). After negotiations failed to produce a solution, Ethiopia mobilized its forces on 29 September 1935.

Crisis   On 2 October 1935 Italian forces invaded Ethiopia. Its response was military resistance and an appeal to the League of Nations the following day. Mussolini pronounced the war justified because of Ethiopian "aggression" and called for national mobilization. The League Council condemned Italian aggression and imposed sanctions on Italy on the 7th.

France, which had suffered severe losses during World War I and had recently concluded an anti-German agreement with Italy and the UK at Stresa (April 1935), feared that strong League action might provoke Italy to leave the alliance and realign with Germany. The Council action, therefore, triggered a crisis for France, and Prime Minister Laval attempted to slow down the imposition of sanctions by a special Committee of Thirteen which had been set up on 9 October to draft specific measures. Their recommendations, issued on 6 November, triggered a crisis for Italy because they included sanctions on oil imports, as well as other vital raw materials. Italy responded in early December by informing France's Prime Minister that such League action would seriously affect French-Italian relations.

Laval took measures to stall the imposition of oil sanctions and succeeded, ultimately, in preventing their adoption, preferring a compromise agreement between the adversaries. UK Foreign Minister Samuel Hoare and Laval began talks on 7 December. France's major response to the crisis was the Hoare-Laval plan, announced on 9 December. The plan called for three areas of Ethiopia, bordering Eritrea and Italian Somaliland, to be ceded to Italy, and a large section of southern Ethiopia to be set aside for exclusive Italian exploitation. Ethiopia was to receive a corridor to the sea and the port of Assab in Eritrea. The plan was uncovered by the press in Britain and published even before it was proposed to the belligerents. The subsequent backlash resulted in Hoare's resignation on 18 December 1935 and the fall of the Laval Government in France on 22 January 1936. On 3 March the new French Prime Minister was able to thwart the final attempt to impose oil sanctions against Italy in favor of an appeal to the belligerents for conciliation. Once the threat of effective League action was over, the crises for Italy and France ended. Hitler's reoccupation of the Rhineland on 7 March diverted League attention from Italy (see Case #18).

Meanwhile, war raged in Ethiopia and escalated with the Italian use of mustard gas, despite League disapproval. Ethiopia appealed to the League, other states and the world at large throughout April 1936. On 2 May Haile Selassie fled into exile through French Somaliland. On 5 May the capital, Addis Ababa, fell to Italy's forces, and Mussolini announced the end of the war and Italian annexation of Ethiopia.

The United States passed the Second Neutrality Act on 29 February 1936, in response to the recommendations for oil sanctions against Italy.

References   Baer 1967; Boca 1969; Carr 1945; Cassels 1968; Chabad 1963; Eden 1962; Feis 1947; Garratt 1938; Haile Selassie 1976; Hallett 1974; Kirkpatrick 1964; Laurens 1967; Laval 1948; Lowe and Marzari 1975; Schaefer 1961; Schuman 1942; Sik 1970; Torres 1941; Villari 1956; Walters 1960; Young 1976; Zimmern 1935.

(17) Marañon I   The first Peru crisis over Marañon lasted from 1 to 30 November 1935.

Background   Ecuador and Peru began to dispute the limits of their territorial inheritances from Spain as early as 1830 when Ecuador became an independent state. The Marañon is an area of 120,000 square miles on the Pacific Coast, lying between the Equator and the Javalry River, and between the Andes and Leticia. During the first hundred years of the dispute the conflict was carried on at three levels – diplomatic, military and demographic. During that time Peruvian settlers, traders and soldiers gradually extended the occupation of the Oriente region; the Ecuadorians maintained a few troops in outposts in the region. Some minor clashes occurred and, in 1910, mediation by the United States, Argentina and Brazil prevented the outbreak of war. In October 1932 there was a clash at the western end of the frontier.

Crisis   On 1 November 1935 Ecuadorian cavalry and police invaded the Peruvian province of Tumbes. The following day Peru delivered a protest note to Ecuador. The Peruvian Congress met in secret session on 13 November. Peru's major response, on the 14th, was to send strong reinforcements, including infantry and planes, to its garrison in Tumbes. Further protests were sent to Ecuador. The crisis terminated on 30 November when the Peruvian Foreign Minister announced that his country had invited Ecuador to submit the question of the disputed territory to arbitration. In 1941–42 the dispute over Marañon once again reached crisis proportions. (see Case #50).

References   Bowman 1942; Davis *et al.* 1977; Ireland 1938; Owens 1964; Veliz 1968; Wood 1966.

(18) Remilitarization of Rhineland

The crisis over Hitler's remilitarization of the Rhineland took place between 7 March and 16 April 1936. The actors were Belgium, Czechoslovakia, France, Poland, Romania, the UK and Yugoslavia.

Background

The international status of the Rhineland, an area separating Germany from France and Belgium, had been determined at Versailles at the end of World War I, and in the Locarno Pact of 1 December 1925. Germany was forbidden to maintain or construct any fortifications either on the left bank of the Rhine or on the right bank to a line drawn 50 kilometers to the east of the river. The Locarno Pact pledged Germany, France and Belgium to non-aggression and pacific settlement. It guaranteed established frontiers and the demilitarization of the Rhineland. If the Reich armed this demilitarized zone, France was legally authorized to declare it an unprovoked act of aggression, and Britain, Italy and Belgium would all be bound to come at once to France's aid. France had secured itself by alliances with Poland and the Little Entente states (Czechoslovakia, Romania and Yugoslavia) which had built their security against German aggressiveness upon these military alliances with France. The Germans claimed that France's 1935 military pact with the Soviet Union, exclusively directed against Germany, was a violation of the Locarno Pact. Hitler proceeded to fulfill his election promises when plans were laid for Germany's reoccupation of the Rhineland.

Crisis

On 7 March 1936 three German battalions entered and occupied the demilitarized zone of the Rhineland, triggering a crisis for Belgium, Czechoslovakia, France, Poland, Romania, the UK and Yugoslavia. The border countries, France and Belgium, had assumed since the end of World War I that the Rhineland would remain permanently demilitarized. Britain had formally obligated itself to protect them. Moreover, it had been a cornerstone of British foreign policy that a threat to France and Belgium was, by nature of their geographic proximity, also a threat to Great Britain. The Little Entente states and Poland, which were now obliged to act in France's defense, perceived their own safety and security to be threatened in the event of France's collapse. Each actor in the Rhineland Crisis sought a pacific solution which might condemn Germany overtly but at the same time allow for a negotiable settlement.

France responded immediately on 7 March with a Cabinet decision to act through the League and consult the Locarno guarantors in order to achieve a German withdrawal; a military solution was rejected as too dangerous. Czechoslovakia also responded that day with a declaration to conform its attitude exactly to that of France in every contingency. The following day Romania and Yugoslavia responded more reticently: they suggested to France that a peaceful solution to the crisis be sought, but refused to commit themselves in the event of a forceful confrontation with Germany or the imposition of economic sanctions. The British responded on 9 March with a Cabinet decision to consult with Hitler, the Locarno Powers and the League Council, in the hope of negotiating a coordinated compromise settlement. A military response and economic sanctions were rejected. On 10 March Belgium's response was contained in a statement by its Prime Minister that it would demand at least a partial restoration of the status quo. He intimated that economic sanctions should be used; but when it became clear that this was not viewed favorably by the other Locarno Powers it was withdrawn. That day, too, Poland declared that the Franco-Polish treaty covered unprovoked aggression against France proper, and as the remilitarization of the Rhineland did not fall into that category, it would not act forcefully in the present crisis or support economic sanctions against Germany.

Members of the League Council began meetings in London on 13 March. On 19 March all members of the Council, with the exception of Germany, endorsed a White Paper condemning German action in the Rhineland as a threat to European unity. The Council proposed the appointment of a committee to recommend measures to be adopted to safeguard peace. Tentative solutions were put forth concerning the partial withdrawal of German troops and the establishment of an international force in a new and narrow demilitarized zone of 20 kilometers between Germany, France and Belgium. They were rejected outright by Hitler who threatened that a punitive resolution by the League Council would be regarded by

Germany as an unfriendly act. This spectre of war, together with Italy's reluctance to cooperate and Germany's veto, finally paralyzed the League completely, and the Council meeting dissolved on 23 March 1936, terminating the crisis for Belgium, Czechoslovakia, Poland, Romania and Yugoslavia. The crisis for France and Great Britain lasted until 16 April as France continued to insist that Britain compensate it for the loss of security on its western border. On 2 April Britain had agreed to hold staff talks with the French on 15 and 16 April. These talks concluded the punitive phase of the crisis; and from that point on no further demands were made directly to Berlin over the Rhineland issue.

Involved in the Rhineland Crisis were the seven crisis actors, along with Germany, Italy and the Soviet Union. Italy, although a guarantor of the Locarno Pact, had moved away from the Western Powers in the ensuing decade and had developed closer ties with Germany. The Soviet Union did not depend upon France's military strength for its security. Indeed Soviet decision-makers perceived that, should the crisis lead to armed conflict, it would be located in Western Europe and would not affect the USSR. As for the US, Secretary of State Hull made it plain that he considered the Rhineland remilitarization to be a European development in which the United States was not involved.

A far-reaching effect of the Rhineland Crisis on Belgium was the termination of the Franco-Belgian treaty of 1920 and Belgium's formal declaration of neutrality in October 1936. More generally, Hitler's first major gamble in international politics succeeded: the Versailles powers acquiesced, paving the way for Munich (see Case #30) and, ultimately, the outbreak of World War II (see Case #38).

References Bullock 1962; Emmerson 1977; Mack-Smith 1981; Schuman 1942; Shirer 1964; Taylor 1966; Weinberg 1980.

(19) Spanish Civil War   The onset of a civil war in Spain set in motion a prolonged international crisis for Britain, France, Spain and the USSR, from 17 July 1936 until 28 March 1939.

Background   The ideological and clerical conflict in the 1920s and 1930s concerning democracy, communism and fascism was the background for the civil war in Spain. On 16 January 1936 a Popular Front was forged by the small Communist Party, the Socialists, the Left Republicans, the Republican Union, the Catalan Left and the Marxist POUM parties of Spain. The Anarcho-Syndicalists of Catalonia and Madrid did not join the Front, which was viewed by all conservatives with alarm. The Popular Front was dominated by middle-class liberals, the Communist elements adhering to a non-revolutionary line. In the general elections a month later the Popular Front won 265 seats of a total of 473. President Zamora was replaced by Manuel Azăna, but reform made slow progress. Strikes, anti-clerical demonstrations and chaos prevailed. The Communists opposed immediate socialization of land and nationalization of industry in favor of a more disciplined evolution. The Socialists promoted a form of proletarian rule. The wealthy and titled saw symptoms of incipient social revolution and secretly mobilized to overthrow the Popular Front. In April 1936 Hans Hellermann became the leader of Spain's Nazi Party which consisted largely of German nationals. By July moral and material help from Italy, Germany and Portugal was being received regularly by the Fascist conspirators. The revolt was to begin in Spanish Morocco and move on the capital Madrid. It began on 16 July.

Crisis   The uprising on the Spanish mainland began on 17 July 1936 and triggered a crisis for Republican Spain. The following day inquiries were made as to the scope of the rebellion and orders were given to the remaining loyal troops in Spanish Morocco to resist. The news of initial Fascist success on 18 July triggered a crisis for the Soviet Union which feared that a Fascist regime in Spain would change the European power balance to the USSR's detriment and Germany's and Italy's favor. Spain's major response, on 19 July, was an order from Prime Minister Giral y Pereira to arm the CNT (Trade Union of the Anarchist Party) and the UGT (General Union of Workers, led by the Spanish Socialist Party, later under Communist control). Giral perceived that these unions formed the only possible effective resistance to the Fascist rebellion which was spreading throughout the country. He ordered the trade unions to enter into active combat against the rebels while appealing to Premier Leon Blum of France to send arms and planes. That day General Franco took command of the Moors and Spain's Foreign Legion.

Giral's appeal to Paris on 20 July triggered a crisis for France which decided to send aid immediately to Republican Spain. The UK crisis was triggered on 30 July when it perceived German and Italian involvement in the civil war in Spain. Italian aircraft en route to Spain were forced to land in Algeria. The major British response, on 2 August, was a unilateral declaration of non-intervention in the Spanish Civil War and the banning of arms to Spain. France followed suit on 8 August. By that time the rebels held the Spanish colonies, the southern coast between Gibraltar and Portugal and some areas in the northwest. On 29 September 1936 the rebel National Defense Council installed Franco in the Palace at Salamanca and named him Head of Government and Generalissimo of the Nationalists' land, sea and air forces.

The Soviets, who had been sending arms and military advisors to Republican Spain but no army units, responded on 4 October by organizing International Brigades of volunteer forces and simultaneously sending an official letter from Stalin to the leader of the Communist Party of Spain expressing support for the Republican regime. Spain's premiership passed to Largo Caballero and then Juan Negrin on 16 May 1937, while the anarchists and Trotskyites were crushed in a bloody rebellion in Barcelona. The Communist "Fifth Regiment" became the model of the People's Army because of its discipline. Thousands of anti-Fascist Italians, Germans, Frenchmen, Americans, Canadians and Britons joined the Republican cause as volunteers in the International Brigades, while their governments declared non-intervention or provided active support to Franco. This, despite a strongly-worded League of Nations Resolution of 29 May, calling for the immediate and complete withdrawal of all foreigners fighting in Spain.

On 23 July 1937 Germany and Italy withdrew from the international naval patrol, which had been set up by members of the Committee on Non-Intervention in April of that year. The Anglo-French naval patrol failed to prevent foreign intervention in the Spanish Civil War because Britain's and France's primary motive was to avoid hostilities with Germany and Italy while pursuing their basic policy of non-intervention. Italy was given a zone off the Mediterranean to patrol, which enabled it to continue sending supplies to the Nationalists in Majorca. By the autumn of 1937 German intervention was somewhat reduced; but Italian forces were operating on a greater scale than ever.

On 15 April 1938 Franco's forces had reached the sea at Vinaroz, thereby cutting off Catalonia from the rest of Republican Spain. On 26 May the Non-Intervention Committee accepted a plan for counting and evacuating volunteers from Spain. By 30 September 1938 the crisis ended for the Soviet Union with the beginning of gradual friendship with Hitler and the decision to withdraw the last of the foreign volunteers in the International Brigades from Spain.

In November 1938 Nazi Germany sent massive arms shipments to Franco which enabled him to launch the Catalonian campaign. This offensive in December 1938 was decisive in finally defeating Republican Spain. Spain's response to this intra-war crisis took the form of resistance to the Fascist offensive on 26 December 1938.

The crisis for Britain and France ended on 27 February 1939 when they simultaneously recognized Franco's regime. On 28 March Madrid finally fell to the Generalissimo's troops, ending both the Republican regime and the crisis for Spain.

The League of Nations began a series of discussions on Spain in 1936. In 1938 a resolution could not be formally passed because of the absence of unanimity. The League was appointed to supervise the withdrawal of volunteers, but it did not contribute to crisis abatement.

References Cameron and Stevens 1973; Churchill 1948; Ciano 1947; Delzell 1970; Deutscher 1949; van der Esch 1951; Payne 1963; Schuman 1942; Thomas 1961; Walters 1960; Wiskemann 1966.

(20) Alexandretta

A lengthy international crisis over Alexandretta began on 9 September 1936 and lasted until 23 June 1939, with France as a crisis actor five times during that period and Turkey once.

Background   The Sanjak of Alexandretta (later called Hatay) is an area between Turkey and Syria which became a part of France's Syria Mandate in 1921. The territory, which included a valuable harbor, had a large Turkish population and had been the subject of negotiation in 1926. In 1936 France began to arrange for the termination of its Syrian Mandate. Turkey considered the Sanjak and port of Alexandretta important to its security and objected to Arab (Syrian) rule over Turks. France maintained that separating Hatay from Syria would mean its dismemberment. In addition, as guardian of the area, France could not risk loss of reputation and prestige among other states. On the other hand, events in Europe preoccupied France and it later looked to Turkey as a potential ally against Germany and Italy, or, at least, as a neutral state.

Crisis   On 9 September 1936 a crisis was triggered for Turkey by the publication of the contents of the Treaty of Alliance between France and Syria which identified the Sanjak of Alexandretta as part of Syrian territory. The major Turkish response was a promise by President Atatürk to his nation, in a speech on 2 November, that Hatay would be returned to Turkey. The matter was brought before the League of Nations by Turkey's Foreign Minister, who also expressed a willingness to enter into direct negotiations with France. On 7 January 1937 the Turks moved troops to the border triggering a crisis for France. France responded on the 22nd by resuming talks with Turkey and welcoming League intervention. On the 27th both agreed to an autonomous government for the region, and the first crisis over Alexandretta ended for Turkey and France.

The manner in which the first agreement was reached encouraged Turkey to reopen the issue. On 3 June 1937 it again sent troops to the border when the French imposed a curfew in Alexandretta because of local disturbances. This triggered a second crisis for France, which responded on the 7th with an agreement to hold direct negotiations in Paris. The matter was brought to the League of Nations by France and Turkey, and an electoral law for the Sanjak was drafted. A Treaty of Amity was signed by the adversaries on 4 July 1937, ending the second crisis for France.

Turkey, still dissatisfied, threatened France with war on 29 October 1937 if new demands for changes in the electoral regulations for the Sanjak were not met. On 16 December 1937 France once more opened negotiations with Turkey and agreed to the demands on 29 January 1938, ending France's third crisis over Alexandretta. On 4 June 1938 Turkey raised its demands to include participation in the military control of the Sanjak and moved its 7th Division from its base at Adana towards the frontier. That day France responded by holding talks with the Turkish Ambassador in Paris. Further negotiations were carried out on 13 June, and the French Cabinet instructed General Huntziger to yield. On 4 July 1938 another Treaty of Friendship was signed between France and Turkey.

On 5 April 1939 a rumor of Turkish annexation was strengthened by Turkish military maneuvers in the Sanjak and a further concentration of troops near the border. France reacted the same day by dispatching a warship to the area and strengthening its troop positions. Turkey demanded the cession of Hatay. Finally, on 23 June 1939, the crisis as a whole ended with a Declaration of Mutual Assistance and an agreement for the final transfer of Hatay to Turkey.

The matter was first brought to the League Council on 7 January 1937. During the course of the crisis the League drafted the Statute of the Sanjak, governing its relations with a future Government of Syria, and the Fundamental Law of the Sanjak, including the Electoral Law. It also sent a commission and observers, but withdrew them on 26 June 1938. The League Commission drafted the Electoral Law and fixed a date for the elections. Elections were not held under League supervision but under Turkish and French military control. Britain pressured France to end the conflict and to yield to Turkey. Protests were made about French concessions to Turkey by Italy, Yugoslavia and Iraq.

References   Clough 1970; Hourani 1946; Kayali 1976; Kilic 1959; Longrigg 1958; Shaw and Shaw 1977; Tamkov 1976; Tibawi 1969; Vere-Hodge 1950; Walters 1960; Ziadeh 1957.

(21) Amur River Incident A crisis between Japan and the USSR took place from 22 June to 4 July 1937.

Background The issue of sovereignty over several small islands in the Amur River between the Soviet Union and Japanese-controlled Manchuria had long been in dispute: the crisis in 1937 was the 185th incident of its kind along this border. Between August 1936 and June 1937 a series of political trials and severe purges took place in the Soviet Union. Some persons who stood trial were executed because of alleged espionage on behalf of the Japanese. Many of the top-ranking Soviet officers stationed in the Far Eastern territories were removed. *Inter alia*, the Japanese wished to test Soviet strength and determination, as well as its readiness for war. On 19 June 1937 a small number of Soviet troops entered the two islets of Sennufu and Bolshoi on the Amur and abducted some gold-miners. The same day Soviet gunboats, which routinely patrolled the area, engaged Manchukuon forces.

Crisis On 22 June Japan's General Staff received reports of Soviet military occupation of the disputed islands. The Japanese responded on the 24th with an order to concentrate troops in the area and a protest to the Soviet Consul-General at Harbin. The trigger to the crisis for the Soviet Union, on 28 June, was a demand, delivered by the Japanese Ambassador in Moscow, that all Soviet forces be evacuated from the islands. On 29 June the Japanese bombed and sank a Soviet gunboat, apparently at the initiative of the local field commander. That day Soviet negotiators indicated a willingness to remove their troops and, on 2 July, the USSR announced that it would comply with Japanese demands. The crisis ended for both actors on 4 July, with the Soviet evacuation of the islands. Four days later the Sino-Japanese War broke out.

References Hane 1972; MacNair and Lach 1955; Morley 1976; Vinacke 1959; See also sources for Case #36.

(22) Marco Polo Bridge The crisis for China and Japan arising from the Marco Polo Bridge incident began on 8 July 1937 and terminated on 16 January 1938.

Background The civil-military conflict in Japan throughout the 1930s was reflected in its foreign policy behavior. The lines between official government policy and policy emanating from field commanders or other military decision-makers were often blurred. Five different Japanese decision-making groups operated simultaneously: the emperor; the civil government; the General Staff in Tokyo; the Kwantung Army Headquarters in Manchuria; and the local field commanders. Since the Mukden Incident of 1931 (see Case #4), Japanese forces had strengthened their grip over Manchuria/Manchukuo and over areas in North China. Japanese garrisons, with China's agreement, had been positioned in locations bordering Peking (Beijing) and were carrying out maneuvers. The Marco Polo Bridge, near Lukouchiao, served two important railways. On the evening of 7 July the Japanese were attacked by Chinese troops. The Japanese commander immediately demanded entry into the neighboring town of Wanping to search for one of his soldiers allegedly captured by the Chinese forces. He was refused entry.

Crisis The trigger for China occurred on 8 July when a reinforced Japanese army unit attacked Chinese forces. China's response, the next day, was to send additional forces to the area to assist the 29th and 37th Chinese divisions stationed there. When the Japanese authorities received reports of the heavy reinforcements moving into the area on 9 July, a crisis was triggered for Japan. Heavy bombardment of Chinese forces ensued. Japan's major response, on the 11th, was to dispatch units of the Kwantung Army, as well as forces stationed in Korea, to the Honan-Hopei border region, into which hostilities had already spread.

Several unsuccessful attempts at a diplomatic settlement, headed by Germany's Trautmann Mission, were made in October. Soon after the initial clashes at Lukouchiao, the two countries were fighting a full-scale war. Points of escalation in the crisis coincide with the history of military campaigns in the Sino-Japanese War.

On 13 December 1937 Nanking fell, terminating China's crisis but not the prolonged Sino-Japanese conflict and only the first stage of their war. This crisis ended for Japan on 16 January 1938 when Japan's Prime Minister stated that Japan would no longer recognize the Chinese Goverment and would now attempt to set up Japanese regimes in different areas of China. The war raged on until the Japanese surrender in 1945.

There were two League of Nations Assembly resolutions, on 28 September and 6 October 1937, which condemned Japanese bombing of several cities in China. Unsuccessful attempts to find a solution were made: by Britain, at the Brussels Conference of November 1937; by France, with a 14 July 1937 statement in favor of peaceful resolution; by Italy, with a similar statement on 21 July; and by Germany, through the Trautmann Mission, which began on 28 October 1937. The US was politically involved through the Roosevelt Quarantine Speech on 5 October. The USSR, which had signed a Treaty of Non-Aggression with China, supplied it with military equipment.

References See sources for Case #21.

(23) Postage Stamp Crisis A postage stamp issued by Nicaragua showing a map of its territory including considerable parts of southeast Honduras created a crisis for both countries from mid-August to 10 December 1937.

Background The boundary between Nicaragua and Honduras had not been settled since 1869, despite several attempts to do so, the last in 1931.

Crisis During the second week of August 1937 Nicaragua issued a postage stamp bearing a map of the Republic which included a considerable part of southeastern Honduras, marked as being "territory in dispute." This triggered a crisis for Honduras, which protested this "affront to her sovereignty" on the 25th. On 30 August Honduras' major response was concentration of military forces along the Nicaraguan border. The possibility of military hostilities triggered a crisis for Nicaragua. Its response, on 3 September, was a refusal to withdraw the stamp, declaring it to be the official map of Nicaragua.

Armed hostilities were prevented by the mediation of Costa Rica, Venezuela and the United States. On 10 December 1937 the two crisis actors signed a Pact of Reciprocal Agreement at San José in Costa Rica, terminating the crisis. The conflict flared up again in 1957 (see Case #121).

References Ireland 1938; Mecham 1961.

(24) Haiti/Dominican Republic A crisis for Haiti began on 5 October 1937 and terminated on 31 January 1938.

Background The Haitian economy had been seriously affected by the Great Depression in the United States, and large numbers of Haitian cane-cutters migrated to the neighboring Dominican Republic, and to Cuba. During 1936 and 1937 a plot by Trujillo, the ruler of the Dominican Republic, to undermine the Goverment of Haiti was uncovered. Both countries had signed the General Convention of Inter-American Conciliation in 1929. When most of the sugar mills in Trujillo's Dominican Republic and Batista's Cuba closed down, the Haitians sought work in other fields. On 2 October 1937 Trujillo declared that Haitian trespassers would no longer be tolerated, while indicating that the slaughter of 300 Haitians which began the day before at Banica would continue. That evening Trujillo ordered a new massacre of Haitian nationals in the vicinity of the Dominican Republic/Haiti border, which continued until 4 October.

Crisis Haitian President Vincent received word of the massacres on 5 October 1937. On the 10th a Note was delivered to the Dominican Republic expressing President Vincent's doubts that the Government of the Dominican Republic could have associated itself with these events and requesting investigation and compensation. An official joint declaration between the two countries in Washington on 23 October stated that relations between them had not been impaired. Nevertheless, as domestic unrest grew, and both countries began concentrating troops at the border, Haitian decision-makers perceived a threat of a Dominican Republic invasion. On 12 November Haiti's major response was to request US, Mexican and Cuban mediation. The Dominican Republic at first refused to cooperate with the commission set up by the three mediating countries, claiming that the magnitude of the dispute did not warrant mediation. On 18 December, four days after Vincent invoked the 1928 Pact and the use of a mediating commission, Trujillo consented to mediation. Negotiations were carried on directly, as well as through meetings in Washington, diplomatic channels, and the good offices of the Pope. Trujillo agreed to the draft settlement with minor revisions; and it was accepted and signed by both countries on 31 January 1938, ending their crisis.

The Haitian Goverment's request to invoke the Inter-American Convention for Conciliation was within the framework of the Pan American Union. The mediation undertaken by the regional organization's commission consisting of representatives from Argentina, Guatemala and Peru, was very effective in abating the crisis and contributed to more rapid termination.

References   Crassweller 1966; Diedrich and Burt 1969; Hicks 1968; Mecham 1961.

(25) Panay Incident   The sinking of the USS *Panay* near Nanking caused a crisis for the United States from 12 to 26 December 1937.

Background   The Sino-Japanese conflict resulted in a mounting threat to the treaty rights and interests of Great Britain, France and the United States in China. On 27 November 1937, as the fighting between the Chinese and Japanese armies drew close to the city of Nanking, US Ambassador Johnson moved most of his staff to Hankow. The few US officials remaining in the capital were to be evacuated by the US gunboat *Panay*, which had been ordered to stand by. On 9 December Embassy personnel boarded the USS *Panay* and, three days later, it docked about 28 miles above Nanking, along with three Standard Oil Co. tankers.

Crisis   A crisis for the United States was triggered on 12 December 1937 when Japanese planes bombed and sank the *Panay*, along with three Standard Oil Co. ships. Japan's Foreign Minister, Hirota, expressed his apologies to the US Ambassador in Japan. In Washington, Japan's Ambassador, Saito, did likewise to Secretary of State Hull. President Roosevelt responded the following day with a message to Tokyo via Secretary Hull, expressing shock at the indiscriminate bombings and requesting that the Emperor be informed of the President's response. Hull urged that Tokyo extend a full expression of regret and compensation. Further, the US demanded guarantees from Japan that such incidents would not occur again.

As reports from China indicated that the Japanese attacks had been deliberate, indignation grew in Washington. On 17 December the US Cabinet met, and strong action was proposed by several members, especially Secretary of the Navy Claude Swanson. Roosevelt expressed concern at Chinese reaction if the assault went unrebuked, and asserted that a stronger response was necessary in order to foil a Japanese plan to force all Westerners out of Japan. An economic blockade was suggested, but no decision made.

On 23 December a US Board of Inquiry reported that the shelling of the *Panay* seemed to have been deliberate and premeditated. The following day, Hirota handed US Ambassador Grew a Note admitting responsibility, offering amends and giving assurances against reoccurrence of such an incident. The crisis ended for the United States with its formal acceptance of the Japanese Note of 26 December. The Roosevelt Administration expressed satisfaction with Japan's apology and the latter's agreement to all US demands.

Toward the end of the crisis a US naval officer was sent to London for technical discussions which would apply in the event that both countries declared war on Japan.

References Borg 1964; Craigie 1946; Grew 1953; Hull 1948; Ickes 1974; Jones 1954; Lee 1973.

(26) Anschluss

The *Anschluss* Crisis between Austria and Germany took place between 12 February and 14 March 1938.

Background Relations between Germany and Austria, after the 1934 *Putsch* attempt (see Case #10), had been governed by the Agreement of July 1936. The interpretation of that agreement, however, was marked by wide differences of opinion on the part of the two states. The Government of Austria hoped to work these out in a meeting with Hitler. Accordingly, on the evening of 11 February 1938 Chancellor Schuschnigg left for Germany accompanied by his Secretary of Foreign Affairs.

Crisis The crisis for Austria began on 21 February 1938 when Hitler presented Schuschnigg with an ultimatum: the Austrian Government was to recognize the Nazi Party and National Socialism as perfectly compatible with loyalty to Austria; the Minister of the Interior would be the Nazi, Seyss-Inquart; an amnesty for all imprisoned Austrian Nazis was to be proclaimed within three days; and dismissed Nazi officials and officers would be reinstated. Finally, the Austrian economy was to be assimilated to that of Germany, and Fischboek was to be appointed Minister of Finance. The Austrian Chancellor signed the papers agreeing to Hitler's demands the same day.

By the end of the first week of the crisis Schuschnigg had decided upon some action to ensure the Austrian Goverment's mastery of its own house. He called for a plebiscite on 13 March in which the Austrian people would be invited to declare whether or not they were in favor of an independent Austria.

The crisis trigger for Germany occurred on 9 March when Hitler was informed of Austria's plans to hold a plebiscite. A surprised Führer, furious at this obstruction of his plans, responded the next day with a decision to invade Austria. A special messenger was sent to Mussolini asking him not to interfere. By the 11th German Army trucks and tanks were already on their way south. Schuschnigg offered to delay the plebiscite, but Goering demanded his resignation and the appointment of Seyss-Inquart as Chancellor. President Miklas at first refused to do so, but at midnight on 11 March he complied as preparations for a German invasion of Austria proceeded seriously. On 13 March Seyss-Inquart secured the passage of a law by the Austrian Government annexing Austria to the Third Reich. On the 14th the crisis ended for both actors when Hitler made his triumphal visit to Vienna. This was accompanied by strong anti-Semitic demonstrations.

While Austria had no illusions about Britain's and France's willingness to act in its favor, it perceived that opposition by Italy might serve as a deterrent to Hitler. When Italy refused to take any action against Germany, Austrian decision-makers had no choice but to comply with Hitler's demands.

References Bullock 1962; Edmondson 1978; Gedye 1939; Gehl 1963; von Papen 1952; Schuman 1942; Shirer 1964; Villari 1956; Weinberg 1980.

(27) Polish Ultimatum

A Polish ultimatum created a crisis for Lithuania from 13 to 19 March 1938.

Background The city of Vilna, which had been awarded to Lithuania after World War I, was occupied by Polish irregular forces since 1920, as ratified by the Conference of Ambassadors. Vilna was annexed to Poland in 1922. An intense campaign was carried out by Lithuania to retrieve Vilna, its capital in medieval times, including a refusal to conduct diplomatic or commercial relations with Poland. In 1936 the Polish Foreign Minister failed in his attempt to restore relations with Lithuania through the League of Nations. Lithuania refused to have its Vilna claim set aside and was willing to open only river traffic and communications, as well as consular facilities. Minority and frontier incidents contributed to the animosity between the two countries. In February 1937 the visit of the Soviet Chief of Staff to Lithuania was followed by rumors of Soviet support for Lithuania's position, but these were denied. The incidents on the border were dealt with by local authorities within the framework of the 1928 Lithuanian–Polish agreement on frontier traffic. On the night of 10–11 March 1938 a Polish soldier was killed by Lithuanian frontier guards. Lithuania proposed solving the incident by a mixed commission of local authorities.

Crisis A crisis for Lithuania was triggered on 13 March when the Polish Government rejected the Lithuanian proposal and issued an official communiqué referring to a pending decision on steps for dealing with the situation existing between Poland and Lithuania. Rumors of Polish military action began to spread through Europe, which indeed had been Poland's initial intention. When Polish Foreign Minister Beck returned to the Cabinet the following day, the military option was postponed. On 17 March Poland handed an ultimatum to the Lithuanian Minister to Estonia. It demanded the restoration of normal relations by 31 March and gave the Lithuanian Government 48 hours to reply. Vilna was not mentioned. The Lithuanian Cabinet met all night, and Parliament was summoned. German advice was sought and that country, having an interest in Memel, counselled Lithuania to accept the Polish demands. German forces moved to the border. The UK and France also advocated Lithuanian compliance. The Lithuanian response on 19 March, to accept the ultimatum, also constituted the termination of its crisis. In subsequent months diplomatic relations and road and rail communications were reestablished. This was followed by a period of relative harmony between the two states. The League of Nations was minimally involved, advising Poland to be reasonable and Lithuania to accept Polish terms. The Soviet Union, while refusing to supply military aid, supported Lithuania by informing Poland that Moscow reserved the right to take action in the event of a Polish attack on Lithuania.

References Cienciala 1968; Gerutis 1969; Walters 1960.

(28) Czech May Crisis The threat of German military hostilities against Czechoslovakia created a crisis for Czechoslovakia, France, Germany and the UK from 19 to 23 May 1938.

Background The determination of Poland and Czechoslovakia to uphold the European status quo as laid down by the Versailles Treaty was opposed by Nazi Germany, which wished to change it in its favor. Britain and France were amenable to changes provided they were not accompanied by military action. In defiance of the Versailles Treaty, Hitler had remilitarized the Rhineland (see Case #18) and was rearming Germany. Austria was annexed to the Reich in March 1938 (see #26). And the widespread perception of Hitler's objectives, the attainment of self-determination for the Germans in the Sudetenland, with the ultimate intent to annex that predominantly German part of Czechoslovakia to the Reich, was reinforced by speeches made by Hitler. The Sudeten Nazi Party, under Konrad Henlein, received open support from Germany. Henlein broke off negotiations with the Czech Government and was present in Berlin during the critical days of the crisis. Elections in the Sudetenland had been scheduled for 22 May, and there was a heightening of turbulence in the area.

Crisis A crisis for Czechoslovakia, France and the UK was triggered on 19 May 1938 when intelligence sources reported that Germany was concentrating troops in Saxony, near the Czech border. These troops were, in fact, carrying out a combined army and air military game near and on the Koenigsbrück military training ground. Czechoslovakia responded on the 20th by declaring a state of emergency and partial mobilization. Britain's and France's response, on 21 May, took the form of strong warnings to Germany, with threats of intervention should Germany attack Czechoslovakia. Hitler, who apparently had no intention of invading Czechoslovakia in the immediate future, was surprised by the Czech response, as well as by the other actors, and perceived them as a threat to Germany. The German response was a decision by its War Council to retreat, as the *Wehrmacht* was not yet ready to meet the British–French–Czech challenge. On 23 May the Czech Ambassador to

Berlin was assured that Nazi Germany had no aggressive intentions towards his country, and the crisis ended for all the participants. The underlying conflict, however, continued unabated and reached a further stage of crisis four months later – the Munich Crisis (see Case #30). There was no USSR intervention in the May weekend crisis. Nor was its aid solicited by Britain and France, despite the fact that the Soviet Union had an alliance with France and Czechoslovakia concerning the latter's independence and territorial integrity.

References   Beloff 1947–49; Braddick 1968–69; Bullock 1962; Butler and Sloman 1975; Schuman 1942; Shirer 1964; Taylor 1979; Wheeler-Bennett 1964.

(29) Changkufeng Incident

A crisis between Japan and the USSR over an incident at Lake Hasan occurred between 13 July and 11 August 1938.

Background   Both Soviet and Japanese border garrisons had been posted in the area of Lake Hasan (Changkufeng) on the Soviet–Manchukuo frontier since the initial Japanese occupation of Manchuria in 1931. Due to the complex terrain there were many areas where the frontier was not clear, including the Changkufeng hill area. In October 1937 there had been a minor clash in the vicinity, but Changkufeng itself was not involved. On 7 July 1938 local Japanese commanders received information of Soviet intentions to occupy the area, and on 11 July about 40 Soviet soldiers appeared atop Changkufeng and began construction of new fortified positions.

Crisis   On 13 July, Imperial Headquarters in Tokyo perceived a crisis for Japan when they received information attesting to Soviet occupation of, and activity at, Changkufeng. The Korean Army Headquarters were also informed on that day. Both armies were preparing for a major campaign at Hangchow in the Sino-Japanese War, and their respective headquarters did not wish an escalation of the situation near Lake Hasan. The Japanese local commanders, seemingly acting independently, met the Soviet activity with military force. The major fighting began on 27 July, but there was no evidence to suggest official sanction by either a supreme military or civil decision-making body in Japan.

On 29 July the Soviets crossed the frontier at Shatsofeng, near Changkufeng, and began to construct positions there. On 31 July the Soviet Union perceived a crisis when its forces were involved in heavy fighting. The Soviets responded with a major counter-attack on 2 August, the same day that Japan's major response occurred: the Japanese Cabinet decided to settle the dispute through negotiation. Indeed, Japan's civilian authorities had been endeavoring to remove any possibility of further military clashes by ordering the withdrawal of Japanese troops from the area. Between 4 and 11 August Ambassador Shigemitsu and Foreign Affairs Commissar Litvinov met to discuss the possibilities of peaceful settlement. By 7 August heavy artillery pieces were being employed by the Soviet forces as fighting continued. On 10 August Litvinov proposed a truce, which came into effect the following day, 11 August, terminating the crisis for both actors.

References   See sources for Case #36.

(30) Munich

The Munich Crisis – for Britain, Czechoslovakia, France and the USSR – took place from 7 September to early October 1938.

Background   The annexation of Austria by Germany in March 1938 (see Case #26) created an immediate threat to Czechoslovakia, which feared that its German-speaking areas would be Hitler's next target. Czechoslovakia sought assurances from France and Britain which refused to give firm guarantees. In April Anglo-French leaders met in London to seek a solution to the problem. In order to avoid the possibility of war with Hitler, the two great powers began to press Czechoslovakia to make concessions over the Sudetenland. In the third week of May rumors reached Prague that large German military forces were gathering near the frontier in Silesia and northern Austria, possibly in preparation for an operation against Czechoslovakia (see Case #28). The activity of the Sudeten German Party (SdP), which was strongly supported by Germany, was intensified. Its leader, Konrad Henlein, presented the party's demands in the Karlsbad Programme on 7 June. In June, July and August there was an intensification of SdP activity. On 18 July the British Government decided to send a mediator to Prague and, on 3 August, Lord Runciman arrived. A "Third Plan" was presented by the Czechoslovak Government on 24 August which proposed a compromise between its original proposals over the Sudetenland and the SdP's demands. As tension in the country built up, Runciman came up with a "Fourth Plan" between 3 and 7 September, leaning strongly towards the earlier Sudeten German demands. The Nazi Party Congress convened at Nuremberg on 5 September.

Crisis   On 7 September 1938 tension in Czechoslovakia escalated when 82 members of the Sudeten German Party were detained in Moravska Ostrava for arms smuggling and other offences against the state. The SdP, for its part, charged the Czech police with violence, and Hitler ordered Henlein to break off all negotiations with the Czechs. That day, too, the *Times of London* published a leading article supporting the "Fourth Plan" as the solution to the Sudeten problem. The arrests on 7 September, which had effectively laid to rest any hope of reaching a compromise solution through the Runciman Mission, triggered a crisis for Czechoslovakia. This was followed by almost daily demonstrations accompanied by acts of violence by the SdP. On the 9th President Beneš addressed the Czech people and attempted to win good will for the "Fourth Plan".

On 12 September a crisis was triggered for Britain and France when Hitler addressed the Nazi Party Congress and demanded self-determination for the Sudeten Germans. That evening riots began in the Sudeten districts. The French and British responses came the following day: British Prime Minister Chamberlain cabled Hitler that he was willing to travel to Germany to seek a solution to the crisis. That day, too, French Premier Daladier requested Chamberlain to arrange a Three-Power Conference to allow the transfer of Sudetenland to Germany. Several French economic and financial decrees were prepared, as well, in case of war. On 15 September Chamberlain met with Hitler at Berchtesgaden. He returned the next day, bringing to his colleagues and the French Government Hitler's plan for the cession of the Sudeten districts to Germany. Anglo-French discussions began in London on 18 September to work out a proposal which Chamberlain could bring to Hitler at their forthcoming meeting in Godesberg.

The Anglo-French Plan, announced on the 19th, called for the immediate transfer to Germany of Sudeten areas with over 50% German inhabitants and the acceptance by Czechoslovakia of a neutralized status, which would require the abrogation of its treaties with the USSR and France. That day a crisis was triggered for the Soviet Union when President Beneš requested USSR affirmation of the Soviet–Czech Pact. The Soviets responded the same day by affirming the Pact on condition of prior French action. On 20 September Czechoslovakia rejected the Anglo-French Plan, but on the 21st Prague reversed its decision and accepted the Plan, after having been served an ultimatum by both Britain and France.

The Godesberg meeting between Hitler and Chamberlain took place on 22 and 23 September. The German leader increased his demands and served an ultimatum for the territorial transfer by 1 October, the date originally set by Hitler in April. President Beneš ordered general mobilization in Czechoslovakia. On the 23rd the USSR warned Poland that it would denounce the Soviet–Polish Pact of Non-Aggression if the Polish Government persisted in sending troops to the Czech–Polish frontier. A partial mobilization in France was ordered on 24 September. On the 25th the British fleet and its auxiliary airforce units were mobilized. Hitler spoke at the *Sportspalast* on the 26th, stating that the Czechs would have to come to terms peaceably with their non-German minorities. Chamberlain sent a message to Hitler that Britain would support France if it were drawn into war over Czechoslovakia. A final appeal to Britain to avoid war was sent by Hitler on the 27th. A conference among Italy, France, Germany and Britain was called.

The signing of the Four-Power Agreement at Munich on 30 September 1938 terminated the crisis for Britain and France. Czechoslovakia was forced to accept the terms. War with Germany had been temporarily avoided. The Soviet termination date was sometime in October, once German troops were in occupation of all the German-claimed territories and war had been averted. Other involved actors were the US – President Roosevelt sent personal appeals on 26 and 27 September to all actors to refrain from the use of force, and Italy – Mussolini attempted on the 28th to aid in the achievement of a peaceful solution.

References See sources for Case #28, and: Bruegel 1973; Eubank 1965; Middlemas 1972; Robbins 1968; Shirer 1985.

(31) Italian Colonial Demands

A crisis for France over this issue began on 30 November 1938 and ended on 31 March 1939.

Background Differences between France and Italy were of long standing. France possessed an important trade route in East Africa through the railroad from Djibouti in Somaliland, where Italy's colonies of Eritrea and Italian Somaliland were located. Corsica, though Italian-speaking, was under French control. Rivalries existed as well over satellites in the post-Hapsburg Empire states of Eastern Europe. Italy's use of the Suez Canal in order to maintain contact with its East African colonies became a source of tension as its objections to the high French-imposed tolls increased. As for the balance of power in Europe, France looked to Italy as a potential ally against Hitler. On 14 April 1935 representatives from France, Italy and Great Britain met at Stresa and aligned themselves formally against Germany. Soon after the Wal-Wal Incident (see Case #12), France signed an agreement with Italy in which small areas were ceded and a settlement of the Italian minority problem in Tunisia was reached. During the Italian war with Ethiopia (see Case #16) France exerted considerable effort not to alienate Italy. When the League Council condemned Italy as the aggressor in Ethiopia in October 1935 French Prime Minister and Foreign Minister Laval was able to prevent the adoption of any substantive sanctions, specifically oil sanctions and the closure of the Suez Canal to Italian shipping. In the period after Italy's annexation of Ethiopia, France made further efforts to improve relations with Italy: it recognized the annexation, signed a commercial agreement on 7 November 1938 and accredited a new French Ambassador to the King of Italy–Emperor of Ethiopia.

Crisis A parliamentary upheaval during Foreign Minister Ciano's speech in Rome on 30 November 1938, which called for retribution over French control of Tunisia, Corsica, Nice, Savoy and Djibouti, turned into a street demonstration which Mussolini addressed from his balcony in the Palazzo Venezia, and triggered a crisis for France. To French protests in Paris and Rome, the reply was that the Italian Government could not be responsible for spontaneous demonstrations which did not reflect its views. An anti-French campaign was begun by the Italian press and, by 5 December, demonstrations and telegrams of support for France had come from Corsica and Tunisia. On 17 December the Italian Governent informed France that their bilateral agreement of January 1935 was now void and that France was obliged to produce new proposals. This was not divulged in Paris until 5 days later. France sent copies of the Italian Note to Germany and Britain and replied on 26 December that, as far as it was concerned, the 1935 Agreement was still intact but that there was a need for new proposals on French and Italian interests in Africa. France's major response, on 2 January 1939, was Prime Minister Daladier's departure for a visit to Corsica, Algeria and Tunisia, where he stated before cheering crowds that France would stand firm in all its territories in the face of any Italian demands or threats. France also reinforced its forces in Africa and in the Mediterranean. On 14 January Chamberlain and Halifax arrived in Rome for Anglo-Italian negotiations. Despite the request of the French Government for no intercession on the Franco-Italian dispute, some British intervention was attempted, but without success.

France and Italy continued to exchange demands and France repeated its intention to defend its territory. The crisis continued until 31 March, on the eve of Italy's invasion of Albania (see Case #35), when Mussolini stated that he would not press demands on France.

The issue did not die down, and throughout the war against Albania the Italian demands remained a source of dispute.

The United States cabled its support to France, while Great Britain and Germany supported Italy.

References Adamthwaite 1977; Carr 1945; Clough 1970; Ebenstein 1973; Nere 1975; Werth 1966.

(32) Czech Annexation

Germany's annexation of Czechoslovakia precipitated a crisis for that country on 14–15 March 1939.

Background The period between Munich and the annexation, October 1938 to March 1939, witnessed national and societal unrest in Czechoslovakia. Slovak and Ruthenian nationalities, supported by Germany and Hungary, were making increasing demands for independence. There was a rapid deterioration in Czechoslovakia's economic situation, apparently generated by the secession of important industrial areas of the Sudetenland and Teschen after September, as a result of the Munich Agreement. This economic and societal disruption formed the basis of Hitler's claim that, as Czechoslovakia was composed of different and dissatisfied nationalities precipitating social unrest which culminated in economic deterioration, it was in fact no longer a viable state. On 17 December 1938 Hitler, assuming no resistance, directed his armed forces to make preparations to occupy the rest of Czechoslovakia. This directive was followed by a final order on 12 March, at the height of the Slovak tension, for the invasion of Czechoslovakia and its incorporation into the Reich. The following day the Czech President, Emil Hacha, requested an interview with Hitler. On 14 March both Ruthenia and Slovakia proclaimed their independence from Czechoslovakia.

Crisis On the morning of 14 March Hitler informed Hacha that German troops had already occupied the important industrial town of Moravska Ostrava and that they were now poised all along the perimeter of Bohemia and Moravia. The crisis for Czechoslovakia had been triggered. Hitler, while ignoring the issue of Slovak independence, stated that, if the Czech President invited the entry of German troops, Czechoslovakia would be allowed to remain autonomous after incorporation into the Reich. If the Czech Army resisted, Czechoslovakia would be annihilated. Faced with this ultimatum, Hacha phoned his government in Prague early in the morning of the 15th and advised capitulation. After receiving their consent, he signed the note of surrender which had been drawn up earlier by the German Foreign Office. The crisis ended at 6 a.m. on 15 March, when German troops poured into Bohemia and Moravia. There was no resistance. The same day they entered Prague. A proclamation of Bohemia-Moravia and Slovakia as German protectorates followed.

The USSR took no action during the critical days of the crisis. Britain declared that its post-Munich guarantee of Czech territorial integrity and independence against unprovoked aggression was no longer applicable because the declaration of Slovak independence had put an end to the state whose frontiers London had promised to guarantee. An official protest from France was that country's only involvement in the crisis.

References Bullock 1962; Deutscher 1949; Mamatey 1973; Schuman 1942; Shirer 1964; Thorne 1967; Vital 1967.

(33) Memel

Germany's demand for the annexation of Memel created a crisis for Lithuania from 15 to 22 March 1939.

Background Memel and its surrounding area, once part of East Prussia, were awarded to Lithuania by the Versailles Treaty, under the supervision of a League High Commissioner, and was formally incorporated in 1923. The city, German-speaking, was made semi-autonomous on 7 May 1924 and was guaranteed by France, Great Britain, Italy and Japan. The surrounding area, Lithuanian-speaking, was placed under Lithuania's sovereignty. Increasing tension between the area's populations followed, especially after the Nazi accession to power in Berlin in 1933.

In 1934 many prominent Germans were arrested in Memel and were accused of planning a Nazi *putsch* there. The Germans retaliated by boycotting Lithuanian agricultural produce. By 1936 the situation had normalized, and a trade treaty was signed between the two countries. The Nazi Party, though illegal, grew in Memel, and more arrests took place in the late spring of 1937. Elections were due to be held in late 1938; and despite Lithuanian electoral law concessions, Nazi strength grew in Memel during the campaign, with the anticipation of a reintegration into Germany after the Austrian *Anschluss* of March 1938 (see Case #26). After the elections, German representation had improved to slightly over 80% of the Memel Diet. The new Lithuanian Government, formed in December 1938, endeavored to be firm on the issue of Memel's autonomy, while Nazification and demands for incorporation into the Reich continued and German pressure increased. In early March 1939 the German press took up a renewed anti-Lithuanian campaign. On the 13th the Lithuanian Prime Minister perceived the danger of a German coup in Memel and related this to the British chargé d'affaires: he anticipated an announcement at the forthcoming meeting of the Memel Diet.

Crisis   On 15 March, when Germany took over Bohemia and Moravia, the remnant of Czechoslovakia (see Case #32), a crisis over Memel was triggered for Lithuania. Nazi party leader Neumann addressed a special meeting of the Memel Diet, pressing for a radical change in the relations between Memel and Lithuania. Rumors of immediate Nazi annexation followed rapidly. At a meeting between the local Lithuanian Governor and German party leaders the Governor refused to consider any concessions. The following day his attitude became more conciliatory and a promise was made to convene the Diet on 25 March.

On 20 March Lithuanian Foreign Minister Urbsys was summoned to Berlin and was handed an ultimatum to return Memel to Germany. He was also warned not to consult any other power. Nonetheless, he spoke to the British, French and Polish Military Attachés, indicating that Lithuania's decision would depend on their willingness to provide aid. Upon his return to Kaunas, German troops were reported moving towards the frontier with Lithuania. Shortly thereafter, Germany demanded an agreement. The Lithuanian Cabinet met on 20 March and accepted the Ultimatum. Two communiqués, issued by Lithuania, were withdrawn upon German disapproval.

The crisis ended on 22 March with the formal approval of an agreement signed in Berlin. Hitler arrived in Memel the following day to an enthusiastic welcome. The agreement safeguarded Lithuanian economic access, a free harbor zone, and a pledge of non-aggression between the two countries. Britain, France and Poland, the other involved actors, denied aid to Lithuania.

References   Cienciala 1968; Gerutis 1969; Sabaliunas 1972; Schuman 1941; Shirer 1964; Walters 1960.

(34) Danzig

A crisis for Poland over Danzig took place between 21 March and 6 April 1939.

Background   The Treaty of Versailles declared Danzig, predominantly German-speaking, to be a free city. Poland was allowed to use the port, it being its only access to the sea. A strip of land lying east of Danzig and the local Polish provinces linked Germany with East Prussia. In 1934 Poland signed a Non-Aggression Pact with Germany, and in November 1937 Hitler officially disavowed his aim of incorporating Danzig into Germany.

On 4 October 1938 the Polish Ambassador in Berlin met with Foreign Minister Ribbentrop. The latter proposed incorporating Danzig into the Reich, granting an extraterritorial railroad and road into Germany, while leaving Poland to maintain a road, railway and free port in Danzig, and guaranteed markets, a recognition of boundaries and an extension of the Polish–German Pact. Poland would also join the Anti-Comintern Pact. Polish Foreign Minister Beck declined and insisted on retaining Polish rights to Danzig while proposing a joint Polish–German guarantee to replace League of Nations protection. On 21 October Hitler began to plan for military action over Danzig. Beck met with Hitler and Ribbentrop in Germany in early January 1939. After the final German takeover in Czechoslovakia (see Case #32) and Hitler's demand to Lithuania for Memel in March 1939 (see Case #33) the issue of Danzig flared up once again.

Crisis Poland's crisis was triggered on 21 March 1939 when Ribbentrop placed Germany's demand for Danzig before Polish Ambassador Lipski. The Polish Foreign Minister sought support against German aggression, especially from Britain, which was at that time trying to establish joint guarantees with France and the Soviet Union. On 21–22 March Anglo-French conversations took place in London. The addition of an economic threat to Romania by Germany induced the UK to try to reach an agreement with its ally for the support of the whole of Eastern Europe, including Polish aid to Romania, if necessary. On 26 March Poland responded to German demands by offering to consider simplifying road and rail communications to East Prussia and by rejecting any extraterritorial highway, as well as the annexation of Danzig to the Reich. Ribbentrop, mentioning Polish interests in the Ukraine, and hinting that Hitler might conclude that there could be no understanding with Poland, asked for further Polish consideration, to which Lipski agreed. Meanwhile, the UK continued to maneuver for a Four-Power declaration, while dropping the Soviet Union from the list, at Poland's request. Britain finally agreed upon a declaration of support for Poland while, at the same time, soliciting Polish support for Romania and Yugoslavia. On 31 March Chamberlain announced in the House of Commons that the UK would offer support to Poland if there was any threat to its independence, and that France had agreed to do likewise. On 3 April Beck journeyed to London for further talks, receiving an official guarantee on 6 April that the UK "would feel themselves bound at once to lend the Polish Government all support in their power." This terminated the crisis for Poland.

The Danzig Crisis of March-April 1939, like those over the German annexation of Czechoslovakia (Case #32), Memel (Case #33), and the Invasion of Albania (Case #35), was an integral part of the intense conflict throughout 1939 which was to culminate in the outbreak of World War II (Case #38). Danzig remained an important issue throughout the summer of 1939 as the city became semi-secretly militarized and war approached. On 1 September Germany invaded Poland.

The Soviet Union negotiated with Britain and France on forging a bloc against Germany, but backed away when other demands were not met by the Western powers. This encouraged Polish suspicions of Moscow's motives and potential actions in support of Germany.

References Bullock 1962; Carr 1945; Cienciala 1968; Debicki 1962; Polonsky 1972; Pounds 1964; Schuman 1941; Shirer 1964; Walters 1960.

(35) Invasion of Albania A crisis for Albania, Britain, France and Greece occurred between 25 March and 13 April 1939.

Background In 1928 a new constitution transformed Albania into a hereditary constitutional monarchy with Ahmed Zog crowned as King. Zog was given broad authority and ruled as a dictator until 1939. In the mid-1920s Albania had turned to Italy for economic and political support and, by the end of the decade, Albania had become an Italian vassal. During the 1930s, on several occasions, King Zog attempted to break away from Italy but was forced to back down when Italian diplomatic, economic and military pressure was applied. By 1938 the Italians had become impatient with Zog and looked for a way to assume direct control over the country.

Crisis A crisis for Albania was triggered on 25 March 1939 when Italy presented a treaty plan, in the form of an ultimatum, proposing the stationing of Italian troops in the main centers and on the frontiers of Albania, along with the full participation of the Italian Minister in Tirana in the Albanian Council of Ministers. The pact was rejected by King Zog and, at the beginning of April, he presented counter-proposals with new concessions. Mussolini was not placated. As Italian/Albanian negotiations were taking place, rumors spread about the completion of Italian military preparations for invasion, with the concentration of army and naval forces in southern Italy. Despite violent anti-Italian demonstrations throughout Albania, Zog issued a public declaration on 3 April denying the worsening of relations with Italy. Following a Cabinet meeting the next day the King indicated to the Greek Minister, then *Doyen* of the Diplomatic Corps, that Italian demands would mean control over all the essentials of Albanian life and the establishment of an Italian protectorate on Greece's borders. Representatives of Britain, France and the Balkan Entente were informed that Italian demands would be rejected by force. Also on the 4th, Mussolini set a deadline of 6 April for the acceptance of Italy's demands. Albania's major response, on the 6th, was a decision by the Council of Ministers to reject the Italian ultimatum; a negative reply was sent the same day. Preparations for resistance were made, including the distribution of arms.

Italian forces invaded Albania on 7 April, triggering a crisis for Britain, France and Greece. Britain, fearing that the situation might undermine its influence and the status quo in the Mediterranean, became concerned about a possible Italian invasion of Greece. France perceived the fall of Albania as a prelude to an Italian–German offensive from the North Sea to Egypt. And the Greek Government was convinced that, once Albania had been annexed, the Italians would invade Corfu.

The crisis for Albania ended on 8 April 1939 when the King and other Albanian officials fled to Greece. The Italians entered the capital that day. On the 9th Greek Prime Minister Metaxas informed the British Minister that the Italians intended to attack Corfu between 10 and 12 April. On the same day two Greek destroyers were manned and made ready for action.

An urgent meeting of the French National Defense Committee was held on 9 April where it was decided to move the French Atlantic Fleet to the Mediterranean, reinforcements to Tunis and French Somaliland, and to call up reservists. The British major response occurred on 11 April, after precautions had been taken in Malta, air services to Italy had been suspended, and military leaves cancelled. That day, at a meeting of the British Cabinet Foreign Policy Committee, a statement was drafted and approved, warning Italy that any aggression against Greek territory would be regarded as a threat to the vital interests of Great Britain.

The crisis for Britain, France and Greece ended on 13 April 1939. The British Prime Minister declared a guarantee of the independence of Greece and Romania. A similar guarantee was made by France's Premier Daladier the same day. These assurances, on 13 April, terminated the crisis for Greece as well. There was no League of Nations activity despite Albania's protest on 8 April. On 13 April the new Albanian puppet regime withdrew from the League.

References   Carr 1945; Ciano 1947; Clogg 1980; Knox 1982; Koliopoulos 1977; Pano 1968; Polo and Pato 1981; Schuman 1941; Shirer 1964; Taylor 1968; Walters 1960; Woodhouse 1968.

(36) Nomonhan

A crisis for the Soviet Union and Japan arising from an incident at Nomonhan occurred between 28 May and 15 September 1939.

Background   Nomonhan is an oasis in the Gobi Desert whose pastures have been used for centuries by Mongol nomads. The territory, partly under Japanese and partly under Soviet control in the 1930s, was inhabited by Mongols. Japanese troops were engaged as allies of Manchukuo, by virtue of the 1932 Japan–Manchukuo Treaty of Mutual Assistance; and Soviet forces were allies of Outer Mongolia under their 1936 Pact of Mutual Assistance. The Manchukuo Government claimed that the Khalha River was the boundary between Manchukuo and Outer Mongolia, whereas the Government of Mongolia declared the boundary lay a number of miles east of the river.

Crisis   On 28 May 1939 a clash took place on the Mongolia–Manchukuo border in which 39 Outer Mongolian planes were shot down and 150 Mongols killed. This triggered a crisis for the Soviet Union which perceived a territorial threat. Moscow warned

Japan on the 31st that the Soviet Union would defend Outer Mongolia's borders as if they were its own. A counter-attack by Soviet forces in the vicinity of Nomonhan on 18 June, accompanied by air attacks on key strategic points in the rear, triggered a crisis for Japan. The Japanese attacked again on 28 June. During July the Japanese Military Attaché in Moscow reported that the Soviets were sending reinforcements to the Far East and that a new offensive was expected around the middle of August. It was thought that Japanese strength in the area would be sufficient to halt an enemy offensive. Fighting continued throughout July; the major Soviet response came on 20 August when Soviet–Mongolian troops inflicted a heavy defeat on the Japanese who were subsequently driven out of the disputed area. The major Japanese response, on 28 August, was a decision to commence discussions with the Soviets in Moscow without delay. All this occurred while Japan's Kwantung Army was planning a major counter-offensive with four fresh divisions. On the 30th an Imperial order was sent to the Kwantung Army to desist from further operations in the Nomonhan area. After several days of negotiations, Foreign Ministers Togo and Molotov reached an agreement on 15 September 1939, providing for a cease-fire along the lines held that day and the setting up of a commission to settle the boundary problem.

References   Dallin 1949; Jones 1954; Morley 1976; Wu 1950.

(37) Tientsin   An international crisis for Britain over Tientsin began on 14 June 1939 and terminated in August of that year.

Background   After Japan's proclamation of "The Greater East Asia Co-Prosperity Sphere," on 3 November 1938, Tokyo concentrated on tightening its hold over the occupied areas of China and on undermining China's currency. Japan put pressure on the International Settlements in Shanghai and Amoy, and the British Concession at Tientsin, maintaining that these foreign enclaves were blocking the absorption of occupied China into "A New Order of East Asia." The Japanese had four main grievances against Britain at Tientsin: the Chinese guerrillas allegedly used the British Concession as a base to launch anti-Japanese attacks and propaganda; circulation of the Chinese currency was allowed; the British banks refused to accept the Japanese-sponsored Peking (Beijing) regime's Federal Reserve Bank notes; and, finally, that silver reserves deposited by Chinese government banks in Tientsin were not reported to the Japanese authorities.

On 9 April 1939 an official of the Peking puppet regime was assassinated within the British Concession in Tientsin. Two of the arrested suspects confessed under Japanese interrogation but retracted when they were handed over to the British. When the British authorities in Tientsin refused to place the suspects under the jurisdiction of the pro-Japanese Peking regime for a trial, Japan sent the UK an ultimatum. Britain proposed an advisory committee to deal with the problem, but Japan refused.

Crisis   On 14 June 1939 a crisis was triggered for Great Britain when Japan imposed a blockade on the British and French Concessions in Tientsin, cutting off supplies and harassing persons entering and leaving the Concessions. Japan then demanded Britain's abandonment of the Chinese National Government and its cooperation with the "New Order." London received information that the Japanese General Staff had plans for war with Britain which were supported by a faction of the Japanese Army.

The Tientsin issue was discussed by the British Cabinet on 14 June, when Foreign Secretary Halifax suggested serious consideration of economic sanctions, but this was postponed. While Halifax advocated retaliatory measures, a report from the Colonial Board of Trade and Foreign Office was issued advising against them. On the 18th a report from Britain's Chief of Staff concluded that it would not be justifiable to take any action which might lead to hostilities with Japan. On 19 June the Foreign Secretary authorized Ambassador Craigie to propose conducting negotiations over Tientsin in Tokyo. This was accepted by Japan on the 23rd. On 15 July Japan's Prime Minister proposed a formula in which British assistance to China would be withheld during the large-scale Japanese military operations. On the 24th the Craigie–Arita Agreement was reached between the two governments providing for British recognition of the "actual situation in China" and stating that British officials and subjects would be instructed to refrain from obstructing the Japanese Army.

The Tokyo conference on the Tientsin issue opened on 27 July, with quick agreement on the proposals dealing with the restoration and maintenance of order in Tientsin. Negotiations reached an impasse on economic issues. The conference was adjourned on 20 August. The following day the British Foreign Office circulated a paper in which Britain declared that, in the event of hostilities with Japan, it would denounce the Anglo-Japanese Commercial Treaty, nationals would be evacuated from North China, and economic steps would be instituted against Japan. On that day, as well, Japan was stunned by the announcement of the German–Soviet Non-Aggression Pact (see Case #38). Japan was at that time engaged in large-scale fighting against Soviet troops at Nomonhan (see Case #36). The Pact enabled the USSR to concentrate on the East Asian situation without fear for its European flank. After the fall of the Hiranuma Government, the silver and currency questions lapsed and the danger of an Anglo-Japanese war became less probable. On 26 August a formula was suggested by the Japanese Embassy in London, to which Halifax agreed on the 29th. The outbreak of war in Europe in September, however, caused the issue to fade, with no clear solution or formal agreement. A British attempt to get American backing resulted in a Roosevelt statement on 26 July giving notice to Japan of America's intention to terminate the US–Japan Commercial Treaty of 1911.

References   See sources for Case #25.

(38) Entry into World War II

The crisis immediately preceding World War II began on 20 August 1939 and ended on 28 September of that year. The following 21 countries were crisis actors: Australia, Belgium, Canada, Denmark, Estonia, Finland, France, Japan, Latvia, Lithuania, Luxemburg, The Netherlands, New Zealand, Norway, Poland, Romania, South Africa, Sweden, Switzerland, the UK and the USSR.

Background   The Czechoslovakia Annexation Crisis of March 1939 (see Case #32) confronted the small states of Europe, especially Poland and Romania, with forebodings of a similar fate. In an effort to build an effective European coalition of anti-German forces, negotiations were initiated between the Western Powers and the Soviet Union. The failure of these negotiations, to a large extent, was due to Poland's and Romania's refusal to allow the entry of Russian troops into their territories, even for the purpose of assisting resistance to a possible German attack.

German–Soviet negotiations had been taking place since June, and on 15 August German Ambassador Schulenberg delivered a message to Soviet Foreign Minister Molotov stating that Ribbentrop was prepared to visit Moscow in order to bring about a permanent change in German–Soviet relations. Hitler wished Ribbentrop to be received at once, for his plans to invade Poland on 26 August were contingent upon Soviet responses. On 19 August the Soviets indicated their agreement to a meeting for the 26th.

Crisis   *Triggers and Responses*

The first country to perceive a crisis was *Latvia*. On 20 August Latvian Foreign Minister Munters received reports of plans for the partition of Eastern Europe between Germany and the Soviet Union. Latvia's representative in Berlin was instructed to obtain a formal statement from the German Government that the security, integrity and independence of the Baltic states would be maintained. Its major response, on 30 August, was a decision at a special meeting of the Latvian Cabinet to introduce a number of defense measures, including mobilization.

On 21 August a crisis was triggered for the *Soviet Union* when Stalin received a personal message from Hitler accepting the Soviet draft for a non-aggression pact and urging an earlier date for the Ribbentrop visit. Stalin interpreted this message as an ultimatum. If the German plan to invade Poland on the 26th was not met by strong action on the part of Britain and France, Germany would be at leisure to deal with the USSR. After short deliberations, Stalin agreed to Ribbentrop's arrival on 23 August. The signing of a non-aggression treaty with Germany on 23 August was the USSR's major response.

On the evening of 21 August word was received in the capitals of Britain, Japan and Poland that negotiations between Germany and the USSR for a non-aggression pact were about to be concluded. In *Britain*, news of the pact was accompanied by reports of German troop movements toward the Polish frontier. At a Cabinet meeting the following day, members decided on partial mobilization and a call to convene Parliament on the 24th. The British were faced with a *fait accompli*, that they could no longer reach an agreement with Moscow, and the existence of the Molotov–Ribbentrop pact did not alter Britain's obligations to Poland. On 22 and 23 August, Notes were exchanged between Chamberlain and Hitler, and on 25 August Hitler demanded that a Polish emissary arrive in Berlin within 24 hours. The British Cabinet considered this unreasonable and refused to recommend to Poland that it comply with this demand. Diplomatic efforts continued until 1 September when German forces crossed the Polish border and began their invasion. On the 2nd Britain sent an ultimatum to Hitler, after no reply had been received to its Note of the previous day, offering to negotiate if German forces were withdrawn from Poland. And on the 3rd Britain declared war on Germany.

Japan's Ambassador to Berlin, Oshima, received the news of the proposed signing of the non-aggression pact on 21 August: he protested to Germany that it would be an act of bad faith and a contravention of the Anti-Comintern Pact. At that time, a full-scale war was raging between Japan and the Soviet Union at Nomonhan (see Case #36), and the Japanese feared that the USSR would take advantage of their strengthened international position to assert added pressure on Japan in Asia. The Hiranuma Cabinet responded by instructing Oshima to make a formal protest to the German Government which was delivered on 26 August.

The impending Ribbentrop journey to Moscow was broadcast by Moscow Radio on 22 August. This news triggered a crisis for Australia, Belgium, Canada, Denmark, Estonia, Finland, France, Lithuania, Luxemburg, The Netherlands, New Zealand, Norway, Poland, Romania, Sweden and Switzerland.

In *Australia*, Prime Minister Menzies stated on the 23rd that if Britain were forced to go to war, it would not be alone. The following day, Menzies issued a declaration confirming the unity in the ranks of the British Empire. The Australian response was Menzies' declaration of war on 3 September.

Belgium's King Leopold, addressing the Oslo Powers (Finland, Sweden, Norway, Denmark, The Netherlands, Belgium and Luxemburg) on 23 August, appealed to the major powers to maintain peace. On the 25th, at a meeting of the Council of Ministers, it was decided to place the Belgian forces at home on a war footing: active divisions and first reserves were mobilized, automobiles and horses were requisitioned, and frontier patrols were posted. That day, the Prime Minister gave the German chargé d'affaires assurances that the actions of the Belgian Government constituted an affirmation of its independence and its wish to stay out of any conflict.

On 23 August *Canada's* Prime Minister, Mackenzie King, declared that Parliament would be summoned the moment the situation required it, stating that the powers of the War Reserve Act would be utilized to place Canada on a war footing. On the 26th Canada's Foreign Minister sent identical appeals to Germany, Poland and Italy urging the avoidance of war and the solving of issues through conference and negotiation. The Canadian major response to the crisis was at an emergency Cabinet meeting on 1 September. Canada vowed to stand by Britain. The mobilization of army and navy forces was to be completed and measures were taken for Canada's defense and the granting of aid to Britain. On the 10th Canada declared war on Germany.

Despite a non-aggression pact signed with Germany in May 1939, the 22 August announcement triggered a crisis for *Denmark*, which sought assurances from both Germany and Britain that its neutrality would be respected. On the 28th these assurances were given by Germany, and on the 30th Britain did likewise. Denmark's major response came on 1 September when the *Rigodag* met to ensure that the Danish forces were adequate to carry out the task of protecting the country's neutrality.

A large concentration of Soviet troops stationed along the Estonian–USSR border posed a serious threat to *Estonia*. In the hope of maintaining German guarantees, Foreign Minister Selter responded to the German–Soviet non-aggression pact by offering congratulations to the German Government and stating his conviction that Germany, according to its non-aggression treaties with Estonia and the Soviet Union, had prepared the ground for ensuring Estonian security.

For *Finland,* the assumption that permanent hostility between Germany and the Soviet Union would maintain a balance of power in the Baltic region was shattered on 22 August. Foreign Minister Errko feared that the signatories of the Pact would turn against neighboring Baltic states at a later date. The German Ambassador to Helsinki was called in on 1 September with a request for assurances that Germany would respect Finland's neutrality; these were given.

In *France*, word of the Pact on 22 August produced a response of partial mobilization. All frontier troops were put on alert on the 23rd, and full mobilization of reserves began on the 24th. Hitler and Prime Minister Daladier exchanged letters on 25 and 27 August. France agreed to come to Poland's aid if it were attacked by Germany. After the attack on 1 September, the French Council of Ministers ordered a general mobilization for the following day. France, like Britain, sent an ultimatum to Hitler on the 2nd, to expire the next day. And on the 3rd France, too, declared war on Germany.

Lithuania viewed the Pact as a threat to its existence, despite the non-aggression pacts which Lithuania, together with Latvia and Estonia, had signed with Germany and with the Soviet Union. Lithuania's response was a declaration of neutrality on 2 September.

Luxemburg attended the Oslo Powers Conference on 23 August which called for peace. Its major response was an appeal on 31 August for the observance of Luxemburg's neutrality.

The response of *The Netherlands* was a Cabinet decision on 25 August to maintain neutrality. The following day the German Minister met with Queen Wilhelmina and conveyed German expectations that The Netherlands would not swerve from the neutrality decision. On the 28th a mobilization order was proclaimed, along with other measures for Holland's security. On 30 August assurances were also received from Britain.

New Zealand, like other members of the British Commonwealth, perceived a crisis on 22 August when the grave threat facing Britain as a result of the Pact became known. The following day, with Cabinet approval, Acting Premier Frazer declared that New Zealand would remain solidly behind Britain should war come. A state of emergency was proclaimed on 1 September.

Ribbentrop's proposed journey to Moscow became known in *Norway* on the 22nd. Norway responded on the 30th with an order for partial mobilization. Assurances of Germany's respect for Norway's neutrality were sought and received on 1 September.

After reports of extensive German military preparations on the 23rd, *Poland* mobilized one-third of its army. On 24 August, Foreign Minister Beck told the British Ambassador that he considered the situation most grave. The following day the Anglo-Polish Agreement was signed. As further German troop concentrations were reported on the border and German troops in Slovakia called upon the population to collaborate against Poland, the Polish Government decided upon general mobilization on 29 August. It was announced on the 30th, despite the advice of the French and British Ambassadors whose countries were still negotiating with Germany. When the invasion took place, Poland's major response, on 1 September, was to fight the invaders while appealing to Britain and France to implement their guarantees.

Romania, caught between the two strongest powers in Europe, viewed the Pact as a grave threat to its sovereignty. Romania particularly feared Russian designs on Bessarabia and the implications for Romania's freedom of movement on behalf of Poland in the event of war. On 27 August Foreign Minister Gafencu told the German Ambassador that Romania was determined to remain neutral even if France and Britain became involved in a war with Germany. On the 28th Romania began to fortify its frontier with the USSR along the valley of the Dniester River.

On 27th August *Sweden* responded to the crisis with a decision to maintain strict neutrality. A partial mobilization had been called on the previous day. On 1 September the King declared that all defense positions would be strengthened.

Switzerland's geographic position, bordering Germany, France, Austria and

Italy, placed it in an especially vulnerable position on 22 August. On the 28th the *Bundesrat* ordered the mobilization of frontier forces and all defense troops. Parliament was summoned the following day for a special session. On 30 August the United Federal Assembly appointed General Henri Guisan as Commander-in-Chief of the Swiss Army. And the following day Switzerland decreed neutrality.

On 1 September Germany invaded Poland, triggering a crisis for *South Africa*. The Herzog–Smuts coalition was split over the question of South Africa's response to the crisis. Herzog advocated neutrality, maintaining that the dispute was among the European powers and did not affect South Africa. General Smuts believed that South Africa should enter the war on the side of Britain. The issue was placed before the House of Assembly. When no solution was forthcoming, Prime Minister Herzog requested the Governor-General to dissolve Parliament and call an election. The request was refused, the Prime Minister resigned, and the Governor-General asked Smuts to form a Cabinet. South Africa's major response was to declare war against Germany on 6 September.

Terminations   *Japan*'s crisis ended on 28 August with the resignation of the Hiranuma Cabinet.

On 31 August the crisis for *Switzerland* terminated when the Federal Council issued a declaration of neutrality after assurances had been received from Germany and Italy. On that day as well, *Luxemburg*'s crisis ended when it, too, received assurances of German observance of its strict neutrality.

On 1 September there were official declarations of neutrality by the Scandinavian countries – *Denmark, Finland, Norway, Sweden*; *Romania*, too, declared neutrality that day, as did *Estonia* and *Latvia*.

Lithuania proclaimed neutrality the next day. Neutrality was declared by *Belgium* and *The Netherlands* on 3 September.

Australia, Britain, France and *New Zealand* declared war against Germany on 3 September.

South Africa joined the war on the 6th, and *Canada* on the 10th.

Germany fought in *Poland* for 17 days and on 17 September the conquest was completed. On that day, the Soviet Union invaded Poland from the east, meeting the advancing German troops near Brest-Litovsk two days later.

The last actor to perceive crisis termination was the *Soviet Union,* on 28 September 1939. Despite the signing of the Pact, bad faith continued to exist between Germany and the USSR until additional agreements were signed on the 28th when the German and Soviet governments divided Poland.

By the end of this crisis, Australia, Britain, Canada, France, New Zealand and South Africa were at war with Germany. Poland had been conquered. The Scandinavian countries, the Baltic states and Romania, Belgium, Luxemburg, Switzerland and Holland had declared neutrality. Japan was at war in Asia with China. And Moscow was serene in the misconception that Germany would not attack the USSR.

References   See sources for Cases #30, #32, #33, #34, #39; and: Grattan 1963; von Rauch 1970; Tarulis 1959.

(39) Soviet Occupation: Baltic   A crisis for Estonia, Latvia and Lithuania occurred between 26 September and 10 October 1939.

Background   The German invasion of Poland on 1 September 1939 was followed by a Soviet invasion of that country on 17 September. By the end of that month Poland had been divided between Germany and the Soviet Union. The Soviets occupied 77,620 square miles of eastern Poland. Lithuania and Slovakia received small parts of Polish territory. On 22 September the Estonian Foreign Minister, Karl Selter, went to Moscow for negotiations on economic issues. While there, a demand was made that Estonia sign a mutual assistance pact which would grant the USSR a naval base and airfields. Foreign Minister Molotov threatened Selter that, if the Estonian Government refused to comply, Soviet demands would be obtained through other methods.

Crisis   On 26 September 1939 Selter informed his government of the Soviet demands, triggering a crisis for Estonia. This was accompanied by extensive flights of Soviet aircraft over Estonian territory and rumors of large Russian troop concentrations along the border. Estonia responded on the 28th by complying with the demands thereby ending its crisis.

On 1 October the Latvian Foreign Minister, Wilhelm Munters, was summoned to Moscow for discussions. He arrived on the 2nd and held conversations with Stalin and Molotov. A crisis was triggered the next day when the Soviets made a series of demands under the threat of war. Lithuania's Foreign Minister, Joseph Urbesys, arrived in Moscow on the 3rd as well, to receive similar demands, triggering a crisis for Lithuania. Latvia, realizing that British or French assistance was out of the question at that time, and aware of the fact that 16 Soviet divisions were concentrated on the Latvian border, responded by signing a mutual assistance pact on 5 October. This marked the end of Latvia's crisis. The pact allowed the USSR to gain control over the Gulf of Riga and several air and naval bases. Thirty thousand Soviet troops were to be garrisoned in Latvia.

Negotiations between the USSR and Lithuania were conducted for a week after the trigger date, with Moscow applying severe pressure. The Soviet–Lithuanian Pact, ending the crisis, was signed on 10 October. It provided for the restoration of the city of Vilna to Lithuania and allowed the USSR to establish air and land bases and to maintain 20,000 troops in Lithuania. Lithuania, while viewing the return of Vilna with much satisfaction, had become a Soviet satellite.

References   Dallin 1960; Gehase 1946; Roi 1948; Sabaliunas 1972; Schuman 1941; Spekke 1951; Svabe 1947; Tarulis 1959.

(40) Finnish War   A crisis for Finland, France, Sweden and the UK, centering on the Finnish-Soviet War, began on 6 October 1939 and terminated on 13 March 1940.

Background   The city of Leningrad is 32 kilometers from the Finnish border, south of the Karelian Peninsula. Treaties signed by the Soviet Union with Estonia, Latvia and Lithuania granted Moscow the right to build bases in the three Baltic states (see Case #39). In addition to a base in Estonia at the southwestern edge of the Gulf of Finland, the Soviets wanted a base at the northern end, along with territorial changes which would protect it from future attack, either by the UK or Germany. From early 1938 until mid-1939 requests for such border changes had been discussed by Soviet diplomats in Helsinki with the Finnish Foreign Minister. Pressure on Finland began once the treaties with the Baltic states had been signed. On 5 October Molotov requested the Finnish Ambassador to the Soviet Union to inform his government that the USSR wished the Finnish Foreign Minister or some high-ranking delegate to come to Moscow to discuss concrete political questions in view of the altered international situation.

Crisis   In the absence of a reply by 6 October strong pressure was applied to the Ambassador of Finland. A crisis was triggered for Finland when its Ambassador in Moscow related the Soviet demands the same day. A negotiator was selected by Finland with clear instructions to convey its determination to stand firm, and Moscow was so informed on 10 October. Finland's major response, the same day, was to call for partial mobilization and evacuation of some cities, along with a practice air raid and blackout in Helsinki. Negotiations took place between 12 and 14 October. Stalin presented his "minimum demands," which included the transfer of islands close to the USSR shore and the port of Itanko, moving the border 35 kilometers farther away from Leningrad; and concessions in the northern peninsula of Rybachi, including the port of Petsamo. The Finnish mission returned to Helsinki for further instructions. On 27 October Finland appealed to Sweden for military aid in case of war. The following day the appeal was rejected by the Prime Minister of Sweden. The last round of negotiations produced lesser Soviet demands, but Helsinki refused to consider them. The negotiators returned to Finland on 14 November.

An incident involving the firing of seven shots occurred in a town on the Soviet side of the Karelian border on 26 November. Moscow accused Finland of violating their Non-Aggression Pact and a vehement press campaign was launched against Finland. The Soviets refused Finland's request to investigate the incident and withdrew its diplomats on 29 November, denouncing the Pact. On the 30th the USSR attacked Finland without a declaration of war. The Finnish Cabinet declared a state of war that day and appointed Marshal Mannerheim Commander-in-Chief of the Armed Forces. The Government resigned on 1 December and was reorganized under a new Prime Minister, Ryti. On the 2nd the Soviet Union set up and recognized a Finnish Democratic Government in captured territory. The same day Finland appealed to the League of Nations, which invited the Soviet Union to attend an Assembly session. Moscow refused on 4 December; and on the 14th the League Assembly condemned the Soviet Union as an aggressor and requested that members give Finland material and humanitarian aid. The Soviet Union was expelled from the League.

During the month of December France and the UK began to consider sending forces to aid Finland, with a view to stopping the flow of Swedish iron shipments through Narvik to Germany. In order to do this, troops had to cross neutral Norway and Sweden. Sweden, physically closer to Finland and politically friendly, saw the situation as dangerous and feared being drawn into the conflict, particularly with Germany. When the first official offer by Britain and France to send troops to Finland via Sweden was made on 27 December 1939, a crisis was triggered for Sweden which (together with Norway) insisted that no troops pass through its territories. On 4 January the German Ambassador to Finland made it clear that Germany would view Allied troops in northern Sweden and Norway as a *casus belli*. The Soviets, who had been surprised at Finnish perseverence and success, finally broke Finland's line on 14 January 1940, triggering a crisis for France and Britain: they were suddenly faced with the real prospect of a Soviet victory in a strategic area and a need to send aid to Finland before the spring thaw shifted the military conditions once more. They responded on 5 February with a finalized plan for action in Finland which was accepted by the Joint Allied Supreme War Council.

Sweden, which had been assisting negotiations between the Finnish Foreign Minister and the Soviet Ambassador to Sweden, became more alarmed over the Allied plans. A press-leaked story about the negotiations and appeals from Finland for aid determined the Swedish major response to the crisis: on 19 February the King of Sweden officially refused to aid Finland. Throughout February and March, Britain and France continued to ignore Sweden's and Norway's refusals to grant passage for their troops and pressed Finland to accept Allied armies on its soil. Finland preferred to continue negotiations for an armistice with the Soviet Union via Sweden.

Moscow, which had originally expected little resistance and popular support for a Communist government in Finland, finally agreed to an armistice while demanding stiffer conditions. The armistice was signed on 13 March 1940, terminating the crisis for all four actors.

Offers to mediate were made by the United States, Italy and Germany.

References   Bullock 1962; Carlgren 1977; Calvocoressi and Wint 1972; Churchill 1948; Jakobson 1961; Maude 1976; Nevakivi 1976; Royal Institute of International Affairs 1947; Ulam 1974; Upton 1964.

(41) Invasion of Scandinavia   The German invasion of Scandinavia generated a crisis for Denmark, France, The Netherlands, Norway and the UK from 8 April to 10 June 1940.

Background   The Soviet–Finnish Winter War, which had ended in March 1940, emphasized the strategic importance of Scandinavia's waterways for both the Allies and Germany (see Case #40). Winston Churchill, then First Lord of the Admiralty, pressed for the mining of Norwegian waters which were the passageway for Swedish ore to Germany. Early in 1940 the German tanker *Altmark*, sailing in Norwegian waters and carrying British prisoners of war, was boarded by the British while moored in Jössingfjord, and the prisoners were released. Both Norway and Germany issued strong protests to London. Norway, which feared German retaliation, emphasized that the British ships had violated its neutrality. The *Altmark* incident accelerated German plans for the invasion of Norway and spurred British Cabinet approval of

Churchill's naval plans. Due to Britain's superior naval strength, Germany decided upon a surprise attack against Norway.

Crisis On 8 April 1940 a crisis was triggered for Norway when it received intelligence reports predicting a German invasion the next day. Several UK vessels did spot and engage the Germans that day, but the British viewed these as isolated clashes. On 9 April the Germans invaded Denmark and Norway, creating a crisis for Britain, Denmark and France. A crisis was also triggered for The Netherlands, which perceived the invasion as presaging an attack on Holland, for it was the first German offensive since the "phony war" of the preceding winter and spring, and was accompanied by perceptions of German plans to attack Western Europe. While Denmark and Norway perceived no more than grave damage at the outset, for Germany demanded free passage only, as the crisis escalated they perceived a threat to their existence in the form of German occupation.

The Norwegian and Danish responses occurred on 9 April. Norway's King Haakon offered to abdicate rather than capitulate. Norway reorganized its defenses and began strong resistance under a new Commander-in-Chief, General Ruge. Denmark held Cabinet meetings with King Christian and, under his leadership, decided not to resist, ending its crisis on the 9th.

The UK and France had been considering the dispatch of troops to aid Norway. The German attack hastened their decision, on 13 April, to do so. Haphazard and insufficient planning prevented the success of the operation. The target areas were too narrow for the ships carrying artillery to land, and the landing sites were changed, confusing the troops. Norwegian forces had tried to keep landing areas and key ports free for the Allies.

On 19 April The Netherlands responded to the crisis by mobilizing its troops and issuing a strong statement of its intention to defend itself against German attack. Holland's tension eased as the German invasion concentrated on Denmark and Norway and, on 27 April, its crisis ended, with military preparations returning to normal.

The Anglo-French forces, together with the Norwegians, resisted for another month. In the interim, on 10 May, Britain's Prime Minister, Neville Chamberlain, resigned and was replaced by Winston Churchill. By the end of May the Allies had been badly beaten and a decision was made to withdraw. The last troops were evacuated on 8 June 1940, following the French defeat in northern France (see Case#42), terminating the intra-war crisis for France and Britain. The King of Norway and his government left the country with the British and French on the 8th and, on 10 June, a member of General Ruge's staff signed an armistice with Germany, ending the last fighting around Narvik and terminating the crisis for Norway.

References Bullock 1962; Calvocoressi and Wint 1972; Carlgren 1977; Churchill 1948; Derry 1952; Olsson 1975; Petrow 1974; Royal Institute of International Affairs 1947; Schuman 1941.

(42) Fall of Western Europe

The crisis over Germany's occupation of Western Europe occurred from 10 May to 22 June 1940. Belgium, Britain, France, Luxemburg and The Netherlands were the crisis actors.

Background On 9 April 1940 German armed forces occupied Denmark and invaded Norway (see Case #41).

Crisis Early in the morning of 10 May 1940 German armies, without warning, invaded Belgium, Luxemburg and The Netherlands, triggering a crisis for those three countries and for France and Britain. The latter were cobelligerent partners in the ongoing European war; the cornerstone of Britain's defense policy had always been that a threat to France was perceived in London as a threat to itself. Thus, on 10 May, they responded by dispatching expeditionary forces into Belgium to cooperate with the Belgian Army in its resistance. Diplomatic negotiations were also carried on. Belgium and The Netherlands responded on the 10th as well with military resistance. In Luxemburg there was no fighting. The Royal Family retired to its castle, refusing to communicate with the German invaders, and its crisis ended on the day of the invasion. In Holland, Rotterdam surrendered to the Germans after a fierce air attack, and the Government, headed by Queen Wilhelmina, escaped to London on 13 May. Holland signed an armistice agreement with the Germans on 15 May 1940.

Between 17 and 21 May German mechanized divisions drove deep into northern France and succeeded in separating British and Belgian forces in Flanders from the main French armies. The fall of Brussels forced the British and Belgian troops back to Ostend and Dunkirk. On 26 May Boulogne fell to the Germans, and King Leopold ordered his army to capitulate. This was done on 28 May, terminating the crisis for Belgium. Two hundred and fifty thousand British troops were evacuated from the beaches of Dunkirk.

A broad attack on France was launched on 5 June. On the 10th Italy declared war against France and Britain. Paris was evacuated on the 13th. And on 17 June the UK crisis ended when it formally withdrew its troops from France and agreed to the latter's making a separate peace with the Germans. On that day Marshal Pétain asked the Germans for an armistice. This was signed on 22 June 1940 ending the crisis for France and leaving three-fifths of the country under German occupation.

An immediate legacy of this intra-war crisis was a near confrontation between Britain and Vichy France as a result of the former's fear that the French fleet concentrated in Toulon would be handed over to Germany. The British signalled their determination to prevent this by sinking the French naval flotilla in Oran, North Africa, on 3 July 1940. The UK remained suspicious of Pétain's intentions throughout the tenure of the Vichy French regime, as evident in the Middle East Campaign Crisis of 1941 (see Case #48).

References Butler 1956; Churchill 1949; Dallek 1979; Nere 1975; Schuman 1941; Shirer 1969; Weinberg 1980.

(43) Burma Road Closure

The closure of the Burma Road by the Japanese created a crisis for the UK from 24 June to 14 July 1940.

Background Throughout the 1930s Britain's support for the Nationalist regime in China was viewed by Japan as hostile to its interests. Britain's involvement in the European War provided Japan with an opportunity to proceed without hindrance to establish the proclaimed "New Order" in Asia. As the tide of the war turned against Britain, Japan increased its pressure.

Crisis On 24 June Japan demanded that Britain cease assistance to Chiang K'ai-shek, withdraw its troops from Shanghai, and close the transit routes for supplies to China through Hong Kong and the Burma Road. A force of about 5000 Japanese troops took up positions along the border of the leased Kowloon territory in Hong Kong. The British perceived that if they yielded to the Japanese demands the security of the British Commonwealth would be compromised. Yet Britain could not afford to risk war with Japan, being already involved in the European and Mediterranean theaters.

Britain's major response, on 27 June, was to seek American assurances that the United States would stand by Britain in resisting Japanese demands, either through an embargo on all exports to Japan or by sending US warships to Singapore. Britain also requested US cooperation in mediating a peace settlement between China and Japan. The United States, while urging the UK to stand firm, rejected any plan for joint action. On the 30th the Hong Kong military authorities ordered the destruction of the frontier rail and road bridges over the Shumchun River. An evacuation of British women and children from Hong Kong to Manila and Australia followed.

A Japanese Foreign Ministry communiqué, on 8 July, demanded British reconsideration. On the 12th Britain informed US Secretary of State Cordell Hull that Japan would declare war at any time unless the British Government closed the Burma Road.

The crisis ended on 14 July 1940 when an Anglo-Japanese agreement was reached in Tokyo whereby all transit of war materials was stopped for three months. Four days later the agreement was communicated to the British Parliament by the Prime Minister and the Foreign Secretary. Britain, perceiving a high probability that Japan would enter the war on the side of the Axis, and unable to meet the threat without American support, yielded to the Japanese demands.

The Burma Road was cleared of Japanese forces in the spring of 1945 following a two-pronged attack on Japanese positions in northern Burma by Chinese troops under the direction of General Stilwell.

References   Boyle 1972; Hull 1948; Jones 1954; Morley 1974.

(44) Romanian Territories   Romania's crises over Bulgarian, Hungarian and Soviet claims on its territories occurred between 26 June and 7 September 1940.

Background   After World War I Romania received disputed territories claimed by several of its neighbors, including the USSR, Hungary and Bulgaria. In July 1935 Romania signed a Pact of Non-Aggression with the Soviet Union which involved tacit recognition of Romania's possession of Bessarabia and was the direct result of Hitler's election victory in Germany and Moscow's preoccupation with the situation in the Far East. The fall of France and the desperate position of Britain in the summer of 1940 (see Cases #42 and #45) caused shifts in the European balance which emphasized Romania's vulnerability. The USSR, in talks with Germany, indicated that it could no longer wait to solve the problem of Bessarabia, which had been Russian from 1812 to 1918. It became clear that, if one power pressed claims on Romania, others would seize the opportunity to follow suit. Both Hungary and Romania viewed Transylvania as an integral part of their history and territory. And Bulgaria had long been voicing its claims to southern Dobruja.

Crisis   On 26 June 1940 Soviet Foreign Minister Molotov handed the Romanian Ambassador in Moscow a 24-hour ultimatum to evacuate Bessarabia. Further, as compensation for the years of loss, the USSR demanded northern Bukovina as well. Romania turned for aid to the Balkan Entente, without success, and to Germany, which advised acceptance of Soviet demands as the territories fell under the Soviet sphere according to the August 1939 Ribbentrop – Molotov agreement. Romania's major response, on 28 June 1940, was to yield. Nevertheless, military preparations and mobilization were also carried out. Advancing Soviet troops went beyond the areas designated in the agreement, and some clashes with Romanian forces occurred. Ultimately, the Soviets withdrew to the agreed boundaries and, on 2 July, the operation was completed, terminating Romania's crisis with the Soviet Union.

Encouraged by the Soviet victory, the Hungarian Nazi Party accused Romania, on 1 July 1940, of evicting Hungarians to make room for Bessarabian refugees and triggered Romania's crisis with Hungary over Transylvania. Hungarian leaders conferred with Hitler and Italy's Foreign Minister Ciano, where they were advised to attack only if there appeared to be no other way to achieve their aims. Romania compromised with a plan for a population exchange and some territorial concessions, but these were rejected. Its major response, on 13 July 1940, was multiple – an offer by King Carol to Hitler for an offensive–defensive alliance, clearly aimed at the possibility of receiving German support against Hungary, and a movement of troops. Hitler replied, on the 15th, that Romania must come to terms with Hungary. On 26–27 July Romania, upon the advice of Hitler and Mussolini, agreed to negotiate.

Meanwhile, in July, clashes occurred on the Bulgarian–Romanian border in connection with the Bessarabian refugees, and another crisis was triggered for Romania, this time with Bulgaria. While Romanian representatives met with Mussolini on 27 July, Hitler proposed negotiations to the Bulgarians. On 4 August 1940 Romania's major response to the Bulgarian crisis was to send a delegate to Germany empowered to open talks with the Bulgarians. A meeting was held on the 19th. As Bulgaria's claim was less drastic and generally justified, agreement was reached quickly. On 21 August, southern Dobruja was transferred. The formal agreement was signed on 7 September 1940 terminating Romania's crisis with Bulgaria.

The Hungarian claims were far more complex. After meetings on 16 and 24 August, negotiations broke off and both sides mobilized. Hungary's decision to invade followed air skirmishes. On 26 August German intervention was suggested by Ribbentrop. The following day, Hitler himself worked out the boundaries and, on the 29th, he called upon Hungary and Romania to send envoys to Vienna. At the meeting Hungarian protests of inadequacies were shouted down while Romania's shock was simply ignored. Neither side had any real choice. After consulting the Crown Council, the Romanian Minister accepted the terms of Hitler's imposed solution on 30 August 1940, terminating the crisis with Hungary. In return, Hungary was obliged to grant its German minority a privileged status, amounting to pro-Reich autonomy. The borders remained stable for several years as the war progressed.

References   Bantea 1970; Fischer-Galati 1969; Gafencu 1945; Macartney 1956-57; Pavel 1944; Waldeck 1943.

(45) Battle of Britain   The battle, an intra-war crisis for Britain, took place from 10 July to 15 September 1940.

Background   A Naval Agreement between the UK and Germany in 1935 and British concessions at Munich in 1938 (see Case #30) led Hitler to expect British cooperation for a quiet Western flank which would enable him to carry out a massive attack on the USSR. After Britain's declaration of war (see Case #38) and Churchill's announcement, after the fall of France (Case #42), that Britain would continue to fight alone, Hitler began to formulate a plan to invade the UK. He envisioned a long and costly campaign requiring at the onset the transport of around 30–40 divisions by sea across the Channel. Since Germany lacked sufficient naval power to compete with Britain, the prerequisite to a successful crossing was absolute air superiority. As German ships began to collect along the coast of France, the *Luftwaffe* initiated its efforts to gain control of the air. After the fall of France and the Dunkirk evacuation, Britain appealed to the United States for military supplies. By the end of June American guns and ammunition had reached British shores. In early July the Germans occupied islands in the English Channel.

Crisis   On 10 July 1940 the *Luftwaffe* began "Operation Eagle" by attacking towns near the coast of Britain. Britain's response to the crisis was immediate, through the RAF counter-attacks. The German assault continued during July and August with fierce RAF opposition. On 8 August German planes bombed airfields and vital industries. On the 15th 1000 German planes ranged as far north as Scotland. The British retaliated with raids on Berlin, Düsseldorf, Essen and other German cities. On 3 September a defense agreement was concluded between Britain and the United States. On the 7th the highest British casualty count occurred. And on 11 September, the British began continuous bombing of continental ports to frustrate German invasion preparations, including the assembling of ships for the future crossing of the Channel.

As time went on it became clear that the *Luftwaffe* would not be able to gain complete air superiority and the original target date for the German invasion ("Operation Sea Lion") was postponed several times. The *Luftwaffe*'s strategy had been to draw Britain's Fighter Command into a major engagement, first over the English Channel and then, on 15 September 1940, in a mass raid on London in an effort to deliver a final assault. The British resisted, preserved the Fighter Command by meeting the German attacks with a minimum of force and pushed the *Luftwaffe* back across the Channel. This victory of 15 September 1940, proving that the RAF was still master of the skies over Britain, marked the termination of Britain's crisis, though night bombing of London and other British cities continued far into the winter.

Once the conditions for a successful German landing had been denied, Germany cancelled the invasion plans. Hitler decided to proceed with an attack in the east without the subjugation of Britain. Italy dispatched an airforce division – after the crisis proper had ended.

References   Bullock 1962; Calvocoressi and Wint 1972; Churchill 1949; Shirer 1964.

(46) East Africa Campaign

Italy and the UK were the crisis actors in an intra-war crisis from 19 August 1940 until 17 May 1941.

Background   On 10 June 1940 Italy declared war on Britain in the belief that the impending collapse of the Allies in Europe would make any serious Italian participation unnecessary. With the expected downfall of the British, Egypt, British Somaliland and British East Africa would be added to Italy's existing possessions covering an immense area in northeast Africa. When Italy entered the war, the reinforcement of British forces through the Mediterranean became extremely dangerous. This threat intensified in July when the collapse of opposition in French Somaliland led to a French–Italian armistice. Large Italian forces had now been released for use against British Somaliland. During July Italy occupied Sudanese and Kenyan frontier posts. On 3 August the Italians crossed the frontier into British Somaliland.

Crisis   On 19 August 1940 the British were forced to evacuate British Somaliland. This setback at the hands of the Italians came as a shock to British public opinion. Although Italian attacks on Aden were now more easily facilitated, the protectorate had no significant strategic value for the UK. Nevertheless, the location of an Italian East Africa on the flank of Britain's vital sea route, the Red Sea, was a threat to Britain's influence among its client states, and the forced evacuation triggered a crisis for the UK. The British responded, months later, on 2 December 1940, with a decision to expel Italy from East Africa. The campaign in North Africa began on 8 December (see Case #53). The East African offensive began in February 1941 when the British advanced from the Anglo-Egyptian Sudan and Kenya into Ethiopia and Eritrea.

On 13 February Kismayu fell, and Mogadiscio (Mogadishu) submitted on the 25th. And on 17 March the Italians abandoned Sigjiga. The British advances had revealed the weakness of the Italian colonial forces, and internal disorder increased greatly. On the 22nd Neghelli in southern Ethiopia was occupied by British and Ethiopian forces.

The crisis trigger for Italy was at the battle of Keren on 27 March 1941. The loss of 3000 men in that battle broke the back of Italian resistance, which now abandoned hope of retaining control over Eritrea. Italy responded on 30 March with a decision to concentrate resistance at Amba Alagi. Mussolini was so informed by the Duke of Aosta, Supreme Commander of all Italian Armed Forces in East Africa. On 3 April the Duke united the remainder of his reserve force with the remnants of the Italian Eritrean army.

On 6 April Addis Ababa capitulated. Prior to the defeat, Mussolini had instructed the Duke not to abandon the capital unless absolutely necessary because it would be politically equivalent to losing the Empire.

On 11 April President Roosevelt announced that the Red Sea and the Gulf of Aden were no longer combat zones within the meaning of American neutrality and US vessels could now carry war supplies to the British Middle East Forces by this route.

The termination of the crisis for both the UK and Italy came on 17 May 1941 when the Duke of Aosta surrendered and signed an armistice agreement. Italian resistance in Eritrea collapsed by June. And before the end of 1941 all of East Africa was under British control.

References   Churchill 1949; Ciano 1947; Collins 1947; Playfair 1954.

(47) Balkan Invasions

The Italian and German invasions of the Balkans created a crisis for Britain, Germany, Greece, Italy, Turkey and Yugoslavia. The duration of the crisis was from 28 October 1940 until 1 June 1941.

Background   The high geostrategic importance of the Balkans for Germany, the USSR and the West stems from the fact that they guard one access to the Mediterranean close to vital areas of the British Empire, namely, the Suez Canal and the Middle East. Together with Turkey and Romania, the Balkans dominate the Dardanelles – the access to the USSR and the Black Sea, and the mouth of the Danube River. They are also rich in natural resources, especially oil. In the summer of 1940, when three countries claimed Romanian territories, Hitler imposed a solution on Romania and Hungary in order to avoid war (see Case #44). On 8 October German troops entered Romania to "protect" the oil fields. Italy had long been interested in Yugoslavia and Greece as guardians of the opposite shore of the Adriatic, and Hitler had cautiously granted Mussolini a free hand in the area. When Italy attacked and occupied Albania in early 1939 (see Case #35), the balance in the area was altered. Mussolini, after a poor showing on the French front, and ignorant of Hitler's plan *vis-à-vis* Romania, wished to present Hitler with a *fait accompli* by occupying Greece.

Crisis   On 28 October 1940 Italy's Ambassador to Greece presented Premier Metaxas with an ultimatum to relinquish Greek bases for use by the Italian Government. One half-hour before the ultimatum expired, Italy attacked Greece from Albania. Greece responded that day by mobilizing its forces and appealing to the UK for help under its guarantee, triggering a crisis for the UK. Britain perceived a threat to the strategic balance in the area and therefore to its entire Middle East empire. Crises were also triggered for Yugoslavia, which feared for its own security should the port of Thessaloniki be occupied by the Italians, and for Turkey, which viewed Bulgaria as capable of seizing the military opportunity to take control of Greek areas of strategic importance to Turkey, as well as a fear of a spillover that would endanger Turkey's neutral status. Yugoslavia and Turkey both responded on 1 November. Yugoslavia held a meeting of its Crown Council and ordered partial mobilization. Turkey's President Inönü announced that his country would stand by its allies and not tolerate a threat to its security. To back this up some Turkish troops were moved to the Bulgarian border – which ultimately freed Greek soldiers, fighting in the vicinity, for campaigns elsewhere in Greece. The UK, which had sent reinforcements to Crete and other Greek Islands on 30 October, decided at a Cabinet meeting on 3 November to increase its military and economic aid to Greece so as to enable that country to resist the Italian offensive.

The attack itself did not go well for Italy. Severe winter conditions and the fierce determination of the Greek forces ground the Italian offensive to a standstill. By the middle of November the Greeks were able to reorganize for an offensive which, by 21 November, had forced the Italians back. The first crisis for Greece and Yugoslavia ended that day. The UK's first crisis ended the following day, with the news of Greek successes on the battlefield.

The Greek offensive of mid-November, which resulted, *inter alia*, in the capture of the strategic town of Koritsa, triggered a crisis for Italy and Germany. Hitler viewed Italian losses as detrimental to his strategy in the area, for Western victories would allow the British access to the Balkans and the Romanian oil fields. Italy responded on 5 December by sending its Ambassador in Berlin to Hitler to request aid in Greece. Although the request was later withdrawn, Hitler had been convinced of the need to salvage the situation there. Accordingly, on 13 December, Germany began to plan for an invasion of Greece in February. It was eventually delayed until April. The proposed Soviet campaign was thus also delayed.

By the beginning of 1941 the military situation had stabilized somewhat. Hitler spent the winter in political maneuvering, easing the tension between Bulgaria and Turkey and countering strong British pressure on Turkey to support Greece. Hitler was instrumental in bringing about the signing of a Bulgarian–Turkish Friendship Pact on 17 February 1941, which terminated Turkey's crisis *vis-à-vis* Bulgaria. On 29 February Bulgaria adhered to the Tripartite Pact (Germany, Italy, Japan) and therewith allowed German troops to assemble on its territory to await the invasion of Greece.

In Yugoslavia much the same German pressure was being applied, together with popular unrest and some civil violence as rival groups maneuvered for dominance in that multinational state. The Regent, Prince Paul, though willing in principle to join the Axis powers, did not wish it to become public knowledge. Nevertheless, he obligated Yugoslavia to provide forces, if necessary, and allowed the passage of German troops. On 4 March 1941 Prince Paul visited Hitler where he experienced strong pressure to adhere to the Tripartite Pact. This triggered a second crisis for Yugoslavia, as Germany threatened to occupy Thessaloniki and hand it over to Bulgaria or Italy. On 24 March 1941 Yugoslavia responded by agreeing to join the Pact, which was done the following day. On the night of the 26th a *coup d'état* took place in Yugoslavia. The new rulers were quick to state that they would adhere to previous policy but the signs were unclear. Hitler, in fury, decided to invade Yugoslavia, as well as Greece, and did so on 6 April 1941, triggering a second crisis for Greece and the UK. Efforts to coordinate military plans between the UK and Greece had met with difficulties. Greece feared that too much British aid would bring Germany into the battle. Britain felt that what was acceptable to Greece was insufficient. Poor coordination and misunderstanding led to poor performance.

On 7 April the British pledged military support to Yugoslavia, and on the 8th the US cabled Belgrade that it would provide material aid. Two days later, with a preliminary UK withdrawal in Greece, Hungary invaded Yugoslavia. The Greek response to the second crisis was a major withdrawal on 12 April. On 17 April Yugoslavia signed an armistice with Germany which terminated its second crisis. And on the 23rd Greece surrendered, ending its crisis and that of Italy as well. The next day the Greek Government requested that the British withdraw, and Bulgaria invaded Greece. The major UK response was a decision on 27 April to withdraw its forces to Crete.

Fighting continued as German forces attacked Crete, which had never been properly fortified. Nonetheless, it took over a month to force a final UK withdrawal from Crete, on 1 June, terminating the crisis for the UK and for Germany. In the final analysis, the Balkan Campaign delayed Operation Barbarossa by at least four weeks, more likely several months (see Case #49).

The US sent a mediator to the Balkans in the spring and invoked the Neutrality Act in the fall of 1940. Australia and New Zealand troops fought alongside the British.

References Barker 1976; Cervi 1971; Churchill 1949, 1950a; Ciano 1947; Creveld 1973; Cruickshank 1976; Kirkpatrick 1964; Miller 1975; Ristic 1961.

(48) Middle East Campaign   Military campaigns in the Middle East triggered intra-war crises for Britain, Germany, Iraq and Vichy France from 29 April to 14 July 1941.

Background At the onset of 1941 the Near and Middle East comprised an area of practical concern to both sides in the European War. With a German/Italian threat to the Suez Canal, the British began to consider the Basra–Baghdad–Palestine route. On 3 April 1941 Rashid Ali staged a coup and reassumed power in Iraq. UK losses in the Balkans and Libya had been reflected in the growth of anti-British sentiment in Iraq, heightened by the fact that Baghdad had become the center of pro-Axis intrigue, leading to British fears of German control over Iraq. The British decided that the situation could be restored only by force. Despite Rashid Ali's assurances that he would honor the 1930 Anglo-Iraqi Treaty, Britain was determined to restore the legitimate government to power in order to safeguard the Allies against Axis intervention in Iraq. On 17 April 1941 a British–Indian military contingent landed in Basra, in accordance with treaty provisions.

Crisis A second British contingent landed on 29 April 1941, triggering a crisis for Iraq. That day Iraq responded by ordering its forces to Habbaniya, the principal British air base there. With Iraqi artillery surrounding the air base and other forces encircling the compound of the British Embassy in Baghdad, on 29 April, a crisis was triggered for Britain. The following day the Iraqi commander demanded the closure of the base. The British replied that any interference with flights would be treated as an act of war. The Ambassador was given full authority to take any steps necessary, including air attacks, to assure the withdrawal of the Iraqis. While Iraq endeavored to take Habbaniya, the British responded with an attack on 1 May. Rashid Ali's early attempts to secure Axis military assistance had been unsuccessful, as Germany was occupied in Greece and in preparing for its attack on the USSR (see Case #49). Despite German pressure, Turkey refused to allow a transit of arms and troops through its territory. The only open channel left was Vichy-controlled Syria.

On 6 May Iraqi forces retreated from the hills overlooking the base. Troops from Palestine relieved the hard-pressed British garrison at Habbaniya. On 12 May Germany came to Iraq's assistance by sending its Syrian-based bombers to attack British airfields in the Mosul/Iraq region. By 30 May the British had succeeded in crushing the rebellion in Iraq. Rashid Ali and his associates fled to Iran, and Iraq sued for an armistice, terminating its crisis. The following day, Germany announced an agreement of military collaboration between the German and Vichy France governments – despite persistent French pressure for German withdrawal from Syrian territory. The crisis ended for Germany when the *Luftwaffe* detachment from Syria was recalled on 6 June 1941.

On the 8th the British Government announced that it would not tolerate Vichy collaboration with the Germans. Free French troops, with support from Imperial forces, entered Syria and Lebanon that day from Palestine, Transjordan and Iraq, and triggered a crisis for Vichy France. It responded on 17 June with an attack on Quneitra and Marjayun, in the Golan Heights and south Lebanon, respectively. As the Allies began closing in on Damascus on the 20th, Vichy France asked the United States to inquire on what terms an armistice might be conducted. On 8 July General Dentz, the Vichy High Commissioner, received authority to negotiate. An agreement was finally reached on 14 July 1941, terminating the crisis for the UK and Vichy France. The latter fell in November 1942, when Germany occupied the rest of France.

References Churchill 1950a; Khadduri 1960; Lenczowski 1962; Nyrop 1971; Palmer 1973; Penrose 1978.

(49) Barbarossa The Soviet Union's crisis over the German invasion lasted from 22 June to 5 December 1941.

Background The Italo-German campaign in the Balkans ended at the end of May 1941 with a greatly-strengthened Axis position. As a result of the conquest of Greece and Crete, the Aegean Sea became unsafe for British ships (see Case #47). On 13 April Soviet and Japanese diplomats signed a Non-Aggression Pact at Moscow. In late May representatives from Finland, Hungary, Romania and Bulgaria met with the German High Command to coordinate plans to invade Russia. Hitler floated a rumor of Soviet intentions to attack Germany as a pretext for his own premeditated designs against the USSR.

Crisis On 22 June 1941 the Germans, in a surprise attack, invaded the Soviet Union along a front of 2000 miles, triggering a crisis for the USSR. Romanian and Finnish troops participated actively with those of Nazi Germany, while Hungary and Bulgaria provided free passage for German troops on their way east. The Soviets responded the same day with fierce resistance, but were soon forced into a slow retreat. Prime Minister Churchill promised that Britain would extend all possible aid to the Soviets. A Mutual Assistance Pact was concluded between them on 13 July. During the month of July Riga, Latvia's capital, and Smolensk were captured by the Germans. On 19 August the Germans claimed all Ukrainian territory west of the Dnieper River, except Odessa, and on 4 September the siege of Leningrad began. During October Axis forces continued their advance and, by the end of the month, the Germans had entered the Crimea on the southern end of the front and had commenced the battle for Moscow. The Soviet Government transferred its headquarters further east, to Kuybyshev.

On 30 October the United States speeded Soviet purchases of promised American supplies by extending the USSR a credit of one billion dollars. This was later supplemented by a Master Lend-Lease Agreement in 1942. In early December the Soviets began a major counter-thrust before the gates of Moscow. On 5 December the German High Command decided to halt operations on the eastern front for the winter because German troops were worn out, short of ammunition, suffering from the cold and beset by logistics problems. The German halt outside of Moscow on 5 December 1941 ended the first stage of Germany's Russian campaign and, with it, the Soviet crisis. Hitler had not fulfilled his objective – defeat of the Soviet Union within three months. Japan adhered to its Pact with the USSR and remained strictly neutral, but two days later launched the Pacific War with an attack on Pearl Harbor (see Case #52).

References   Bullock 1962; Calvocoressi and Wint 1972; Churchill 1950a; de Gaulle 1971; Palmer 1973.

(50) Marañon II   Ecuador perceived a crisis with Peru over the territory of Marañon from 5 July 1941 to 29 January 1942.

Background   The 100-year dispute between Peru and Ecuador over the territory of Marañon erupted into a crisis in 1935 but ended with the issues unresolved (see Case #17). In December 1938, at the Eighth Conference of American States, several unofficial attempts were made to achieve a settlement – none was successful. During 1939–40 there were numerous border incidents. Relations between Ecuador and Peru deteriorated and, towards the end of 1940, there were rumors of Peruvian troop movements in two directions towards Ecuadorian positions in the east and west. Ecuador increased the number of military posts and built roads for greater maneuverability. By December 1940 the danger of war with Peru was fully recognized by Ecuador.

Crisis   On 5 July 1941 Peruvian agricultural workers, accompanied by civil guards, entered Ecuador and opened fire on an Ecuadorian patrol. Fighting spread to several frontier posts and included Peruvian artillery and air attacks. Argentina, Brazil and the United States proposed a joint effort by all American states to establish peace, but Chile refused to support it. A plan for each side to withdraw 15 kilometers from the recognized boundary was accepted by the adversaries whose representatives arrived in Washington for separate talks with Under-Secretary of State Sumner Welles – to no effect.

On 23 July, as hostilities were renewed along a 50-kilometer front, Argentina, with US support, renewed its appeal to cease hostilities. Ecuador began to mobilize on the 23rd, but agreed to a cease-fire on the 26th. Peru demanded that Ecuador annul the mobilization decree. After much deliberation Ecuador complied on 31 July, despite the fact that an Ecuadorian victory was likely in view of the fact that the Peruvian Army was highly disorganized and desertion among its soldiers was commonplace. On 2 August the mediating powers proposed a 15-kilometer withdrawal of all troops behind the status quo boundaries of 1936 and the placing of observers. Ecuador accepted, but Peru did not reply. A cease-fire was carried out in the western zone, but in the Oriente, where there were no observers, Ecuador reported continued Peruvian advances. On 2 October military commanders of Ecuador and Peru agreed to the "Talara Truce" in which a neutral zone was established between the two lines in the provinces of Guayas, El Oro and Loja. The situation in the Oriente was not affected. And on the 4th Lima proposed a boundary line which corresponded to the most advanced Peruvian posts.

The third Conference of Foreign Ministers of the American States met in Rio de Janeiro on 15 January 1942, where informal negotiations were carried out by the Foreign Ministers of Ecuador and Peru. A protocol was signed on 29 January describing the boundary zones between the two countries and ending the fighting between them. The boundary was considerably more favorable to the Peruvian position.

References   See sources for Case #17.

(51) Occupation of Iran   Iran's crisis over the Anglo-Soviet invasion of its territory began on 25 August 1941 and ended on 29 January 1942.

Background Iran's neutrality at the onset of World War II was opposed by the UK and the Soviet Union because of that country's rich oil reserves and the Allied need for strategic bases and communication routes. They particularly objected to the large number of Germans in Iran and demanded their expulsion by August 1941. Iran refused to comply, maintaining its right to control its own internal affairs.

Crisis The Anglo-Soviet invasion on 25 August 1941 triggered a crisis for Iran which promptly ordered its army to resist the attack. When resistance collapsed within 48 hours, Reza Shah abdicated in favor of his son Muhammad Reza. A decision was reached on 28 August, at an extraordinary session of the Cabinet, to cease fire and to continue diplomatic negotiations already in progress. Soviet troops occupied the north of the country, while the British occupied the south, joined, in 1942, by American troops. Negotiations with Britain and the Soviet Union continued throughout the year. While the British assumed a more flexible position, the Soviets proceeded to increase their demands upon Iran. During the course of the negotiations Iran sought direct United States intervention. While the US refused to participate in the talks at that time, it did serve as a mediator and was instrumental in bringing about a Treaty of Alliance between Iran and the UK/USSR. The treaty was signed on 29 January 1942, ending Iran's crisis.

References See sources for Case #71.

(52) Pearl Harbor The Japanese attack on the US Pacific Fleet at Pearl Harbor constituted a crisis for the United States, Australia, Canada, Germany, Italy, Japan, The Netherlands, New Zealand, Thailand and the United Kingdom. The duration of the crisis was from 26 November 1941 until 7 June 1942.

Background Japan's quest for an empire in the Far East, symbolized by the proclamation of the "Greater East Asia Co-Prosperity Sphere," began with the invasion of Manchuria in 1931 (see Case #4). During the 1930s the Imperial Army spread southward into China. Later its attention shifted to the Western colonial empires in Southeast Asia (Malaya, Indonesia, etc.). These countries could supply Japan's need for raw materials so as to reduce its dependence on other countries, notably the United States, for such strategic commodities as petroleum, rubber and iron.

In 1941 both the United States and Britain stood in the way of complete Japanese control of the Far East and Southeast Asia. The United States had vested interests in the region since the early part of the century, and its army and navy occupied important bases around Manila Bay in the Philippines. The Americans considered the Philippines a vital link in the defense line for the protection of the west coast and continental United States. The British had long controlled Malaya and Borneo, with Singapore serving as one of the most important UK bases for imperial defense.

The fall of France in 1940 (see Case #42) had removed one of Japan's obstacles – in French Indochina – and by 1941 the Konoye Government had worked out an arrangement with Vichy France for the use of French territory as a military corridor and base. The Dutch Government and royal family fled to London with the fall of The Netherlands on 12 May 1940. However, its Government-in-Exile, together with the Dutch East Indies Government (headed by the Governor-General), continued to run the affairs of Indonesia, which was rich in oil and rubber.

During 1940 the United States exerted economic pressure on Japan. On 25 July the President prohibited the export of petroleum, petroleum products and scrap metal without license. A few days later an embargo was imposed on the export of aviation fuel to all countries outside the Western Hemisphere except for use by American planes. The embargo was expanded to scrap iron and steel after the signing of the Germany–Italy–Japan Tripartite Pact on 26 September 1940. After Japan landed troops in French Indochina on 24 July 1941, talks between Japan and the United States were broken off and all Japanese assets in the United States were frozen, effectively cutting Japan off from its most important markets and sources of raw materials.

In August Prime Minister Konoye sought a meeting with President Roosevelt but none was arranged. Later that month, at a joint army–navy meeting, the heads of the Japanese armed forces agreed in principle that, if diplomacy did not bring results by mid-October, the use of force against the US would be unavoidable; and they subsequently stated that the decision for war or peace must be made by 15 October. Between 25 September and 15 October Konoye was unsuccessful in gaining political control over the Supreme Command of the Armed Forces. The Cabinet resigned on 16 October and Konoye was replaced, on the 18th, by General Tojo, who retained the position of War Minister.

To America's surprise, Tojo decided to continue the diplomatic efforts and sent a second envoy, Kurusu, to Washington to help the resident Ambassador, Nomura, in his efforts to reach an agreement. Meanwhile, secret plans for the military campaign against the United States continued. During the first two weeks of November the Japanese Embassy in Washington received a steady stream of messages which would eventually make up two Japanese proposals, A and B. These messages were deciphered by US Naval Intelligence, through MAGIC, thus informing the Americans of a new Japanese deadline of 25 November for acceptance of the final proposal. (The deadline, the Americans discovered, was postponed to 29 November.) Japan's proposals were rejected by Secretary of State Cordell Hull.

Crisis On 26 November 1941 Hull presented the two Japanese Ambassadors with a Ten Point Plan, viewed by Japan as an ultimatum and triggering a crisis for it. At the same time that Nomura and Kurusu were talking with Hull, Nagumo's task force had been at sea for 24 hours en route to Pearl Harbor. However, it was still in Tojo's power to stop them. On 1 December Japan's major response was a decision for war, but negotiations with the United States continued until 7 December.

The attack on Pearl Harbor, on 7 December 1941, triggered a crisis for the United States as well as Australia, Britain, Canada, The Netherlands and New Zealand. The Americans suffered 2403 deaths and over 1000 wounded. The United States responded on 8 December with a declaration of war. The British responded to the attack on a friendly state, as well as to the attack on Malaya the same day, by declaring war on Japan. Canada did likewise on the 8th. The Netherlands' response, on 8 December, was to mobilize the army in The Netherlands East Indies and to declare a state of emergency.

The trigger for Thailand's crisis was a Japanese attack on its territory on 8 December. After only 5 hours of fighting, the Thai Government surrendered and announced that it would allow Japanese forces to pass through its territory. Japan, it was contended, would respect Thailand's territorial integrity. On 8 December, too, when the United States and its allies declared war on Japan, a crisis was triggered for Italy and Germany. The following day Australia and New Zealand responded to the crisis with similar declarations of war. On 10 December Thailand announced that it would not fight together with the Allied forces, thereby ending its crisis. And on 11 December Italy and Germany declared war on the United States. On the 21st a 10-year alliance was signed at Bangkok between Japan and Thailand: the Thai Government agreed to aid Japan and declared war on Britain and the United States on 25 January 1942.

On 25 December 1941 British and Canadian forces in Hong Kong surrendered to the Japanese. In January the Japanese forces occupied The Netherlands East Indies. Singapore fell on 15 February 1942 when the Japanese, having penetrated Malaya, landed from the north. Sixty thousand prisoners were taken. The fall of Singapore, signalling apparent victory for Japan, terminated the crisis for it and the Axis allies, Germany and Italy. The British surrender terminated the UK crisis, in defeat.

From 27 January to 1 March the Battle of the Java Sea took place – Allied naval units were largely destroyed, and the way was opened for the Japanese conquest of the East Indies. The end of the crisis for The Netherlands was its formal surrender on 5 March 1942. In March the British evacuated Rangoon, allowing Japan to occupy Burma; the Burma Road was subsequently closed. The Battle of the Coral Sea began on 7 May. Allied naval and air power frustrated a possible Japanese invasion of Australia by destroying 100,000 tons of Japanese shipping between New Guinea and the Solomon Islands. On 8 May, with the reduction of danger, the crisis ended for Australia and New Zealand. And on 4 June a Japanese naval force attacked Midway Island and was dispersed, with heavy losses, by American air and naval units. The crisis for Canada and the United States ended on 7 June 1942.

The United States approached the Pan American Union on 10 December 1941, but no activity followed.

References   Butow 1961; Churchill 1950a; Dallek 1979; Prange 1981; Toland 1970; Vandenbosch 1959; Watt 1967; Wohlstetter 1962.

(53) El Alamein   The North African Campaign, beginning with the Battle of El Alamein, was an intra-war crisis for Italy and Germany from 23 October 1942 to 13 May 1943.

Background   In the summer of 1941 a number of military victories were achieved by the Axis powers in North Africa. The British had been considerably weakened by their dispatch of 60,000 troops to Greece and had been forced to abandon recent conquests in Libya. On 21 June German General Rommel, commanding eight Italian divisions along with the Afrika Corps, captured Tobruk, the key to British defenses in North Africa. By the end of the month Rommel had moved towards the British-held stronghold at El Alamein in Egypt. When fuel shortages became extreme, the Italians were forced to halt their advance.

Crisis   On 23 October 1942 the British Eighth Army, commanded by General Montgomery, attacked from its position at El Alamein and broke through the Axis lines, triggering a crisis for Italy and Germany. The battle, which turned the tide of the war in North Africa, lasted 16 days.

A major British attack on 1–2 November succeeded in breaking through the southern sector of the front and overrunning the Italian divisions in the area. Rommel contacted Hitler's headquarters and informed him of his intention to withdraw while opportunity still prevailed. On 3 November Hitler ordered Rommel to stand fast and use all men and weapons available to defend the Axis position; the Italian response was similar. Rommel adhered reluctantly to the order. By the time permission for withdrawal was given the following day it was too late to save anything but the motorized divisions of the Panzer Army.

On 8 November an Anglo/American Force, commanded by General Eisenhower, disembarked in French Morocco and Algiers in an amphibious operation hitherto unequalled in history. Within three days Vichy French resistance had collapsed. The British headed towards Tunisia. Tobruk was reoccupied on 12 November and Benghazi on the 20th – by British forces advancing from Egypt into Libya.

From 17 to 27 January Churchill, de Gaulle and Roosevelt met in Casablanca. Eisenhower took command of the unified Allied North African operations. The British Eighth Army broke through the Mareth Line into southern Tunisia and met the advancing American Second Army Corps on 8 April. The termination of the crisis for Italy and Germany was 13 May 1943 when all German and Italian troops in North Africa surrendered.

References   Churchill 1950b; Ciano 1947; Liddell-Hart 1953; Mussolini 1949; Shirer 1964; Woodward 1962.

(54) Stalingrad   Germany's intra-war crisis over Stalingrad occurred from 19 November 1942 to 2 February 1943.

Background   The city of Stalingrad was cut off from its Soviet hinterland, both in the north and the south, in August 1942. On 14 September 1942 German forces launched another heavy attack on the city. Their summer offensive appeared on the point of succeeding, but they had overstretched their lines. Soviet forces counter-attacked northwest of Stalingrad on the 19th, and a day and a half later they opened a second attack southeast of the city.

Crisis   On 19 November 1942 the USSR launched a massive counter-offensive at Stalingrad, triggering a crisis for Germany. The following day Germany responded with a personal order from Hitler to stand fast. During the course of the crisis this "no retreat" decision was repeated several times – after Field Marshal Manstein's request to withdraw on 25 November and General Zeitzler's similar appeal during December. The German operation, "Winter Gale," began on 12 December, but the Germans suffered defeat after defeat. Soviet forces recaptured Velikye-Luki on 1 January and entered Mozdok on the 3rd to relieve Leningrad from a 17-month siege. On 8 January 1943 the Soviets presented Hitler with an ultimatum to surrender at Stalingrad, which was refused. On the 10th the last phase of the Battle of Stalingrad began with an enormous artillery bombardment. Another Soviet demand for German surrender was made on the 24th, again refused by Hitler. On 31 January Soviet forces captured Field Marshal Paulus, the commander of the German forces at Stalingrad. Twenty-two German divisions were cut off at Stalingrad and reduced to 80,000 men. They were forced to capitulate on 2 February 1943, ending Germany's crisis in defeat. The second Soviet winter offensive lasted three months, with the Germans and their allies losing more than 500,000 men, killed or captured.

References   Ciano 1947; Freidin and Richardson 1956; Gilbert 1950; Jukes 1985; Schroter 1958; Seaton 1970; Shirer 1964.

(55) Fall of Italy

The Allied invasion of Italy triggered an intra-war crisis for Germany and Italy from 10 July to 11 September 1943.

Background   The Anglo-American campaign in North Africa resulted in a crushing defeat for Germany and Italy in May 1943 (see Case #53).

Crisis   American, British and Canadian forces launched an attack on Sicily on 10 July 1943, triggering a crisis for Italy: its mainland was threatened; and there was an imminent danger of the collapse of Mussolini's Fascist regime. Italy's leader perceived capitulation as a threat to Italy's existence as a Great Power, in fact, as a power at all. Mussolini met with Hitler on 19 July in the hope of obtaining Hitler's consent to Italy's early withdrawal from the war; no concessions were granted. The Italian response, on 24 July, was the dismissal of Mussolini by the King, at a meeting of the Fascist Grand Council, and the appointment of a new government under Marshal Pietro Badoglio. The Council, which had not met since 12 September 1939, criticized Mussolini for leading the country into disaster. The majority of the party leaders were convinced of the advisability of a conclusion of a separate peace and a return to constitutional monarchy.

The news of Mussolini's dismissal, on 25 July, triggered a crisis for Germany. Armistice proposals by Italy, expected within a week to 10 days, would jeopardize German strategic control of northern Italy and expose the Reich's southern flank. The following day Hitler ordered German forces into northern Italy. On 18 August Italian resistance in Sicily collapsed following thousands of casualties on both sides. Allied troops landed on the boot of southern Italy on 2 September. The next day an armistice agreement was signed between Italy and the Western Powers, ending hostilities between the Anglo-American forces and those of the Badoglio regime. German and Italian forces evacuated Sicily on 8 September, terminating Italy's crisis with the Allies. On the 10th Italian forces surrendered to the Germans after they were defeated in the battle around Rome. The crisis ended for Germany on 11 September when all Italian territory, including Rome, was declared by the German Army to be a theater of war under German military control.

Mussolini, who had been held prisoner near Rome, was rescued by German troops, and proclaimed the establishment of a Republican Fascist Party in northern Italy, in alliance with the German Army of Occupation.

References   Churchill 1951; Deakin 1962; Liddell-Hart 1953; Mussolini 1949; Shirer 1964.

(56) German
Occupation of Hungary

Hungary's intra-war crisis with Germany lasted from 13 to 19 March 1944.

Background After Italy's capitulation to the Allies in September 1943 (see Case #55), Germany began to consider the possibility of a similar fate for Hungary and Romania, and plans were made for German occupation of both countries. While Romania was perceived to be a lesser problem, it was known that Hungary had begun to send out feelers for an armistice agreement with the Allies. German plans for the occupation of Hungary were operationalized on 12 March, as Soviet forces moved rapidly toward the Hungarian frontier.

Crisis The concentration of German troops around Vienna and on the Hungarian frontier triggered a crisis for Hungary on 13 March 1944. Two days later, Hitler demanded that Hungary's Regent, Horthy, meet with him. While Horthy deliberated his decision, fearing his detention and arrest while Germany occupied Hungary, the Allies decided finally to seek an armistice with Hungary and therefore dropped a US Mission into that country, on 17 March, to discuss terms of surrender. By 18 March Horthy had decided that he was compelled to see Hitler at any cost, and set out to do so.

Horthy was detained for one day, under the pretext of an air raid, and allowed to reach the Hungarian frontier as German troops began their invasion. On 19 March Hungary was occupied by Germany with no real resistance. The US Mission was turned over to the German forces, and Hungary's capitulation ended its crisis.

References Fenyo 1972; Macartney 1956-57; Shirer 1964; Speer 1970; Werth 1964.

(57) Soviet Occupation
of East Europe

Soviet offensives into Eastern Europe in 1944–45 created an intra-war crisis for Romania, Germany and Hungary from 26 March 1944 to 13 February 1945.

Background Romanian oil fields had been protected by Germany since 1939, and on 23 September 1940 Romania became a member of the Tripartite Pact (Germany, Italy, Japan), fighting alongside Germany against the Soviet Union. As the tide turned at the Battle of Stalingrad (see Case #54), Soviet troops began major offensives into Eastern Europe. In December 1943 the United States and the USSR, followed by Britain, warned Romania, Bulgaria and Hungary that Germany's defeat would mean a defeat for those countries as well. Romania's King Michael began to try to find ways to arrange an agreement with the Allies. By the end of March Soviet troops were marching towards Romania's borders.

Hungarian peace-feelers throughout 1943 provoked German suspicions; and that country was occupied by Germany on 19 March 1944, at the time that Hungarian Regent Horthy was meeting with Hitler (see Case #56). The economic situation in Hungary was severe from 1943, along with increased repression, as a result of the German occupation.

Crisis A crisis was triggered for Romania on 26 March with the arrival of Soviet forces at its border, threatening defeat and occupation. A USSR announcement on 2 April declared that the Soviet Union did not wish to take over Romanian territory; nor did it aspire to create a new social order there. Soviet troops would enter the country only as needed to continue the resistance to enemy forces. On the 4th the Allies began mass bombings of Romania, especially oil production installations. One week later Soviet armistice terms were rejected by Romania. By 5 May oil production was down to half of its previous level.

Romania's major response, on 23 August, was King Michael's acceptance of armistice terms preferred covertly by the Soviet Union. An amnesty was declared for political prisoners, and a Government of National Union was set up: Romania would henceforth fight alongside the Allies. The Romanian response triggered a crisis for Germany, with the loss of an ally, and the threat of the Soviet thrust extending to Germany itself. The German response, the same day, was an order to seize the Romanian oil fields and the nearby harbor of Constanta, and to set up a pro-German Government in Romania. On the 25th Germany bombed Bucharest while negotiations between the Soviets and the Romanians continued. On 12 September an armistice was signed in Moscow, ending the crisis for Romania.

Within a week Soviet forces approached the borders of Bulgaria, Yugoslavia and Hungary. And on 27 September they expelled the Germans from Romania, ending Germany's crisis over Romania in defeat.

A crisis for Hungary was triggered on 22 September with an invasion by Soviet and Romanian forces. Hungary attempted to contact the Allies that day, and again on 10 October, when a provisional armistice was arranged in Moscow conditional on Hungary's joining the war against Germany. Hungary responded on 15 October with Horthy's proclamation of an armistice. Some Hungarian troops, however, joined the German forces. Hungary's response triggered another crisis for Germany, which responded on the 16th by placing Horthy under protective custody; and, as the Hungarians surrendered, German forces took over Budapest. Horthy finally signed the appointment of Szalasi, head of the pro-Nazi Arrow Cross movement, as Prime Minister.

By December 1944 the Red Army had begun a siege of Budapest, completely encircling the city by the 26th. The battle lasted two more months and, on 13 February, Budapest fell, terminating the crisis for both Germany and Hungary in defeat, with the latter effectively out of the war.

Bulgaria held a series of negotiations with the Soviet Union and eventually withdrew from the Axis and entered the war against Germany.

References   Bullock 1962; Fenyo 1972; Ionescu 1964; Macartney 1956–57; Shirer 1964.

(58) D-Day

An intra-war crisis was triggered for Germany with the Allied landing in Western Europe on 6 June 1944. It lasted until Germany's surrender on 7 May 1945.

Background   By 1944 the tide of war had definitely turned in the Allies' favor. The end of Axis resistance in North Africa had been achieved by 13 May 1943 (see Case #53). The Soviets had defeated the Germans at Stalingrad and at Kursk-Orel and were advancing rapidly through Eastern Europe (see Cases #54 and #63). German divisions in southern Italy had been forced to retreat (Case #55). And the war in the Pacific was proceeding successfully for the Americans (Case #59). For many months careful and elaborate plans for the invasion of France had been made by the Supreme Headquarters of the Allied Expeditionary Forces, commanded by General Eisenhower. The chief base for the concentration of men and war materials was Britain and the plan of the campaign had been rehearsed and prepared to the finest detail.

Crisis   An intra-war crisis was triggered for Germany on 6 June 1944 when British, American and Canadian forces invaded Nazi-occupied Western Europe. The German response was immediate: wherever they encountered Allied troops they fought back, hoping to prevent a firm Allied foothold on the Normandy coast. Within one week, however, a strip of beach 60 miles long had been occupied and artificial harbors were constructed – to offset the lack of port facilities for disembarkation. With the capture of Cherbourg on 27 June the Allies gained a major port. Throughout the summer they advanced into France and Belgium and, on 2 September, the American First Army crossed the German frontier. The advance was halted when an Allied attempt to outflank the Westwall through the flat Dutch territory in the north failed, and survivors of an Allied airborne division, which had been dropped in Holland at Arnhem, had to be withdrawn. On 16 December the Germans broke through US defense lines in the Belgian and Luxemburg sector. The Battle of the Bulge inflicted heavy losses, and the Allied forces were driven back to the Meuse. The gap was closed by the end of September when the Allies rallied to attack on both sides of the "bulge."

With the beginning of 1945 the Allied drive into Germany from the west co-ordinated with the rapid and powerful Soviet offensive from the east (see Case #63). President Roosevelt, Prime Minister Churchill and Marshal Stalin met at Yalta in the Crimea on 7 February to plan the final defeat and occupation of Germany. The US First and Third Armies crossed into Germany in February and March, and the British and Canadians opened an offensive southeast of Nijmegen, Holland. By 12 April the US Ninth Army had reached the Elbe River. On that day, too, President Roosevelt died. Soviet forces fought their way into Berlin on the

25th, and on the 26th the armies of the US and USSR met on the Elbe at Torgau. On 29 April German resistance in northern Italy broke and on 1 May the Battle of Berlin began. A German radio announcement from Hamburg declared that Hitler had died that day. On 7 May a group of German army leaders sent envoys to Reims where they signed terms of surrender, ending the crisis for Germany and the war in Europe.

References Calvocoressi and Wint 1972; Churchill 1951, 1953; Eisenhower 1948; Liddell-Hart 1970; Palmer 1973; Weigley 1981.

(59) Saipan

The defeat at Saipan precipitated an intra-war crisis for Japan between 9 and 18 July 1944.

Background The war in the Pacific had been turning against Japan since the Battle of Midway in June 1942 (see Case #52). Towards the end of 1943 and the beginning of 1944 Japanese sea lanes came under continuous attack from the American and British navies. Although the Japanese leadership understood the gravity of the situation, the Japanese press continued to inform the public of the war's progress – in Japan's favor. In February 1944 the largest carrier-launched air armada in history attacked Japan's strategic Caroline Islands base at Truk, sinking 19–26 ships and destroying about 200 planes. Prime Minister Tojo carried out a major reorganization and consolidation of his Cabinet on 19 February. He assumed the post of Chief of the Army General Staff and appointed Navy Minister Shimada as Chief of Naval General Staff. For the first time in Japanese history administrative and command posts were held by the same persons.

Severe restrictions were placed on Japanese society. There was mobilization and reorganization of labor and business. Air raid defense networks were built, and entertainment centers were closed. As the presssure of the Allied forces grew, so did the opposition to Tojo within the Japanese élite. In June American forces delivered a series of devastating attacks upon Saipan, Tinian, Guam and Rota in the Marianas. The strategic cordon of defense which Japan had created around the home islands vanished rapidly. The American invasion of Saipan (Operation Forager) began with a bombardment of Japanese positions on 13 June 1944. The island's strategic importance was due to the fact that long-range American bombers, if installed on airstrips there, could threaten the Japanese people in their cities and towns.

Crisis The defeat at Saipan on 9 July 1944 triggered another intra-war crisis for Japan which perceived a threat of grave damage to its population centers. On 13 July Tojo sought advice from the Lord Privy Seal, Marquis Kido, who had been Tojo's supporter for the position of Prime Minister. The Marquis Kido presented the Prime Minister with three conditions aimed at changing the nature and style of his government. He demanded the separation of the War Minister and Army Chief of Staff posts, the replacement of the Navy Minister, and the formation of a United Front Cabinet which would include members of the senior statesmen-group (*Jushin*), consisting of former Prime Ministers.

During the next four days Tojo made unsuccessful attempts to reorganize his Cabinet. Most ex-Prime Ministers refused to join and demanded Tojo's resignation. On 18 July Tojo's resignation terminated this crisis for Japan.

References See sources for Case #52.

(60) Iran

A crisis for Iran over Soviet demands for oil concessions took place from 26 September to 9 December 1944.

Background In August 1941 Soviet troops occupied northern Iran, and British troops, joined by Americans in January 1942, occupied the south (see Case #51). In January 1942 Britain, the US and the USSR signed the Tripartite Treaty of Alliance in which the three powers undertook to respect Iran's sovereignty and to withdraw from that country within six months after the cessation of hostilities with the Axis powers. Contrary to this treaty, the USSR showed signs of continuing its occupation in order to keep northern Iran and its oil resources within the sphere of Soviet influence.

At that time there were only two authorized oil concessionaires in Iran: the Anglo-Iranian Oil Company in the southwest, and the Kavir-i-Khurian Company near Semnan, owned jointly by the Soviet Union and an Iranian group. The publication, in August 1944, of a general Anglo-American agreement for oil concessions in the southeast aroused criticism by the Communist-dominated *Tudeh* Party in a *Majlis* (Parliament) debate, and apparently disturbed the Soviets to a point at which they decided to revive their claims to oil concessions in northern Iran.

Crisis   A crisis was triggered on 26 September 1944 when the Soviet Assistant Peoples' Commissar for Foreign Affairs, Kavtaradre, during a visit to Teheran, demanded oil concessions in five northern Iranian provinces. The Soviet demand was viewed by nationalist elements in Iran's Government as being detrimental to Iran's national interests, as well as an infringement upon Iran's sovereignty. Iran's response was a decision to reject all (British, American and Soviet) demands for oil concessions. Whereas Britain and the United States accepted the Iranian decision, the USSR rejected it and questioned the integrity of Iran's Prime Minister Sa'id. This was followed by a violent press campaign by the *Tudeh* Party attacking Sa'id's policies and demanding his resignation. The campaign led to mass demonstrations in Teheran and other cities against Sa'id. In Teheran, Soviet Army trucks carried considerable numbers of *Tudeh* Party members to a demonstration in front of the *Majlis*, while Soviet Army detachments with tanks protected the demonstrators against any counter-action by Iranian troops. The presence of Soviet troops paralyzed any activity on the part of the Iranians. Sa'id resigned on 8 November and a new government was formed by Mortera Quli Bayat. This new government was also attacked by the *Tudeh* Party in demonstrations and through the press. On 2 December the *Majlis* passed a law forbidding any minister to grant or negotiate oil concessions with foreign governments without parliamentary approval. The crisis ended when Kavtaradre and his delegation left Iran for Moscow on 9 December. The United States, whose political activity did not specifically oppose Soviet claims, disappointed Iran which had looked towards the US as a friendly third power.

References   See sources for case #71.

(61) Leyte and Luzon   The American invasion of the island of Leyte in the Philippines created a crisis for Japan from 20 October to 26 December 1944. Similarly, the invasion of Luzon created a crisis for it from 9 January to 24 February 1945.

Background   The Japanese anticipated an early American invasion to retake the Philippines, and, in the summer of 1944, they began developing defense plans which included air and navy support. By September 1944 Japan had suffered serious reverses on both military and diplomatic fronts (see Case #59).

Crisis   On 20 October 1944 US invasion groups landed on the island of Leyte, opening the campaign for the reconquest of the Philippines and triggering a crisis for Japan: Tokyo perceived a strategic threat to the home islands if the Philippines fell to the Americans. Japan's response, on 23 October, was to withdraw its fleet from Philippine waters once they had failed to halt the invasion. The Japanese Navy suffered a loss of 40 ships sunk, 46 damaged and 405 planes destroyed. The Philippines had been earmarked by Japan as the first in a series of decisive battles which were slated to end in Japan's overwhelming triumph. When the army agreed to concentrate its forces in a bold effort to rout the Americans, Prime Minister Koiso and the Japanese people were led to believe that a Japanese victory in Leyte would turn the tide of the war. After the defeat, Japan no longer had a fleet or airforce that could mount an offensive. Japan was losing planes and pilots faster than they could be replaced. On 24 November the first large-scale B-29 raids on Japan began. These destroyed major Japanese aircraft factories. On 26 December the US announced the successful completion of the Leyte Campaign, granting control of the Pacific to the Allies.

After the defeat at Leyte, Japanese political and military leaders concentrated their hopes for victory on Luzon. As the situation deteriorated in the Philippines, the Emperor called a meeting of the *Jushin* (senior statesmen) on 6 January to seek their opinion on the future course. While the Japanese military had already lost the war, some of the *Jushin* advised, Japanese spirit could not be destroyed! For want of a better solution, they now proposed a concentration of their forces against the US in the hope that a victorious battle would permit Japan to end the war on more favorable terms.

On 9 January the Americans invaded Luzon, triggering a new crisis for Japan. The Sixth Army had gained an element of surprise by selecting an undesirable part of the coastline for landing. A combination of Allied artillery, air bombardment and the dogged advance of the infantry gradually led to progress. Although the Japanese forces were cut off from retreat in Manila, they continued to refuse to surrender. Other US forces sought to secure Manila Bay. Finally, on 24 February, the Allied occupation of Manila was completed.

References See sources for Case #52.

(62) Greek Civil War I A crisis for Britain over Greece lasted from 3 December 1944 to 15 January 1945.

Background After the withdrawal of the German occupation forces from Greece in October 1944, there was an intense struggle for power among Greece's political factions. The British, who were determined to impose a settlement which would ensure stability and their strong presence in the country, were in direct opposition to Greece's Communists. The Caserta Agreement, signed on 20 September 1944, called for all guerrilla forces in the country to be placed under Greek Government command, headed by British General Scobie.

Crisis The crisis trigger for Britain was an exchange of fire between Greek Communist demonstrators and the police on 3 December 1944. This touched off a violent civil war which was perceived by Britain as a threat to its influence in the international system. More specifically, a Communist takeover in Greece would virtually end all British influence in the region. Prime Minister Churchill responded the next day by ordering General Scobie to intervene with his forces and to open fire if necessary. Churchill flew to Athens on 24 December in an effort to bring the various factions together and settle the crisis. British and Greek troops succeeded in driving the Greek Communists out of Athens.

The crisis for Britain ended on 15 January 1945 with the implementation of a truce agreement. The United States was not active in this crisis, though Churchill and Roosevelt corresponded regularly. State Department criticism of British intervention was viewed unfavorably by Churchill. On the other hand, USSR inactivity was viewed favorably by him because it meant that Stalin was living up to the terms of the "spheres of influence" agreement struck at an earlier meeting in Moscow. The civil war in Greece erupted into another crisis for Britain in 1946 (see Case #75).

References See sources for Case #75.

(63) Final Soviet Offensive An intra-war crisis for Germany took place from the beginning of the final Soviet offensive on 11 January until Germany's surrender on 7 May 1945. This crisis overlapped with the German crisis over the continuing Allied advance in Western Europe in 1944–45 (see Case #58). Both ended with Germany's capitulation.

Background   The campaign was planned by the Soviets as a separate and well-defined offensive. The aim was to strike at the heart of the Third Reich. The Russian homeland had been liberated from Nazi conquest by July 1944 and, by 29 August, Soviet forces had reached the border of East Prussia. At this point they halted and deliberately did not penetrate German territory. Instead, concentration centered on the Baltic peninsula and the Balkans. These areas were liberated in October and December of 1944. In January 1945 the Soviets turned their full attention to the planning of a two-pronged attack against East Prussia in the north and Silesia in the center.

Crisis   An intra-war crisis for Germany was triggered on 11 January 1945 when the first part of the Soviet offensive began with a thrust from Poland into Silesia. For the first time Germany proper was threatened. The German response was immediate: they used every means available to them in order to halt the Soviet advance. On 13 January the second Soviet thrust advanced from Lithuania into East Prussia. By 1 February East Prussia had been conquered and the Soviets advanced into Silesia capturing a long and broad front inside the eastern border of Germany along the Oder River from Zehden in the north to Ratibor in the south. By the end of March they were holding the entire area of eastern Germany. On 25 April 1945 the Soviets entered Berlin.

Meanwhile the Allies were advancing in western Germany (see Case #58), and the two armies met on the 25th. Thereafter, both armies converged on those parts of Germany which had not yet been conquered until the Third Reich finally collapsed and surrendered on 7 May 1945 to the Allied and Soviet Commands.

References   Calvocoressi and Wint 1972; Churchill 1953; Clark 1965; Werth 1964.

(64) Iwo Jima   The Battle of Iwo Jima was an intra-war crisis for Japan from 19 February to 16 March 1945.

Background   The island of Iwo Jima, located among a volcanic group of islands midway between the Marianas and Japan, was of high strategic salience to the armies of both adversaries. Japan used it as a staging base for damaging raids on grounded US B-29s in the Marianas, and the Americans found it imperative to capture the island, destroy the airbase and establish a position 750 miles from Yokahama. Iwo Jima received the longest and most intensive US pre-invasion bombardment of any objective in the Pacific. Regular air raids had begun in August 1944 and, soon thereafter, they were a daily occurrence. Nevertheless, Japanese defenses were not destroyed. After the fall of Saipan (see Case #59), the Japanese determined to convert Iwo Jima into an impregnable fortress. As the bombs fell, they dug deeper underground.

Crisis   An intra-war crisis for Japan was triggered on 19 February when the US launched a massive invasion of Iwo Jima. Firing from concealed points, the Japanese resisted the American advance yard by yard in a stubborn and protracted battle which cost the US 19,938 casualties, including 4198 dead. On 8 March the Japanese began one of their most concerted counter-attacks. It caught the US Marines off guard and they, in turn, rallied for a great flanking movement which pressed the Japanese back towards the sea. Japanese losses were very high. The last phase of the battle began on 11 March with a more rapid American advance. On 16 March one of the last segments of opposition was pushed into a small region on the northern end of the island where the Japanese fought defiantly until the end. Other pockets were eliminated, with difficulty. The crisis for Japan ended in defeat on the 16th.

The following day the Americans raised the US flag on the island of Iwo Jima.

References   See sources for Case #52.

(65) Communism in Romania   A crisis between Romania and the Soviet Union lasted from 24 February to 6 March 1945.

Background   The Soviet August 1944 offensive against Germany prompted a palace revolt in
Bucharest on 23 August 1944, and Romania became part of the Allied war effort
against Germany (see Case #57). Predominant Soviet influence in Romania was
recognized by the Allies in September 1944. Following the palace coup there was a
succession of governments. Radescu was appointed Prime Minister in December
1944. The domestic political situation during his tenure was very fluid and the
country became increasingly paralyzed between the Right and Left. Disturbances
occurred in factories, with Communist attempts to take over workshop committees.
In February 1945 unrest steadily mounted, with violent criticisms in the Soviet
media. The Romanian press was suppressed.

Crisis   The Soviet crisis was triggered on 24 February 1945 when rioting erupted in
Bucharest. That evening Premier Radescu broadcast a call to resist all foreign
attempts at intervention in Romania's affairs. The USSR response was the dispatch
of Deputy Foreign Minister Vyshinsky to Bucharest on 27 February. Moscow
demanded that Radescu be replaced immediately on the grounds that he was
incapable of maintaining order. When King Michael refused to consider this,
Vyshinsky issued an ultimatum to appoint the "democratic choice" as Premier,
Petru Groza, the Soviet candidate for the position. He also informed the King that
his refusal would be interpreted as a hostile act against the Soviet Union. Simultaneous with Vyshinsky's ultimatum, the Soviet Command in Bucharest moved
Romanian troops from the capital to the front, eliminating the King's chances of
resistance while one million Soviet troops remained within striking distance of the
capital. This ultimatum, on 28 February, triggered a crisis for Romania. Soviet
demands were complied with on 1 March. The termination date for both crisis
actors was 6 March 1945. when Groza was installed as Prime Minister after the
King had overcome domestic opposition.

References   Bishop and Crayfield 1948; Byrnes 1947; Fischer-Galati 1969, 1970; Ionescu
1964.

(66) Okinawa   Japan's intra-war crisis over the island of Okinawa took place from 1 April to 21
June 1945.

Background   By the spring of 1945 both time and space for Japan had run out. US victories in
the Philippines (see Case #61) and Iwo Jima (see Case #64) had completely chiseled
away the outer walls of Japan's outposts of defense, and the route to final victory
was thoroughly controlled by Allied air and naval power. On 21 March a United
States aircraft carrier, penetrating Japanese inland waters, attacked principal units
of the Japanese fleet, damaging 15 warships and destroying 475 planes. Japanese
suicide attacks had become a calculated tactic as the US proceeded to plan for the
occupation of Okinawa, 325 miles from Japanese cities.

Crisis   On 1 April US Marines and Army troops invaded Okinawa and triggered another
intra-war crisis for Japan. A Japanese attempt to check this amphibious operation
resulted in the sinking by American aircraft of the Japanese battleship *Yamato*, two
cruisers and three destroyers. On 5 April the Koiso Cabinet collapsed in Tokyo.
That day, as well, the Soviets announced that they would not renew their Neutrality
Pact with Japan. One of the most extensive suicide assaults of modern warfare was
launched by Japan on 6 April. A 5-hour battle ensued in which 135 *Kamikazi* pilots
sank six vessels and damaged 18 others. Heavy fighting in April brought the
adversaries to a stalemate. Toward the end of the month a Japanese counter-attack
was launched. American advances were slowed down both by the strong resistance
and the heavy rains. On 9 June the new Prime Minister, Suzuki, announced that
Japan would continue to defend itself to the end and that unconditional surrender
was out of the question. Official resistance on Okinawa ended on 21 June 1945.
    The Okinawa campaign was the climax of Japan's final resistance; it left little
room for doubt as to the outcome of the Pacific War.

References   See sources for Case #52.

(67) Trieste I   The first international crisis over Trieste took place from 1 May to 11 June 1945. Great Britain, the United States and Yugoslavia were the crisis actors.

Background   With the crumbling of German resistance, the military issues which had necessitated cooperation between the Soviet Union and the Western allies were rapidly being superseded by political and ideological disputes related to the post-war settlement. At this juncture the fundamental differences in their economic systems, political regimes, ideological beliefs and historically competing interests, as well as the diverse immediate concerns of each actor, led to the breakdown of the Grand Alliance. It gave way rapidly to intense competition and potential conflict over spheres of influence in war-ravaged Europe. By the spring of 1945 these differences began to crystallize in the form of increasingly evident political objectives behind military directives.

Churchill urged the Americans to seize as much territory in Europe as possible. Trieste, located on the Adriatic coast along the Italian–Yugoslav border, reflected the emerging clash of interests between East and West. As German troops retreated from Italy, Anglo-American forces reached the northeast – to find that Tito had preceded them with his Yugoslav Partisans.

Crisis   On 1 May 1945 a crisis was perceived by Britain when Churchill received a cable from the Supreme Allied Commander in the Mediterranean reporting the presence of Tito's forces in Trieste. The following day the news reached the United States and triggered a crisis. That day, too, the Anglo-Americans occupied Trieste triggering a crisis for Yugoslavia.

Tension in the Trieste area mounted during the next week as the Yugoslavs began setting up a local administration and carrying out political purges while restricting the movements of Anglo-American forces. On 11 May Truman cabled Churchill suggesting that Tito be informed (through their respective Ambassadors in Belgrade) that the Yugoslav Government must immediately agree to the control of its forces by the Supreme Allied Commander in the Mediterranean. Churchill agreed, and a directive was issued to the Joint Chiefs of Staff. Yugoslavia's response was to reject the Allied demands on 17 May. The American and British response, on 21 May, was taken in conjunction with earlier inquiries by Truman to the Joint Chiefs of Staff regarding possible military measures should Tito refuse to yield. Field Marshal Alexander's troops, reinforced by American units, crossed into the Yugoslav-occupied zone of Trieste. Later that day Yugoslavia announced its willingness to negotiate. The Anglo-American forces were far too strong for Yugoslavia to consider military resistance, especially as the USSR remained a non-participant in the crisis.

Talks were held at Devin at the end of May between General Morgan of the Allies and Yugoslav Army representatives, and later in Belgrade among representatives of the three governments. The crisis ended without violence, when Yugoslavia withdrew its troops on 11 June 1945, two days after it yielded to UK/US demands. Italy was an involved actor. The crisis served to intensify the conflict over Trieste, for Yugoslavia was an aggrieved party and later became involved in a series of tense situations which eventually escalated to a renewal of crisis in 1953 (see Case #106).

References   Auty 1970; Churchill 1953; Duroselle 1966; Grew 1953; Novak 1970; Truman 1955.

(68) Syria/Free French Forces   France and Syria were actors in a crisis involving French control over Syria, from 17 May to 3 June 1945.

Background   Syria's independence was formally recognized by France and Britain in 1941. France, however, remained the Mandatory Power until the end of World War II and allowed Syria to maintain a militia, but not an army. The *Comité Français de Libération Nationale* (CFLN), under the leadership of General Charles de Gaulle, had been recognized by Britain and the United States as the French Government-in-Exile. On 25 August 1944 de Gaulle entered Paris and the CFLN was then recognized as the Provisional Government of the French Republic, with Charles de Gaulle as President.

With the defeat of Nazi Germany in May 1945, the President and Assembly of Syria appealed to France for a new treaty which would curtail French privileges in Syria and transfer control over security and foreign affairs from the French Mandatory Power to the Government of Syria. France wished to delay this step until the formal establishment of the United Nations. Sporadic riots and strikes against the French in Syria began on 8 May. In order to retain control, and as a security measure, de Gaulle ordered French troops into Syria.

Crisis A crisis was triggered for Syria on 17 May 1945 when three French battalions landed in Beirut and proceeded to Syria in order to secure positions in Damascus and other major cities. On 28 May the Syrian militia, accompanied by rioting citizens, attacked all French posts in the country. De Gaulle accused the British of supplying arms to the Syrians. The riots triggered a crisis for France, which responded the same day by firing on the militia and bombing major Syrian cities. Within two days of fighting an estimated 400 soldiers and civilians lay dead in Damascus, along with countless injured.

After the outbreak of violence, the British intervened and demanded that France agree to a cease-fire and evacuate its positions in the Syrian cities, and that all French forces return to their barracks. Churchill intimated to de Gaulle that, if the French did not comply, the consequences might be collisions between British and French forces. A disagreement between France and Britain over the authority of British General Paget, the Commander-in-Chief of all Allied Forces in the Middle East, had precipitated the British ultimatum. Churchill regarded the French forces to be still officially under the supreme command of General Paget until the end of the Pacific War, while de Gaulle assumed that Paget had completed his function once the war in Europe was over.

De Gaulle considered rejecting the British ultimatum, even in the light of the possibility of hostilities between French and British forces, but the French Parliament and press vehemently opposed French resistance. On 3 June France complied with the ultimatum and evacuated its positions ending the crisis. On 1 June the USSR sent a memorandum to de Gaulle expressing concern about developments in the Middle East. The US was approached by de Gaulle on the 2nd to participate in a conference to settle the crisis in Syria, as well as all other Mandate questions in the Middle East, including Palestine and Iraq. Washington, however, refused to involve itself in an issue which it considered to be exclusively of British and French concern. Moreover, the idea of an invitation to the USSR to the conference prompted President Truman to reject the idea. British troops replaced the French until 1946 when the United Nations cancelled the French Mandate and acknowledged the Syrian Republic's full sovereignty.

References Churchill 1953; de Gaulle 1971; Longrigg 1958; Palmer 1973; Willis 1968.

(69) Kars–Ardahan   The Kars–Ardahan Crisis lasted from 7 June 1945 to 5 April 1946. Turkey alone was a crisis actor, while the US, USSR and UK were deeply involved.

Background The territories of Kars and Ardahan are located in northeast Turkey bordering Soviet Armenia. At the end of World War II long-standing Soviet designs on the Turkish Straits were revived when the USSR requested a revision of its 1925 Treaty with Turkey – due to changed conditions. A Soviet press campaign was launched against Turkey.

Crisis On 7 June 1945, at a meeting in Moscow with the Turkish Ambassador, Foreign Minister Molotov submitted a set of Soviet proposals to revise the 1936 Montreux Convention on the Straits. The demands, including the return of the Kars and Ardahan territories, triggered a crisis for Turkey. Ambassador Sarper informed the Turkish Government, which apprised Great Britain on 12 June. In Washington the UK Ambassador proposed a joint US–UK *démarche*, to be presented before the scheduled July Potsdam Conference; this was rejected by the US at that time. Later in June, and in early July, information about the massing of Soviet forces on the Greek and Turkish frontier was relayed to Washington. The USSR, in exchanges with the US, presented its territorial demands for parts of Turkish Armenia, emphasizing the need for adequate security on the Black Sea coast, with free passage for Soviet warships and the right to close the Straits to all ships should it so desire. On 2 July Turkey responded by requesting aid from the UK and the US, impressing upon the Americans the dangerous situation in which the US was being placed. This succeeded in getting Washington's agreement to bring the matter before Stalin at Potsdam.

When Churchill refused to consider Stalin's demands for bases in Turkey, Truman proposed a revision of the Montreux Convention under a three-power guarantee, to ensure free passage through the Straits for the ships of all states in peace and war. Discussion was postponed. As US concern about Soviet ambitions increased, Washington decided on a show of force. On 5 April 1946 the US Navy announced that the body of the deceased Turkish Ambassador to the US would be returned to Istanbul via the battleship *Missouri*, with full escort. This move, pointing to assured US support, terminated the crisis for Turkey.

The situation remained stable throughout the summer until a renewal of Soviet demands triggered another crisis for Turkey in August 1946 (see Case #74).

References   See sources for Case #77.

(70) End of World War II   Japan's final intra-war crisis began with the dropping of the atom bomb on 6 August and terminated with its formal surrender on 2 September 1945.

Background   Prime Minister Koiso, who had succeeded Tojo in July 1944, resigned on 8 April 1945. He was replaced by Admiral Suzuki whose mission was to bring the war to an end, though the Japanese Government and people were still committed publicly to continued resistance.

After the collapse of Germany in May (see Cases #58 and #63) the Japanese were left without allies, and British and American efforts concentrated on the Pacific theater. US aircraft destroyed or immobilized the remnants of the Japanese Navy and shattered Japan's industry. American battleships shelled densely populated cities, and the Air Force dropped 40,000 tons of bombs on Japanese industrial centers in one month. Japanese morale began to disintegrate. On 20 June the Emperor summoned the Supreme War Council and indicated his wish to seek peace with the Allies and to approach the Soviet Union with a request for mediation. The Potsdam Conference began on 17 July 1945 with Churchill, Stalin and Truman participating. The final text of their communiqué, dated 26 July, called for Japan's unconditional surrender, while avoiding all mention of the future of the Emperor, implying that the Allies would determine whether he would remain after the surrender. Japanese military forces would be disarmed and Japan would be deprived of its imperial conquests. The Potsdam Declaration specified that Japan would be welcomed back into the international community and that the occupation would end after the Allies had accomplished their objectives and the Japanese had chosen a responsible government by democratic means. "The alternative for Japan is prompt and utter destruction." Japan's Prime Minister, Foreign Minister and Navy Minister were in favor of accepting the terms, but the War Minister and the Chief of Staff were opposed.

Crisis   A grave crisis was triggered for Japan on 6 August when an atomic bomb was dropped on Hiroshima. Three-fifths of the city was destroyed. A second threat to Japan's existence occurred on 8 August when the Soviet Union declared war on Japan and launched a powerful invasion of Manchuria. Japan responded on the 9th after another bomb had been dropped on Nagasaki, with an appeal by the Inner Cabinet to the Emperor for a final expression of his wish. The Emperor opted for peace. On the 10th Japan made an offer of surrender on the basis of the Potsdam Declaration, but on condition that it did not comprise "any demand which prejudices the prerogatives of His Majesty as a Sovereign Ruler."

The US Government refused to accept any such conditions and replied that, from the moment of surrender, "the authority of the Emperor and the Japanese Government to rule the state shall be subject to the Supreme Commander of the Allied Powers." After long consideration Japan, once again following the lead of the Emperor, decided to surrender despite the rejection of conditions which had been considered essential. On 15 August the Emperor told the Japanese nation that the war was at an end. The Suzuki Cabinet resigned, and the formal terms of surrender were signed on 2 September aboard the USS *Missouri* in Tokyo Bay, ending the war and the final crisis for Japan. The Japanese home islands were placed under the rule of a US Army of Occupation, the Emperor remained as Head of State, and the Japanese political and police officials continued to function. The capitulation of Japanese forces in China took place on 9 September and China regained sovereignty over Inner Mongolia and Manchuria, as well as the islands of Formosa and Hainan. Hong Kong was reoccupied by the British, who accepted the formal Japanese surrender at Singapore on 12 September 1945.

References   Brooks 1968; Buchanan 1964; Butow 1961, 1968; Feis 1966; Hane 1972; Iriye 1981; Kase 1969; Knapp 1967; Kolko and Kolko 1972; Sansom 1948; Shigemitsu 1958; Truman 1955.

(71) Azerbaijan

There were four crisis actors in the Azerbaijan Crisis, Iran, the Soviet Union, the United Kingdom and the United States. The time span was 23 August 1945 to 9 May 1946.

Background   The Communist-dominated *Tudeh* Party of Iran objected to an Anglo-American agreement for oil concessions in southeast Iran. A Soviet demand for oil concessions in five northern provinces was made known on 26 September 1944 (see Case #60). That crisis ended for Iran when the Soviets apparently withdrew their claims, and a USSR delegation to Teheran left the city without obtaining Iranian consent for the concessions.

Crisis   A crisis for Iran erupted on 23 August 1945 when the *Tudeh* Party attempted to take over the city of Tabriz, the Azerbaijani capital and headquarters of Soviet occupation forces. Supported and protected by Soviet troops, the *Tudeh* occupied several government buildings and issued a manifesto demanding administrative and cultural autonomy for Azerbaijan. The following day the Iranian Government sent a *gendarme* force to reassert central authority over the insurgents. The *gendarmes*, however, were denied entry to the Soviet zone of occupation. The tension eased towards the end of September when the *Tudeh* Party withdrew from government buildings, the Iranian governor regained his authority, and communications with Teheran were restored. Iran's first crisis in this cluster appeared to have faded some time in September, under Soviet instructions to the *Tudeh* Party. The United States was inactive.

The trigger to Iran's second crisis, on 16 November 1945, was a Soviet-supported rebellion by Iran's Democratic Party for the autonomy of Azerbaijan. The Iranian Government responded by sending an armed force to Tabriz on about 17 November; they were, however, stopped near Qasvin by a Soviet military force.

The 16 November rebellion also triggered a crisis for the UK which perceived a threat to its influence in the Middle East. Britain delivered a Note to the Soviet Union on the 26th asking it to withdraw its troops from Iran by 2 March 1946. A similar Note had been sent 2 days earlier by the US setting 1 January 1946 as the date for withdrawal. During the Moscow Conference of Foreign Ministers, on 19 December 1945, Foreign Secretary Bevin and Secretary of State Byrnes tried to settle the Iranian problem with Stalin. Bevin proposed that a joint commission of the Big Three be sent to Iran to investigate the Azerbaijan problem, but it was rejected by the USSR.

Disenchanted by the outcome of the Moscow Conference and unable to do anything within Iran because of Soviet interference, the Iranian Government lodged a complaint with the Security Council on 19 January 1946. Britain's major response, on 25 January, was to introduce in the Security Council a resolution calling for bilateral negotiations between Iran and the USSR. On the 30th the

Security Council passed the modified resolution which also requested the parties to inform the Council of the results. On 19 February Iranian Premier Qavam left for Moscow in an unsuccessful attempt to negotiate a solution.

During Qavam's negotiations in Moscow the deadline arrived for the evacuation of foreign troops from Iran. All American troops had withdrawn by 1 January 1946 and Britain had declared that its troops would be out by the stipulated date of 2 March. By contrast, Radio Moscow announced on 1 March that, except for the northern provinces, Soviet forces would remain in other parts of Iran pending clarification of the situation. In fact, Moscow began to pour new forces into Iran: on 4 and 5 March Soviet troops and armored columns moved outward from Tabriz in three directions – toward the Turkish and Iraqi frontiers and toward Teheran.

The movements of Soviet troops in Iran, combined with an intensive Soviet diplomatic and propaganda offensive against Turkey, the main bastion against the USSR's advance into the Middle East, triggered a crisis for the United States on 4 March: its global and regional influence were threatened. The US responded, on the 7th, with a decision by Byrnes to send a sharply worded protest to Moscow and to instruct the US delegation to the Security Council to take a firm position on the Iranian case. The Note, which was far stronger than any previous American communication to the Soviet Union, was delivered in Moscow on 9 March and triggered a crisis for the USSR. It called for explanations of Russian troop movements and of the continued presence of Soviet troops in Iran. The Soviet Government, in a Tass Agency broadcast on 14 March, stated that Washington's report of troop movements was incorrect.

The State Department followed up its Note by declaring the same day that the US would bring the dispute to the Security Council if the differences between the Soviet Union and Iran were not settled before the forthcoming Council meeting on 25 March, and if Iran itself did not raise the issue at the UN forum. In fact, on 18 March Iran did request the Security Council to place the Azerbaijan issue on its agenda. When the Soviets failed to keep the Iranian case off the Council's agenda, they attempted to postpone the debate until 1 April. When this too was defeated, the Soviet delegate, Gromyko, left the Council chamber.

The strong position adopted by the US, the resistance of Iran, world public opinion, and the publicity of the Security Council meetings led the Soviet leadership to decide on 24 March to announce to the Council, two days later, that an agreement between the USSR and Iran had been reached, and that Soviet troops would be withdrawn from Iran within 5–6 weeks if no unforeseen circumstances occurred. After that announcement the Iranian case was temporarily removed from the Security Council agenda. On 4 April 1946 Prime Minister Qavam concluded an agreement with the Soviets which declared that Iranian territory would be evacuated within six weeks of 24 March, that a joint Soviet–Iranian oil company would be established (to be ratified by the *Majlis* within seven months after 24 March), and that Moscow recognized Azerbaijan as an internal problem of Iran. Finally, on 9 May 1946, Soviet troops left Iran, terminating the Azerbaijan Crisis for Britain, Iran, the US and the USSR.

References   Byrnes 1947; Chubin and Zabih 1974; Hamilton 1962; Lenczowski 1949, 1962, 1978; Ramazani 1964, 1975; Rossow 1956; Shwadran 1973; Werth 1964; Zabih 1966.

(72) Indonesia Independence I

The first of three crises over Indonesia's struggle for recognition began on 29 September 1945 and terminated on 25 March 1947. The crisis actors were Indonesia and The Netherlands.

Background   Indonesia, a colony under the Dutch Crown, was occupied by Japan from 1942 until 17 August 1945 when Indonesian national leaders proclaimed its independence and established a provisional government of the new Republic.

Crisis   A crisis for The Netherlands was triggered on 29 September 1945 when the Supreme Allied Commander for Southeast Asia announced that his troops would maintain law and order in The Netherlands East Indies until a lawful government was again functioning, and that Indonesian leader Ahmad Sukarno was to continue to direct civil administration in those areas not occupied by Allied forces. This was regarded by The Netherlands as *de facto* recognition of the Provisional Indonesian Government and, therefore, a grave threat to the survival of the Dutch empire. The Hague responded on 1 October with an official statement that The Netherlands would not recognize nor negotiate with Sukarno.

Indonesia's crisis was triggered on 2 October by the arrival of a Dutch administrator and the landing of additional Dutch forces, interpreted by the Indonesians as a Dutch effort to restore colonial rule. Severe fighting ensued between nationalist and Dutch and British forces. On 13 October 1945 Indonesia responded with a declaration of war against The Netherlands and the prohibition of the sale of food to the enemy. The British were accused of promoting the return of the Dutch administration. In late 1946 British forces were withdrawn. The fighting continued, along with prolonged negotiations, until the signing of the Linggadjati Agreement on 25 March 1947, which provided for a transitional regime until 1 January 1949 at which time the Dutch Government would transfer authority to an independent Republic of Indonesia. The agreement, which terminated the first international crisis over Indonesia's independence, provided for a truce and stabilization of existing military positions, the establishment of a Truce Supervisory Committee composed of Dutch, British and Indonesian representatives, and the creation of the United States of Indonesia linked to The Netherlands.

The UN Security Council was involved because of a joint USSR/Ukrainian complaint on the issue of Dutch military intervention. Draft resolutions calling for on-the-spot investigation and limitation, and withdrawal of British forces, were rejected.

References Agung 1973; Crouch 1978; Dahm 1971; Fifield 1958; Gerbrandy 1950; Kahin 1952; van der Kroef 1951; Reinhardt 1971; Taylor 1960.

(73) Communism in Poland

A crisis for the USSR lasted from 30 June 1946 to 19 January 1947.

Background The post-World War II situation in Poland was extremely tense as thousands of armed men, belonging to various underground movements, aimed at sabotaging the Communist-controlled Lublin coalition government established in 1944. The presence of Soviet troops added to the complex environment.

Crisis On 30 June 1946 the Provisional Government of Poland held a pre-election referendum which pointed to the fact that the strongest political force in the country was Mikolajczyk's Peasant Party. This triggered a crisis for the USSR which feared Poland's withdrawal from the Soviet bloc. The Polish Communist leaders were summoned immediately to Moscow for consultations. The major Soviet response came on 28 August when, at a meeting in Moscow with leaders of both the Polish Communist Party and the Peasant Party, Stalin dictated the results of the forthcoming elections in Poland, demanding that Mikolajczyk ally his party with the Polish Communists.

On 19 January 1947 elections were held and were predictably won by the alliance of the Communist and Peasant parties, despite charges of gross irregularities. As Poland's potential defection from the Soviet bloc had been prevented, the Soviet crisis was over.

The UK and the US were involved diplomatically with notes and statements *vis-à-vis* the elections and border issues. There was no violence.

References Brzezinski 1967; Dziewanowski 1959; Korbonski 1965; Leslie 1980; Mikolajczyk 1948.

(74) Turkish Straits

A second post-World War II crisis over the Straits, arising from renewed Soviet demands for a revision of the Montreux Convention, occurred for Turkey and the United States between 7 August and 26 October 1946.

Background   In June 1945 the Soviets demanded territories and bases in northeast Turkey, as well as a revision of the 1936 Montreux Convention governing the Straits (see Case #69).

Crisis   The crisis trigger for Turkey and the United States was a Note from the USSR on 7 August 1946, requesting a revised international regime for the Straits, Simultaneously, the Soviets began naval maneuvers in the Black Sea and a concentration of forces in the Caucasus. Turkey viewed this as additional pressure from the Soviets for bases on its territory. On 11 August Moscow broadcast the content of a series of documents allegedly found in the archives of the German Foreign Office which recorded violent anti-Soviet statements by Turkey's former Premier and President Inönü. Ankara denied the authenticity of these documents two days later. The US major response occurred on 20 August 1946: after meetings between President Truman and his top advisors, Washington opted for a show of force by sending army and naval forces into the area. With US backing, Turkey was able to give a firm response on 22 August resisting the Soviet demands, while expressing a willingness to participate with all the original signatories in a conference to revise the Montreux Convention. Another Soviet Note followed on 24 September, milder in tone. On 9 October the United States sent a Note to the Soviet Union reaffirming its support for Turkey. The UK did the same.

Increased American and British naval activity in the region preceded Turkey's total rejection of Soviet demands, sent in a Note to Moscow on 18 October. On the 26th the USSR relented: word was passed to London that, in Soviet opinion, a conference on the Straits at that time was premature, thereby terminating the crisis for both actors. Moreover, once Soviet troops had begun to withdraw from Iran (see Case #71), there was a growing feeling in Turkey that the USSR would not use violence to achieve its goal relating to the Straits. And no violence was used by any crisis actor.

References   See sources for Case #77.

(75) Greek Civil War II

Greece experienced an international crisis during the first phase of a lengthy civil war; the crisis began on 13 November 1946 and ended on 28 February 1947.

Background   The Communist attempt to seize power in Greece in December 1944 was crushed by British forces. Many of the guerrillas escaped to Yugoslavia, Albania or Bulgaria, all of which provided sanctuary and military support (see Case #62). The civil war continued in the north of Greece with few lulls in the fighting.

Crisis   On 13 November 1946 a major attack was launched by Greek guerrillas at Skra. The seriousness of the situation triggered a crisis for Greece which feared for the legitimacy of its political system. Aid to the Greek Communist rebels by the Communist regime in Yugoslavia made that country Greece's principal adversary. A full-scale military operation against the rebels was launched by the Greek Army on 18 November. On 3 December Greece responded with an appeal to the Security Council.

UN activity took the form of a fact-finding mission authorized by the Council. The mission found that infiltration across Greece's frontiers was indeed taking place. The crisis may be said to have ended on 28 February 1947, the day on which the United States Government invited Greek officials to draft a letter asking for aid. Two weeks later President Truman requested Congress to provide economic and military assistance to the Athens regime (see Case #77).

The outcome may be designated a compromise because the conflict continued for more than two years after the termination of Greece's crisis with neighboring states aiding Greek Communist guerrillas. The Greek civil war ended on 10 July 1949 when Tito announced the closing of Yugoslavia's border to Greek guerrillas. One month later the Greek Army launched an offensive and, within two weeks, the guerrillas were crushed. Prior to Tito's action the Army had been unable to suppress the Greek Communists, despite its military superiority.

References Berle 1975; Chandler 1959; Kousoulas 1953; McNeil 1957; Miller 1967; Woodhouse 1976; Xydis 1963.

(76) Communism in Hungary

A crisis between Hungary and the Soviet Union began on 10 February and terminated on 1 June 1947.

Background The Soviet Army liberated Hungary from German occupation at the end of World War II and was the dominating factor in the Allied Control Commission which administered the country after 1945. With Soviet support, the Hungarian Communist Party began to organize itself as a political force. In 1947 the Government of Hungary was a coalition of the Smallholder, Social-Democratic, National Peasant and Communist parties. Although the Smallholders had obtained a majority, the party was obliged by the Soviet-led Allied Control Commission to form a coalition and grant the Communists the key post of Ministry of the Interior, thus enabling them to control the police. In December 1946 a conspiracy to overthrow the regime was uncovered, with the Secretary-General of the Smallholders Party, Béla Kovacs, being implicated. An investigation by Hungarian police began.

Crisis The trigger to the Soviet crisis was the environmental change created by the signing of the Peace Treaty on 10 February 1947: it called for the withdrawal of occupation forces from Hungary within six months. The Soviets perceived this to be a threat to their control of the country and responded on 26 February with the arrest of Kovacs on charges of undermining the security of the Soviet occupation forces. This act triggered a crisis for Hungary which viewed Kovacs' arrest as a physical challenge to the élite and the regime. In March there was another purge of the Smallholders Party extending to members of Parliament and ministers in the Government. When Prime Minister Nagy was away from Hungary, on vacation in Switzerland, the Soviet authorities presented the Hungarian Government with a record of the Kovacs interrogation wherein Nagy was named as a fellow conspirator. When Nagy refused to return to the country for fear of arrest, he was asked to resign. This was accompanied by threats to the safety of his son, still in Hungary. Nagy decided to do so on 30 May. His resignation constituted Hungary's major response during the crisis. The termination for both crisis actors was his formal resignation on 1 June 1947. Hungarian political resistance had been broken (see Case #119).

The United States and Great Britain asked for a three-power inquiry into Kovacs' arrest. Notes with the USSR were exchanged.

References Kertesz 1950; Kovrig 1970; Lahav 1976; Nagy 1948; Schoenfeld 1948; Seton-Watson 1956; Vali 1961.

(77) Truman Doctrine

An international crisis culminating in the proclamation of the Truman Doctrine lasted from 21 February to 22 May 1947. It involved three crisis actors: Greece, Turkey and the United States.

Background Soviet demands for the transfer of Turkish territories in 1945 and 1946 deepened US suspicion about USSR intentions in the eastern Mediterranean (see Cases #69 and #74). In Greece, civil war was raging, with support and bases for Greek Communists being supplied by Yugoslavia, Albania and Bulgaria (see Case #75). Thus societal unrest and mass violence were rampant in Greece. Labor strikes erupted in the cities. And on 30 January 1946 martial law was declared. Britain, struggling to restore economic stability at home following the massive dislocations of World War II, decided it could no longer bear the burden of military and economic aid to Greece and economic assistance to Turkey.

Crisis The UK announcement on 21 February 1947 of its intention to discontinue aid to Greece and Turkey by 31 March triggered a crisis for the United States, Greece and Turkey. For the US, the issue was fear of Soviet hegemony in the eastern

Mediterranean region, while Greece and Turkey perceived a threat to the stability of their political systems. Turkey felt obliged to keep its army fully mobilized in order to discourage and forestall Soviet aggression. Its major response, on 21 February, was to request aid from the US. Similarly, upon the advice of President Truman, Greece responded to the UK announcement by sending a formal Note to Washington on 27 February requesting American aid. Truman then requested Congress, on 12 March 1947, to grant military and economic assistance to Greece and Turkey in order to offset Communist threats. The crisis for the three actors ended when an aid bill was signed on 22 May 1947. This marked the proclamation of the Truman Doctrine with a US offer of aid to countries threatened by the Communist bloc during the first stage of the Cold War.

There was no discussion about Turkey in the United Nations, but the Security Council did establish a commission to investigate Greek border violations. The report, issued in May 1947, called for an end to external assistance to Greek Communist guerrillas. The recommendation and, with it, UN activity, was vetoed by the USSR.

References Acheson 1969; Berle 1975; Bisbee 1951; Chandler 1959; Forrestal 1951; Harris 1972; Howard 1974; Kilic 1959; Robinson 1963; Seton-Watson 1956; Shaw 1977; Truman 1955; Vere-Hodge 1950.

(78) Marshall Plan

A crisis for the Soviet Union and Czechoslovakia over the Marshall Plan occurred between 4 and 10 July 1947.

Background Severe winters in 1945 and 1946 and a drought in 1947 had caused great economic hardship in Czechoslovakia. The food supply was severely reduced and all goods originally destined for domestic consumption had to be exported. Both unemployment and citizen discontent were rising rapidly. Consequently, when an invitation was issued by France and Great Britain to Czechoslovakia to attend a conference in Paris dealing with the Marshall Plan and US conditions for aid, it was readily accepted and a delegation was sent.

Crisis The announcement of the Marshall Plan in June 1947 and the favorable response by the Eastern and Central European states to the American initiative posed a threat to the Soviet Union. The crisis trigger for the USSR was the Czech Cabinet's unanimous acceptance of the Anglo-French invitation on 4 July. A delegation consisting of Czech Prime Minister Gottwald, together with Democratic Party Ministers of Justice and Foreign Affairs, Dritna and Masaryk, flew to Moscow for scheduled talks. The USSR response to the Marshall Plan threat was conveyed to the Czech members of the delegation on 9 July by Stalin who delivered an ultimatum calling for immediate Czech withdrawal from the Marshall Plan talks in Paris. Stalin told the delegation that Czech participation would be viewed as an "unfriendly act." This triggered a crisis for Czechoslovakia, which was virtually surrounded by Soviet troops. It responded the following day by compliance to Soviet wishes. The Czech ministers in Moscow telephoned their Cabinet colleagues in Prague and requested them to rescind the earlier decision to participate in the Paris meetings. The Czech Cabinet met at 4:00 a.m. and did so. The 10th of July was the termination date for both actors in the 1947 Marshall Plan Crisis. There was no violence.

(For the related Czech regime crisis in 1948 see Case #84 Communism in Czechoslovakia.)

References Kolko 1972; Korbel 1959, 1977; Szulc 1971.

(79) Indonesia Independence II

The second crisis over The Netherlands' opposition to Indonesia's declaration of independence occurred between 21 July 1947 and 17 January 1948 (see Case #72 for the first Netherlands/Indonesia crisis over Indonesian Independence).

Background   The Linggadjati Agreement of 25 March 1947 called for the transfer of power by The Netherlands to Indonesia on 1 January 1949. The agreement was regarded by many Dutch colonials as too progressive and inadequate in its provisions for the protection of Dutch interests. The Indonesians, on the other hand, felt that Prime Minister Sjahrir had gone too far in conceding to Dutch demands; he resigned on 3 July 1947 as internal pressure mounted.

Crisis   The second Indonesia crisis was triggered on 21 July 1947 when The Netherlands, dissatisfied with the deteriorating relations between the two countries, authorized the launching of military action. The response, on 22 July, was an appeal to India for aid and foreign intervention. India, and later Australia, brought the issue to the Security Council. Its discussion on 31 July, with the implied danger of international intervention, was the trigger for a Netherlands crisis. That day, the Dutch Representative to the Security Council denied international jurisdiction over what he termed a police action in an internal Dutch matter. He set forth The Netherlands' conditions for reopening talks. The crisis ended on 17 January 1948 when US involvement helped to bring about the Renville Agreement calling for a military truce and adopting the UN Good Offices Committee's recommendation for a plebiscite.

The Security Council adopted two resolutions. In the first, submitted by China and Australia, the Council noted with satisfaction the Dutch Government statement affirming its intention to recognize a sovereign, democratic United States of Indonesia in accordance with the provisions of the Linggadjati Agreement. Further, the Security Council requested that member governments having consular representatives in Batavia (Djakarta) supervise the carrying out of the cease-fire orders and report their findings. The second resolution, submitted by the United States, expressed Security Council resolve to render its good offices to the parties in order to assist in the pacific settlement of the dispute through a committee of three members – one each from the disputing parties and the third to be appointed by the first two.

UN intervention in the crisis clearly implied that the crisis was international, and not a matter of Dutch domestic jurisdiction. It was considered a great political victory for the Republic of Indonesia, increasing its international prestige. The Renville Agreement included a military truce along the Van Mook line – the position held by the Dutch after 21 July 1947 – and a number of political principles. Holland's acceptance suggested the possibility that the Dutch would not evacuate the territories it administered and that Indonesian guerrilla forces would be removed from these areas. Nevertheless, there was a guarantee that plebiscites would be held in the Dutch-occupied territories in 6–12 months under supervision of the Good Offices Committee, which would remain in Indonesia to supervise the implementation of the agreement by both parties.

References   See sources for Case #72, and Miller 1967.

(80) Dominican Republic/Cuba   This Caribbean crisis had only one actor, the Dominican Republic, and lasted from 26 July until 28 September 1947.

Background   President Trujillo, the dictator of the Dominican Republic since 1930, had seized control of all the instruments of power (army, courts, press, economy) and had crushed all opposition. The result was a large number of political exiles from the Dominican Republic seeking shelter in neighboring states such as Cuba and Guatemala. They in turn were joined by exiles, mercenaries, adventurers and criminals from other states in the region. This group was known as the "Caribbean League."

These states, with Cuba as the most supportive, supplied weapons, training, bases, and money, as well as ideological support to the League's activities. The crisis, therefore, was the result of a military threat to the Trujillo regime by the Caribbean League, with Cuba taking the lead. The exiles began gathering at Cayo Confites (Cuba) as early as January 1946, with the Cuban Government providing training and support.

Crisis   By 26 July 1947 the Trujillo regime perceived the exiles to be a serious military threat. Dominican precautions in the form of blackouts were instituted on that day. The Dominican Republic's major response occurred on 18 August when Trujillo voiced the possibility of war breaking out, and suggested setting up an international commission to investigate the matter. The Dominican armed forces were also put on alert. On 28 September the Cubans disbanded the revolutionary forces at the same time as the US began to play a more active role, including a prohibition on the purchase of US weapons. The immediate threat subsided, but the conflict was to continue for several more years, with later involvement of the OAS, and a crisis erupting in 1949 (see Case #94).

References   Atkins and Wilson 1972; Crassweller 1966; Espaillat 1963; Furniss 1950; de Galindez 1973; Mecham 1961; Nanita 1951; Pattee 1967; Pochando 1974; Szulc 1971; Wiarda 1969, 1970; Wilgus 1963.

(81) Junagadh

The crisis between India and Pakistan over Junagadh, one of three which accompanied the partition of the subcontinent, took place from 17 August 1947 to 24 February 1948.

Background   The rulers of all princely states geographically contiguous to India or Pakistan, with the exception of Junagadh, Kashmir and Hyderabad, had signed an Instrument of Accession to India or Pakistan by 15 August 1947, the date of the transfer of power from Britain to the new Dominions of India and Pakistan (see Cases #82 Kashmir I and #88 Hyderabad). The three crises over these states occurred against a setting of an unparalleled transfer of 15,000,000 people – Hindus and Sikhs fleeing from Pakistan to India and Muslims in the reverse direction. It is estimated that one million people were killed in the ensuing riots during the transfer. In Junagadh, the Muslim Nawab ruled over a population of whom 80% were Hindu. Further, the state had no contiguity with Pakistan by land, and its distance by sea was about 300 miles.

Crisis   The news of Junagadh's accession to Pakistan on 17 August 1947 triggered a crisis for India. New Delhi responded on 25 October by approving a plan to occupy Mangrol and Babariawad with civil personnel accompanied by a small military force. This triggered a crisis for Pakistan on 1 November 1947. After the Nawab left Junagadh, its government formally requested India to assist in the administration. Accordingly, instructions were issued on 9 November, marking the termination of India's crisis. Pakistan's response occurred on 11 November in the form of a reply by Liaquat Ali Khan to a cable from Nehru requesting a discussion on Junagadh. The Pakistani Prime Minister contended that, since Junagadh had already acceded to Pakistan, there was no room for discussion and that India's action was a clear violation of Pakistani territory. However, Pakistan was in no position to defend Junagadh. Its crisis ended on 24 February 1948 when a plebiscite was held in Junagadh, reinforcing India's control over the state.

　　The UK was a deeply-involved actor. Lord Mountbatten, India's Governor-General, held talks in Lahore with Liaquat Ali Khan and received Pakistan's agreement to hold a plebiscite in Junagadh.

References   See sources for Case #82.

(82) Kashmir I

The first crisis over Kashmir between India and Pakistan lasted from 24 October 1947 to 1 January 1949.

Background   The last Viceroy of British India visited Kashmir in July 1947 in an effort to convince the Maharajah to accede to either India or Pakistan. At that time Kashmir had a Hindu ruler, with an overwhelming Muslim population, approximately 75% of more than four million. The great importance of this territory for Pakistan lay in the fact that the upper regions of four of the rivers upon which Pakistan depended for irrigation were either inside Kashmir or on the border. The location of Kashmir, contiguous to India and Pakistan, Chinese-controlled Tibet and the Afghanistan-controlled narrow Wakhan corridor leading to the Soviet Union, endowed it with strategic importance.

In 1847 the British sold the Vale of Kashmir to the Dogra ruler of Jammu who, in turn, acknowledged British paramountcy. In 1947 it was run along orthodox Hindu lines. If the disposition of Kashmir had been made according to the principles applied to British India, the state – with the possible exception of a Hindu-majority area in Jammu adjacent to the Indian Punjab – would have gone to Pakistan. However, the power of decision rested with the Maharajah. Accession to a democratic India had no appeal for him, but the future looked even less promising in a Muslim Pakistan. Furthermore, he was suspicious of the British and resisted Mountbatten's efforts to make a definite decision. Hoping to achieve independence, the Maharajah arrested most of the state's politicians in mid-1947 and tried to arrange standstill agreements with both India and Pakistan.

The communal rioting throughout Punjab spread to Jammu, where Hindu and Sikh refugees attacked Muslims. In September a Muslim revolt against the Government of Kashmir occurred in the western part of the state. A provisional Azad (free) Kashmir Government was established by the rebels. At this point, with much of the northern and northwestern part of the subcontinent in near chaos, Muslim tribesmen from the North West Frontier Province of Pakistan invaded Kashmir. Pakistan aided these tribesmen by allowing them to use its territory as a base and enabling them to pass through to Kashmir.

Crisis   The trigger to India's crisis was the arrival on 24 October 1947 of a desperate appeal from the (Hindu) Maharajah of Kashmir asking for help in putting down an invasion by Kashmiri Muslims. India responded on 26 October, only after receiving Kashmir's formal accession, by ordering an airlift of troops, equipment and supplies into the area. This triggered Pakistan's crisis on 27 October. On 6 February 1948 rebel forces launched an attack on the key junction of Naushara. At this point Pakistani officers realized that the Azad Kashmir forces could not hold the Indian Army. They decided to maintain the Pakistani Seventh Division in position behind the front. The major response was on 17 March 1948, long after Pakistan had become involved in a related crisis over Junagadh (see Case #81), when Pakistan launched an unsuccessful attack on Poonch which resulted in an Indian spring offensive. The crisis over Kashmir ended for both India and Pakistan with a UN-mediated cease-fire on 1 January 1949. The conflict over Kashmir remains unresolved.

India referred the issue to the UN, charging Pakistan with complicity in the tribal invasion, and asked the Security Council to have Pakistan halt its assistance to the tribesmen fighting in Kashmir. Pakistan charged New Delhi with genocide. Resolutions were adopted on 15 and 17 January 1948 calling upon the parties to refrain from aggression. A UN Commission for India and Pakistan was established to investigate and mediate the dispute. After much delay UNCIP submitted a three-part resolution proposing a cease-fire, Indian and Pakistani withdrawals, with India retaining forces in Kashmir to maintain order, and a plebiscite. Pakistan refused. A cease-fire resolution of the Security Council was finally accepted by both parties in December 1948 and took effect on 1 January 1949. Since then two-thirds of Jammu and Kashmir has been occupied by India and one-third by Pakistan, with a UN Observer Group to monitor the cease-fire.

References   Blinkenberg 1972; Brecher 1953; Brines 1968; Das Gupta 1958; Gupta 1966; Keesing's 1973; Korbel 1954; Lamb 1966; Menon 1956; Muhammad Ali 1967; Nehru 1956.

(83) Palestine Partition   The prelude to the Israel Independence Crisis lasted from 29 November until 17 December 1947. There were four crisis actors: Egypt, Iraq, Lebanon and Syria.

Background   The situation in Palestine in 1946–47 reflected the intensified struggle of the Jews for a national homeland after the European Holocaust, and the Arab objection to it. Serious fighting between Jews and Arabs had broken out intermittently over many years. Jewish resistance to British control became increasingly strong. The Arab states stated their determination to object by force to any plan which would authorize the creation of a Jewish state.

Crisis The trigger for all four actors was the UN General Assembly Resolution on 29 November 1947 calling for the partition of Palestine into two independent states, one Arab, the other Jewish. Egypt, Iraq, Lebanon and Syria, together with Jordan, met in Egypt for four days beginning on 8 December. The crisis ended on 17 December when the Arab League approved a decision of the earlier summit meeting and proclaimed its determination to maintain Palestine as an Arab state and to recruit an army of volunteers from the different League members. No further action was taken until May 1948 (see Case #86). The UK and Jordan were involved actors. The other Arab states objected to Jordan's territorial plans to annex all of Palestine when the British Mandate ended.

References See sources for Case #86.

(84) Communism in Czechoslovakia

The Czech regime crisis for Czechoslovakia and the USSR occurred from 13 to 25 February 1948.

Background The 1946 elections in Czechoslovakia resulted in a coalition government in which the Communists were the most numerous single party. Klement Gottwald, the Communist leader, became Prime Minister, and Jan Masaryk, son of the first President and a liberal belonging to no party, was appointed Foreign Minister. A campaign of intimidation against non-Communist ministers of the Czechoslovak Cabinet began in the autumn of 1947. Elections were scheduled for May 1948. A pre-election poll commissioned by the Ministry of the Interior pointed to a Communist Party defeat, although there were indications of genuine Czech sentiment toward the USSR as liberators and protectors against Germany. There was, as well, some popular sympathy with Soviet economic goals. The desperate state of the national economy, increasing police malpractice, threats from the trade unions and other political disturbances were present in Czechoslovakia in January and February 1948. In January the Czech coalition government accused the Czech Secret Police of direct cooperation with the Soviet Secret Police. On 13 February all non-Communist regional commanders of the police in Prague were suddenly retired or transferred. The Cabinet ordered the Communist Minister of the Interior to reinstate the non-Communist police. As a result of the non-implementation of this order, 12 members of the Cabinet resigned in protest.

Crisis The Cabinet resignations triggered a crisis for the USSR on 13 February 1948. The Soviets, fearing that early elections would adversely affect Communist supremacy in Czechoslovakia, responded on the 19th by dispatching Deputy Foreign Minister Zorin to Prague – ostensibly to supervise an incoming shipment of Soviet wheat. He immediately called upon Czech President Beneš suggesting that the USSR was interested in seeing Prime Minister Gottwald succeed in solving the Cabinet crisis. This constituted the trigger for a Czech crisis. The Czech response, and the termination of the crisis for both actors, occurred on 25 February when Beneš, fearing Soviet military intervention, yielded to Zorin's and Gottwald's pressure and accepted the resignations of non-Communist Cabinet Ministers – despite his own reluctance and demonstrations outside the President's Palace.

The bloodless coup enabled the Communist Party to retain control of Czechoslovakia. It was alleged that Soviet troops participated in the coup directly or indirectly. On 10 March 1948 Jan Masaryk was found dead – a suicide or a victim of assassination – on the ground below his apartment in the Foreign Ministry. Czechoslovakia maintained that the coup was an internal matter and refused to participate in UN deliberations. Subsequent draft resolutions before the Security Council were vetoed by the Soviet Union.

References See sources for Case #78, and Stirling 1969.

(85) Soviet Note to Finland I

Finland was in a state of crisis with the USSR from 22 February until 6 April 1948.

Background On 9 February 1948 there was a meeting of representatives of the Nordic states. The Soviet Union felt that Nordic cooperation, backed by the West and, specifically, by the United States, posed a threat to Soviet hegemony in northern Europe.

Crisis On 22 February the Soviet Union sent a Note to the Finnish Government requesting a meeting of high-level officials for the purpose of concluding a treaty of mutual friendship, cooperation and non-aggression. Such a treaty would effectively prevent Finland from adopting a pro-Western stance. Finland responded on 8 March 1948 by sending a delegation to Moscow.

The crisis ended on 6 April 1948 with the signing of a treaty. There was no violence and no evidence of any actions on the part of the Soviet Union or Finland which would indicate an increase in perceived probability of military hostilities. No overt threats were made by the Soviet Union. In fact, the negotiations seemed to proceed smoothly and all parties appeared satisfied with the outcome. However, a message from Stalin was construed as containing an implied threat of Soviet military action if Finland did not comply with Moscow's proposal. The crisis led to a basic change in Finland's foreign policy orientation and created the phenomenon of "Finlandization," namely, curtailing the freedom of action in international relations of a formally sovereign state aligned with Western values in the emerging global cold war.

References Finnish Political Science Association 1969; Maude 1976; Vloyantes 1975.

(86) Israel Independence

The crisis over Israel's independence began on 15 May 1948 and terminated on 20 July 1949. There were six crisis actors: Egypt, Iraq, Israel, Jordan, Lebanon and Syria.

Background The Arab–Jewish conflict over Palestine dates back at least 40 years, but only reached crisis proportions when the UN Partition Plan was approved in November 1947 (see Case #83). Arab attacks on Jewish settlements in Palestine preceded the British evacuation, but regular Arab armies did not enter the area until the end of the Mandate.

Crisis The trigger for all five Arab actors was the creation of the State of Israel through its proclamation of independence on 14–15 May 1948. Plans for a combined army of Arab League forces, to be organized under an Iraqi commander, fell through, and directives were sent to each country to dispatch regular forces to Palestine. All the Arab states perceived a value threat – the loss of territory considered an integral part of the Arab world – and responded by invading Israel on 15 May – Syria and Lebanon in the north, Jordan and Iraq in the east, including Jerusalem, and Egypt in the south. Israel responded to the threat to its existence by dispatching its newly formed army to fight on all fronts. A struggle for power among Arab states and their fear that Jordan (whose King Abdullah had been negotiating with the Jews) would enlarge its area to include all of Palestine and part of Syria, also contributed to the Arab decision to fight. Iraq, the only crisis state which did not border Israel, maintained a very strong anti-Israel position, partly to divert its population's attention from internal problems and partly as an extension of its struggle with Egypt for Arab leadership.

The termination dates vary. Fighting ended in the north on 30 October 1948 for Lebanon and Syria in defeat, but it was their Armistice Agreements with Israel, on 29 March and 20 July 1949, respectively, which marked the termination dates for those two countries. For Iraq, unlike the four other Arab states, there was no formal agreement to end the war, but fighting effectively ceased after 18 July 1948. Fighting ended for Egypt with the defeat in Sinai on 7 January 1949; and an Armistice Agreement was signed on 24 February 1949. The war ended for Israel after it captured the southernmost city of Eilat and the Israeli Government ratified the Cease-Fire Agreement with Egypt on 10 March 1949. The last Armistice Agreement was signed with Syria on 20 July 1949. Although the war with Jordan ended earlier, the danger of renewed hostilities did not end until Parliament ratified the Cease-Fire Agreement on 11 March 1949 and Jordan signed an Armistice Agreement with Israel on 3 April 1949.

The UN was intensely involved in this crisis, arranging several truce agreements and inducing all the Armistice Agreements, through the mediation of Count Folke Bernadotte (later assassinated) and Under Secretary-General Ralph Bunche. Both superpowers and the UK were involved actors.

References   Abdullah 1978; Abidi 1965; Baaklini 1976; Bethell 1979; Ben Gurion 1969, 1971; Bowyer-Bell 1969; Cattan 1969; Glubb 1957; Goiten 1965; Hadawai 1964, 1967; Khouri 1968; Lenczowski 1962; Longrigg 1953; al-Marayati 1961; Pollak and Sinai 1976; Safran 1969; Savegh 1956; Shimoni 1977; Sykes 1973; Torrey 1964, Zayid 1965.

(87) Berlin Blockade   The crisis actors in the first of three international crises over Berlin were Britain, France, the Soviet Union and the United States. It began on 7 June 1948 and ended on 12 May 1949.

Background   Escalation of tension between the Western Powers and the Soviet Union centered around the issue of occupied Germany. The Potsdam Agreement of 1945 divided Germany into four zones, but decreed that the country was to be treated as one economic unit under the Allied Control Council. The final breakdown of this agreement occurred when the Soviet representative walked out of a meeting of the Council on 20 March 1948. On 1 April the Russians temporarily restricted Western access to Berlin by the imposition of a "baby blockade." The UK, the US and France met once more in June.

Crisis   On 7 June 1948 the Western Powers published the recommendations of the March 1948 London Conference, to which the Soviet Union had not been invited, to integrate their zones in Germany. This triggered a crisis for Moscow which perceived a basic threat to its influence in Europe. The USSR responded on 24 June by blockading all Western transportation into and out of Berlin. The Soviets also cut off all electric current, coal, food and other supplies to West Berlin. This triggered a crisis for the United States, Britain and France; the future of Germany and, with it, their influence in Europe was at stake. The response by the Western Powers, on 26 June 1948, was to step up the airlift to Berlin, which had begun two months earlier, and to continue with plans for the rehabilitation of Germany as part of Western Europe. Talks to break the diplomatic deadlock began in August. By 21 March 1949 the blockade had been almost completely lifted. A full agreement was reached on 12 May, the termination date for all four crisis actors; it left Germany split into two embryonic states – the Federal Republic of Germany (FRG) and the German Democratic Republic (GDR).

A UN Security Council Resolution calling for the lifting of the blockade and the resumption of talks was vetoed by the Soviet Union. A neutral commission was set up to study the currency problem, but it failed to get agreement of the Four Powers. Talks were held in the winter of 1949 between the Soviet and American Representatives to the UN. The status of Berlin evoked a second crisis in December 1957 (see Case #127).

References   Acheson 1969; Balfour 1968; Bohlen 1973; Davison 1958; Fischer 1951; George and Smoke 1974; Grosser 1964; La Feber 1976; Murphy 1964; Paterson 1973; Shlaim 1983; Sowden 1975; Tanter 1974; Truman 1955; Ulam 1971, 1974; Windsor 1963; Young 1968.

(88) Hyderabad   India experienced a crisis over Hyderabad from 21 August to 18 September 1948.

Background   Hyderabad was the second largest princely state in the subcontinent, after Jammu and Kashmir (see Case #82). It is located in the geographic center of India and, in 1948, 80% of its population was Hindu while most of the political élite were

Muslim. The Nizam of Hyderabad did not view with favor accession to distant Pakistan. Nor did predominantly Hindu India attract him. He therefore opted for independence a few days after the British left. The Indian Government stated that Hyderabad was far too important to India's territorial integrity and economic needs to be permitted to choose independence. Throughout late 1947 and early 1948 tension and communal violence mounted. India, insisting that the Nizam liberalize his government and curb the violence, organized an economic blockade. The Nizam then loaned Pakistan some of his Government of India securities which it began to cash, despite promises not to do so while the Standstill Agreement between Hyderabad and India continued to operate. These developments, coupled with border raids and frequent attacks on trains passing through the state territory, had pushed the Standstill Agreement into the background. Hyderabad raised the question of arbitration on the alleged breaches of the Agreement, but the infringements had become relatively unimportant in the context of the grave and increasing deterioration of law and order within the state.

Crisis   India's crisis over the state of Hyderabad, which had proclaimed independence, was triggered on 21 August 1948 with Hyderabad's request for UN discussion of both India's economic blockade and incidents of violence in the area. India's reply to a grave threat to its territorial integrity came on 9 September after efforts to facilitate Indian troop movements through the state failed. A decision was taken to send troops into Hyderabad to restore law and order: this was implemented on the 15th. The crisis terminated on 18 September 1948 when an Indian military governor was appointed and a military administration was installed.

On 23 September the Nizam sent a cable to the Security Council withdrawing the Hyderabad case from its agenda. Pakistan continued to press for discussion, but it was ultimately dropped. Hyderabad's complaint to the Security Council was included in the Council's provisional agenda. India argued that because Hyderabad was not an independent state, it had no right to seek international legal intervention in what was purely a domestic affair. There was no substantive consideration of the question at the UN.

References   See sources for Case #82.

(89) China Civil War   The international crisis resulting from the civil war in China involved Nationalist China and the United States as crisis actors from 23 September 1948 to 8 December 1949.

Background   Chiang Kai-shek's Nationalist (*Kuomintang*) Government emerged from World War II in disarray due to the Chinese Communist resumption of the civil war, combined with severe inflation and economic difficulties. President Roosevelt, and after him President Truman, advocated political unification of the Nationalist Government and the Communists. Accordingly, Truman sent George Marshall to China to mediate between the two parties, while giving active US assistance to the Nationalists. The mediation mission, which lasted for 13 months, ended in failure, despite a cease-fire in 1946, when fighting resumed in Manchuria. US pressure on *Kuomintang* (KMT) leaders to bring the Communists into the Chinese Government took the form of an arms embargo on China. By January 1947 Marshall concluded that there was no hope of accomplishing Chinese unification. He left China to assume the post of Secretary of State. Partial withdrawal of American soldiers began.

As the situation in China deteriorated during April and May 1947, the US decided to lift the arms embargo on 26 May and the process of partial withdrawal came to an end. In an attempt to reappraise US/China policy, a fact-finding mission, headed by General Wedemeyer, was sent to China. The Wedemeyer Report recommended a 5-year program of large-scale US economic aid to be administered by the Nationalist Government with US guidance, along with an American supervisory force of 10,000 soldiers. Secretary of State Marshall, determined not to adopt any measure of military aid which might lead to US intervention in China, shelved the report. On 18 February President Truman signed a Foreign Assistance Act granting economic aid to China.

The military campaigns in mainland China during 1948 were of decisive importance. The Communists attacked in Manchuria and in Shantung and occupied Supingchieh, the gateway to Changchun.

Crisis   On 23 September 1948 the strongly fortified city of Tsinan, Shantung's capital, fell to the Chinese Communists, triggering a crisis for the United States: the city was lost after the defection of an entire division of Nationalist soldiers. For the United States the Nationalist setback posed in increasingly acute form the threat of loss of US influence in China and the question of granting large-scale military aid, including the eventual use of American armed forces, to a government which had lost the confidence of its own troops and its own people. By the autumn of 1948 the whole of northeast China had fallen into Communist hands.

US decision-makers undertook an extensive policy review in October, and on the 26th the US responded to the crisis with a decision not to commit military aid to Nationalist China, despite the near-certain consequences of Communist victory in the civil war. This decision ended the crisis for the United States.

Early in January 1949 the Nationalist military strength was broken. Throughout that year the Communists gradually achieved control over the mainland. In the spring Nationalist forces began retreating to Taiwan.

The proclamation of the People's Republic of China (PRC) on 1 October 1949 expanded Nationalist China's internal crisis to international proportions. The response and termination occurred on the same date, 8 December 1949, when the Nationalists formally established the Republic of China (ROC) on the island of Taiwan, thereby tacitly acknowledging the PRC. The United States backed Nationalist claims to be the sole representative of the people of China at the United Nations until 1971.

On 8 December 1949 the United Nations General Assembly passed a resolution calling on all states "to refrain from (a) seeking to acquire spheres of influence or to create foreign controlled regimes within the territory of China; (b) seeking to obtain special rights or privileges within the territory of China."

The Soviet involvement was political; substantial Soviet forces had been withdrawn from China by October 1948. Three subsequent crises erupted over PRC/ROC disputes over the Taiwan Straits and the larger issue of the unresolved China civil war, in 1954, 1958 and 1962 (see Cases #110, #133, and #158).

References   Bianco 1971; Chiang Kai-shek 1957; Donovan 1977; Fairbank 1972, 1976; Kalicki 1975; Latourette 1952; Schurmann and Schell 1967–74; Truman 1955; Tsou 1963; United States Department of State 1967.

(90) Costa Rica/ Nicaragua

A crisis for Costa Rica took place from 11 December 1948 until 21 February 1949.

Background   Civil war broke out in Costa Rica after the dictatorship of Picardo, which supported the incumbent President Calderon, opposed the election in February 1948 of Seno Ulate as President. Ulate fled the country, and Picardo was subsequently overthrown. He left Costa Rica for Nicaragua on 20 April. The country was then governed by a 10-man military junta headed by José Figueres.

Crisis   A crisis for Costa Rica was triggered on 11 December 1948 by an invasion of about 1000 men, primarily Nicaraguan National Guardsmen, and a number of supporters of Calderon. The response, on the same day, was an order for immediate mobilization, the imposition of martial law, and the movement of troops to the frontier with Nicaragua. In addition, Costa Rica appealed to the UN Security Council and protested to the Nicaraguan Government which denied the charges. Fighting continued until mid-December when Costa Rican troops recovered the La Cruz area, which had been occupied by the invaders, and forced them back to the Nicaraguan border.

On 14 December the OAS appointed and dispatched an Inquiry Commission to the disputing states to investigate the facts. The report, on 24 December, stated that the invasion had been led by Costa Rican political exiles and criticized Nicaragua for not having prevented it. A military commission was appointed to supervise the activity on the Costa Rican–Nicaraguan border. The crisis ended on 21 February 1949 when the two countries signed a treaty of friendship.

References See general list and de Lima 1971.

(91) Indonesia Independence III

The last of three interrelated crises between The Netherlands and Indonesia over the latter's independence (see Cases #72 and #79) occurred between 19 December 1948 and 27 December 1949.

Background The Linggadjati and Renville Agreements of 25 March 1947 and 17 January 1948, respectively, had recognized the *de facto* authority of the Indonesian Republic over Java, Sumatra and Madura. The Dutch, nevertheless, created autonomous regions and states on those islands, thus violating the agreements. Tension began to mount again in 1948, and negotiations reached a deadlock when the Dutch tried to force a one-sided agreement. It became clear to the Indonesians that The Netherlands would once more attempt to solve the problem unilaterally by the use of force.

Crisis A crisis for Indonesia was triggered on 19 December 1948 when Dutch forces occupied Djakarta and other cities in Java and Sumatra, while capturing eminent Republican political leaders. The trigger for The Netherlands' crisis was an anti-Netherlands report to the Security Council by the Good Offices Committee on 23 December 1948, threatening the Hague empire in Southeast Asia. Indonesia responded on 25 December 1948 by setting up an emergency government in Sumatra and appealing to Nehru who officially transmitted the Resolution adopted by the 2nd New Delhi Conference to the Security Council with strong recommendations for action. Holland responded on 27 December by deciding to reject the Security Council's call for an immediate cease-fire and the transfer of sovereignty to Indonesia after free elections. On the 30th it refused to cease fire and release political prisoners. International pressure, the 2nd New Delhi Conference, an Arab League resolution calling for a Dutch cease-fire, and intense US pressure finally convinced the Dutch to comply. On 27 December 1949 the crisis ended for both actors, when Queen Juliana signed a formal act transferring sovereignty over the Dutch East Indies to the Republic of Indonesia. The Soviets supported Indonesia politically throughout the 1945–49 conflict between Indonesia and The Netherlands. The US, on the other hand, progressed from supporting The Netherlands to pressuring them to sign the Renville Agreement, to securing Dutch compliance by threatening to suspend US aid.

References See sources for Cases #72 and #79.

(92) Sinai Incursion

A crisis for Egypt, Israel and the UK occurred during the first Arab–Israel War and lasted from 25 December 1948 to 10 January 1949.

Background The first of many Arab–Israel wars had begun on 15 May 1948 (see Case #86), with the end of the British Mandate, Israel's proclamation of independence and the invasion by five Arab states. Egypt's refusal to negotiate an armistice agreement led Israel to increase its efforts to conquer southern territories.

Crisis On 25 December 1948 Israeli forces launched an attack on the Egyptian Army in the south, crossing into the Egyptian-held Sinai peninsula and triggering crises for Egypt and Britain. After an unsuccessful attempt to rally Arab League states to its aid, Egypt responded to this territorial threat on 31 December by appealing to the UK to press for a Security Council resolution demanding Israeli withdrawal. Britain, relying on its unrenewed 1936 treaty with Egypt, triggered a crisis for Israel by sending an ultimatum, via the US Embassy, on the 31st, demanding the evacuation of Egyptian territory no later than 8 January 1949. Israel responded to this threat of military intervention by changing the direction of its forces while still remaining in Sinai. The crisis was escalated further when Israel shot down five British planes over Israeli territory which had been sent to observe the Israeli withdrawal from Sinai. Britain reacted strongly by sending military reinforcements to its base in Aqaba, Jordan, on 7 January. That day Israel ordered its troops out of the area. This withdrawal was completed by 10 January 1949, the termination date for all three crisis actors.

References See sources for Case #86.

(93) Pushtunistan I Afghanistan's demand for an independent Pathan state was followed by a propaganda campaign between the two countries in March 1949. The exact date of the

Background The crisis in 1949–50 was the first in a series of crises between these two states (see Cases #114 and #148). After the 1947 partition of British India into India and Pakistan, Afghanistan demanded the creation of a separate state for the Pushtu-speaking people located on the Pakistani side of the border between Afghanistan and Pakistan. This demand was rejected by Pakistan as undermining its unity.

Crisis Afghanistan's demand for an independent Pathan state was followed by a propaganda campaign between the two countries in March 1949. The exact date of the crisis trigger for Afghanistan is uncertain: it occurred when the Pakistani Government arrested Communist infiltrators into its North West Frontier Province and initiated efforts towards more effective control of that region, while rejecting any Afghanistan claims to the territory. On 27 March it was reported that Afghanistan had moved two divisions and part of its airforce to the Pakistani frontier. On 2 April Afghanistan recalled its diplomatic representatives to Pakistan. Tension between the two countries increased following an incident on 12 June when a Pakistani plane bombed the village of Moghulgai, 2100 yards from the frontier. After an investigation by a joint Afghanistan–Pakistan Commission, Pakistan took responsibility for an unintentional flight and offered to pay compensation, ending Afghanistan's crisis on 31 July 1949.

On 12 August a large group of Afridi Pathans met on the Pakistani side of the Durand Line – the internationally recognized Afghanistan–Pakistan frontier – and established a Pushtunistan Assembly. When Pushtunistan's independence was proclaimed, it was immediately recognized by Afghanistan.

The tension level remained low for several months. The beginning of 1950 signalled the start of new propaganda campaigns between the two countries. The pro-Pushtunistan movement in Afghanistan strengthened during the spring and summer. Tribal unrest was prevalent and demands for the separation of Pathanistan increased.

The trigger for Pakistan occured on 30 September 1950, more than a year after the termination of Afghanistan's crisis, when Afghan troops invaded Pakistan. Pakistan responded with troops and aircraft and succeeded in driving the Afghan forces across the border on 5 October 1950, which marked the termination date of Pakistan's crisis.

References Burke 1973; Dupree 1980; Feldman 1967; Franck 1952; Fraser-Tyler 1967; Hussain 1966; Spain 1954.

(94) Luperon This mini-crisis involved one actor only, the Dominican Republic. It started on 19 June 1949 and terminated two days later.

Background Tension in the Caribbean region was high, and there had been several attempts by the Caribbean League to overthrow Trujillo, the Dominican Republic's authoritarian ruler (see Case #80).

Crisis On 19 June 1949 a planeload of fifteen mercenaries from Guatemala landed at Luperon in the Dominican Republic. The plane was destroyed by the Dominican Navy, and the expedition was crushed immediately. Although this did not represent a large-scale military threat, Trujillo took the incident seriously and on 21 June sent a protest note to Cuba, along with threatening words to Guatemala – the Dominican Republic's major response to a perceived threat to its political regime. On that date the Cuban Government announced its determination to stop the enlistment of men to fight as mercenaries, and the crisis terminated, although tension in the area remained high until December 1951, the culmination of all OAS activity to settle the disputes in the region.

References   See sources for Case #80.

(95) Soviet Bloc/Yugoslavia

A crisis for Yugoslavia began on 19 August 1949 and subsequently faded without a precise termination date.

Background   Relations between the Soviet Union and Yugoslavia began deteriorating soon after World War II. In January 1948 the Soviet Union communicated its displeasure over what it perceived as Yugoslavia's increasingly independent domestic and foreign policy. In the next few months there were further Russian charges and Yugoslav denials of disloyalty to international Communism. In the summer of 1948 Yugoslavia was expelled from the Soviet-dominated Cominform.

Crisis   On 19 August 1949 the Yugoslav Government received an ultimatum from Soviet Foreign Minister Molotov which was perceived as a possible prelude to a military invasion; there was, in fact, a show of force by the Soviet division in Yugoslavia, but Moscow acted so as to avoid involvement in military hostilities against Tito's regime. Yugoslavia responded the same day by placing its forces on alert and conducting military maneuvers along the border. The crisis gradually faded.

In November 1951 Yugoslavia lodged a formal complaint with the UN against the "hostile actions" by the Soviet Union and its Eastern European allies. The General Assembly passed a resolution noting Yugoslavia's readiness to seek a peaceful solution. US involvement consisted of economic aid to Yugoslavia. Sanctions by the Cominform were imposed on Yugoslavia and, later, by the Comecon. This crisis led to a basic shift in Yugoslavia's foreign policy orientation and marked a precedent for what became known as the Brezhnev Doctrine almost two decades later (see Case #194 Prague Spring).

References   See general list, especially *Keesing's* and *New York Times*.

(96) Korean War I

The first international crisis related to the Korean War began on 25 June and ended on 30 September 1950. There were four crisis actors: the People's Republic of China (PRC), the Republic of China (Taiwan), South Korea (ROK) and the United States.

Background   After setting up dependent but Korean-led regimes in their respective occupation zones in 1945, the United States and the Soviet Union subsequently evacuated South and North Korea. There was constant tension, and minor incidents were reported in 1949. That year, too, General MacArthur and Secretary of State Acheson had defined Korea as beyond the US defense perimeter in East Asia. The Chinese Communist regime was preoccupied with internal reconstruction after the civil war (see Case #89), and plans were made for a probable invasion of Formosa in 1950. During June 1950 Kim Il-Sung, the leader of North Korea, initiated an all-out campaign for the peaceful reunification of Korea, through general elections. This constituted a challenge to Synghman Rhee's regime in the south.

Crisis   On 25 June North Korean forces crossed the 38th Parallel, triggering a crisis for South Korea and the United States. Rhee responded the same day with an appeal to the US for military aid. On 27 June President Truman responded by authorizing US forces to fight alongside troops of the ROK. He also reacted to the critical situation developing between the two Chinas by ordering the Seventh Fleet to the Formosa Straits and by establishing a naval blockade there. This was the trigger for the PRC whose plans for the invasion of Formosa were further complicated by a possible combined US/Taiwan invasion of the mainland. The PRC response, on 28 June, was contained in a speech by Chou En-lai accusing the US of aggression. Taiwan, still fearful of a Chinese Communist invasion as PRC forces were massed along the coast, perceived Chou's speech as a threat with possible grave consequences and responded the following day with a general mobilization.

A US-sponsored resolution at the Security Council was passed by a vote of 9 to 0, with Yugoslavia abstaining and the Soviet Union absent – its delegates had walked out of the Council. The resolution condemned the North Korean attack, demanded the immediate cessation of hostilities and the withdrawal of North Korean forces to the 38th Parallel. A second Security Council Resolution, on 27 June (7 to 1, with India and Egypt abstaining and Yugoslavia opposed), called on UN members to provide assistance to South Korea. And on 7 July, after US and ROK forces had come under heavy attack and had been driven southward, the Security Council passed a third resolution by 7 to 0, with India, Egypt and Yugoslavia abstaining: it urged all members to contribute forces to a UN Unified Command. US General MacArthur was appointed to lead the combined forces.

The PRC crisis faded in July as events in the area merged into the ongoing Korean War. The Soviet Union provided air cover for Shanghai and other cities against possible bombing from Taiwan. There had been no specific United Nations action concerning the PRC/Taiwan crisis.

By 29 September 1950 UN forces had restored control of South Korea to the Rhee Government and the crisis ended for South Korea and the United States. The following day the crisis ended for Taiwan with the reduction of the conflict.

References Academy of Sciences of the Democratic People's Republic of Korea 1961; Acheson 1951a, 1951b, 1969, 1971; Berger 1957; Caridi 1968; Clark 1954; Collins 1969; Dean 1954; Eisenhower 1963; Halle 1967; Hoopes 1973; Kaplan 1981; Kennan 1967; Kim Il-Sung 1976; Knapp 1967; La Feber 1976; Leckie 1963; O'Ballance 1969; Oliver 1952; Paige 1968; Public Information Association of (South) Korea 1973; Rees 1964; Ridgway 1967; Simmons 1975; Spanier 1959; Stone 1952; Truman 1955, 1956; U.S. Department of Public Information 1950; U.S. Department of State 1951; Whiting 1960; Yoo 1965.

(97) Korean War II   A second international crisis of the Korean War lasted from 1 October 1950 to 10 July 1951. The crisis actors were the People's Republic of China, North Korea, South Korea, the Soviet Union and the United States.

Background On 25 June 1950 forces of the People's Democratic Republic of Korea (North) invaded the Republic of Korea (South). The United Nations set up a unified command under US General MacArthur. In August the PRC warned the United Nations that it would retaliate if US forces crossed the 38th Parallel, which was the official boundary between North and South Korea. On 29 September 1950 the UN forces handed control of South Korea to the civilian government and the first crisis in the Korean War ended (see Case #96).

Crisis On 1 October 1950 South Korean forces crossed the 38th Parallel and advanced rapidly, triggering a crisis for North Korea. On the 7th, US forces crossed the 38th Parallel, triggering a crisis for the People's Republic of China and the Soviet Union. North Korea's Kim Il-Sung responded on 10 October by deploring South Korea's "aggression" and declaring North Korea's determination to defend itself. The Soviets responded in mid-October by placing its forces both in the Soviet Far East and in Manchuria on alert, pending further penetration by the US into North Korea which might bring US troops closer to the Soviet border. The Chinese major response was a decision to dispatch thousands of "People's Volunteers" into North Korea (secretly from Manchuria) on 16 October and to cross the Yalu River. Confirmation of the presence of Chinese forces in Korea was received in Washington on 31 October, triggering a crisis for the United States. By late November the Chinese had begun successful major attacks against UN forces. The US response, on 30 November, was a statement by President Truman announcing that the United States was prepared to use whatever weapons it had in its arsenal to defeat Chinese troops.

PRC and North Korean forces recrossed the 38th Parallel on 26 December 1950. That, along with heavy fighting in Seoul, triggered a crisis for South Korea. On 3 January 1951 UN and South Korean forces abandoned the capital, which was captured the following day. The reversal of the tide of battle terminated the crisis for the Soviet Union. Differences between President Truman and General Mac-Arthur over the expansion of the conflict led to MacArthur's dismissal in the early spring of 1951. The UN forces recaptured Seoul on 14 March 1951. There was a PRC counter-attack in late April, but by June the fighting stabilized around the 38th Parallel. Cease-fire and armistice negotiations began on 10 July 1951, terminating the crisis for North and South Korea, the PRC and the United States.

Soviet vetoes had effectively blocked UN Security Council action during the crisis and, therefore, the General Assembly became increasingly involved. On 7 October 1950 the Assembly created the UN Commission for the Unification and Rehabilitation of Korea. When the Security Council was unable to do so, a new resolution, the Uniting for Peace Resolution, was passed on 3 November, granting the General Assembly authority to take action on threats to peace and security. In December the Assembly created the UN Korean Reconstruction Agency and a three-man group on a cease-fire. And on 1 February 1951 a resolution was passed by the General Assembly declaring the PRC to be an aggressor and demanding the withdrawal of its forces from Korea.

References   See sources for Case #96.

(98) Tel Mutillah

The crisis over the village of Tel Mutillah between Israel and Syria began on 15 March 1951 and ended on 14 May of that year.

Background   This crisis was the first traumatic event to follow the Israel War of Independence (see Case #86). Its origins lay in the extended conflict over sources of the Jordan River and claims to territory considered "No Man's Land" on the Israel/Syrian border.

Crisis   Syria perceived a threat on 15 March 1951 when Israel declared its intentions to drain the Hula swamp in the valley north of Lake Tiberias (Sea of Galilee) in order to use the land for agriculture. Syria's initial response was to attack the town of El-Hamma on 4 April which resulted in the death of an Israeli policeman. This triggered a crisis for Israel which responded the following day with an aerial retaliation raid on Syrian targets. Syria's major response to the threat posed by Israel's Hula project was an attack on the Tel Mutillah outpost on 2 May. After several unsuccessful counterattacks, Israel finally captured the outpost from the Syrians, only to be thrown back with heavy losses in an assault by Syrian irregulars. Fighting continued until Israel halted the Syrians on 6 May. The matter was raised before the Security Council which called for a cease-fire accepted by both sides on 14 May 1951.

References   Ben Gurion 1969; Seale 1965; Shimoni 1977.

(99) Punjab War Scare

A crisis for India and Pakistan began on 7 July 1951 and ended some time the following month.

Background   Protests against a number of alleged Pakistani violations of the Kashmir Cease-Fire Agreement of 1 January 1949 (see Case #82) were made to the UN Security Council by India in the latter half of June 1951. In a letter from India's Representative to the UNSC on 25 June, it was stated that the Indian Government saw the incidents as being "very grave," especially when "coupled with the fanatical war propaganda that is daily growing in volume in Pakistan which justify the suspicion that they are part of a planned program calculated to lead, if unchecked, to an outbreak of hostilities between the two countries." The Pakistani Minister of

Kashmir Affairs maintained that there was nothing new or extraordinary in the incidents mentioned by India.

Crisis India's crisis was triggered on 7 July 1951 when Pakistan moved a brigade to within 15 miles of the Kashmir district of Poonch. These military movements, along with the perception of talk of *jihad* and the growing evidence of political instability in Pakistan, led Prime Minister Nehru to respond on 10 July with an order to move Indian troops to the Punjab border and to Jammu and Kashmir. Leaves for Indian army officers were cancelled. Nehru's response constituted the trigger to Pakistan's crisis. Acting upon advice by Pakistan's Chief of Staff, Ayub Khan, that Pakistan was unprepared for war, Prime Minister Liaquat Ali Khan decided to attempt to manage the crisis through diplomatic channels. His major response, on 15 July, was to inform a press conference that the heavy concentration of Indian troops was within easy striking distance of Pakistan's borders. He requested that Nehru remove the threat and added that Pakistan "would not allow itself to be intimidated or influenced by any threat of force." In addition, on 27 July, four battalions of the Pakistan National Guard were sent to reinforce the Pakistani Army on the border. Prolonged correspondence between Nehru and Liaquat Ali Khan took place from 15 July throughout August.

The crisis wound down sometime in August when the withdrawal of forces by both armies began. Violence was not employed by either country as a crisis management technique.

US activity was limited to an expression of concern. There was no Soviet activity. Dr. Frank Graham, the UN-appointed Representative for India and Pakistan, that is, Kashmir, was in the area from 30 June to the end of July and had discussions with Nehru, Liaquat Ali and other officials, but was ineffective in abating the crisis.

References Ayub Khan 1967; Gopal 1979.

(100) Suez Canal This crisis lasted from 30 July 1951 to 30 January 1952 and involved two crisis actors, Egypt and the United Kingdom.

Background At the end of World War II Egypt had demanded the abrogation of the 1936 Anglo-Egyptian Treaty on the Suez Canal and its unification with Sudan. When Britain promised self-determination to Sudan, Egypt's relations with the UK worsened, and talks between the two countries to renew the Treaty allowing a British presence in the Canal Zone ran into difficulties. A shift towards radicalization in Egypt's political life occurred.

Crisis On 30 July 1951 a crisis was triggered for Egypt by Britain's reaffirmation of its rights to the Canal under the 1936 Treaty and a call for US support. Cairo viewed this as an implied threat of force and an explicit threat to Egypt's sovereignty over the Canal Zone. Egypt's response, on 8 October 1951, which triggered a crisis for Britain, was a draft proposal to the Egyptian Parliament calling for the abrogation of the Treaty and demanding British evacuation of the Suez Canal Zone. Britain responded on 16 October by declaring a state of emergency for its forces in Egypt and a decision to reinforce troops in the Canal Zone, as well as to prohibit the export of arms to Egypt. Attempts to force the evacuation of British troops by a popular resistance movement caused prolonged and serious clashes. Guerrilla warfare in Egypt against the British continued for some time until the country was in near-total disorder. Egypt's crisis ended on 27 January 1952 when King Farouk appointed a new government. The crisis for Britain ended on 30 January when the Egyptian Prime Minister called upon the British Ambassador and agreed to resume talks.

The United States strongly supported the British position. Egypt appealed to the UN in November 1951, and an inquiry committee was set up. On 18 February 1952, subsequent to the crisis, a report was published which denied Egyptian allegations of Britain's use of forced labor to build its bases in Egypt. The Political Committee of the Arab League passed a resolution on 3 September 1951 expressing full support for Egypt.

References Acheson 1969; Blake 1975; Childers 1962; Duff 1969; Eden 1960; Egyptian Ministry of Foreign Affairs 1951; Farnie 1969; Great Britain Foreign Office 1951; Hoskins 1950; Marlowe 1954; Morrison 1960; Moussa 1955; Royal Institute of International Affairs 1952; Sadat 1957; Schonfeld 1952, 1969; Vatikiotis 1969; Watt 1957.

(101) Catalina Affair

The crisis for Sweden began on 16 June 1952. The exact termination date is unknown, but was probably sometime in July 1952.

Background Sweden, separated from the USSR by Finland and the Baltic Sea, maintained its neutrality during the Soviet invasion of Finland in 1939 (see Case #40) and, subsequently, during World War II. Swedish–Soviet relations after 1945 were cautious, but correct. In February 1952 a spy ring working in the service of the USSR was uncovered in Sweden.

Crisis On 16 June 1952 two Soviet fighters shot down a Swedish Catalina flying boat which was taking part in a search for a Swedish training plane that had disappeared with its crew of eight men 3 days earlier. In response, Sweden placed its army on alert on the 18th. An exchange of notes between the two countries followed. On 19 June several members of the Soviet Embassy in Stockholm left Sweden to return to Moscow. The following day the Swedish Foreign Minister interrupted a visit to Italy to return home. There was no precise termination date: it was determined as some time in July after the fourth and last Note relating directly to the crisis was sent by Sweden. There was no reply from the USSR, implying a tacit understanding to let the matter drop.

  The incident was condemned by the United States in a statement by Secretary of State Dean Acheson.

References A. H. H. 1952; Swedish Royal Ministry for Foreign Affairs 1957.

(102) Burma Infiltration

A crisis for Burma over Chinese Nationalist troops on its territory occurred between 8 February 1953 and 15 October 1954.

Background In 1949 *Kuomintang* (KMT) forces of Chinese Nationalists, who had retreated to southern China during the Chinese Civil War (see Case #89), crossed into Burma as the Chinese Communists consolidated their position in the south. KMT forces, commanded by General Li Mi, occupied part of the Burmese state of Kengtung which adjoined China and Thailand and became an intolerable nuisance to Burma because of their alliance with, and supply of arms to, the local insurgents. They also served as a possible provocation for a Chinese Communist incursion into Burmese territory and drew 12,000 Chinese forces into an uncomfortable proximity to the border. By 1952 air drops and supplies from foreign air bases became frequent and blatant.

Crisis On 8 February 1953 a crisis was triggered for Burma when local insurgents combined with 300 KMT troops to attack Loikaw, the capital of the state of Kayah. Additional attacks occurred on the 11th and 27th at other Burmese locations. Documents showed that the intention of the KMT was to overthrow the Union of Burma Government. Burma contended that the KMT forces were being supplied by Nationalist-held Taiwan, with tacit US agreement. Prime Minister U Nu responded to the threat of his regime on 2 March with a statement that his government intended to take the KMT question to the United Nations. On 17 March Burma notified the United States that their assistance agreements would be terminated by June. This step was taken so that the government would not be accused of complacency on the KMT issue due to its obligations to Washington. Burma submitted a complaint to the Secretary-General of the UN on the 25th, and on the 31st requested that it be placed on the General Assembly agenda for debate. A resolution was introduced on 17 April condemning the Nationalist Chinese Government and indicating necessary steps to disarm and withdraw the KMT troops from Burma. On the 21st the General Assembly adopted a resolution condemning the presence of foreign troops in Burma and insisting upon their withdrawal. The US proposed a conference with Burma, Nationalist China and Thailand, to discuss the withdrawal of the KMT forces. A four-nation Joint Military Commission under UN auspices was formed and met on 22 May 1953. Negotiations, as well as serious clashes between Burma and KMT troops, continued throughout the summer. Burma withdrew from the talks on 17 September. Eventually 7000 KMT troops were airlifted to Nationalist China between November 1953 and May 1954. On 30 May General Li Mi announced the formal dissolution of his Yunnan anti-Communist army and, on 30 July, the Joint Military Commission announced that its program had been completed. About 6000 guerrillas remained in Burma.

Burma submitted a new request to the Secretary-General on 20 August, and on the 29th of September a report on the situation was submitted to the UN stating that Burma viewed the continued presence of Chinese Nationalist troops in its territory as a threat. On 15 October 1954 the Burmese Representative acknowledged that the partial removal of KMT troops "represented the limit of what could be accomplished by international action." The crisis terminated that day with a Burmese statement that the removal of foreign troops from its territory would be its responsibility alone.

KMT troops, with US and Taiwan aid, continued their operations in Burma until 1961 when they were finally driven into Thailand and Laos by the Burmese Army.

References   Burma Ministry of Information 1953; Johnstone 1963; Maung 1969.

(103) Invasion of Laos I   The crisis began on 24 March 1953 and faded, with no specific termination date. The two actors were France and Laos.

Background   The invasion of Laos fell within the sphere of the first Indo-China War which had begun after the Japanese evacuation and reestablishment of French control following World War II. Within Laos there were Communist-oriented guerrilla groups, the Pathet Lao, who cooperated with the Vietminh guerrillas of Vietnam. The northern frontier of Laos was occupied by Vietminh forces in December 1952 and, for the next three months, they massed along the border. By mid-March their strength had grown to four divisions.

Crisis   The trigger for France occurred on 24 March when the massing of Vietminh troops reached its peak. The trigger for Laos was the launching of a Vietminh offensive on 5 April. The French response was on 13 April when it evacuated the first major town along the Laos border. The major response by Laos was 13 April, when it ordered a general mobilization and appealed to the UN to halt the invasion. On the 27th Prince Souphanouvong declared the formation of a Free Laotian Government. Vietminh forces surrounded the airfield and the fortified camp on the Plaine des Jarres and advanced towards the two Laotian capitals of Vientiane (administrative) and Luang Prabang (royal). French–Laotian troops, supplied by an extensive airlift from Saigon, clashed with the Vietminh at Sam-heva. The widely-dispersed Vietminh garrisons began withdrawing to Vietnam by mid-May, leaving behind guerrilla forces of Laotian resistance. The French proceeded to recapture the abandoned position. On 2 June two columns of French–Laotian forces advancing north and south reestablished contact between the provinces of Vientiane and Xiengkhouang. Fighting erupted and subsided and finally led to the Navarre military plan and the Battle of Dien Bien Phu the following year (see Case #109), with no precise termination date for this crisis.

The only regional organization activity was a communiqué on 25 April by NATO citing the invasion of Laos as an example of continuing Communist aggression.

References   Buttinger 1967; Goldstein 1973; Gravel 1971; Gurtov 1967; Hammer 1954; Le Bar 1960; Stevenson 1972.

(104) Korean War III   The third international crisis of the Korean War began on 16 April and ended on 27 July 1953. The crisis actors were North and South Korea, the PRC and the USA.

Background   The Korean War had been in progress since June 1950 when North Korean forces attacked South Korea leading to the creation of a UN command which fought alongside the South Korean Army. The PRC entered the battle in October 1950; and, on 10 July 1951, armistice talks began between North and South Korea (see Cases #96 and #97).

   In January 1953 Eisenhower succeeded President Truman in the White House. Primary US concerns in Korea were the release of the prisoners of war and an end to the stalemate. On 2 February the President mentioned the possibility of removing the Seventh Fleet from the Formosa Straits which had been serving as an effective barrier to Chinese Nationalist plans to invade the mainland. In addition, Stalin's death on 5 March left a power vacuum in the USSR, the PRC's closest ally during this period. Armistice and POW negotiations at Panmunjom continued with little progress, as a reported 46,000 PRC and North Korean troops held prisoner in South Korea stated that they did not wish to return to their respective homelands. While the Communists demanded their return, the UN sought ways not to force them to do so.

Crisis   On 16 April 1953 the PRC–North Korean forces began a new offensive against UN troops at Pork Chop Hill and Old Baldy. In the setting of the political discussions at Panmunjom and the general lull in the fighting, this new attack became a crisis trigger for the United States. Washington responded on 22 May when Secretary of State Dulles threatened the PRC, via India's Prime Minister Nehru, with the possible use of nuclear weapons to break the deadlock in Korea. This American response triggered a fresh crisis for the PRC and North Korea. Their combined response, on 8 June, was an agreement at Panmunjom for the voluntary repatriation of POWs, which broke the political deadlock. The softening of the Communist position, on 8 June, triggered a crisis for South Korea, which, fearing an American withdrawal, viewed any agreement on the POW issue as a possible compromise to its plans for a reunification of the Korean peninsula. The South Korean response, on 18 June, was the unauthorized release of about 25,000 prisoners of war who had declared their preference not to return to either the PRC or North Korea. This act, while angering the US, did not succeed in halting the negotiating process. An Armistice Agreement was signed on 27 July 1953 terminating the crisis for all four actors.

   The Agreement established a demarcation line and a demilitarized zone, a Military Armistice Commission to resolve violations of the Agreement, and a commission to supervise troop withdrawals.

References   See sources for Case #96.

(105) East Berlin Uprising   A crisis for the Soviet Union over East Berlin riots began on 17 June and terminated on 11 July 1953.

Background   Following Stalin's death in March 1953, greater attention was devoted to consumer goods by the USSR, and East Germany's Ulbricht was advised to follow suit. Nevertheless, on 28 May 1953 an increased quota system was introduced in East Germany. This prompted a strike by construction workers on 16 June, a spontaneous demonstration directed against the ruling party on strictly economic grounds. Towards the end of the day, although the government had agreed to roll back the new quotas, there was a shift of a political nature: a general strike was called for the following day.

Crisis   On 17 June 1953 workers went on strike and marched in East Berlin and 250 other towns. Economic grievances took on political overtones, while throngs of people rioted. The demonstrators were joined by criminal elements freed from prisons. A state of emergency was declared and martial law was introduced. The USSR response, on the same day, was to send tanks and Soviet troops stationed in bases inside East Germany to East Berlin where they were supported by East German paramilitary police. These forces succeeded in quelling the rebellion.

The Soviets looked upon these riots as a dangerous precedent and a threat to their East European bloc. On 11 July martial law was lifted, putting the official seal on a gradual process that also involved reducing the strengthened Soviet presence. Moscow's crisis ended with that act. The Western Powers limited themselves to issuing diplomatic notes on the need to cease hostilities and urging German reunification.

References Baring 1972; Blake 1975; Duff 1969.

(106) Trieste II There were two crisis actors in the second international crisis over Trieste – Italy and Yugoslavia. The crisis was triggered on 8 October and ended on 5 December 1953.

Background Both Italy and Yugoslavia held strong claims to the city of Trieste. After World War II the city was demilitarized and divided into two zones, one controlled by an Allied (UK–US) military government and the other by Yugoslavia. In a Memorandum of Understanding between Italy, Britain and the US, Rome was given a larger share in the administration of the Allied-controlled zone (see Case #67).

Crisis On 8 October 1953 Britain and the United States announced their intention to terminate the Allied Military Government in Trieste, to withdraw their troops and to relinquish the administration to the Italian Government. This triggered a crisis for Yugoslavia which responded two days later by lodging a formal protest with London and Washington and informing the UN. The frontier was closed, the Yugoslav military reserves were called up and warships moved into the area. Those acts on the 10th triggered Italy's crisis. Italy's major response, on 17 October, was to place three divisions facing the Yugoslav frontier on emergency posting.

The decision by the US and UK to withdraw was postponed while diplomatic efforts continued to convene a conference. On 5 December 1953 an agreement was announced in Rome and Belgrade for the simultaneous withdrawal of Italian and Yugoslav forces from the common border. This terminated the crisis for both actors. The final outcome of the dispute took the form of a Memorandum of Understanding, signed on 5 October 1954 by the US, UK, Italy and Yugoslavia, granting the northern zone's administration to Italy and the southern zone to Yugoslavia.

References See sources for Case #67 and Clissold 1970; Donelan and Grieve 1973; Eden 1960.

(107) Qibya There was one crisis actor – Jordan. The crisis was triggered on 14 October 1953. It had no exact termination date.

Background After the Arab–Israel War of 1948–49 (see Case #86), Arab refugees who had fled Palestine were placed in camps in Jordan where anti-Israel sentiments flourished. Infiltrations from Jordan into Israel began in 1951. In October 1953 the situation was exacerbated when Jordanian infiltrators murdered an Israeli woman and her two children.

Crisis On 14 October 1953 a Jordan crisis was triggered when the Israel Defence Forces retaliated against the village of Qibya in Jordan, killing 69 civilians and destroying 45 houses. Jordan responded on the 16th by conferrring with the US and Britain, lodging a complaint with the Security Council, and calling for a meeting of the Arab League. This resulted in condemnation of Israel by both forums. Israel public opinion prompted its leaders to decide to refrain from attacks on civilian targets in the future. Infiltrations stopped for a while, but were resumed after a few months.

References Blechman 1972; Shimoni 1977; Shwadran 1959.

(108) Guatemala   Guatemala, Honduras and the United States were actors in a crisis from 12 December 1953 until 29 June 1954.

Background   Agrarian reform and foreign investment control were instituted in Guatemala in 1951, with growing influence of the Communist Party. The US perceived this development as a threat to its influence in Latin America.

Crisis   The Guatemala Crisis was triggered on 12 December 1953 when it received information concerning a US decision to support an anti-government "liberation" movement. The following month, in January 1954, Guatemala responded by a decision to obtain arms from the Soviet bloc in order to arm a workers' militia. This information, confirmed to the United States on 10 February 1954, triggered a crisis for the US. Soviet arms began reaching Guatemala on 15 May and were viewed by the US as a grave development. On 18 May Honduras, in the midst of a general strike causing substantial damage to its economy, perceived Guatemalan infiltration, along with rumors about arms reaching Honduran strikers via Guatemala, as a threat. Honduras responded on 25 May by recalling its Ambassador to Guatemala. After unsuccessful efforts by the US to resolve the situation through conferences, negotiations and promises to review Latin American economic problems, its major response occurred on 18 June when the US proclaimed a complete embargo of arms shipments to Guatemala and backed an invasion led by Castillo Armas against the Arbenz Government, then in power in Guatemala. Guatemala appealed to the Security Council and the Inter-American Peace Committee for assistance, accusing Honduras (and Nicaragua) of aggression, but the Security Council passed a resolution calling for no UN intervention until an investigation had been completed by the Organization of American States (OAS). When the Guatemalan Army refused to engage the Armas forces in fighting, Arbenz resigned. After an interim Diaz-led military junta stayed in control for two days, a new junta, led by Colonel Morzon, was set up on 29 June 1954 and suppressed the "Arbencista" political élite. This marked the termination date for all three crisis actors.

References   Alexander 1954a, 1954b, 1957; Ball 1969; Braden 1971; Eisenhower 1963; Galich 1968; Gillin and Silvert 1956; Grant 1955; Hammond and Farrell 1975; Maitz 1959; Mecham 1961; Pike 1955; Roberts 1972; Rosenthal 1962; Schneider 1959; Shapira 1978; Silvert 1954; Slater 1967; Szulc 1971; Taylor 1956; Toriello 1955; Whitaker 1954; Wise and Ross 1964; Ydigoras 1963.

(109) Dien Bien Phu   The crisis over Dien Bien Phu for France, the US and the UK lasted from 13 March to 21 July 1954.

Background   France's strategy in the first Indochina War (1946–54) changed in early 1953 when a new commander, Henri Navarre, arrived in its Southeast Asia colony. Laos had been invaded by the Communist Vietminh (see Case #103), and the French sought proof of their ability to remain in Indochina before the scheduled May 1954 Geneva Conference on Indochina. The new strategy consisted of regrouping and reinforcing local forces and areas held by the French and opening areas held by the Vietminh. This plan was not successful. Dien Bien Phu was in a flat valley surrounded by Vietminh-occupied hills on the entrance road to Laos and at the crossroads of three other roads. Throughout the winter of 1953–54 the French fortified the area. The plan was to draw the Vietminh forces to Dien Bien Phu for a showdown battle. Both forces underestimated the strength of their adversary.

Crisis   On 13 March 1954 the Vietminh launched their first major offensive against Dien Bien Phu, triggering a crisis for France. By 17–18 March the surrounding French defensive positions had been taken. France's major response, on the 20th, was an appeal to its allies for increased aid and strong military action. This triggered a crisis for the United States – the threat of direct and immediate US involvement in the war. French General Ely met with the US Joint Chiefs of Staff on 21 and 24 March and with President Eisenhower on the 22nd. Matters involving the supply of US bombers and ground strategy were discussed. The US response was on 29 March when Secretary of State Dulles, stressing the importance of Indochina to US security, proposed that the US and its allies meet the Communist threat with "united action." The next day the second Vietminh offensive began.

Strategy discussions were held by the US Joint Chiefs from 29 March to 3 April. A plan was proposed for limited tactical nuclear airstrikes of Vietminh positions around Dien Bien Phu by the Seventh Fleet then positioned in the Philippines. The President rejected this proposal. The need to strengthen France's will to fight was stressed. There was also a plan to dispatch seven armored divisions – contingent upon the US being allowed to train the Indochinese forces. This did not appeal to either the UK or France.

The UK crisis was triggered on 11 April with Dulles' arrival in London, posing a danger of direct British participation in the Indochina War. The same day another attack brought Vietminh forces within a quarter of a mile of the French stronghold, cutting off the use of its airstrip and preventing the evacuation of the wounded, as well as the arrival of supplies. In London Dulles reiterated that his plan for "united action" was not designed to prejudice the upcoming Geneva talks on Indochina, scheduled to begin on 8 May. On 13 April Dulles and Prime Minister Eden issued a statement referring to a regional collective defense arrangement, under the UN Charter, which would be considered at the Geneva Conference. A similar US–France statement was issued the next day.

On 21 April General Navarre informed Paris that Dien Bien Phu could not hold out unless there were allied air attacks on Vietminh supply routes. Dulles, in Paris at the time for a NATO meeting, met with Eden and heard Prime Minister-Foreign Minister Bidault's request for air strikes. The US refused to act without UK cooperation, which Eden would not grant. US aid was formally requested by France on 25 April. A plan was formulated by Dulles and the French Ambassador to London to push for a UK decision.

An emergency British Cabinet meeting ended with a decision that the UK would take no action before the Geneva Conference, along with a promise to consider a collective defense scheme in the area after the conference. On 26 April Eisenhower stated that, in view of the absence of a joint Allied response, the US would not send ground forces, and no unilateral action would be taken. The UK crisis ended on 27 April with a speech by Churchill to the House of Commons stating that there would be no British military action in Indochina before the Geneva Conference. Eisenhower made a similar statement on the 29th. On 7 May Dien Bien Phu fell and the US crisis ended. The following day a formal cease-fire was instituted. The crisis for France persisted until the signing of a bilateral armistice agreement between France and the Vietminh. A final declaration, on 21 July 1954, provided for the partition of Vietnam into north and south, along with a call for elections and unification two years hence.

A regional collective defense scheme, first considered at the beginning of April 1954, became the basis for SEATO.

References Eisenhower 1963; Hammer 1954; Hoopes 1973; O'Ballance 1964; Randle 1969.

(110) Taiwan Straits I There were three crisis actors in this first international crisis over the Taiwan Straits, each experiencing two foreign policy crises: Nationalist China (ROC or Taiwan), the People's Republic of China (PRC), and the United States. The crisis began in early August 1954 and ended on 23 April 1955.

Background The conflict over the Taiwan Straits began in 1949 after the Communist victory in China's civil war and the split between the PRC and the Nationalists on Taiwan (see Case #89). Neither side was content with this arrangement: each aimed at a reunification of China, with the PRC advocating a Communist regime while Chiang Kai-shek wished to see the Mao Tse-tung Government removed from the mainland.

Crisis The trigger for the PRC's first crisis in this cluster was the formation of the US-sponsored Southeast Asia Treaty Organization (SEATO) in August 1954, subsequently denounced by Chou En-lai in a speech on 11 August 1954 in which he emphasized the justice of any Communist attempt to reunify China. On 3 September 1954 the PRC bombarded the Nationalist-held offshore islands of Quemoy and Matsu. This triggered a crisis for the United States and Taiwan. Nationalist China's response, on 7 September, took the form of air strikes against the Chinese mainland. On the 12th the US responded by deciding to send the Seventh Fleet to the area and appealing to the UN. The PRC's first crisis faded some time in November after Taiwan's bombing of the mainland had stopped. On 2 December 1954 a defense treaty was signed between the US and Taiwan, by which time the PRC had eased off the bombardment, ending the crisis for both the US and Taiwan.

The signing of a US–Taiwan Defense Pact on 2 December 1954 triggered a second crisis for the PRC. Its response, on 10 January 1955, was heavy bombardment of the Tachen Islands. This, in turn, triggered a second crisis for the US and Taiwan. The latter responded some time in January 1955 by returning fire and staging battles on the three islands of Tachen, Quemoy and Matsu. Taiwan subsequently evacuated the Tachen Islands. The US responded to the crisis with a request by President Eisenhower to Congress on 24 January to grant him a free hand in controlling the situation in the Taiwan area. The termination of Taiwan's second crisis occurred on 25 March 1955, after completion of the fortification of Quemoy and Matsu, with US help. The crisis for the US and the PRC ended on 23 April when Chou En-lai offered to negotiate in the face of an increasing US commitment and the reduced prospects for a successful PRC invasion. Taiwan did not participate in the talks.

During the course of the crisis there was a shift from the plane of Communist–Nationalist confrontation to primary interaction between the PRC and the USA. American strategy was directed at building an alliance network of anti-Communist states. The Secretary-General of the UN conducted talks, as did the Security Council, but no resolution was passed and the UN had no effect on the abatement of the crisis. Although the formation of SEATO was the first trigger to the crisis, that regional organization was entirely inactive during the crisis.

In 1958 the same three states experienced another cluster of crises over the issue of Quemoy and Matsu (see Case #133).

References   Branyan and Larsen 1971; Bueler 1971; Dulles 1972; Eisenhower 1965; George and Smoke 1974; Hsieh 1962; Kalicki 1975; MacFarquhar 1972.

**(111) Costa Rica/
Nicaragua II**

The crisis for the two states lasted from 8 to 20 January 1955.

Background   Hostilities began in 1948 when José Figueres led a revolt that overthrew Picardo's dictatorship in Costa Rica. Nicaragua was accused of aiding Costa Rican political exiles. While Nicaragua had a well-trained army of about 7500 men, Costa Rican defense was entrusted to the National Police Force (see Case #90).

Crisis   On 8 January 1955 Costa Rican President José Figueres received information that Venezuela had sent a fleet of 10 military transports, fully manned, into Nicaragua. Costa Rica appealed to the OAS, mobilized volunteer reserve troops, and placed its army on stand-by alert. Three days later Costa Rican rebels crossed the frontier from Nicaragua and captured a town 30 miles north of the capital city San José. Costa Rica proclaimed a state of emergency and broke diplomatic relations with Nicaragua.

The OAS Council met in an emergency session on 11 January and voted to send a fact-finding mission to Costa Rica. On the 14th the mission reported that there were serious indications that the rebels were being supplied with arms from Nicaragua and that foreign aircraft had flown over Costa Rica, strafing and bombing cities. The Council then called upon Nicaragua to stop the flow of arms to the rebels and voted to send observers to the area. The Council decided further, on 16 January, to grant the Costa Rican request for aircraft. Four F-51 Mustang fighter-planes were delivered from the United States. This triggered a crisis for Nicaragua.

President Somoza responded on the 19th by reinforcing Nicaragua's borders and stepping up military flights. Costa Rican forces drove the rebels from the captured territory and forced them back across the Nicaraguan border.

The crisis ended on 20 January 1955 when both states agreed to an OAS plan for demilitarized zones along the border. Whereas Figueres considered the termination as a victory for Costa Rica and credited the OAS and the United States, Nicaragua's Somoza was disappointed that the attempt to overthrow Figueres had failed and considered Costa Rica to be in a stronger position than at the beginning of the crisis.

References   See source for Case #90.

(112) Baghdad Pact

Egypt's crisis over the Baghdad Pact began on 24 February and ended in mid-October 1955.

Background   In February 1954 a Syrian Army coup, with Iraqi involvement, ousted a pro-Egyptian regime in Damascus headed by Shishakli. However, Iraqi hopes for a pro-Western Syria were not realized. An agreement between Turkey and Pakistan and bilateral military aid agreements between the US, Turkey and Iraq, were signed in April 1954. The United States and Pakistan signed a similar agreement the following month. Iraq announced its intention to join a pro-Western alliance and endeavored to prevent possible isolation in the Arab world by attempting to persuade other Arab states to join as well. On 16 January 1955 Egypt called for an emergency meeting of the Arab League, claiming that no member should become party to an agreement with the Western Powers and that such a pact would likely undermine Arab sovereignty and independence. Cairo was unsuccessful in its efforts to have Iraq expelled from the Arab League.

Crisis   On 24 February 1955 the UK, Iraq, Iran, Turkey and Pakistan created a regional anti-Soviet defense arrangement known as the Baghdad Pact, triggering a crisis for Egypt: Nasser viewed the Pact as a challenge to his leadership in the Arab world and a direct threat from the US and UK to overthrow his regime. At the end of February Egypt and Syria announced their intention to exclude Iraq from a new Arab alliance with Saudi Arabia and Yemen. Egypt's response, on 15 March, was a denunciation of the Pact and an accusation that the West was introducing Great Power rivalry and the Cold War into the Middle East, thus dividing the Arab world and threatening Egypt with encirclement. Egypt began to forge counter-alliances with Jordan, Lebanon and Syria; and the division of the Arab states into rival camps hardened.

The crisis ended in mid-October 1955 when Syria and Egypt concluded a Mutual Defense Pact. In July 1958 a coup in Iraq overthrew the monarchy and established a military dictatorship (see Case #132). Iraq subsequently left the Baghdad Pact.

The United States participated in the negotiations and provided economic assistance, but never formally joined the Pact. The Soviet Union provided arms and weapons to Egypt and Syria.

References   Bowie 1974; Dekmejian 1971; Finer 1964; Hofstadter 1973; Lacouture 1973; Love 1969; Nutting 1967; Robertson 1964; Thomas 1970.

(113) Gaza Raid

The crisis between Egypt and Israel began on 28 February 1955 and ended on 23 June 1956.

Background   During the early 1950s Israel suffered from repeated terrorist attacks by infiltration into Israeli territory, particularly from Gaza which was then controlled by Egypt. Five reprisal raids into Egyptian territory were carried out by Israel from 1950 to 1955.

Crisis   Israel's retaliatory raid into Gaza on 28 February 1955, in which 39 Arabs were killed and 32 injured, triggered a crisis for Egypt. On 20 March Egypt appealed to the UN Security Council and the Arab League. Its major response, on 20 April, was a request by Nasser to Chou En-lai to contact Moscow about supplying arms to

Egypt. The crisis ended for Egypt on 28 September 1955 when, with Soviet approval, an arms agreement was signed with Czechoslovakia.

This marked the trigger for Israel's crisis. By 11 December 1955, when an agreement between France and Israel for the purchase of French Mystères was signed, Israel had answered cumulative terrorist attacks by four more raids into Egyptian territory. On 5 April 1956 a large raid into Gaza resulted in 59 deaths and 93 wounded. However, Israel's major response was a letter to the Prime Minister of France on 12 April 1956 requesting massive amounts of arms . Another agreement was signed for six more French Mystères on 23 April. The termination date for Israel's crisis was 23 June 1956 when a third arms deal was signed with France which would provide substantial French arms to Israel, and enable Israeli decision-makers to correct the imbalance in military capability which had occurred as a result of the Czech arms agreement with Egypt and Syria.

The Security Council passed a resolution condemning Israel for the Gaza Raid. The Secretary-General visited the area in the hope of mediating between the two parties, but the UN did not contribute to crisis abatement. The Arab League held discussions, but did not pass any resolution.

References Bar-Zohar 1967; Brecher 1974; Dayan 1966; Lacouture 1973; Love 1969.

(114) Pushtunistan II High tension between Afghanistan and Pakistan in the border area was further revived from 27 March to November 1955 after a relative hiatus following a crisis in 1950 (see Case #93).

Background This crisis was another stage in the ongoing conflict over Afghanistan's demand for the creation of an independent Pushtu (Pathan) state, the territory of which at that time was under Pakistani sovereignty.

Crisis The crisis began on 27 March when information reached Afghanistan of the Pakistani Government's proposal to incorporate the areas of Pushtu-speaking people on the North West Frontier into a unified province of West Pakistan. Afghanistan's major response was a broadcast by Prime Minister Daud voicing his government's protest and a formal Note protesting the proposed merger. This reached Karachi on 29 March and triggered a crisis for Pakistan. The issue was further escalated by an attack on the Pakistan Embassy in Kabul on the 30th. Pakistan responded to the crisis on 1 April with a declaration by Prime Minister Mohammed Ali that Pakistan would not tolerate any intervention in its domestic affairs and would not rest until amends were made for the attack on Pakistan's embassy. Further Pakistani steps were taken on 1 May – the breaking off of diplomatic relations, the closing of the borders and the termination of economic relations, including the closing down of all Afghan trade agencies in Pakistan. The latter had a severe effect on Afghanistan as it was dependent on Pakistani ports for trade. Afghanistan announced a mobilization and declared a state of emergency. By 9 September the two countries had reached an agreement whereby Afghanistan promised to make amends for the insult to the Pakistani flag. On 14 October a united West Pakistan was declared which included areas of the North West Frontier that bordered Afghanistan. The "One Unit Scheme" terminated the crisis for Pakistan.

The diplomatic issue regarding the Pakistani Embassy in Afghanistan was solved by a formal ceremony of reopening in Kabul in November 1955, terminating the crisis for both actors. After diplomatic and economic relations were restored, the prior issue of independence for the Pushtuns was once more brought to the fore. Although the protracted conflict over Pushtunistan continued, the high level of tension was reduced by reciprocal visits in August 1956 of Pakistan's Prime Minister and Afghanistan's President when intentions to improve relations were declared (see Case #148).

References See sources for Case #93.

(115) Goa I   The first Goa crisis for Portugal began on 10 August and lasted until 6 September 1955.

Background   After the British withdrawal from India in 1947 Portugal continued to reject all Indian requests for the reunification of its enclaves on the west coast of India into the Republic of India. This led to the closing of the Indian Legation in Lisbon in June 1953.

Intensification of nationalist agitation within India, as well as within Portugal's enclaves, began in mid-1954 and resulted in mass arrests, curfews and expulsions. In July of that year Dadra, Nagar Haveli and Damao were seized by Free Goan volunteers. The Indian Government refused passage to Portuguese forces to reinstate control over these areas. The mass entry of volunteers into Goa in May and June became the symbol of a campaign for the peaceful liberation of Goa.

Crisis   On 10 August 1955 it was announced that, despite Nehru's disapproval, Indian volunteers would march into Goa in a peaceful mass invasion on 15 August, India's Independence Day. This announcement triggered a crisis for Portugal which responded by moving army units to the Indian–Goan border and sending its Chief of Staff to Goa. Prime Minister Cunha called upon the Indian Government to ban the march.

On 15 August about 3000 Indian demonstrators marched across the Goan border. Portuguese police and soldiers opened fire killing 20 and wounding many more. Lisbon protested to New Delhi on the 17th, accusing it of violating Portugal's sovereignty. India broke diplomatic relations with Portugal on the 19th.

On 4 September the All-India Congress Committee declared that in the present situation it would be inappropriate for Indian nationals to enter Goa. This crisis ended on 6 September when Indian Prime Minister Nehru stated in Parliament that India had no intention of taking any war-like measures over Goa. A second crisis over Goa erupted in 1961 (see Case #156).

References   Brecher 1968; Kaul 1967; Kay 1970; Marshall 1961; Maxwell 1970; Rao 1963; Rubinoff 1971; Salazar 1956; Wright 1962.

(116) Suez Nationalization   Britain and France were the two actors in a crisis over Egypt's nationalization of the Suez Canal. The crisis lasted from 26 July until 6 November 1956.

Background   Egypt had voiced its concern about the continued presence of British forces in the Canal Zone on several occasions during the early part of 1956. Cairo had also declared its support for the FLN (Algerian nationalists) in their struggle for independence from France.

Crisis   A crisis was triggered for both London and Paris on 26 July 1956 when Egypt proclaimed the nationalization of the Suez Canal. On the 30th multilateral talks were initiated – the US, Australia and the two crisis actors – in order to find a peaceful solution. When these talks, as well as an appeal by Britain and France to the United Nations, did not result in satisfaction of the aggrieved parties, bilateral talks between France and Israel were initiated in August. Britain joined its two allies at a conference at Sèvres held between 22–25 October. The major response by Britain and France was a decision on 24 October to launch a joint military attack, along with Israel, on Egypt's Sinai Peninsula. Israel invaded on 29 October and British and French intervention followed two days later (see Case #120).

When, on 5 November, the Soviet Union threatened to bomb London and Paris if the situation were not rectified, Britain and France complied at once and agreed to a cease-fire which came into effect the following day, 6 November – the termination date for both crisis actors.

The US, too, though countering the Soviet threat, pressed its allies to withdraw their forces. The UN was intensely active, culminating in a decision by the General Assembly to send Emergency Forces to police Sinai and Gaza, from which all foreign forces were to be withdrawn.

References   Adams 1958; Bar-Zohar 1964; Barker 1963; Beaufre 1969; Bowie 1974; Childers 1962; Dayan 1976; Eden 1960; Epstein 1964; Farnie 1969; Finer 1964; Love 1969; Macmillan 1971; Neustadt 1970; Nutting 1967; Pineau 1976; Robertson 1964; Thomas 1970.

(117) Qalqilya   A crisis for Jordan and Israel took place from 13 September until mid-October 1956.

Background   Infiltration into Israeli territory from neighboring Arab states occurred with great frequency during the six years prior to the Sinai Campaign. Acts of reprisal against the Arab state from whose territory infiltrators crossed into Israel were numerous and swift (see Cases #98, #107 and #113). Most recently, during July and August 1956, dozens of Israelis were killed or wounded as a result of several infiltrations of *feda'yun* (guerrilla) groups from Jordan.

Crisis   On 13 September 1956 Israeli forces <u>blew up</u> a police station in the Jordanian village of Garandal. King Hussein's response, the following day, was a decision to visit Iraq to consult Prime Minister Nuri Sa'id about the possible stationing of Iraqi troops in Jordan. After several other incidents from Jordan, including the firing on Israeli archaeologists meeting at a border settlement, Israel carried out another reprisal on the Jordanian village of Husan. A third reprisal raid took place on 10 October at Qalqilya in response to a Jordanian ambush of an Israeli bus.

On the 12th Iraq issued a statement that it was ready to send troops to Jordan immediately, if requested to do so. This triggered a crisis for Israel. Foreign Minister Meir responded the next day be declaring that the stationing of Iraqi troops in Jordan would be a threat to Israel's integrity and that in such an event Israel would retaliate. In addition, Israel's ambassadors to the major powers were called home for consultation and a request was made to convene the UN Security Council.

Israel's crisis ended on 15 October with a Jordanian declaration that Iraqi forces would not enter Jordan at that time, but would do so if Israel attacked. The crisis for Jordan faded at the end of October. At that time RAF planes from Cyprus flew over Jordan in a symbolic gesture to reinforce the Jordan regime which had been undermined by the Qalqilya raid.

The UN Secretary-General met with the representatives of the powers and the two crisis actors and warned of Security Council intervention if peace did not prevail in the area. After the raid on Qalqilya, General Burns, the Head of the UN Observer Forces, attempted to stop the fighting but was not successful.

References   See sources for Case #107.

(118) Poland Liberalization   This crisis had two actors, Poland and the USSR. It began in early October 1956 and ended on the 22nd of that month.

Background   During the summer and autumn of 1956 the Soviet Union faced threats to its hegemonial position in Eastern Europe, particularly in Hungary and Poland where economic stagnation was accompanied by increasing demands for greater political freedom internally as well as more independence from Soviet dictation in foreign policy. On 28 June a demonstration of Polish workers in Poznan turned into a riot which was brutally suppressed by the Polish Government with hundreds killed or wounded. The Polish leadership eventually took decisions which gradually led to the rehabilitation of Wladsylaw Gomulka, a member of the Politburo purged in 1948 for Titoism. Politically, he was one of the few people acceptable to the Polish masses.

Crisis   The trigger to the crisis for the Soviet Union was Gomulka's return to power in early October 1956, which the Soviets perceived as a threat to their hegemony. Moscow's response was a decision on 17 October to send a delegation to attend the Polish Warsaw Party Plenum. When this decision became known in Poland on the

18th, a reciprocal crisis was triggered. Poland's response, the next day, took the form of a threat by Gomulka to broadcast the news that Soviet troops were marching on Warsaw, a fact confirmed by Khrushchev. Such a broadcast could have led to widespread demonstrations. Seven Soviet divisions were put on the alert and patrols along the East German border with Poland were increased. Khrushchev finally relented and ordered a halt to Soviet troop movements when he perceived that Warsaw was in control of the situation and would not allow anti-Soviet demonstrations. Moreover, the veiled threat of the USSR was determined sufficient to keep the Polish leadership within acceptable boundaries.

The crisis over Poland's liberalization ended on 22 October 1956 with the close of the meetings of the Polish Plenum. Khrushchev, now back in Moscow, telephoned his best wishes to Gomulka. The crisis outcome was a compromise. While Gomulka remained in power, the Soviets retained effective control over Poland.

References   Crankshaw 1966; Kaplan 1981; Lewis 1959; Ulam 1971, 1974.

(119) Hungarian Uprising

There were two crisis actors, Hungary and the USSR. The crisis began on 23 October and ended on 14 November 1956.

Background   Threats to USSR hegemony in Eastern Europe began to appear in the summer and fall of 1956. A crisis over Poland occurred in October (see Case #118). At that time, Hungary was ruled by a Soviet-backed government headed by Communist leader Matyas Rakosi. There was growing unrest due to a severe economic situation, lack of democracy and the aggravating presence of Soviet troops.

Crisis   On 23 October approximately 200,000 Hungarian demonstrators, including workers, students and soldiers, massed in Budapest and other major cities. They called for the withdrawal of Soviet troops, the return of Imre Nagy to power, progress towards democratization, and the development of Soviet–Hungarian relations on the basis of absolute equality. This was the trigger for the Soviet crisis, a perceived threat to unity in the Soviet bloc. Moscow responded on 1 November with a decision to remove the new government by military action.

A crisis was triggered for Hungary the same day: the Nagy Government received reports of massive Soviet armor and tank formations crossing the Hungarian frontier. Hungary responded immediately by announcing its withdrawal from the Warsaw Pact. A message was also sent to the UN Secretary-General requesting that the issue of Hungarian neutrality be placed before the General Assembly. On 4 November the General Assembly passed a resolution calling for Soviet withdrawal from Hungary, but this had no effect on the Soviet Union's actions or the termination of the crisis.

The crisis ended in defeat for Hungary on 4 November when the Soviets removed the Nagy Government by force and installed in power a more compliant puppet regime. Nagy was later shot.

The Soviet crisis ended on 14 November with the end of Hungarian armed resistance.

The US issued a protest against Soviet interference in Hungary, but acquiesced in the reassertion of Moscow's hegemony in Budapest.

References   Goodspeed 1967; Irving 1981; Lasky 1957; Meray 1959; United Nations Special Committee on the Problem of Hungary 1957; Vali 1961.

(120) Suez-Sinai Campaign

The six crisis actors were Egypt, France, Israel, the Soviet Union, the United Kingdom and the United States. The crisis began on 29 October and ended on 12 March 1957.

Background   Israel had been subjected to increased terrorist infiltrations from Egypt-controlled Gaza and the Sinai Peninsula and was concerned about the flow of arms to Egypt from Czechoslovakia in 1955–56 (see Case #113). Britain and France perceived a threat from Egypt's declaration to nationalize the Suez Canal (see Case #116). A decision was made by the three countries in October 1956 to invade Sinai.

Crisis Crises for Egypt and the USSR were triggered by an Israeli invasion of Sinai on 29 October 1956. Two days later British and French forces landed in the Canal Zone. Egypt's major response, on 30 October, was military opposition to the invasion; a call for general mobilization, and an appeal to the Soviet Union. The major response by the Soviet Union, on 5 November, took the form of a harsh Note to the three invading powers and the United States, referring to the "dangerous consequences" of the aggressive war in Egypt, warning that London and Paris lay under the threat of Soviet missiles and indicating the USSR's intention to use force if the situation were not rectified immediately. This created intra-war crises for Britain, France and Israel, all of which perceived a threat of grave damage to their urban centers and population at large. It also triggered a crisis for the United States, threatening its international influence.

Britain and France complied at once and on 6 November announced their intention to withdraw all their forces from the Canal Zone. This marked the termination of the crisis for these two countries. The US responded on 6 November by accusing the Soviets of exploiting the situation in Sinai for their own interests and by declaring a semi-alert. They also indicated that the US would not stand idly by if London and Paris were bombed. The Soviet Note was received in Israel just after its Prime Minister had broadcast a victory speech to his nation. Israel conferred with France, but when no commitment of French military support against the Soviet threat was forthcoming, it acquiesced. Israel's major response was a declaration on 8 November that it would evacuate Sinai providing negotiations with the UN over the setting up of an emergency force in Sinai were satisfactory. This terminated the crisis for the superpowers. The process of Israel's withdrawal, with periodic eruptions of high tension, lasted four months: its crisis – and with it the Suez–Sinai Crisis as a whole – ended on 12 March 1957 when that process was completed.

UN activity centered on the dispatch of an emergency force to the Sinai Peninsula. NATO, as the regional security organization of Western Europe, was also involved through a strong counter-threat by the NATO Supreme Commander on 13 November.

References See sources for Case #116 and Ben Gurion 1963, 1969; Brecher 1974; Bromberger 1957; Dayan 1966; Eayrs 1964; Eban 1972; Eisenhower 1965; Golan 1958; Goodspeed 1967; Johnson 1957; Mackintosh 1962; Middle East Research Center, Cairo 1956; Nutting 1958; Smolansky 1974.

(121)
Nicaragua/Honduras The crisis for Honduras and Nicaragua lasted from 26 February until 9 May 1957.

Background In 1906 the Spanish monarch ruled in favor of Honduras in a dispute over territory between that country and Nicaragua. Nicaragua refused to accept this arbitration and continued to claim sovereignty over the disputed area (see Case #23).

Crisis A crisis for Nicaragua occurred on 26 February 1957 when Honduras began to organize the administration of the disputed area, including some sections in which Nicaragua had been exercising *de facto* control. On 18 April, after Nicaragua had strengthened its presence in these areas, Nicaraguan troops crossed the Coco River and occupied Morocon, on the Honduran bank of the river. This triggered a crisis for Honduras, which responded by putting its army on alert and issuing orders to clean up the area around Morocon. The Honduran Ambassador to the OAS requested a special meeting of the Council to deal with Nicaraguan "aggression." A five-man investigating committee was appointed. On 1 May the Morocon area was recaptured by combined Honduran ground and air forces. Nicaragua's President Somoza ordered general mobilization.

By 5 May the OAS Committee had succeeded in getting both parties to sign a cease-fire agreement. However, fighting continued as Honduras accused Nicaragua of breaking the truce. The crisis did not end until 9 May 1957 when a truce-cum-troop withdrawal plan was finally accepted by both actors.

US activity was channelled through the OAS.

References de Lima 1971; Wainhouse 1966.

(122) Jordan Regime   A crisis over a threat to the regime of King Hussein occurred from 4 April to 3 May 1957.

Background   In October 1956 leftist nationalist parties won the parliamentary elections in Jordan, placing Suleiman al-Nabulsi as Prime Minister. Jordan joined a military alliance with Egypt, Syria and Saudi Arabia. The treaty between the UK and Jordan was annulled in March 1957, and diplomatic relations were established with the USSR which included the acceptance of an offer of Soviet aid. The British Commander of Jordan's Arab Legion, Glubb Pasha, was dismissed and was replaced by General Ali Abu Nuwar, who favored closer ties with Nasserist Egypt. His country's increasingly rapid movements towards the Left alarmed King Hussein. The United States became concerned about a possible threat to the independence of Jordan and to the pro-Western regional alliance system, established by the Baghdad Pact (see Case #112).

Crisis   The trigger to Jordan's crisis was an attempt on 4 April to overthrow the King. Hussein accused Syria and Egypt of aiding anti-Hussein elements within Jordan. On 10 April Hussein responded by dismissing the entire leftist Cabinet. Riots and demonstrations followed but were controlled by suppressing all the political parties. Ali Abu Nuwar, the Chief of Staff, was dismissed and the King succeeded in persuading army officers to support him. The United States, as well as Saudi Arabia, came to the King's assistance with military and economic aid. Units of the Sixth Fleet were sent to the eastern Mediterranean, and their departure, on 3 May 1957, indicated that the crisis for the Hashemite Kingdom seemed to have ended.

The Soviet Union covertly supported the anti-Hussein plot.

References   See general list and Shimoni 1972.

(123) Tunisia/France I   Tunisia's crisis started on 31 May and ended on 27 June 1957.

Background   France, reluctant to give up its position as an imperial power, attempted to retain its North African colonies, especially Algeria. Following Tunisia's independence from France in 1956, the French were granted the right to maintain military bases on Tunisian soil. However, Tunisian sympathy for Algeria's struggle for independence created hostile feelings towards the French military presence. Moreover, President Bourguiba saw this as a threat to his regime. France, frustrated by its inability to crush the Algerian FLN, accused Tunisia of providing sanctuary for retreating Algerian guerrillas, thus creating further tension between France and Tunisia which erupted in sporadic clashes.

Crisis   The trigger to Tunisia's crisis was a clash on 31 May 1957 between French troops and Tunisian soldiers and National Guards, in which seven Tunisians were killed. This took place on the Algerian–Tunisian frontier where about 2000 Algerian refugees had crossed into Tunisia. Tunisia responded the next day by issuing a strong protest to France, along with a call for negotiations concerning the evacuation of French forces from Tunisia and an order forbidding the movement of French troops without the Tunisian Government's authority.

Negotiations between France and Tunisia led to an announcement on 27 June that approximately 10,000 of the 25,000 French troops stationed there would be transferred to Algeria during the following six months with the remainder confined to military bases. This marked the end of the crisis. Another one broke out in February 1958 (see Case #129).

References   See general list and Ling 1967.

(124) Syria/Turkey Border   The three crisis actors were Syria, Turkey and the United States. The crisis began on 18 August and ended on 29 October 1957.

Background   Syria and the USSR signed a trade agreement in November 1955 and a cultural agreement in August 1956. The Syrian Defense Minister visited Moscow in July with an extensive military shopping list, which had been accepted. Some armed clashes and border incidents took place between Turkey and Syria in the summer of 1957.

Crisis   On 18 August a number of changes in high-ranking positions were made in Syria. Among them was the appointment of a Communist as Chief of Staff. This triggered a crisis for the United States and Turkey who feared that Syria had now moved irrevocably into the Soviet camp. The major response of Turkey, on 21 August, was a series of frantic meetings with its neighbors – Iraq, Jordan, Lebanon and Saudi Arabia. On 7 September the United States reaffirmed the Eisenhower Doctrine, whereby the US would come to the assistance of any Middle East state threatened by "international communism." This triggered a crisis for Syria. Syria responded on 8 September, after an emergency Cabinet session, by announcing that it did not intend to attack any Arab state. Following Bulganin's severe warning to Turkey, Premier Menderes replied, on 21 September, that Turkey had no aggressive intentions against Syria.

A Soviet naval squadron which had been visiting Syria left on 2 October. On the 7th Khrushchev once again accused Turkey of planning to attack Syria; there were 30,000 Turkish troops taking part in NATO exercises. The United States shipped arms to Jordan and held Sixth Fleet maneuvers off Syria, but its activity in the crisis was mainly political – diplomatic messages and speeches reaffirming its commitments to Turkey. On 29 October 1957 Khrushchev appeared at a reception held at the Turkish Embassy in Moscow, thereby signalling the termination of the crisis for all three actors. This surprise move was apparently due to domestic motives: Marshal Zhukov had been dismissed, ostensibly as a consequence of his blunder in Syria, but in reality as a result of his challenge to Khrushchev's power. Syria requested UN discussion of the crisis, but this was officially shelved a few days after Khrushchev's appearance at the Turkish Embassy.

NATO's Supreme Commander warned the USSR not to attack Turkey.

References   Eisenhower 1965; Mackintosh 1962; Macmillan 1971; Smolansky 1974.

(125) Ifni   Spain's crisis in North Africa began on 23 November 1957 and faded with no precise termination date.

Background   Ifni, a small Spanish enclave in southern Morocco on the Atlantic coast, was ceded to Spain in 1869 and occupied in 1934. In 1956, when Morocco became independent, Spain ceded to the new kingdom the part known as Spanish Morocco on the Mediterranean coast but retained Spanish West Africa and the tiny enclave of Ifni. For several months prior to this crisis, armed bands of the Army for the Liberation of Sahara (AOL) had crossed into Ifni to harass Spanish forces. The AOL were also active in aiding Algeria in its struggle for independence from France. Spain requested Morocco to impose its authority on the armed bands and replace them with units of the regular Moroccan Army. Since no response was received, Spain decided to reinforce its garrison in Ifni.

Crisis   On 23 November 1957 large-scale fighting broke out between Spanish troops stationed in Ifni and Moroccan irregulars, following an attack by the latter. Spain's major response to the threat to its territory occurred one day later – heavy bombing of the invading forces by the Spanish Air Force. Moroccan troops were sent to take up positions around Ifni. Several of the AOL camps were dismantled. Spain then threatened to carry the fighting into Agadir, a Moroccan town north of Ifni. Negotiations among several militant Saharan groups and King Mohammed V of Morocco, in the spring of 1958, enabled the King to solidify his authority and permitted Morocco to exercise a restraining influence over guerrilla operations. The AOL gradually withdrew from Ifni, with no specific termination date for the crisis. In January 1969 a treaty was signed in Fez whereby Spain ceded Ifni to Morocco.

References   Ben Ami 1977; Payne 1967; Welles 1965; Whitaker 1961.

(126) West Irian I   There was one actor only, The Netherlands. The crisis began on 1 December 1957 and faded until it erupted into a new crisis almost four years later.

Background   In order to prevent last-minute obstacles to the Dutch–Indonesian agreement of 1949 concerning the transfer of power from The Netherlands to the Republic of Indonesia (see Case #91), the issue of West Irian (West New Guinea) had been left open. In November 1957 talks were held between Australian and Dutch leaders on practical measures for improving their joint administration of West Irian. Indonesia, which had begun a campaign for its liberation, viewed this as an attempt to influence the peaceful outcome to Indonesia's claim to West New Guinea.

Crisis   A crisis was triggered for The Netherlands on 1 December 1957 when Indonesia's Minister of Information authorized a general strike of all Indonesian workers employed by Dutch enterprises. This was followed by a ban on all Dutch publications and on KLM landings. A large number of Dutch businesses was seized by groups of Indonesian workers and youth. The Dutch response, on 3 December, was a statement by the Prime Minister pledging the safeguarding of Dutch national interests in Indonesia. On 5 December the Indonesian Minister of Justice announced that some 50,000 Dutch nationals would be expelled, and that all Dutch consulates, with the exception of the one in Djakarta, would be closed. On the 6th The Netherlands Government called for an urgent session of the North Atlantic Council which met but did not issue an official statement. This was followed on 9 December by an Indonesian decree placing all Dutch-owned estates and plantations under the control of the Indonesian Government. Another Netherlands attempt to gain international support was made on 23 December with a letter to the UN Secretary-General asking that the situation be brought before the General Assembly and the Security Council. In the meantime two Dutch navy destroyers were dispatched to reinforce troops already in the New Guinea area.

There is no clear termination date. The issue lingered on at below-crisis level until 1961 (see Case #153).

References   See sources for Cases #72 and #79.

(127) Berlin Deadline   The crisis over the Berlin deadline began on 15 December 1957 and lasted until 15 September 1959. Crisis actors were Britain, France, the Soviet Union, the United States, and West Germany.

Background   Since the end of World War II, Berlin had been administered as four zones by the victorious powers, Britain, France, the Soviet Union and the United States. The Berlin Blockade Crisis occurred in 1948 (see Case #87). An abortive East Berlin uprising took place in 1953. (see Case #105). The crises of 1956 in Poland and Hungary (see Cases #118 and #119) caused further apprehension in the Kremlin about the appeal of West Berlin for East Berliners and East Germans generally, offering them a haven from the rigors of socialism as practiced in East Germany. West Germany's role within NATO and its extensive rearmament were of primary concern to the Soviet Union. In the summer and fall of 1957 the USSR demonstrated new missile and rocket capabilities. In response, the United States proposed sending tactical nuclear weapons and intermediate-range ballistic missiles to Europe.

Crisis   On 15 December 1957 NATO Foreign Ministers passed a resolution to station intermediate-range ballistic missiles armed with nuclear warheads in Europe, including Germany, but under American control. This triggered a crisis for the Soviet Union which perceived a grave potential physical threat if West Germany had nuclear weapons within its grasp. Moscow first tried to manage the crisis by calling for a nuclear-free zone in Central Europe, along with conventional force reductions and measures to prevent surprise attacks in Europe. It also announced unilateral troop reductions. The Kremlin then proposed a summit conference and threatened to deploy ballistic missiles in East Germany, Czechoslovakia and Poland, if NATO would not agree to the Soviet proposals. When none of the above had any effect on Western determination to rearm Germany, Khrushchev decided upon harsher measures. In a speech on 10 November 1958 he announced that the Soviet Union intended to turn over control of East Berlin, including all access routes to West Berlin, to East Germany (German Democratic Republic or GDR), thus forcing the West to recognize and to deal with East Germany. There was no reaction from the West.

The crisis trigger for West Germany, France, the UK and the US was a Soviet Note handed to the four Western Ambassadors in Moscow on 27 November 1958 proposing that West Berlin be demilitarized and declared a "Free City" whose status would be guaranteed by the Western Powers, the Soviet Union and, perhaps, the United Nations. If no agreement could be reached on this proposal within six months, the Soviet Government would turn over to the GDR full sovereignty over East Berlin, including access routes to West Berlin. At a press conference the same day, Khrushchev denied that the six months constituted an ultimatum, but stated that Moscow did indeed intend to carry out its proposals; and should the West use force against the Ulbricht regime, the USSR was committed militarily to the defense of East Germany as a Warsaw Pact ally.

After several rounds of negotiations among the three Western Powers, their joint response, on 14 December 1958, was a communiqué which rejected the Soviet Note and its repudiation of the obligations to the Western Powers to maintain the status quo in Berlin and *vis-à-vis* the access routes. After approval by the NATO Council, the formal replies of Britain, France and the United States were presented to Moscow on 31 December. West Germany's reply was presented on 5 January 1959. On 7 January the East German Government announced its support for the Soviet proposal. On 10 January the Soviet Union presented a draft of a peace treaty with Germany to all countries who fought Germany between 1939 and 1945. And on 16 February the four Western Powers, including West Germany, sent replies with NATO approval, counterproposing a Foreign Ministers' Conference to deal with the problem of Germany. Moscow agreed to a Foreign Ministers' Conference for the 2nd of March, but the proposed agenda was unacceptable to the West. The Soviet Union also demanded a summit conference for the end of April.

Further negotiations for lower- and higher-level conferences took place among the crisis actors. The UN Secretary-General attempted conciliation. On 19 March Khrushchev revealed his willingness to accede to a Foreign Ministers' Conference on 11 May if the agenda were limited to Berlin and a German peace treaty, implying the need for a summit meeting to discuss the larger issues of disarmament and European defense. This was made formal in Notes dated 28 March 1959. On 30 March the Soviet Union formally agreed to a May conference, in return for US agreement to a summit conference the following year. Still suspicious of Soviet intentions, the United States began to reinforce its combat and support units in Europe and US transport planes prepared for an airlift. In May, as the deadline of the six months from 27 November approached, US aircraft carriers with nuclear weapons aboard were redeployed in the Mediterranean and Marines were alerted for rapid movement to West Berlin. An interim agreement was signed on 3 August 1959 when President Eisenhower visited Khrushchev in Moscow. The formal agreement was signed on a return visit to Washington on 15 September, the crisis termination date for all the actors. The agreement called for the banning of all atomic weapons and missiles from Berlin and the limiting of Anglo-French-American forces in the city. Negotiations on Germany would be resumed.

References Crankshaw 1966; George and Smoke 1974; Ulam 1974.

(128) Formation of UAR The two crisis actors were Iraq and Jordan. The crisis began on 1 February and ended on 14 February 1958.

Background An announcement by King Hussein of Jordan in April 1957 of the discovery of a Syrian–Egyptian plot against him led to the dismissal of the entire Jordanian Cabinet and a political swing to the Right (see Case #122). As a result Jordan's relations with Syria and Egypt worsened, and a violent anti-Jordan campaign of defamation ensued in those countries.

In Iraq, since Nuri Sa'id's return to power in 1954, close collaboration with the West existed simultaneously with a repressive domestic regime. Discontent among the politically-articulate elements of the population grew – Arab nationalists, Liberals, Communists, traditionalists and army officers. And as the popularity of Egypt's Nasser increased, the Iraqi regime looked for ways to counter Egyptian influence on its citizens.

Crisis A crisis was triggered for Iraq and Jordan when the merger of Egypt and Syria into the United Arab Republic (UAR) was proclaimed on 1 February 1958. This was perceived by the Hashemite rulers, King Hussein of Jordan and King Feisal of Iraq, as an act to incite the revolutionary pan-Arab movement and the Arab peoples to rise against existing Arab governments in order to join the UAR. The merger changed the Middle East subsystem: the Syrian Republic ceased to exist, and the new UAR was controlled by Nasser, giving it a population larger than all other Arab states combined. Hussein suggested a meeting with Feisal, which would include King Ibn Sa'ud of Saudi Arabia, to discuss the possibility of a similar union. On 11 February an Iraqi delegation arrived in Amman. Their response was a joint proclamation on 14 February 1958 establishing the Arab Federation. This marked the end of the crisis for both Iraq and Jordan. Saudi Arabia sent a representative to the talks but did not sign the proclamation. At first Nasser accepted the formation of the Federation, but two weeks later he attacked it as an arrangement between reactionaries who lacked the support of their subjects

There was no violence during this Middle East crisis.

References Cremeans 1963; Hussein 1962; Kerr 1970; Lenczowski 1962; Saint John 1960; Shimoni 1972; Stephens 1971.

(129) Tunisia/France II Tunisia faced a crisis with France on 8 February 1958. This crisis ended on 17 February, but another erupted on 24 May and lasted until 17 June 1958.

Background Following Tunisia's independence from France in 1956, the French were granted the right to maintain military bases on Tunisian soil. France's presence, together with Tunisia's sympathy for Algeria's struggle for independence, caused tense relations which reached crisis proportions in May 1957 (see Case #123). The outcome of that crisis was unsatisfactory to both sides, and the tension between them remained high.

Crisis The crisis was triggered on 8 February 1958 when French medium-range bombers attacked a village along the Tunisian–Algerian border, killing 69 Tunisians. Although this action was not authorized by Paris, the French Government defended it. Tunisia's multiple response came later that day, following an emergency Cabinet meeting: the Tunisian Ambassador to France was recalled; all French troop movements in Tunisia were henceforth forbidden unless approved by Tunisian authorities, and the evacuation of all French forces from Tunisia was once more demanded. Tunisia also decided to appeal to the UN Security Council. The United States, faced with the dilemma of supporting France as a NATO partner and promoting US regional influence in North Africa by supporting Tunisia, was not interested in encouraging Security Council discussions and resolutions, always subject to a Soviet veto.

The debate in the Security Council ended when the US and Britain offered their good offices in an attempt to resolve the dispute. The first Tunisian crisis ended on 17 February 1958 when France and Tunisia accepted this offer and agreed to begin direct negotiations. However, the French National Assembly refused to support the government's decision to resume direct talks with Tunisia and, in May, tension increased as clashes broke out once more.

The trigger to Tunisia's second 1958 crisis with France occurred on 24 May following clashes at Remada. Once again the Tunisians responded by complaining to the UN Security Council, on 29 May. The Security Council debate was suspended on 2 June following an appeal by President de Gaulle to President

Bourguiba to settle the differences between the two countries. The crisis came to an end on 17 June following direct negotiations, when France agreed to withdraw all its forces from Tunisia except those at Bizerta.

References   See sources for Case #123.

(130) Sudan/Egypt Border

There was one crisis actor, Sudan. The crisis occurred between 9 and 25 February 1958.

Background   Egypt claimed two areas lying north of the 22nd Parallel which had been administered by Sudan since 1902.

A plebiscite on the formation of the United Arab Republic (Egypt and Syria) was scheduled for 21 February. Forthcoming Sudanese elections were to be held six days later. On 1 February 1958 the Egyptian Government sent a Note to the Sudanese Government charging Sudan with making arrangements for elections in areas north of the 1899 frontier.

Crisis   On 9 February 1958 a crisis was triggered for Sudan when it received reports that Egyptian Army units were being sent to the disputed area. There were several strands to Sudan's response: a statement on 18 February in reply to an Egyptian Note received that day, declaring Sudan's determination to defend its sovereign territory; the dispatch of Sudanese troops to the area; and a complaint to the UN Secretary-General the next day.

The Security Council met on 21 February but did not pass a resolution. However, Egypt, realizing that its case did not carry much weight, moved to settle the dispute expeditiously. On 25 February the Sudan Government announced that the Egyptian flag had been taken down at Abu Ramada and that Egyptian forces had been removed. The crisis ended on 25 February without violence.

References   See general list and Shimoni 1972.

(131) Indonesia-Aborted Coup

A crisis for Indonesia took place from 21 February until 20 May 1958.

Background   A series of bloodless army coups in regional districts of Indonesia served to undermine Djakarta's power. Nationwide martial law was imposed in March 1957. The dispute between Holland and Indonesia over West Irian had not been resolved in the UN in their November discussions (see Case #126). An aborted attempt on President Sukarno's life took place on 30 November 1956. On 3 December labor groups began seizing Dutch enterprises in Indonesia: within a fortnight virtually all were under military control. That month 46,000 Dutch nationals were repatriated. Tension between the President and regional powers was high. By 10 February 1958 opposition in the outer islands had erupted. An ultimatum demanding central government changes was rejected by the Djakarta Cabinet the following day. On the 15th a revolutionary state was proclaimed. US sympathies lay with the anti-Communist secessionists, and there is evidence that US military aid had arrived in West Sumatra before the ultimatum, along with the presence of US intelligence officers. Sukarno returned to Indonesia on 16 February and called for Cabinet deliberations to consider the issue of the civil war, compounded by an apparent threat of possible US intervention.

Crisis   The first indication of an Indonesian perception of a threat of foreign involvement was Sukarno's rejection of rebel demands on 21 February 1958: in his call for measures against the rebels, he cited his conviction that the rebels were acting as instruments of foreign powers who wished to force Indonesia to join one bloc or another. Indonesia's major response was a military move against the rebels in central Sumatra on 22 February, with airforce bombings and strafings. During the course of the fighting from 7 to 12 March crack government paratroops occupied Pakanbahru, where US personnel were located at oil fields. This step was taken partly out of fear that the US might send in Marines. The Seventh Fleet, situated off-shore, caused great anxiety in Djakarta, where anti-American sentiments were at a fever pitch. By mid-April two key rebel towns had fallen. Following the fall of Padang, the US began an effort to improve relations with Indonesia. US Ambassador Jones's initiatives met with positive Indonesian responses. On 20 May, in the form of an official statement, Dulles formally reiterated the US position of not being involved in what was an internal Indonesian affair. The statement set in motion a chain of events pointing to a *rapprochement* between the two states and marks the end of Indonesia's crisis.

The rebellion lasted until 4 April 1961, after prolonged guerrilla warfare with several thousand casualties.

References   Feith 1962; Feith and Lev 1963; Kahin 1963; Kosut 1967; Lev 1966; Mozingo 1976.

(132) Lebanon/Iraq Upheaval   Riots in Lebanon and a coup in Iraq precipitated an international crisis for four actors, Jordan, Lebanon, the UK and the US, lasting from 8 May to the end of October 1958.

Background   A crisis in Lebanon occurred during a situation of continuing unrest in the Middle East. The US, in an effort to counter a Soviet threat to American interests, tried to unify the pro-Western Arab states through the Eisenhower Doctrine in January 1957, pledging US aid to any Middle East state attacked by "international communism." It was publicly supported by Lebanon alone. President Nasser's strong anti-Western policy was strengthened by the Union of Syria and Egypt in February 1958 which weakened Saudi Arabia and Lebanon, while bringing Iraq and Jordan closer together in an Arab Federation set up at the same time (see Case #128).

In Iraq discontent focused on the Baghdad Pact of 1955 (see Case #112). A conspiratorial group of "Free Officers" hostile to the monarch laid plans for a coup and elected Brigadier Abd-ul-Karim Qassem as Chairman of the Executive Committee.

Crisis   A crisis for Lebanon was triggered on 8 May 1958 by the murder of a reformist editor of a pro-Communist Beirut newspaper, a vocal critic of President Chamoun's Western orientation, including his attempt to amend the Lebanon constitution in order to run for a second term. Opposition elements believed the Government was responsible for the assassination. Full-scale rioting ensued. On the 12th the Lebanese Army took over security in Beirut, Tripoli and other areas. Lebanon's major response was multiple: Foreign Minister Malik accused the UAR of massive interference in Lebanon's internal affairs. Chamoun sent a message to Eisenhower inquiring as to American action if he were to request US assistance; on 21 May Lebanon officially complained to the League of Arab States whose attempt to settle the dispute took the form of a neutral resolution without any call for concrete action; and on 22 May Chamoun brought the matter to the UN Security Council. Its discussions on 6 and 11 June resulted in a Swedish-sponsored resolution to dispatch an Observer Group to Lebanon to determine if there was infiltration from Egypt or Syria across the Lebanon border. The first report, submitted on 3 July, indicated no border infiltration. Lebanon criticized the report as being inconclusive and misleading, adding that the observers were insufficient in number to cover the entire border area and their activity was, therefore, ineffective to the point of exacerbating the crisis and delaying its termination.

On 14 July, after Iraq's decision to send a brigade to Jordan resulted in a coup in Baghdad against the Hashemite monarch, a crisis was triggered for the United States. The same day American Marines were ordered to Lebanon in an attempt to end the violence and stabilize the area.

The coup in Baghdad, followed by the dispatch of US troops to Lebanon, triggered a crisis for Jordan and Britain. King Hussein appealed to the UK for help on the 16th; and, the following day, London decided to dispatch troops to Jordan. By 31 July the situation in Lebanon was sufficiently calm to allow a special presidential election. When Security Council action was effectively blocked by a Soviet veto, an Emergency Session of the General Assembly was called for 8 August. After 15 meetings, a mild resolution was adopted. The Five-Power Summit

Conference called for by Khrushchev did not take place. Events in Lebanon remained unstable; and it was not until 14 October that tension dissipated with the acceptance of the new government in Lebanon by all political factions, marking the end of the crisis for Lebanon and the US.

The crisis faded for the UK and Jordan towards the end of October 1958. At that time Hussein voiced his perception of crisis abatement. The crisis ended with no agreement among the adversaries.

Soviet involvement was political in the main, but naval vessels did move westward through the Baltic during the crisis, interpreted as an attempt to prevent the victory of the pro-US Lebanese forces.

References   Agwani 1965; Dowty 1984; Eisenhower 1965; Goodspeed 1967; Hoopes 1973; Hussein 1962; Kaplan 1981; Macmillan 1971; Miller 1967; Penrose 1978; Qubain 1961; Shwadran 1959.

(133) Taiwan Straits II   A second international crisis in the Taiwan Straits, from 17 July to 23 October 1958, comprised three actors: Taiwan, the United States and the People's Republic of China.

Background   East Asia again became a theater of armed conflict between Communist and anti-Communist forces in 1958, breaking an informal truce that prevailed in the region since 1955 (see Case #110). The unresolved issue of "one China" erupted once more, at the same time as a new crisis in the Middle East, when US forces landed in Lebanon, British forces entered Jordan, and the Iraq monarchy was overthrown (see Case #132). The PRC was critical of Soviet silence on Middle East and East Asian events and decided to test Soviet and American resolve by building up its forces in the coastal areas opposite the offshore islands of Quemoy and Matsu.

Crisis   By 17 July 1958 the massing of mainland China's military forces near the offshore islands had triggered a crisis for Taiwan. Khrushchev arrived in Beijing for conversations with Mao from 31 July to 3 August. On the 23rd of August, when the PRC began bombarding Quemoy and Matsu, a crisis was triggered for the United States. Taiwan responded that day by returning fire. The US responded, two days later, by threatening to move into the area with the reinforced Seventh Fleet, a decision implemented with some restriction on the 27th. This, in turn, triggered a crisis for the PRC.

Between 2 and 4 September the US Administration met to frame a detailed policy position. On the 4th the PRC responded to the crisis by announcing the extension of its territorial waters to 12 miles offshore, thereby blockading Quemoy and Matsu. This threat to US ships supplying the islands was promptly rejected by the US in a statement by Secretary of State Dulles, who strongly implied that the US would intervene if Quemoy were invaded, and that such an intervention might involve the use of nuclear weapons. Chou En-lai suggested that ambassadorial talks between the PRC and the US be resumed.

On 7 September Khrushchev sent a letter to Eisenhower in which he warned that "an attack on the PRC is an attack on the Soviet Union." Nevertheless, one week later it was clear that the Soviets intended to remain aloof from the crisis. Talks between the PRC and the United States were resumed in Warsaw on 14 September, ending the crisis for the latter. On the 30th the crisis ended for the PRC when Secretary Dulles declared that the US favored the evacuation of Nationalist Chinese forces from the offshore islands if the PRC would agree to a cease-fire. Taiwan's crisis termination date was 23 October, when Chiang and Dulles issued a joint communiqué: this constituted a tacit understanding between Taiwan and the PRC, for there was a clear indication that an invasion of the mainland would not be supported by the US. Washington recommended a redefinition of Nationalist China's objectives.

The Soviet position was clarified in a Tass statement on 5 October which excluded military support for Beijing's efforts to liberate Taiwan. However, while publicly disavowing Soviet military intervention in the crisis, Moscow extended covert aid in support of the PRC.

The General Assembly held discussions, but no resolution was passed.

References See sources for Case #110.

(134)
Cambodia/Thailand

A crisis for Thailand and Cambodia took place from 24 July 1958 to 6 February 1959.

Background Relations between these two Southeast Asia countries had been tense for centuries; for long periods Thailand occupied Cambodian territory. Ideological differences, mixed border populations and extreme suspicion on both sides persisted. The temple of Khao Phra Viharrn, a place of worship for the Cambodian Khmer, was accessible only through Thai-held territory, and even then with much difficulty. Prince Sihanouk of Cambodia claimed that the territory surrounding the temple was part of Cambodia, according to a Franco-Siamese treaty of 1907, while the Thai Foreign Minister claimed it belonged to Thailand, according to the geographic principle of "natural watershed."

Crisis A crisis for Thailand was triggered on 24 July 1958 when diplomatic relations were established between Cambodia and the PRC. Thailand, fearing Communist infiltration, declared a state of emergency on the Cambodian border on 8 August. Negotiations followed, with a final Thai offer to allow Cambodian visitors to the site of the temple. Cambodia rejected the offer. When the negotiations broke down, Thailand's response took a military form: on 1 September 10 bridges on the Thai–Cambodian border were blown up in order to prevent infiltration. This triggered a crisis for Cambodia which feared Thai involvement in its internal affairs and perceived Thai ambitions to rule all Buddhist countries in Indochina once more. On 7 September several thousand Thais marched to the Cambodian Embassy in Bangkok. Cambodia's response was a *de facto* suspension of diplomatic relations on 24 November 1958. The following day Thailand closed the border between the two countries, withdrew its Ambassador from Phnom Penh, and suspended air service between the capitals. The United Nations was introduced into the crisis when Cambodians asked Secretary-General Hammarskjöld to appoint a UN Mediator. Baron Johan Beck-Friis, a retired Swiss diplomat, mediated between the adversaries and, on 6 February, a joint communiqué announced the reopening of the frontier and the return of the respective ambassadors to each other's capital.

Subsequent events were an appeal to the International Court of Justice in October 1959 by Cambodia and a rejection of its verdict by Thailand.

References Armstrong 1964; Ayal 1961; Blanchard 1958; Darling 1960; Insor 1963; Leifer 1961–62, 1962; Silcock 1967; Vella 1955.

(135)
Mexico/Guatemala
Fishing Rights

A crisis between these two actors lasted from 29 December 1958 to 1 February 1959.

Background Mexico observed a 9-mile territorial water limit off its shores while Guatemala regarded its own territorial waters as extending to 12 miles. Mexican fishermen had been fishing for shrimp in what Guatemala considered its territorial waters.

Crisis On 29 December 1958 the President of Guatemala articulated his perception of a crisis stemming from an economic threat from Mexico and warned it of impending attack if its fishermen did not leave Guatemalan waters. Guatemala's response, and the trigger for Mexico, occurred on 31 December when Guatemalan planes strafed three Mexican shrimp boats off the Pacific Coast, killing three fishermen and wounding 14 others. Mexico's response was a severe protest to Guatemala on 3 January 1959. The crisis ended for Mexico on 12 January 1959, the day 200 Mexican shrimp boats began fishing in the same general area of the incident, after receiving an official promise from the Guatemalan Government that its planes would not attack them. The termination date for Guatemala was 1 February 1959, the day the President of Mexico proposed a peaceful settlement with Guatemala and requested information about its terms for a settlement.

References See general list, especially *Keesing's* and *New York Times*.

(136) Cuba/Central America I

This crisis involved four actors: the Dominican Republic, Haiti, Nicaragua and Panama; and it lasted from 25 April until some time toward the close of 1959.

Background The Batista dictatorship in Cuba collapsed on 1 January 1959 when Castro established control. The new Cuban Government welcomed exiles from Latin American countries and aided them in organizing revolutionary activities. All four actor-cases derived from invasions in which exiles and the Cuban armed forces tried to establish a revolutionary government in each of the states noted above. In all, a grave economic situation existed and domestic unrest was prevalent.

Crisis The first to experience a crisis was Panama where a boat carrying 80–90 foreign invaders landed on 25 April 1959. Panama responded the following day by requesting assistance from the OAS, which agreed to supply arms, as well as to send an inquiry committee. Castro, recognizing OAS disapproval, denounced the invaders on 28 April and sent two government officials to persuade the invaders to surrender. They did so on 1 May. The following day an OAS international naval patrol off the Panama coast was authorized. The crisis terminated for Panama on 4 May 1959 when the naval and aerial patrols were called off and the OAS investigating committee returned to Washington.

On 1 June a small force of Nicaraguan exiles from Costa Rica landed in two areas of Nicaragua. An emergency session of the OAS was held on 2 June and a fact-finding mission was sent two days later to Costa Rica and Honduras. President Somoza accepted the Costa Rican expression of neutrality and did not view the latter as the source of threat to Nicaragua. On 11 June the rebellion was crushed as a result of a swift military response by Nicaragua. On 13 June Somoza accused Castro of personally preparing the master plan for the overthrow of the Nicaraguan Government. The crisis ended on 14 June 1959 when a victory parade was held in Nicaragua.

The third in this series of mini-crises was an invasion of the Dominican Republic on 14 June 1959, which met with military resistance. The economic situation in the Dominican Republic was particularly grave, with mounting terror and government repression. On 24 June Trujillo declared that the invasion, assisted by the Cuban Navy, had been repelled. A complaint was lodged against Cuba at the OAS on 2 July, but because of an unfavorable OAS attitude towards the Trujillo regime, the Dominican Republic did not request an emergency session. Tension remained high for several more months and dissolved slowly at the end of 1959.

Haiti was invaded on 13 August 1959, during a period of extreme instability and terror. The response occurred on the 16th with a Note to the OAS Foreign Ministers charging Cuba with responsibility. And on 5 September the Haiti Government announced the surrender of the invaders.

The OAS was actively involved throughout this multiple crisis, assisting each state in its confrontation with the Cuban threat. Fact-finding missions were sent. Superpower involvement was relatively limited. The USSR announced its support of Castro. The US sought to maintain stability in the area by organizing a naval mission to patrol the Caribbean waters and authorizing it to shoot in order to bar any Communist-led invasion attempt.

References Atkins and Wilson 1972; Bayo 1967; Bonsal 1971; Castillero and Reyes 1962; Crassweller 1966; Diederich and Burt 1969; Dreier 1962; Duff and McGamant 1976; Galich 1968; Halperin 1972; Rosenthal 1962; Rotberg and Clage 1971; Szulc 1963; Veliz 1968; Ydigoras 1963.

(137) India/China Border I

A border crisis for India and the PRC began on 25 August 1959 and ended on 19 April 1960.

Background The basis of India's claim to the North East Frontier Agency (NEFA) was the Simla Agreement of 1914 between British India and the semi-autonomous Tibet Government, and the accompanying McMahon Line. Although initialed by the representative of the central Chinese Government, this agreement was not formally ratified by China then or later. The border issue was accentuated in 1958 when the

Chinese completed the construction of the Aksai Chin road in the west, linking Tibet to Sinkiang.

Crisis On 25 August 1959 Indian patrols in the region of Longju, NEFA were perceived by the PRC as challenging its version of where that border village lay – on the Indian or Chinese side. The PRC response that day was to attack Indian positions at Longju. Information about this attack triggered India's crisis on 28 August. Prime Minister Nehru informed the *Lok Sabha* that a Chinese detatchment of 200–300 men had crossed into Indian territory at Longju 3 days earlier. At the same time he revealed correspondence between the two governments since 1954 on alleged Chinese border violations and other issues in Sino-Indian relations. On 20 October 1959 another incident at the Kongka Pass in the Ladakh area of northeast Kashmir occurred. In addition, Premier Chou En-lai explicitly refused to recognize the existing McMahon Line and claimed large tracts of NEFA territory.

India's response, on 1 November 1959, was an announcement by Nehru that the Indian Army would assume control of the border posts in Ladakh from police detachments. Nehru described those border incidents as challenges by China to India's territorial integrity. PRC suggestions for negotiations were followed by a series of letters between Nehru and Chou En-lai. A meeting between the two leaders, convened on 19 April 1960, ended this initial crisis. The meetings led to the establishment of a Joint Officials Committee to examine relevant documents and to report points of disagreement and agreement.

Superpower involvement was limited to diplomatic activity. The United States expressed strong sympathy for India's attempts to resolve the issue peacefully. The Soviets adopted a neutral position, which was viewed unfavorably by the PRC.

References Clubb 1972; Galbraith 1969; Hoffmann 1988; Maxwell 1970; Thornton 1973; Vertzberger 1978, 1984; Whiting 1972, 1975.

(138) Shatt-al-Arab I A crisis for Iran and Iraq over their joint waterway lasted from 28 November 1959 to 4 January 1960.

Background An international agreement in 1937 determined, in accord with previous Ottoman Turkey/Iran agreements, that the Shatt was wholly Iraqi territory except for a length of three miles opposite Abadan, where the frontier was to run along the *thalweg* (the line of greatest depth) of the river. According to the treaty, Iraq would collect transit dues from passing ships and would be responsible for the upkeep of the waterway. After the overthrow of the Hashemite Kingdom in Iraq, in July 1958, the Shah of Iran began, once more, to express his dissatisfaction with the 1937 agreement.

Crisis The trigger for Iraq was a press conference held on 28 November 1959 where the Shah described the status quo concerning the Shatt-al-Arab as "intolerable." Prime Minister Qassem's response, the trigger for Iran, was a reiteration of Iraq's claim to the waterway on 2 December. On 23 December Iran placed its military forces on full alert; previously Iran had been moving troops to the Iraqi border. By the last week in December both actors had expressed a willingness to negotiate their differences. The termination date for both of them was 4 January 1960 when an Iranian ship was allowed to pass through the Shatt unmolested.

The US and Great Britain proposed mediation talks, and the USSR broadcast propaganda directed against Iran.

References Chubin and Zabih 1974; Dann 1969.

(139) Rottem The crisis for Egypt and Israel occurred between 15 February and 8 March 1960.

Background Acts of terror in Israel by infiltrators crossing the border from Syria, and a subsequent Israeli retaliation raid in early February 1960 preceded this crisis. At that time Egypt and Syria constituted a single political entity, the United Arab Republic.

Crisis On 15 February 1960 President Nasser received a message from the Soviet Embassy in Cairo claiming that Israel's troops were massing on its northern border, with an intention to attack Syria. In order to offset this danger, Egypt began secret troop maneuvers across the Suez Canal in Sinai towards the Israeli border, on the 19th. On 23 February Israeli intelligence notified Prime Minister (and Minister of Defense) Ben Gurion that the major part of the Egyptian Army had crossed the Canal and was situated near Israel's southern border. The following day Israel responded by moving its forces southward in army maneuvers, termed *Rottem* by the Israel Defense Forces. Egypt's crisis ended on 1 March 1960 when its forces began to return to their bases west of the Canal. One week later, on 8 March, Israel's Prime Minister departed for an official visit to the United States. This act indicated a reduction of tension and the end of Israel's crisis.

The Soviet Union was politically involved in support of the UAR.

References Rabin 1979; Schiff and Haber 1976.

(140) Ghana/Togo Border   A crisis for Ghana lasted from early March to 1 April 1960.

Background In 1956 a majority of voters in a plebiscite held in the Trust Territory of British Togoland voted to accede to Ghana instead of to the adjoining area under French jurisdiction. Counter-demands were made for the reunification of the two Togos and the creation of a Togolese state within its pre-1914 German colonial frontiers. In October 1958 the announcement by France that Togo would receive its independence in April 1960 revived the dispute. In October 1959 and again in January 1960 Prime Minister Nkrumah of Ghana called for the integration of the two countries after Togo's independence. The future Prime Minister of Togo, Sylvanus Olympio, rejected the idea of a merger with Ghana.

Crisis A crisis for Ghana was triggered in early March 1960 when a draft constitution for the Republic of Togo was uncovered by Ghanaian goverment agents. It laid claim to the territory of the formerly-British Togoland which had been incorporated into Ghana as the Volta region. Furthermore, a plot by irregular forces, inhabitants of the Volta region trained in Togo, to infiltrate and attack Ghana in the last week of March was uncovered. After France ignored a formal Ghanaian protest requesting that it take immediate action to prevent the territory under its administration from serving as a base for an armed attack against Ghana, Nkrumah convened an emergency meeting of his Cabinet. Cabinet members were asked to approve the following decisions taken by an *ad hoc* committee on 14 March: to strengthen security forces in the Volta region; to arrest opposition leaders and those involved in the plot, and to issue a public statement. Annual army exercises were carried out in the Volta region between 22 and 28 March and an additional army battalion was sent to the region in April.

After the date of the expected invasion passed without incident the tension began to subside. The termination date was 1 April when a decision was made to send top-level Ghanaian delegates to Togo's independence celebrations. Subsequent to the crisis, a meeting between Nkrumah and Olympio was held on 12 June 1960 where agreement was reached on a union for economic and political cooperation.

References Austin 1963; Dei-Anang 1975; Oliver 1972; Thompson 1969; Touval 1972; Widstrand 1969.

(141) Assassination Attempt/Venezuela President   A crisis between Venezuela and the Dominican Republic occurred from 24 June to mid-September 1960.

Background Diplomatic relations with the Dominican Republic were broken by Venezuela in June 1959. In February 1960 a charge against the Dominican Republic of flagrant violations of human rights was made to the OAS by the Venezuelan Government.

Crisis   An assassination attempt on Venezuelan President Betancourt triggered the crisis on 24 June 1960. Dominican Republic complicity was suspected when it was learned that the plot was organized by Venezuelan exiles living there. In addition, the Dominican Republic radio reported the assassination attempt 15 minutes after it occurred. On the 25th Venezuela accused Trujillo of initiating it. This triggered a crisis for the Dominican Republic which feared a Venezuelan attack on its territory. The Dominican Republic promptly denied all charges. Its major response, on 27 June, was to place the Dominican armed forces on alert and to call for general mobilization. The Congress met in emergency session the following day.

Venezuelan counter-measures consisted of placing its army on alert and issuing another formal accusation against the Dominican Republic. On 30 June a state of emergency was declared in Venezuela after Trujillo accused Venezuela of preparing for war in order to overthrow his regime. Venezuela's major response, on 1 July, was to call for an emergency session of the OAS and to press for a resolution of sanctions against the Dominican Republic. President Betancourt stated that, if no measures were taken against Trujillo by the OAS, Venezuela would act unilaterally. An investigation committee was appointed by the OAS on 8 July. On 20 August a resolution was passed condemning the Dominican Republic's "acts of aggression and intervention." It called upon the members of the OAS to break off diplomatic relations with the Dominican Republic and to impose an arms embargo, along with partial economic sanctions. This terminated the crisis for Venezuela.

During the OAS debate the United States attempted unsuccessfully to have a more conciliatory resolution passed, fearing a replacement of the Trujillo Government by a Communist regime. The US then complied with the resolution by witholding the Dominican Republic's sugar quota and breaking off diplomatic relations.

On 5 September, at an urgent meeting of the Security Council, the USSR called for a resolution to act upon OAS sanctions, but it was not passed. The crisis for the Dominican Republic faded in September.

References   Atkins and Wilson 1972; Crassweller 1966; Wainhouse 1966.

(142) Congo I: Katanga   The two crisis actors were Belgium and the Congo. The crisis lasted from 5 July 1960 to 15 February 1962.

Background   The Belgian Congo was granted independence on 30 June 1960. Lumumba became the first Prime Minister and Defense Minister and Kasavubu the first President. The country had been plagued by tribal fighting and serious disorders. A treaty of friendship and cooperation was signed in Leopoldville between the Congo and Belgium.

Crisis   The trigger for Belgium, on 5 July 1960, was a mutiny among soldiers of the Congolese *Force Publique* which rapidly turned into a general assault against Belgian and other European residents. Belgium responded on the 8th by announcing its intention to send troop reinforcements to the Congo. A crisis was triggered for the Congo two days later when Belgian troops went into action. Lumumba decried Belgium's alleged violation of their friendship treaty. A request to President Eisenhower to restore order was denied. Tshombe announced Katanga's independence on 11 July, triggering a second Congo crisis. That day, too, Lumumba responded by appealing to the UN. Belgium announced on the 13th that it would not withdraw its troops. The Soviet Union issued a statement condemning what it termed Western and NATO aggression against the Congo. On 14 July the UN Security Council passed a resolution to establish a UN military force in the Congo and requested the withdrawal of Belgium's forces. Lumumba demanded the withdrawal of Belgian diplomats as well and declared a state of war between the two countries.

Lumumba's forces began receiving aid from the USSR and the split between him and Kasavubu increased. Internal developments in the Congo prevented a quick solution. On 14 September 1960 Colonel Mobutu announced that the army was taking control. A new central government was finally formed on 9 February 1961. An announcement of Lumumba's death was made on 13 February. On 21 March the UN Secretary-General's Conciliation Committee on the Congo recommended a federal form of government to preserve the country's unity and integrity. On 1 August President Kasavubu invited Adoula, a moderate, to form a new government.

The UN passed a resolution calling upon the Secretary-General to organize and dispatch an emergency military force. Pressure was exerted by the US to bring Tshombe and Adoula together. And on 18 December 1961 a provisional cease-fire was announced which led to the Kitona Agreement of 21 December, with a unilateral declaration by Tshombe that the Katanga secession was over, and a pledge to recognize the indivisible unity of the Congo Republic. The crisis ended for both actors on 15 February 1962 when the Katanga Assembly ratified Tshombe's declaration and agreed to end its secession.

References van Bilsen 1962; Dayal 1976; Gerard-Libois 1966; Goodspeed 1967; Hoskyns 1965; Lefever 1965, 1967; Miller 1967; Okumu 1963; Tondel 1963; Wigny 1961.

(143) Mali Federation A crisis for Mali and Senegal occurred from 20 August to 22 September 1960.

Background The Mali Federation, consisting of Senegal, the Soudan (later, Mali), Upper Volta and Dahomey, was created in June 1959 and became independent one year later. Upper Volta and Dahomey left the Federation immediately thereafter, and the two remaining countries decided to appoint a federal president with wide authority. This appointment was the cause of a bitter dispute between Senegal and the Soudan over control of the presidency. Elections never took place because the Federation ended one week before the scheduled elections. Senegal, whose political system tolerated open opposition, among them Soudan supporters, perceived itself to be in danger of being placed in a permanent minority despite the constitutional balance built into the Federation. It warned the Soudan to stop intervention into Senegal's internal affairs.

Crisis A crisis was triggered for Mali, then known as the Soudan, on 20 August 1960 when Senegal President Senghor declared its independence from the Federation. Mali's President, Modibo Keita, proclaimed a state of emergency and called upon France to intervene. The Mali response, the same day, triggered a crisis for Senegal, whose President, on 20 August, broadcast an impassioned speech accusing Mali of desiring the colonization and enslavement of the Senegalese people. A state of emergency was declared in Senegal, the army took control of the capital, Dakar, and all Mali ministers, as well as soldiers who had been stationed in Senegal, were returned to Bamako, the capital of Mali, the following day. France, which had ignored Keita's call for intervention, recognized Senegal's independence on 11 September 1960.

On 22 September the Soudan ended the Federation and proclaimed its independence, adopting the name of Mali. When the Federation ceased to exist, the crisis ended for both actors.

Discussions were held in the Security Council, but no resolution was passed. The USSR gave political support to Mali.

References Carter 1962; Crowder 1962; Foltz 1965; *Keesing's* 1972; Snyder 1965.

(144) Cuba/Central America II This crisis occurred from 9 November to 7 December 1960, with two actors, Guatemala and Nicaragua.

Background In 1959 Panama, Nicaragua, the Dominican Republic and Haiti were confronted with crises involving Cuban-supported rebels (see Case #136). Each state succeeded, with OAS support, in repelling the invaders. In Guatemala, domestic political and economic instability was present, with high unemployment, demonstrations, strikes and rapid inflation.

Crisis   Nicaragua was invaded once more on 9 November 1960 when exiles crossed into its territory from Costa Rica and captured two small towns. Martial law was imposed and troops were rushed to the area. And on 13 November dissident units of the Guatemalan Army seized a port 70 miles northeast of Guatemala City. President Ydigoras responded on 14 November by stating that the government had proof of Cuban involvement and appealed to the US to dispatch naval and air patrols. The revolt in Guatemala collapsed on the 16th.

The Nicaraguan response was an appeal to the United States on 17 November. That day President Eisenhower announced that surface and air units of the United States Navy would act to prevent invasions by Communist-directed elements. The crisis for both Nicaragua and Guatemala ended when the US President, having received assurances from both governments that coastal defense was no longer required, ordered the withdrawal of the Caribbean patrol on 7 December 1960. During the crisis Guatemala and Nicaragua submitted a joint complaint about Cuban interference to the OAS. This was denied by Cuba, which protested the US naval presence in the area, describing it as a violation of the principle of non-intervention and an act of aggression. Soviet and Chinese newspapers and broadcasts took a similar stand.

References   See sources for Case #136.

(145) Ethiopia/Somalia   A crisis for Ethiopia began on 26 December 1960 and subsequently faded after about a year, with no fixed termination date.

Background   A 1954 agreement between Britain and Ethiopia confirmed the 1897 annexation of the Huad region by Ethiopia but also granted grazing rights to Somali tribes in that area. On 5 June 1960 Ethiopia announced that the 1954 agreement would become invalid upon Somalia's independence on 3 July. The Somalia Government published a manifesto on 30 August calling for a Greater Somalia which would include British- and Italian-held territories of Somalia, as well as parts of Ethiopia and Kenya which were inhabited by Somalis; it also charged that the agreement of 1897 with Ethiopia violated the treaties of protection Britain had concluded with northern Somali tribes in 1885. The All-African People's Solidarity Organization Conference of January 1960 and the Afro-Asian People's Solidarity Organization Conference of April 1960 adopted resolutions supporting Somalia's struggle for independence and unification. By the end of 1960 several serious clashes had occurred. Although friction between grazing tribes and Ethiopian authorities contributed to the crisis, the conflict concerned Somalia's right to self-determination and its ambition for territorial expansion. This was a challenge to Ethiopia's sovereign integrity as it felt that to grant privileges to one tribe in its multinational state would open the door for other requests. The prospect of an independent Somalia Republic alarmed Ethiopia. Somalia, on the other hand, was threatened by disintegration and felt that it was not bound to accept colonial boundaries.

Crisis   On 26 December 1960 7000 Somali tribesmen surrounded an Ethiopian police garrison and launched a heavy attack. The Ethiopian response to a perceived territorial threat occurred on the 29th when military units, including the air force, invaded Somalia forcing the tribesmen to retreat. A strong protest was sent from Ethiopia to Somalia. The crisis continued with accusations, violence and clashes for several months thereafter. During January 1961 Ethiopia bombed Somalia; there were clashes between their forces in Huad; Somalia postponed an oil shipment to Ethiopia, and the leader of the nationalist movement in Somalia warned of an imminent war. On 5 February there was a Somali invasion of Ethiopia with propaganda distributed in the disputed province. The All-African People's Conference of 1961 decided in favor of Ethiopia. In May, at the Monrovia Conference, an appeal was made to both sides to renew the efforts for a settlement. On 25 August talks were held between President Osmon of Somalia and Haile Selassie at the Non-Aligned Conference in Belgrade. On 31 August clashes were reported once again between Somali tribesmen and Ethiopians. And on 27 September there was an official complaint from Somalia that the dispute was not yet solved.

Clashes between the two states occurred again in 1964 (see Case #175) and continued until 1967 when an agreement was finally reached. The superpowers maintained a neutral position in the 1960 crisis.

References   Austin 1963; Castango 1960; Dei-Anang 1975; Farer 1976; Hoskyns 1969; Lewis 1963; Oliver 1972; Spencer 1977; Touval 1963, 1971, 1972; Widstrand 1969.

(146) Pathet Lao Offensive I

The first Pathet Lao crisis for Thailand and the United States began on 9 March and ended on 16 May 1961.

Background   From December 1960 supplies and equipment from the Soviet Union had been airlifted to the Pathet Lao. This aid included heavy weapons and combat specialists.

Crisis   A crisis was triggered for the United States on 9 March 1961 when Pathet Lao troops, with Vietminh support, launched a major offensive breaking through the Laotian government defenses in central Laos, severing the key road junction between Vientiane and Luang Prabang. The Laotian troops retreated and, within days, the two cities were threatened by Communist and neutralist troops. President Kennedy felt forced to consider armed intervention in order to stabilize the situation in Laos. It had become evident that, if Laos were to be abandoned, the Communists would hold the north–south road along the Mekong lowlands from which stronger pressure would be mounted against South Vietnam, Cambodia and Thailand. US troops were ordered to be ready to move into Laos; a helicopter air base was established in Thailand; supplies and ammunition were stocked at forward bases along the Mekong River; and the task force on Okinawa, specially trained for combat in Southeast Asia, was put on alert. In addition, the Seventh Fleet was sent to the Gulf of Siam. On 23 March Kennedy gave a televised news conference in which he warned that USSR and North Vietnam support of the Pathet Lao increased the probability of war, and that the shape of the necessary response would be carefully considered by the United States and its SEATO allies. At the same time, Kennedy supported UK proposals for a joint US–USSR appeal for a cease-fire followed by an international conference on Laos.

The situation in Laos deteriorated during April. On the 10th the Pathet Lao forces' advance toward the Mekong River threatened to divide Laos, triggering a crisis for Thailand. Thai troops were sent to the areas bordering Laos. On the 20th, when Communist forces advanced to within 10 miles of Takhek, the Thai Prime Minister declared that the Thai Army was ready to go into action immediately if Takhek were attacked. On 28 April some token US forces were ordered into Laos, and the (military) advisors serving in Laos were ordered into uniform and sent into battle with the Laotians. Impressed by the singularity of the US position, the USSR agreed to co-sponsor the UK proposal on 24 April. On 3 May a cease-fire went into effect, and on 16 May the Geneva Conference on Laos opened, terminating the crisis for both the US and Thailand.

The SEATO Council met on 27 March at the request of the US. A communiqué was issued stating that, if peaceful efforts failed SEATO would take appropriate action. Another session was held on 29 April and a resolution was passed supporting US–USSR proposals for a cease-fire.

References   Adams and McCoy 1970; Brandon 1970; Dommen 1971; *Facts on File* 1973–74; Fall 1969; Gravel 1971; Herring 1979; Hilsman 1967; Johnson 1971; Kahin and Lewis 1967; Lewy 1978; Nuechterlein 1965; Schlesinger 1965; Sorensen 1965; Toye 1968.

(147) Bay of Pigs

Cuba and the United States were the adversaries in a crisis from 15 to 24 April 1961.

Background   A series of incursions into Caribbean and Central American states, in which Cuba was perceived to be involved, took place in 1959–60 (see Cases #136 and #144). In addition, the United States had become increasingly concerned about the strong ties which had developed between Cuba and the USSR. Relations between the US and Cuba were strained; and the latter appealed to the Security Council at the end of 1960 charging the US with plans to mount an invasion of Cuba using Cuban exiles trained in Guatemala. Diplomatic relations between the two countries were broken on 3 January 1961. In early April 1961 President Kennedy authorized an invasion of Cuba by the exiles, reasoning that, in the event of a failure, the remaining force would be able to establish guerrilla bases in the Cuban mountains. Support, or non-objection to the invasion plans, was given to Kennedy by the CIA, the Defense Department and the Joint Chiefs of Staff of the United States.

Crisis On 15 April 1961 Cuban military and civilian centers were bombed by exiles flying US-provided B-26 aircraft, triggering a crisis for Cuba. The US crisis was triggered the same day when Cuba, at a meeting of the UN General Assembly, charged the United States with complicity in planning and financing the air attack. On 17 April Cuba responded with a declaration of a state of "national alert," an order to Cubans to fight, and a second appeal to the General Assembly charging the US with aggression. While the United States Ambassador to the UN denied the charge, the US proceeded with support for the invasion on 18 April by an anti-Castro force made up of Cuban exiles.

A Note from the USSR to the US on 18 April warned of a possible chain reaction to all parts of the globe arising from the invasion and reasserted Soviet support to Cuba to repel the attack. The US responded that day through President Kennedy's answer to the Soviets: Kennedy emphasized that the US "intends no military intervention" in Cuba, but would act to protect the Hemisphere in case of military intervention by an outside force. The crisis ended for Cuba on 19 April when it defeated the invading force whose remnants were unable to escape to the mountains. It ended for the United States on the 24th when, reversing earlier disclaimers of US involvement, the White House issued a statement by President Kennedy bearing sole responsibility for the events leading to the Bay of Pigs fiasco.

A weak resolution was passed by the General Assembly calling upon all members to take action to remove the tension.

US/Cuba relations continued to deteriorate, the latter being heavily supplied with weapons by the Soviet Union. In 1962 the much graver crisis over missiles in Cuba occurred (see Case #162).

References See sources for Case #162 and Bonsal 1971; Government of Cuba 1964; Dominguez 1978; *Facts on File* 1964; Fontaine 1975; Johnson *et al.* 1964; Meyer and Szulc 1962; Mezerik 1962.

(148) Pushtunistan III This ongoing dispute between Afghanistan and Pakistan escalated to crisis proportions again during the period from 19 May 1961 to 29 January 1962 (see Cases #93 and #114).

Background There was a decrease in tension between the two states during the late fifties, but border clashes and tribal incidents continued through the period 1956–61.

Crisis The first crisis in this phase of the conflict over Pushtunistan occurred on 19 May 1961 when Pakistan became aware of the violent infiltration of 1000 Afghan troops into its territory. The response was bombing by the Pakistan Air Force, on 21 May, of areas along the border which it claimed were occupied by Afghan troops. This was categorically denied by an Afghanistan Embassy spokesman in Karachi. The crisis dissolved during June.

On 23 August 1961, in a Note to the Afghanistan Government, the Pakistan Foreign Ministry demanded the closure of Afghan consulates and trade agencies which it claimed were being used for anti-Pakistani and other subversive activities. This triggered a crisis for Afghanistan. Kabul responded on 30 August that it would consider diplomatic relations as broken unless Pakistan withdrew its demands. This triggered a second crisis for Pakistan because it feared that harsh measures on its part would throw Afghanistan into the camp of the Soviet Union. Pakistan responded on 2 September by issuing a White Paper claiming that Afghanistan's policy of "expansionism" was the main cause of the hostilities. Diplomatic relations were severed on the 6th. United States' efforts in October to settle the dispute did not bear fruit immediately. However, on 29 January 1962 President Kennedy's special envoy, L. T. Merchant, succeeded in making possible the delivery of goods from Pakistan to Afghanistan, and the frontier was temporarily reopened, ending the crisis for both actors. During the course of the crisis the Soviet Union supplied economic aid and weapons to Afghanistan. Diplomatic relations were not reestablished until 24 January 1964.

References   Dupree 1980; Fletcher 1966; Hussain 1966; Spain 1954.

(149) Kuwait Independence

A crisis for Kuwait and Britain lasted from 25 June to 13 July 1961.

Background   Kuwait was granted independence by Britain on 19 June 1961, accompanied by a defense treaty between the two countries.

Crisis   The trigger for Kuwait occurred on 25 June 1961, when Iraq's Prime Minister claimed that Kuwait was an integral part of Iraq. Kuwait responded on the 30th by a formal request to Britain for assistance under the provisions of their defense treaty. This triggered a crisis for the UK. On 1 July Britain responded by rapidly building up its troops and airborne forces in Kuwait: within one week the British forces numbered 6000. Kuwait appealed to the UN Security Council which held discussions, but a proposed resolution was vetoed by the USSR. An Egyptian appeal for the withdrawal of British troops did not secure a Security Council majority. In July 1961 the League of Arab States accepted Kuwait as a member, in the face of Iraqi protests, and established a Pan-Arab force, consisting mostly of Jordanians and Saudi Arabians, to defend Kuwait.

The crisis ended on 13 July when the Iraqi Military Attaché in the UK denied Iraqi intentions to attack Kuwait and an alleged concentration of Iraqi troops on the border. With the recognition of the Arab world, the Amir of Kuwait requested British troops to leave; the evacuation was completed by October 1961. Iraq, which had boycotted the Arab League after its admission of Kuwait, withdrew its claim in the autumn of 1963. After the downfall of General Qassem, Iraq's ruler, in February 1963, it recognized Kuwait's independence.

References   Bartlet 1977; Bogdanor and Skidelsky 1970; Fitzimmons 1964; Macmillan 1973; Northedge 1974.

(150) Bizerta

This crisis involved two actors, France and Tunisia. It began on 17 July and ended on 29 September 1961.

Background   France continued to maintain a number of military bases in its former colony of Tunisia after Tunisia's independence in 1956. This caused tense relations which reached crisis proportions in 1957 and 1958 (see Cases #123 and #129). As a result, France reduced its military presence to one large base at Bizerta.

Crisis   In spite of a vague promise by President de Gaulle to President Bourguiba that France would evacuate the base, the French began construction in July 1961 of an additional runway designed to increase its military capability. On 17 July Bourguiba triggered a crisis for France when he issued an ultimatum giving the French approximately 48 hours to open negotiations on a timetable for withdrawal from Bizerta, or face a Tunisian-imposed blockade. France's response was a decision on the 18th to take military action; and on the 19th, when the Tunisians tried to block a French attempt to resupply the base, French paratroops and other forces launched a military assault against Tunisian positions, triggering a crisis for Tunisia. Tunisia's response was multiple: on 20 July it appealed to the UN Security Council and also attempted to meet French violence with violence of its own. France was condemned in resolutions by the Security Council and the General Assembly. An Arab League resolution was also passed authorizing action by member states in the form of volunteer military forces for Tunisia. However, none of these contributed to the abatement of the Bizerta Crisis. The crisis ended on 29 September with an agreement between France and Tunisia that restored the status quo prior to Bourguiba's ultimatum.

References See sources for Case #123.

(151) Berlin Wall

This crisis was of direct concern to six actors: France, the FRG (West Germany), the GDR (East Germany), the UK, the US and the USSR. It began on 29 July and ended on 17 October 1961.

Background After World War II, the US, France and the UK were parties to an uneasy agreement with the Soviet Union regarding the administration of Germany and its capital, Berlin. Crises between the superpowers had occurred in 1948–9 and 1957–9 (see Cases #87 and #127). In October 1960 Khrushchev, after cancelling a summit meeting with Eisenhower, set April 1961 as the deadline for the USSR signing a separate peace treaty with East Germany. Kennedy's meeting with Khrushchev in Vienna in the spring of 1961 had no positive results. On returning to Moscow, Khrushchev repeated his ultimatum while Kennedy announced to the American people that the US would fight to defend its rights in Berlin and the freedom of West Berliners. He also called up military reserve units.

Crisis A crisis for East Germany and the Soviet Union can be dated to 29 July 1961 with the acute perception that the flow of East German refugees to the West had reached alarming proportions. On 13 August the Soviets responded with an announcement by Khrushchev that the USSR might have to call up reserves if the US continued to send reinforcements to Berlin. The trigger to a crisis for the US, UK, West Germany and France occurred at dawn on 13 August with East Germany's crisis response, the erection of a wall between East and West Berlin in order to close the border between East and West Germany. This terminated East Germany's crisis because it ended the flow of refugees to the West. West Germany responded on 16 August by a call from West Berlin's Mayor Brandt to the West for effective action. An emergency session of the West German parliament was held the next day. On the 17th and 18th the US, UK and France responded by strengthening the Berlin Garrison – 15,000 US troops were rushed to the city. On 22 August GDR forces announced the establishment of a No-Man's Land of 100 meters on each side of the Wall. West Berliners were warned to keep clear of that zone. Western forces began to patrol the area to the west, while East German forces kept watch over their side.

The crisis ended for the US, UK, France, West Germany and the USSR with the Soviet 22nd Party Congress when Khrushchev pronounced the Four Powers' Statute as invalid, signalling Soviet intention to keep the city divided. After that, no further dramatic developments occurred with respect to Berlin.

Both NATO and the Warsaw Treaty Organization were active in the crisis, each backing its own protagonists in the dispute.

The issue of Berlin remains unsolved: the Western allies failed to demolish the Wall, but they were determined to hold West Berlin and reaffirm its inviolability. This was communicated to the people of West Berlin in a speech by President Kennedy during his August 1963 visit.

References Anderson 1962; Barker 1963; Crankshaw 1966; Dulles 1972; Eisenhower 1963, 1965; Filene 1968; George and Smoke 1974; Kulski 1966; La Feber 1976; McClelland 1968; Macmillan 1972; Merritt 1968; Schick 1971; Schlesinger 1965; Slusser 1973; Smith 1963; Sorensen 1965; Tanter 1974; Thomas 1962; Ulam 1974; Windsor 1963; Young 1968.

(152) Vietcong Attack

A crisis for South Vietnam and the United States in Indochina took place from 18 September to 15 November 1961.

Background For several years prior to this crisis Vietcong groups, backed by the North Vietnam regime, had been brought together for attacks on civilian and military centers in South Vietnam. By September 1961 these attacks had trebled in number. Vietcong guerrilla forces were situated in the northern marshlands of South Vietnam. When approached by South Vietnam government forces, they disappeared across the border into North Vietnam making their capture extremely difficult.

Crisis A crisis for South Vietnam and the United States was triggered on 18 September 1961 when Phuoc Vinh, the provincial capital of Phuoc Thanh, only 55 miles from Saigon, was captured and held for a day by the Vietcong. Before government troops arrived, the provincial governor was publicly beheaded, and arms and ammunition were captured and removed. This attack had a shattering effect on the South Vietnam regime, despite the quick success in forcing the Vietcong to retreat. The United States, whose influence in Southeast Asia had been threatened by North Vietnam and, therefore, Soviet gains, was reluctant to increase its commitment to the area.

In view of the dangerously deteriorating situation South Vietnam President Diem responded on 29 September by requesting a bilateral defense treaty with the United States. On 11 October President Kennedy and his advisors decided to send National Security Advisor Walt Rostow and General Maxwell Taylor to Vietnam to assess the political and military feasibility of US intervention. A state of emergency was proclaimed in South Vietnam on 19 October. In a report to the President on 3 November, Rostow and Taylor recommended a significant expansion of US aid to South Vietnam, as well as the dispatch of an 8000-man logistical task force. On 11 November a joint recommendation from the Secretaries of State and Defense (Rusk and McNamara) to the President stated that a decision to commit ground forces in South Vietnam could be deferred. The US major response, on 15 November, was a National Security Council decision for a limited commitment of aid and advisors to South Vietnam – several hundred specialists in guerrilla warfare, logistics, communication and engineering, to train South Vietnam forces. Aircraft and other special equipment would be sent as well. That decision also ended the crisis for the US and South Vietnam.

The Rostow–Taylor trip to South Vietnam was assailed by Moscow and North Vietnam as a prelude to US military intervention in Southeast Asia. On the regional level, SEATO's military advisors met from 3-6 October and issued a communiqué on the 6th to the effect that practical measures were being taken to increase the effectiveness of SEATO defenses.

References See sources for Case #146.

(153) West Irian II There were two actors in this crisis, Indonesia and The Netherlands. It began on 26 September 1961 and ended on 15 August 1962.

Background The dispute over the territory of West Irian (West New Guinea) began when Indonesia attained its independence in 1949 and reached crisis proportions in 1957 (see Case #126). Following an Indonesian decision to liberate West Irian, Sukarno appealed to the USSR for political and military support, which was granted. A new Dutch plan was designed stressing the idea of self-determination for the Papuans.

Crisis The crisis for Indonesia began on 26 September 1961 when the Dutch Foreign Minister submitted a proposal to the UN for the decolonization of West Irian and the transfer of sovereignty to its people, with the UN assuming its administration temporarily. Indonesia, which viewed the proposal as a means of consolidating Dutch administration and thus keeping Indonesia out of West Irian indefinitely, responded on 19 December 1961 by inaugurating a triple command for the liberation of New Guinea, decreeing general mobilization. In order to focus world attention, a small-scale infiltration into West Irian was begun. This triggered a crisis for The Netherlands.

Active participation by the UN Secretary-General and an announcement by President Kennedy of the US intention to seek a solution actively persuaded The

Netherlands to respond on 3 January by announcing its decision, of the previous day, to drop the demand that Indonesia accept the principle of self-determination for the Papuans as a condition for negotiations. Once the US had abandoned its neutral position for a policy of active mediation, which also meant that Holland would lose Australian support, a solution became possible. According to an agreement signed by Holland and Indonesia on 15 August 1962, the termination date of the crisis, the UN would supervise the evacuation of Dutch military forces and take over administration of the area until it could be handed over to Indonesia not later than 1 May 1963.

The USSR supplied arms to Indonesia.

References Agung 1973; Crouch 1978; *Facts on File* 1967; Jones 1971.

(154) Breakup of UAR   The duration of Egypt's crisis was from 28 September to 5 October 1961.

Background A number of high-ranking right-wing Syrian officers in the army of the United Arab Republic formed an alliance with civilian politicians connected with the Syrian business class. Secret talks were held between these Syrians and Nasser's representative, Vice-President Field Marshal Amer, where strong dissatisfaction with the UAR was expressed.

Crisis A coup in Syria, which occurred on the night of 27–28 September 1961, triggered a crisis for Egypt on the 28th. The restoration of Syria's independence was demanded, and this was viewed by Nasser as a threat directed at Egypt's influence in the Middle East subsystem. Nasser immediately ordered the UAR armed forces to suppress the rebellion. Two thousand paratroops supported the First Army, followed by the entire UAR navy and more troop reinforcements in ships. The following day, the ports of Aleppo and Latakia were taken by the rebels. When Nasser learned this, he ordered the ships to turn back arguing that the reconquest of Syria was almost impossible unless a substantial part of the Syrian Army remained loyal to the UAR. Egypt's primary crisis management technique was negotiations with Syrian leaders, but Cairo was unable to persuade them to continue Syria's merger with Egypt. The crisis terminated on 5 October when the end of the Union was admitted to have taken place. Nasser announced that he would not oppose the application of the new Syrian regime for readmission into the United Nations and the Arab League.

After the termination of the crisis, on 9 and 10 October, respectively, the USSR and US recognized the new regime in Syria.

References See sources for Case #128.

(155) Soviet Note to Finland II   A second crisis for Finland *vis-à-vis* the USSR occurred between 30 October and 24 November 1961; the earlier one was in 1948 (see Case #85).

Background Cold war tensions resulting from the erection of the Berlin Wall in August 1961 (see Case #151) and the breakdown of the disarmament talks in September contributed to Soviet concern about the January 1962 presidential and parliamentary elections in Finland. Five coalition parties had united to back the candidacy of Olair Honka for President and presented a serious challenge to incumbent President Kekkonen. The Soviets perceived the possibility of Kekkonen's defeat as a political threat which would affect Finland's neutrality and its general pro-Soviet foreign policy. Finland, always sensitive to the wishes of its giant neighbor, perceived a military threat from the Soviet Union if it deviated too much from previous policy.

Crisis On 30 October 1961 a Note was sent by the Soviet Union to Finland calling for consultations between the two governments "to ensure the defense of both countries from the threat of a military attack by Western Germany and allied states." The Finnish response, on 7 November, was a decision to send Foreign

Minister Karzalaimen for talks with Soviet Foreign Minister Gromyko. Further negotiations between Kekkonen and Khrushchev resulted in the termination of the crisis on 24 November 1961 postponing military consultations between the two countries. In 1962 Kekkonen was re-elected to the presidency.

References See general list and Vloyantes 1975.

(156) Goa II   A second crisis for Portugal over Goa lasted from 11 to 19 December 1961.

Background There had been relative inactivity since Portugal's first crisis with India over Goa in 1955 (see Case #115). In April 1961 a bill was passed by the Indian Parliament enabling the merger of Dadra and Nagar Haveli with the Indian Union. During the debate Nehru stated that he didn't rule out sending the Indian Army into Goa. He repeated this warning in October. Meanwhile, Indian public opinion began demanding that more active steps be taken toward the integration of Goa.

Tension between India and Portugal escalated with the reported build-up of Portuguese military strength in Goa and, on 17 and 24 November, Indian ships were shot at from the Portuguese island of Anjadev. India announced, on 5 December, that precautionary troop movements were taking place. On 8 December Portugal charged that the Indian build-up threatened peace in the area and suggested that international observers be sent. Portugal appealed to the Security Council on 9 December.

Crisis Portugal's crisis was triggered by a Nehru statement on 11 December that Indian patience was at an end and that he hoped the Portuguese would withdraw from Goa. Portugal responded the same day by informing the UN Security Council that Indian forces were massing along the border and were ready to invade Goa. On 12 December Portugal announced that it had decided to evacuate European women and children from the disputed area in view of an imminent Indian attack: information received by Portugal anticipated an attack on 15 December. On that day UN Secretary-General U Thant sent a message to the Prime Ministers of India and Portugal requesting them not to allow the situation to deteriorate and proposing negotiations. Salazar acceded to the Secretary-General's request, but Nehru replied with a demand that Portugal leave Goa.

On 18 December 1961 Indian troops entered Goa. Portugal called for an urgent meeting of the Security Council. A resolution was introduced calling for a cease-fire, Indian withdrawal and a peaceful settlement but it was defeated by a Soviet veto. The United States strongly criticized India's action. President Kennedy sent a message to Nehru urging that no force be used. US Ambassadors in Delhi and Lisbon had succeeded in postponing the invasion date a number of times.

The crisis for Portugal ended on 19 December 1961 with the entry of Indian troops and the signing of a surrender agreement ending four centuries of Portuguese rule over Goa.

References See sources for Case #115.

(157) Mauritania/Mali   A crisis for Mauritania lasted from 29 March 1962 to 18 February 1963.

Background The border between Mauritania and Mali had been the subject of dispute since 1944. Nomadic tribes from both states crossed back and forth over the border. Prior to the independence of both countries, in 1960, conferences on future boundaries were held, but immediately after independence relations between the two states deteriorated. Guerrillas, thought to be organized by Morocco and based in Mali, carried out actions in Mauritania: there were several attempted assassinations of Mauritanian officials as well. In early 1962 Mauritania changed its position on the border question, successfully overcoming internal Moroccan-supported opposition.

Crisis On 29 March 1962 six people were accused of murdering French officers at Nama in eastern Mauritania. Mali was accused of harboring a Moroccan terrorist group which aimed at ridding Mauritania of the French in order to facilitate Moroccan territorial claims in the area. The response, on 6 April, was a presidential declaration that Mauritania would not allow any attempt against the integrity of the country. On 7 June 1962 the Mauritanian UN Representative charged that Moroccan terrorists, trained in bases in Mali, had raided border outposts in his country.

A political settlement was reached by the Presidents of the two countries at Kayes, Mali, on 18 February 1963. The nationals of both states were guaranteed nomadic rights and the use of wells in disputed areas. Compromise agreements were reached, although Mali gained more territory than Mauritania.

References Gerteiny 1967; Moore 1965; Touval 1963, 1972; Widstrand 1969; Zartman 1963, 1965, 1966.

(158) Taiwan Straits III   The PRC was the sole crisis actor. This crisis lasted from 22 April to 27 June 1962.

Background Since the end of the Chinese Civil War in 1949 Nationalist China (Taiwan) and Communist China (PRC) both claimed sovereignty over the whole of China. Armed forces of the PRC were situated in Fukien Province directly opposite those of Taiwan which were deployed on the islands of Quemoy and Matsu. During the three years before this crisis there had been agricultural disasters and a significant increase of consumer goods shortages on the Chinese mainland. There was a mass exodus of Chinese across the borders; from Sinkiang into Soviet Central Asia and from Kwangtung into Hong Kong. In addition, during the period preceding the crisis there was tension along China's border with India. Beginning in January 1962, a series of bellicose statements by high Nationalist officials alerted decision-makers in the PRC that Chiang Kai-shek might be preparing an invasion of the mainland.

Crisis The trigger for the PRC was an Easter message by Chiang Kai-shek to his people, on 22 April 1962, which contained threats to invade the mainland. This was followed by a conscription of additional manpower to Taiwan's army. On 1 May a special new tax was imposed in order to support the "return to the mainland." Further, from 22 May more Nationalist statements were issued indicating plans for an invasion. On 29 May the PRC's Foreign Minister, Ch'en Yi, divulged the existence of specially-trained agents who, together with anti-Communist elements on the mainland, would join forces if a decision were made by Chiang Kai-shek to drop paratroops into Communist China. Ch'en Yi intimated that there would be US support for this venture.

Alarmed by the possibility of American intervention, the response of the PRC was a considerable troop build-up in Fukien Province beginning on 10 June. On 23 June a meeting was held between US and PRC Ambassadors in Warsaw where American Ambassador John Cabot denied that the US would actively support a Taiwan invasion. On 27 June President Kennedy, at a news conference, reiterated American policy: the US would defend Taiwan against a PRC threat, but its policy was peaceful and defensive only. This was an indirect assurance that the US would not support a Taiwanese attempt to invade the mainland. That statement marked a tacit conclusion to the third Taiwan crisis.

References Brugger 1977; Cheng 1972; Hilsman 1967; Hinton 1966; Kennedy 1964; Leng and Chiu 1972; Mendel 1970; Simmonds 1970; Yahuda 1978.

(159) Pathet Lao Offensive II   The duration of this crisis for Thailand and the United States was from 6 May to 12 June 1962. A first Pathet Lao offensive took place one year earlier (see Case #146).

Background Following the cease-fire of May 1961, talks in Geneva began on the problem of Laos. Negotiations proceeded slowly with such issues as the seating of the Pathet Lao delegation as a full representative, and the frequent breaking of the cease-fire which threatened the continuation of the talks in general. The Kennedy–Khrushchev meeting in Vienna on 3-4 June 1961 resulted in a joint statement calling for a neutralized Laos and an effective cease-fire. Difficulties among the three Laotian factions – pro-Communist, pro-West, non-aligned – prevented the forming of a coalition government. Negotiations reached a deadlock in early 1962. This was followed by an increased Pathet Lao military presence in the Nam Tha area bordering Thailand. In February Pathet Lao forces, with Vietminh support, began a siege of the capital of Nam Tha. On 13 February Thai troops were deployed to strategic areas near the Laotian border. At a news conference the following day, President Kennedy expressed concern about the situation. By the end of April there was no progress in the negotiations, and new fighting had broken out.

Crisis A crisis for Thailand and the United States was triggered on 6 May 1962 when a heavy Pathet Lao attack was launched against Nam Tha. Laos government forces retreated without resistance across the Mekong River into Thai territory, abandoning northwest Laos to the Communists and thereby opening the way for the Pathet Lao to move to the northern border of Thailand. On 11 May Thailand's Prime Minister Sarit ordered several units of the Thai armed forces to reinforce defenses along the border with Laos. The United States' response, on 12 May, was an order by President Kennedy to send the Seventh Fleet to the Gulf of Siam and to put US armed forces elsewhere in the Pacific and at home on standby alert. At the request of the Thai Government 1000 US Marines, in Thailand for SEATO exercises, were moved to the Laotian border on 14 May. On the 15th Kennedy announced that 4000 more US troops had been ordered into Thailand to protect its territorial integrity. The US deployment put a stop to the Pathet Lao drive, and its political pressure was successful in reopening negotiations.

The crisis ended on 12 June 1962 for both actors when the three Laotian princes (Souvanna Phouma, Boum Oum and Souphanouvong) signed an agreement on their participation in a Government of National Union, indicating a tacit understanding between Thailand and the US, on the one hand, and North Vietnam, on the other.

Regional organization activity was multiple. An emergency meeting of the SEATO Council requested that members send token military forces to Thailand on 16 May: all agreed, with the exception of France. The USSR's involvement was political. Ambassador Dobrynin and US Secretary of State Rusk met on 15 May and agreed on the need to maintain the cease-fire and establish a neutral and independent Laos. The USSR condemned the movement of US troops to Thailand as aggression.

References See sources for Case #146.

**(160) India/China
Border II**

A second border crisis between India and China, leading to full-scale war, began on 8 September 1962 and ended on 23 January 1963.

Background Border clashes between India and China erupted into an international crisis in August 1959 (see Case #137). From 1960 to 1962 the dispute continued at a lower level of intensity until Chinese forces began to take control of more disputed territory in the Aksai Chin region. India demanded a return to the status quo ante as a condition for negotiations. The PRC refused and began to concentrate military forces on the northeast (NEFA) border. India continued with its Forward Policy in which military patrols attempted to establish posts in territories held or claimed by the Chinese.

Crisis On 8 September 1962 Chinese forces crossed the Thag La Ridge on the McMahon Line, triggering India's perception of a threat to its territorial integrity, with a limited time to respond militarily due to the imminent approach of winter. The following day India began to plan "Operation Leghorn" to bring about the eviction of the Chinese. The beginning of its implementation on 4 October triggered a c̶ for China which perceived an imminent Indian military campaign beyond bord̶ incidents. On the same day China informed the Soviet Chargé d'Affaires of India's plans. The PRC responded on 20 October with a massive simultaneous attack on the western and eastern sectors of the disputed frontier. That day Nehru received a letter from Khrushchev expressing concern at reports that India intended to settle the dispute militarily, warning of the inherent dangers, and urging India to accept the Chinese proposals for talks. India's major response, on 24 October, was to take up the military option and to reject the PRC suggestion for mutual withdrawal to the 7 November 1959 "line of actual control," which would leave China in control of large tracts of disputed territory. On 29 October the US Ambassador in New Delhi offered American military aid to India. So too did Britain.

An intra-war crisis for India was triggered on 16 November with a second Chinese offensive. On the 19th Nehru appealed to President Kennedy to dispatch immediately 15 bomber and fighter squadrons to provide air cover for Indian cities against an anticipated Chinese attack. An American aircraft carrier was ordered to leave its base in the Pacific and head towards Indian waters. Shortly thereafter the defeat of the Indian Army was completed.

The crisis ended for China on 21 November when the PRC announced a unilateral cease-fire and, from 1 December, a withdrawal of Chinese forces 20 kilometers behind the actual control lines of 7 November 1959 (see Case #137), in both the Aksai Chin (western sector) and the McMahon Line (eastern sector).

Six Asian and African non-aligned states (Burma, Ceylon, Indonesia, Cambodia, Ghana and the UAR) attempted mediation at the Colombo Conference in early January 1963. By the time India's *Lok Sabha* approved their proposals, on 23 January, the PRC had implemented its unilateral withdrawal, a *de facto* cease-fire was in place, and the crisis ended for India.

Australia, Canada, the UK and the US sent aircraft and other military equipment to India. The USSR and Pakistan were peripherally involved.

References See sources for Case #137.

(161) Yemen War I The four actors in the first phase of the Yemen War were Egypt, Jordan, the Republic of Yemen and Saudi Arabia. This international crisis lasted from 26 September 1962 to 15 April 1963. (For related crises occurring through 1967 see Cases #176, #179 and #186.)

Background The Imam Ahmad, who had been the absolute ruler of Yemen since 1948, died on 19 September 1962 and was succeeded by his son the Imam Muhammad al-Badr. One week later his monarchy was toppled by a *coup d'état* carried out by a group of officers headed by Colonel Abdullah Sallal and aided by exiled Yemenis in Egypt who, prior to the coup, sent men and materials to uphold the new regime. Abdul Rahman al-Beidani, an exiled Yemeni diplomat living in Cairo, was named first Prime Minister of the Republic of Yemen.

Crisis The coup, on 26 September, triggered a crisis for Saudi Arabia and Jordan. Both countries feared the possibility that the fall of the monarchy in Yemen would spread to their own kingdoms. They responded on 1 October with a delivery of arms to the Royalists led by the former Imam. This triggered a crisis for Egypt and the Republic of Yemen. On 4 October the Republican regime ordered a general mobilization. Egypt, after sending a team to observe the situation on 13 October, decided to dispatch several thousand troops to Yemen by mid-November.

Civil war broke out between the Republicans in the south, aided by Egypt, and the Royalists in the north, aided by arms and men from Jordan and Saudi Arabia. On 4 November Mecca Radio announced that Egyptian aircraft had attacked five Saudi villages. That day, too, a military alliance between Jordan and Saudi Arabia was revealed. On the 10th a Joint Defense Pact between the Republic of Yemen and the UAR was signed. Following the UAR raids on Saudi Arabia, a Saudi decision was made to carry out reprisal raids against Yemen. When the Republican Government got word of this (via Jordanian officers who fled to Egypt), they warned of air attacks on the two countries.

The US reacted by sending a warship to Jiddah as a warning against further Yemeni or UAR attacks on Saudi Arabia. Word was also given to Yemen that, in the event of an attack by the two states, all US military aircraft would be withdrawn and the United States would adopt a neutral attitude. President Kennedy offered his good offices to bring about a peaceful solution and announced US recognition of the Republican Government on 19 December. Further UAR bombing of Saudi Arabia resulted in a Saudi call for general mobilization. Ralph Bunche, UN Under-Secretary-General for Special Political Affairs, visited Yemen from 1 to 4 March on a fact-finding mission on behalf of U Thant.

On 15 April 1963 Jordan recognized the Republic of Yemen and withdrew from the war. A disengagement agreement, that day, marked the termination of this international crisis and the first phase of the Yemen War.

References Dawisha 1975; Hassouna 1975; Heikal 1975; Ismael 1970; Kerr 1970; Kimche 1966; Little 1968; Mahjub 1974; O'Ballance 1971; Sadat 1978; Schmidt 1968; Shimoni 1977; Stephens 1971; Stookey 1982.

(162) Cuban Missiles There were three crisis actors, Cuba, the Soviet Union and the United States. The crisis lasted from 16 October to 20 November 1962.

Background After the 1961 Bay of Pigs abortive invasion (see Case #147), Cuba became one of the central issues of American foreign policy: the US viewed Cuba as a potential source of Communist-oriented subversive activities in all Latin America. When the US discovered the presence of Soviet military personnel in Cuba on 7 September 1962, it called up 150,000 reservists. The Soviets mobilized on the 11th. Although persistent rumors circulated concerning the deployment of Soviet missiles in Cuba, Soviet Ambassador Anatoly Dobrynin denied the charges, and Premier Khrushchev gave his personal assurances that ground-to-ground missiles would never be shipped to Cuba. On the eve of the Missile Crisis, Washington did not openly challenge the Soviet statements concerning the defensive character of the weapons being sent to Cuba.

Crisis The US crisis was triggered on 16 October when the CIA presented to President Kennedy photographic evidence of the presence of Soviet missiles in Cuba. The US responded with a decision on the 20th to blockade all offensive military equipment en route to Cuba. When this was announced on 22 October, a crisis was triggered for the USSR and Cuba. An urgent meeting of the Security Council was requested by both the US and Cuba on the 22nd. The following day a Soviet request for an urgent debate was received by the UN. On the 23rd as well, the Soviets accused the United States of violating the UN Charter and announced an alert of its armed forces and those of the Warsaw Pact countries. That day Cuba responded by condemning the US blockade and declaring its willingness to fight.

A resolution was adopted on the 23rd by the OAS calling for the withdrawal of the missiles from Cuba and recommending that member-states take all measures, including the use of force, to ensure that the Government of Cuba would not continue to receive military materiel. On 24 October the Security Council adopted a resolution requesting the Secretary-General to confer with the parties: U Thant began mediation by proposing that the Soviet Union and the United States enter into negotiations, during which period both the shipment of arms and the quarantine be suspended.

Moscow's major response to the crisis was a letter to Kennedy from Khrushchev on 26 October offering the removal of Soviet offensive weapons from Cuba and the cessation of further shipments in exchange for an end to the US quarantine and a US assurance that it would not invade Cuba. The situation was exacerbated on the 27th when a US U-2 surveillance plane was shot down. That day another Khrushchev letter was received in Washington offering the removal of Soviet missiles from Cuba in exchange for the removal of US missiles from Turkey. US mobilization and aerial reconnaissance flights were stepped up. And on the 27th President Kennedy sent the Soviet Premier an acceptance of the proposals contained in the letter of 26 October while making no reference to Khrushchev's second letter of the 27th. The following day Khrushchev notified the US Government that he had ordered work on the missile sites in Cuba stopped. He agreed to ship the missiles back to the USSR and promised that UN observers would be allowed to verify the dismantling of the sites. At the same time he warned Washington that U-2 reconnaissance flights over Cuba must be stopped as well.

The crisis continued at a lower level of intensity for several more weeks due to Cuban President Castro's demands concerning a US pledge not to invade his country. On 30 October U Thant began talks in Havana, and Kennedy agreed to lift the quarantine for the duration of the talks. When Cuba rejected UN inspection, the US resumed the quarantine and air surveillance.

The Kremlin sent Deputy Premier Anastas Mikoyan to Cuba on 2 November to try to persuade Castro to allow UN inspection. When this proved unsuccessful, a US–USSR agreement was reached on 7 November allowing US inspection and interception of Soviet ships leaving Cuba and the photographing of the missiles. The following day the superpowers negotiated the removal of the IL-28 bombers which Castro had claimed were Cuban property. Castro's agreement was conveyed to the US on 20 November 1962, which terminated the Missile Crisis for all three actors. The US naval quarantine was lifted immediately, but aerial surveillance continued until the agreement was completely carried out.

Regional/security organizations involved were the OAS and NATO, and the Warsaw Treaty Organization. President Kennedy sent Dean Acheson to Paris on 23 October to brief the Permanent Council of NATO on US measures against Cuba. Involved actors included members of the Warsaw Pact whose forces were put on alert and Latin American states which offered military assistance to the US.

References Abel 1966; Allison 1971; Bender 1975; Brzezinski and Huntington 1964; Chayes 1974; Crankshaw 1966; Daniel and Hubbel 1963; Dinerstein 1976; Divine 1971; Draper 1965; *Facts on File* 1964; George and Smoke 1974; Goldenberg 1965; Halper 1971; Horelick 1964; Kennedy 1962, 1964, 1969; Langley 1970; Pachter 1963; Plank 1967; Rush 1970; Schlesinger 1965; Sorensen 1965; Wohlstetter 1965; Young 1968.

(163) Malaysia Federation

Indonesia and Malaysia were crisis actors over the issue of the Malaysia Federation from 11 February 1963 until 9 August 1965.

Background Throughout the 1950s Great Britain had attempted to create a viable political structure that would include Brunei, Sarawak, Sabah, Singapore and Malaya. Plans for a Federation of Malaysia conflicted with territorial claims of the Philippines and, more seriously, of Indonesia. Hostility was first expressed in December 1962 when Indonesia covertly backed a revolt in Brunei for independence from the UK. The rebellion was quelled within 10 days. Following this revolt, Indonesia's support became more open.

Crisis The trigger for Malaysia's first crisis was President Sukarno's declaration on 11 February 1963 that Indonesia opposed a Malaysia Federation. Malaysia responded two days later by announcing an immediate expansion of its armed forces. Talks between the UK and the five participating entities resulted in an agreement in London, on 9 July 1963, for the establishment of the Federation of Malaysia, which was signed by all except Brunei. This triggered the first crisis for Indonesia. The response, on 11 July, was a sharp statement of opposition claiming a violation of a 14 June 1963 agreement that a federation would only be established after the UN ascertained the wishes of the people involved. The crisis for both actors was terminated on 5 August when a summit conference of Indonesian, Malaysian and Philippine Heads of State agreed that the UN would assess the views of the people.

The second crisis for Indonesia was triggered on 14 September 1963 by the publication of the results of an election indicating the people's preference for a Malaysia Federation. Indonesia responded the following day by declaring that it would not recognize the Federation and recalling its ambassador from Kuala Lumpur. This triggered the second crisis for Malaysia, which responded, on 17 September, by severing diplomatic ties with Indonesia and the Philippines. The US sanctioned Indonesia by suspending economic aid, and sending Attorney-General

Robert Kennedy to mediate, with no results. Following this, the International Monetary Fund withdrew its offer of promised credit. The Soviet Union gave Indonesia only lukewarm political support. China supported Indonesia throughout the crisis.

As the issue of confrontation faded, so did the crisis. The termination date of the crisis was 9 August 1965, when Singapore seceded from Malaysia. Although Malaysia survived, Indonesia viewed that act as the beginning of the break-up of the Federation. Malaysia, too, perceived a victory in this crisis because Indonesia's confrontation policy ended without destroying the Federation.

References See sources for Case #153.

(164) Jordan Internal Challenge

A crisis for Israel over domestic tension in Jordan lasted from 21 April to 4 May 1963.

Background The formation (abortive) of a federation among Egypt, Syria and Iraq in 1962 was perceived by King Hussein to be basically anti-Jordan. Riots by the Palestinians in the West Bank, demonstrating sympathy for the Federation, followed immediately. As these intensified, the stability of the Jordan regime became threatened. The King replaced the Prime Minister, censored newspapers, cut off links to the outside world and ordered the army to surround the Palestinian refugee camps. This was a domestic crisis for Jordan. However, a threat to the stability of the Jordanian King's regime had long constituted a major concern for Israel, to the point of military intervention if necessary to prevent the takeover by more radical Arab leaders.

Crisis Israel's perception of threat, time pressure, and war likelihood concerning Egyptian-supported anti-Hussein developments in Jordan was evident on 21 April 1963 when an urgent meeting between Prime Minister and Defense Minister Ben Gurion and his Chief of Staff took place. The same day Israel responded with a concentration of forces in Jerusalem and along the border with Jordan. During the next two weeks tension gradually abated as the King's forces succeeded in bringing the situation under control. King Hussein's statement on 4 May, inferring that Jordan's internal riots had been quelled and that stability was restored, marked the termination of this crisis: Israel then gradually pulled back its forces.

The United States supplied military equipment to Israel and Jordan.

References See general list and Shimoni 1977.

(165) Dominican Republic/Haiti

The Dominican Republic and Haiti were the actors in a crisis from 26 April to 3 June 1963.

Background The Dominican Republic's dictator, Trujillo, was assassinated in 1960 and members of his family fled to Haiti. Newly-elected President Bosch feared that Trujillo's exiled relatives would try to regain power in the Dominican Republic. An attempt on the lives of the children of Haiti's dictator Duvalier (Papa Doc) aroused suspicions of Dominican Republic complicity: the conspirators had sought refuge in the Dominican Republic Embassy in the Haitian capital of Port-au-Prince.

Crisis On 26 April 1963 Haitian policemen forcefully entered the Dominican Republic Embassy and took hostages. This violation of diplomatic immunity triggered a crisis for the Dominican Republic. The next day Dominican Republic President Bosch responded by issuing a 24-hour ultimatum to Haiti which triggered a reciprocal crisis. Bosch also appealed to the OAS and proposed a joint democratic Latin American force to oust Duvalier. On the 28th Haiti severed diplomatic relations with the Dominican Republic. The following day the Dominican Republic began stationing troops along its border with Haiti.

An OAS fact-finding mission arrived in Haiti on 30 April. On 5 and 6 May the crisis reached its peak. OAS officials shuttled between the two countries in an attempt at de-escalation. By 10 May the possibility of a Dominican Republic invasion of Haiti had lessened considerably. On the 14th Duvalier released the hostages, terminating the crisis for the Dominican Republic. On 3 June Haiti's crisis ended with the publication of the final report by the OAS Committee which recommended that no further action be taken against Haiti. The US, fearing for the lives of foreign citizens in Haiti, sent a naval task force. This was withdrawn after the final report of the OAS, and normal relations with Haiti were restored.

The UN Security Council met on 8-9 May at Haiti's request and discussed the issue but left action to the regional organization.

References See general list, especially *Facts on File* 1963, and Tomasek 1968.

(166) Algeria/Morocco Border A border crisis between Algeria and Morocco lasted from 1 October to 4 November 1963.

Background The dispute centered around areas of the Sahara held by Algeria which Morocco claimed had been part of the Moroccan state in precolonial times. Algeria countered that the disputed territory had been administered by the French and was liberated by the National Liberation Front (FLN), along with the rest of Algeria. A revolt in Algeria exacerbated the situation.

Crisis On 1 October 1963 Algerian President Ben Bella announced that Moroccan troops had taken up positions in the disputed territory. Further, he charged, the Moroccans were supplying aid to rebel leader Ait Ahmed, a former member of the Algerian National Assembly, then situated in the nearby region of Kabylia. Algeria responded to this threat on 8 October when its forces clashed with Moroccan troops. This constituted the crisis trigger for Morocco, which subsequently withdrew. On 14 October Morocco responded by reinforcing its troops and reoccupying the last outposts.

Efforts at negotiation were initiated by Algeria, but Morocco also called for a peaceful settlement. The final agreement, signed on 30 October by both parties, was worked out through the mediation of Ethiopian Emperor Haile Selassie and Mali President Modiba Keita. However, fighting continued for several more days until a Malian officer observing the truce succeeded in bringing the fighting to an end on 4 November 1963.

In the agreement Morocco obtained Algeria's consent to an examination of the border problem and an undertaking to cease propaganda attacks against it. Algeria obtained Moroccan withdrawal from the positions occupied during the fighting and an agreement to settle the dispute within the framework of the Organization of African Unity.

In addition to the OAU, the Arab League was also active in the crisis, but neither regional organization contributed to crisis abatement. The active role of the OAU occurred in the later stages of negotiation and reconciliation after the termination of the crisis. While Algeria perceived Morocco to be the only adversary, Morocco perceived Cuba and the United Arab Republic as partial to Algeria in the dispute.

References Touval 1972; Zartman 1966.

(167) Venezuela/Cuba The duration of Venezuela's crisis with Cuba was one month, from 1 November to 1 December 1963.

Background During 1963 Venezuela's internal situation began to verge on civil war. There was a marked increase in Communist guerrilla attacks on major targets within Caracas itself. President Betancourt had announced emergency legislation against Venezuela's left-wing parties and ordered the arrest of leading Communists, following an assassination attempt. Betancourt's drive against the Left on the domestic scene was matched by attempts in his foreign policy to isolate Cuba and invoke OAS sanctions against the Castro regime. This policy was actively encouraged by the US. Presidential elections in Venezuela were scheduled for 1 December 1963.

Crisis   On 1 November 1963 the Venezuelan Government discovered a significant arms cache on the Paraguana Peninsula, one of Venezuela's quiet, secluded beaches. A plan of operation to capture Caracas and prevent the elections of 1 December was also discovered. On 29 November the Cuban origin of the arms was confirmed. Venezuela took the matter to the OAS Council for action under Article 6 of the Rio Treaty. The crisis ended on 1 December with the successful conclusion of the presidential election. The OAS agreed to investigate Venezuela's charges on 3 December, after the termination of Venezuela's crisis: six months later the OAS voted in favor of sanctions against Cuba which, by that time, was no longer a member of the regional organization of the Americas.

References   See general list and Parkinson 1974.

(168) Kenya/Somalia   Kenya experienced a crisis with Somalia from 13 November 1963 until 4 March 1964.

Background   In March 1963 Britain announced that it would grant internal self-government to the British colony of Kenya after the local parliamentary elections of 18-26 May 1963. Despite a demand from the Somali population residing in the Northern Frontier District (NFD) to secede from Kenya and unite with Somalia, it was also announced that the NFD would become the seventh region of Kenya. On 18 March Somalia severed diplomatic relations with Britain. On 1 June Jomo Kenyatta became Kenya's first Prime Minister. The elections were boycotted by the Somali tribesmen of the NFD. In addition, Somali secessionists carried out a series of protest raids in the territory. The Kenyan Government banned non-essential travel to the area and issued a statement to the effect that Kenya would not give up an inch of the area.

Crisis   A statement by Kenyatta referred to 33 attacks by Somali raiders on military and police posts in the NFD since 13 November. This, therefore, marked the crisis trigger for Kenya. The Vice-President of Kenya's eastern region, Ahmed Farah, stated on 20 November that Somalia was preparing to attack Kenya and had already secretly distributed arms to Kenya's Somalis. Kenya, he warned, should be ready for war with Somalia after independence on 12 December 1963. Fearing a full-scale insurrection in the north, Kenyatta issued an order on 28 November that he wanted all Somali raiders captured, dead or alive.

Kenya's major response, on 25 December, was a proclamation of a state of emergency along the 440-mile NFD. A 5-mile prohibitive zone was established along the entire frontier. The next day Kenyan troops were placed on full alert; and on the 29th the border with Somalia was completely sealed. British troops stationed in Kenya were also sent to back up Kenya's security forces. On 28 December a military delegation from Ethiopia arrived to confer with Kenyan officials on the Somali border crisis, and a mutual defense treaty was ratified.

In February 1964 Kenya requested that the dispute be placed on the agenda of the OAU Council of Ministers. On 12 February an OAU resolution was passed detailing steps to settle the dispute and requesting the sides to refrain from propaganda. On 25 February 1964 the Kenyan state of emergency in the NFD was extended for another two months; but by the time of the 4 March elections the crisis had ended. Secessionist Somalis in the NFD participated in the election for the regional assembly, thus indicating their willingness to drop their secessionist demands.

The superpowers maintained a neutral position, but Somalia was receiving military aid from the Soviet Union and therefore regarded it as an ally.

By mid-1967 a Zambian initiative to mediate the continued low-level conflict succeeded when Kenyan and Somali leaders promised to cease provocative acts and restore normal relations.

References   Castango 1964; Touval 1972.

(169) Cyprus I   During the period from 30 November 1963 to 10 August 1964 Cyprus, Greece and Turkey were crisis actors in the first of several international crises over the Mediterranean island-state.

Background   The Zurich and London Conferences of 1959 worked out arrangements for Cypriot independence, subject to the terms of a series of interrelated agreements known as the Zurich–London Accords. According to these Accords, the interests of both the Greek and Turkish communities in Cyprus were recognized and safeguarded under a republican form of government, with several provisions insuring the fair participation of both autonomous communities in legislative functions. Once Cyprus became independent, however, each community became suspicious of the other's intentions. The Turkish minority, feeling that it did not receive all of the rights granted by the constitution, made frequent use of its legislative veto power. President Makarios, who felt that effective operation of his government was being hampered, acted often without legislative approval.

Crisis   The trigger for Turkey's first crisis, and the beginning of this international crisis, was its receipt on 30 November 1963, along with Great Britain and Greece, of a copy of a memorandum from the President of the Cypriot Republic, Archbishop Makarios, to Vice-President Kutchuk containing 13 proposals for the amendment of the constitution which would change Cyprus into a unitary state with guarantees for the Turkish minority. The trigger for Greece and Cyprus was an announcement on 6 December 1963 by Turkish Foreign Minister Erkin, rejecting the amendment proposals as totally unacceptable. Further, the Turkish Government threatened to intervene in Cyprus if the constitution was altered in any way, triggering a threat of grave damage for Cyprus decision-makers. Within this tense atmosphere, an incident on 21 December, involving a Greek police patrol which insisted on searching a Turkish car, sparked the outbreak of fighting between the Greek and Turkish communities in Nicosia which spread quickly to other areas in Cyprus. Three days later the Greek Cypriot forces were on the verge of completely overrunning the Turkish section of the capital. And on 24 December the Turkish Cypriots appealed to Turkey for assistance. Turkey replied that, if the fighting continued, it would intervene under the terms of the Treaty of Guarantee.

Turkey's major response, on 25 December, took the form of orders to the Turkish army contingent in Cyprus to move out of its camps and take positions controlling the road to Kyrenia. The Turkish fleet left the Istanbul area for the eastern Mediterranean; its armed forces were put on alert; more troops were moved into areas which were in easy striking distance of Cyprus; and Turkish aircraft flew over Nicosia.

The Greek response, the same day, was an announcement that, if Turkey intervened in Cyprus, Greece would do likewise. Makarios, hoping to gain Security Council condemnation of the Zurich–London Accords, accused Turkey of interference in the internal affairs of Cyprus, at a session of the Security Council on 27 December. No resolution was passed at that time.

On 28 December Britain's Commonwealth Secretary, Duncan Sandys, met with Greek and Turkish Cypriot leaders, as well as with the Ambassadors of Greece and Turkey in Cyprus. A cease-fire and the setting up of neutral zones on 29 December terminated the first crisis for Turkey. The United States participated in the cease-fire talks. NATO, which was repeatedly warned by the USSR to keep out of the internal affairs of Cyprus, met in emergency session in Paris.

The London Conference began on 15 January 1964. A British proposal for an international peace force composed of units from NATO countries was ultimately accepted by Makarios if the forces were from the UN only. USSR Premier Khrushchev protested NATO involvement in a letter to the UK, US, France, Greece and Turkey, on 7 February. In the middle of February fighting once again threatened to break out. The Security Council convened in emergency session on 14 February and adopted a resolution in March to establish a UN Peace-Keeping Force in Cyprus. It was formed on 27 March 1963, terminating Greece's crisis.

A second crisis for Turkey began on 27 May 1964 when conscription orders to the Cypriot National Guard for all men between the ages of 18 and 59 were announced. It was also learned that Cyprus was purchasing heavy arms from abroad. Despite British, Greek and Turkish protests that these acts were in violation of Cyprus's constitution, the conscription bill was passed on 1 June. Turkey's response on 4 June was a statement of its intention to provide security for Turkish Cypriots. Conscious of the implications in a US warning the same day not to invade Cyprus, Turkey announced on 5 June that it had abandoned plans to land forces in Cyprus; this marked the end of Turkey's second crisis.

During June tensions rose again with the return of General Grivas to Cyprus. The Turkish and Greek Prime Ministers were invited to Washington for talks in late June. Proposals by the US special mediator Dean Acheson were rejected by Greece. During July the UN mediator held talks in Geneva with the Greek and Turkish Ambassadors.

On 4 August Greek Cypriot patrol boats fired on vessels in the Turkish Cypriot harbor of Kokkina triggering another crisis for Turkey. During the next two days a number of Turkish Cypriot villages fell to Greek Cypriot forces, largely because of the restrictions placed upon the United Nations forces by Makarios. Turkey responded on 7 August with an appeal to the Security Council and a warning to Makarios of possible retaliation; and Turkish planes flew over Cyprus. Turkey's response triggered Greece's second crisis. The following day, on 8 August, Greek Cypriot troops attacking Kokkina were bombed by the Turkish Air Force. On 9 August Greece responded by issuing an ultimatum to Ankara that, if attacks did not cease within 36 hours, Greek Cypriots would be assisted with all military means at Greece's disposal. Greek planes flew over Cyprus that day. On 9 August the Security Council adopted a cease-fire resolution. The NATO Council met as well. Makarios appealed to the USSR and received a promise of Soviet support if the island were invaded. Turkey was warned to stop its military operations. President Johnson sent urgent appeals to Cyprus, Greece and Turkey to settle the crisis peacefully. An unconditional cease-fire was accepted by Cyprus and Turkey on 10 August, ending the crisis for them and for Greece. Continuing tension escalated into another international crisis with the same actors in November 1967 (see Case #190).

References Bitsios 1975; Ehrlich 1974; Miller 1967; Salih 1978; Stephens 1966.

(170) Jordan Waters The crisis for the five actors, Egypt, Israel, Jordan, Lebanon and Syria, started on 11 December 1963 and ended on 5 May 1964.

Background The dispute between Israel and the neighboring Arab states concerning the utilization of the Jordan waters was long-standing. Since the mid-forties several plans had been drawn up for its resolution but only one, the "Revised" Unified Johnston Plan of 1955, was approved and agreed upon at the technical level by both Israel and the Arab states. However, at a meeting of the Arab League Political Committee, it was rejected in principle because of its supposed bias to Israel. After the Sinai Campaign in 1956 (see Case #120) all further hopes of Arab–Israeli acceptance of any regional water proposal were destroyed and both sides felt free to proceed in developing their own unilateral water projects.

In 1958 Jordan started working on a water scheme, and in 1959 Israel began the National Water Carrier plan for carrying water to the Negev by pumping it from Lake Tiberias. During the early months of 1960 concern by the Arab states, particularly Syria, deepened, claiming that Israel's water scheme would endanger Arab security because Israel could now settle larger numbers of immigrants, thereby increasing its potential military power.

Under Syrian pressure a conference of Arab Chiefs of Staff was held in Cairo from 7 to 10 December 1963 in order to draw up a common Arab strategy against the Israeli diversion plan, due to be completed at the end of 1963. The Conference also agreed to prepare an agenda for the forthcoming December meeting of the Supreme Arab Defense Council.

Crisis A crisis for all four Arab states (Egypt, Jordan, Lebanon and Syria) was triggered on 11 December, the day after the Arab Chiefs of Staff conference, when Israel's Minister of Labor stated that the National Water Carrier would be operated despite pressure from the Arab states or any other country. Nasser responded on 23 December 1963 by proposing a meeting of all Arab Heads of State to consider

Israel's plan to divert the Jordan waters. Realizing the Arab armies were not capable of defeating Israel, Nasser hoped to check the trend towards war which was being proposed by Syria. A Summit Conference was held on 13-16 January 1964 in Cairo under the auspices of the Arab League and attended by all 13 members of the League. At the Conference it was decided unanimously not to go to war with Israel but to divert the three tributaries of the Jordan River and to set up a joint (unified) military command to protect the Arab states. An official communiqué at the end of the Conference, on 16 January, represented the response to the crisis by Egypt, Jordan, Syria and Lebanon.

The announcement of the Summit Conference decisions on 16 January triggered a crisis for Israel which perceived a grave threat to its vital water supplies. On 19 January Israel responded by an official Cabinet statement repeating its determination to carry out the plans for using the waters of the Jordan River.

Both superpowers, as well as the United Nations, issued strong warnings to Israel and the Arabs against using armed force.

The crisis ended on 5 May 1964 when it was officially announced by Israel that the project was completed and that it would go into operation in the summer of 1964. The announcement set off an outburst of indignation in the Arab press at the failure of the Arab governments to stop the project, but no further action was taken by them.

References   Alexander and Kitrie 1973; Brecher 1974; Jansen 1964; Kadi 1966; Kerr 1970; Khouri 1964, 1968; Mehdi 1964; Nimrod 1965a, 1965b, 1965c; Saliba 1968; Stevens 1965.

(171) Dahomey/Niger   On 21 December 1963 a crisis began for Dahomey and Niger, lasting until 4 January 1964.

Background   Civil disorder preceded a military revolt in Dahomey which replaced President Hubert Maga with the Commander of the Army, Colonel Soglo. A provisional government was set up on 29 October 1963. There was also a sharp increase in labor strikes and regime repression prior to the onset of the crisis. Since 1960 the Government of Niger was in the hands of the authoritarian President Hamani Diori, a friend and ally of Dahomey's former President. The conflict originated from a dispute over ownership of the tiny island of Lete on the Niger River which forms the frontier between the two countries.

Crisis   On 21 December 1963 the National Assembly of Niger alleged that Dahomey was preparing to send troops to occupy Lete Island. Niger's response to this perceived threat, and the trigger for Dahomey, was an announcement on 22 December of the imminent expulsion of 16,000 Dahomeyans residing and working in Niger. President Soglo, on 27 December, responded with an order to close Dahomey's rail and road links to Niger, thus cutting off the Dahomeyan port of Cotonou from landlocked Niger. Both sides sent forces to the border. On 4 January delegations from both countries met at the frontier and issued a joint communiqué reopening the road and withdrawing forces. This was the result of mediation efforts by several neighboring countries, Gabon, Togo and Nigeria, and a proposal by the President of the Union Africaine et Malagache, President Yameogo of Upper Volta.

References   See general list, especially *Africa Diary, Africa Recorder* and *Keesing's*.

(172) Rwanda/Burundi   A crisis between Rwanda and Burundi began on 21 December 1963 and ended some time in April 1964.

Background   Relations between Rwanda and Burundi had been strained since precolonial times. Both were traditional sacred kingdoms ruled by a *Mwami*. Each kingdom was populated by three ethnic groups: the Tutsi, the Hutu and the Twa. The Tutsi traditionally dominated politics and social life in both kingdoms.

The Belgian-administered UN Trust Territory of Rwanda-Urundi achieved independence as two separate states on 1 July 1962: the southern part became the Kingdom of Burundi, and the northern part became the Republic of Rwanda. Attempts by the UN to bring about the creation of a single independent state had failed.

Between 1960 and 1964 some 200,000 members of the Tutsi tribe left Rwanda and settled in the border regions of neighboring states, the Congo, Uganda, Burundi and Tanganyika. Many of the Tutsi, however, had not given up the hope of returning to Rwanda to reestablish the monarchy (officially abolished on 2 October 1961) and thus reestablish their traditional position as political rulers over the majority Hutu.

Early in December 1963 the Burundi Government dispersed a group of about 5000 Tutsi refugees who had gathered on the border with Rwanda apparently intending to unleash an armed attack against their former homeland.

Crisis On 21 December 1963 a crisis was triggered for Rwanda when a band of about 5000 Tutsi exiles, armed with bows and arrows and a few rifles, invaded Rwanda from Burundi territory. The Rwanda Government responded the same day by meeting the invasion with force, broadcasting a warning to the Hutu population to be "on the alert" for Tutsi invaders, and by dividing the country into nine emergency regions. By 27 December the attack had reportedly been repulsed, but the level of tension had not decreased. Bitter attacks were directed against the remaining Tutsi population in Rwanda, which appeared to have been condoned and even supported by the government. These massacres created an international problem which immediately involved the UN.

A crisis for Burundi was triggered on 22 January 1964 when it was reported that troops of the Rwanda Army had violated Burundi territory and "massacred" a number of Burundi inhabitants in the border area. The Burundi response was an appeal, on 28 January 1964, to the UN and the OAU to intervene and "to put an end to provocations by Rwanda." King Mwambutsa of Burundi also wrote to UN Secretary-General U Thant to complain of the frontier violations by Rwanda. The crisis ended some time in April, without a formal agreement: by then the threat of military hostilities had been reduced sufficiently for President Kayibanda of Rwanda to allow some of the Tutsi emigrés back into the country.

The overthrow of the King (*Mwami*) in Burundi in November 1966 facilitated a final agreement in March 1967 whereby all Tutsi refugees could return to their homes after giving up their arms.

UN activity was limited to dealing with the refugee problem: a Special Representative was appointed for this purpose by the Secretary-General. The OAU was minimally involved through its good offices.

References See sources for Case #171.

(173) Panama Canal A US/Panama crisis over the Panama Canal took place from 9 to 12 January 1964.

Background The treaty giving the US control over the Panama Canal was signed in 1903. Panamanian opposition to the treaty, in effect for about 30 years, centered around the full sovereignty of the US over the Canal Zone, Panama's inability to fly its flag in the area, and inadequate payment, according to Panama, for United States' use of the Canal. On 9 January 1964 a group of Panamanian students entered the Canal Zone and attempted to raise their national flag.

Crisis The crisis for Panama began when Canal authorities called upon US General O'Hara to deal with anti-American demonstrators following the Panamanian attempt to raise the flag on 9 January. US forces were ordered to secure the Canal Zone and disperse the demonstrators. When these forces were attacked and injured, they fired upon the Panamanians. The result was 26 dead and 100 wounded. Panama President Chiari responded by breaking diplomatic relations with the United States the same day. Chiari filed a complaint with the OAS and with the UN Security Council. On 10 January the United States was formally advised of this, triggering a US crisis. The same day President Johnson responded by sending a high-level delegation to Panama. Johnson telephoned Chiari who demanded a complete revision of all treaties affecting US/Panama relations. Johnson insisted that order must be restored to the Canal Zone first. He requested the OAS Peace Committee to investigate the matter.

It took several days to persuade the Panamanian President to agree to Johnson's terms. When he gave the order to do so, on 12 January, the crisis ended for both countries.

References Bloomfield 1967; Geyelin 1966; Gurtov 1974; Johnson 1971; La Feber 1978; Minor 1974; Stebbins 1966.

(174) East Africa Rebellions

A crisis for Britain occurred in several East African states from 19 to 30 January 1964.

Background On 12 January 1964 a *coup d'état* took place in Zanzibar, a former British colony. Western observers claimed that there had been Communist involvement. At that time Tanganyika, at Zanzibar's request, sent a group of armed police. The UK sent naval reinforcements to the coast off Dar-es-Salaam.

Crisis On 19 January a crisis was triggered for the UK when soldiers of the First Battalion Tanganyika Rifles mutinied against their British and Tanganyikan officers. The European officers were captured and replaced by Africans. The rebel troops demanded an interview with President Nyerere, better pay and the removal of the European officers. The Tanganyikan Minister of the Interior appealed to the UK to intervene in order to help control the rioting and looting. In the meantime British troops were moved from Aden to Kenya to protect British nationals in Tanganyika in case of a threat. On 21 January, in a broadcast by President Nyerere, the nation was informed that Tanganyika's internal crisis was over.

On 23 January soldiers of the Uganda Rifles mutinied and held their British officers prisoner. The UK received a request for aid from Prime Minister Obote, and responded the same day by landing troops in Entebbe. Another request for British troops came from Tanganyika on 24 January when fighting broke out again. Troops were also rushed from Kenya to Tanganyika. Also on the 24th a brief revolt broke out in Kenya, and British troops stationed there, along with those offshore, were rushed to the scene.

On 27 January Nyerere of Tanganyika called for an emergency OAU meeting, but it did not meet. The British troops stayed in the area until 30 January when calm once more prevailed in the three former British colonies, Kenya, Tanganyika and Uganda.

References See general list, especially *Keesing's*.

(175) Ogaden I

A crisis between Ethiopia and Somalia over Ogaden in the Horn of Africa lasted from 7 February until 30 March 1964.

Background Ethiopia's eastern frontier was established by treaties with Italy and Britain at the end of the nineteenth century. The treaties included the ceding to Ethiopia of the Maud territory which contained a vast population of the nomadic Somali people. The Italians occupied Ethiopia in 1935 (see Case #16). Full sovereignty was restored in 1942 after the British invasion. In 1946 the Ogaden and Maud territories were returned to Ethiopia after having been under British military administration. Italy regained authority over Italian Somaliland. Several attempts to reach agreement over the territorial dispute before Somalia's independence in 1960 failed, and its boundary with Ethiopia was still not demarcated. Economic conditions were severe in Somalia preceding the crisis. In November 1963 the Soviet Union concluded a military aid deal with Somalia.

Crisis   A crisis for Ethiopia was triggered on 7 February 1964 when military forces of the Republic of Somalia reportedly carried out a mass attack on the Ethiopian frontier post at Tog Wajeleh. Ethiopia responded the next day in a number of ways: military resistance at the frontier post; a declaration of a state of emergency in the border region; a call for an immediate meeting of the OAU; and a strong protest by Ethiopia's Foreign Minister to the Soviet Chargé d'Affaires in Addis Ababa. In addition, Emperor Haile Selassie addressed a message to all Heads of African states informing them of the incident. Military clashes reportedly continued until 10 February. The Ethiopian retaliation on the 8th and military action on Somali territory triggered a crisis for Somalia. Its response, on the 9th, was also multiple: resistance to the Ethiopian attack; a declaration of a state of emergency throughout Somalia; the dispatch of an accusation of Ethiopian penetration into Somali territory to the Ethiopian Embassy in Mogadishu, and notification of the conflict to the OAU. Somalia perceived the OAU members, many of whom experienced border disputes with their neighbors, as insensitive to its territorial claims. Success for Somalia, it was felt, would constitute a precedent which would threaten the existence of several other newly-independent African states. Somalia looked upon the UN as a more friendly forum for its complaints and, therefore, on 10 February, Somalia requested a meeting of the Security Council, if the OAU failed to end the border dispute. Secretary-General U Thant appealed to the parties to settle the dispute peacefully. A cease-fire was agreed upon on 16 February but did not hold.

The crisis ended on 30 March 1964 with a formal agreement for a cease-fire concluded in Khartoum. A joint border commission was established. Sporadic fighting, however, continued after the agreement. The territory in question was retained by Ethiopia after the crisis ended. Tensions were to escalate into a crisis again (see Case #251).

References   Farer 1976; Hoskyns 1969; Lewis 1963; Perham 1969; Spiegel and Waltz 1971; Touval 1963, 1972; Widstrand 1969.

(176) Yemen War II   Egypt, the Republic of Yemen and Saudi Arabia experienced intra-war crises from mid-May until 8 November 1964.

Background   Fighting among the adversaries broke out immediately after the cease-fire of April 1963 (see Case #161) and continued throughout the year. President Sallal visited the Soviet Union in March and the PRC in June 1964. President Nasser visited Yemen in April 1964. Jordan, which had at first supported the Yemen Royalists, gradually withdrew as its ties with Egypt became closer. It was not a crisis actor in any of the ensuing clusters of crises pertaining to the war in Yemen. Reports by UN Secretary-General U Thant indicated a reduction in Egyptian forces in the area and an increase in supplies to the Royalists for the period preceding this crisis. The military situation had been fairly quiet, and the report indicated a military stalemate. Republican and UAR forces controlled the mountains, coastal plain and the south of Yemen, while Royalists carried on guerrilla warfare in the mountain and desert areas of the north and east.

Crisis   In mid-May 1964 a retaliation attack was launched by the Royalists, triggering a crisis for Egypt and Republican Yemen. Their response, in August, was the successful Horadeh offensive to seal the border with Saudi Arabia and thus prevent supplies from reaching Yemen. This triggered a crisis for Saudi Arabia. By 11 September the UN Yemen Observer Mission (UNYOM) had terminated its activities and left Yemen. The Saudi Arabian response to the crisis was Prince Feisal's visit to Alexandria on 11 September 1964 for talks with Nasser. Ben Bella of Algeria and Aref of Iraq served as mediators. Peace talks were held in early November and a cease-fire came into effect on 8 November 1964, the termination date for all three actor-cases.

References   See sources for case #161.

(177) Gulf of Tonkin   The first international crisis of the Vietnam War (1964–75) began on 2 August 1964. It ended for the United States on the 7th. North Vietnam's crisis faded some time later in August.

Background   Until the North Vietnam attack on US naval vessels in the Gulf of Tonkin, the American presence in Southeast Asia was limited to military and economic aid to Thailand, Cambodia and South Vietnam. In June 1962 direct US armed intervention to stabilize the deteriorating situation in Laos was considered but found to be unnecessary when the deployment of US forces in Thailand and the dispatch of the Seventh Fleet to the Gulf of Siam succeeded in halting the Pathet Lao attack in Laos and led to the reopening of negotiations for a Government of National Union (see Case #159). American policy in Vietnam was based upon the maintenance of a separate state in South Vietnam. Any support to the insurgency in the south by North Vietnam was viewed as external aggression. The US supported the repressive Ngo Dinh Diem regime in Saigon against rebellion, but the growth of insurgency in the south was rapid. Southerners, regrouped in North Vietnam, began to return to join the expanding military strength of the Vietcong.

During 1962 the United States undertook a major military build-up in Vietnam. American helicopter crews took an active part in the war. There was a sharp rise in the incidence of terrorism by the Vietcong directed against the civilian population. The Buddhist uprising against the Diem Government, accompanied by acts of suicide by Buddhist monks, dramatized the situation and brought about US political pressure against Diem.

On 1 November 1963 Diem was murdered, and a Military Revolutionary Council took power under General Duong van Minh. At that time less than half the territory of South Vietnam was under effective Saigon control. President Kennedy's assassination followed shortly thereafter. In the 1964 presidential campaign, Johnson reassured the public that Americans would not be sent to fight in Vietnam. Nevertheless, he would never permit Communist expansion there. Across the Pacific, on 25 July 1964, Hanoi Radio charged that Americans had fired on a North Vietnamese fishing craft. On 30 July it accused South Vietnamese naval vessels of again raiding its fishing boats in the Gulf of Tonkin and, with the protective cover of an American destroyer, bombarding two North Vietnamese islands.

Crisis   A crisis for the United States was triggered on 2 August 1964 when the American destroyer *Maddox* was attacked by North Vietnamese torpedo boats in the Gulf of Tonkin off North Vietnam. Hanoi admitted to this attack, but insisted that a second attack never occurred. However, the United States' version was that a second attack was launched on 4 August against two American destroyers. Neither suffered any casualties or damage. The American response was prompt. Shortly after the alleged second attack, on 4 August, President Johnson ordered an air attack against North Vietnamese gunboats and their supporting facilities, which became the trigger to a crisis for North Vietnam. Its major response was a verbal protest against the United States. On the 5th Johnson asked Congress to pass a resolution to approve all necessary action to protect American armed forces and to assist nations covered by the SEATO treaty. The Gulf of Tonkin Resolution, giving the President broad war powers in defense of US and allied interests in Southeast Asia, was passed on 7 August terminating the crisis for the US. The mass bombing of North Vietnam ceased in early August, and North Vietnam's perception of crisis faded shortly thereafter.

The United States requested a Security Council meeting and also called for a session of SEATO, as well as informing its NATO allies of events through high-level consultations. Nothing concrete emerged from these meetings. No clear agreement between Hanoi and Washington was reached. The outcome of the crisis led to an escalation of tension in the area. The USSR provided political support to Hanoi.

References   Gelb and Betts 1979; Gravel 1971; Johnson 1971; Kahin and Lewis 1967.

(178) Congo II

The formation of a rebel regime and the taking of hostages in Stanleyville led to a crisis for Belgium, the Congo (later, Zaire), the United States and the USSR lasting from 4 August to 30 December 1964.

Background
On 29 September 1963 President Kasavubu disbanded Congo's parliament after a series of increasingly repressive measures were passed against the political opposition. The deterioration of economic and social conditions, along with repression, led to societal unrest which manifested itself in tribal fighting, raids and other arbitrary acts of violence – mainly in East Katanga and Upper Congo. Large-scale uprisings, led by the National Liberation Committee (NLC), occurred during January and April 1964. On 30 June the UN Emergency Force, which had been set up in 1960, left the Congo. In July of that year Kasavubu requested Moise Tshombe to form a new government. The Governments of Congo-Brazzaville, Burundi and Mali were accused of giving support to the NLC, as were the USSR and China which were providing arms and military training. Rebel activities against the central government increased, and large areas in the eastern part of the country, including Stanleyville, were under control of the rebel forces.

Crisis
The trigger to the Congo's crisis was the formation of a Revolutionary Council in Stanleyville on 4 August 1964, with the NLC Leader Christophe Gbenye as President, after rebel forces had occupied the city. The Congo's response, on the 6th, was an appeal by Premier Tshombe to the United States and Belgium for direct military aid. Tshombe also took his case to the OAU, which resolved to set up an *ad hoc* committee to examine the situation and to act as a mediator among the rival African countries which supported the rebels.

The trigger for the United States and Belgium occurred on 26 September when Gbenye, who was holding 1500 white foreign civilians as hostages in Stanleyville, announced that they would not be allowed to leave the city. Their safety was made contingent upon a cease-fire, the eschewing of bombings by the central government, and the termination of Western support. This was accompanied by threats of physical harm against the hostages if those conditions were rejected. The US's, and Belgium's, major response, on 22 November, was to dispatch paratroops to a British base in the Congo to prepare for a military rescue of the hostages. On the 24th an emergency NATO meeting, requested by Belgium, expressed sympathy and support for the Western countries.

The paratroops occupied Stanleyville on 24 November and rescued the hostages within a few hours. The Congo Government coordinated an attack on the rebels for the same time as the rescue mission. Control was handed back to the central government on 29 November, marking the termination date for Belgium and the United States.

A crisis for the USSR was triggered by the Belgian/US rescue mission on 24 November. The Soviets feared that Tshombe's pro-Western regime would crush the rebels and thus reduce Soviet influence in the area. Its response, on the 26th, was to accuse the US, Belgium and Britain of aggressive intervention. The Soviet crisis ended on 17 December when its Embassy in Kinshasa was closed down.

Discussions were held at the Security Council between 9 and 30 December. It adopted a resolution after the crisis ended, on 30 December, calling for a cease-fire in the fighting between the rebels and the central government, the removal of mercenaries and a stop to foreign intervention. This terminated the Congo's crisis and the international crisis as a whole.

In early 1965 President Kasavubu dismissed Premier Tshombe and was himself ousted in a *coup d'état* led by General Joseph Mobutu on 25 November 1965. Relations between Congo–Brazzaville and Congo–Kinshasa remained poor until 1970, when diplomatic relations and river traffic were finally restored.

References
Clark 1968; CRISP 1966; Epstein 1965; Gappert and Thomas 1965; Hoare 1967; Hoskyns 1969; Kitchen 1965; Miller 1967; Nkrumah 1967; Reed 1965; Schlesinger 1973; Spaak 1971; Talon 1976; Tshombe 1967; United States Department of State 1965.

(179) Yemen War III   This phase of the long war in Yemen, as crises for Egypt, Saudi Arabia and Yemen, lasted from 3 December 1964 to 25 August 1965.

Background   The peace talks, which were held in Sudan, led to a cease-fire on 8 November 1964, as well as an agreement to set up a National Congress to deal with the fundamental differences between the Republicans and the Royalists (see Case #176). By 20 November an announcement was made postponing the Congress and on 13 December it was postponed indefinitely. The Royalist Foreign Minister, Ahmed al-Shami, made it clear that, if Royalist demands were not accepted, they would renew the fighting. The political confusion in Yemen was further intensified in December by an open split among the Republicans.

Crisis   On 3 December 1964 a Royalist offensive, backed by Saudi Arabia, began, eventually reoccupying most of the territory captured by the Republicans. This triggered a crisis for the UAR and Yemen. Their major response, on 10 January 1965, was the resumption of fighting. There were heavy casualties on both sides. The Information Minister of the Royalist Government alleged on 23 January that Egyptian aircraft had dropped gas bombs, the crisis trigger for Saudi Arabia.

A Royalist request to the International Red Cross to investigate the charges was refused on the grounds that the use of gas was not forbidden by any International Red Cross Convention. Fighting continued in the southeastern region, as well as in northern Yemen. Egyptian attempts in March and May to cut the Royalists' supply routes from Saudi Arabia failed. A strong Royalist offensive near Haral (Saudi frontier) on 7 June was repulsed. Yemen's Republican Government lodged a complaint with the UN on 26 July, accusing Saudi Arabia of aiding the Royalists and claiming that, without Saudi support, the Royalists would have been defeated long before. Reports of large-scale Saudi and Iranian support were frequent from February 1965.

Negotiations for a peace settlement, with Jordanian, Kuwaiti and Algerian mediation, began in May 1965. After prolonged consultation in Cairo among the Republican leaders, President Sallal announced on 18 July a compromise agreement between the dissident Republicans and reaffirmed the proposals of the Khamner Conference. On 22 July President Nasser said that the UAR had reopened negotiations with Saudi Arabia concerning Egyptian troop withdrawal.

An agreement, signed by President Nasser and King Feisal on 24 August, provided for an immediate cease-fire, the ending of Saudi aid to the Royalists, the withdrawal of UAR forces, the establishment of a Provisional Yemen Government, and the holding of a plebiscite in November 1966. On 25 August 1965, the crisis termination date, the Royalists stopped fighting and the Egyptian forces began their withdrawal.

References   See sources for Case #161.

(180) Pleiku   This crisis for North Vietnam and the United States lasted from 7 February to 2 March 1965.

Background   North Vietnamese firing on an American destroyer in the Gulf of Tonkin, on 2 August 1964, was the opening gambit of US involvement in the Vietnam War. On 7 August the Gulf of Tonkin Resolution was passed by Congress granting the US President broad war powers (see Case #177). In the following six months fighting took place between South and North Vietnam with minimum US participation. In the United States a debate ensued regarding American commitments to the Saigon Government which, on 27 January 1965, had been taken over by a military coup.

Crisis   An intra-war crisis for the United States was triggered on 7 February 1965 when Vietcong guerrillas staged a night raid against American army barracks at Pleiku, killing eight Americans and wounding 126. An intra-war crisis for North Vietnam was triggered the same day, 12 hours later, when President Johnson authorized air strikes against the North following a meeting of the National Security Council. North Vietnam's major response, on the 10th, was an attack on Qui Nhan. The US response, on 13 February, was a decision in favor of measured and limited air action jointly with South Vietnam against selected military targets in North Vietnam. For the United States, the immediate military consequences of the attack were superseded by political-diplomatic considerations related to America's commitment to maintain its influence in Southeast Asia.

The Pleiku Crisis may be said to have ended on 2 March 1965, the day on which the first of the US air strikes was actually carried out; this action constituted a unilateral act and a transition from one phase to another in the evolution of US involvement in Vietnam. There was no clear outcome to the crisis: the US was pulled deeper into the morass of Vietnam; the North Vietnamese suffered from increased US bombing.

There was minimal UN activity: Secretary-General U Thant called for all sides to negotiate but his efforts were unsuccessful. The Soviets extended military aid to North Vietnam.

References   See sources for Case #177

(181) Rann of Kutch   This crisis between India and Pakistan, one of several since 1947, lasted from 8 April until 30 June 1965.

Background   The conflict between India and Pakistan can be traced to the 1947 partition of the Indian subcontinent and, in non-state terms, much longer. The princely state of Kutch had acceded to the Indian Union, but Pakistan claimed the northern part of the Rann of Kutch as part of its territory. Incidents occurred in 1956, but Indian control over the disputed territory was quickly restored. A border clash took place in March 1965.

Crisis   A crisis was triggered for Pakistan on 8 April 1965, when India launched an attack on a Pakistani police post in the disputed part of the Rann of Kutch. The same day Pakistan responded by a counter-attack, triggering a crisis for India. Pakistani forces outfought the attacking Indian troops. India's response occurred on 26 April when its army was placed on alert. Pakistan claimed that Indian armed forces had been moved close to Pakistan's West Punjab border, apparently in preparation for an attack. Britain called for a cease-fire based upon the restoration of positions held by each side as of 1 January 1965. This was followed by intense trilateral negotiations, involving New Delhi, Islamabad and London, ending in a cease-fire agreement on 11 May. The crisis for India and Pakistan was not terminated until 30 June when both parties agreed to all the terms of the cease-fire: mutual withdrawal of forces; direct negotiations, and arbitration, if all else failed to settle the dispute.

Moscow expressed the hope that India and Pakistan would exercise restraint and settle the dispute in a manner safeguarding the interests of both states. A US declaration deplored the fighting and offered American help in restoring peace to the subcontinent. India charged that Pakastani forces were using American equipment, and US–Indian relations deteriorated. Beijing supported Pakistan throughout the crisis (see Case #183).

References   Barnds 1972; Brines 1968; Choudhury 1968; Lamb 1966.

(182) Dominican Republic   A crisis for the United States began on 24 April and ended on 31 August 1965.

Background   In December 1962, more than a year after Trujillo's assassination, the first free elections in 38 years were held in the Dominican Republic. Juan Bosch was inaugurated as President in February 1963. In September of that year military officers, alleging Communist control of the civilian center, staged a coup. Donald Reid y Cabral acted as puppet President while real power lay in the hands of a three-man military junta.

Crisis   A crisis was triggered for the United States on 24 April 1965 when Bosch supporters overthrew the junta. Civil war broke out immediately. US Embassy personnel cabled President Johnson that American lives were in danger. The United States responded on 28 April with a decision to send paratroops and marines to the island. All foreign citizens were evacuated. The next day, Johnson assigned US military units the task of restoring order.

   While fighting continued, intense diplomatic activity was taking place within the OAS and the UN, as well as bilateral US/Dominican Republic negotiations. An OAS resolution called for a cease-fire, mediation, and the dispatch of an Inter-American Peace Force to the Dominican Republic. In the Security Council, Cuba and the USSR charged the United States with military intervention in the internal affairs of the Dominican Republic. A mild Security Council resolution called for a cease-fire and authorized the Secretary-General to take appropriate action. U Thant appointed Dr José Antonio Mayobri as his Personal Representative. Mayobri began mediation efforts with US and Dominican delegates to the OAS.

   "The Act of Dominican Reconciliation," signed on 31 August 1965, ended four months of civil war and, with it, the international crisis. All sides compromised by agreeing on Garcia-Godoy as Provisional President. Further military incidents occurred in 1965 and 1966. Free elections were held once more, in June 1966, in which Dr. Joaquín Balaguer was elected President of the Republic.

References   Barnet 1968; Draper 1968; Evans and Novak 1967; Herring 1968; Johnson 1971; Miller 1967; Parkinson 1974; Spiegel and Waltz 1971; Stuart 1975; Wilson 1966.

(183) Kashmir II   The second India–Pakistan crisis over Kashmir occurred between 5 August 1965 and 10 January 1966 (see Case #82).

Background   The Rann of Kutch Crisis between India and Pakistan ended on 30 June 1965 (see Case #181). On 2 July Pakistan's President, Ayub Khan, ordered the withdrawal of all Pakistani troops from the frontiers with India; and shortly thereafter similar instructions were issued to Indian forces.

Crisis   Another 1965 crisis for India was triggered on 5 August when Pakistani "freedom fighters" began infiltrating into the Vale of Kashmir with a view to creating a large-scale uprising against Indian control over most of the former princely state. On 25 August India sent several thousand troops across the 1949 Kashmir cease-fire line, capturing most of the areas through which the infiltrators came, and triggering another crisis for Pakistan. The latter responded on 1 September by dispatching an armored column across the cease-fire line in southern Kashmir and threatening the vital road linking the capital city of Srinagar with the plains of India. India's major response was to invade West Pakistan on 5 September. Two days later China denounced Indian "aggression" against Pakistan and alleged Indian provocation on the border of Sikkim and Tibet. An intra-war crisis was triggered for India on 16 September, when China issued an ultimatum that, unless the Indian Government dismantled all military bases near the Chinese border and stopped all intrusions into China, it would have to bear full responsibility for the grave consequences. India responded on the 17th by rejecting Chinese allegations while hinting at a willingness to make minor concessions. Although India reported Chinese troop movements to within 500 meters of Indian positions on the 18th, by 21 September China had withdrawn its ultimatum by an announcement on Beijing Radio that India had complied with the Chinese demands. This crisis for India was thus resolved on 21 September 1965.

   The threat of Chinese intervention stimulated the superpowers to seek a rapid termination of the war between India and Pakistan. New efforts were made through the Security Council. A resolution, to which both parties agreed, was drawn up on 17 September, and the UN Observer Mission, in Kashmir since 1949, was strengthened. However, this did not mark the termination of the crisis, for both armies still faced each other across the Punjab border, each occupied one another's territory, and a series of violations of the cease-fire agreement occurred.

On 17 September Soviet Premier Kosygin proposed a conference in Tashkent between Pakistan's President Ayub Khan and India's Prime Minister Shastri. The conference, held between 4 and 10 January 1966, ended with a declaration affirming the intentions of both parties to restore diplomatic, economic and trade relations, to withdraw troops to the internationally-recognized borders, and to repatriate prisoners of war. The crisis ended on 10 January 1966.

On 8 September 1965 US Secretary of State Rusk had informed the Senate that the US had suspended military aid to both countries and no new commitments of economic assistance to either party had been made. Since the US was the sole supplier of arms to Pakistan, while India received arms from several sources, including the USSR, the embargo was especially effective against Pakistan.

UN Secretary-General U Thant visited the area but was unable to persuade either side to take a more flexible position. However, the Security Council Resolution of 17 September was agreed to by India on the 20th and by Pakistan on the 22nd.

References See sources for Case #181.

(184) Guinea Regime A crisis for Guinea began on 9 October 1965 and ended some time in December of that year.

Background Guinea's independence from France in October 1958 was followed by a severe curtailment of French aid and expertise. In the year prior to this crisis the political climate in Guinea was constantly troubled, the standard of living had dropped, and consumer goods were expensive and irregularly supplied. Many Guineans fled the country in search of more favorable economic conditions.

In July 1965 a meeting was held in Paris among the Presidents of the Ivory Coast (Houphouet-Boigny), Niger (Diori), and Upper Volta (Yaméogo), with Tshombe from the Congo and two French Ministers. According to Guinea's President, Sekou Touré, this group decided to provide funds and other aid to Guineans who wished to remove him from the presidency. Three attempts to overthrow the Guinean Government between February and October 1965 were uncovered and halted.

Crisis The crisis trigger for Guinea was internal: on 9 October 1965 the statutes of a new opposition party to the only authorized party in Guinea were deposited with the Guinean Minister of the Interior. On 12 October Mamadou Touré, leader of the Parti de l'Unité Nationale de Guinée, was arrested, and disorders in Guinea's second town, Kankan, were suppressed. Guinea's formal complaint to the OAU, on 17 November, alleged that subversive acts were being financed by the Ivory Coast, with a view to a *coup d'état* in Guinea. Houphouet-Boigny publicly refuted Sekou Touré's charges. On 7 December Guinea allegations against France were reiterated in the Political Committee of the United Nations General Assembly, which offered its good offices.

By mid-December Sekou Touré had succeeded in overcoming the threat to his regime, and the crisis ended through a tacit understanding by the parties.

References See general list, especially West Africa.

(185) Rhodesia UDI A declaration of independence by the white minority regime in Southern Rhodesia precipitated a crisis for Zambia from 5 November 1965 to 27 April 1966.

Background During 1964 and 1965 evidence mounted that the white regime in Southern Rhodesia planned to issue a Unilateral Declaration of Independence (UDI). Newly-independent Zambia (formerly Northern Rhodesia) viewed the possible establishment of a hostile white state, independent of the UK, as a threat to its existence: being landlocked, Zambia was totally dependent on Rhodesia for rail routes to ports, sources of coal and oil, and power from the jointly-owned hydroelectric stations at the Kariba Dam on the Rhodesian border.

Crisis   The trigger to Zambia's crisis was a Rhodesian proclamation of a state of emergency on 5 November, granting the government in Salisbury sweeping powers. Zambia perceived this to be a prelude to a Rhodesian Declaration of Independence. The next day, Zambia issued a final warning to Rhodesia of the consequences of such an action. Rhodesian troops were moved to the Zambian border on 9 November. And on the 11th independence was declared.

Zambia's response, the next day, combined the dispatch of troops to the Zambezi River, a promulgation of emergency regulations, and limited economic sanctions against Rhodesia: Rhodesian currency and money orders would not be negotiable in Zambia as of 13 November. And on the 17th Zambia's President Kaunda began sustained pressure on Britain for an immediate military response or, at least, British guarantees for Zambia's supply of Kariba power. Zambia also pressed for an emergency meeting of the Security Council. British objections frustrated these attempts for intervention by the global organization, but the Security Council did pass a resolution condemning UDI, urging non-recognition by member-states, and appealing to them to refrain from rendering any assistance to Rhodesia.

On 20 November, at an OAU meeting in Dar-es-Salaam, representatives from Egypt, Kenya, Nigeria, Tanzania and Zambia debated the setting up of a multi-national African army; but as a result of Zambian opposition, no action was taken. After initial British refusal to exert military pressure on Rhodesia, the UK finally offered to send ground troops to Zambia for protection against invasion. Zambia, which viewed this suggestion as designed to prevent, rather than prepare for, military action against Rhodesia, refused. On 23 November discussions began on a proposal to station Royal Air Force units at Zambia's three international air fields, in order to deter a Rhodesian air attack. The following day, Zambian troops were withdrawn from the border, and the UK Prime Minister, Harold Wilson, announced that Britain and Zambia had agreed to the provision of RAF planes and personnel for Zambia's air defense. By the time the Extraordinary Meeting of the OAU Council of Ministers convened, on 3 December, to consider the severance of diplomatic relations with Britain by several states, the RAF was being installed at Zambia's airfields. On the 28th Zambian ministerial missions visited Washington and Moscow with a view to securing superpower support for a more vigorous response to UDI and increased assistance to Zambia. A UN oil embargo on Rhodesia (and therefore, Zambia) led to the mounting of an Anglo-American-Canadian oil airlift to Zambia in early January.

The success of the 1948-49 Berlin-style airlift to Zambia, and the development of alternative surface supply routes, encouraged Wilson to believe that UDI could end "within weeks, not months," providing that Zambia imposed complete sanctions and broke entirely with Rhodesia. Wilson promised massive external support and a tougher British policy on Rhodesia, but these promises were adjusted during February and March 1966. And, finally, London reneged altogether on 27 April, following the British general elections, which returned a commanding majority for Labour. On that day the crisis ended for Zambia; although betrayed by Wilson's announcement of the initiation of "talks about talks" with Rhodesia's Prime Minister Smith, Zambia's existence was no longer in peril.

The completion of a pipeline from Dar-es-Salaam on the Indian Ocean, almost three years later, reduced Zambia's dependence on Rhodesia for oil, coal and electricity.

References   Anglin 1988; Good 1973; Hall 1973; Sklar 1974.

(186) Yemen War IV   The last phase of the long war in Yemen took place between 14 October 1966 and 26 September 1967 and encompassed three crisis actors: Egypt, the Republic of Yemen and Saudi Arabia.

Background   On 23 November 1965 Yemeni Republican and Royalist delegations, together with observers from Egypt and Saudi Arabia, met to discuss the nature of the plebiscite agreed upon at Jiddah (see Case #179). The parties failed to reach agreement on any of the items on the agenda. Intermittent fighting continued. A new agreement for a peace settlement in Yemen was reached at Kuwait on 19 August 1966 but was never put into effect. The long war was renewed.

Crisis   On 14 October 1966 air raids began on Royalist-controlled villages in the northern mountains, a main target being the headquarters of the Royalist Government-in-Exile. Two Saudi villages were also bombed, the crisis trigger for Saudi Arabia. On 24 October intelligence reports that a strong concentration of Royalist tribesmen was gathering for an attack on the town of Sa'da triggered another intra-war crisis for Egypt and Yemen. The Yemeni response, on 30 October, was a combined attack on Saudi troops and the Royalist Homdon tribe. Egypt's response was the use of poison gas in bombings of Halhal, a Royalist-held town, on 27 December 1966. Other gas bombings by Egypt were reported in January. Egyptian expeditionary forces had reached 50,000 to 60,000 men.

The Saudi response to the crisis occurred the next day – a combined Royalist – Saudi attack on Yemen President Sallal's Residence and a military post in the Yemen capital, San'a. The Saudi Arabian delegate to the UN complained to the Secretary-General and warned that Saudi patience was at an end. On 28 February 1967 U Thant, whose attempt at good offices was the principal UN activity, stated that he was powerless to deal with the matter. Jordan and Tunisia withdrew their recognition of the Yemen Republic. A UN General Assembly resolution of 5 December 1966 condemned the use of poison gas as contrary to international law, as well as to the policies of governments throughout the world.

The Republicans remained seriously divided during the early months of 1967. Military action was confined to sporadic Egyptian air raids on Royalist villages, in which poison gas bombs were reported to have been dropped. In March there were reports of a serious split among the Royalists. A reconciliation was reached on 10 April when a Royalist Government-in-Exile was formed. The Six Day War Crisis in May and the outbreak of war between Israel and the UAR beginning 5 June (see Case #189) produced a profound transformation of the situation in Yemen. Egypt began withdrawing large numbers of troops, but a counter-offensive by them and Republican troops was launched in July. A Republican delegation visited Moscow to discuss Soviet military and economic aid to Yemen.

Under an agreement concluded in Khartoum between President Nasser and King Feisal, on 31 August 1967, Egyptian forces were to be withdrawn. The termination date of the crisis was 26 September when Egyptian forces began the final evacuation of Yemen. Saudi Arabia subsequently withdrew as well, but the civil war between North and South Yemen simmered for another two years. An unwritten agreement was finally concluded whereby a number of Royalist leaders would be appointed to the Presidential Council and the Government. The Republican regime was officially recognized by Saudi Arabia, the UK and France in July 1970.

References   See sources for Case #161.

(187) El Samu   The two actors in this crisis, a prelude to the Six Day War (see Case #189), were Israel and Jordan. It began on 12 November 1966 and ended on the 15th of that month.

Background   A series of border infiltrations and terrorist attacks on Israel emanating from Jordan took place from the summer of 1966 onwards.

Crisis   On 12 November an Israel crisis was triggered when an army command car was blown up by a mine near the Jordanian border. Three soldiers were killed and six wounded. In an effort to deter Jordan from further aid to the Palestinian infiltrators, Israel responded the following day with a commando raid on the village of El Samu, in Jordan, where Palestinian supporters were concentrated. Jordan's response to the raid was mobilization of its army. Heavy fighting took place and Israel withdrew a few hours later. Jordan appealed to the Security Council and issued an internal state of alert, especially against possible riots on the West Bank. Jordan ended the state of alert on the 15th, terminating the crisis for both countries.

The Secretary-General of the UN met with the Ambassadors of both actors, but the UN did not resolve the crisis.

References   See sources for Case #189.

(188) Ché Guevara   Guerrilla activity, led by Cuban revolutionary Ché Guevara, caused a crisis for Bolivia from 23 March to 10 October 1967.

Background   In October 1966 Ché Guevara left Cuba on a secret mission – to establish a guerrilla training camp in Bolivia to bring about the overthrow of the Bolivian Government. La Paz newspapers began reporting the presence of guerrilla forces in the Santa Cruz region in early March 1967. There was no comment on these reports by Bolivian authorities.

Crisis   An ambush by guerrillas of a large Bolivian army patrol in the Santa Cruz region on 23 March 1967 triggered a crisis for Bolivia. The incident was reported by Bolivian President Barrientos in a broadcast to the nation on the 27th. Bolivia feared that the pro-Cuban guerrilla movement might serve as a catalyst to revolt and would spread anti-government sentiment in the country. On 30 March Bolivian troops were moved to the southeast region, more forces were mobilized, and clashes with the guerrillas ensued. Bolivia's major response, the next day, was a request to the United States for arms and aid. A policy of containment was decided upon, and on 1 April Barrientos flew to the area in which 3000 Bolivian soldiers had encircled the guerrillas until an effective fighting force could be trained. On 11 April the US sent 40 advisors to train anti-guerrilla forces, in addition to modern weapons, including helicopters.

Bolivia decreed a state of siege on 2 June, suspending constitutional guarantees, after Bolivian students and miners staged demonstrations in support of the guerrillas. Towards the end of June the Bolivian Government confirmed officially that Ché Guevara was in command of a force of well-trained Cubans in southeast Bolivia. Bolivia appealed to Argentina to send troops to assist in the counter-insurgency operation but received supplies and arms only.

The OAS Foreign Ministers Conference met in Washington on 21 September, at Venezuela's request. At the meeting Bolivian representatives made public captured guerrilla documents, diaries and photographs. US Secretary of State Dean Rusk urged the OAS to tighten the diplomatic, economic and political isolation of Cuba. The OAS passed a resolution condemning Cuban subversive activities in the Western Hemisphere.

On 10 October Barrientos announced that Ché Guevara had been killed by government troops on the 8th and that his death had ended the guerrilla movement in Bolivia.

References   See general list.

(189) Six Day War   The six actors in this Middle East crisis were Egypt, Israel, Jordan, the Soviet Union, Syria and the United States. It began on 17 May and ended on 11 June 1967.

Background   Tension along the Israel–Syria border had been increasing since the autumn of 1966 due to the stepping up of attacks by Palestinian guerrillas based in Syria. On 7 April 1967 six Syrian MIGs were downed in an air battle over the Israel–Syria border. Israel repeatedly warned Syria that a massive reprisal would be inevitable if Damascus did not stop active support of Palestinian raids into Israel. On 14 May both Syria and Egypt announced a state of emergency based upon Soviet-inspired reports that Israel was concentrating troops on its northern border.

Crisis   Two hostile acts by Egypt on 17 May 1967 triggered a crisis for Israel: an overflight of Israel's nuclear research center at Dimona, and the dispatch of two additional Egyptian divisions into Sinai (others had crossed the Canal in the preceding two days). On the 18th UN Secretary-General U Thant acceded to President Nasser's demand, two days earlier, to withdraw the United Nations Emergency Force (UNEF) from Sinai. (It had functioned since the 1956 Suez–Sinai Campaign – see Case #120.) Army reserves were mobilized in Israel and Egypt on the 19th and

21st. And on 23 May Egypt announced the closure of the Straits of Tiran, thus blockading the Israeli port of Eilat. The British and United States Governments termed this act a violation of international law, while the Soviet Union blamed Israel for the dangerous situation in the Middle East. Efforts by the US and UK to form a naval flotilla failed. The US Sixth Fleet moved towards the Eastern Mediterranean. The Security Council met at the request of Canada and Denmark. On 30 May a Defense Pact was signed between Jordan and Egypt.

Israel's major response to its crisis was a decision on 4 June to launch a preemptive strike. This was implemented by an air attack on Egypt's air force bases on 5 June, destroying Egyptian air power and triggering a crisis for Jordan and Egypt. Despite an Israeli assurance to Jordan via the United Nations that, if Jordan kept out of the war, Israel would not initiate any military action against its eastern neighbor, Jordan responded the same day by opening fire on Jerusalem and bombing Netanya. Israel destroyed the small Jordanian Air Force and, by noon of 7 June, captured the Jordan-controlled Old City of Jerusalem. Egypt's response, on 5 June, was to launch a counter-attack against Israel.

The crisis trigger for the United States was a message from Premier Kosygin on 6 June threatening Soviet intervention. The crises for Syria and the Soviet Union were triggered on the 9th by Israeli advances on the Golan Heights. Syria responded immediately by bombarding Israeli border settlements. The next day the Soviets responded with a "hot line" telephone call from Kosygin to Johnson threatening Soviet action unless Israel halted operations at once. The major US response was an immediate order by President Johnson to change the course of the Sixth Fleet and to cut the 100-mile restriction from the Syrian coast to 50 miles, signalling that the US was prepared to resist Soviet intervention in the Arab–Israel war. Syria accepted a cease-fire on 10 June. The following day the cease-fire came into effect for all the other actors, terminating the 1967 Middle East Crisis.

Five East European states, together with the Soviet Union, severed diplomatic relations with Israel, namely, Bulgaria, Czechoslovakia, Hungary, Poland and Yugoslavia. The UN helped to escalate the crisis, by the removal of UNEF, but it also contributed to the more rapid termination of the crisis through the efforts of the Security Council and cease-fire resolutions.

References Bar-Zohar 1970; Brecher 1980; Bull 1976; Burdett 1970; Dayan 1976; Draper 1968; Eban 1977; Higgins 1969; Hussein 1969; Johnson 1971; Khalidi 1975; Kimche and Bawly 1968; Lall 1970; Laqueur 1968; O'Ballance 1972; Rafael 1972; Safran 1969; Shiloah Center 1971; Velie 1969; Wilson 1971.

(190) Cyprus II

One of several international crises over the Mediterranean island-state, among Cyprus, Greece and Turkey, broke out on 15 November 1967 and ended on 4 December of that year.

Background The cease-fire of August 1964 (see Case #169) was breached in 1967 in a clash between Turkish–Cypriot and Greek–Cypriot forces.

Crisis The crisis trigger for Turkey was an attack by the Greek–Cypriot National Guard against two Turkish–Cypriot villages on 15 November 1967. Turkey responded on the 17th with a resolution by its Grand National Assembly which authorized the government to decide upon the number and destination of armed forces to be dispatched to the area to deal with any new situation which might occur and to call for General Grivas, head of the Greek forces in Cyprus, to be sent home. This constituted the crisis trigger for Cyprus and Greece. The Greek response was to recall Grivas for consultations on 19 November. Greece also indicated that it was ready to negotiate. On 22 November UN Secretary-General U Thant sent a message to the three states urging them to avoid war. Cyprus, on 24 November, called for an urgent meeting of the Security Council, which subsequently met and discussed the situation. Discussions between Greece and Turkey took place with Cyrus Vance, former US Deputy Secretary of Defense, as mediator. An agreement was reached on 1 December 1967 between Turkey and Greece. Cyprus signed on 4 December. Greece agreed to withdraw all troops from Cyprus that exceeded the number specified in the London and Zurich agreements of 1959–60. Turkey cancelled large-scale preparations for an invasion of Cyprus.

References   Adams and Cottrell 1968; Crawshaw 1978; Foley and Scobie 1975; Patrick 1976; Volkan 1979.

(191) Pueblo   A crisis for the US began on 22 January and ended on 23 December 1968.

Background   The USS *Pueblo* was an intelligence ship which had been stationed off North Korea purportedly on an oceanographic research mission, with orders to stay at least 14 miles off the coast of North Korea. Representatives of the US and North Korea had been engaged in negotiations at Panmunjom since the end of the Korean War in 1953, but were unsuccessful in areas other than the exchange of prisoners. Relations between North Korea and the USSR were strained, and the former wished to assert its influence in East Asia. Guerrillas from North Korea infiltrated into Seoul and attacked the South Korea Presidential Palace in January 1968.

Crisis   The trigger for the US crisis was the seizure of the *Pueblo* on 22 January 1968 by North Korean patrol and torpedo boats. That day the US aircraft carrier *Enterprise* and its task force were diverted from their course toward the North Vietnam coast and ordered into the Sea of Japan. At the Panmunjom Armistice Talks the Americans demanded the return of the *Pueblo* and its crew. This demand was refused, with North Korea claiming that the *Pueblo* was spying in its territorial waters. The US insisted that the *Pueblo* was 25 miles off the North Korean coast. The Soviets refused a request by the US Ambassador in Moscow to use their good offices to bring about the *Pueblo's* release. An appeal was also made to the Security Council. The major response of the US was to call up army and airforce reservists ✓ on 25 January. The next day the Soviet Union, which supported North Korea's claim that the *Pueblo* was in its territorial waters, sent a trawler to shadow the *Enterprise.* A second request for USSR intervention, made by US Ambassador Thompson, was rejected. *Inter alia* the incident provided the means for an improvement of relations between the Soviet Union and North Korea.

By 3 February the US was able to reach agreement with the North Koreans to continue to use the Panmunjom talks as a vehicle for negotiating the end of the *Pueblo* Crisis. The US then withdrew the *Enterprise* and its task force, and the military threat decreased. The admission of spying by the *Pueblo* commander was broadcast by North Korea on 16 February. It was rejected by the US as fabricated.

Negotiations continued for 10 months until an acceptable compromise was reached on 23 December 1968. The US representative, Major-General Woodward, signed an apology stating that the *Pueblo* had been in North Korean waters and acknowledged that the confessions of its commander and, later, some crew members were genuine. Before signing it, however, Woodward read a public statement disavowing the apology. The crew was returned to South Korea, but the ship was never recovered. The UN was ineffective in abating the crisis.

References   Armbrister 1970; Druks 1971; Johnson 1971; Kaplan 1981; Koh 1969; Murphy 1971.

(192) Tet Offensive   The Tet Crisis for South Vietnam and the United States began on 30 January and ended on 31 March 1968.

Background   A major escalation in the Vietnam War had occurred in February 1965 when American planes bombed North Vietnam in retaliation for a Vietcong raid against US installations at Pleiku (see Case #180). Buddhist monks in South Vietnam had launched a peace movement and had called for the withdrawal of all foreign troops from North and South Vietnam and a reunification of the Vietnam nation. The United States opposed a negotiated settlement at that time. On 2 March 1965 American bombers attacked North Vietnam. A changed American policy aimed at compelling the enemy to negotiate on Washington's terms. By the end of 1966 American military personnel in South Vietnam had increased to 375,000. The escalation of the air war proceeded steadily. In early 1965, too, the USSR and China began to provide economic assistance and military equipment to Hanoi. The military operations had gradually been expanded to include the adjacent countries of Southeast Asia. The US bombed the Ho Chi Minh Trail in Laos and retreating enemy troops in Cambodia. Bombing was stopped briefly on two occasions in an effort to bring about negotiations, but Hanoi's demand to seat the NFL (Communist-controlled National Liberation Front) of South Vietnam at the conference table as a full and equal partner was rejected by the US. Raids were resumed with greater American involvement in Vietnam.

In 1967 an important shift in Soviet policy occurred, indicating a desire to end the war. Each side began by softening its position, leading to cautious optimism. In the summer of 1967 a North Vietnamese offensive undermined that appraisal. North Vietnam's attempt to turn the tide of the war and to place Hanoi and the Vietcong in a stronger position for negotiations led to an attack on a US Marine outpost near the Demilitarized Zone between the two parts of Vietnam on 21 January 1968. The Vietcong announced a three-day truce from the 27th, but South Vietnam revealed its decision to continue the bombing of the North. During the Tet (lunar New Year) holiday the Vietcong launched its biggest offensive.

Crisis On 30 January 1968 an attack on Saigon, Hué and 36 of the 44 provincial capitals in South Vietnam, along with military installations and district towns, triggered an intra-war crisis for South Vietnam. The South Vietnamese responded on 2 February by urging an extension of the bombing of North Vietnam which would cover all military objectives. After heavy fighting the North Vietnamese were repelled from all the towns into which they had infiltrated. A state of martial law in the south was declared by President Thieu. In Saigon a 24-hour curfew was imposed so that the South Vietnamese Army could drive out the North Vietnamese unhindered by the civilian population. American infantry and tanks were rushed to the city on 1 February and an American general assumed control of the whole operation. The main Vietcong forces withdrew on 3 February; but on the 18th another attack was launched in and around the capital. Fighting continued until the 24th, when the Vietcong troops were expelled once more. This terminated the Tet Crisis for South Vietnam. The US ordered more combat troops into the area.

A pessimistic report on 27 February by the Chairman of the JCS, General Wheeler, on the situation in Vietnam, shocked Washington and triggered a US crisis. President Johnson's major response to the Tet Offensive was an announcement on 31 March that he had ordered a halt to the bombing of North Vietnam and an appeal for negotiations. This policy decision was identified as the termination date for the US intra-war crisis, for it marked the beginning of a fundamental change in Washington's appraisal of the Vietnam War. The Vietcong was defeated militarily, but scored a psychological and political victory. Its belief that a massive offensive against the cities and towns would demonstrate the weakness of the government in the south and bring about a general uprising of civilians proved wrong and caused its military defeat; but the battle raised public opposition in the US to a new level of intensity. The President and his advisors were shocked by the suddenness and magnitude of the Tet Offensive; and this proved to be a turning point on the American path to disengagement from Vietnam five years later.

A mediation proposal by the UN Secretary-General during the Tet Crisis proved ineffective. The Warsaw Treaty Organization condemned South Vietnam and the US. Soviet involvement included active military personnel in the anti-aircraft operations by the North and the supply of arms to Hanoi.

References Adams and McCoy 1970; Brandon 1970; Dommen 1971; Herring 1979; Johnson 1971; Lewy 1978.

(193) Karameh   This crisis between Israel and Jordan lasted from 18 to 22 March 1968.

Background From 15 February to mid-March 1968 Israel reported 37 sabotage raids from Jordan causing death and injuries among Israeli soldiers and civilians.

Crisis A crisis for Israel was triggered on 18 March when an Israeli school bus went over a mine near the Jordan border; two children were killed and 28 wounded. Defense Minister Dayan issued a warning to Jordan to prevent further border crossings by

Palestinian *fedaiyun*. The bus incident and Dayan's warning also triggered a crisis for Jordan: King Hussein stated that on that day he perceived a threat of invasion from Israel. Israel's response was a raid on the village of Karameh, a *fedaiyun* base in Jordan, on 21 March. There was also an appeal to the United Nations. The Jordanian response was to dispatch armed forces to the site. Heavy fighting followed, with severe losses on both sides. Israel's crisis ended when it withdrew IDF forces, on 21 March. Jordan's crisis ended the following day, when it reopened the Allenby bridge linking the Israel-occupied West Bank and Jordan. UN activity took the form of a discussion in the Security Council; no resolution was passed.

References   See general list.

(194) Prague Spring   There were six actors in the Prague Spring Crisis: Bulgaria, Czechoslovakia, East Germany, Hungary, Poland and the Soviet Union. It lasted from 9 April to 18 October 1968.

Background   During late 1967 domestic unrest and political conflict within the Czechoslovak Communist Party led to the overthrow of Antonin Novotny as First Secretary of the Communist Party on 5 January 1968 and as the President on 23 March 1968. Alexander Dubček, his successor as party leader, proposed an "Action Program" which was accepted by the Czechoslovak Party Central Committee. The Program proposed solutions to the Czech economic crisis, the Slovak question, the rehabilitation of party leaders sentenced during the purges of the 1950s, and a way to deal with the dissent of students and intellectuals. Censorship was abolished, economic controls and central planning by the government were reduced and restructured, and new members were appointed to political posts. A more independent foreign policy was pledged, but it would conform to the interests of the Warsaw Treaty Organization (WTO) in general and the USSR in particular.

Polish leader Wladyslaw Gomulka and East German leader Walter Ulbricht feared that the infection of liberalism, already in its early stages in their countries, would spread and undermine their respective positions. In the Soviet Union apprehension increased that the "Prague Spring" would encourage Ukrainian nationalist sentiment, and the possibility emerged that liberalization would spill over into neighboring states. Furthermore, the unity and strength of the Warsaw Pact as a whole was seen to be in jeopardy with Czechoslovakia's decreased reliability as an ally. The possibility of military intervention in Czechoslovakia alarmed Hungary and Bulgaria which perceived a threat to their own political regimes.

Warsaw Pact delegates met in Dresden in March 1968 to discuss the situation. Military exercises of the WTO were decided upon, and these were held in June 1968.

Crisis   The publication of Czechoslovakia's "Action Program" on 9 April 1968 triggered a crisis for East Germany and Poland. A crisis was triggered for Bulgaria and Hungary on 8 May after they had participated in a meeting with delegates from the Soviet Union, Poland and East Germany: it was at that time that Bulgaria and Hungary became seriously alarmed over the situation in Czechoslovakia, since military intervention now appeared as a very real possibility. The stability of East Europe, including Bulgaria's own regime, seemed at stake. Hungary was concerned over the possibility of having to participate in a military attack initiated by the Soviet Union and East Germany.

An open letter in Prague on 27 June, "Two Thousand Words," which called for the speeding up of Czech democratization and criticizing the conditions inside the Czechoslovak Communist Party prior to the January reforms, triggered a crisis for the Soviet Union: Moscow interpreted this letter as proof that the political situation in Czechoslovakia was out of control. Due to increasing tension, the Warsaw Pact Command delayed removing its troops from Czechoslovakia upon completion of the military exercises held there.

The responses of Hungary, Bulgaria, Poland and East Germany were contained in an ultimatum to Czechoslovakia on 15 July. A letter, signed by the USSR and the four East European states, singled out the "Two Thousand Words" manifesto as a threat to the vital interests of the whole Communist community. When the Czech Head of Defense and Security criticized the Warsaw Pact structure, the USSR demanded his dismissal. Dubček acceded, signalling that military resistance was no longer a realistic option for Czechoslovakia. Intense diplomatic negotiations followed at a meeting held between Czech leaders and nine of the 11 members of the Soviet Politburo. The result was verbal promises to resolve the crisis, confirmed on 3 August by the Bratislava Declaration. WTO troops were withdrawn from Czechoslovakia but remained concentrated along its borders.

Ulbricht met with Dubček on 12 August and reported to the Soviet Politburo that the Czech leaders were unwilling to live up to the terms of the Bratislava agreement. Reports about the enthusiastic reception in Prague of Yugoslav President Tito and Romanian Party Leader Ceauşescu irritated the Soviets, who feared Czech influence on other Pact members which might undermine their loyalty to the Soviet Union. The major Soviet response to the crisis, the invasion of Czechoslovakia, was decided on 17 August after three days of talks among military leaders of East Germany, Poland and the USSR.

Dubček, who continued to disregard unmistakeable signs of a new Soviet debate on Czechoslovakia and who did not wish to create anti-Soviet feelings, did not inform the Czech President, Svoboda, about warnings received from Hungarian leader Kádár or those contained in a letter from the Soviet Politburo on 19 August. The invasion of Czechoslovakia began on 20 August. It was the crisis trigger for Czechoslovakia and the termination date for Bulgaria, Hungary, East Germany and Poland. The Warsaw Pact armies acquired total control of Czechoslovak territory within 36 hours. The Czech response, on the 21st, was compliance. Svoboda flew to Moscow for talks with the Soviet leadership and pressed for the release of Czech leaders Dubček, Cernik and Smrkovský, who had been taken prisoner during the invasion. With Czech promises to control and arrest "counter-revolutionary" elements, the Moscow Protocol was signed on 18 October 1968 legalizing the presence of Soviet troops in Czechoslovakia and terminating the crisis for the USSR and Czechoslovakia.

The destruction of the Czech reform movement was viewed as a victory by Bulgaria, East Germany, Poland and the USSR. However, Hungary was not pleased by the triumph of the hardliners within the Soviet bloc, since it might threaten Hungary's own progressive movement.

A UN Security Council draft resolution censuring the invasion as a violation of the UN Charter was vetoed by the Soviet Union on 21 August. US President Johnson condemned the Soviet actions and cancelled all diplomatic activities scheduled with the USSR regarding future SALT I talks. NATO Foreign Ministers discussed the situation on 8 October, but no meaningful decisions were taken.

References Bethell 1969; Bohlen 1973; Dawisha 1978, 1984; Golan 1971; Grey 1967; Johnson 1971; Paul 1971; Shawcross 1970; Szulc 1971a; Valenta 1979a, 1979b; Westwood 1973; Wolfe 1970.

(195) Essequibo Territory

A crisis for Guyana, in a long-standing dispute with Venezuela, occurred from 9 July to some time in August 1968.

Background An 1899 Arbitration Tribunal awarded Great Britain approximately 45,000 miles of the 53,000 square miles of disputed territory between British Guiana and Venezuela. The boundary was demarcated in 1905. Until 1962, when Britain announced Guyana's forthcoming independence, Venezuela accepted the territorial status quo. Thereafter it began pressing for a revision of the boundary, insisting that the disputed area, which represented 62% of Guyana's entire territory, be returned to Venezuela. After independence in 1966, Guyana protested a Venezuelan occupation of the island of Ankokoin in the Guyuni River, half of which had been awarded to British Guiana. In February 1966 a mixed commission was established by Britain, Venezuela and Guyana to seek a satisfactory solution to the boundary dispute within four years.

Crisis On 9 July 1968 Dr. Raúl Leoni, President of Venezuela, issued a decree which annexed to Venezuela the territorial waters lying from three to 12 miles along the coast of the Guyana Essequibo. Venezuelan naval craft were later reported patrolling outside the three-mile limit. Guyana's response was a protest note to Venezuela, a complaint to UN Secretary-General U Thant, protests to Latin American members of the United Nations, and a complaint by Guyana's Foreign Minister to President Johnson. It was reported that, although the US wanted to maintain a neutral position in the dispute, it did appeal to Venezuela to revoke the decree. Guyana declared Venezuela's decree to be null and void and announced that it would resist an invasion by Venezuela. The crisis faded in August 1968.

The UN Secretary-General offered his good offices to settle the dispute. Barbados expressed concern about Venezuela's contemplated use of force, in a note from its Prime Minister to the Foreign Minister of Venezuela.

References Ince 1970.

(196) Pre-War of Attrition

A crisis for Israel took place between 7 September and 7 November 1968.

Background By 11 June 1967, at the end of the Six Day War (see Case #189), Israel was in control of territory more than three times the size of the state when the war began, bringing with it a marked improvement in its defensible frontiers. Among them were the Suez Canal and the entire Sinai Peninsula which created a large, armed territory inaccessible to Egypt.

Soviet arms shipments to Egypt began again immediately after the Six Day War. By the autumn of 1968 Egypt's weaponry was restored to its pre-June 1967 strength. Israel was totally dependent on the United States for heavy weapons, notably planes and tanks, as a result of a French embargo imposed in early June 1967.

Crisis On 7 September 1968 a crisis was triggered for Israel when Egypt launched a heavy artillery attack on Israeli military outposts along the east side of the Suez Canal, known as the Bar-Lev Line. Its major response, on 31 October, was a decision to destroy an Egyptian power station at Naj Hamadi. This display of force achieved a quick termination to the crisis. On 7 November Egypt decided to postpone further military activity and to create civilian and military units to guard likely targets of an Israeli attack on the Nile Valley. Several months of tranquillity followed, until March 1969 when Nasser launched the War of Attrition to compel Israel's withdrawal from the Sinai Peninsula (see Case #200).

References See sources for Case #200.

(197) Beirut Airport

A crisis for Lebanon began on 28 December 1968. The crisis terminated sometime in January 1969.

Background On 26 December 1968 the Lebanon-based PFLP (Popular Front for the Liberation of Palestine) attacked an Israeli civilian plane at Athens International Airport. One passenger was killed. Israel's policy had long been to retaliate against the host country in the hope of compelling the Arab state to restrain Palestinian attacks on Israeli citizens and property.

Crisis The crisis trigger for Lebanon was Israel's retaliation raid on Beirut International Airport on 28 December 1968, destroying 13 jetliners belonging to the Middle East Airlines, and other Lebanese-owned planes. There was no loss of life. The Lebanese security forces did not intervene. Lebanon's major response, the following day, was a complaint against Israel to the Security Council. Two days later

Lebanon declared a state of alert and mobilized reserve forces. The raid on Beirut accentuated Lebanon's civil tensions and triggered an internal political crisis in that country. The international crisis ended some time in January 1969.

There was widespread condemnation of the Israeli raid, including a protest by the Vatican. On 7 January 1969 France reiterated its policy of a total embargo of all military supplies destined for Israel. The US offered aid to Lebanon and put its Sixth Fleet on low-level alert. The Soviet Union confined its political activity to statements at the United Nations. The Security Council passed a resolution condemning Israel.

References See general list.

(198) Vietnam Spring Offensive

A North Vietnam countrywide offensive into South Vietnam led to an intra-war crisis for South Vietnam and the United States from 22 February until 8 June 1969.

Background The 1968 Tet Offensive (see Case #192) broke the stalemate that had characterized the Vietnam War since 1966. Thereafter US policy underwent several changes. President Johnson restricted US bombing to south of the 20th Parallel and offered to begin negotiations with North Vietnam, which responded favorably. Agreement was reached to begin talks in Paris. In October 1968 the US announced that all air, naval and artillery attacks against North Vietnam would be halted on 1 November. The US also agreed to allow representatives of the (South Vietnam) Vietminh National Liberation Front to participate in the talks, despite South Vietnam objections. Nevertheless, while war raged in the area, all parties maintained inflexible positions at the talks. On 20 January 1969 Richard Nixon was installed as President of the United States.

Crisis On 22 February 1969 Hanoi launched an offensive into South Vietnam, the day before a scheduled Nixon visit to Europe, triggering a crisis for the US. According to Nixon, the offensive was a deliberate test, clearly designed to take the measure of the new Nixon Administration. On 23 February Nixon ordered the bombing of sanctuaries in Cambodia but cancelled the order 2 days later upon the recommendation of National Security Advisor Kissinger. On 4 March orders were once more given, only to be retracted on the 7th. Meanwhile US casualties were mounting. Finally, as the North Vietnam attack continued and American casualties remained intolerably high, Nixon reverted to his earlier decisions and, on 15 March, orders were given to bomb Cambodian sanctuaries (Operation "Menu"). These orders were carried out three days later, terminating the US crisis on 18 March. Thereafter there was a steady decline in US casualties in South Vietnam.

The secret bombing of Communist sanctuaries in Cambodia put military pressure on the North Vietnamese. Nevertheless, they were still able to launch a major attack throughout South Vietnam on 12 May 1969: it contained the largest number of strikes since the Tet Offensive of 1968. These attacks contributed to a crisis for South Vietnam. The crisis was accentuated by Nixon's 14 May speech in which he elaborated an eight-point peace plan for Vietnam which included the setting of a precise timetable for withdrawal and a cease-fire under international supervision. Saigon's fears about US intentions and a possible change in the military balance, which would threaten South Vietnam's existence, caused President Thieu to object strongly to US proposals for withdrawal from South Vietnam. On 17 May Thieu responded by calling for a meeting with Nixon in order to coordinate a common policy. Nixon and Thieu met on 8 June on Midway Island. Nixon's assurances that day of steadfast American support terminated the crisis for South Vietnam. After the meeting Nixon announced the redeployment of 25,000 US troops from Vietnam. Although Thieu was appeased by US guarantees, he perceived the withdrawals as an irreversible process which would end with the departure of all American forces from Vietnam.

There was no UN activity, although Secretary-General U Thant issued a statement applauding the peace efforts of both sides.

SEATO and CENTO meetings took place in May at which the Vietnam War was reviewed.

References *Facts on File* 1973-74; Kalb and Kalb 1974; Kissinger 1979; Nixon 1978; Shaw-cross 1979.

(199) Ussuri River   The People's Republic of China and the Soviet Union were involved in a border crisis from 2 March to 20 October 1969.

Background The ideological rivalry between the USSR and the PRC surfaced with Khrushchev's accession to power in the Soviet Union in 1955. At the conference of world Communist parties in 1960, an open split developed. For a decade before this crisis there had been a series of clashes along the Sino-Soviet border. Border talks in 1964 had been unilaterally suspended by China. In 1965 the USSR initiated a military build-up along China's borders. The impact of China's traumatic Cultural Revolution was still fresh. There had been large population transfers in China from urban to rural areas. The Prague Spring Crisis had terminated with a Soviet bloc invasion of Czechoslovakia in August 1968 (see Case #194). And by March the following year Soviet preoccupation with Berlin had subsided, allowing Moscow to concentrate on China. On 16 February 1969 the Chinese were aware that Soviet forces along the Ussuri River had been placed on the highest alert.

Crisis A crisis for the USSR was initiated by a Chinese ambush of Soviet troops on 2 March 1969. Its response, which triggered a crisis for China, was a massive military attack against Chinese forces stationed along the Ussuri River, on 15 March. China responded militarily on the day of the attack. There were considerable casualties on both sides. Tension continued along the border, but there were no further military incidents. Following the clashes, there were mass demonstrations in Beijing and in Moscow. On 29 March the USSR issued the first of a series of moderate diplomatic notes urging China to negotiate. A joint Sino-Soviet Commission to regulate navigation on border rivers reconvened on 11 May and reached agreement on 8 August. On 13 August, when the Soviets threatened to bomb the Chinese nuclear facilities situated several thousand miles away in the remote province of Sinkiang, Beijing agreed to negotiate on the larger border problems between the two countries.

After the Sinkiang threat, a brief meeting took place on 11 September between Premiers Kosygin and Chou En-lai. Negotiations on the topic of Sino-Soviet border disputes began on 20 October, which marked the crisis termination date for both actors. The talks proved to be inconclusive, and while the conflict continued, the polemics had been considerably toned down. US activity was limited to political statements. The Warsaw Treaty Organization met, but it had no effect on abating the crisis. The UN remained aloof.

References Berton 1969; Borisov and Koloskov 1975; Gelber 1970; Hinton 1971, 1975, 1976; Horn 1973; Jacobsen 1974; *Keesing's* 1970; Levine 1969; Lowenthal 1971; Maxwell 1973, 1978; Powell 1973; Rhee 1970; Shapiro 1969; Simon 1973; Sulzberger 1974; Tai-Sung-An 1973.

(200) War of Attrition I   Israel was the sole crisis actor from 8 March to 28 July 1969.

Background During the Six Day War of 1967 (see Case #189) Israel had captured all of the Sinai Peninsula, and remained there as an occupying army. In the autumn of 1968 Egyptian leaders reached the conclusion that the strategic balance had turned in their favor permitting a limited military confrontation with Israel along the Canal. Accordingly, Egyptian artillery bombarded Israeli positions on the east bank of the Canal in September and October (see Case #196).

Crisis Commencing on 8 March 1969, intense and sustained Egyptian artillery fire was directed toward Israeli positions along the Canal. After heightened losses in the months of May, June and July, Israel's major response was a decision on 20 July to escalate the crisis by introducing air raids into Eygpt. Toward the end of July, as a consequence of Israeli Air Force actions, Egypt was forced to a reappraisal: an

Egyptian offensive to cross the Canal was now out of the question. Israeli threat perceptions declined and air raids were suspended on 28 July, the termination date of Israel's crisis. UN Observer Forces and Big Four talks under the auspices of the UN contributed marginally to crisis abatement. The Soviet Union supplied arms and missiles to Egypt and influenced it to abandon plans for a cross-Canal military operation. The US was politically involved as well.

References   Bar-Siman-Tov 1980; Brecher 1974; Dayan 1976; Eban 1977; Whetten 1974.

(201) EC-121 Spy Plane   A crisis for the United States over this plane incident lasted from 15 to 26 April 1969.

Background   The previous crisis between the United States and North Korea was the North Korean seizure of the USS *Pueblo* and capture of its crew in what the US claimed was international waters. It began on 22 January 1968, but was not concluded until December of that year, less than four months before the outbreak of a new crisis between the two countries (see Case #191).

Crisis   On 14 April 1969 a United States Navy EC-121 reconnaissance plane with 31 men aboard was shot down by a North Korean aircraft over the Sea of Japan. In a radio broadcast North Korea claimed that the plane was flying deep into its territorial airspace. The US countered with the statement that the plane had never left the international airspace over the Sea of Japan. In the US an *ad hoc* group of the National Security Council was formed to recommend to the President alternative ways to deal with the crisis. This group was the beginning of the Washington Special Action Group (WSAG), organized to assist in crisis management.

The options presented to President Nixon ranged from diplomatic protests to strong military retaliation, for US credibility and its influence as a superpower were at stake. The US response was an order by President Nixon to resume the reconnaissance flights, accompanied by armed escorts, and the redisposition of the strong American naval force into the Sea of Japan. The Soviet Union became involved early in the crisis when the Nixon Administration requested Moscow's assistance in the search for the plane and missing crewmen. On 22 April the USSR issued a mild protest against American activity in the Sea of Japan. The crisis ended on 26 April when the US naval task force was moved from the Sea of Japan into the Yellow Sea, after no further incidents occurred.

References   Hersh 1983; Kalb and Kalb 1974; Kaplan 1981; Kissinger 1979; Nixon 1978.

(202) Shatt-al-Arab II   The second crisis for Iran and Iraq over the Shatt-al-Arab lasted from 15 April to 30 October 1969.

Background   The lower part of the Shatt-al-Arab River serves as a border between Iraq and Iran. According to an agreement concluded in 1937, the Shatt is almost completely within Iraq's sovereignty. Questions of dues and general procedures caused continued tension between the two states, and a crisis occurred between them in 1959-60 (see Case #138). Negotiations to reach agreement were deadlocked in 1968.

Crisis   Iran's crisis was triggered on 15 April 1969 when its Ambassador to Baghdad was informed by Iraq's Deputy Foreign Minister that Iraq regarded the Shatt-al-Arab as part of its territory and requested ships flying Iran's flag to lower their flag when entering the estuary. Furthermore, no Iranian nationals were to be aboard. If the demands were not met, Iraq would use force and would not allow vessels destined for Iranian ports to use the river. Iran responded on 19 April by declaring the 1937 treaty null and void and demanded its renegotiation. Iran's Deputy Foreign Minister warned that any violation of Iran's sovereign rights would be met with full retaliation. The nullification of the 1937 treaty was the crisis trigger for Iraq. On 20 April Iraq responded by reiterating the validity of the treaty and reserved the right to take legal and legitimate action. Iran then concentrated its forces around Khorramshahr and Abadan and put its navy on full alert, while Iraqi forces were placed on alert at the port of Basra.

On 22 April, as a show of force, Iran sent a freighter through the Shatt, escorted by naval craft and protected by an umbrella of jet fighters. It was the first Iranian vessel to pass through the Shatt flying Iran's flag since the outbreak of the crisis. An Iraqi naval launch allowed the vessel to go through. This act of compliance constituted the Iraqi response to the crisis. Another escorted Iranian vessel passed through the Shatt unmolested on the 25th.

On 28 April Iraq circulated a document to UN delegates complaining of Iran's actions in the Shatt-al-Arab. This charge was answered on 5 May by Iran which appealed to the UN Secretary-General to send a representative to Iran in order to witness the influx of Iranians expelled from Iraq who had been subjected to inhumane treatment by Iraqi authorities. Notes were also sent to the Security Council. During October the addresses to the General Assembly by the Foreign Ministers of both states contained accusations against one another in the Shatt-al-Arab Crisis. The CENTO Ministerial Council conferred in Teheran on 26 and 27 May and issued a signed communiqué by Britain, Pakistan, Iran, Turkey and the US, disclosing discussion of the dispute.

The crisis ended on 30 October 1969 when the Information Ministers of Iran and Iraq decided to terminate the propaganda campaign against each other with the hope that this would prepare the atmosphere for a settlement between the two countries. Several Middle East states attempted to mediate: Jordan, Kuwait, Saudi Arabia and Turkey. Whereas Iraq was ready to accept mediation, Iran viewed these efforts unenthusiastically. A full-scale war between Iran and Iraq, catalyzed by the Shatt-al-Arab dispute, was to break out in September 1980.

References Chubin and Zabih 1974; Ramazani 1972; Shimoni 1977.

(203) Football War A crisis between El Salvador and Honduras began on 15 June and terminated on 30 July 1969.

Background Honduras, a sparsely-populated country, was the domicile of large numbers of Salvadorans who had left overcrowded El Salvador in the decade preceding this crisis. Salvadorans slipped over the border into Honduras to farm, squat or work on the banana plantations. Reports of their ill-treatment were brought to the attention of El Salvador. In Honduras the economic situation was bleak, with societal unrest increasing. The first football game between teams of the two countries in the elimination rounds of the 1970 World Cup Championship was played in the Honduras capital, Tegucigalpa, on 8 June 1969. Following the opener, Salvadoran players complained of suffering at the hands of their hosts. Violence in the stadium followed. In the next game, on 15 June in San Salvador, Honduran players were subjected to reciprocal treatment by their hosts, and riots broke out once again.

Crisis The aftermath of the soccer game, combined with reports from large numbers of Salvadoran refugees fleeing from Honduras and alleging maltreatment and confiscation of property, triggered a crisis for El Salvador on 15 June 1969. El Salvador declared a state of alert and appealed to the OAS. On 26 and 27 June diplomatic relations between the two countries were broken. Tension, accompanied by incidents along the border, continued until El Salvador's major response: troops crossed into Honduras on 14 July. Honduras responded to that trigger on the same day by air attacks on Salvadoran cities and ports. A cease-fire, due to effective OAS negotiation, came about on 18 July. By this time casualties on both sides exceeded 2000.

El Salvador's victories led to the conquest of sizeable chunks of Honduran territory from which it refused to withdraw after the cease-fire. Subsequent threats of OAS sanctions against El Salvador convinced it to do so. A compromise settlement was accepted by both sides, and this came into effect on 30 July 1969, marking the termination of the crisis.

The US embargo on arms to both countries was perceived by Honduras as favoring the better-equipped Salvadoran Army. At the same time, there was

American pressure on El Salvador to withdraw from the Honduran territory it had invaded. Costa Rica, Guatemala and Nicaragua attempted to mediate at the beginning of the crisis, but without success.

References   Cable 1969; Holly 1979.

(204) Cairo Agreement   Syria's acquiescence in Palestinian Arab guerrilla activity caused a crisis for Lebanon from 22 October to 3 November 1969.

Background   The political equilibrium within Lebanon was endangered when Palestinian Liberation Organization (PLO) guerrilla groups, based in Lebanon or infiltrating from across the Syrian border, stepped up their sabotage operations against Israel, bringing about retaliations in 1968. For some time clashes between forces of the Lebanon Government and Palestinian guerillas had been taking place. The clashes always centered around the issues that occupied Lebanon in the late 1960s and throughout the 1970s, namely, the PLO's right to maintain bases in Lebanon and its demands to be allowed to operate from Lebanese soil against targets in Israel. Following an Israeli raid on Beirut's International Airport (see Case #197), political upheavals in April 1969 left Lebanon with a caretaker government for seven months. Syrian intervention posed an ever-present threat to its political regime.

Crisis   On 22 October 1969 Syria triggered a crisis for Lebanon by closing its border with Lebanon and concentrating military units there. That day the PLO announced that serious clashes had occurred with Lebanese government forces after an attack on its bases in the south along the Israel border. Lebanon, while continuing its military response against the guerrillas, began meetings with representatives of Egypt and Jordan on the 24th. Syria was also approached by Lebanon for negotiation in a phone conversation between the two Presidents a day earlier. The crisis ended on 3 November when an agreement was reached betweeen the Lebanese Army and Government and the PLO in Cario, with the mediation of President Nasser. The Cairo Agreement contained a *modus operandi* for the guerrilla groups, limiting their bases to the southeastern corner of Lebanon. Sabotage operations against Israel were also limited and some army control was imposed. The United States and the Soviet Union gave political support to Lebanon and Syria, respectively.
Syria's border with Lebanon was reopened 11 days after the Cairo Agreement.

References   See general list.

(205) War of Attrition II   The three crisis actors in the final phase of the War of Attrition, from 7 January to 7 August 1970, were Egypt, Israel and the Soviet Union.

Background   The War of Attrition began on 8 March 1969, following a preliminary Egyptian shelling in September–October 1968 (see Cases #196 and #200). The intensity of violence had been reduced on 28 July 1969 as a result of an Egyptian reappraisal of prospects for a cross-Canal operation. By the end of 1969 fighting had gradually escalated leading to an Israeli consideration to launch deep penetration air raids into Egypt after its air force had successfully destroyed SAM-2 and Egyptian anti-aircraft systems in October.

Crisis   The Israeli decision to launch deep penetration air raids triggered a crisis for Egypt on 7 January 1970. Nasser, anxious not to lose the War of Attrition and afraid that the raids might produce domestic pressure which would endanger his regime, decided to appeal to the Soviet Union. The major Egyptian response was Nasser's visit to Moscow, starting on 22 January, to request Soviet intervention, including advisors, and the introduction of a sophisticated defense weapons system in Egypt. Nasser's threat to resign if his requests were not met was the trigger for the Soviet crisis. Its major response, on 25 January, was to grant Egypt larger military support. On 19 March Soviet anti-aircraft systems were placed in Egypt near the Canal, triggering a crisis for Israel.

Israel responded on 24 March by intensive bombing of the missile sites. One escalation point was a dogfight between Israeli and Soviet planes on 18 April, the only direct Israeli encounter with Soviet military personnel. A cease-fire took effect on 7 August, based upon a Security Council resolution and the acceptance of US Secretary of State Rogers's Plan "B" to bring about a peaceful solution. The plan remained unfulfilled. In addition to diplomatic activity, the US employed an on-again, off-again policy of sale of Phantom jets to Israel in the hope of pressuring it to accept the Rogers' Plan. Big Four talks involved the two superpowers, along with the UK and France. The Arab League held a conference in Rabat in December 1969, prior to the outbreak of the crisis, but the LAS had no impact on its course or outcome.

References   See sources for Case #200.

(206) Invasion of Cambodia

An intra-war crisis over Cambodia occurred from 13 March to 22 July 1970. The crisis actors were Cambodia, North Vietnam, South Vietnam and the United States.

Background   Despite Cambodia's declaration of neutrality in the on-going war in Indochina, eastern Cambodia was being used by the Vietcong (National Liberation Front or NFL) and North Vietnamese as a base for launching military operations against South Vietnam. From March 1969 the United States had been secretly bombing enemy sanctuaries in Cambodia. As a result, the Vietcong began to move deeper into Cambodia, bringing them into increasing conflict with Cambodian authorities. The situation, coupled with Cambodia's deepening economic crisis, placed ruling Prince Sihanouk in a precarious position. On 8 March, and again on 11 March 1970, while Sihanouk was in France for medical treatment, there were violent demonstrations in Phnom Penh demanding the removal of Vietcong and North Vietnamese troops from Cambodia. These demonstrations were denounced by Sihanouk. On 12 March the two houses of the Cambodian Parliament met in a joint session and adopted a resolution condemning the presence of the Vietcong and North Vietnamese on Cambodian territory and demanding that the Cambodian Army be expanded. On 12 March an announcement was made suspending the trade agreement that allowed the Vietnamese to use Sihanoukville port and purchase supplies in Cambodia.

Crisis   A crisis for North Vietnam was triggered on 13 March 1970 when the Cambodian Foreign Ministry sent notes to the Vietcong Provisional Government and to the North Vietnam Government demanding that all Vietcong and North Vietnamese troops be withdrawn from Cambodia within 48 hours. Sihanouk left Paris for meetings in Moscow with President Podgorny and Premier Kosygin in order to get their support in persuading Hanoi and the NFL to curb their activities in Cambodia. On 18 March he travelled to Beijing for the same reason. That day the Cambodian National Assembly deposed Prince Sihanouk. The following day it declared a state of emergency suspending a number of civil liberties. On the 21st Cheng Heng became the new Head of State.

The crisis trigger for Cambodia came on 23 March when Sihanouk issued a proclamation dissolving the new government in Cambodia and announcing his intention of forming a Government of National Union and a National Liberation Army. Mass demonstrations in support of Sihanouk began on 26 March, with the Cambodian armed forces being placed on alert. Vietcong troops moved deeper into Cambodia; and on 31 March, North Vietnam responded to the crisis by attacking a Cambodian regiment 100 miles northeast of Phnom Penh and five miles from the frontier, marking the beginning of the combined Vietcong, North Vietnamese and Sihanoukist invasion of Cambodia. By early April these forces had reached the Svay Rieng province known as "Parrots Beak," which was surrounded by South Vietnamese territory on three sides.

The crisis trigger for South Vietnam occurred on 10 April, when Cambodian troops were forced to evacuate border positions in Parrots Beak. Cambodia's major response to the crisis came on 14 April, when Premier Lon Nol stated that, due to the gravity of the situation, the Cambodian Government was prepared to accept foreign aid from all sources. A request was sent to the United States the next day and again on 20 April.

The US crisis began on 21 April when Communist forces attacked the town of Takeo cutting the road connecting it with Phnom Penh. The US response, on 28 April, was a decision by President Nixon to send American troops into Cambodia. South Vietnam's response was to send troops into Cambodia on 29 April. US troops remained in Cambodia until 30 June 1970, the termination date for North Vietnam and the United States. The crisis for Cambodia and South Vietnam ended on 22 July with the beginning of the South Vietnamese withdrawal from Cambodia.

Although President Nixon termed the campaign a complete success, the situation in Cambodia remained more or less the same. South Vietnam obtained a victory in Parrots Beak, and North Vietnam obtained a strong foothold in Cambodia.

The UN was approached by Cambodia on 30 March. Secretary-General U Thant proposed peace negotiations, but this had no effect on ending the crisis.

References   Gordon and Young 1970, 1971; Kalb and Kalb 1974; Kissinger 1979; Nixon 1978; Shawcross 1979; Sihanouk 1970.

(207) Black September   This Middle East crisis took place from 15 to 29 September 1970. There were four crisis actors: Israel, Jordan, Syria and the United States.

Background   Autonomous Palestinian guerrilla forces, encamped in Jordan, were creating serious internal problems for King Hussein throughout 1970. In June major fighting occurred in Amman between the PLO and the Jordan Legion. The King was forced to agree to full freedom of movement for the guerrillas. During the summer of 1970 there were more sporadic clashes. On 1 September Palestinian guerrillas sought to assassinate King Hussein for a second time in a period of three months. Fighting broke out immediately between Palestinians and King Hussein's forces in Jordan. After an unsuccessful attempt to hijack an Israeli plane on 4 September, the Popular Front for the Liberation of Palestine (PFLP) hijacked two civilian aircraft on the 6th, belonging to Switzerland and the United States, and forced them to land on a desert strip outside Amman. Three days later a BOAC plane was rerouted to join the other two. The PFLP hijackings were attempts to force the release of terrorist prisoners held in Switzerland and England.

The Rogers-initiated cease-fire in the War of Attrition between Egypt and Israel had been accepted and came into effect in early August 1970. Israel, which had withdrawn from the UN-sponsored Jarring talks because of cease-fire violations by Egypt, aided by the Soviet Union, was pressing the United States for increased sophisticated military aid. In September the US uncovered Soviet intentions to build a nuclear submarine base in Cuba (see Case #208).

Crisis   A crisis for Syria and the United States was triggered on 15 September 1970 by King Hussein's announcement of a drastic change in his Cabinet which would now include military personnel. His intention to confront the PLO challenge seemed clear. The US feared the loss of an ally if Hussein were overthrown, and Syria perceived a decline in its influence in the region if the Palestinians were defeated. Syria responded on 19 September by invading Jordan. This triggered a crisis for Jordan and Israel. Jordan's response was immediate; it engaged in battle with the Syrian forces the same day and appealed to the United States for aid. Israel, at a Cabinet meeting on 20 September, decided upon military action, if necessary, in order to prevent a Palestinian victory in Jordan, which was perceived as a grave threat to Israel's security. The United States response was a decision on 21 September to provide umbrella support to Israel if the USSR and Egypt became involved; and Secretary of State Rogers, together with Israel's Ambassador to the US (and former Chief of Staff) Rabin, worked out a possible joint plan of military action. This plan was approved by President Nixon. For Syria and the United States, the crisis escalated with the entry of the Jordanian Air Force against the Palestinians. All Syrian tanks were withdrawn from Jordanian territory by 22 September. As a result the Palestinian guerrillas were forced to leave Jordan, and they subsequently built strongholds in southern Lebanon.

The League of Arab States met in Cairo at Nasser's initiative, and a Jordan-Syria cease-fire agreement was signed on 27 September. While Hussein's victory was acknowledged, the agreement was a face-saving gesture for Syria because its forces had already been withdrawn, following a US-backed Israeli threat to intervene militarily in support of Jordan. A declaration was issued supporting the rights of the Palestinians. The cease-fire was implemented on the 29th, which marked the termination date for all the crisis actors.

During the course of the crisis the US placed airborne divisions in Germany and the US on semi-alert, ships of the Sixth Fleet were reported to be heading towards Lebanese shores, and the aircraft carrier *Saratoga* was ordered to the eastern Mediterranean. The USSR involvement in the crisis consisted of political statements calling for a cease-fire and warning against outside intervention while pressuring Syria to pull out of Jordan. The Soviets also monitored US naval operations off the Syrian coast. Three additional surface combatants were redeployed into the Mediterranean.

References Blechman and Kaplan 1978; Cooley 1973; Dowty 1978, 1984; Kalb and Kalb 1974; Kissinger 1979; O'Neill 1978; Quandt *et al.* 1973; Quandt 1977.

(208) Cienfuegos Base This crisis for the United States occurred from 16 September to 23 October 1970.

Background U-2 intelligence flights over Cuba had been conducted by the US since the Missile Crisis of 1962 (see Case #162). In 1968 a Soviet naval squadron visited Cienfuegos in Cuba. On 2 and 9 September 1970 two more Soviet naval visits took place. The Soviet Ambassador in Washington, Dobrynin, met with National Security Advisor Kissinger in August to determine US intentions in light of the 1962 agreement on Cuba. In September U-2 planes picked up the first information on Soviet construction of a nuclear submarine base at Cienfuegos.

Crisis Kissinger informed President Nixon on 16 September that US intelligence flights had substantiated reports about construction of the Soviet base, the trigger for a US crisis. Nixon warned Foreign Minister Gromyko that the US was monitoring events carefully. On 25 September the story broke in the US press. The US major response, that day, was a warning from Kissinger to Dobrynin and a demand for an explanation. Dobrynin's answer, on the 27th, was that there had not been a violation of the 1962 agreement since no offensive weapons had been installed at Cienfuegos. At another meeting with Kissinger on 5 October, Dobrynin reaffirmed the validity of the 1962 agreement. Kissinger asked for a definition of a "base". On 13 October a Tass communiqué denied that the Soviet Union was building a base in Cuba. Reports in the US confirmed that a submarine tender had left Cienfuegos. On 22 October Gromyko, at a meeting with Nixon, reaffirmed the 1962 agreement once again. U-2 photos revealed a slowdown, and later a halt, in construction. On 23 October the US crisis ended when Washington received Soviet assurance that construction had been halted and that the Soviet naval force had left Cienfuegos.

The dispute continued until the spring of 1971, but tension decreased substantially, and the docking of Soviet submarines at other Cuban harbors was not perceived as a military threat to the United States.

References Gonzalez 1972; Kalb and Kalb 1974; Kissinger 1979; Quester 1971.

(209) Portuguese Invasion of Guinea A crisis for the Republic of Guinea took place from 22 November to 11 December 1970.

Background Guinean President Sekou Touré alleged Portuguese assassination attempts on his life during January and July 1964 and October 1970. Portugal accused the Republic of Guinea of harboring guerrillas wishing to oust Lisbon from the neighboring colonial territory of Portuguese Guinea.

Crisis On 22 November 1970, the trigger date, Radio Conakry of the Republic of Guinea announced an invasion by mercenaries from several sanctuaries, especially from the colonial territory of Portuguese Guinea. The same day, President Sekou Touré responded with force and an appeal for troops from the United Nations. The termination date of the crisis was 11 December 1970, the day the Organization of African Unity (OAU) passed a resolution, initiated by Ethiopia, Egypt, Libya and Sudan, condemning Portugal and demanding reparations to Guinea. There was a subsequent tacit agreement to end the invasion.

The Security Council met from 22 to 24 November and called for the cessation of the attack and decided to send a special mission to Guinea. The mission visited Guinea from 25 to 29 November. Its report, confirming the invasion of 350-400 men on 22 November and alleging support from an outside power, which seemed to be Portugal, was published on 4 December. The report also stated that the invasion was aimed at the overthrow of Sekou Touré, the freeing of Portuguese prisoners in the Republic of Guinea, and the weakening of the PAIGC whose guerrilla forces were active in Portuguese Guinea. Portugal rejected the UN report and denied participation in the invasion.

On 25 November Sekou Touré appealed to all friendly countries for military support. Kenya, Mali, Nigeria and Sierra Leone offered to send troops. Tanzania, Zambia and the US sent economic aid. Egypt sent arms and ammunition. Algeria and Libya were also reported to have sent military supplies. Political support for Guinea came from China, India, Ivory Coast, Senegal, and the Soviet Union. Portuguese Guinea became Guinea Bissau after it achieved independence in 1974.

References See general list, especially *Africa Diary* and *Africa Recorder*.

(210) Invasion of Laos II This intra-war crisis (Vietnam War) lasted from 8 February until 25 March 1971. The two crisis actors were Laos and North Vietnam.

Background A major North Vietnamese offensive was expected in 1972. US and South Vietnamese military planners therefore scheduled an invasion of Laos, in order to cut off the Ho Chi Minh Trail through which the North Vietnamese transported supplies to their strongholds in South Vietnam and Cambodia. The invasion was to be carried out by South Vietnamese troops with US air support. Although Laos had been neutralized by the Geneva Protocols of 1954 and 1962, there were thousands of North Vietnamese troops operating there, along with the Pathet Lao Communist guerrillas. During the crisis President Nixon announced that action to cut off the Ho Chi Minh Trail had been under consideration since 1965.

Crisis The South Vietnam–US invasion of Laos began on 8 February 1971. This triggered a crisis for Laos, whose borders and neutrality had been violated, and for North Vietnam, against which the invasion was directed. The major response by Laos was a declaration of a state of emergency on 12 February. North Vietnam, too, responded on that day by beginning the first wave of a counter-offensive. A day earlier the International Control Commission had convened at the urgent request of Canada in order to initiate an investigation into the violation of Laotian neutrality by foreign forces. The Commission reached no conclusion.

At that time Paris was hosting talks among the US, South and North Vietnam. South Vietnam stated that there could be no negotiations while North Vietnamese troops remained in Laos.

From the beginning to the middle of March South Vietnamese forces launched a drive to move further into Laos. On 7 March Tchepone, a key town in the Trail network, was captured. It was recaptured after a second major counter-offensive was launched by North Vietnamese troops on 12 March. The US began to airlift South Vietnamese troops out of Laos by mid-March. This was completed by 25 March, the termination date for both crisis actors.

Soviet activity was limited to declarations against the US and South Vietnam. The United States gave South Vietnam air support but announced that it would not use any ground forces. It repeatedly denied support to a possible South Vietnam invasion of the North. The only UN activity was an appeal by Secretary-General U Thant for Laos-Pathet Lao negotiations.

References   Goldstein 1973; Kissinger 1979; Nixon 1978; Stevenson 1972.

(211) Bangladesh   The crisis over Bangladesh took place from 25 March to 17 December 1971; Bangladesh, India and Pakistan were the crisis actors.

Background   When the British withdrew from the Indian subcontinent in 1947, West and East Pakistan were separated by 1000 kilometers of Indian territory. Since 1958 Pakistan was ruled by a military junta led by Ayub Khan and, later, Yahya Khan. The overwhelming victory of the Awami League in the 1970 East Pakistan elections for representatives to the Pakistan National Assembly placed Pakistan's political structure in jeopardy, especially the supremacy of the military-controlled executive over representative institutions, and West Pakistan's dominance over East Pakistan. Negotiations between the two principal political leaders, West Pakistan's Zulfikar Ali Bhutto and the Awami League's Sheikh Mujibar Rahman, including an offer of the prime ministership to the latter, failed to break the impasse.

In mid-February 1971 a decision was made by the military rulers in West Pakistan to suppress the growing fervor of East Bengali nationalism. Military personnel were posted to the East. On 1 March President Yahya Khan postponed the opening of the Assembly. This was protested by the Awami League which launched a non-cooperation movement on the 6th. A declaration of Bangladesh's independence was scheduled for 6 March, but on that day Yahya Khan announced that the National Assembly would convene on 25 March. While the West Pakistani military build-up in East Pakistan continued, the Awami League took over civil administration of the region.

Crisis   On 25 March a crisis for Bangladesh (still formally known as East Pakistan) was triggered by a West Pakistani Army attack on the student dormitories of Dacca University. The response, on the following day, was a declaration of independence by Bangladesh. This triggered a crisis for Pakistan, which responded the same day by outlawing the Awami League and suppressing the East Pakistani revolt with violence. While fighting raged over the spring and summer, an estimated nine million refugees fled from Bangladesh to India, causing severe economic problems there. A number of these refugees were then trained and armed by India to fight the West Pakistanis.

Throughout the autumn of 1971 there were minor clashes between the Indian and Pakistani armies. The situation reached crisis proportions for India when, on 12 October, orders were given to concentrate Pakistani troops on the Indian Punjab border. On 21 November the Indian Army crossed into West Pakistan, causing another crisis for Pakistan, already at war with Bangladesh. Pakistan responded on 3 December with an air attack on Indian airfields in Kashmir. Indian forces poised on the East Pakistan border overwhelmed the Pakistani troops in the seceding territory within a fortnight. The war ended on 17 December 1971 with Pakistan's surrender and the emergence of a new sovereign state on the Indian subcontinent.

The UN, approached by Bangladesh in March 1971, declared the problem an internal matter for Pakistan. The Security Council was the most active UN organ; it discussed the situation several times but was unable to pass a resolution, due to a Soviet veto. During the war between Pakistan and India the General Assembly succeeded in passing a resolution calling for a cease-fire, which, although ignored by India, did have a marginal effect on abating the crisis. The most important Soviet activity was the signing of a Friendship Treaty with India in August 1971, providing support by a superpower in case of war with Pakistan. The USSR moved naval vessels in the direction of the Bay of Bengal on 15 December, as a symbol of support for India. It also moved troops closer to the Sino-Soviet border in order to deter Beijing from becoming involved. Besides considerable United States political activity, its Seventh Fleet was moved into the Bay of Bengal on 13 December 1971, in support of Pakistan.

References   Anderson and Clifford 1973; Ayoob and Subramanyam 1972; Chopra 1971; Costa 1972; Gandhi 1972; Haendel 1977; Jackson 1975; Jain 1974a, 1974b; Misra 1973; Payne 1973; Rahman 1972; Sen Gupta 1974.

(212) Chad/Libya I   The first of four Chad/Libya crises in the 1970s lasted from 24 May 1971 to 17 April 1972, with these two Sahara states as the crisis actors.

Background   Along with many other French colonies in Equatorial Africa, Chad achieved its independence in 1960. The new state was home to many ethnic groups, the largest being the Black African and Christian Saras in the south, with many Muslim tribes in the north. Neither the French colonial regime nor the Sara-based Chad Government exercised effective control in the north. The Chad regime itself was unstable for more than a decade, with frequent repression of political opponents. In 1968 French troops were called in to suppress a rebellion. Chad's relations with its northern neighbor, Libya, worsened in 1969, following the overthrow of King Idris and the assumption of power by Muammar Qaddhafi. The Libyan leader did not conceal his country's claim to a large part of northern Chad, the Aouzou Strip, which had been ceded to Italy by France in the 1930s, but the treaty of cession had not been ratified by the French National Assembly. Nor did he conceal his goal of hegemony *vis-à-vis* Chad's political regime.

Crisis   Half of the portfolios in the Chad Government were granted to Muslim politicians on 24 May 1971. This attempt at Christian-Muslim reconciliation created a crisis for Libya by threatening its future influence in the domestic affairs of its southern neighbor. The pro-Libyan FROLINAT (Front for the National Liberation of Chad) rejected the Chad Government's offer. On 27 August Libya responded to the threat by backing a coup against President Tombalbaye. Although it failed, the coup attempt triggered a crisis for Chad, which responded the same day by severing diplomatic relations with Libya and immediate expulsion of Libya's diplomats. The perceived threat to its regime having been overcome, Chad's crisis ended the following day. On 17 September Libya recognized FROLINAT's claim to being the legitimate Government of Chad. However, persistent pressure on Libya by France, the sole involved actor, bore fruit: on 17 April 1972 Libya resumed relations with Chad, marking the end of this international crisis, a short-term victory for Chad.

Later that year, on 28 November, Tombalbaye agreed, under pressure, to the cession of the mineral-rich Aouzou Strip to Libya, which had occupied that territory in April; and in December 1972 Chad and Libya signed a Treaty of Friendship.

References   See general list and Haley 1984; Neuberger 1982.

(213) Caprivi Strip   Zambia's crisis over the Caprivi Strip occurred from 5 to 12 October 1971.

Background   South Africa and Zambia share a common border along the Caprivi Strip, a long narrow strip of land in the far northeast corner of South Africa-ruled Southwest Africa (Namibia). Large operational bases in the area are maintained by South African Defense and Police forces against guerrilla infiltration. Economic conditions in Zambia deteriorated towards the end of 1970 when world copper prices were forced down.

Crisis   A crisis was triggered for Zambia on 5 October 1971 when South African Prime Minister John Vorster announced that a Union police vehicle along the Zambian border had been blown up by a landmine. He placed responsibility on Zambia, charging that it had made Zambia's territory available for "this sort of aggression." Units of the South African security forces crossed into Zambia in order to pursue alleged perpetrators. On 8 October Zambia requested a special session of the UN Security Council to discuss the "numerous violations of South African forces against the sovereignty, airspace and territorial integrity of Zambia." Zambia's President Kaunda announced that compulsory national service and Home Guards would reinforce the regular army as part of the country's defense system.

A Security Council resolution on the 12th, condemning South Africa and calling on it to respect the sovereignty of Zambia, terminated the crisis, although Zambia viewed the resolution as "watered down" and insufficient.

There was no agreement between the parties.

References See general list and Pettman 1974.

**(214)
Uganda/Tanzania I**

A crisis for Uganda and Tanzania began on 20 October and ended on 25 November 1971.

Background On 25 January 1971, while Uganda President Milton Obote was out of the country, a coup took place and General Idi Amin assumed power. Obote took refuge in Tanzania where he was joined by about 1000 loyal Ugandan soldiers. Other Ugandans fled to southern Sudan. Amin viewed Tanzania and Sudan as possible jump-off points for military operations against his regime. Sharp hostility existed between Tanzanian President Nyerere and Amin. On 7 July Amin closed the border with Tanzania, alleging that guerrillas had infiltrated from Tanzania into Uganda. Further allegations, in early August, pointed to Tanzanian violations of Ugandan airspace and tank and troop movements into Ugandan territory. On 24 August Amin announced that his troops had clashed with Chinese-led Tanzanian forces. More reports of troop movements and bombings followed, and by the end of September accusations were steadily exchanged between the two countries.

Crisis A crisis for Tanzania began on 20 October 1971 when it was announced that Ugandan Air Force jet fighters had destroyed a Tanzanian military camp which was perceived by Amin as a base for ex-President Obote and his men. On 24 October Uganda claimed that Tanzania had mobilized its forces on the border between the two states. The Tanzanian response was a statement by the Minister of Information and Broadcasting the next day, objecting to the Ugandan threat to destroy Tanzanian bases established north of the Kagera River and declaring its intention to meet with resistance any troop movements in that area. Amin responded on 1 November with a declaration of his determination to defend "every inch of Ugandan territory." There is evidence that both Uganda and Tanzania had moved troops to the border.

On 21 November Amin reestablished air and telephone communications with Tanzania. The crisis ended for both actors on 25 November. Nyerere, though still refusing to recognize Amin, announced his intention to reduce the number of troops on the border. These acts represented a semi-formal agreement.

References Gukiina 1972; Kyemba 1977; Low 1973; Martin 1974.

**(215) Vietnam – Ports
Mining**

North Vietnam, South Vietnam and the United States were crisis actors in a Vietnam intra-war crisis which lasted from 30 March to 19 July 1972.

Background The period preceding the 1972 Vietnam Ports Mining Crisis was marked by periodic escalation in fighting, the invasion of Cambodia and military confrontations between government forces and the Pathet Lao in Laos. The acknowledged US policy since 1969 had been the replacement of American troops by South Vietnamese forces. Periodic announcements of substantive US troop withdrawals undermined, to a great extent, the political strength of the US at the Paris Peace Talks, conducted between Henry Kissinger and the North Vietnamese representatives Lê Dúc Thọ and Xuan Thee. This crisis occurred during a US Presidential election year. At the same time there were on-going demonstrations in the United States against the war in Vietnam.

Crisis North Vietnam launched another spring offensive in South Vietnam on 30 March 1972, triggering a crisis for South Vietnam and the United States. South Vietnam, perceiving a threat of a further loss of territory, responded the same day with defensive fighting. The US immediately renewed B-52 bombing of the Hanoi–Haiphong industrial complex. Despite these bombings, the North Vietnamese undertook further escalation on 24 April by initiating a renewed attack on South Vietnamese troops in the Central Highlands and forcing them to withdraw. The major US response was an order by President Nixon on 8 May to mine all North Vietnamese ports in an effort to prevent military shipments from reaching North Vietnam by sea. The announcement of the mining and blockade of the ports triggered a crisis for North Vietnam. Its response to the threat of isolation from crucial sources of supplies was a statement at the Paris Peace Talks on 9 May declaring the American act to be the gravest step so far in the escalation of the war, and that North Vietnam would never accept an American ultimatum. At the same time, North Vietnamese delegates appealed to all governments and peoples of fraternal socialist countries to persuade the US to negotiate seriously at the Paris Talks.

The USSR and China played constructive roles in abating the crisis. Diplomatic talks between the US and the USSR, including a summit meeting held in Moscow in May, resulted in intensive Soviet and Chinese pressure on North Vietnam.

The crisis ended for all actors on 19 July 1972 with renewed talks in Paris: the negotiations shifted to a serious exchange of views, with a promise of compromise.

In a letter from United States UN Ambassador George Bush to the President of the Security Council on 8 May 1972, US actions were reported to be measures of collective self-defense. Secretary-General Waldheim held a series of meetings at the Security Council between 8 and 10 May and advocated an active UN role in ending hostilities. However, he received no support and thus on 19 May the Security Council merely issued a statement calling on all parties to act with utmost restraint. Almost three years later North and South Vietnam were reunited under a Communist regime.

References   Gelb and Betts 1979; Herring 1979; Kalb and Kalb 1974; Kissinger 1979; Lewy 1978; Nixon 1978; Quandt 1977.

(216)
Uganda/Tanzania II

A second crisis for Uganda and Tanzania began on 17 September 1972 and ended on 5 October of that year.

Background   Military clashes between Uganda and Tanzania were reported for much of 1971. The two countries verged on a wider confrontation when Ugandan Air Force planes attacked border placements in Tanzania, triggering a crisis from 20 October until its termination on 25 November 1971 (see Case #214).

Crisis   On 17 September 1972 1000 supporters of ex-President Obote in Tanzania invaded Uganda from Tanzania; no Tanzanian soldiers were among them. Idi Amin responded the following day by moving forces to the border region to meet the invasion and by bombing the town of Bukoba in Tanzania, triggering a crisis for Tanzania. Tanzania responded the same day by moving its Fourth Battalion of over 1000 men to the border. Its crisis management technique was mediation, both through the OAU and Somalia.

The termination date for both actors was 5 October 1972, when they signed an agreement wherein both announced their intention to remove forces from the border area and to cease all military hostilities. Moreover, the two sides agreed to stop all hostile propaganda against each other and "to refrain from harboring or allowing subversive forces to operate in the territory of one state against the other."

References   See sources for Case #214.

(217) North/South
Yemen I

A major battle between North and South Yemen triggered a crisis for the two states from 26 September to 28 November 1972.

Background Relations between North and South Yemen deteriorated in 1971 as the latter adopted a more radical pro-Soviet policy while the former established increasingly friendly relations with Saudi Arabia. The situation in North Yemen was further complicated by rivalry between the traditionalist Fadi tribes of the northern provinces and the more progressive peoples of the southern provinces who looked for support to South Yemen. Irregular forces operating from Saudi Arabia made a series of unsuccessful raids into South Yemen between October 1970 and June 1971. A series of clashes on the border of the two Yemeni states occurred between February and May 1972. The USSR provided military aid and advisors to both sides. Each country accused the other of troop build-ups along the border. During the summer of 1972 the long-standing border dispute resulted in a series of armed clashes.

Crisis A major battle on 26 September 1972 over the border town of Qa'taba spread over a 45–75-mile front and triggered a crisis for both North and South Yemen. Fighting continued until 13 October when a cease-fire was concluded by an Arab League Mission which was to provide military observers to monitor the cessation of hostilities. Nevertheless, fighting continued until 19 October when a new cease-fire agreement was reached.

A peace agreement and an agreement on unification were initialled in Cairo on 28 October by representatives of the two countries. The two Presidents signed an agreement on unification on 28 November 1972 in Tripoli, Libya, terminating the crisis for both countries. Colonel Qaddhafi was reported to have taken an active part in the discussions. During the crisis Kuwait, Algeria and Libya attempted mediation.

Air services were resumed between North and South Yemen two days later. The cease-fire lasted until May 1973, when fighting broke out again (see Case #225), and full-scale war erupted in 1979 (see Case #271).

References See general list and Abir 1974; Hassouna 1975.

(218) Christmas Bombing This intra-war crisis for North and South Vietnam and the United States began on 23 October 1972 and ended on 27 January 1973.

Background The Port Mining Crisis, which occurred from March to July 1972, had ended in renewed and serious peace negotiations at Paris (see Case #215). These talks broke down once more; and, when a deadlock could no longer be avoided, it was followed by an escalation in hostilities on the battlefield.

Crisis The trigger for South Vietnam occurred on 23 October 1972 when it learned of agreements reached between the delegates of the United States and North Vietnam at the Paris Talks. The response, the next day, was a public refusal to comply with these agreements. Fighting in Vietnam and negotiations in Paris were carried on simultaneously. But on 4 December 1972 North Vietnam rejected all US proposals and withdrew its acceptance of early changes already agreed upon while making new demands. This triggered a crisis for the US. Secretary of State Kissinger surmised that North Vietnam was now willing to risk a break in the talks. When additional meetings on 6, 11 and 13 December ended in stalemate, the US concluded that Hanoi had in effect made a strategic decision to prolong the war, abort all negotiations and seek an unconditional victory.

On 14 December the US responded with an order by President Nixon to renew the aerial bombing of the Hanoi–Haiphong military complex and the mining of North Vietnamese ports. Massive bombing began on 17 December and triggered a crisis for North Vietnam, which responded on the 26th by signalling a willingness to return to serious negotiations without preconditions. On the 26th the US bombed the Hanoi railway station, killing 283 people and wounding 266. North Vietnam proposed 8 January 1973 for meetings in Paris. The crisis ended for all three actors on 27 January, with the formal signing of the Peace Accords in Paris.

As with so many crises during this long war and protracted conflict, the USSR was marginally involved – politically.

References See sources for Case #215.

(219) Zambia   A Zambia crisis with Rhodesia took place from 19 January to 3 February 1973.

Background On 9 January 1973 the UDI Rhodesian Government closed the border with Zambia except for copper exports (90% of all exports from Zambia). Rhodesian Prime Minister Ian Smith accused Zambia of harboring terrorists who were allegedly responsible for incidents threatening Rhodesian citizens. Preceding and immediately following the closure there had been several border incidents between the two countries.

Crisis On 19 January 1973, after Zambian troops and police fired on a South African police motorboat on the Zambezi River, the Government of Zambia perceived that Rhodesia might use this incident as an excuse to launch a military attack on Zambia. The same day, in response to this trigger, Defense Minister Grey Zulu declared that Zambian forces had been moved to the border. On 24 January Zambia requested an urgent session of the Security Council and accused Rhodesia, with South African aid, of violating Zambia's sovereignty and territorial integrity. On the 27th President Kaunda sent a letter to Secretary-General Waldheim stating that Zambia would not tolerate violations of its territory by Rhodesia or South Africa. The Security Council met on the 29th (at that time, Rhodesia and South Africa were under UN economic sanctions and South Africa's formal status at the UN had been reduced). The crisis ended on 3 February, when Rhodesia, satisfied that its objectives had been achieved, reopened the border with Zambia.

On 10 March, after the termination of the crisis, the Security Council passed a resolution calling upon Britain to convene a conference to bring about self-determination and independence to Rhodesia and called upon Rhodesia to release all political prisoners.

References See general list, especially *Africa Contemporary Record* and *Africa Research Bulletin*.

(220) Libyan Plane   The appearance of a Libyan plane over Israeli-occupied territory created a 30-minute crisis for Israel on 21 February 1973.

Background Several weeks prior to this event, Israel's Cabinet had been alerted to a terrorist plot to hijack an airliner which would be packed with explosives and crashed into an Israeli center of population.

Crisis On 21 February 1973 a plane was spotted on Israeli radar heading in the direction of Israel's nuclear plant in Dimona. Apparently a Libyan Boeing-727 with 113 passengers on board had strayed over the eastern side of the Suez Canal, then occupied by Israel. Israeli fighter planes immediately intercepted the intruding aircraft, demanding identification. Twenty minutes of sustained warnings and signals to the pilot brought no results. Orders were requested from higher military officers. The Army Chief of Staff, General Elazar, ordered the air force to shoot down the plane. Israel responded to the crisis by so doing. When the plane crashed, 30 minutes after it had been spotted, the crisis for Israel was terminated.

Immediately thereafter the Israelis learned that the plane had been a civilian airliner from Libya and that it had represented no security threat to it. There were very few survivors. Most of the passengers were Egyptian, some German. The pilot was French. Israel subsequently paid compensation to the families of the dead. Following the crisis Israel was condemned by most members of the international system. France conducted a separate investigation. There was no UN or super-power activity during the crisis because of its brevity.

References See general list, especially *Keesing's* and *New York Times*.

**(221) Iraq
Invasion-Kuwait**

A crisis for Kuwait began on 20 March and ended on 8 June 1973.

Background Iraq's territorial designs on Kuwait were of long standing (see Case #149). By 1973 Iraq's pressure on Kuwait to make territorial concessions that would enable an Iraqi creation of a new base for petroleum and military operations in the Persian Gulf had increased. A year earlier Kuwait had refused a large loan to Iraq. The USSR supported Iraqi claims to two Kuwaiti islands as it was expected that Iraq would permit the USSR to establish a naval facility there. Soviet support of Iraq was perceived by Kuwait, Iran and other Western-aligned states in the Middle East as threatening, and Kuwait's growing *rapprochement* with Iran and Saudi Arabia disturbed Iraqi decision-makers.

Crisis On 20 March 1973 Iraqi troops crossed the border into Kuwait, with a view to annexing part of the disputed territory along their 99-mile border. Kuwait immediately sent troops, but they were defeated by the superior Iraqi forces who then occupied the Kuwaiti outpost of Sametah where a number of huts were established. When Kuwait surrounded these huts with mosques, the Iraqi forces were contained. The next day, at an emergency session of the Kuwaiti Cabinet and Parliament, a decision was taken to negotiate rather than fight. Kuwait's insistence on Iraqi withdrawal, and the latter's refusal to do so, brought mediation efforts by Arab League Secretary-General Riad to a standstill. On 6 April the two Foreign Ministers met, after which Iraqi forces were withdrawn and an announcement was made by both parties that they accepted the Palestine Liberation Organization leader, Yasser Arafat, as mediator. The debate centered around Kuwait's refusal to concede or to lease the islands to Iraq. The following day Kuwait offered a substantial investment in Iraqi development projects and special treatment for Iraqis residing in Kuwait.

The crisis ended on 8 June 1973 when an agreement was reached between the two states which included an Iraqi increase of fresh water supplies to Kuwait from the Shatt-al-Arab, but there were no concessions on the islands. Following the agreement both Kuwait and Saudi Arabia completed substantial arms deals with the US and UK, respectively, while Iraq obtained increased arms supplies from the USSR.

Mediation attempts were made by Egypt, Lebanon and Syria; and Iran and Saudi Arabia offered military support to Kuwait. There were reports of 15,000 Saudi troops in Kuwait shortly after the beginning of the crisis.

References See general list, especially *Keesing's* and *New York Times*.

(222) Israel Mobilization

A crisis for Israel in its relations with Egypt began on 10 April 1973 and ended in late June of that year.

Background After the Arab defeat in the 1967 War (see Case #189), the Egyptians began to rebuild their armed forces, in conjunction with efforts to find a diplomatic solution to Arab (mainly Egypt's and Syria's) dissatisfaction over Israeli control of the Sinai Desert, the Golan Heights, the West Bank and East Jerusalem. Anwar al-Sadat succeeded Nasser as President of Egypt in 1970 and persuaded Moscow to resupply weapons on a large scale. In early 1973 newly-appointed Egyptian Chief of Staff Ahmed Ismail visited Moscow and conducted negotiations for additional Soviet arms. His visit to Washington, however, was less successful. In February President Nixon emphasized that the United States had no intention of putting pressure on Israel to withdraw from the Sinai Peninsula and all other territories captured during the Six Day War. Shortly thereafter news of US agreement to supply Israel with 48 Phantoms and 36 Skyhawks was leaked to the press. Egyptian coordination with the Syrians began in February 1973, and a joint attack was scheduled for May of that year. At the beginning of April Sadat stated publicly that Egypt was preparing for war with Israel. He also announced a large Egyptian army exercise.

Crisis On 10 April 1973 Israel's Chief of Staff, David Elazar, received intelligence reports of an intended Egyptian attack slated for 15 May: further, that Iraq and Libya had each sent 16 fighter planes to Egypt. Israeli intelligence maintained, however, that Sadat would back down before the actual launching of the war. This estimate was not accepted by Elazar. Israel responded by placing its army on alert on 13 April and by cancelling all leaves. War preparations began, and reserve units were called into active service.

Some time toward the end of June, after the Nixon–Brezhnev talks on the 22nd, Israel became convinced that Egypt did not intend to go to war at that time, and the crisis came to an end. Sadat subsequently explained that the postponement of the war was due to a scheduling of a second summit conference in Washington for May. Elazar came under severe criticism by Israel's Finance Minister for the economic cost of the April mobilization, while the Israel intelligence estimates were vindicated. This proved to be a crucial factor in Elazar's reluctance to order general mobilization and misconceptions that characterized Israeli thinking just before the successful Egyptian attack on 6 October 1973 (see Case #224).

References Bartov 1978; Herzog 1975; Insight Team of the *Sunday Times* 1974; Meir 1975.

(223) Cod War I The first crisis between the UK and Iceland over cod fishing rights began on 14 May and ended on 13 November 1973.

Background In 1972 a dispute between Iceland, on the one hand, and Great Britain and West Germany, on the other, centered around Iceland's unilateral extension of its territorial waters from a 12-mile limit to 50 miles. This severely curtailed the fish catch available to other countries. Several incidents occurred as a result of the harassment of British and West German trawlers by Icelandic gunboats. Further incidents of ramming and exchanges of fire were reported in March and April 1973.

Crisis On the night of 14 May 1973 Icelandic gunboats fired on British trawlers triggering a crisis for the UK. On the 16th British fishermen threatened to leave the disputed waters if protection were not assured. London responded on 19 May by dispatching Royal Navy ships to Icelandic waters, triggering a crisis for Iceland. The following day, Iceland banned RAF aircraft from landing at the Keflavik NATO Base, while protesting to the UK. Talks between the two Prime Ministers began on 2 October. On 13 November 1973 the Parliament of Iceland approved an agreement whereby Iceland set aside certain areas within the newly-accepted 50-mile limit for British fishermen, terminating the crisis for both actors.

Two regional/security organizations, NATO and the Council of Europe, were involved, but neither was effective in abating the crisis. The US limited its involvement to a statement about the dispute. A proposal for mediation came from Norway. USSR involvement was more substantial, however. Continued NATO use of the Keflavik Air Base, which was necessary for the implementation of important NATO anti-submarine warfare operations, was already an issue in Icelandic politics. Iceland's request to the USSR for a show of force during the crisis was answered by a special Soviet naval exercise: ten Russian ships and ten submarines were dispatched as a signal to Britain. There was also a reported request from Iceland to the Soviet Union for a gunboat to strengthen Iceland's coastguard. A second "Cod War" crisis occurred between Iceland and the UK in 1975–76 (see Case #233).

References See general list and Kaplan 1981.

(224) October-Yom Kippur War The October-Yom Kippur War Crisis began on 5 October 1973 and ended on 31 May 1974. The crisis actors were Egypt, Israel, the Soviet Union, Syria and the United States.

Background The West Bank of the Jordan River, the Gaza Strip, and the entire Sinai Peninsula had been occupied by Israel since the Six Day War of June 1967 (see Case #189). In 1969 Egypt launched a War of Attrition against Israeli forces in the Sinai (see Case #200). In 1970 a cease-fire was accepted by both sides with plans to put into effect a US plan for peace in the region (see Case #205). The plan was never implemented. In April 1973 Israeli forces were put on alert, including a large mobilization, when its leaders suspected Egyptian mobilization and war exercises to be a prelude to an invasion of Israel (see Case #222). The invasion never took place.

On 13 September 1973 Israel and Syria fought an air battle in which 13 Syrian MIGs and one Israeli Mirage were shot down. When Syria did not react immediately to this dramatic defeat, Israel became suspicious that Damascus was planning a more basic action. IDF forces in the north were strengthened, and precautionary measures were also taken in the south. Syria's massing of three infantry divisions, tanks and artillery, and a mobilization of Syrian reserves in the north, along with the evacuation of Soviet military advisers and their families from Damascus and Cairo, were all noted by Israeli intelligence. The Israel Defense Forces (IDF) was put on the highest state of alert. Nevertheless, Israeli intelligence, as late as 3 October 1973, perceived the outbreak of war to be very unlikely. This erroneous judgment was based upon two Israeli misperceptions: that Egypt's inferior air power would not permit it to launch a war against Israel, and that Syria would not "go it alone," without Egyptian active participation.

Crisis On 5 October 1973 a movement of Egyptian forces towards the Suez Canal and a change from a defensive to an offensive posture triggered a crisis for Israel. At the same time, Israel's intelligence service reported an impending Egyptian attack across the Canal scheduled for the following day. Israel immediately raised the IDF alert level and strengthened its forces along the northern and southern borders. The War began on 6 October with a simultaneous attack by Egyptian and Syrian forces. By 10 October, after heavy losses, Israeli forces succeeded in reversing the tide of battle in the north, triggering a crisis for Syria. Syria's response was multiple: it stepped up resistance, called upon Egypt to increase military pressure on Israel in the south, and appealed to the Soviet Union for aid. During the next three days Israeli forces advanced 10 kilometers beyond the 1967 cease-fire lines into Syrian territory.

On 12 October Israeli Prime Minister Meir agreed to a cease-fire in place. Its rejection by Egypt and Syria triggered a crisis for the United States which feared a possible confrontation with the USSR. All seven Soviet airborne divisions had been placed on an increased state of readiness. The heavy Soviet commitment to the Arabs, in the form of resupplying arms by air and sea, indicated to Washington that Moscow would not tolerate an unambiguous Arab defeat, comparable to that in 1967.

The successful Egyptian operation to cross the Suez Canal was followed on 14 October by a large-scale tank battle in which Egypt suffered a severe defeat. On the 16th the Israelis crossed the Canal threatening to surround the Egyptian Third Army. A crisis for Egypt was triggered on the 18th when Sadat became aware of the worsening position. Egypt's response was to pressure the Soviet Union to obtain a cease-fire agreement, which was accepted by Israel and Egypt on 22 October. When the Egyptians continued their attempt to destroy Israeli tank concentrations in order to open up an escape route for the Third Army, fighting broke out once more, with Israel strengthening its positions on the Egyptian side of the Canal.

Israeli violations of the 22 October cease-fire agreement triggered a crisis for the Soviet Union. Moscow responded on the 24th with a movement of naval vessels and a Note from Brezhnev to Nixon containing a clear warning that, unless the Israeli onslaught on the west bank of the Suez Canal was stopped at once, the USSR might intervene unilaterally. The US responded with mounting pressure on Israel to stop fighting and to allow non-military supplies to reach the Third Army. At the same time, Nixon issued a sharp reply to Moscow: most of the the US armed forces, including the Strategic Air Command with its nuclear capability, were put on a high state of alert, namely "Defensive Condition 3."

The crisis escalated further when, on 25 October, a Soviet freighter arrived in Alexandria reportedly carrying nuclear weapons. Finally, on 26 October 1973, a

US–Soviet-sponsored Security Council resolution calling for a cease-fire was accepted by all the parties.

Talks between Egypt and Israel, with the active participation of US Secretary of State Kissinger, continued for two months and concentrated on withdrawal to the post-Six Day War lines, the problem of the encircled Third Army, and the exchange of prisoners. A one-day symbolic Geneva Conference was convened on 21 December. Israel agreed to withdraw to 20 kilometers from the Canal and the size of both forces was reduced. A Disengagement Agreement was signed on 18 January 1974, ending the crisis for Egypt.

The negotiations between Israel and Syria took much longer. Kissinger mediated once more. Israel's demand for a complete list of all Israeli prisoners-of-war was negotiated by Kissinger in February 1974. In March Syria announced that it had decided to resume the war immediately. Shelling of Israeli-held positions in the north and firing back and forth continued throughout the spring of 1974. On 2 May the US Secretary of State began a month of shuttle-diplomacy, travelling between Damascus and Jerusalem, with side trips to Riyadh, Amman and Cairo.

In the final agreement Israel returned parts of the Syrian town of Quneitra but kept control over two of the three strategic hills in the area where heavy weapons were forbidden. A UN buffer zone was established. The Israeli demand that Syria commit itself to a cessation of all terrorist activities was refused. As in the case of the Israel–Egypt Agreement, a US Memorandum of Understanding was given to Israel. The Agreement was announced on 29 May and was signed on 31 May 1974, terminating the crisis for Israel, Syria, the Soviet Union and the United States.

The superpowers, as crisis actors, were involved at a high level. Each supplied massive arms and equipment, as well as political support, to its client state. The cease-fire agreements were worked out between their representatives. Premier Kosygin arrived in Cairo on 16 October to persuade Egypt to accept a cease-fire. Kissinger visited Moscow on 19–20 October and hammered out a draft resolution for the Security Council, calling for an immediate cease-fire. The Council adopted this resolution within hours and authorized the creation of a UN force to police the Golan Heights.

References Aruri 1975; Bandmann and Cordova 1980; Bartov 1978; Brecher 1980; Dayan 1976; Dowty 1984; Eban 1977; Freedman 1975; Golan 1974, 1976, 1977; Heikal 1975; Herzog 1975; Kalb and Kalb 1974; Kissinger 1982; Meir 1975; Monroe and Farrar-Hockley 1975; Nixon 1978; Quandt 1977; Sadat 1978; Schiff 1975; Shimoni 1977.

(225) South Yemen–Oman

South Yemen's active military assistance to Omani rebels created a crisis for Oman from 18 November 1973 to 11 March 1976.

Background Fighting in Oman's eastern province of Dhofar between rebels and the Sultan's army began in 1963. After independence in 1967 South Yemen increased support to the rebels. By 1970 the insurgents' control extended to all of Dhofar. The traditional Sultan was deposed by his son in July 1970. This was followed by a lull in the fighting and the more liberal Sultan was able to gain some tribal support. After the British withdrawal from the Persian Gulf in 1971, the area was character-ized by a power vacuum. Oman independence was proclaimed at the end of 1971. In 1972 the Omani forces, strengthened by British, Iranian and Jordanian troops, along with financial aid and arms from Saudi Arabia and the United Arab Emirates, succeeded in turning the campaign in their favor.

The focal point of tension between Oman and South Yemen had been the latter's support to the insurgents, along with Iraq, both in training (with arms supplied by the People's Republic of China) and active participation in fighting. Rights over the Kuria Muria Islands, located off the Dhofar coast, were also in dispute. Clashes occurred on the South Yemen/Oman border in 1972, mainly as a result of an incursion into Dhofar by left-wing guerrillas operating from South Yemen. On 15 April 1973 Iran sent additional forces to Oman.

Crisis On 18 November 1973 the Oman Government announced that a military post had been attacked by South Yemen aircraft and that South Yemen forces were actively engaged in the fighting in Dhofar. Oman's response, on 22 December, was a successful military campaign to free the Muscat–Salala road held by the rebels. Oman's growing economic strength had enabled it to purchase large quantities of military equipment and to expand the army. On 28 January 1975 it was reported that guerrilla supply lines from South Yemen had been blocked. The rebels were completely cut off from supplies by October, and by the end of 1975 the insurgents had been driven out of their last strongholds in Dhofar and had crossed into South Yemen. A cease-fire, with Saudi mediation, was signed by South Yemen and Oman on 11 March 1976.

In May 1974 the League of Arab States had created a Conciliation Commission which attempted to mediate, but without success. An LAS proposal for an international force to replace the non-Arab troops was refused by the Sultan, who was willing to welcome it only if the Arab force consented to fight alongside the existing forces.

Oman received military assistance from the United States. As South Yemen relations with the Soviet bloc improved, the USSR increased arms supplies to the rebels.

References   Lapidoth 1982; Litwak 1981; Owen 1973; Peterson 1981; Stookey 1982.

(226) Cyprus III   This crisis lasted from 15 July 1974 until 24 February 1975. As in earlier crises over Cyprus (see Cases #169, #190), there were three actors: Cyprus, Greece and Turkey.

Background   The 1960 agreement among Britain, Greece and Turkey for the maintenance of the status quo in Cyprus was undermined once more when a terrorist group, EOKA-B, advocating *enosis* (union with Greece), planned a coup against President Makarios. On 2 July, in a letter to the Greek Government, the President accused Greek officers in the Cypriot National Guard of plotting his assassination and demanded their removal. New policies were introduced by Cyprus to reduce their influence.

Crisis   On 15 July 1974 a military coup was engineered in Nicosia by officers from Athens and parliamentary rule was overthrown, triggering a crisis for Cyprus. Makarios escaped to London and Nikos Sampson was installed as President. Heavy fighting followed. The Cypriot response, on the 19th, was an appeal to the UN Security Council and to Britain for assistance. The 15 July coup also triggered a crisis for Turkey which then proceeded to mount a counter-police action. On 20 July, after rejecting pleas from the US, UK and the global organization for restraint, Turkey invaded Cyprus. Soon some 40,000 Turkish troops were in control of the territory stretching from Kyrenia on the north coast to Nicosia. Fighting was extensive, and there were thousands of casualties. A crisis was triggered for Greece with the invasion on 20 July.

The superiority of the Turkish forces and the geographic distance between Greece and Cyprus prevented a Greek counter-attack: and the disastrous failure of the Greek military junta's attempt to precipitate *enosis* toppled the regime in Greece. On 23 July a civilian government was restored in Athens. Sampson resigned as President of Cyprus, and Glafkos Clerides was installed as Acting President. Peace negotiations opened on 25 July attended by representatives from the UK, Greece and Turkey and an observer from the USSR. An agreement was signed on 30 July confirming a cease-fire and establishing a security zone between the Greek and Turkish forces. Talks, however, broke down on 4 August, and Turkish forces advanced to occupy the entire northern part of Cyprus. Human rights violations against the Greek population were reported. Once Turkey had achieved its military objectives, it called for a cease-fire on 16 August which went into effect immediately. Following a series of talks between Archbishop Makarios and Clerides during November, Makarios returned to Cyprus on 7 December 1974. In February 1975 a Turkish–Cypriot Federated State was proclaimed and, on 24 February, a Constituent Assembly for Turkish Cyprus was convened, ending the crisis for Turkey, Cyprus and Greece, the latter two by acquiescing in this unilateral act.

The UN played an active role in the third international crisis over Cyprus. An emergency meeting of the Security Council convened immediately after the coup on 15 July. Several resolutions, calling for a cease-fire, an end to foreign military intervention in Cyprus and respect for its sovereignty, and the resumption of negotiations as well as cooperation of the parties with UN forces, were passed. The abortive cease-fire agreements of 22 and 30 July were to come into effect under UN auspices. The UN Forces in Cyprus (UNFICYP) supervised the cease-fire of 16 August. Talks between Acting President Clerides and the Turkish Cypriot leader, Denktash, were also held under UN auspices. On 13 December the UNFICYP mandate was extended for another 6-month period.

The US, beset by the Watergate domestic political crisis at home, was nevertheless active in efforts to mediate among the parties. Cyprus and Greece maintained that the absence of US pressure on Turkey to stop military action encouraged it. And when American military aid to Turkey was stopped in December, relations between those two countries deteriorated. NATO was not active in the crisis. Greece, protesting that security organization's inability to restrain Turkey, withdrew its forces from NATO.

The Soviet Union made several military moves during the crisis. A Soviet task force moving towards Cyprus was reinforced at sea, and seven airborne divisions were put on alert. More than a decade later, the partition of Cyprus remained intact.

References Kaplan 1981; Kissinger 1982; Nixon 1978.

(227) Final North Vietnam Offensive

The final crisis for South Vietnam and Cambodia during the long war in Indochina occurred from 14 December 1974 to 30 April 1975.

Background Civil wars in Cambodia and Vietnam persisted after the United States formally withdrew its forces in 1973. The US continued to supply economic and military aid to the governments of both Cambodia and South Vietnam. Some US advisers stayed in the area. By the end of 1974 forces of the Khmer Rouge in Cambodia and the Vietcong and North Vietnamese Army in South Vietnam had increased their activities in preparation for a final offensive.

Crisis The trigger for South Vietnam occurred on 14 December 1974 with the beginning of the North Vietnamese offensive. For Cambodia, the crisis was triggered on 1 January 1975 with the launching of a major Khmer Rouge offensive. Several areas in Cambodia were lost and recaptured as fighting raged between the two sides. On 17 February Cambodia responded with a counter-offensive. The South Vietnamese response was multiple: continued fighting, a request for aid to the US, and a tactical retreat instigated by President Thieu on 11 March. On 17 April the Cambodian capital of Phnom Penh fell to the rebels, forcing the government to flee and marking the end of Cambodia's last crisis in the Vietnam War. Meanwhile, North Vietnamese troops pressed on with their offensive as the South Vietnamese Army retreated towards Saigon. Thousands of refugees fled before the advancing troops, clogging the roads and filling the ports and airports. Saigon fell on 30 April. ending the crisis for South Vietnam.

US involvement took the form of aid to both governments. Despite special appeals to Congress on 28 January by President Ford and, subsequently, by Secretary of State Kissinger, Congress decided to cut aid to both Cambodia and South Vietnam. Assistance was given to Vietnamese refugees; and by the end of the crisis US activity was limited to evacuating American citizens. UN involvement was confined to calls for a cease-fire and the activities of the UN High Commissioner for Refugees.

References See sources for Case #215.

(228) Mayaguez

The *Mayaguez* episode was a crisis for Cambodia and the United States from 12 to 15 May 1975.

Background American prestige was at a low point in the wake of the US withdrawal from Southeast Asia and the collapse of US-supported regimes in Cambodia and Vietnam. In Cambodia the Khmer Rouge had emerged victorious from the civil war. While US relations with China had improved considerably since 1971, relations with the new Government of Cambodia were hostile.

Crisis On 12 May 1975 a US-registered cargo ship, the *Mayaguez*, was seized off Cambodian coastal waters by the Khmer Rouge, triggering a crisis for the United States. The ship was taken into custody, together with its crew, with no word of their fate. Washington looked upon this incident as a challenge to US influence in Southeast Asia. Following demands for the return of the ship and crew, on the 12th, the US threat, on 13 May, to use force if necessary, triggered a crisis for Cambodia. The decision to use military force, taken on the 14th by President Ford at the fourth and final meeting of the National Security Council to deal with this issue, was the major American response to the Mayaguez Crisis. Cambodia's response, also on the 14th, was a statement accusing the US of interfering in its internal affairs and threatening reprisals. A few minutes after fighting began, the Cambodians released the ship and crew, ending the crisis for the United States. Nevertheless, even after Cambodia's acquiescence, serious clashes took place between Khmer Rouge forces and US Marines in the vicinity of Koh Tong, an island thought to be in the area where the *Mayaguez* crew was being held. The amount of force applied by the US was massive, and heavy casualties were reported on both sides.

The crisis for Cambodia ended on 15 May when the US ceased its military operations. UN involvement was minimal: the Secretary-General offered his good offices to settle the dispute, but this had little effect. In addition to the two crisis actors, the PRC became involved when Cambodia requested Beijing to conduct limited negotiations on its behalf.

References Head *et al.* 1978; Paust 1976; Poole 1976.

(229) Angola   Angola, Cuba, South Africa, the Soviet Union, the United States, Zaire and Zambia were direct participants in a crisis from 12 July 1975 until 27 March 1976.

Background On 24 April 1974 the Portuguese dictatorship was overthrown. The new regime announced its intention to grant independence to all of Portugal's colonies in Africa. The Alvor Agreement, signed on 15 January 1975, formally granted independence to Angola, to take effect on 10 November 1975 after elections in October. A transitional government was to be composed of representatives of: the FNLA (National Front for the Liberation of Angola), supported by the PRC, USA and Zaire; the Marxist-oriented MPLA (Popular Movement for the Liberation of Angola), supported by the Soviet Union and Cuba, and popular in the cities and among the north-central tribes; and the UNITA (National Union for the Total Independence of Angola), which had a strong popular base in the south and received support from South Africa and Zambia. There was to be a unified security force under a Portuguese High Commissioner. The Alvor Agreement broke down as early as March 1975, with major fighting between the FNLA and MPLA erupting in late April. Portugal declared martial law on 15 May. President Kenyatta of Kenya mediated a cease-fire on 21 June, but it was broken immediately.

Crisis On 12 July 1975 Soviet-backed MPLA forces attacked the FNLA headquarters in Luanda triggering a crisis for Zaire, which backed the FNLA, and for Zambia, when the essential Benguela railroad was closed down. Zaire began sending small-scale commando units into Angola in mid-July to aid the FNLA. By that time the Soviet Union had started providing massive aid to the MPLA, causing alarm in Zaire, Zambia and South Africa, as well as in the United States which had been providing covert aid to both the FNLA and the UNITA movements.

Zambia responded on 27 July with an appeal to the US for aid. Hydroelectric power projects, built jointly by South Africa and Portugal, were located on the Kunene River bordering Southwest Africa (Namibia). Clashes between the

UNITA and MPLA began approaching the power projects on 8 August, triggering a crisis for South Africa, which sent small units of troops to the projects on the 11th and 12th. On the 15th the FNLA captured the major port of Lobito, triggering a crisis for Cuba, the Soviet Union and the MPLA. Cuba and the USSR were concerned that South African intervention would result in the defeat of the MPLA in the struggle for power and influence in Africa. Cuba's response, on 20 August, was a decision to greatly increase military aid to the MPLA (which was later to be recognized as the official Government of Angola). More South African troops were sent to the district capital on 21–22 August. On the 21st the UNITA declared war on the MPLA, after concluding an alliance with the FNLA. A USSR decision, on the 31st, was similar to that of Cuba – increased aid to Angola. On 1 September the MPLA (Angola) responded with a major offensive and succeeded in reversing its losses, triggering a crisis for the United States. Cuban troops began to arrive on the 3rd. On 11 September Zaire sent in two full battalions to strengthen the FNLA. President Mobutu approached the US for aid, and diplomatic activity was initiated with other African states. The US response on 25 September was to increase covert aid to Zaire, to be funnelled to the UNITA/FNLA groups: President Ford requested that Congress increase emergency aid to Zaire.

South Africa's response to the escalating crisis, on 23 October 1975, was the dispatch of a strike force into Angola to aid the FNLA/UNITA: it was successful in recouping earlier losses. A further escalation for Zaire, Zambia, the US and South Africa was the arrival of a large number of Cuban troops to fight alongside the MPLA, together with massive arms supplies to Angola from the Soviet Union. On 10 November the remaining Portuguese personnel were withdrawn from Angola. Both the MPLA and the FNLA/UNITA declared independence. The former was recognized by the USSR, Soviet-bloc allies, including Cuba, and some African states. The latter was never officially recognized.

The US crisis terminated on 19 December 1975 when Congress refused to grant aid to Zaire or to support the FNLA/UNITA. An earlier appeal by Secretary of State Kissinger to the NATO Foreign Ministers' Council for support to the FNLA/UNITA was also denied. The crisis for Zambia ended after an MPLA victory had become more apparent. On 18 February 1976 Zambia announced that it would recognize the State of Angola but not the MPLA Government. This was done on 22 February, after negotiations. The crisis for Angola, Cuba and the USSR ended on 24 February 1976 after UNITA, on the 12th, announced its decision to retreat and revert to guerrilla warfare, followed by a similar announcement by the FNLA on the 24th. On 28 February Zaire announced its decision to recognize the Angola Government after talks between Mobutu and MPLA head, Neto. South Africa, after extensive negotiations via British Foreign Secretary Callaghan and the Soviet Ambassador to London, achieved MPLA guarantees for the security of the hydroelectric projects and the safety of the personnel there. On 27 March South Africa announced a complete troop withdrawal from Angola.

There was heavy involvement in the crisis. Cuba, the Soviet Union, the Congo (Brazzaville) and Yugoslavia actively supported the MPLA. The United States, the PRC, North Korea and Zaire aided the FNLA; the latter, in addition to extensive diplomatic activity, provided bases. Zambia, active diplomatically as well, supported UNITA. And Tanzania engaged in political-diplomatic activity and provided ports for Soviet arms to be unloaded for the MPLA. Diplomatic efforts were sustained by the Ivory Coast, Kenya, Uganda and Nigeria.

The OAU used several different procedures in an attempt to settle the conflict; all were unsuccessful. In January 1975 it supported the Alvor Accords. In July it called once more for a cease-fire and a National Unity Government for Angola. OAU conciliation commissions were sent to the area in July and October 1975. On 10–13 January 1976 the OAU held an emergency summit meeting on Angola which broke down on the 13th with members divided evenly on their stands *vis-à-vis* the crisis. By 2 February 1976 a majority of OAU members had recognized the MPLA Government, automatically extending OAU recognition. Angola was admitted to the regional organization on 10 February 1976. By 22 February 70 countries, including those belonging to the EEC, had granted recognition.

The global international organization was less active. The good offices of Secretary-General Waldheim were used to relay MPLA guarantees to South Africa. The UN sent an inquiry and conciliation mission into Portuguese territory on 14 October 1975. On 10 March 1976 Kenya requested an emergency Security

Council session on South Africa's "act of aggression." It took place from 26 to 31 March and, despite South Africa's claim that its troops had already left Angola, a resolution was passed condemning South Africa and demanding that it respect the territorial integrity of Angola, as well as to cease the use of Southwest Africa for military incursions.

Washington had been supplying aid covertly to the FNLA since the Kennedy Administration. In January 1975 an interagency National Security Task Force on Angola was set up. In December the State Department instructed Gulf Oil to suspend royalty payment of $125 million to the MPLA-controlled Finance Ministry. During the Angola Crisis there were widespread strikes and unemployment in the United States in the aftermath of Vietnam and Watergate. These legacies prompted Congress to decide to withdraw aid to Zaire, thereby extricating the US from the crisis in southern Africa.

Angola was viewed by both the Soviet Union and Africans as a watershed in American attitudes to US military intervention in the Third World. The initial Soviet position on Angola was to favor the right of all three rival Angolan movements to participate in the transitional government, but that changed early in 1975. Sino-Soviet rivalry was a major feature of Moscow's approach to the Angolan conflict. Soviet MIG-21s, tanks and missiles were airlifted into Angola for the MPLA, and Soviet naval movements took place outside Angolan waters. With Cuban assistance, Moscow was able to help its local ally, the MPLA, to establish itself as Angola's legitimate government. Nevertheless, the opposing FNLA and UNITA factions remained in control of a considerable portion of Angola's territory and continued to pose a military challenge to MPLA and Cuban troops.

References   Barratt 1976; Bender 1978; Carter and O'Meara 1977; Davis 1978; Dominguez 1978; Ford 1979; Grieg 1977; Hodges 1976; Kaplan 1981; Kitchen 1976; Larrabee 1976; Legum 1975, 1976; Lemarchand 1981; Marcum 1976; Mazrui 1977; Nyerere 1977; Stevens 1976; Stockwell 1978.

(230) Moroccan March-Sahara

Spain and Morocco were the crisis actors from 16 October to 14 November 1975.

Background   The territory of Western Sahara, bordering Morocco on the northeast and Mauritania on the west and south, had been under Spanish colonial rule since the beginning of the twentieth century. In 1965 the United Nations passed a resolution calling on Spain to liberate Spanish Sahara. Franco refused. In 1974 Morocco, interested in obtaining the rich phosphate mines, claimed the territory. In August 1974 Spain enacted a statute proclaiming internal autonomy as the first stage of decolonization. Morocco objected and called for immediate Spanish withdrawal, UN supervision and the repatriation of some 20,000 refugees then in southern Morocco. In October Morocco and Mauritania took the question of sovereignty to the International Court of Justice (ICJ), through the UN Committee on Non-Self-Governing Territories, to determine if Morocco or Mauritania had any legal claim to Western Sahara. Algeria, advocating Saharan independence, was concerned about Moroccan expansion, while Libya declared its willingness to fight Spain for the liberation of the disputed territory. On 16 October 1975 the Court ruled that, despite some links, neither Morocco nor Mauritania had a valid claim to sovereignty over Western Sahara.

A secret agreement to split the territory between Morocco and Mauritania was reached by them on 1 October 1975, after a Spanish announcement that a referendum would be held during the first half of 1976. On 15 October a UN Mission for Decolonization Committee reported sentiment for independence in Western Sahara. The Polisario, an independent liberation movement in Sahara, was formed in 1968. Originally based in Mauritania, it later moved to Algeria.

Crisis   On 16 October 1975 King Hassan of Morocco declared that he interpreted the ICJ's reference to Saharan "links" to Morocco as justification for Moroccan claims to sovereignty over the area and, therefore, he intended to march with 350,000 civilians into Western Sahara to hasten its integration into his kingdom. This triggered a crisis for Spain which, fearing a military clash, attempted to stop the proposed march by appealing to the Security Council. On 28 October Spain imposed emergency measures in order to prevent hostilities. Morocco's crisis was triggered on 2 November when Algeria and Spain announced that the March would be countered by force. That day, Spain's Acting Head of State, Prince Juan Carlos, flew to Sahara. The following day he returned to Spain to hold talks with the Moroccan Prime Minister. A Moroccan minister was also sent to Algeria and 20,000 Moroccan troops were moved to the Saharan border.

Spain's major response, on 5 November, was to withdraw its forces eight miles from the border. The March, Morocco's major response to the crisis, began on 6 November, but was halted by King Hassan on the 10th. The termination of the crisis for both actors was an agreement signed on 14 November 1975 as a result of trilateral negotiations among Mauritania, Morocco and Spain. The agreement divided Western Sahara between Morocco and Mauritania and left Spain a share in the valuable Bu Craa phosphate mines. It provided for Spanish withdrawal on 28 February 1976. Sahara was to be administered jointly by the three countries.

The Security Council met on 20 October 1975 and passed a resolution on the 22nd calling for restraint by all the parties. It also called upon the Secretary-General to begin negotiations which were conducted between 26 and 28 October. The Council convened twice more, on 2 and 8 November. Secretary-General Waldheim's mediation efforts contributed substantially to crisis abatement. The US Assistant Secretary of State was sent to the area in early November and contributed marginally to a settlement.

The signing of the tripartite agreement was to trigger a crisis for Algeria (see Case #232).

References Franck 1976; Fraenkel 1976; Gretton 1980; Henderson 1976; Joffe 1976; Lalutte 1976; Marks 1976; Mercer 1976a, 1976b; Ramchadani 1977.

(231) Belize I   A crisis for Britain over Guatemala's threats to annex the British self-governing colony of Belize occurred between 1 and 30 November 1975.

Background Guatemalan claims to Belize and threats to annex that territory once it became independent were discussed at the UN General Assembly for about 10 years prior to this crisis. The UK retained responsibility for the defense of Belize but, in all other aspects, the colony was self-governing. In 1972 Guatemala threatened to invade Belize, but the incident de-escalated without violence.

Crisis On 1 November 1975 Britain perceived a likely military invasion of Belize following increased Guatemalan military activity which took the form of a movement of troops and patrol boats near the Belize border. Its response, on 5 November, was the dispatch of additional forces to strengthen the British garrison in Belize. A declaration by Guatemala that it intended to annex Belize was reported on the 7th. Talks were held during a visit by Edward Rowlands, UK Minister of State at the Foreign Office, to Guatemala and Belize. An agreement was reached on 30 November, terminating the crisis. The two countries would resume talks about the future of Belize in February 1976. Troops were subsequently withdrawn on both sides.

The UN Trusteeship Council adopted a resolution on 20 November urging the resumption of negotiations between the UK and Guatemala. An earlier offer of UN arbitration had been rejected by Guatemala. Two years later a second UK crisis occurred over Belize (see Case #248).

References See general list, especially *The Economist, Keesing's, New York Times* and *Times of London.*

(232) Sahara   The second crisis over Western Sahara, with Algeria, Mauritania and Morocco as crisis actors, began on 14 November 1975 and faded sometime near the end of April 1976.

Background   The Moroccan March into Western Sahara began on 6 November 1975 (see Case #230). On 14 November an agreement was signed between Morocco and Mauritania dividing the territory of the Sahara between them. Spain's scheduled withdrawal was to be on 28 February 1976; it would retain a share in the valuable phosphate mines.

Crisis   The agreement of 14 November 1975 to divide Western Sahara triggered a crisis for Algeria where Polisario bases were situated. Clashes between troops from Morocco and Mauritania with Polisario guerrillas and regular Algerian troops began in December. A crisis for Mauritania was triggered on 10 December with the first major Polisario offensive, allegedly aided by Cuban and North Vietnam "volunteers." Mauritania responded the same day with force. The very strong resistance to its occupation of Western Sahara came as a surprise.

On 27 January 1976 Algerian troops launched a major attack on Moroccan forces in response to the agreement to divide Western Sahara between Morocco and Mauritania. This triggered a crisis for Morocco which responded with force and increased efforts to occupy more of the disputed territory. Spain withdrew two days ahead of schedule, on 26 February. The following day the Polisario declared its independence as the Saharan Arab Democratic Republic. The SADR was recognized on 6 March by Algeria, whose crisis was thus terminated. Relations with Algeria were broken by Morocco and Mauritania on the 7th. Other African countries, together with North Korea, also granted immediate recognition to Saharan independence, but Morocco and Mauritania remained adamant in their demand for a division of Western Sahara between them.

On 14 April Morocco's crisis ended with the signing of a convention with Mauritania, fixing the borders of the divided territory. In early April King Hassan had sent emissaries to a number of governments explaining Morocco's position. Clashes still continued, however, particularly between Mauritanian and Polisario troops; these gradually faded by the end of April. New tensions would break out once more in June.

Mediation was attempted by Egypt and Libya. Spain was also an involved actor. The OAU debated the issue from 26 February to 1 March 1976 and passed a compromise resolution leaving the decision to the individual members whether or not to recognize the Saharan Arab Democratic Republic. A joint effort was made by the OAU and the League of Arab States in sending the League's Secretary-General, Mahmoud Riad, to the area, but no solution was found.

Mediation was also attempted by the UN Secretary-General and his appointee, the Swedish Ambassador to the UN, Olof Rydbeck, during March and April, but it was stymied because of the refusal of any of the parties to compromise on their positions. The United States supplied aid to Morocco. And a Moroccan plane, shot down by a Soviet SAM-3 missile, gave evidence of covert Soviet aid to Algeria and the Polisario. Four years later, in July 1980, Sahara was accepted into OAU membership following recognition by 36 of the 49 member-states.

References   See sources for Case #230.

(233) Cod War II   Disputes over fishing rights in waters contiguous to Iceland precipitated a crisis for the UK and Iceland from 23 November 1975 to 1 June 1976.

Background   In November 1973 an agreement was reached between Iceland and the UK which set the former's territorial waters as 50 miles offshore, within which certain areas were set aside for British fishermen (see Case #223). On 15 July 1975 the Government of Iceland announced its intention to extend its territorial waters to 200 miles off the Icelandic coast, as of 15 October; further, all foreign vessels would be forbidden to fish inside the new limit. During November Icelandic gunboats harassed British trawlers fishing for cod within the 200-mile limit. A number of similar incidents occurred.

Crisis   On 23 November British trawler skippers warned the UK that they would withdraw from Iceland's 200-mile zone unless they were assured of Royal Navy protection. On the 25th the British Government, convinced of the danger to the welfare and safety of the fishermen, decided to dispatch frigates to the Icelandic waters, triggering a crisis for Iceland. Iceland's Foreign Minister termed this UK move as "unmasked armed violence" and initiated talks between the two governments. The Foreign Ministers met in December 1975, and the Prime Ministers in January 1976. When these talks did not achieve progress, Iceland broke diplomatic relations with Britain on 18 February. Britain maintained the presence of the Royal Navy in Icelandic waters throughout the crisis, in order to protect the trawlers engaged in uninterrupted fishing. On 1 June 1976 an interim agreement between the two countries was signed in Oslo, allowing British trawlers fishing rights within the 200-mile zone, while limiting their number to an average of 24 trawlers a day.

Discussions were held in the Security Council from 2 to 11 December 1975 and talks between the two disputants were held under UN auspices. NATO and the Nordic Council discussed the military and economic issues of the crisis and met with the Icelandic and British leaders.

References   See general list.

(234) East Timor   The disputed territory of East Timor generated a crisis for Indonesia from 28 November 1975 to 17 July 1976.

Background   The three most important political parties in Portuguese East Timor were Fietilin, which demanded immediate independence, UDT, which favored eventual independence with the continuation of ties to Portugal, and Apodeti, which wanted integration into Indonesia. After the Portuguese Government announced its intention to relinquish control over all overseas territories, the UDT held high-level talks with Indonesian officials and announced, on 6 August 1975, that the party had decided to follow a political line acceptable to Indonesia. On 11 August the UDT carried out a coup in East Timor and demanded immediate independence from Portugal. Fighting between Fietilin and UDT factions broke out immediately. On 27 August the Governor of East Timor admitted that the Portuguese authorities had lost control of the situation. The Portuguese Administration then abandoned East Timor and retreated to the offshore island of Atauro. Portugal rejected Indonesia's offer to move in and restore order. As fighting intensified in September, an announcement was made by the Defense Ministry in Jakarta, on 9 September, that Indonesia would refuse to accept any Portuguese move to hand over East Timor to a government dominated by Fietilin, which at that time controlled a major part of the East Timor territory. This was followed by an announcement by the Foreign Minister that Indonesia had the right to intervene in East Timor if war endangered its territory. Border clashes increased in October and, on the 11th, Fietilin announced that a transitional administration had been established.

Crisis   The crisis trigger for Indonesia was the Fietilin declaration of East Timor's independence on 28 November 1975. Indonesia feared that an independent East Timor would encourage internal secessionist movements in Sumatra, West Irian and the South Moluccas, as well as aid Communist infiltration and influence in the area. On 29 November the pro-Indonesian political parties in East Timor declared it to be a part of Indonesia. That day, too, Portugal rejected all declarations of independence and, on 30 November, formally requested help from the UN to settle the problem. The major Indonesian response, on 7 December, was a large-scale invasion of East Timor. Portugal severed relations with Indonesia and requested a meeting of the Security Council. A second invasion was launched on 25 December, with heavy fighting between Fietilin and Indonesian forces continuing throughout December.

In March 1976 the East Timor Provisional Government announced its intention to integrate the island with Indonesia. This was followed by an Indonesian declaration that its troops would be withdrawn. The integration was approved by the East Timor People's Assembly on 31 May and, on 17 July 1976 the crisis for Indonesia ended when President Suharto signed a bill formally incorporating East Timor into Indonesia. At that time, the Indonesian forces had achieved control of the entire coastal area but not much of the interior.

The UN General Assembly passed a resolution on 12 December 1975 calling for withdrawal of Indonesian forces. On the 12th the General Assembly condemned Indonesian military intervention; and it, too, called for withdrawal. The UN Security Council met five times between 15 and 22 December 1975. On the 22nd it passed a resolution calling on Indonesia to withdraw its forces from East Timor without delay and urged that a special representative of the Secretary-General be sent to assess the situation. This was done in late January 1976, but he was unable to establish contact with the Fietilin. On 22 April another resolution with the same content was adopted. None of these resolutions helped to abate the crisis.

References Kamm 1981; Lawless 1976; Leifer 1976; Nichterlein 1977; Viviani 1976.

(235) Lebanon Civil War I The civil war in Lebanon created a crisis for Syria from 18 January to 30 September 1976.

Background The civil war in Lebanon began in April 1975: it was the culmination of years of gradual social dislocation of Lebanese society which developed into a polarization of the indigenous Christian and Muslim communities and signalled the possibility of the disintegration of Lebanon. Syria has always maintained that Lebanon and Syria are integral parts of Greater Syria and that the division of the two countries was artificially created by France to serve its colonial interests. Thus a possible partition of Lebanon was perceived by Syria as a threat to its vital security interests: first, as undermining Syria's image as the guardian of Arab nationalism and unity; and secondly, as giving Israel a pretext to move into Southern Lebanon and occupy the area up to the Litani River. Syria's primary interest, in 1975, was to mediate among the conflicting parties in Lebanon. Towards the end of that year victories of the Christian militias seemed to heighten the possibility of a partition of Lebanon. On 7 January 1976 Syria threatened to intervene militarily after the Christians began a concerted drive to clear the region of "alien" elements.

Crisis On 18 January 1976 Lebanese Christian forces triggered a crisis for Syria when they overran al-Karantina and al-Maslakh, the predominantly Muslim towns in the "Christian Heartland," and proceeded to expel their residents. The following day Syria responded by dispatching to Lebanon the Yarmouk Brigade of the Syrian-controlled Palestine Liberation Army, in response to appeals by Lebanese leftist Muslim leaders. On the 19th, as well, Syria sent a delegation to Lebanon to try to impose an effective cease-fire. Shortly after coming to the rescue of the Muslim Lebanese and Palestinians, Syrian threat perceptions began to change. They no longer saw the Christians as a catalyst to a Lebanese partition; rather, it was now the Muslim leftists and their PLO allies who, on the momentum of successive victories, threatened the fragile Lebanese equilibrium. On 28 March Syria decided to place an embargo on all arms supplies to the leftist-PLO coalition. By 9 April Syria was sending clear signals to the leftists that Syrian troops concentrating on the Lebanese border would be brought into use if their intransigence persisted. On 1 June Syrian troops poured into Lebanon in order to force a resolution of the conflict. The immediate – and successful – goal was the relief of some Christian villages under siege. The Syrian advance against the Muslim leftist-PLO forces continued throughout the summer. On 28 September Syria decided to inflict a military defeat on them to be followed immediately by peace talks in which the Syrian point of view would be imposed. A massive offensive smashed all Palestinian forces in the Lebanese mountains. By 30 September all opposition in Lebanon to Syria's hegemony had been overcome and partition had been averted.

An Arab Deterrent Force was subsequently authorized by the Arab League, composed of 20,000 to 30,000 Syrian troops. Shortly after, Syria reverted to its traditional pro-Palestinian stance, supporting the latter against the Israeli-backed Christian militias.

Secretary-General Waldheim offered his good offices for UN mediation, but it was refused. US political activity consisted of verbal approbation of Syrian actions and serving as a conduit between Syria and Israel, relaying intentions and information. The USSR supported Syria until the 1 June invasion – to which it was strongly opposed. Arms deliveries to Damascus were halted. Syria's careful efforts not to provoke Israel by crossing the "Red Line" of the Litani River kept the latter out of the Lebanon fighting. During the crisis an Iraqi troop movement to the Syrian border precipitated another crisis for Syria from 9 to 17 June (see Case #239).

References Dawisha 1978, 1980; Heller 1980; Rabin 1979; Vocke 1978.

(236) Uganda Claims Ugandan claims to Kenyan territory caused a crisis for Kenya from 15 to 24 February 1976.

Background Disputes between Uganda and the two other members of the East African Community, Kenya and Tanzania, had occurred for 5 years prior to this crisis. In 1971 and 1972 confrontations took place between Uganda and Tanzania over Idi Amin's allegations of Tanzanian support for exiled Ugandans (see Cases #214, #216). During the next several years Idi Amin's behavior became more aggressive. There was a gradual deterioration of relations between Uganda and Kenya since 1975.

Crisis On 15 February 1976 a crisis was triggered for Kenya when Idi Amin announced that large parts of Kenya and the Sudan historically belonged to Uganda and that he was investigating the possibility of claiming these territories. The disputed area extended to within 20 miles of Nairobi, Kenya's capital. Amin stated further that, despite his preference for peace, he would consider engaging Kenya in war in order to recover the territory. Should Uganda's access to the sea be denied by any country (Kenya or Tanzania), war would be the result. The following day another Amin statement, while withdrawing an actual claim to the areas, guaranteed the security of any Ugandans within that territory who sought independence. He also intimated that he was connected with the Luos secession movement in western Kenya. Kenya responded on 17 February when President Kenyatta addressed a mass rally, stating Kenya's readiness to fight to protect its territorial integrity. Amin cabled the OAU Secretary-General setting forth Ugandan claims, along with vague threats accompanying a denial of any intention to go to war. The OAU never met to discuss the issue. Amin approached the UN as well, but there was no activity by the global organization either. In Kenya protests were held in the town of Kakamega. On 20 February Kenyatta cancelled two ministerial meetings of the East African Community and refused to participate in any further Community work until the issue between Uganda and Kenya was settled. On 23 February dock workers in Mombassa boycotted Ugandan cargo.

 The crisis ended on 24 February when Kenyatta received a message from Amin disavowing any intention to seize territory from Kenya or Sudan. A telephone conversation between the two Presidents was reported the following day dealing with matters other than territorial claims.

References See general list, especially *Keesing's*.

(237) Operation Thrasher The first of several international crises concerning the struggle for black majority rule in Rhodesia erupted on 22 February and ended in April 1976. Mozambique and Rhodesia were the crisis actors.

Background According to figures published by the Central Statistical Office in Salisbury, Rhodesia, there were, in June 1975, a total of 277,000 "Europeans" in Rhodesia, 6,000,000 "Africans," 10,000 "Asians" and 20,400 "Coloureds." In November 1965 Rhodesia had proclaimed a Unilateral Declaration of Independence (see Case #185). Opposition from African states was fierce, and condemnation followed from the UN, the OAU and the vast majority of states in the international community. The UK undertook a commitment to the principles of a peaceful solution and a negotiated settlement which would lead to majority rule in Rhodesia. Systematic guerrilla activity began in Rhodesia in December 1972, but was restricted to the northeast. When the campaign extended throughout the whole country in 1976, Rhodesia became involved in a full-scale war. The scale of operations also changed, as large groups of guerrillas entered Rhodesia, operating from Mozambique, Botswana and Zambia. The Zimbabwe African People's Union (ZAPU), headed by Joshua Nkomo, was based in Zambia. Its military wing was the Zimbabwe People's Revolutionary Army (ZIPRA). The Zimbabwe African National Union (ZANU), headed by Robert Mugabe, was based in Mozambique. Its military wing was the Zimbabwe African National Liberation Army (ZANLA). Together they formed the African National Council (ANC) whose office was situated in Botswana.

The Heads of State of the "Frontline States" – then Botswana, Mozambique, Tanzania and Zambia – met in Mozambique on 7 and 8 February 1976. There they reaffirmed the need for an armed struggle to achieve majority rule in Rhodesia. On the 8th, Mozambique President Machel threatened to invade Rhodesia. Constitutional talks between Rhodesian Prime Minister Smith and Nkomo, representing the ANC, were resumed on 10 February.

Crisis   The first clash involving Rhodesian security forces, which triggered a crisis for Rhodesia, was a 3-hour battle on 22 February 1976 with "unidentified" forces from across the Mozambique border. Further guerrilla activity was reported in the Chipinga district, 180 miles south of the northeastern border, on the 24th. Rhodesia responded that day by launching Operation Thrasher with an attack on ZANLA bases on its southeastern border with Mozambique, causing the death of a number of people and extensive damage, which in turn triggered a crisis for Mozambique. Machel described the attack as an act of war and stated that Mozambique forces had shot down Rhodesian aircraft and helicopters, a claim which was not backed by other sources. The Mozambique response was to meet the Rhodesian forces with violence, an announcement of 3 March that all communications with Rhodesia had been banned, and the imposition of sanctions – including the confiscation of all Rhodesian property and assets in Mozambique in accordance with earlier UN and OAU resolutions. On the 8th, Mozambique closed its border with Rhodesia and the country was put on a war footing.

The crisis for Rhodesia faded in March 1976 with a temporary halt in guerrilla activities. The Smith–Nkomo talks ended in deadlock on 19 March with each side blaming the other. The crisis ended in April for Mozambique with a decision to set up a joint institute for the training of defense and police forces with Tanzania and Zambia.

The Security Council met in March and adopted a resolution on the 17th condemning Rhodesia. Mozambique's Foreign Minister appealed to the Council for $57 million in aid to meet the direct consequences of the loss of revenue from the imposition of sanctions against Rhodesia. Another Security Council resolution on 6 April strengthened the sanctions. The OAU supported the UN sanctions and granted military aid to the guerrillas.

United States' involvement was political – several statements by Secretary of State Kissinger favorable to Mozambique. The Soviet Union supplied weapons to ZIPRA and ZANLA.

References   See sources for Case #276.

(238) Nouakchott I   A Polisario attack on Mauritania's capital city caused a one-day crisis for Mauritania on 8 June 1976.

Background   The former Spanish territory of Western Sahara had been occupied by Morocco and Mauritania following the conclusion of a tripartite agreement with Spain in November 1975 (see Case #230). The Algerian-backed Popular Front for the Liberation of Saguia el Hamra and Rio de Oro (Polisario), which had been struggling for control over the territory for several years, continued to wage guerrilla war against both states. Polisario was originally based in Mauritania, where it received government support; but it later moved to Algeria which became the Front's faithful ally. When Western Sahara was formally handed over to Morocco and Mauritania on 28 February 1976, the Saharan Arab Democratic Republic was established in the name of Polisario. Algeria recognized the Polisario regime, but Mauritania and Morocco did not, signing an agreement on 14 April fixing the borders of the divided Western Sahara between the two countries. Clashes continued between Mauritania and Polisario (see Case #232), as the latter concentrated its attacks on Mauritania, which was viewed as being the weakest link in the chain.

Crisis On 8 June 1976 a force of 600–700 Polisario guerrillas attacked the Mauritanian capital city of Nouakchott, threatening Mauritania's political regime: the attack took the form of a lightning mortar and machine-gun offensive with several mortar shells falling around the Presidential Palace of Ould Daddah, causing turmoil and panic in the city. The Mauritanian response came immediately after the firing when troops reportedly crushed the attacking forces, killing Polisario leader El-Ouali. The remaining Polisario troops withdrew after an hour, thus terminating the crisis on the day of the attack. The conflict in Western Sahara had assumed the nature of a war with the failure of the Polisario–Algerian efforts for the independence of the territory. Nouakchott was attacked a second time in March 1977 (see Case #249).

References See general list, especially *Africa Contemporary Record, Africa Diary, Africa Recorder* and *New York Times*.

(239) Iraqi Threat   An Iraqi troop concentration on the Syrian border caused a crisis for Syria from 9 to 17 June 1976.

Background Events in the Middle East Core in 1976 were complex. A civil war was raging in Lebanon, with Syrian military participation in the attempt to avert a partition of Lebanon (see Case #235). Syria's 1974 Disengagement Agreement with Israel (see Case #224) had facilitated an uneasy truce between the two countries, with Syria maintaining a division on its border in the Golan Heights. Iraqi relations with the rival Ba'ath regime in Syria were openly tense. In addition, disputes between Iraq and Syria's ally, Iran, over the Shatt-al-Arab had never been solved (see Cases #138, #202). In June 1976 Syria's preoccupation with events in Lebanon afforded Iraq an opportunity to attempt to weaken President Assad's regime.

Crisis On 9 June 1976, in a sudden and surprise action, Iraq moved troops to its border with Syria, triggering a crisis for the latter. Part of Syria's army was engaged in a heavy offensive in the civil war in Lebanon, with much of its forces occupied with protecting Syria's border with Israel. A tacit agreement with Israel was sought to allow Syria to transfer troops from the Golan Heights. When this was achieved Syria responded on 13 June by removing the division from the Golan Heights and placing it on the Iraqi border. On 17 June the crisis ended when President Assad, the highest Syrian decision-making authority, signalled the decline of threat perception by leaving the country for a 3-day visit to France. In a short while, the forces of both Iraq and Syria withdrew from the border and resumed their original positions.

References See general list.

(240) Entebbe Raid   Israeli hostages held in Uganda caused a crisis for Israel from 30 June to 4 July 1976.

Background Terrorist activity against Israel by the Palestine Liberation Organization (PLO) took several forms, including the hijacking of planes, from Israel's national carrier or other airlines carrying Israeli passengers. By instituting strict security controls, these acts diminished in number. However, the security conditions at some airports remained less than stringent. One of these was Athens. On 27 June 1976 an Air France plane en route from Tel Aviv to Paris was hijacked, shortly after a stopover in Athens, by an armed group belonging to the Popular Front for the Liberation of Palestine (PFLP), including persons from Germany's terrorist organization, Bader-Meinhof. The plane was forced to fly to Libya where it spent 9 hours. Later it reached Entebbe, Uganda's airport. The passengers, many of whom were Israelis, were taken to the airport's former terminal building and divided into two groups –

Israelis and Jews, and members of other nationalities. The latter were released shortly thereafter and the French crew remained with the former.

Crisis On 30 June a crisis was triggered for Israel when it perceived that Uganda's President, Idi Amin, had no intention of pressing for the release of the Jewish and Israeli passengers. Israel began to consider a military operation for their rescue. A decision to that effect was made on 1 July. On the 3rd three Hercules transport planes carrying Israeli commando troops landed in Entebbe, fought Ugandan soldiers in a one-hour battle and succeeded in rescuing the hostages still being held at the airport. On the 4th the crisis ended when the rescue team, together with the hostages, landed safely in Israel after a stop for fuel at Nairobi Airport.

During the hour that the surprise attack took place, Uganda's highest-level decision-maker was unaware of the events. After the rescue, Amin blamed Kenya for aiding Israel and instituted several economic measures against that country. In Arab League discussions Israel was condemned for the raid on Uganda but no resolution was passed.

References Rabin 1979; Ya'akobi 1980.

(241) Sudan Coup Attempt A Libyan-backed attempt to overthrow President Numeiri caused a crisis for Sudan from 2 to 15 July 1976.

Background With Sudan's independence on 1 January 1956 the predominantly Muslim region in the north was united with the non-Muslim Sudanese in the south. Regional diversity persisted in the post-independence period, with the most acute domestic problem being the question of Sudan's southern provinces, where open rebellion to the regime began in 1963. Harsh military action caused a large number of southern Sudanese to take refuge in neighboring countries. A guerrilla war began in January 1964. The unrest in the south was one of the main reasons for the bloodless military coup staged by a group of army officers under Colonel Numeiri in May 1969 which invested absolute powers in a National Revolutionary Council. Numeiri formally recognized southern autonomy and attempted to include southern political leaders in the government. Negotiations with the Anya-Nya guerrilla organization, based in Uganda, were begun in 1971. The following year the civil war ended in Sudan, but hostilities in the south persisted. Relations between Sudan and Libya were strained. The former, together with Egypt and Saudi Arabia, were in the Western camp; Libya was strongly supported by the USSR. Libyan forces in Chad was another bone of contention between Libya, which wished them to remain, and Sudan, which advocated their withdrawal (see Case #212). Libya's leader, Qaddhafi, took advantage of Sudan's north/south problem, and Numeiri's absence from the country, to encourage an attempt to overthrow Sudan's government.

Crisis Minutes after President Numeiri arrived at Khartoum airport, on his return from a visit to the United States and France, on 2 July 1976, grenades exploded in many parts of the city, and armed civilians advanced on the airport. The coup was suppressed by loyal government troops after some loss of life and considerable damage to property. Sudan accused Libya of designing the coup attempt and of an act of armed aggression: Libya, Numeiri claimed, provided training, arms, ammunition and transport to the rebels. A complaint was lodged by Sudan in the Security Council on 4 July, and on the 6th Sudan broke off diplomatic relations with Libya. The crisis ended for Sudan with the signing of a joint Defense Agreement between Egypt and Sudan on 15 July: Libya was defined as the common enemy in the agreement.

The OAU and the Arab League were both involved in this crisis, although neither regional organization had any effect on the outcome: the latter urged President Numeiri to withdraw his complaint to the Security Council with a promise that his accusations against Libya would be investigated. The UN was inactive, as were both superpowers.

References See general list and Nelson 1979.

(242) Aegean Sea A crisis for Greece occurred from 7 August to 25 September 1976 over the dispute with Turkey about rights to resources in the Aegean Sea.

Background The long-standing adversarial relationship between Greece and Turkey flared up when a Turkish geological exploration was planned for certain areas of the Aegean Sea. Greece claimed sole rights to the resources of the continental shelf of its Aegean islands. This claim was disputed by the Government of Turkey. In mid-July 1976 it became known in Greece that the Turkish exploration would begin. On the 19th Greece threatened military reprisals if Turkey violated Greek jurisdiction in the Aegean Sea. This threat was ignored by Turkey which subsequently dispatched a seismic ship toward the disputed area.

Crisis A crisis for Greece was triggered on 7 August when it learned that the Turkish research ship had entered Greek disputed waters. Greece filed a complaint with Turkey. The major response, on 12 August, was to declare a state of alert for all Greek troops along the Greece–Turkey border, and almost all of the Air Force was moved to advance bases. The Greek Navy began patrolling the eastern Aegean, where the Turkish vessel continued to take seismic soundings. In addition, negotiations with the Turkish Foreign Minister were carried out through United States auspices, a complaint was registered with the Security Council, and an appeal was made to the International Court of Justice. NATO called upon the two countries to exercise restraint. The Security Council passed a resolution calling upon them to resume negotiations for a peaceful solution. So too did the Soviet Union.

In September the Turkish Navy announced that the research ship would cease to operate; and on 25 September it returned to Turkish waters terminating the crisis for Greece. Turkey's decision-makers did not perceive a crisis at that time. In September the United States agreed to sell Turkey military equipment, including planes.

References See general list.

(243) Nagomia Raid A Rhodesian "hot pursuit" operation precipitated a second crisis for Mozambique on 9 August 1976 ending in November of that year.

Background In March 1976 President Samora Machel announced the closure of his country's borders with Rhodesia and the country was put on a war footing (see Case #237). A sharp rise in guerrilla activity had increased Rhodesian "hot pursuit" operations which had been taking place since Rhodesia's war spread to its eastern border with Mozambique. Early in August guerrilla attacks on Rhodesian security forces occurred at a camp at Ruda.

Crisis On 9 August 1976 Rhodesian forces raided a guerrilla camp at Nagomia, Mozambique, and triggered a crisis for that state: it was reported that more than 300 Zimbabweans were killed. This dramatic operation, in which, according to Mozambique sources, approximately 600 were killed, was the largest raid across the border by Rhodesia. Mozambique responded on 11 August with a 30-minute mortar attack by government troops on a white residential suburb in Umtali, Rhodesia, close to the Mozambique border. Mozambique requested an investigation by the UN High Commission on Refugees which subsequently reported that the Pungwe camp on the Nagomia road was a refugee camp containing 8000 black Rhodesians and that many women and children were among the 500 dead counted by UN officials. Rhodesia, on the other hand, produced captured documents on 29 August to provide evidence that the camp was a military base for several thousand Rhodesian African nationalist guerrillas. Further attacks on Mozambique territory were reported during August.

On 6 September the "Front Line States" (then Botswana, Mozambique, Tanzania and Zambia) met in Dar-es-Salaam to coordinate their defense policies.

Secretary of State Kissinger arrived in the area on 13 September, and soon thereafter agreements were concluded for $10 million in US aid to Mozambique. Mozambique's Foreign Minister addressed the General Assembly on 5 October 1976. And, at a meeting in November 1976, an Inter-State Defense Commission decided to organize joint action for the defense of the Front Line States. This ended the crisis for Mozambique.

The USSR, which had been supplying semi-military, medical and other aid to the guerrillas, published a condemnation of Rhodesia in *Pravda* in August.

References See sources for Case #276.

(244) Syria Mobilization A Syrian Army advance towards southern Lebanon precipitated a crisis for Israel from 21 November to 13 December 1976.

Background In an attempt to avoid the partition of Lebanon during the latter's civil war, Syrian troops entered Lebanon in January 1976 (see Case #235). By September Syria had defeated Palestinian and Lebanese Muslim leftists and remained in control of large areas of the country. In the middle of October a summit meeting of the Heads of State of Arab countries took place in Riyadh, Saudi Arabia. On 18 October a comprehensive peace plan for Lebanon was signed, setting up an Arab Deterrent Force, consisting almost entirely of Syrian troops. By 20 November Syria controlled all the key points in Lebanon with the exception of the area south of the Litani River bordering with Israel. A tacit agreement was reached with Israel marking the Litani as the "Red Line," whereby both countries avoided confrontation.

Crisis On 21 November, as Syrian forces pushed towards South Lebanon, Israel perceived a crisis, recognizing that Syria might break the tacit "Red Line" agreement, thereby undermining Israel's influence in Lebanon. Israel responded the following day by concentrating infantry and tanks along its northern border with Lebanon. In Jerusalem Prime Minister Rabin met with US Ambassador Lewis to discuss the situation on 23 November, while in Washington talks were held between Ambassador Dinitz and US Secretary of State Kissinger. The Syrians halted at the Litani River. By 13 December the situation stabilized and the tacit agreement between the two countries was restored.

References See general list, especially *Ha'aretz* and *Ma'ariv*.

(245) Operation Tangent The extension of Rhodesian military operations against African guerrillas to include the border area with Botswana caused a crisis for Botswana from 20 December 1976 to 31 March 1977.

Background In February 1976 Rhodesia launched Operation Thrasher to deal with military incursions by Mozambique-based guerrillas into its territory (see Case #237). During that year a number of guerrilla operations were mounted from Botswana staging camps. Rhodesian security forces increased dramatically their incursions into Botswana which issued a public accusation on 12 August. In November a villager was killed and several bombs exploded in Francistown at the office of the African National Council (ANC). On 15 December Rhodesian forces raided a village on the border and kidnapped three Botswana citizens. Three days later fire was exchanged between Botswana police and Rhodesian troops. And on the 20th Botswana claimed that its territory had been violated by Rhodesian forces 31 times since the beginning of November 1976.

Crisis On 20 December 1976 the Rhodesian Government announced the definition of a new operational military zone – Operation Tangent – in the northwest and west covering the Botswana border area. This announcement triggered a crisis for Botswana, particularly because it maintained a police force only, and had no army. Botswana responded by declaring the 30-kilometer border with Rhodesia a protected area, imposing a curfew, and appealing to the UN Security Council on 21 December. It also set up a Police Mobile Unit to patrol the border and expanded it in January 1977. The Security Council met on 14 January and condemned Rhodesian incursions into Botswana, demanding the cessation of all hostile acts. The Council accepted a Botswana invitation to send a mission to assess its needs and requested the Secretary-General to organize immediately financial and other forms of assistance to Botswana and to report back to the Council not later than 31 March. The UN mission, which visited Botswana in February, reported that there was evidence of Rhodesian incursions and stated that Botswana's difficulties had been increased severely by the influx of refugees. The report recommended a $50 million grant over 3 years, half for reinforcing the Police Mobile Unit and the rest for the care of the refugees. On that day, 31 March 1977, Botswana decided to establish a formal army. The UN report terminated the crisis.

The USSR offered economic aid to Botswana.

References See sources for Case #276.

(246) Shaba I

An invasion of Zaire by former Katangan exiles based in Angola brought about a crisis for Zaire and Angola from 8 March to 26 May 1977.

Background Rebel forces in the Congo fled across the border to Angola and Zambia after Colonel Mobutu instigated a successful coup in Zaire in November 1965 (see Case #178). In Angola members of the Congolese National Liberation Front (FLNC) were trained and aided by personnel and equipment from the Soviet Union and Cuba. During 1966 and 1967 armed rebellion in Angola received assistance from Zaire, while Portugal supported separatist sentiments in that country. Border incidents and clashes intensified as guerrilla independence movements became stronger. These conflicts continued throughout the Angolan Civil War (see Case #229), with Zaire, on a number of occasions, complaining to the UN Security Council of rebel incursions from Angolan territory into its southern province of Shaba.

Crisis On 8 March 1977 Shaba was invaded by former Katangan exiles residing in Angola, triggering a crisis for Zaire. A crisis for Angola was triggered the same day when President Mobutu accused Angola, together with Cuba and the USSR, of being involved in an attempt to overthrow his regime. Angola feared an attack on its territory from Zaire and an internationalization of the conflict. Zaire responded with force on the day of the attack but, aware of its inability to repel the invaders alone, an appeal for help was sent to African states, Belgium and the United States. Morocco dispatched 1500 troops by a French-supplied airlift. Pilots and mechanics were sent from Egypt. Non-lethal aid was supplied by the US. The Angolan response was a statement on 11 March by the Defence Ministry disclaiming any responsibility for the invasion. On that day the FLNC announced in Paris that the object of the invasion was to overthrow Mobutu's regime.

With the help of Moroccan troops and French advisors the Zairian Army was able to stop the advance of the invading forces and, subsequently, to reoccupy all the towns and villages. The Moroccans completed their mission on 22 May and withdrew, as did the Egyptians on the 25th. When the foreign troops left Zaire, Angola's fear of internationalization of the conflict subsided and its crisis terminated on 25 May. The following day, Zairian troops recaptured the last town held by the secessionist rebels in Shaba, ending Zaire's crisis.

References See general list, especially *Africa* and Hul 1977.

(247) Mapai Seizure

Rhodesian raids into guerrilla camps inside Mozambique caused a third crisis for that country from 29 May to 30 June 1977.

Background Beginning in March 1976 Rhodesian troops and aircraft repeatedly raided across the 1200-kilometer border with Mozambique in order to harass Zimbabwean guerrillas before they could infiltrate into Rhodesia, and to strike at economic targets in a bid to drive home to the Maputo regime the high cost of its support for the Zimbabwean insurgents (see Cases #237, #243).

Crisis On 29 May 1977 the Rhodesian Military Command announced that security forces, with air support, had entered southwest Mozambique and overrun guerrilla bases. The attack triggered a crisis for Mozambique; and on the same day its Minister of Defense stated that the Rhodesian military operations had been directed at military installations. On 30 May, after more raids, Mozambique announced a counter-offensive. The following day the crisis escalated when the chief of Rhodesia's armed forces announced that troops had occupied the town of Mapai and were prepared to stay in Mozambique as long as was necessary in order to destroy the ZANLA (military wing of ZANU, Zimbabwe African National Union) terrorists in the area.

The Rhodesian actions drew particularly strong condemnations from the international community. On 1 June UN Secretary-General Waldheim condemned it, as did the US and the UK. Even South African Prime Minister Vorster issued a statement of concern that the Rhodesian action would lead to increased Communist (Cuban) activity.

The Rhodesian troops withdrew from Mapai on 1–2 June, but the tension level remained high. On 18 June Mozambique President Machel accused Rhodesia of waging open warfare against his country and requested a meeting of the UN Security Council. The Council passed a resolution at the end of June condemning Rhodesia for aggression against Mozambique. The resolution also requested immediate and substantial material assistance to enable Mozambique to strengthen its defense capability in order to safeguard its sovereignty and territorial integrity. This resolution, on 30 June, terminated the crisis for Mozambique.

References See sources for Case #276.

(248) Belize II Guatemalan claims to Belize caused a second crisis for the UK from 25 June to 28 July 1977.

Background Belize's independence from Britain had been delayed for many years because of Guatemalan threats to invade the territory once it became independent, claiming historic rights to its annexation. In 1975 Britain perceived a threat that Guatemala would invade Belize (see Case #231). The issue has been discussed in the United Nations General Assembly year after year. In the early summer of 1977 the possibility of independence for Belize once more precipitated Guatemalan action. On 17 June Guatemala's Defense Minister stated that his country's forces were waiting for word from the President to begin the recovery of Belize.

Crisis On 25 June 1977 Guatemalan troops were deployed to the Belize border area and reservists were called up. This action triggered a crisis for the UK which was responsible for Belize's security. It was followed by a statement from President Garcia on 1 July affirming Guatemala's rights to the territory. The UK responded on 6 July by dispatching air, infantry and naval forces to the area. HMS *Achilles* took up position in Belizean waters, and British troops were moved to within two miles of Guatemala's border. At the request of the United States, British Minister of State Edward Rowlands visited Washington to hold talks with Secretary of State Cyrus Vance. Vance then held separate talks with Guatemala's Foreign Minister Adolfo Molina and a Belizean delegation led by Premier George Price. It was decided that Rowlands would visit Guatemala. He did so from 26 to 28 July. A communiqué was issued on the 28th in which both sides agreed to take steps to reduce the border tension adding that there would be no sudden move to independence for Belize, thus terminating the UK crisis over Belize.

The United States welcomed the outcome of the talks.

Independence for Belize was proclaimed in 1981.

References See general list, especially *Keesing's, New York Times* and *Times of London*.

(249) Nouakchott II   A Polisario invasion of Mauritania's capital city on 3 July 1977 precipitated a crisis for Mauritania lasting until late that month.

Background The conflict over Western Sahara began in 1975 (see Cases #230, #232). A Polisario attack on Nouakchott took place in June 1976 (see Case #238). During the following year, the Moroccan and Mauritanian armies had undergone major expansion to deal with the increasing frequency and severity of the Polisario attacks: the former from 60,000 to 90,000 and the latter, reportedly, from 3000 to 12,000 men. On 13 May 1977 the Moroccan–Mauritanian Supreme Defense Committee was established to deal with the Sahara problem. Its first meeting took place the following month.

Crisis Polisario forces, backed by Algeria, attacked the capital city of Mauritania on 3 July 1977, triggering a crisis for Mauritania. The Polisario claimed to have caused heavy losses and damage; Mauritania reported one civilian and one soldier killed. On 12 July the Mauritanian Permanent Representative to the United Nations sent a letter of protest to the President of the Security Council accusing Algeria of responsibility for both the attack on Nouakchott and an assault on the Mauritanian Ambassador in Paris, and requested an urgent meeting of the Council – but no UN activity took place. On 15 July Mauritania responded by a reorganization of key positions in its armed forces. The following day the city of Zouerate was attacked by the Polisario, and on 18 and 19 July Morocco airlifted 600 troops to Mauritania. Towards the end of July the reorganization of the Mauritanian Army had been completed and the threat to the regime was reduced, terminating the crisis for Mauritania.

The OAU met between 2 and 5 July in Gabon and arranged for a special meeting on Western Sahara for October 1977.

References See sources for Case #238.

(250) Libya/Egypt Border   Border clashes between Egypt and Libya created a crisis for these two states from 14 July to 10 September 1977.

Background The problem of undemarcated boundaries between Egypt and Libya was long-standing. The personal enmity between President Sadat and Colonel Qaddhafi increased after the conclusion of the October 1973 War between Egypt and Israel, when the Libyan leader accused Sadat of working towards a thaw in Egypt–Israel relations, as well as developing stronger ties with the United States. Egypt, on the other hand, resented the increasing Muslim fundamentalism in Libya and feared the spread of Soviet influence then prevalent in that country. For several years the two African neighbors had accused each other of acts of sabotage and had carried on an almost unbroken propaganda campaign.

Crisis A crisis was triggered for Libya when Egyptian armed forces attacked a Libyan border police fort on 14 July 1977. The Libyan response, on 19 July, was artillery fire on a Egyptian border post killing nine soldiers and capturing 14. This triggered a crisis for Egypt. On the 21st Egyptian forces, supported by tanks and aircraft, crossed the border into Libya. During August intermittent clashes continued, with each side accusing the other of aggression. The matter was brought before the Arab League, and representatives of the Palestine Liberation Organization succeeded in mediating the crisis. On 10 September Egyptian and Libyan troops withdrew from the border, terminating the crisis for both actors.

The United States provided arms and weapons to Egypt, as did the Soviet Union to Libya. Libya brought the matter before the United Nations, but no discussion took place.

References See general list and Oliver and Crowder 1981.

(251) Ogaden II   War between Ethiopia and Somalia over the disputed territory of Ogaden precipitated a crisis for both states from 22 July 1977 to 14 March 1978.

Background   Since Somalia's independence in 1960 the creation of a "Greater Somalia," which would include Djibouti, the Northern Frontier District of Kenya and, above all, the Ogaden on Ethiopia's eastern border with Somalia, had been a stated aim of the Somali Government. A crisis erupted in 1964 between Somalia and Ethiopia over rights to Ogaden (see Case #175). The water and grazing resources of the Ogaden were essential to the nomadic people of both countries. In Ethiopia the anti-monarchical revolution of 1974 had brought about the upsurge of competing regional nationalisms. Brutal repression was being practised by the Mengistu regime. Ten out of Ethiopia's 14 provinces were in a state of armed insurrection against the Derge, whose failure to master the revolt in Eritrea, together with the hostility of Ethiopia's neighbors, afforded Somalia an opportunity to realize the long-held aim of the liberation of the Ogaden.

Crisis   On 22 July 1977 Somalia mounted a full-scale attack into the Ogaden, triggering a crisis for Ethiopia. Within days most of the disputed territory was completely overrun, and Somali troops pushed on to capture a score of Ethiopian posts on the outskirts of the Ogaden. Ethiopia responded on 7 August by severing diplomatic relations with Somalia. By October 90% of the Ogaden was captured and Somalia had reached the threshold of victory. At that time the Soviet Union came to the aid of Ethiopia in the form of an airlift of weapons, and after Somalia broke relations with the USSR and Cuba, the Soviets poured air and military personnel into Ethiopia. The counter-offensive of Ethiopian and Cuban troops began on 21 January 1978 and triggered a crisis for Somalia. Jijiga, which had fallen to the Somalis in September 1977, was retaken in March 1978, and by the 10th the Somalis were a fleeing and broken force. The dramatic breakthrough was reported to have been masterminded by the Cubans and Soviets. On 9 March Somalia announced its intended withdrawal from the Ogaden, conceding victory to the Ethiopians. The withdrawal was complete on 14 March 1978 and terminated the crisis for both actors.

References   Cheg 1979; Kaplan 1981; Laitin 1979; Legum and Lee 1977; Lewis 1980; Mayall 1978; Schwab 1978; Sheik-Abdi 1977; Spencer 1977; Valenta 1981.

(252) Rhodesia Raids   Rhodesian air raids on ZIPRA bases in Zambia brought about a crisis for that country from 31 August 1977 until 14 August 1978.

Background   Despite ongoing discussions in search of an acceptable constitutional settlement to the Rhodesian conflict, the situation deteriorated in 1977. In May of that year the British Government released information which claimed that Prime Minister Smith had proposed to take preemptive action against guerrilla attacks on the grounds that a build-up of African forces was taking place on the Zambian side of Rhodesia's border. Zambia was the home base for the Zimbabwe African People's Union (ZAPU) headed by Joshua Nkomo, and its revolutionary army ZIPRA. On 16 May Zambia's President Kaunda said that a state of war existed with Rhodesia. On 8 July he stated that his country had approached one or two other states, presumably Cuba and Somalia, for aid. Earlier, on 8 June, Rhodesia accused Zambia of a rocket attack and threatened to disconnect Zambia's power from Rhodesia's Kariba hydroelectric station. In August an increasing number of incidents was reported on Rhodesia's borders with Zambia and Botswana. On the 27th it was reported from Zambia that air strikes were feared. In the light of tensions since May and the growing fears in late August, the first incident to take place would have been sufficient to escalate the situation to crisis proportions.

Crisis   On 31 August a crisis was triggered for Zambia when Rhodesian jet bombers strafed the border district of Luanshya causing casualties and damage to property. Kaunda's response, on 3 September, was several days of blackout and curfew in Lusaka, Zambia's capital, and in other cities. On the 7th the blackout and curfew were extended indefinitely when Kaunda invoked full powers under the state of emergency which had existed since Rhodesia's declaration of independence in 1965 (see Case #185). On the 11th the President accused Rhodesia of using napalm which was denied the following day by the Combined Operational Headquarters in Rhodesia. The curfew was lifted on 20 September.

A period of highly tense conflictual relations between the two states followed. Escalation occurred on 6 March 1978 when Rhodesian forces entered Zambian territory in force with aircraft, helicopters and ground troops attacking the Luanshya district in what the Smith regime described as "hot pursuit." A secret meeting between Prime Minister Smith and ZAPU leader Nkomo in Lusaka on 14 August 1978 terminated the crisis for Zambia. The meeting, held under the auspices of President Kaunda, indicated an easing of tension. Smith attempted to bring Nkomo into his domestic settlement via changes in the Executive Council of Rhodesia, with local black representation. The Council was set up in March 1978, but had been losing support among Rhodesia's black population.

The UN Security Council met on 15–17 March 1978 and adopted a resolution reaffirming sanctions against Rhodesia, which Zambia had been carrying out fully at great sacrifice. The OAU held discussions without passing a resolution. The United States and Britain attempted to seek implementation of the Anglo-American proposals for a constitutional settlement leading to internationally recognized independence for Rhodesia.

The Zambian railway to Rhodesia was reopened on 6 October 1978.

References See sources for Case #276.

(253) Vietnam Invasion of Cambodia A crisis over Vietnam's invasion of Cambodia occurred from 24 September 1977 to mid-January 1978. Cambodia and Vietnam were crisis actors.

Background The roots of the conflict between Vietnam and Cambodia can be traced to the latter's lengthy struggle to maintain an independent existence against the steady encroachment of the Vietnamese. In March 1970 Cambodia attempted to expel North Vietnamese and Vietcong army concentrations from its territory (see Case #206). Fighting began immediately after the fall of Phnom Penh to the Khmer Rouge in April 1975 (see Case #227). From that time there were continuing disputes over boundary lines imposed by the French colonial administration concerning some islands in the Gulf of Siam possessing oil potential, and more importantly, threats to the survival of the diminishing Cambodian state. The conflict was exacerbated by the reluctance of North Vietnam's Army to withdraw from acknowledged Cambodian territory after 1975. The border conflict between Cambodia and Vietnam escalated in 1977. In April Cambodian forces staged heavy raids into Vietnam. In May Vietnam unilaterally extended its territorial waters to 12 miles and established a 200-mile "exclusive economic zone" that encompassed islands and archipelagos outside those territorial waters. These acts directly affected islands contested by Vietnam and China, as well as those in dispute between Vietnam and Cambodia. Cambodia charged Vietnam with an intrigue to reconstitute the Union Indochinoise established by France, as well as an attempt to instigate an internal coup in Cambodia against the regime. Vietnam countered by accusing Pol Pot of plans to reconquer Saigon and the Mekong Delta which had belonged to Cambodia some 300 years before. In late April 1977 Cambodian troops stepped up their assaults along the border. Vietnam militia guarding the area were forced to withdraw. In September the Khmer Rouge launched another series of raids and penetrated deep into Vietnam, while the latter continued systematic incursions into Cambodia. Cambodia alleged the participation of foreign nationals – Russians and Cubans – as advisors to Vietnam's artillery companies and tank squadrons. By mid-September Vietnam's policy of minimum military reaction changed.

Crisis The crisis for both Cambodia and Vietnam was triggered on 24 September 1977. Cambodia reported an invasion by several Vietnam divisions supported by hundreds of tanks, artillery pieces and aircraft. Vietnam alleged that four divisions of Cambodian forces had launched attacks along the entire border of the Tayninh province where over 1000 civilians had been killed or wounded. In December

Vietnam responded with a punitive assault by six divisions 50 miles into Cambodia. After inflicting a substantial defeat, Vietnam troops pulled back, with some units remaining in Cambodia to support subsequent diplomatic approaches. Cambodia moved 13 of its 17 divisions to hold the border against a renewed invasion. On 13 December Phnom Penh broke off diplomatic relations with Hanoi and quietly abandoned its Moscow Embassy as well, thereby emphasizing the link between the Indochina dispute and the Sino-Soviet conflict. Vietnamese Embassy personnel were ordered to leave Cambodia and air services between the two countries were to be suspended as of 7 January 1978. A Vietnamese offer to negotiate, on 3 January, was rejected by Cambodia.

There were contradictory reports concerning the fighting in January. Cambodia claimed to have expelled the Vietnamese after a major victory on 6 January, while Vietnam continued to report incursions into its territory. The Vietnamese invasion halted in mid-January and its forces were gradually withdrawn, terminating the crisis for both actors. From the second half of January until June 1978 the Vietnam forces remained largely on the defensive, repelling repeated Cambodian raids across the border.

Beijing, which had been providing substantial military and economic aid to Cambodia since 1975, urged both sides to resolve the dispute through negotiation. North Korea, too, supported Cambodia. The Soviet bloc and Albania supported Vietnam, while Laos, Yugoslavia and Romania remained neutral. The divisions in the Communist world were thus widened, and the USSR took the opportunity provided by the dispute to denounce the PRC. Attempts to mediate were made by both the USSR and the PRC. Concentration on aid programs – the USSR to Vietnam and Laos, the PRC to Cambodia – continued throughout the crisis.

References Bellows 1979; Bui Diem 1979; Duncanson 1979; Galbraith 1980; Hung 1979; Jackson 1978, 1979; Jencks 1979; Kallgren 1979; Kershaw 1979; van der Kroef 1979a, 1979b; Leifer 1979; Leighton 1978a, 1978b; Pike 1978, 1979; Poole 1978; Tai-Sung-An 1978; Thien 1978; Yahuda 1977, 1979.

(254) French Hostages As part of the ongoing conflict over the independence of Western Sahara, French citizens working in Mauritania were held hostage by the Polisario. This created a crisis for Algeria and France from 25 October to 23 December 1977.

Background The Mauritanian town of Zouerate was attacked by Polisario guerrillas on 1 May and 16 July 1977 (see Case #249). Zouerate was an important mining settlement housing a fairly large French community, consisting mainly of engineers and their families. In the May attack two French citizens were killed and six others taken prisoner. France, which had been supplying Morocco and Mauritania with arms and instructors, evacuated 450 women and children and issued a strong protest calling on Algeria to use its good offices to free the hostages. In May Mauritania and France considered the reactivation of the military defense agreements which the former had terminated in January 1973. France brought the matter before the United Nations, but all attempts to release the prisoners met with little success due mainly to Polisario's unwillingness to cooperate.

Crisis On 25 October 1977 a crisis was triggered for France when two French engineers, working on the Mauritanian railway 60 kilometers west of Zouerate, were taken prisoner. The abduction of the two engineers, together with the six taken on 1 May, gave rise to a serious threat to French citizens working in Mauritania. The following day a five-man War Cabinet met in France; it included President Giscard d'Estaing, the Foreign and Defense Ministers, the Chief of Staff and the Minister of Cooperation. And on the 28th eight alleged members of the Polisario were expelled from France.

France's major response, and the crisis trigger for Algeria, was the placing of French paratroops on alert on 29 October, amid rumors that French troop-carrying aircraft had departed for Senegal. Algeria feared that the French would attack targets on Algerian soil which housed major Polisario bases and training camps. On the 30th Algeria responded with a *démarche* from Foreign Minister Bouteflika to the Ambassadors from the five permanent members of the UN Security Council, drawing their attention to the risks of French intervention in the area and the subsequent danger to international security. On 1-2 November DC-8 and Transall transport planes flew to Dakar with approximately 300 reinforcements for the 1100 French troops stationed in Cape Vert, Senegal. During the first two weeks in November French instructors were sent to Mauritania to establish communication facilities. From 1 to 7 November a French Foreign Ministry official, Claude Chayets talked with Polisario leaders in Algiers, and from 5 to 6 November a second official visited the Algerian capital. On 7 November the FLN, Algeria's sole legal political organization, staged a demonstration against French threats of intervention – reportedly one of the largest since Algeria's independence from France in 1962. From 12 to 18 December French Jaguar aircraft strafed Polisario columns in Mauritania.

Negotiations with the Polisario succeeded in freeing the hostages who were handed over to UN Secretary-General Kurt Waldheim in Algiers on 23 December 1977, ending the crisis for Algeria and France.

At France's request, the General Assembly met on 31 October. The Secretary-General offered his good offices and a resolution was adopted on 9 November calling upon all members to respect Western Sahara's right to self-determination.

References See sources for Case #238.

(255) Chimoio Tembue Raids Rhodesian attacks on bases of the Zimbabwe African National Liberation Army (ZANLA) in Mozambique triggered an intra-war crisis for Mozambique from 23 November 1977 to 22 March 1978.

Background Rhodesia's full-scale war against the Rhodesian guerrilla movements' struggle to obtain black majority rule in that country began in 1976 with a Rhodesian attack on bases inside Mozambique (see Case #237). Another "hot pursuit" operation in August of that year ended with Mozambique's joining Botswana, Tanzania and Zambia in setting up joint action for the defense of the Front Line States (see Case #243). After the Mapai Seizure of May-June 1977 (see Case #247), there was a decline in activity on the Mozambique border. However, in November 1977 the raids of Rhodesian forces into Mozambique were reported to be the heaviest since the guerrilla war had begun. Serious food shortages prevailed prior to the crisis.

Crisis On 23-24 November 1977 Rhodesian forces attacked the main operational headquarters of ZANLA near Chimoio in Mozambique. This was followed by raids on a base at Tembue, on 25-26 November. These attacks triggered a crisis for Mozambique. Salisbury announced that 1200 ZANLA terrorists had been killed, expressing regret at the possibility of civilian deaths, but emphasizing that Rhodesia was at war and that civilians, particularly women and children, should not be in such camps. On 1 December Prime Minister Smith added that the raids had been essential to stop heavy attacks which had been planned against Rhodesia. ZANLA leader Robert Mugabe denied that the Chimoio camp was a guerrilla base. On 23 December 1977, and on 14-15 February 1978, Rhodesia made public documents claimed to have been seized during the raids listing women guerrillas with their weapons, adding there had been armed clashes between ZANLA and ZIPRA (Zimbabwe People's Revolutionary Army) units. President Machel visited Nigeria and Angola for talks between 13 and 17 December, and on the 18th, upon his return to Mozambique, he met with leaders of the Front Line States to discuss joint strategy. At that meeting the Presidents of Angola, Mozambique, Tanzania and Zambia drew up a four-point declaration expressing their support for some aspects of the Anglo-American plan to develop a clear timetable for achieving majority rule in Rhodesia, while reaffirming the unity of their group and its commitment to the Patriotic Front in its "liberation **war**." The 18 December meeting terminated the crisis for Mozambique.

The OAU Ministerial Committee met in January 1978 to discuss the matter.

The Rhodesian raids were officially condemned by Britain and the United States. And the UN General Assembly passed a resolution calling for assistance to Mozambique. Several months before the Rhodesian raids, army and ammunition to aid the guerrillas had been received in Mozambique from both the PRC and the Soviet Union, though the USSR was not directly involved during the crisis.

References   See sources for Case #276.

(256) Beagle Channel I   The century-old dispute over the Beagle Channel erupted into a crisis for Argentina and Chile on 5 December 1977 and ended on 20 February 1978.

Background   Since the mid-nineteenth century Argentina and Chile contested the ownership of three tiny islands, Lennox, Nueva and Picton, located at the eastern entrance to the Beagle Channel, a waterway 150 miles long and 3–8 miles wide in the southern tip of South America. The islands are inhabited by Chilean shepherds and patrolled by Argentinian torpedo boats. The two countries signed an agreement in 1972 referring the dispute to the International Court of Justice which awarded the islands to Chile on 2 May 1977. Argentina's access to the Atlantic, its Antarctic bases, and to the potential resources of oil, minerals and fish in the South Atlantic and Antarctic regions was in jeopardy.

Crisis   On 5 December 1977 the Argentina Government delivered a formal Note objecting to the terms of the court ruling. More importantly, it called up army reservists in the Mendoza border region the same day, triggering a crisis for Chile. Negotiations between Chile and Argentina ended on 28 December and all further meetings were cancelled. Chile's response, on 5 January, was a speech by President Pinochet stating that his government would henceforth pursue a more aggressive and pragmatic foreign policy. That day it was also reported that Chilean soldiers were being massed between Puerto Natales and Punta Arenas and that tank and infantry maneuvers were in progress with Chilean warships patrolling the Magellan Straits. This activity triggered a crisis for Argentina. Argentinian vessels sailed for the Beagle Channel area and remained offshore on 8 January. Two days later Argentina's naval commander, while observing maneuvers, stated that the navy was ready for action; the air force commander inspected airfields on the Chilean border. The same day President Videla interrupted a vacation to return to Buenos Aires for consultations with the junta.

Throughout January Argentina and Chile continued their preparations for a military confrontation. On 19 January Videla and Pinochet met in Mendoza to discuss matters of joint concern, especially the area in dispute. When Argentina once more rejected the ruling by the International Court of Justice, a second meeting between the two Presidents was postponed. However, on 20 February they did meet once more and signed the "Act of Puerto Montt" under which a joint negotiating committee was set up and given 180 days to resolve the dispute. The crisis ended for both actors that day with no change in the status quo. The United States tried to persuade both parties to reduce tension and seek a solution through diplomatic means.

Toward the end of the 180 days a second crisis over the Beagle Channel occurred (see Case #266).

References   See general list and Gwyne 1979.

(257) Chad/Libya II   Libya's involvement in Chad's internal war caused a second crisis for those two actors between 22 January and 27 March 1978.

Background   In April 1972, prior to the agreements between Chad and Libya in November-December of that year (see Case #212), Libya occupied the Aouzou Strip, a large part of northern Chad long controlled by pro-Libyan Muslim rebels and reputed to contain uranium and oil deposits. Chad President Tombalbaye was overthrown in an army coup on 14 April 1975 and was replaced by Felix Malloum, who pledged national unity by peaceful means. Within the opposition FROLINAT, Hissene Habré was ousted from the leadership by Goukouni Oueddei, who led the loosely-organized Command Council of the Northern Armies. In April 1976 a

Qaddhafi-supported mutiny and planned assassination of President Malloum failed. Throughout 1977 there were continuous pro-Libyan attacks against Chad troops, with Libyan involvement reaching its peak in the summer, when FROLINAT forces occupied territory south of the Aouzou Strip.

Crisis As in 1971, Libya perceived a threat to its influence in Chad – and was confronted with a crisis – as a result of a domestic Chadian agreement, on this occasion, between Hissene Habré and President Malloum signed in Khartoum on 22 January 1978 with the help of Sudan's mediation: it provided for a national unity goverment, the establishment of a constituent assembly, an amnesty for all political prisoners, and the reorganization of Chad's armed forces. Libya's major response, on the 28th, was active support for a FROLINAT offensive against Faya-Largeau, the administrative center of the province of Borkou-Ennedi-Tibesti, in northern Chad.

This act triggered a crisis for Chad. President Malloum responded by severing diplomatic relations with Libya on 6 February. A Chad appeal to the UN Security Council on the 8th, to condemn Libya's involvement in the renewed fighting, as well as its occupation of the Aouzou Strip, had to be withdrawn and a cease-fire accepted because of the loss of half the Chad Army and the fall of Faya-Largeau to FROLINAT forces on 19 February. Libya halted the advance of its proxy on the Chad capital because of strong pressure by France, then an important arms supplier to Libya, and partly to avoid a clash with French military forces in Chad.

The crisis ended for Libya on 24 February when, at the first Sebha Conference, attended by Qaddhafi, Malloum, Niger's President and the Vice-President of Sudan, Chad and Libya agreed to settle their differences in a "new fraternal spirit," to resume diplomatic relations, to hold a peace conference between the Chad Government and FROLINAT on 21 March, and to establish a joint military committee to supervise affairs in Chad during the interim period, thereby institutionalizing Libyan intervention in Chad.

Chad's crisis and the second Chad/Libyan international crisis as a whole ended on 27 March 1978, following a second Sebha Conference and a comprehensive agreement announced in Benghazi that day: under the Benghazi Accords, Chad agreed to recognize FROLINAT; both agreed to abide by the cease-fire, to allow free movement throughout Chad, and to assist a Libya–Niger military committee in implementing the Accords. Most important, Chad agreed to the termination of foreign (French) military bases and military presence in Chad. However, the Benghazi Accords were short-lived, and other Chad/Libya crises were soon to erupt (see Cases #261 and #273).

References See general list and Haley 1984, Neuberger 1982.

(258) Lebanon Civil War II

Christian-Lebanese opposition to Syrian military activity in Lebanon caused a crisis for Syria from 7 to 20 February 1978.

Background On 19 January 1976 Syrian forces entered Lebanon to aid Lebanese Muslim factions fighting Maronite Christians, in an effort to prevent the partition of Lebanon. In June of that year the Syrians came to the aid of some Christian villages under siege. Shortly thereafter a Syrian-dominated Arab Deterrent Force supported Muslim and PLO leftists against the Israeli-backed Christian militias (see Case #235).

From 1976 to 1978 the civil war in Lebanon continued sporadically, with Syria in control of many parts of Lebanon – either directly or indirectly through client forces. The Christian-controlled Lebanese Army resisted Syria's presence in Beirut.

Crisis On 7 February 1978 Syrian troops attempted to set up a checkpoint barrier near barracks of the Lebanese Army in south Beirut. Lebanese Army resistance, resulting in a serious clash and the death of 20 Syrian soldiers with many others taken hostage, triggered a crisis for Syria. The following day Syria retaliated strongly. Its army was reinforced with an additional 2000 men, and heavy fighting took place. When the fighting subsided, Syrian control of the Muslim areas in Beirut remained unchallenged and its presence in Lebanon became the determining factor in Lebanon's civil war. The decline in threat from the Lebanese Christians was signalled by Syrian President Assad's departure for a visit to the USSR, on 20 February, terminating the crisis for Syria.

In March 1978 Israel invaded southern Lebanon and withdrew in June of that year (see Case #260).

References   See general list, especially *Keesing's* and *New York Times*

(259) Sino/Vietnam War   Cambodia, the PRC, Thailand and Vietnam were crisis actors in the Sino/Vietnam War. The crisis lasted from 9 February 1978 to 15 March 1979.

Background   The long-standing conflict between Vietnam and Cambodia was a result of many factors: ethnic hatred, traditional hostility, territorial disputes and ideological differences. A Vietnam invasion of Cambodia in September 1977 terminated in January 1978 with a gradual, partial withdrawal of the Vietnam forces (see Case #253). A treaty of economic and defense cooperation between Vietnam and Laos, which was signed in August 1977, transformed Laos into a Vietnamese satellite, another step in Vietnam's efforts to gain control over all of Indochina. In Vietnam the demoralization of the population and a serious refugee problem in an economically-strategic area, together with Cambodian attacks which had penetrated deep into the country, exacerbated the tense situation. Cambodia was troubled by the continued presence of Communist Vietnam troops in the eastern part of its territory. By the end of 1977 China was airlifting substantial quantities of ammunition to Cambodia while modern military equipment was being shipped to Hanoi from the USSR. Beijing's perception of threat from a new arena of Soviet encirclement, as well as from Vietnam's regional ambitions, increased as border incidents between China and Vietnam escalated. While reluctant to challenge USSR prestige in the area to the point of risking direct Soviet intervention, the PRC was nevertheless determined to resist what it considered Soviet-inspired Vietnamese expansionism. In particular, the PRC objected to Vietnam's attempt to gain control over the PRC's client, Cambodia.

The scale of tension on Thailand's border with Cambodia was much smaller than the latter's conflict with Vietnam. Nevertheless, uncertain borders, poor communication between Phnom Penh and its forces, the lack of discipline among the Khmer Rouge troops, provocative Thai military action, smuggling operations, ideological factors, and the presence of an enormous Cambodian refugee camp in Thailand all contributed to poor relations between Cambodia and Thailand. Despite the agreement to normalize Thai-Cambodian relations, signed on 2 February 1978, Cambodian troops, often acting in collaboration with Thai guerrilla Communists, continued to make frequent raids into Thailand.

Crisis   On 9 February 1978 an increase in Cambodia's raids into Thai border villages triggered a crisis for Thailand. Mass assaults on police posts in the frontier zone and savage destruction of small nearby population centers took place with no serious obstacles on the part of the Thai Army or its border police units. The Thai Government, while opting for diplomatic measures to control Cambodia, responded on 10 April in a statement by its Premier vowing swift and drastic retaliation. With the heightening of the Cambodia-Vietnam conflict and a Cambodian invasion directed at the Vietnamese port of Ha Tien, the scale of incidents in Thailand was reduced.

Vietnam's Air Force began systematic attacks against Cambodia in June 1978. After China cut off all aid to Vietnam, the latter joined the Soviet bloc's economic union, COMECON, on 29 June. Six months later it signed a Treaty of Friendship and Alliance with the Soviet Union. On 12 July China tightened border controls in order to stem the influx of refugees which had reached 169,000 of the Hoa people fleeing Vietnam for China. Moreover, a significant military build-up occurred along the Sino/Vietnam border. The two countries edged towards full-scale war during the summer of 1978, while fighting continued during the autumn, followed by a break during the rainy season. The November Treaty of Friendship with the Soviet Union, which provided Vietnam with practical assistance in the event of an attack, and the continued drain on Vietnam's resources eventually led its government to a decision for an all-out invasion of Cambodia.

A crisis for Vietnam was triggered by a Cambodian intrusion on 15 December 1978. Vietnam responded with a massive and rapid strike into Cambodia on 25 December, triggering a crisis for Cambodia and the PRC. Cambodia responded on the 31st with a request to the UN to condemn Vietnam and to demand that it cease "aggression" and that all Soviet aid and assistance to Vietnam be stopped. The Cambodian Foreign Minister also requested an urgent meeting of the Security Council. Vietnam's conquest of Cambodia was completed in less than a fortnight. On 7 January 1979 a puppet regime was installed in Phnom Penh, terminating the first crisis for Vietnam, as well as for Cambodia and Thailand.

The PRC response to Vietnam's invasion of Cambodia on 25 December was to dispatch Chinese troops into Vietnam and to occupy a number of towns in the border area on 17 February. This Chinese action triggered a second crisis for Vietnam. When Chinese troops met with stronger than anticipated opposition, the advance was halted and not resumed until the 23rd, after the invasion force had been enlarged to 200,000. The Vietnam response was the launching of two counter-attacks into Chinese territory on 23 February. Fighting subsided on 5 March after the PRC capture of a provincial capital. A PRC government statement on that day announced that the Chinese troops had attained their goals and would withdraw to Chinese territory. The same day the Government of Vietnam issued a decree proclaiming general mobilization. Chinese troops were withdrawn from Vietnam by 15 March 1979, terminating the crisis for the PRC and the second Vietnam crisis.

The Security Council overruled Soviet and Czechoslovak objections and agreed to convene a formal meeting on 11 January. Soviet proposals were rejected and Prince Sihanouk was invited to address the meeting. A draft resolution was submitted on the 15th but was not adopted because of a Soviet veto. On 17 February Vietnam urged the Secretary-General to take appropriate measures to put an end to Chinese aggression, but did not request a formal session. On the 22nd the US, Britain, Norway and Portugal requested an urgent meeting to consider the situation in Southeast Asia. The five ASEAN countries circulated a draft resolution calling for a halt to all hostilities in Indochina; it, too, was vetoed by the Soviets. Indonesia, the Philippines, Malaysia and Thailand condemned the Vietnam invasion of Cambodia in December 1978.

The United States supported Cambodia at the Security Council. North Korea sent pilots to fight alongside Cambodia and the PRC. The USSR sent arms and aid to Vietnam, while Thailand, Singapore and Indonesia halted aid to Vietnam, as did Australia, Britain, Denmark and Japan. The Vietnam invasion of Cambodia succeeded in toppling the Pol Pot regime but failed to destroy its army, thereby initiating a protracted guerrilla war. The PRC, while shown to be unable to prevent the toppling of a regime to whose support it was publicly committed, succeeded in giving Vietnam a credible warning. China emerged in a stronger political position because of no active USSR participation in the war and no damage to the normalization of US/PRC relations which had been concluded in December 1978.

References See sources for Case #253.

(260) Litani Operation An Israeli retaliatory invasion caused a crisis for Lebanon from 14 March to 13 June 1978.

Background PLO bases in Lebanon, supplied with Soviet weapons, had long been in operation as training camps for Palestinian guerrillas making frequent, mostly unsuccessful, incursions into Israeli territory. On 11 March 1978 11 Palestinians entered Israel by sea and attacked vehicles on the main highway 11 kilometers north of Tel Aviv. Thirty-five Israelis were killed and another 70 wounded before Israeli police, in a fierce clash, killed or captured all of the terrorists.

Crisis   Israeli troops, supported by the air force, crossed into southern Lebanon in a major attack against PLO bases, triggering a crisis for Lebanon on 14 March 1978. On the 17th Lebanon requested the Security Council to discuss the Israeli invasion. The Council met on the 19th and called for Israel's immediate withdrawal, along with the placement of a UN peace-keeping force in the area occupied by Israel. Lebanon's Foreign Minister met with ambassadors in Beirut to explain Lebanon's position. The hostilities ended at the end of March, but Israeli forces remained in Lebanon until 13 June 1978 when the last stage of the withdrawal was carried out. This terminated the crisis for Lebanon.

The Soviet Union and the United States were involved politically. Vice-President Mondale acknowledged Israel's right to defend its borders against terrorist incursions, but called for an Israeli withdrawal. The United States supported the Security Council resolution. The Soviet Union condemned the Israeli invasion and abstained in the Council vote. UNIFIL (the United Nations Interim Force in Lebanon), established in 1978, remained in southern Lebanon through the Lebanon War of 1982 and for years thereafter.

References   See general list.

(261) Chad/Libya III   France, Libya and Chad were crisis actors in the third eruption during the protracted Chad/Libya conflict, from 15 April to 29 August 1978.

Background   The Benghazi Accords on 27 March 1978 provided a brief respite in the ongoing struggle between President Malloum's regime and the Libya-backed rebels led by Goukouni Oueddei for control over the territory and government of Chad (see Case #257). The cease-fire authorized by the Benghazi Accords for 10 April broke down almost at once.

Crisis   On 15 April FROLINAT forces, led by Goukouni Oueddei, seized Salal and advanced south to within 100 miles of Chad's capital, Ndjamena. This created a crisis for France by threatening its continued influence in Equatorial Africa generally and, in particular, its secure access to the uranium resources of neighboring Niger, vital for France's *force de frappe*. France responded on the 26th, to an appeal by Malloum, with an airlift of 1700 troops, a heavy bombardment of rebel convoys, and the creation of a defense perimeter around the capital, thereby preventing the fall of Malloum's regime.

French intervention in April-May 1978 and its success in halting Goukouni's advance was perceived by Libya in mid-May as a serious threat to its hegemony in Chad. Qaddhafi responded with an invasion on 22 June by 800 Libyan troops who overran several provinces in northern and central Chad. Libya's escalation of hostilities, in turn, created a crisis for Chad. President Malloum responded on 20 July with an appeal to the OAU to denounce Libya's intervention and to press for the withdrawal of Libya's forces from Chad's territory.

While an OAU Commission was investigating Chad's charges, France and Libya concluded a secret agreement in late July 1978 providing for a *de facto* partition of Chad at the 14th Parallel into two spheres of influence. The formation of a virtual condominium over Chad ended the crisis for these two actors. Chad's crisis ended on 29 August when an agreement was reached in Sudan's capital creating a National Unity Government, with Habré as Prime Minister and Malloum continuing as President and their military forces formally integrated.

References   See sources for Case #257.

(262) Cassinga Incident   Fighting between South African forces and guerrillas based in Angola led to a crisis for South Africa and Angola from 3 to 17 May 1978.

Background   For much of the period since the SWAPO (South-West Africa People's Organization) guerrilla war against South African forces stationed in Namibia began in 1966, its raids had been carried out from neighboring states. Since its civil war in

1976, Angola had become the main staging center for SWAPO raids (see Case #229). In the early months of 1978 there was an intensification of SWAPO activity. South African troop losses were reported in periodic clashes in the northern Namibian border region. In February 1978 Angola complained to the UN Secretary-General of South African violations of its territory and air space.

Crisis A SWAPO attack on the Ruacana hydroelectric power station in Namibia's border area with Angola on 3 May triggered a crisis for South Africa. The South African Foreign Minister and the Army Chief of Operations reported that a raid of approximately 700 South African troops into Angola, on 4 May, was a response to the upsurge of guerrilla activity and the SWAPO raid the day before.

Angolan sources stated that South African troops occupied the town of Cassinga, 230 kilometers north of the border, which South Africa claimed to be SWAPO's main operational center. The town of Chetequera was also attacked. South Africa's raid was the largest since the 1975–76 period when its forces were involved on the side of UNITA (National Union for the Total Independence of Angola) in the Angolan civil war. In the operations at Cassinga, which lasted for 12 hours, six South African soldiers and about 1000 refugees were reportedly killed; in addition to ground forces, aircraft were alleged to have been involved. Angolan troops met the attacking forces.

On 5 May Angola appealed to the United Nations for support. The following day a resolution was passed by the Security Council unanimously condemning South Africa and warning that "more effective measures might be taken." With the resolution, and the end of the raid, the crisis ended for Angola on 6 May. The Ambassadors of Canada, France, the UK, the USA and West Germany in South Africa formed a committee, known as the Contact Group, to investigate and propose solutions to the problem. On 17 May, for the first time since the raid, the South African Foreign Minister met with the Contact Group. This meeting, signalling a major reduction in stress, terminated the crisis over Cassinga for South Africa.

US activity was confined to the political realm: on 6 May the United States expressed grave concern and urgently requested South Africa to explain its behavior; the US also participated in the Contact Group. The USSR was a major supplier of arms to Angola through Cuba, as well as arms and advisors to SWAPO. The OAU condemned South Africa on 9 May 1978 and called for the withdrawal of South African troops from Namibia.

References See general list, especially *Africa Contemporary Record*, *Africa Research Bulletin* and *Keesing's*.

(263) Shaba II A second invasion of Shaba from Angola created a crisis for Angola, Belgium, France, the USA and Zaire from 11 May to 30 July 1978.

Background Shaba, located in southern Zaire, was first invaded by Katangan exiles operating from Angola in March 1977 (see Case #246). From May 1977 to May 1978 the rebels concentrated on organizing and strengthening their forces.

Crisis Katangan rebels invaded Shaba on 11 May 1978 triggering a crisis for Zaire. Zaire accused Angola of harboring the rebels and threatened to retaliate, triggering a crisis for Angola the same day. During the ensuing four days killings and massacres occurred on the part of both the rebels and the Zairian Army, whose respective leaders had lost control of their forces. President Mobutu called for intervention by Belgium, France, Morocco, the PRC and the United States in order to quell the insurgents. In addition, he accused the Governments of Algeria, Angola, Cuba, Libya, the Soviet Union and Zambia of supporting, training and actively fighting alongside the rebels.

On 14 May a crisis was triggered for Belgium, France and the United States when their governments were informed of a massacre of French and Belgian citizens working in the mines, and of the danger facing the white community in Zaire. The United States viewed the events in Zaire as threatening its influence in the international system, and on 16 May responded with a decision to deploy an airlift to carry foreign troops to the battleground. The French response, on 17 May, was a decision by President Giscard d'Estaing, together with the Foreign and Defense Ministers and the Chief of Staff, to dispatch French troops to Zaire. Belgium, too, decided on the 18th to send troops. The foreign troops arrived in Zaire on the 19th, airlifted in American planes. That day, at the UN, Zaire accused Angola of aggression. However, the issue was not brought up for discussion in the Security Council since it was claimed that the dispute was an African affair.

The tide of battle turned with the intervention of foreign forces. Within two days Belgian troops had evacuated those persons who wished to leave the Shaba area. On 22 May the crisis ended for the United States and Belgium as Belgian forces began to withdraw from the area. French troops assumed a larger burden of the fighting. They occupied the towns around Kolwezi and cleared the area on 25 May, terminating the crisis for France. An African force, consisting of soldiers from Morocco, Senegal and Zaire, took over from the French and the Belgian forces on 4 June. On the 10th Angola's major response to the crisis took the form of an announcement by President Neto that the incursion by FLNC rebels across Angola's borders would be halted and any Zairian troops crossing the border into Angola would be disarmed. Angola also denied any Soviet involvement in the invasion. By the end of June all foreign troops had left the area.

Presidents Mobutu and Neto held talks during July ending with the Brazzaville Agreement on 30 July 1978; the latter informally undertook to stop FLNC infiltrators across the Zaire border.

References   See sources for Case #246.

(264) Air Rhodesia Incident   The shooting down of a Rhodesian plane precipitated a crisis for Rhodesia and Zambia from 3 September to 31 October 1978.

Background   War between Rhodesia and Zambia, Mozambique and Botswana had been raging since 1976 when Rhodesia set up a War Council to supervise the destruction of guerrilla bases in those countries. From August 1977 to August 1978 relations between Zambia and Rhodesia were highly conflictual (see Case #252). That crisis ended when Rhodesia's Prime Minister agreed to bring black representation into an Executive Council for Rhodesia, including Joshua Nkomo, the Rhodesian guerrilla leader based in Zambia. Despite apparent easing of tensions, a very serious escalation of guerrilla warfare occurred in the late summer of 1978.

Crisis   On 3 September an Air Rhodesia Viscount civilian aircraft was shot down from Zambia by ZAPU (Zimbabwe African People's Union) guerrillas near Kariba, in Rhodesia's border area with Zambia, triggering a crisis for Rhodesia. Ten survivors were reportedly murdered on the ground after the plane had crashed. The plane was shot down by a heat-seeking SAM-7 missile, the first time such advanced weaponry had been used in the fighting. Zambia, anticipating a Rhodesian retaliation, appealed to Britain to restrain Rhodesia from attacking. The United States and Britain urged Prime Minister Smith of Rhodesia not to retaliate. The UN Secretary-General condemned the guerrilla attack. Within Rhodesia, where the incident had caused great indignation, Smith announced, on 10 September, that martial law legislation would be introduced. Four days later Smith rejected the possibility of including ZAPU leader Nkomo in any internal settlement and objected to British and American support for the Zimbabwean guerrillas. Zambia complied with a Rhodesian demand to ground all civil aviation.

Smith visited the United States on 7 October. On the 10th all racial discrimination in Rhodesia was formally abolished. The same day the Security Council passed a resolution, at India's initiative, condemning the United States for allowing Smith into the country. On 19 October Rhodesia launched a major offensive against targets in Zambia – triggering a crisis for the latter. The raid was mainly against ZAPU bases, and 300 followers of Nkomo were reportedly killed. Zambia responded with military resistance and minor clashes with the raiders. President Kaunda declared, on 23 October, that his country was militarily weaker than

Rhodesia and was unable to fight back. Kaunda also had 18 foreigners arrested on suspicion of aiding Rhodesia. The statement of acquiescence of 23 October terminated the crisis for Zambia. Rhodesia's crisis ended on 31 October with an extension of martial law to half the country. The crisis ended in stalemate for both countries with no change in the status quo.

References   See sources for Case #276.

(265) Nicaraguan Civil War   The international crisis over the civil war in Nicaragua involved Costa Rica and Nicaragua as actors from 10 September 1978 to 17 July 1979.

Background   During 1978 there was severe unrest in Nicaragua, with widespread demonstrations and strikes in opposition to President Somoza's dictatorial regime. On 22 August the National Palace was temporarily seized by left-wing guerrillas of the Sandinista National Liberation Front who were supported by Costa Rica. The internal situation worsened in early September when regime repression increased, and the Sandinistas called for a national insurrection against Somoza. On the 9th heavy fighting broke out between the Nicaraguan National Guard and the Sandinista supporters.

Crisis   A crisis was triggered for Nicaragua on 10 September by a large-scale guerrilla attack from Costa Rica at the border town of Penas Blancas. According to Somoza, the 300-man invasion force was part of a plan to overthrow his regime, with the complicity of the Costa Rican Government, President Cararo and other high officials. Nicaragua responded the same day with a counter-attack and the reorganization of the National Guard to meet attacks throughout the country. The following day Somoza declared a partial state of siege.

A crisis for Costa Rica was triggered on 12 September by Nicaraguan bombing of its territory and "hot pursuit" by Nicaraguan forces across the border. The threat for Costa Rica was of limited damage to population and property. The following day the state of siege in Nicaragua was extended throughout the country. The Costa Rican response to the crisis was the signing of a mutual aid and cooperation agreement with Venezuela on 15 September, a day after the latter had sent four jet bombers to Costa Rica on a goodwill visit. Costa Rica had no official army; its defense was handled by a Civil Guard. Panama, too, sent arms to Costa Rica. On 16 September Nicaragua recalled its ambassadors from Costa Rica, Panama and Venezuela, and later, from Colombia.

On 18 September the Permanent Council of the OAS accepted a proposal to convene a meeting of Foreign Ministers to consider the situation in Nicaragua. At meetings which took place in Washington between 21 and 23 September, a resolution was passed affirming the principle of non-intervention and reaffirming Nicaraguan sovereignty over its internal affairs; and a decision was reached to send an investigation team to Nicaragua. A statement by the United States Department of State expressed concern at reported atrocities committed by the Nicaraguan National Guard. On 25 September the insurgents were defeated and factories and businesses reopened in Nicaragua, terminating its first crisis. On that day, too, Somoza announced that Nicaragua would accept US mediation.

On 29 September Nicaragua's President agreed to a mediation team sponsored by the OAS, the mediating countries being the Dominican Republic, Guatemala and the United States. Its first meeting was held on 16 October. However, by mid-January 1979, mediation efforts collapsed. And on 8 February the US ended all military aid to Nicaragua.

Following clashes between Costa Rican Civil Guards and Nicaraguan National Guards on 21 November 1978, Costa Rica severed diplomatic relations with Nicaragua and began a call-up of 2500 men. A resolution was passed by the UN General Assembly on 15 December condemning Nicaragua for repressive activities against its population and demanding that Nicaragua cease all acts endangering the security of its neighbors. UN activity made it difficult for Somoza to contend that his government was a victim of foreign Communist aggression; and his regime became isolated. On the 27th Somoza threatened to invade Costa Rica if that country continued to assist the guerrillas. On 30 December Somoza met with the

Presidents of El Salvador, Guatemala and Honduras, all of whom had been supporting him in the fight against the Sandinistas.

Sporadic fighting continued until 27 May 1979 when a second crisis was triggered for Nicaragua by an invasion of guerrillas from Costa Rica. Nicaragua responded the same day by repelling the invaders. The US continued to refuse to sell arms to Nicaragua, and, according to Somoza, convinced Israel to impose an arms embargo as well.

At the end of May Nicaragua called upon the Permanent Council of the OAS to invoke the Rio Treaty in response to the Costa Rican invasion. Costa Rica requested the same OAS action against Nicaragua on 3 June. The following day the OAS Council met and passed a resolution calling for the replacement of President Somoza's dictatorship by a democratic regime. A US proposal to dispatch a peace-keeping force to Nicaragua was rejected by the OAS. Despite the embargo, US military equipment found its way into the conflict zone. Heavy fighting continued throughout June. Towards mid-July the OAS agreed to a proposal whereby General Somoza would resign, a cease-fire would take place, and the revolutionary junta would assume power in Nicaragua. No agreement was reached between Somoza's Government and the Sandinistas. The President fled Nicaragua on 17 July 1979, ending the crisis for Costa Rica and Nicaragua.

The Sandinistas, in coalition with liberal democrats, assumed power in Nicaragua. During the Carter Administration a $75 million loan was granted to Nicaragua, but the final payment was suspended by President Reagan in January 1981 when relations between the two countries deteriorated: the State Department charged that the Sandinista Government was aiding guerrillas in El Salvador; Managua denied the charges.

References   Gordon and Munro 1983; LeoGrande 1979; Sweroza and Cox 1980.

(266) Beagle Channel II   A second crisis for Argentina and Chile over the Beagle Channel lasted from 16 October 1978 to 8 January 1979.

Background   The first crisis over the Beagle Channel ended in February 1978 with a moratorium of 180 days in an attempt to settle the dispute (see Case #256). During that period six rounds of negotiations took place, with little progress. As the 2 November deadline drew near, Argentina began overt military preparations.

Crisis   On 16 October a crisis was triggered for Chile when Argentina called up 50,000 reserves; tank and troop movements, with minor clashes, were also reported near the Chilean border. Chile responded on the 24th by sending troops to the border and cancelling naval maneuvers with the US and Peru, due to take place 1500 miles north of Chile, in the event that Argentina might try to occupy the disputed islands in the Beagle Channel.

On the day of the deadline, 2 November, the two states announced that they had reached an agreement on joint economic development of the Beagle region, but that the distribution of the maritime zones had still not been resolved. Chilean Foreign Minister, Herman Cubillos Sallato, proposed mediation by a friendly government. Argentina agreed on the 8th. On 11 December Sallato met with Argentina's Foreign Minister, Carlos Washington Paston, to designate a mediator. Pope John Paul II was chosen, but the talks collapsed after an Argentinian plan was rejected by Chile.

On 16 December a crisis was triggered for Argentina when Chile put 45,000 troops on full alert. It responded on the 21st with a complaint to the UN Security Council that Chile was creating a military imbalance in the disputed area by illegally deploying troops and artillery. The same day Chile asked for an urgent meeting of the OAS to prevent Argentina from attacking the islands; and the Pope announced that he would act as mediator. The offer was accepted by both states. On the 26th Cardinal Sumore arrived in Buenos Aires to start a mediation mission. The crisis ended for both actors with the signing of the Declaration of Montevideo, in which the two parties accepted the Pope's mediation and committed themselves not to use force in their relations with one another. The Security Council discussed the problem but did not pass a resolution. On 10 November 1978 the United States called on the OAS to offer its services to the parties in order to avoid a violent conflict, but it did not become more deeply involved in the crisis despite US and Chilean requests. The issue remained unresolved until 1984 when a Vatican-mediated treaty was signed between Argentina and Chile. The accord granted Chile sovereignty over the islands, but limited its maritime rights to the Pacific waters, while Argentina won control of the waters on the Atlantic side of the Beagle Channel.

References   See sources for Case #256.

(267) Fall of Amin   Uganda, Tanzania and Libya were the actors in a crisis leading to the fall of Uganda's President Idi Amin, from 30 October 1978 to 10 April 1979.

Background   In 1971 General Idi Amin seized power in Uganda in a coup which overthrew the regime of President Milton Obote who then took refuge in Tanzania. From that time onward relations between the two countries were hostile as Amin perceived President Nyerere of Tanzania as supporting a military overthrow of his regime. Crises between the two countries occurred in 1971 and 1972 (see Cases #214, #216). During the years that followed no overt clashes occurred, but there were mutual accusations of troop movements. In October 1978 serious mutinies erupted in various Ugandan army barracks near the Tanzanian border. The mutineers were reported to have fled into Tanzania.

Crisis   On 30 October Ugandan troops invaded Tanzania and occupied the Kagera Salient, triggering a crisis for Tanzania. Idi Amin announced that he had annexed the area north of the Kagera River. A large Ugandan force followed the invading troops. Tanzania's resistance in the Salient on 31 October triggered a crisis for Uganda, but the Tanzanian major response was a counter-offensive launched on 11 November. Uganda responded on the 13th by withdrawing its forces from the Kagera Salient. By late November President Nyerere made it known that Tanzania would not be satisfied until Amin was overthrown. Sporadic fighting continued until the end of January 1979 as Tanzanian forces pushed across the Ugandan border. As they began to advance northwards into Uganda, the tense border situation exploded in a series of violent exchanges. By mid-February the Tanzanian advance had come within 150 kilometers of Kampala. At that stage, Libya, an ally of Amin's Uganda, renewed its mediatory efforts, with little success. As Amin's position became more vulnerable, the Ugandan leader appealed to "all friendly countries" to come to his rescue with troops and military equipment. On 25 February the Government of Libya perceived the possible downfall of Amin as a threat to its influence in the region. It responded to this crisis on 4 March by sending troops to Kampala to join an earlier contingent which had arrived in Entebbe, together with supplies, in mid-February.

Despite the new equipment and foreign reinforcements, Uganda suffered defeat after defeat until, by 25 March, Tanzanian artillery was firing on Kampala and Entebbe. On 6 April Tanzanian and anti-Amin Ugandan forces moved to the outskirts of Kampala; and, on the following day, they captured Entebbe. On 9 April it was reported that Libya paid to the Ugandan National Liberation Forces (UNLF, the combined exiled anti-Amin forces) the equivalent of $20 million to allow Libya's expeditionary force to pull out of Uganda without being attacked. The crisis ended for Libya in defeat.

The following day Amin fled from the capital, and the crisis ended for Uganda and Tanzania.

Amin's appeals to the OAU, the Arab League and the UN, on 4 November 1978, to force the Tanzanians to stop fighting had failed, as did the mediation attempts by Kenya, Nigeria and Zambia. Discussions in the OAU *ad hoc* committee on inter-state conflicts were also fruitless; and on 2 March 1979 the OAU admitted that its efforts to reach a cease-fire had failed. UN Secretary-General Waldeim appealed to Tanzania and Uganda to stop fighting and offered his good offices to seek a solution.

United States involvement was political: on 6 March 1979 the State Department accused Libya of direct military involvement; this followed a statement by Secretary of State Vance calling for the withdrawal of Ugandan troops from the Kagera Salient at the onset of the crisis. A *Pravda* statement on 12 November 1978 accused Tanzania of aggression: the USSR had been a supplier of weapons and advisors to Amin's Uganda prior to the crisis, but there was no increase of this activity during the crisis. In March 1979 the Soviet Union reportedly withdrew advisors and military supplies from Uganda.

References See general list.

(268) Angola Invasion Scare A South African troop build-up precipitated a crisis for Angola from 7 to 14 November 1978.

Background In May 1978 South Africa invaded Angola after a guerrilla attack on the Ruacana hydroelectric power station in Namibia (see Case #262). On 22 October Angolan, SWAPO (South-West Africa People's Organization), Cuban and East German forces launched a major offensive against UNITA (National Union for the Total Independence of Angola) in the southern and central part of Angola.

Crisis On 7 November 1978 the Angolan Minister of Defense stated that intelligence reports had reached him of a major build-up of South African forces along the border with Namibia; further, that South Africa planned a large incursion into Angola. The same day Angola responded with a general mobilization of the Angolan Army (about 200,000 men) and a curfew in the five largest urban centers. On 8 November the South African military command issued a statement denying any intention of invading Angola. But, on the 10th, a bomb explosion in Angola's second largest city, Muambo, gave rise to the fear of an imminent South African attack. The next day Angola's President Neto accused South Africa of fighting an undeclared war against Angola and closed its airspace to South African overflights.

South African statements claimed that the Angolan perception of war was the result of UNITA successes in the 22 October campaign, and that Angola wished to detract attention from its domestic problems. The crisis ended with a statement on 14 November by South African Prime Minister Botha, denying any intention to invade Angola. UN activity took the form of an appeal to all governments on 14 November, by the UN Special Committee on Apartheid, to help Angola repel South African "aggression." Angola accused the Security Council of ineffective measures to stop the threat of invasion.

References See sources for Case #262.

(269) Tan Tan A Polisario attack on the Moroccan town of Tan Tan triggered a crisis for Morocco on 28 January 1979. The crisis faded in March of that year.

Background The Polisario, an independence movement for the Western Sahara, based in Algeria, was formed in 1968. In 1975 an agreement was signed between Morocco and Mauritania dividing the territory of Western Sahara. Spain ended its colonial rule there in February 1976, triggering an attack by Algerian forces on Moroccan troops. The Saharan Arab Democratic Republic was proclaimed by the Polisario in March and recognized by Algeria (see Cases #230, #232).

On 10 July 1978 the Government of Mauritania, under President Mokhtar Ould Daddah, was overthrown in a bloodless coup led by Lieutenant-Colonel Mustapha Ould Mohammed Salek. Mauritania's involvement in the Saharan conflict had resulted in serious economic difficulties. The Polisario immediately announced a unilateral cease-fire in Mauritania and entered into peace talks with that country. Concentration of activities by the Polisario then moved against Moroccan troops stationed in the northern section of the disputed territory.

By the fall of 1978 the Polisario raids began to creep closer to southern Morocco, and in September a group of guerrillas carried out a spectacular raid 70 kilometers into Moroccan territory. Morocco appealed to the UN, without success. On 27 December Algerian President Houari Boumédienne died: he had been viewed by the Polisario as one of its main sponsors and supporters, and a source of political, military and ideological strength. His death gave rise to a series of Polisario offensives which were termed "Houari Boumédienne Attacks." In December alone, it was reported that Morocco lost 600 troops. On 1 January 1979 Colonel Salek of Mauritania spoke of his support for the right of self-determination for all peoples. Shortly thereafter he announced that he had asked Morocco to withdraw all its forces from Mauritania by March 1979. More serious Polisario attacks in Morocco occurred on 16 and 17 January 1979.

Crisis On 28 January Polisario forces attacked Tan Tan, a garrison town, air force base and convoy assembly point 40 kilometers inside Moroccan territory. Fighting continued for three days as the Moroccan forces in the area resisted and ultimately succeeded in defeating the invaders. King Hassan sent his top military advisor to the area and summoned other military officers to a meeting in Marrakesh. On 2 February Morocco's Foreign Minister Boucetta stated, in a message to his Algerian counterpart, Bouteflika, that Morocco did not intend to exercise its "right of pursuit." Morocco's major response, on 8 March, was an announcement by King Hassan that he had decided to establish a Defense Council, comprising two members of each political organization or party, to deal with the Saharan situation which he said had reached the "limit of the intolerable." The Moroccan Chamber of Representatives approved the King's decision and adopted a declaration which recommended that the government should exercise its "right of pursuit" and should mount retaliatory operations whenever Moroccan territory was the object of military aggression.

The crisis faded sometime later, during March, with a temporary halt in Polisario activities.

References See sources for Case #230.

(270) Raids on ZIPRA Rhodesian raids on guerrilla bases in Angola and Zambia occurred during a crisis for these three actors from 12 February to 31 May 1979.

Background The transitional Rhodesian Government established in April 1978 made little progress towards reaching an understanding with the Patriotic Front with no cease-fire in sight. By the beginning of 1979 Rhodesia's security forces reportedly totalled 50,000, including a 10,000-man army. In February 1979 guerrilla attacks on power and transport installations in Rhodesia increased.

Crisis On 12 February 1979 a Rhodesian Viscount aircraft on a flight from Kariba to Salisbury was shot down by a SAM-7 missile, and all 59 passengers and crew were killed. (A similar incident had occurred in September 1978 and had precipitated a crisis for Rhodesia and Zambia (see Case #264).) In response to the downing of the plane by Zambia guerrillas, Rhodesian forces attacked Zimbabwe People's Revolutionary Army (ZIPRA) bases in Zambia on 23 February. These strikes did not bring an immediate response from Zambia. Three days later seven Rhodesian planes bombed a ZIPRA base near Luso in Angola, marking a new phase in the Rhodesian war, with Angolan territory now becoming a legitimate target for Rhodesian raids. The attack triggered a crisis for Angola, which responded the following day with a strongly-worded statement condemning Rhodesia, as well as South Africa, for its apparent aid. (The latter was thought to have provided Mirage planes for the attack.) March 1979 was marked by repeated skirmishes on all fronts.

On 13 April Rhodesian commandos attacked guerrilla bases in Zambia, including ZAPU leader Joshua Nkomo's house in Lusaka, as well as other targets in the city and country. This triggered a crisis for Zambia which responded on the 16th with a declaration by President Kaunda of a curfew on parts of the country close to the national railway line. On the 22nd Kaunda announced that Zambia would be receiving new weaponry.

On 10 May 1979 Angola's President Neto met with Kaunda and concluded an agreement that, in the face of the threat from Rhodesia, an attack on one country would be considered an attack on both. A Joint Security Force was to be set up to repel Rhodesian or South African incursions into their respective territories. This pact marked the termination of the crisis for Angola, while for Zambia the crisis ended two days later with the lifting of the curfew which had been imposed on 16 April. The crisis ended for Rhodesia on 31 May with the change of government: on that day Ian Smith handed over the reins of government to Bishop Abel Muzorewa.

The UN Security Council met on 8 March 1979 to discuss the strengthening of sanctions against Rhodesia, while condemning the forthcoming Rhodesian elections as insufficient in the provision for black representation in government.

The Ministerial Council of the OAU met between 1 and 3 March and adopted a resolution condemning Rhodesia.

References   See sources for Case #276.

(271) North/South Yemen II   War between North and South Yemen involved those two states as actors in a crisis from 24 February to 30 March 1979.

Background   In the period following their 1972 crisis (see Case #217) relations between the Yemen Arab Republic (YAR) in the north and the People's Democratic Republic of Yemen (PDRY) in the south oscillated between statements of friendship and calls for unity, alternating with expressions of hostility accompanied by border clashes. After the assassination of North Yemen's President in June 1978 there was a sharp rise of tension between the two states, and relations with the PDRY were severed. The following month both Heads of State were killed within days of each other. Accusations and counter-accusations of murder and penetration across each other's border followed. Despite Palestine Liberation Organization (PLO) leader Yasser Arafat's attempt at mediation in September, serious border incidents continued, with both sides massing troops along the frontier. In December the YAR sent troops to restore control over some villages on the border. Localized clashes escalated into open hostility as the YAR charged the PDRY with training saboteurs, harboring foreign troops from Cuba, Ethiopia and the USSR, and having aggressive designs against it. The PDRY rejected these accusations, claiming the YAR had made open declarations of war. Renewed attempts by Iraq, Kuwait, Syria and the PLO to ease the tension and stop border clashes were made during the first half of February 1979.

Crisis   On 24 February 1979 North Yemen asserted that South Yemen had launched a three-pronged attack across the border, while the latter maintained it was successfully repulsing an attack launched by North Yemeni forces and had penetrated into the YAR capturing border towns. North Yemen called for an emergency meeting of the League of Arab States (LAS) to discuss South Yemen's "aggression" and appealed to the United States for arms.

Saudi Arabia placed its armed forces on a state of alert on the 28th. The Saudis, while remaining a staunch ally and supporter of North Yemen, also wished to improve their relations with the PDRY and sought to preserve the military balance in the area.

That day, as well, the United States announced a speed-up of delivery of Saudi-financed American arms to North Yemen. This move reflected, at least in part, the profound impact of the Iranian revolution and a fear that Yemen would be the next target in a Soviet plan to dominate the region. The USSR was the main supplier of arms and weapons, directly, or indirectly through Cuba, to South Yemen.

On 2 March mediation efforts by Iraq, Syria and Jordan succeeded in bringing about an agreement to a cease-fire to begin the next day. Nevertheless, fighting continued for two weeks after the 3 March agreement. On the 5th the LAS adopted a resolution calling for a cease-fire and agreed to form a follow-up committee to supervise its implementation and work towards normalizing relations between the two adversaries. A meeting in San'a between the Chiefs of Staff of both Yemens on 16 March resulted in a second cease-fire agreement and its observation. The withdrawal of YAR and PDRY troops began on the 18th and was completed the next day. The Presidents of both states arrived in Kuwait on the 28th. On the 30th they announced a provisional agreement to unite their countries, terminating the crisis. With the beginning of the unity talks after the Kuwait summit, a new atmosphere prevailed – both Yemens abstained from public accusations, and propaganda ceased immediately.

References See general list and Peterson 1981; Stookey 1982.

(272) Raids on SWAPO South African raids on SWAPO bases in Angola caused a crisis for Angola from 6 to 28 March 1979.

Background The South-West Africa People's Organization (SWAPO) had carried on guerrilla warfare against South African troops in Namibia since 1966. In 1978 activity was intensified, and a crisis occurred from 3 to 17 May (see Case #262). In November of that year Angola perceived the possibility of a South African invasion (see Case #268). Guerrilla activity against South Africa reached its highest intensity in January 1979.

Crisis On 6 March air and ground attacks by South African forces on SWAPO targets in southern Angola triggered a crisis for Angola. The attacks lasted until the 15th, the targets being mainly arms dumps and supplies; some villages were attacked as well, and minor clashes were reported. Angola accused South Africa of using napalm, but there was no verification of this claim. On 16 March Angola approached the United Nations for help. The Security Council met between 20 and 28 March and passed a resolution on the 28th condemning South Africa and demanding an immediate end to provocative acts; it also called for "aid to strengthen the defensive capabilities" of Angola. The resolution terminated the crisis for Angola's decision-makers.

The United States abstained from the Security Council vote.

Following the crisis, in April, President Neto announced to the Angolan people that he planned to increase the size of the armed forces. In October 1979 South African troops invaded Angola once more (see Case #277).

References See sources for Case #262.

(273) Chad/Libya IV Another crisis for Chad, France and Libya in Equatorial Africa occurred from 12 April to 10 November 1979.

Background Shortly after the formation of a National Unity Government for Chad on 29 August 1978 (see Case #261), fighting erupted once more between government and rebel forces. Rivalries among the latter and mass killings of minority Muslims in the south aggravated the situation. The Malloum–Habré coalition government broke down in February 1979. Thousands of Christian Saras were reported slaughtered in the capital by Habré's followers. By the end of February, FROLINAT leader Goukouni's forces entered Ndjamena. And by 11 March, when the first Kano Conference on national Chad reconciliation opened, there were four competing power centers, led by Goukouni, Habré, Asil and Kamougue. France and Nigeria pressed Goukouni and Habré to share power. And this was done in a new Provisional State Council (GUNT), formed on 23 March, in accordance with an agreement a week earlier: Goukouni became interim Head of State, following Malloum's resignation that day; and in mid-April, after an inconclusive second Kano Conference, from 3 to 11 April, Goukouni took the Interior portfolio, with Habré as Defense Minister. While they had yielded to Libya–Nigeria pressure at Kano to enlarge GUNT, they reneged upon their return to Chad.

Crisis It was the *volte-face* by Goukouni and Habré that triggered a crisis for Libya on 12 April 1979, the onset of Chad/Libya IV. While there was some minor Libyan troop activity in the north, beginning on the 13th, and Libyan support for a secessionist movement in southern Chad, its major response did not come until 25 June, following another inconclusive reconciliation conference, at Lagos, Nigeria, on 26–27 May. The four factions represented in the Provisional State Council were absent from Lagos, but dissidents, backed by six of Chad's neighbors (Cameroun, Central African Republic, Niger, Nigeria, Libya and Sudan), demanded the formation of a new, enlarged National Unity Government by 25 June. When this call went unheeded, Libya sent 2500 troops into northern Chad aimed at Faya-Largeau. The Libyan invasion, in turn, triggered a crisis for both Chad and France the same day. The former appealed to Paris not to withdraw its forces from Chad. France agreed, and French reconnaissance planes and bombers played a crucial role in the Chad counter-offensive which forced the Libyans to retreat.

A second Lagos Conference, the fourth concerned with Chad in 1979, met in mid-August, with all eleven Chad factions represented, along with all Chad's neighbors and also Benin, Congo, Liberia and Senegal. The upshot was an agreement providing for: a cease-fire to be monitored by a peace force with contingents from states not bordering on Chad, headed by the OAU Secretary-General; demiliterization of Ndjamena; amnesty for all political prisoners; the merger of all factional militias into a national army; and the formation of a broad-based transitional National Unity Government. When that government was established, on 10 November 1979, the crisis ended for all three actors, Chad, France and Libya.

Yet the complex civil and international conflict over Chad continued: five years after the end of Chad/Libya IV, Qaddhafi and French President Mitterand met and agreed to withdraw all their forces from Chad; France did so in September 1984, but 3500 Libyan troops were reported remaining in northern Chad.

References See sources for Case #257.

(274)
Goulimime-Tarfaya
Road

A Polisario attack on a road in Morocco led to a crisis for Morocco and Algeria from 1 to 25 June 1979.

Background King Hassan of Morocco drove Spain from the Western Sahara by mobilizing more than 350,000 Moroccans in a peaceful "Green March" into the territory in 1975 (see Case #230). Madrid split the territory between Mauritania and Morocco for temporary administration. This was challenged by the leftist Polisario, which used Algerian territory as a staging area and had been largely financed and armed by Algeria and Libya (see Cases #232, #238, #249 and #254). The dispute is partly traceable to a long-standing rivalry between Morocco and Algeria for dominance of the Maghreb, the Arabic-speaking region of northern Africa, stretching from Mauritania to Libya. Mauritania's President Ould Daddah was deposed by the army and that country, under pressure from Polisario attacks, began pulling out of the Western Sahara conflict in 1979. Morocco carried on.

Crisis A large-scale Polisario military operation inside Moroccan territory, on the Goulimime – Tarfaya road, triggered a crisis for Morocco on 1 June 1979. The targetting of an important mineral area within Morocco was quite rare. An additional incident took place on 4 June, north of Zag. The Moroccan response was multiple, including violence. Its troops met the Polisario guerrillas, losing about 20 soldiers with a number of others wounded. On 6 June King Hassan announced that he had ordered the Moroccan Army, in future, to exercise its "right of pursuit" whenever lives of Moroccan citizens were endangered; that decision had been taken by the Moroccan Chamber of Representatives in March (see Case #269). The next day Hassan appealed to the OAU. Moreover, the ambassadors of the five permanent members of the Security Council were summoned to the Foreign Ministry and told that Morocco would not stand by "with arms folded" against repeated aggression. And, on the 15th, Morocco requested an urgent meeting of the Security Council.

The "right of pursuit" claim made by the King on 6 June triggered a crisis for Algeria which feared incursions into Algerian territory. On the 10th Algeria appealed to the President of the OAU, Sudan's Numeiri. Ambassadors of the permanent members of the Security Council were summoned to Algeria's Foreign Ministry as well.

A major Polisario offensive took place at Tan Tan on 13 June. This city had been the victim of an earlier attack in January 1979 (see Case #269).

The Security Council met and discussed the issue from 15 to 25 June; no resolution was passed. On the 25th Morocco requested the indefinite suspension of the UN debate, having perceived the lowering of tensions after the incidents at the beginning of the month. Polisario attacks into Morocco had been temporarily stopped and it did not exercise its "right of pursuit" into Algeria. Morocco's request ended the crisis, but there was no agreement between the adversaries. The OAU "Committee of Wise Men" (Sudan, Mali, Nigeria, Guinea and the Ivory Coast) met on 23 June to discuss the conflict and set forth recommendations.

There was no superpower involvement during the 1979 crisis. However, the Polisario were armed with Soviet-made anti-aircraft missiles, tanks and artillery, while the United States supplied King Hassan with large amounts of military equipment, including jet fighters and radar.

In subsequent years Morocco adopted a simple military strategy of building massive walls of sand across the Sahara Desert, advancing steadily and bringing nearly one-third of the territory and almost all of the population inside their ramparts. Since 1981 the Polisario has been unable to breach the advancing walls. Despite military losses, the Polisario has scored important diplomatic victories: it was admitted into the OAU in 1982 and, in November 1984, the Sahrawi Arab Democratic Republic was seated as a full-fledged member. Morocco quit the OAU. It was supported by Zaire which suspended its participation.

References   See sources for Case #238.

(275) Soviet Threat to Pakistan

Soviet statements implying USSR intervention in the advent of war between Afghanistan and Pakistan created a low-threat crisis for Pakistan from 1 June to 3 July 1979.

Background   Hostile relations between Afghanistan and Pakistan date to Pakistani independence in 1947 when Afghanistan demanded the creation of a separate Pushtu state in part of Pakistan's North West Frontier Province. Several crises occurred over this issue, in 1949, 1955 and 1961 (see Cases #93, #114 and #148). Between 1976 and 1978 Kabul dropped its insistence on self-determination for the Pushtu peoples on the Pakistan side of the border, and an active search for a settlement began. After the Marxist coup in Afghanistan in April 1978 clashes between Afghan government forces and anti-Communist rebels led to a large-scale influx of refugees into Pakistan. The nature and length of the border made it almost impossible for Pakistan to control the border crossings.

Crisis   A crisis was triggered for Pakistan by a statement in *Pravda* on 1 June 1979 accusing it of allowing Afghan rebel groups to attack Afghanistan from its territory, and indicating that the USSR would not remain indifferent. Pakistan, although perceiving its military strength as sufficient to cope with direct Afghan threats, viewed a Soviet-backed and -protected Afghanistan with alarm. The Soviet statement, which charged Pakistan with willingly providing border sanctuaries to the Afghan rebels, made it clear that Moscow would intervene in the event of war between Afghanistan and Pakistan. Pakistan responded the same day with a denial of Soviet allegations, adding that it adhered strictly to the five principles of peaceful coexistence and calling for a resumption of normal relations between Pakistan and Afghanistan.

On 11 June Tass charged that the US was training Afghan rebel forces in Pakistan. This was denied by a spokesman for the US Department of State.

The dialogue between Afghanistan and Pakistan was renewed on 1 July when Afghan Foreign Minister Shah Mohammad Dost arrived in Pakistan for talks with President Zia-ul-Haq.

The crisis ended on 3 July with a joint decision to continue the talks: the two parties agreed to prepare the ground for a summit meeting between the Presidents. It was also agreed that the refugees in Pakistan would return to Afghanistan as soon as possible, on a voluntary basis.

Agreement between the two parties did not alter the situation. The flow of Afghan refugees into Pakistan continued, as did attacks on Afghanistan by rebels operating from Pakistani sanctuaries. A summit meeting never took place. Six months later the USSR invaded Afghanistan, and imposed a pro-Soviet regime. Afghan anti-Communist guerrillas engaged in warfare against Soviet forces lasting more than 7 years.

References   Cheema, 1983; Ziring 1980.

(276) Rhodesian Settlement

Black majority rule in Zimbabwe (formerly Rhodesia) terminated a crisis for Botswana, Mozambique, Rhodesia and Zambia which had occurred from 15 July 1979 to 4 March 1980.

Background   Guerrilla warfare against Rhodesia began in 1972 and expanded to conventional war in 1976. Operations were carried out from bases in Botswana (see Case #245); Mozambique (see Cases #237, #243, #247 and #255); and Zambia (see Cases #252, #264 and #270).

On 13 April 1979 Rhodesian forces captured 14 people in Francistown, Botswana, which had been occupied by ZAPU (Zimbabwe African People's Union), destroying the ferry between Botswana and Zambia, allegedly used for supplies to ZIPRA (the military wing of ZAPU). Clashes between Rhodesian and Mozambiquean forces, which were better equipped than those of Botswana, were frequent in 1979. The attacks were primarily on economic targets. Some of the more serious recorded attacks took place on 9–10 February, on the Mapai–Pafuri road; on 20 February, on the Chimoio guerrilla base; the 14 March bombing of Chokene, and the 18–21 April bombings of Mozambique army positions in the Gaza Province.

In Zambia, as well, raids were numerous. Zambia was the target several times in 1979: 26 June, 1 and 20 July, 23 August and throughout the month of October.

After the elections in Rhodesia in April 1979 a new government led by Bishop Abel Muzorewa took office on 31 May. Muzorewa quickly made it clear that his government intended to continue the policy of preemptive attacks on guerrilla bases and economic targets in Botswana, Mozambique and Zambia. The war inside Zimbabwe–Rhodesia escalated quite rapidly with reports of about 1000 people being killed each month. The number of guerilla forces operating within the country during July was estimated at about 12,000. Early in July Muzorewa visited the US and UK in order to seek recognition for Zimbabwe and to get the economic sanctions lifted.

Crisis   A crisis for Rhodesia was triggered internally on 15 July 1979 when a large number of security forces, loyal to Ndabamingi Sithole, the leader of the opposition ZANU Party (Zimbabwe African National Union), were killed – apparently by regular Rhodesian forces. Internal events, peaking with the massacre, made it clear to Muzorewa that his regime did not have the ability to cope with the issues at hand. Further, on 18 July the High Court ruled that seven MPs of the Zimbabwe Democratic Party could take their seats in Parliament, thereby causing Muzorewa to lose parliamentary control. On 25 July UK Prime Minister Margaret Thatcher announced that legal independence and sovereignty recognition would not be forthcoming as long as the government and constitutional structure of Muzorewa's Zimbabwe-Rhodesia remained unchanged.

From 1–8 August the Commonwealth Heads of Government met in Lusaka, Zambia and decided on an all-party conference to end the Rhodesian conflict. The conference would be held in London in September. Invitations were sent to the

Zimbabwe-Rhodesian Government and to members of the Patriotic Front, along with a draft outline for a new constitution for Zimbabwe.

The trigger to Botswana's crisis was the attack by Rhodesian troops and helicopters on ZIPRA bases at Francistown on 8 August. The response was immediate – an air attack on the helicopters returning to Rhodesia.

On 15 August Rhodesia responded to its crisis by accepting the invitation issued at the end of the Lusaka Conference: Prime Minister Muzorewa's decision was based upon the need to stop the internal challenges to his regime and to achieve some political stability. An intra-war crisis for Mozambique was triggered on 5 September when important economic targets in the Limpopo Valley were attacked by Rhodesian forces. Severe damage caused a reduction in the country's capacity to wage war. Mozambique responded the same day with strong resistance by its army. Fighting in the valley continued until 10 September, and attacks on other targets were reported on the 13th, as well as on 27 September to 1 October, 11–13 and 18–20 October.

British Foreign Secretary Lord Carrington opened the constitutional conference on Rhodesia at Lancaster House on 10 September.

During October Muzorewa sent a message to Zambia's President Kaunda in which he threatened to take measures other than military if Kaunda did nothing to stop ZIPRA infiltration into Zimbabwe-Rhodesia. Indeed, this threat was realized on 5 November when trains carrying maize shipments to Zambia were prevented from passing through Rhodesia. By the 15th some progress had been made at Lancaster House: agreement on transitional arrangements for Rhodesia had been reached; and the British Government had proposed the establishment of a Cease-Fire Commission on which military commanders of both sides would be represented.

Despite apparent political progress, Rhodesia expanded its economic pressure on Zambia with a series of major military attacks: a crisis for Zambia was triggered on 17 November when Rhodesian forces attacked a bridge on the main road to Tanzania; Zambian villagers were killed, and another vital bridge linking Zambia to Malawi and Mozambique was blown up. On the 20th President Kaunda responded by declaring a full alert, cancelling all military leaves and announcing a call-up of reserves. On 12 December Lord Soames, newly-appointed Governor of Rhodesia for the interim period, arrived in Salisbury to oversee the cease-fire, elections and the transfer of government.

The end of the crises for Botswana and Mozambique was the cease-fire which took effect on 21 December. The crisis ended for Zambia on 31 January 1980 when its borders with Zimbabwe were reopened – once the situation had stabilized. And on 4 March 1980, with the election of Robert Mugabe, former leader of the Mozambique-based ZANU, as Prime Minister of the new state of Zimbabwe, the crisis terminated for that country as well.

United Nations activity consisted of a Security Council resolution, passed on 23 November 1979, condemning Rhodesia for its raids into Zambia and calling for full compensation. A condemnation of Rhodesia was also issued by the OAU. The United States supported the Lancaster House discussions. The Soviet Union provided military aid and advisors to ZIPRA.

Following the elections in Zimbabwe, internal unrest persisted, especially in Matabeleland – where Joshua Nkomo, former leader of ZANU/ZIPRA, enjoyed the total support of his fellow Ndebele tribesmen.

References See general list, especially *Africa Contemporary Record*, *Africa Diary*, *Africa Recorder*, *Africa Research Bulletin* and *Kessing's*, and Wiseman and Taylor 1981.

(277) Raid on Angola A South African incursion into Angola caused a crisis for the latter from 28 October to 2 November 1979.

Background During 1978 South Africa triggered two Angolan crises (see Cases #262 and #268). And in March 1979 a third crisis occurred as a result of South African raids into Angola (see Case #272). In September 1979 Augustino Neto, who had led Angola to independence and had been its President since 1975, died. A day after his death Angola reported a South African attack on several economic targets in southern Angola by troops stationed in Namibia. Then, on 13 October, reportedly for the first time, Angolan forces crossed into Namibia.

Crisis   On 28 October South African troops attacked roads and bridges 190 kilometers inside Angola, in the Sierra da Leba area. Angola responded on the 31st with an appeal to the United Nations. The Angolan Ambassador to Belgium, Almeida, and the Angolan Politburo were particularly vocal in their accusations of South African hostile activity.

On 2 November Angola's crisis ended when the Security Council adopted a resolution condemning South Africa and calling for an immediate withdrawal. The United States abstention in the vote was perceived unfavorably by the Angolan decision-makers. There was no change in the Angola–South African relationship after the crisis ended, no reports of South African withdrawal from Angola at the end of the raids; the stalemate continued.

There was no regional organization activity during the crisis, though earlier, on 6–20 July, the OAU Council of Ministers, as well as the OAU Heads of State and Government, had met to discuss the ongoing dispute between South Africa and Angola.

Negotiations towards Namibian independence continued for many years without success.

References   See sources for Case #262.

(278) US Hostages in Iran   A crisis for the United States and Iran over American hostages held in Iran lasted from 4 November 1979 to 20 January 1981.

Background   On 11 February 1979 an Islamic fundamentalist movement led by Ayatollah Khomeini established a new regime in Iran to replace the exiled Mohammed Riza Shah. During the course of government efforts to crush the power of the clergy – 90% of Iran's population belonged to Shiite Islam – Ayatollah Khomeini had been exiled from Iran in 1963, after leading students in a protest march against the Shah. The Shah's regime was protected by the *Savak* – a secret police force known for its methods of torture – and was bitterly opposed by many Iranians. The United States was viewed by anti-Shah Iranians as propping up the Shah, exploiting Iran's oil, profiting from the enormous sale of arms, and helping the *Savak*.

Two factions joined forces to overthrow the Shah: a coalition between the clergy, masses of the Muslim faithful, and the traditional merchants of the bazaar; and the emerging class of Westernized nationalist students and intellectuals. On 26 October 1979, four days after the Shah had been admitted to a New York hospital, young Iranian revolutionaries met and planned a sit-in at the United States Embassy in Teheran. The previous week the Provisional Government of Prime Minister Mehdi Bazargan had turned marching demonstrators away from the American Embassy.

Crisis   On 4 November a crisis was triggered for the United States when some 400 students broke away from one of Teheran's frequent demonstrations and stormed the US Embassy. US Marines held them back for a time with tear gas while diplomats within tried to shred secret documents. Minutes later the students occupied the Embassy, indicating that this had been done in order to protest the admission of the Shah to the United States for medical care. As support for the students grew, a decision was made to put the US hostages on trial if Washington did not return the Shah to Iran. This demand was rejected by the US two days later. On the 6th, as well, the Provisional Bazargan Government collapsed.

In the following days President Carter sent two representatives, Ramsey Clark and William Miller, to Iran to seek to secure the release of the hostages. Khomeini would brook no compromise on his demand that the Shah be returned for trial. On 10 November all Iranian students illegally present in the United States were ordered to leave. Two days later US oil purchases from Iran were discontinued. The following day American and British naval vessels began maneuvers in the Arabian Sea. Iran called for a meeting of the Security Council on 13 November. All Iranian assets in the United States were frozen the following day, and the US initiated action against Iran in the International Court of Justice. On 20 November Iran suddenly released all black and female American hostages. An internal political struggle began there between the students and the clergy, on the one hand, and the secular political leaders, on the other.

After receiving medical treatment in the US, the Shah went to Panama on 15 December. On that day as well, the International Court ordered the return of the Embassy in Teheran to US control, while the Iranians declared that the trial of the hostages would certainly take place. The US approached the Security Council for economic sanctions, but the Soviet Union (and East Germany) voted against the draft resolution, thus preventing its approval.

Major efforts at negotiation began in January 1980. The UN set up a five-member commission under Secretary-General Waldheim to inquire into Iran's grievances. The US, in an effort not to provoke Iran further, delayed imposing formal economic sanctions on 6 February. On the 18th President Bani-Sadr authorized a visit by the UN commission. However, when it arrived in Iran on the 23rd, Khomeini announced that the hostage issue would be decided by the new Iranian *Majlis* (Parliament), to be elected in March. The Ayatollah also called upon the students not to allow members of the commission to see the hostages until the commission's report was published. On 10 March the UN commission met with the Revolutionary Council. When the commission members felt they had reached an impasse, they gave up. Parliamentary elections in Iran were postponed on 22 March. The same day, at a meeting of the United States National Security Council, Carter authorized a plan to rescue the hostages. The US broke diplomatic relations with Iran on 7 April. And on the 11th the fateful US decision was taken to send an airborne rescue mission to Iran. US helicopters landed in Iran on 24 April. However, a collision between two helicopters, causing the death of eight American soldiers, led Carter to abort the mission.

The US attempt to rescue the hostages by military means triggered a crisis for Iran on 24 April 1980. By the end of the month Iran had responded by dispersing the hostages among 16 different locations. Secretary of State Vance resigned on the 27th and was replaced by Edmund Muskie. The Shah died on 27 July in Egypt.

In September a German diplomat in Washington informed Muskie that a close associate of Khomeini wanted to meet urgently in Bonn with senior representatives of the US Government to work out conditions for the release of the hostages. A week later Sadegh Tabatabai met with US Deputy Secretary of State Warren Christopher. The former agreed, on 22 September, to inform Khomeini of US proposals, but on that day war between Iran and Iraq broke out, and the hostage issue was set aside. In November, two days preceding the presidential elections in the United States, the Iranian Parliament adopted the conditions outlined by Khomeini for the release of the hostages. Algeria was asked to serve as the mediator.

In December Iran demanded $24 billion from the US to cover its claims on frozen Iranian assets and property taken by the Shah and his family. However, by early January 1981 the claim had been reduced to $9.5 billion. Christopher flew to Algiers to work out a complex international agreement with Algeria's Foreign Minister, Mohammed Ben Yahia. The final documents were signed in Algiers on 20 January; and later that day word was received in Washington that the hostages had been freed – 35 minutes after Ronald Reagan was installed as President of the United States.

Unsuccessful negotiation and mediation efforts were made throughout the crisis by Swiss and West German diplomats, as well as by private citizens. The Pope and Yasser Arafat of the PLO also tried to mediate between the two adversaries.

References See General list, especially *Keesing's* and *New York Times*, and Brzezinski 1983; Carter 1982; Vance 1983.